Southern Georgia Canoeing

A Canoeing and Kayaking Guide to the Streams of the Western Piedmont, Coastal Plain, Georgia Coast and Okefenokee Swamp

Bob Sehlinger
Don Otey

Menasha Ridge Press Birmingham, Alabama

First Edition, Third Printing
Printed in the United States of America
Published by Menasha Ridge Press
P.O. Box 59257
Birmingham, Alabama 35259-9257

Library of Congress Cataloging in Publication Data

Sehlinger, Bob, 1945–

Southern Georgia Canoeing: A canoeing and kayaking guide to the streams of the western Piedmont, Coastal Plain, Georgia coast and Okefenokee Swamp.

Bibliography: p. Includes index.

1. Canoes and canoeing—Southern Georgia—Guide-books.

2. Southern Georgia—Description and travel—Guide-books.

I. Otey, Don, 1950– joint author.

II. Title.

ISBN 0-89732-007-7

Cover photo by James Valentine. Courtesy of Graphic Arts Center Publishing, Portland, Oregon.

This book is dedicated to three special friends,

Helen & Wilbur Otey, Jr.,

who also happen to be very good parents, and

Cyril Sehlinger,

who has never parented anyone (as far as is known) but has managed nonetheless to live surrounded by lovely ladies and to have this book dedicated to him.

Acknowledgments

Though many individuals and organizations contributed toward the writing of this guide, there were a special few whose enthusiasm and dedicated efforts actually made the work possible. We wish to thank, therefore, Marty Otey for her tireless assistance and support; Harold Golden, Associate District Chief of the Water Resources Division of the Georgia District, U.S. Geological Survey, who granted us access to the U.S.G.S. data base and allowed us to camp in his office for a week while we were computing technical data; Gary DeBacher, who assisted with the research of several streams and served as general adviser to the entire project; Bill Conger, friend, outdoorsman, and mathematician, who supervised the computation of technical data; Jerry Penland, whose river research assistance was invaluable; Jim and Jeanette Greiner and their wonderful staff at Wildwater, Ltd., on the Chattooga, who provided Bob Sehlinger with a base of operations during his field research; *Brown's Guide to Georgia*, which unselfishly provided dozens of professional quality photographs for inclusion in the guide; and Russ Rymer, who, like Gary DeBacher, lead us to some beautiful little streams we had overlooked and supplied the data necessary to include them in the guide.

The following is a partial list of yet more wonderful folks who contributed significantly to the finished product:

River Research

John Lott
Toby Thomas
Gerald Marshall
Bob Brooksher
Eddie Jones
Terry Bramlett
Ben Parker
Liz Cornish
Preston Justice

Technical & Editorial Assistance

Mary Joscelyn
Kathy Jackson
Donna Brown
Marilyn Marshall
Ann George
Rita Mirus
Tara Cope

Data Collation

U.S. Geological Survey
Mary Bergner
Phillip Allen
Rod Smith

Photography

Fred Brown
Robert Harrison
Dick Murless
Wilderness Southeast
Georgia Department of Industry and Trade
Okefenokee National Wildlife Refuge

Special Assistance & Advice

Ron Odom, Georgia Senior Biologist for Endangered Species
Oscar Dewberry, Regional Game Supervisor
BMC Stephen Taylor, U.S. Coast Guard
BMC C. D. Harmon, U.S. Coast Guard
U.S. Forest Service
Lloyd Culp, Okefenokee National Wildlife Refuge
Max Walker, Georgia Department of Natural Resources
Rob Holland, U.S. Army Corps of Engineers
Juanita Guinn
Buckhorn Mountain Shop
SAGE Outfitters
High Country Outfitters
Georgia Department of Transporation

Contents

Introduction

1 Paddler Information 2

Rating the Paddler—Rating the River
Hazards and Safety
Legal Rights of Landowners
Ecological Cosiderations

2 Stream Dynamics 12

Understanding Hydrology
The Water Cycle
Rainfall and Weather in Georgia
Water Temperature
Stream Evolution and Morphology
Volume, Velocity and Gradient

3 Georgia's Land and Water 18

Physiographic Regions of Georgia
Water and Rivers in Georgia
Georgia Streamflow
The Major Drainages of Georgia
Water Quality in Georgia

The Streams

4 Streams of the Western Piedmont 35

5 Streams of the Coastal Plain 91

6 Waters of Special Mention 265

Appendixes 277

Commercial Raft Trips and Expeditions
Commercial River Outfitters
Canoeing Organizations
Where to Buy Maps
Fish and Game Offices
Other Paddling Guides
Camping Sites
Fauna of Georgia

Glossary 290

Index 292

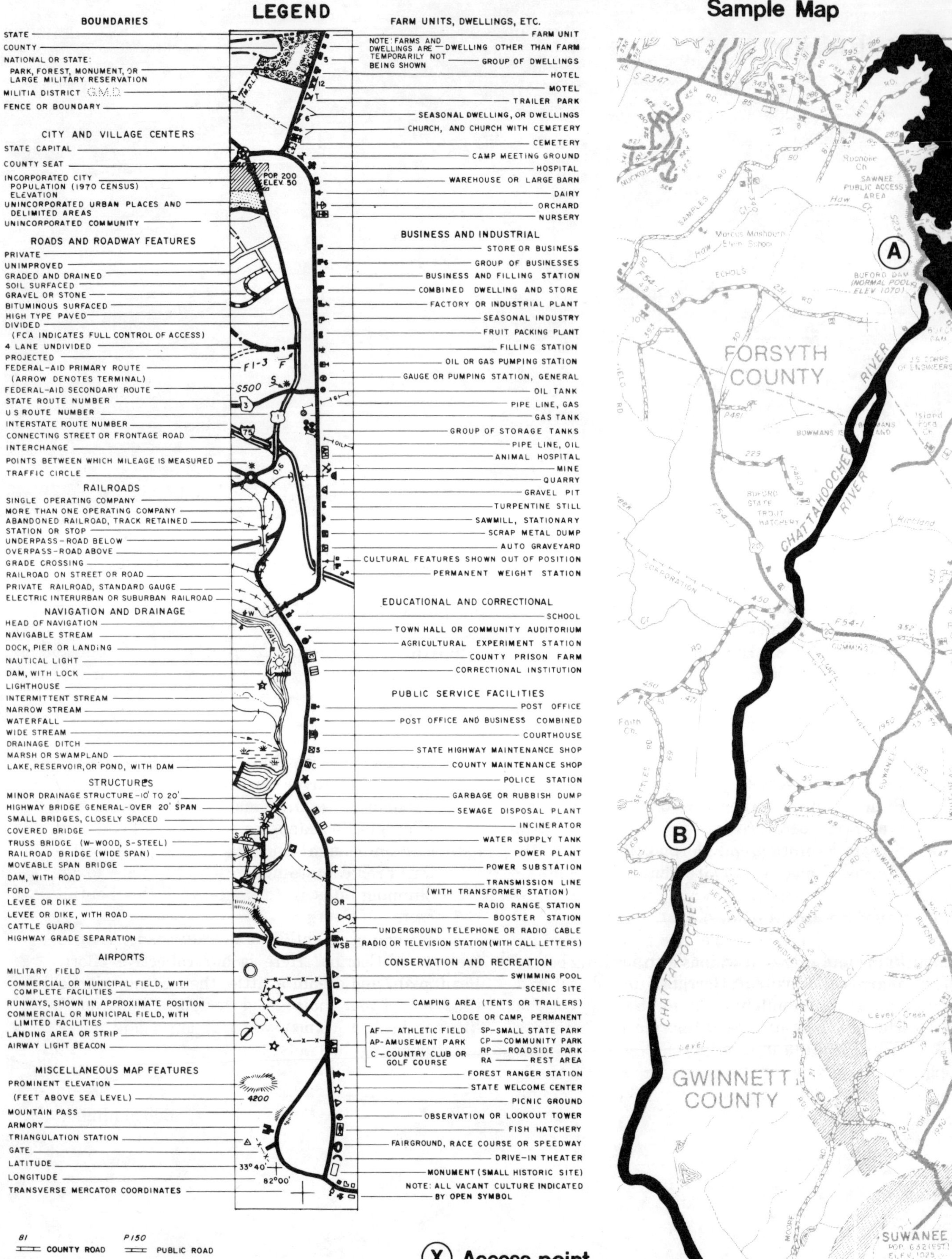

LEGEND
BOUNDARIES
STATE
COUNTY
NATIONAL OR STATE:
PARK, FOREST, MONUMENT, OR LARGE MILITARY RESERVATION
MILITIA DISTRICT G.M.D.
FENCE OR BOUNDARY
CITY AND VILLAGE CENTERS
STATE CAPITAL
COUNTY SEAT
INCORPORATED CITY
POPULATION (1970 CENSUS)
ELEVATION
UNINCORPORATED URBAN PLACES AND DELIMITED AREAS
UNINCORPORATED COMMUNITY
ROADS AND ROADWAY FEATURES
PRIVATE
UNIMPROVED
GRADED AND DRAINED
SOIL SURFACED
GRAVEL OR STONE
BITUMINOUS SURFACED
HIGH TYPE PAVED
DIVIDED
(FCA INDICATES FULL CONTROL OF ACCESS)
4 LANE UNDIVIDED
PROJECTED
FEDERAL-AID PRIMARY ROUTE
(ARROW DENOTES TERMINAL)
FEDERAL-AID SECONDARY ROUTE
STATE ROUTE NUMBER
U.S ROUTE NUMBER
INTERSTATE ROUTE NUMBER
CONNECTING STREET OR FRONTAGE ROAD
INTERCHANGE
POINTS BETWEEN WHICH MILEAGE IS MEASURED
TRAFFIC CIRCLE
RAILROADS
SINGLE OPERATING COMPANY
MORE THAN ONE OPERATING COMPANY
ABANDONED RAILROAD, TRACK RETAINED
STATION OR STOP
UNDERPASS-ROAD BELOW
OVERPASS-ROAD ABOVE
GRADE CROSSING
RAILROAD ON STREET OR ROAD
PRIVATE RAILROAD, STANDARD GAUGE
ELECTRIC INTERURBAN OR SUBURBAN RAILROAD
NAVIGATION AND DRAINAGE
HEAD OF NAVIGATION
NAVIGABLE STREAM
DOCK, PIER OR LANDING
NAUTICAL LIGHT
DAM, WITH LOCK
LIGHTHOUSE
INTERMITTENT STREAM
NARROW STREAM
WATERFALL
WIDE STREAM
DRAINAGE DITCH
MARSH OR SWAMPLAND
LAKE, RESERVOIR, OR POND, WITH DAM
STRUCTURES
MINOR DRAINAGE STRUCTURE-10' TO 20'
HIGHWAY BRIDGE GENERAL-OVER 20' SPAN
SMALL BRIDGES, CLOSELY SPACED
COVERED BRIDGE
TRUSS BRIDGE (W-WOOD, S-STEEL)
RAILROAD BRIDGE (WIDE SPAN)
MOVEABLE SPAN BRIDGE
DAM, WITH ROAD
FORD
LEVEE OR DIKE
LEVEE OR DIKE, WITH ROAD
CATTLE GUARD
HIGHWAY GRADE SEPARATION
AIRPORTS
MILITARY FIELD
COMMERCIAL OR MUNICIPAL FIELD, WITH COMPLETE FACILITIES
RUNWAYS, SHOWN IN APPROXIMATE POSITION
COMMERCIAL OR MUNICIPAL FIELD, WITH LIMITED FACILITIES
LANDING AREA OR STRIP
AIRWAY LIGHT BEACON
MISCELLANEOUS MAP FEATURES
PROMINENT ELEVATION
(FEET ABOVE SEA LEVEL)
MOUNTAIN PASS
ARMORY
TRIANGULATION STATION
GATE
LATITUDE
LONGITUDE
TRANSVERSE MERCATOR COORDINATES
POP. 200
ELEV. 50
F1-3
S500
4200
33°40'
82°00'
FARM UNITS, DWELLINGS, ETC.
FARM UNIT
NOTE: FARMS AND DWELLINGS ARE TEMPORARILY NOT BEING SHOWN
DWELLING OTHER THAN FARM
GROUP OF DWELLINGS
HOTEL
MOTEL
TRAILER PARK
SEASONAL DWELLING, OR DWELLINGS
CHURCH, AND CHURCH WITH CEMETERY
CEMETERY
CAMP MEETING GROUND
HOSPITAL
WAREHOUSE OR LARGE BARN
DAIRY
ORCHARD
NURSERY
BUSINESS AND INDUSTRIAL
STORE OR BUSINESS
GROUP OF BUSINESSES
BUSINESS AND FILLING STATION
COMBINED DWELLING AND STORE
FACTORY OR INDUSTRIAL PLANT
SEASONAL INDUSTRY
FRUIT PACKING PLANT
FILLING STATION
OIL OR GAS PUMPING STATION
GAUGE OR PUMPING STATION, GENERAL
OIL TANK
PIPE LINE, GAS
GAS TANK
GROUP OF STORAGE TANKS
PIPE LINE, OIL
ANIMAL HOSPITAL
MINE
QUARRY
GRAVEL PIT
TURPENTINE STILL
SAWMILL, STATIONARY
SCRAP METAL DUMP
AUTO GRAVEYARD
CULTURAL FEATURES SHOWN OUT OF POSITION
PERMANENT WEIGHT STATION
EDUCATIONAL AND CORRECTIONAL
SCHOOL
TOWN HALL OR COMMUNITY AUDITORIUM
AGRICULTURAL EXPERIMENT STATION
COUNTY PRISON FARM
CORRECTIONAL INSTITUTION
PUBLIC SERVICE FACILITIES
POST OFFICE
POST OFFICE AND BUSINESS COMBINED
COURTHOUSE
STATE HIGHWAY MAINTENANCE SHOP
COUNTY MAINTENANCE SHOP
POLICE STATION
GARBAGE OR RUBBISH DUMP
SEWAGE DISPOSAL PLANT
INCINERATOR
WATER SUPPLY TANK
POWER PLANT
POWER SUBSTATION
TRANSMISSION LINE (WITH TRANSFORMER STATION)
RADIO RANGE STATION
BOOSTER STATION
UNDERGROUND TELEPHONE OR RADIO CABLE
RADIO OR TELEVISION STATION (WITH CALL LETTERS)
WSB
CONSERVATION AND RECREATION
SWIMMING POOL
SCENIC SITE
CAMPING AREA (TENTS OR TRAILERS)
LODGE OR CAMP, PERMANENT
AF— ATHLETIC FIELD
AP- AMUSEMENT PARK
C - COUNTRY CLUB OR GOLF COURSE
SP-SMALL STATE PARK
CP—COMMUNITY PARK
RP—ROADSIDE PARK
RA — REST AREA
FOREST RANGER STATION
STATE WELCOME CENTER
PICNIC GROUND
OBSERVATION OR LOOKOUT TOWER
FISH HATCHERY
FAIRGROUND, RACE COURSE OR SPEEDWAY
DRIVE-IN THEATER
MONUMENT (SMALL HISTORIC SITE)
NOTE: ALL VACANT CULTURE INDICATED BY OPEN SYMBOL
Sample Map
A
B
FORSYTH COUNTY
GWINNETT COUNTY
CHATTAHOOCHEE RIVER
CHATTAHOOCHEE
SAWNEE PUBLIC ACCESS AREA
Roanoke Ch
BUFORD DAM (NORMAL POOL ELEV 1070)
U.S. CORPS OF ENGINEERS
Marcus Mashburn Elem. School
BOWMANS ISLAND
BUFORD STATE TROUT HATCHERY
SAMPLES
ECHOLS
NUCKOLS
HITT
LANIER
CUMMING
SUWANEE
SETTLES
BRIDGE
Faith Ch.
Level Creek Ch.
Richland
F54-1
P481
SUWANEE
POP. 682 (EST.)
ELEV. 1025

81 COUNTY ROAD　　P150 PUBLIC ROAD

Numbering system of County Roads and Public Roads is indicated along roadband.

(X) **Access point**

Introduction

Having scouted and written about a fair number of rivers, I began my exploration of Georgia with no special enthusiasm. The Chattooga I had known and loved for some time, but it seemed a lonely jewel in a crown of mediocrity. Don Otey, my partner in this effort and native of Gainesville, Georgia, raised an unceasing chorus of praise for the Peach State, but then he didn't have to spend the summer in the hot, Coastal Plain river swamps. To me, southern Georgia was a steamy, sweltering giant with features of monotonous sameness inhabited by mosquitoes and yellow flies. The cool Chattooga seemed continents away and no rivers ran beneath the ample table of Pittypat's Porch.

That was then. No, I won't tell you that I discovered a paradise in the Plains, but I was able to jar myself out of my ignorant lethargy and wholly open my heart to one of the most incredible paddling environments I have ever encountered. Southern and central Georgia, you see, are anything but monotonous. Capped to the north with verdant mountains and ridges, it widens into a rolling belt of fertile farms and luxurious forests situated as if on a giant plain that stretches out to the sea. On the Atlantic coast a thousand islands, floating languidly in a glittering tidewater marsh, beckon the paddling explorer. And between the mountains and the sea is a little (or a lot) of everything: secluded jungle streams with burgundy red water flowing over dazzling white sand banks; lazy cypress and gum-shaded swamps; restless, driving rivers with great, wide shoals; intimate valleys covered with hardwoods; sandy bluffs; bubbling springs; dense pine forests; and an incredibly beautiful and varied array of flora and fauna.

To know the streams of southern and central Georgia is to love them, not just for their variety, but also for their pristine beauty, exotic uniqueness, and, paradoxically in the South's most developed state, their wilderness flavor and tranquil remoteness. Almost every stream is protectively cradled in a forested wilderness corridor only occasionally interrupted by the encroachment of civilization. And though several streams have been polluted and dammed, the natural heritage of Georgia's waterways still predominates; there's still a place to get away from it all on the rivers of the South's heartland.

So add one more enthusiastic cheerleader for the streams of Georgia. Here is our collective effort. Read, plan, and dream a little, then go experience the rivers of your choice. And though we hope you'll like the book, we know you will enjoy and never forget paddling the trails of Georgia.

Bob Sehlinger

How to Use Stream Information

For each stream in this guide you will find a general description and at least one stream data list and map. By definition, a stream is flowing water and may be a river, creek, or a branch or fork of a river; therefore lakes are not included here. The streams are grouped roughly by geological region, that is, western Piedmont and Coastal Plain. Only the southern portions of the lengthy Chattahoochee, Savannah, and Oconee rivers are found in this book. For a description of the northern portions of these rivers, see the companion book, *Northern Georgia Canoeing: A Canoeing and Kayaking Guide to the Streams of the Cumberland Plateau, Blue Ridge Mountains and Eastern Piedmont.* Long rivers such as the Ocmulgee, Flint, and Chattahoochee appear in more than one chapter, and there is a separate chapter for special waters such as the Georgia Coast and Okefenokee Swamp.

Stream Descriptions

The descriptions that accompany the maps and data lists are intended to give you a feel for the stream and its surroundings and are presented in general, nontechnical terms.

Stream Data

Each stream data list provides the necessary technical and quantitative information for each of the streams listed, as well as some additional descriptive data. Occasionally certain facts will be covered in both the general description and in the data list for added emphasis. Listed below are fuller explanations of many of the categories found on the data lists.

Each list begins with the specific stream **section** to which the data apply and the **counties** in which the stream is located.

Suitable For. While most streams described in this book are best suited to *day cruising*, some provide the opportunity for *canoe camping*. A few, because of their convenient access and configuration, are designated as being good for *training* runs.

Appropriate For. This item was included strictly for convenience. For a better idea of whether or not a listed stream is for you, evaluate yourself according to the paddler self-evaluation format on pages 4–5 and match your numerical score with the numerical point rating of the river. For definitional purposes, *families* connotes adults of various skill levels who want to take nonswimming adults or children in the canoe with them. We always assume that personal flotation devices (PFD's), e.g., life jackets, will be worn by all parties on moving water. We also assume that no passengers will be carried in whitewater.

Beginners are paddlers with a knowledge of strokes and self-rescue who can maneuver their boat more or less intuitively on still water (lakes and ponds). True *intermediates* meet all beginner qualifications, have a working knowledge of river dynamics, have some ability in rescuing others, and (for our purposes) are competent and at home on Class II whitewater. *Advanced paddlers* (not experts) are paddlers who possess all the foregoing qualifications in addition to specialized rescue skills, and who are competent and at home on Class III and IV whitewater. *Experts* are paddlers who easily exceed all the above qualifications. Needless to say, these definitions could be refined or elaborated ad infinitum. They are not intended to be all-inclusive but rather to give you a reasonable idea of how to classify yourself and how experienced practitioners of the sport may tend to classify you.

Months Runnable. The months given are based on the average rainfall for a year. Different sections

---

Section: Moultrie to Florida border

Counties: Colquitt, Thomas, Grady; Gadsden (FL)

Suitable For: Cruising, camping

Appropriate For: Families, beginners, intermediates, advanced
Months Runnable: November through July and all year during wet years
Interest Highlights: Scenery, wildlife

Scenery: Beautiful

Difficulty: International Scale I
Numerical Points 5

Average Width: 40-60 ft.
Gradient: Slack to slow
Velocity: 2.09 ft./mi.

Runnable Water Level: Minimum 175 cfs
Maximum Up to flood stage

Hazards: Strainers, deadfalls

Scouting: None required

Portages: Around deadfalls

Rescue Index: Accessible but difficult

Mean Water Temperature (°F)

Jan 51	Feb 52	Mar 57	Apr 64	May 72	Jun 77
Jul 81	Aug 80	Sep 75	Oct 66	Nov 60	Dec 53

Source of Additional Information: Albany Game and Fish Office (912) 439-4252

Access Point	Access Code
A	1357
B	2368
C	2357
D	1368
E	1367
F	1357
G	1357
H	1357
I	1357
J	1357
K	1357
L	2357

Access Key
1 Paved Road
2 Unpaved Road
3 Short Carry
4 Long Carry
5 Easy Grade
6 Steep Incline
7 Clear Trail
8 Brush and Trees
9 Launching Fee Charged
10 Private Property, Need Permission
11 No Access, Reference Only

of rivers may be runnable at different times. Some rivers are not necessarily runnable at a given time of year but are only runnable after a heavy rainfall or when a dam or powerhouse is releasing enough water.

Interest Highlights. This category includes special *scenery, wildlife, whitewater, local culture and industry, historical locations,* and unusual *geology.*

Scenery. Taste is relative, and in the absolute sense ours is no better or worse than anyone else's. Our preference is that you form your own conclusions about the comparative beauty of the streams listed in this guide. Knowing, however, that it takes a long time to run all of the state's major drainages, we were presumptuous enough to include a comparative scenery rating based strictly on our own perceptions. The ratings run from *unattractive,* to *uninspiring,* through gradations of *pretty* and *beautiful,* to *spectacular.* To indicate how capricious taste is, some popular canoeing streams in surrounding states are rated:

Tuckasegee River (North Carolina) .... Pretty in spots to pretty
Nantahala River (North Carolina) .... Pretty to beautiful in spots
Hiwassee River (Tennessee) .... Beautiful in spots to beautiful
Suwannee River (Georgia) .... Beautiful
Conasauga River (Tennessee) ...... Exceptionally beautiful
Chattooga River, Section IV (Georgia) .... Spectacular

Difficulty. The level of difficulty of a stream is given according to the International Scale of River Difficulty and according to the river evaluation table on page 3. Both ratings are relative and pertain to the stream described under more or less ideal water levels and weather conditions. For streams with two International Scale ratings, the first represents the average level of difficulty of the entire run and the second (expressed parenthetically) represents the level of difficulty of the most difficult section or rapids on the run. Paddlers are cautioned that changes in water levels or weather conditions can alter the stated average difficulty rating appreciably.

Average Width. Rivers tend to start small and enlarge as they flow toward their confluence with another river. Pools form in some places, and in other places the channel may constrict, accelerating the current. All of these factors affect the width and make the average width a very approximate measure.

Velocity. This represents the speed of the current, on the average, in nonflood conditions. Velocity can vary incredibly from section to section on a given stream depending on the stream's width, volume, and gradient at any point along its length. Velocity is a partial indicator of how much reaction time you might have on a certain river. Paddlers are known to describe a high velocity stream as "coming at them pretty fast," meaning that the speed of the current does not allow them much time for decision and action.

Rivers are described here as *slack, slow, moderate,* and *fast.* Slack rivers have current velocities of less than a half mile per hour; slow rivers have velocities over a half mile per hour but less than two miles per hour. Moderate velocities range between two and four miles per hour, and fast rivers are those that exceed four miles per hour.

Gradient. Gradient is expressed in feet per mile (ft/mi) and refers to the steepness of the stream bed over a certain distance. It is important to remember that gradient (or "drop" as paddlers refer to it) is an average figure and does not tell the paddler when or how the drop occurs. A stream that has a listed gradient of 25 feet per mile may drop gradually in one- or two-inch increments (like a long, rocky slide) for the course of a mile, or it may drop only slightly over the first nine-tenths of a mile and then suddenly drop 24 feet at one waterfall. As a general rule, gradient can be used as a rough indicator of level of difficulty for a given stream (i.e., the greater the gradient, the more difficult the stream). In practice, gradient is almost always considered in conjunction with other information.

Runnable Water Level: Minimum. This represents the lowest water level at which a given stream is navigable. For purposes of continuity and because of disagreement in many instances between depth markers on the same stream, most water levels are expressed in terms of volume as cubic feet per second (cfs). The use of cfs is doubly informative in that knowledge of volume at a gauge on one stream is often a prime indicator of the water levels of ungauged runnable streams in the same watershed or for other sections of the gauged stream, either up- or downstream.

Maximum. In this book, "runnable" does not mean the same thing as "possible." The maximum runnable water level refers to the highest water level at which the stream can be safely run (this may vary for open and decked boats). With few exceptions (which can only be run when flooded), this categorically excludes rivers in flood.

Hazards. Hazards are dangers to navigation. Because of the continuous action of the water, many of these hazards may change and new ones might appear. *Low-hanging trees*, which can be a nuisance, may become *deadfalls*, and *strainers*. Human intervention creates hazards such as *dams, low bridges, fences* (an especially dangerous "strainer"), and *powerboat traffic*. Some watersheds have soils that cannot retain much water and the streams in that watershed may have a *flash-flood* potential. Additionally, geologically young rivers, usually whitewater rivers, may have *undercut rocks, keeper hydraulics, difficult rapids,* and a *scarcity of eddies.*

Scouting. In this guidebook we attempt to list spots on specific rivers where scouting is required, i.e., recommended for the continuation of life and good health. Because many hazards may change in a short period of time, we also subscribe to the rule of thumb that you should scout any time you cannot see what is ahead (whitewater or flatwater and even on familiar rivers); that small, turning drop that you have run a thousand times may have a big log wedged across it today.

Portages. We adhere to the rule that dams should be portaged. Additionally, portages are recommended for certain rapids and other dangers. The fact, however, that a portage is not specified at a certain spot or rapid does not necessarily mean that you should not portage. It is the mark of a good paddler to be able to make safe and independent decisions about his or her own ability to run a given river or rapid.

Rescue. Many of the streams in this book run through wild areas. A sudden serious illness or injury could become an urgent problem if you can't get medical attention quickly. To give you an idea of how far you may be from help, a brief description is given of what might be expected. *Accessible* means that you might need up to an hour to secure assistance, but evacuation is not difficult. *Accessible but difficult* means that it might take up to three hours to get help and evacuation may be difficult. *Remote* indicates it might take three to six hours to get help; *and extremely remote* means that you could expect to be six hours from help and would need expert assistance to get the party out.

Water Temperature. This figure is the average temperature for each month of the year computed

Table 1: Conversion Table
Degrees Celsius (°C) to degrees Fahrenheit (°F)*
(Temperature reported to nearest 0.5°C)

°C	°F	°C	°F	°C	°F	°C	°F	°C	°F
0.0	32	10.0	50	20⁰	68	30.0	86	40.0	104
0.5	33	10.5	51	20.5	69	30.5	87	40.5	105
1.0	34	11.0	52	21.0	70	31.0	88	41.0	106
1.5	35	11.5	53	21.5	71	31.5	89	41.5	107
2.0	36	12.0	54	22.0	72	32.0	90	42.0	108
2.5	36	12.5	54	22.5	72	32.5	90	42.5	108
3.0	37	13.0	55	23.0	73	33.0	91	43.0	109
3.5	38	13.5	56	23.5	74	33.5	92	43.5	110
4.0	39	14.0	57	24.0	75	34.0	93	44.0	111
4.5	40	14.5	58	24.5	76	34.5	94	44.5	112
5.0	41	15.0	59	25.0	77	35.0	95	45.0	113
5.5	42	15.5	60	25.5	78	35.5	96	45.5	114
6.0	43	16.0	61	26.0	79	36.0	97	46.0	115
6.5	44	16.5	62	26.5	80	36.5	98	46.5	116
7.0	45	17.0	63	27.0	81	37.0	99	47.0	117
7.5	45	17.5	63	27.5	81	37.5	99	47.5	117
8.0	46	18.0	64	28.0	82	38.0	100	48.0	118
8.5	47	18.5	65	28.5	83	38.5	101	48.5	119
9.0	48	19.0	66	29.0	84	39.0	102	49.0	120
9.5	49	19.5	67	29.5	85	39.5	103	49.5	121

*°C = 5/9 (°F - 32) or °F = 9/5 (°C) + 32.

over a minimum ten-year period. Because it represents an average, actual water temperatures on a given day may vary considerably from the stated average. The statistic is included to help paddlers determine the need for special warm- or cold-weather clothing or equipment. At water temperatures below 50°F a wet suit is recommended in case of an upset. Table 1 presents equivalent Celsius and Fahrenheit temperatures.

Sources of Additional Information. Various sources of additional information on water conditions are listed. Professional outfitters can provide both technical and descriptive information and relate the two to paddling. TVA and the various hydraulics branches of the respective district Corps of Engineers' offices can provide flow data in cfs but will not be able to interpret the data for you in terms of paddling. Other sources listed (forest rangers, fish and wildlife officers, police departments, etc.) will normally provide only descriptive information, e.g., "The creek's up pretty good today," or, "The river doesn't have enough water in it for boating."

Access Code. Access codes correspond to the letter-denoted access points on accompanying maps. The code is usually four digits, but it may be more or less. Each digit relates to a description of the actual access point on the river. For example, the access code 1357 indicates that (1) a paved road goes to the river; (3) it is a short carry from your vehicle to the water's edge; (5) you don't have to carry down a steep hill or embankment; and (7) there is a clear trail, road, or path to the river. The number 9 means that the access is on private land and permission must be secured to put in or take out a boat. Absence of the number 9 does not necessarily mean that the access is public, it could mean that the landowner has historically granted access and that it is not essential for each boater to secure permission individually. It could also mean that the landowner is nonresident or extremely difficult to locate. The rule of thumb is to respect property.

Maps

The maps in this book are not intended to replace topographic quadrangles for terrain features. Rather, they are intended to illustrate the general configuration of the stream, its access points, and the surrounding shuttle network of roads.

The scale of these maps, unless otherwise stated, is one inch (the approximate length of the end portion of your thumb) equals one mile, and north is at the top of the page. A legend explaining the map symbols is found inside the front cover. A general map of Georgia counties and the rivers described in this book is found inside the back cover.

Some of the maps are congested to the point that access letters may not represent exact location, but are only in the general vicinity. You may have to scout the area before launching. Approximate river miles and car shuttle miles from one access point to the next are provided with the maps.

Additionally, the names of the 7½-minute topographic quadrangles on which the streams appear are provided with the maps. To order these maps, see the address list in "Where to Buy Maps" in the Appendix.

Southern Georgia Canoeing

A Canoeing and Kayaking Guide to the Streams of the Western Piedmont, Coastal Plain, Georgia Coast and Okefenokee Swamp

Chapter 1

Paddler Information

Rating the River—Rating the Paddler

For several years concerned paddlers have sought to objectively rate rivers. Central among their tools has been the International Scale of River Difficulty. While certainly a useful tool, and by no means outdated, the International Scale lacks precision and invites subjective, judgmental error. A more objective yardstick is the recently developed difficulty rating chart that is based on a point system. While more cumbersome, it does succeed in describing a river more or less as it really is. Gone is the common confusion of a single rapid being described as Class II by the veteran while the novice perceives a roaring Class IV. Also eliminated is the double standard by which a river is rated Class III for open canoes but only Class II for decked boats. Instead, points are awarded as prescribed for conditions observed on the day the river is to be run. The total number of points describes the general level of difficulty.

Once the basic difficulty rating is calculated for a river, however, how is it to be matched against the skill level of a prospective paddler? The American Whitewater Affiliation relates the point system for rivers back to the International Scale and to traditional paddler classifications.

This helps, but only to the extent that the individual paddler understands the definitions of "Practiced Beginner," "Intermediate," "Experienced," and so on. If paddlers find these traditional titles ambiguous and hard to differentiate, they will probably classify themselves according to self-image. When this occurs, we're back to where we started.

Correctly observing the need for increased objectivity in rating paddlers as well as in rating rivers, several paddling clubs have developed self-evaluation systems where paddlers are awarded points that correspond to the point scale of the river rating chart (Table 2). Thus an individual can determine a point total through self-evaluation and compare his or her skill, in quantified terms, to any river rated through use of the chart. The individual paddler, for instance, may compile 18 points through self-evaluation and note that this rating compares favorably with the difficulty rating of 17 points and unfavorably with a difficulty rating of 23 points. It should be reiterated here, however, that river ratings obtained from the river difficulty chart pertain to a river only on a given day and at a specific water level. Generalized ratings, when given, represent the difficulty of the river under ideal weather and water conditions.

The most widely publicized of the *paddler* self-evaluations was created by the Keel-Haulers Canoe Club of Ohio. This system brings the problem of matching paddlers with rivers into perspective but seems to overemphasize nonpaddling skills. A canoe clinic student who is athletically inclined but almost totally without paddling skill once achieved a rating of 15 points using the Keel-Haulers system. His rating, based almost exclusively on general fitness and strength, incorrectly implied that he was capable of handling many Class II and Class III rivers. A second problem evident in the system is the lack of depth in skill category descriptions. Finally, confusion exists in several rating areas as to whether the evaluation applies to open canoes, decked boats, or both.

To remedy these perceived shortcomings and to bring added objectivity to paddler self-evaluation, Bob Sehlinger has attempted to refine the paddler rating system. Admittedly the refined system is

Table 2: Rating the River

	Secondary Factors Factors Related Primarily to Success in Negotiating			Primary Factors Factors Affecting Both Success and Safety			Secondary Factors Factors Related Primarily to Safe Rescue				
Points	**Obstacles, rocks and trees**	**Waves**	**Turbulence**	**Bends**	**Length (feet)**	**Gradient (ft/mile)**	**Resting or rescue spots**	**Water Velocity (mph)**	**Width and depth**	**Temp °(F)**	**Accessibility**
0	None	Few inches high, avoidable	None	Few, very gradual	<100	<5, regular slope	Almost anywhere	<3	Narrow (<75 feet) and shallow (<3 feet)	<65	Road along river
1	Few, passage almost straight through	Low (up to 1 ft) regular, avoidable	Minor eddies	Many, gradual	100–700	5–15, regular slope		3–6	Wide (<75 feet) and shallow (<3 feet)	55–65	<1 hour travel by foot or water
2	Courses easily recognizable	Low to med. (up to 3 ft), regular, avoidable	Medium eddies	Few, sharp, blind; scouting necessary	700–5,000	15–40, ledges or steep drops		6–10	Narrow (<75 feet) and deep (<3 feet)	45–55	1 hour to 1 day travel by foot or water
3	Maneuvering course not easily recognizable	Med. to large (up to 5 ft), mostly regular, avoidable	Strong eddies and cross currents		>5000	>40, steep drops, small falls	A good one below every danger spot	>10 or flood	Wide (>75 feet) and deep (>3 feet)	<45	>1 day travel by foot or water
4	Intricate maneuvering; course hard to recognize	Large, irregular, avoidable; or med. to large, unavoidable	Very strong eddies, strong cross currents								
5	Course tortuous, frequent scouting	Large, irregular, unavoidable	Large scale eddies and crosscurrents, some up and down								
6	Very tortuous; always scout from shore	Very large (>5 ft), irregular, unavoidable, special equipment required					Almost none				

SOURCE: Prepared by Guidebook Committee—AWA (From "American White Water," Winter, 1957)

Table 3: Ratings Comparisons

International Rating	Approximate Difficulty	Total Points (from Table 2)	Approximate Skill Required
I	Easy	0–7	Practiced Beginner
II	Requires Care	8–14	Intermediate
III	Difficult	15–21	Experienced
IV	Very Difficult	22–28	Highly Skilled (Several years with organized group)
V	Exceedingly Difficult	29–35	Team of Experts
VI	Utmost Difficulty-Near Limit of Navigability		

more complex and exhaustive, but not more so than warranted by the situation. Heavy emphasis is placed on paddling skills, and description has been adopted from several different evaluation formats, including a non-numerical system proposed by Dick Schwind.*

*Schwind, Dick; "Rating System for Boating Difficulty," *American Whitewater Journal,* Volume 20, Number 3, May/June 1975.

Rating the Paddler

Instructions: All items, except the first, carry points that may be added to obtain an overall rating. All items except "Rolling Ability" apply to both open and decked boats. Rate open and decked boat skills separately.

1. Prerequisite Skills. Before paddling on moving current, the paddler should:

a. Have some swimming ability.
b. Be able to paddle instinctively on nonmoving water (lake). (This presumes knowledge of basic strokes.)
c. Be able to guide and control the canoe from either side without changing paddling sides.
d. Be able to guide and control the canoe (or kayak) while paddling backwards.
e. Be able to move the canoe (or kayak) laterally.
f. Understand the limitations of the boat.
g. Be practiced in "wet exit" if in a decked boat.

2. Equipment. Award points on the suitability of your equipment to whitewater. Whether you own, borrow, or rent the equipment makes no difference. *Do not* award points for both *Open Canoe* and *Decked Boat.*

Open Canoe

0 Points — Any canoe less than 15 ft. for tandem; any canoe less than 14 ft. for solo.

1 Point — Canoe with moderate rocker, full depth, and recurved bow; should be 15 ft. or more in length for tandem and 14 ft. or more in length for solo and have bow and stern painters.

2 Points — Whitewater canoe. Strong rocker design, full bow with recurve, full depth amidships, no keel; meets or exceeds minimum length requirements as described under "1 Point"; made of hand-laid fiberglass, Kevlar®, Marlex®, or ABS *Royalex*®; has bow and stern painters. Canoe as described under "1 Point" but with extra flotation.

3 Points — Canoe as described under "2 Points" but with extra flotation.

Decked Boat (K-1, K-2, C-1, C-2)

0 Points — Any decked boat lacking full flotation, spray skirt, or foot braces.

1 Point — Any fully equipped, decked boat with a wooden frame.

2 Points — Decked boat with full flotation, spray skirt and foot braces; has grab loops; made of hand-laid fiberglass, Marlex®, or Kevlar®.

3 Points — Decked boat with foam wall reinforcement and split flotation; Neoprene spray skirt; boat has knee braces, foot braces, and grab loops; made of hand-laid fiberglass or Kevlar only.

3. Experience Compute the following to determine *preliminary points,* then convert the preliminary points to *final* points according to the conversion table.

Number of days spent each year paddling
Class I rivers × 1 = ______
Class II rivers × 2 = ______
Class III rivers × 3 = ______
Class IV rivers × 4 = ______
Class V rivers × 5 = ______
Preliminary Points Subtotal___
Number of years paddling
experience______ × subtotal =
Total Preliminary Points ______

Note: This is the only evaluation item where it is possible to accrue more than 3 points.

Table 4: Conversion Table

Preliminary Points	Final Points
0–20	0
21–60	1
61–100	2
101–200	3
201–300	4
301–up	5

4. Swimming

0 Points — Cannot swim
1 Point — Weak swimmer
2 Points — Average swimmer
3 Points — Strong swimmer (competition level or skin diver)

5. Stamina

0 Points — Cannot run mile in less than 10 minutes
1 Point — Can run a mile in 7 to 10 minutes
2 Points — Can run a mile in less than 7 minutes

6. Upper Body Strength

0 Points — Cannot do 15 push-ups
1 Point — Can do 16 to 25 push-ups
2 Points — Can do more than 25 push-ups

7. Boat Control

0 Points Can keep boat fairly straight
1 Point Can maneuver in moving water; can avoid big obstacles
2 Points Can maneuver in heavy water; knows how to work with the current
3 Points Finesse in boat placement in all types of water, uses current to maximum advantage

8. Aggressiveness

0 Points Does not play or work river at all
1 Point Timid; plays a little on familiar streams
2 Points Plays a lot; works most rivers hard
3 Points Plays in heavy water with grace and confidence

9. Eddy Turns

0 Points Has difficulty making eddy turns from moderate current
1 Point Can make eddy turns in either direction from moderate current; can enter moderate current from eddy
2 Points Can catch medium eddies in either direction from heavy current; can enter very swift current from eddy
3 Points Can catch small eddies in heavy current

10. Ferrying

0 Points Cannot ferry
1 Point Can ferry upstream and downstream in *moderate* current
2 Points Can ferry upstream in *heavy* current; can ferry downstream in *moderate* current
3 Points Can ferry upstream and downstream in *heavy* current

11. Water Reading

0 Points Often in error
1 Point Can plan route in short rapids with several well-spaced obstacles
2 Points Can confidently run lead in continuous Class II, can predict the effect of waves and holes on boat
3 Points Can confidently run lead in continuous Class III; has knowledge to predict and handle the effects of reversals, side currents, and turning drops

12. Judgment

0 Points Often in error
1 Point Has average ability to analyze difficulty of rapids
2 Points Has good ability to analyze difficulty of rapids and make independent judgments as to which should not be run
3 Points Has the ability to assist fellow paddlers in evaluating the difficulty of rapids; can explain subtleties to paddlers with less experience

13. Bracing

0 Points Has difficulty bracing in Class II rivers
1 Point Can correctly execute bracing strokes in Class II water
2 Points Can correctly brace in intermittent whitewater with medium waves and vertical drops of 3 ft. or less
3 Points Can brace effectively in continuous whitewater with large waves and vertical drops (4 ft. and up)

14. Rescue Ability

0 Points Self-rescue in flatwater
1 Point Self-rescue in mild whitewater
2 Points Self-rescue in Class III; can assist others in mild whitewater
3 Points Can assist others in heavy whitewater

15. Rolling Ability

0 Points Can only roll in pool
1 Point Can roll 3 out of 4 times in moving current
2 Points Can roll 3 out of 4 times in Class II whitewater
3 Points Can roll 4 out of 5 times in Class III and IV whitewater

Hazards And Safety

Hazardous situations likely to be encountered on the river must be identified and understood for safe paddling. The lure of high adventure has in part explained why there are so many more paddlers these days. Unfortunately, an alarming number were not prepared for what they encountered and lost their lives.* They didn't use good judgment or just didn't understand the potential dangers. In some cases the use of alcohol has been a factor in bad judgment, just as it is in driving and private flying. In swiftly moving water you need all your faculties to handle the rapid, critical decisions.

*Paddling Fatality Facts: (1) Over three-quarters of the operators in canoe/kayak accidents have not had any formal instruction; (2) 86 percent of fatalities occurred within 90 minutes of departure on an outing; (3) approximately 74 percent of the victims encountered water temperatures less than 70°F. (From a presentation by the U.S. Coast Guard at the 1976 American Canoe Association instructors' conference in Chicago.)

American Whitewater Affiliation Safety Code

The American Whitewater Affiliation's safety code is perhaps the most useful overall safety guideline available.

I. Personal Preparedness and Responsibility

1. **Be a competent swimmer** with the ability to handle yourself underwater.
2. **Wear a life jacket.**
3. **Keep your craft under control.** Control must be good enough at all times to stop or reach shore before you reach any danger. Do not enter a rapid unless you are reasonably sure you can safely navigate it or swim the entire rapid in the event of capsize.
4. **Be aware of river hazards and avoid them.** Following are the most frequent killers.
   a. **High Water.** The river's power and danger and the difficulty of rescue increase tremendously as the flow rate increases. It is often misleading to judge river level at the put-in. Look at a narrow, critical passage. Could a sudden rise in the water level from sun on a snow pack, rain, or a dam release occur on your trip?
   b. **Cold.** Cold quickly robs your strength, along with your will and ability to save yourself. Dress to protect yourself from cold water and weather extremes. When the water temperature is less than 50°F, a diver's wet suit is essential for safety in event of an upset. Next best is wool clothing under a windproof outer garment such as a splashproof nylon shell; in this case one should carry matches and a complete change of clothes in a waterproof package. If after prolonged exposure a person experiences uncontrollable shaking or has difficulty talking and moving, he or she must be warmed immediately by whatever means available.
   c. **Strainers.** Brush, fallen trees, bridge pilings, or anything else that allows river current to sweep through but pins boat and boater against the obstacle. The water pressure on anything trapped this way is overwhelming, and there may be little or no whitewater to warn of this danger.
   d. **Weirs, reversals, and souse holes.** Water drops over an obstacle, then curls back on itself in a stationary wave, as is often seen at weirs and dams. The surface water is actually going *upstream,* and this action will trap any floating object between the drop and the wave. Once trapped, a swimmer's only hope is to dive below the surface where current is flowing downstream or to try to swim out the end of the wave.
5. **Boating alone is not recommended.** The preferred minimum is three craft.
6. **Have a frank knowledge of your boating ability.** Don't attempt waters beyond this ability. Learn paddling skills and teamwork, if in a multi-person craft, to match the river you plan to boat.
7. **Be in good physical condition** consistent with the difficulties that may be expected.
8. **Be practiced in escape** from an overturned craft, in self-rescue, and in artificial respiration. Know first aid.
9. **The Eskimo roll should be mastered** by kayakers and canoeists planning to run large rivers or rivers with continuous rapids where a swimmer would have trouble reaching shore.
10. **Wear a crash helmet** where an upset is likely. This is essential in a kayak or covered canoe.
11. **Be suitably equipped.** Wear shoes that will protect your feet during a bad swim or a walk for help, yet will not interfere with swimming (tennis shoes recommended). Carry a knife and waterproof matches. If you need eyeglasses, tie them on and carry a spare pair. Do not wear bulky clothing that will interfere with your swimming when water-logged.

II. Boat and Equipment Preparedness

1. **Test new and unfamiliar equipment** before relying on it for difficult runs.
2. **Be sure the craft is in good repair** before starting a trip. Eliminate sharp projections that could cause injury during a swim.
3. **Inflatable craft should have multiple air chambers** and should be test inflated before starting a trip.
4. **Have strong, adequately sized paddles or oars** for controlling the craft and carry sufficient spares for the length of the trip.
5. **Install flotation devices** in non-inflatable craft. These devices should be securely fixed and designed to displace as much water from the craft as possible.
6. **Be certain there is absolutely nothing to cause entanglement** when coming free from an upset craft; e.g., a spray skirt that won't release or that tangles around the legs; life jacket buckles or clothing that might snag; canoe seats that lock on shoe heels; foot braces that fail or allow feet to jam under them; flexible decks that collapse on boater's legs when trapped by water pressure; baggage that dangles in an upset; loose rope in the craft or badly secured bow and stern lines.
7. **Provide ropes to allow you to hold on to your craft** in case of upset and so that it may be rescued. Following are the recommended methods:
   a. **Kayaks and covered canoes** should have 6-inch diameter grab loops of ¼-inch rope attached to bow and stern. A stern painter 7 or 8 feet long is optional and may be used if properly secured to prevent entanglement.
   b. **Open canoes** should have bow and stern lines (painters), securely attached, consisting of 8 to 10 feet of ¼- or ⅜-inch rope. These lines must be secured in such a way that they will not come loose accidentally and entangle the boaters during a swim, yet they must be ready for immediate use during an emergency. Attached balls, floats, and knots are not recommended.

c. **Rafts and dories** should have taut perimeter grab lines threaded through the loops usually provided on the craft.

8. **Respect rules for craft capacity** and know how these capacities should be reduced for whitewater use. (Life raft ratings must generally be halved.)
9. **Carry appropriate repair materials:** tape (heating-duct tape) for short trips, a complete repair kit for wilderness trips.
10. **Car-top racks must be strong and positively attached** to the vehicle, and each boat must be tied to each rack. In addition, each end of each boat should be tied to the car bumpers. Suction-cup racks are inadequate. The entire arrangement should be able to withstand all but the most violent accident.

III. Leader's Preparedness and Responsibility

1. **River conditions.** Have a reasonable knowledge of the difficult parts of the run, or, if making an exploratory trip, examine maps to estimate the feasibility of the run. Be aware of possible rapid changes in river level and how these changes can affect the difficulty of the run. If important, determine approximate flow rate or level of the river. If the trip involves important tidal currents, secure tide information.
2. **Participants.** Inform participants of expected river conditions and determine whether the prospective boaters are qualified for the trip. All decisions should be based on group safety and comfort. Difficult decisions on the participation of marginal boaters must be based on group strength.
3. **Equipment.** Plan so that all necessary group equipment is present on the trip: 50- to 100-foot throwing rope, first aid kit with fresh and adequate supplies, extra paddles, repair materials, and survival equipment, if appropriate. Check equipment as necessary at the put-in, especially life jackets, boat flotation, and any items that could prevent complete escape from the boat in case of an upset.
4. **Organization.** Remind each member of individual responsibility in keeping the group compact and intact between the leader and the sweep (a capable rear boater). If the group is too large, divide into smaller groups, each of appropriate boating strength, and designate group leaders and sweeps.
5. **Float plan.** If your trip is into a wilderness area, or for an extended period, your plans should be filed with appropriate authorities or left with someone who will contact them after a certain time. Establishing of checkpoints along the way from which civilization could be contacted if necessary should be considered; knowing the location of possible help could speed rescue in any case.

IV. In Case of Upset

1. **Evacuate your boat immediately** if there is imminent danger of being trapped against logs, brush, or any other form of strainer.
2. **Recover with an Eskimo roll** if possible.
3. **If you swim, hold on to your craft.** It has much flotation and is easy for rescuers to spot. Get to the upstream side of the craft so it cannot crush you against obstacles.
4. **Release your craft if this improves your safety.** If rescue is not imminent and water is numbingly cold, or if worse rapids follow, then strike out for the nearest shore.
5. **When swimming rocky rapids,** use backstroke with legs downstream and feet near the surface. If your foot wedges on the bottom, fast water will push you under and hold you there. Get to slow or very shallow water before trying to stand or walk. Look ahead. Avoid possible entrapment situations: rock wedges, fissures, strainers, brush, logs, weirs, reversals, and souse holes. Watch for eddies and slackwater so that you can be ready to use these when you approach. Use every opportunity to work your way to shore.
6. **If others spill, go after the boaters. Rescue boats and equipment only if this can be done safely.**

V. International Scale of River Difficulty

(If rapids on a river generally fit into one of the following classifications, but the water temperature is below 50°F, or if the trip is an extended one in a wilderness area, the river should be considered one class more difficult than normal.)

Class I Moving water with a few ripples and small waves; few or no obstructions.

Class II Easy rapids with waves up to 3 feet, and wide, clear channels that are obvious without scouting; some maneuvering is required.

Class III Rapids with high, irregular waves often capable of swamping an open canoe; narrow passages that often require complex maneuvering; may require scouting from shore.

Class IV Long, difficult rapids with constricted passages that often require precise maneuvering in very turbulent waters. Scouting from shore is often necessary, and conditions make rescue difficult. Generally not possible for open canoes; boaters in covered canoes and kayaks should be able to Eskimo roll.

Class V Extremely difficult, long, and very violent rapids with highly congested routes that nearly always must be scouted from shore. Rescue conditions are difficult and there is significant hazard to life in event of a mishap. The ability to Eskimo roll is essential for kayaks and canoes.

Class VI Difficulties of Class V carried to the extreme of navigability; nearly impossible and very dangerous; for teams of experts only, after close study and with all precautions taken.

Injuries and Evacuations

Even allowing for careful preparation and attention to the rules of river safety, it remains a fact of life that people and boats are somewhat more fragile than rivers and rocks. Expressed differently, accidents do occur on paddling trips, and *all* boaters should understand that it can happen to them. Although virtually any disaster is possible on the river, there seem to be a small number of specific traumas and illnesses that occur more frequently than others. These include:

1. Hypothermia
2. Dislocated shoulder (especially common in decked boating)
3. Sprained or broken ankles (usually sustained while scouting or getting into or out of the boat)
4. Head injuries (sustained in falls on shore or during capsize)
5. Hypersensitivity to insect bite (anaphylactic shock)
6. Heat trauma (sunburn, heat stroke, heat prostration, dehydration, etc.)
7. Food poisoning (often resulting from sun spoilage of foods on a hot day)
8. Badly strained muscles (particularly of the lower back, upper arm, and the trapezius)
9. Hand and wrist injuries
10. Lacerations

What happens when one of the above injuries occurs on the river? Many paddlers are well prepared to handle the first aid requirements but are unfortunately ill prepared to handle the residual problems of continued care and evacuation. The following is an excerpt from *Wilderness Emergencies and Evacuations* by Ed Benjamin, Associate Program Director at SAGE, School of the Outdoors in Louisville, Kentucky, "When a paddler is injured during a river trip he can usually be floated out in a canoe. Unfortunately, however, circumstances do sometimes arise when the victim is non-ambulatory, or when lack of open canoes or the nature of the river preclude floating the injured party out. In such a situation the trip leader would have to choose between sending for help or performing an overland evacuation."

When sending for help, send at least two people. Dispatch with them a marked map or drawing showing your location as exactly as possible. (Yes, that means pencil and paper should be part of every first aid kit). Also send a note giving directions for finding you plus information on the nature of your emergency and the type of assistance you require. Have your messengers call the proper agencies, such as local police, a rescue squad, the U.S. Forest Service, the state police, plus any unofficial parties such as professional river outfitters who could lend special expertise to the rescue. This having been done, the messengers should be instructed to report the situation simply and factually to the families of the persons involved.

Many paddlers, unfortunately, do not know where they are except in relation to the river, and all too few carry topographical maps. Rescuers need to know exactly where you are in terms of the land, roads, etc. A helicopter pilot will not make much sense of the information that your victim is on the left bank below Lunchstop Rapid. Establish shelter for yourselves and your victim; any rescue is going to take a long time. In the time it takes your messengers to walk out, organize help, and return to you, many hours or perhaps days will pass. Psychologically prepare yourself for a long wait. To expedite the rescue attempt, build a smoky fire to help your rescuers locate you.

Many people believe that if they are ever hurt in the wilderness, a helicopter will come fly them out. This is not necessarily so. Only if you are near a military air base or a civilian air rescue service do you have a good chance of getting a helicopter. Even if one is available, there are several serious limitations to this type of rescue. A rescue helicopter will not fly in bad weather, over a certain altitude, or at night. A helicopter needs a clear area about 150 feet in diameter that is reasonably level on which to land. Moreover, the pilot will probably need some sort of wind indicator on the ground such as a wind sock or a smoky fire. All helicopters are not the same; most do not have a cable on which to raise a victim, and all have limitations on where they may hover. If a helicopter is successful in landing near you, do not approach the craft until the crew signals you to do so, and then only as the crew directs. In most situations the availability or usefulness of a helicopter is doubtful. More likely you will be rescued by a group of volunteers who will drive to the nearest roadhead, reach you on foot, and carry the victim out on a litter. Be advised that volunteer rescue teams are usually slow and sometimes lack adequate training (particularly for a river or climbing rescue). Occasionally you may encounter a top-notch mountain rescue team, but this is rare.

If help cannot be obtained, or if you have a large, well-equipped group, it may be possible to carry the victim out yourself. A litter can be improvised from trees, paddles, packs, etc. Any litter used should be sufficiently strong to protect your victim from further injury. If you do attempt to evacuate the victim yourself, be advised that overland evacuations (even with the best equipment) are extremely difficult and exhausting and are best not attempted unless there are eight or more people to assist. When carrying a litter, a complement of six bearers is ideal. Not only does this spread the load, but, if one bearer loses footing, it is unlikely that the litter will be dropped. Bearers should be distributed so that there are two by the victim's head, two by the feet, and one on each side in the middle. Those carrying at the head of the victim must pay careful attention to the victim. An unconscious victim requires constant checking of vital signs. A conscious victim will be uncomfortable and frightened and will need reassurance. Bear in mind also that a day warm enough to make a litter carrier perspire may be cool enough to induce hypothermia in an unmoving victim. Always have one bearer set the pace and choose the safest and easiest route. Go slow and easy and be careful. Always use a rope to belay the litter from above when ascending or descending a slope—a dropped litter can slide a long way. Paddlers should insist that their partners learn first aid. First aid gear (including pencil and paper), extra topographical maps, and rope should be carried in the sweep boat.

Hypothermia

Hypothermia, the lowering of the body's core temperature, and death from drowning or cardiac arrest after sudden immersion in cold water are two serious hazards to the winter, early spring, and late fall paddler. Cold water robs the victim of the ability and desire to save him- or herself. When the body's temperature drops appreciably below the normal 98.6°F, sluggishness sets in, breathing is difficult, coordination is lost to even the most athletic person, pupils dilate, speech becomes slurred, and *thinking irrational.* Finally unconsciouness sets in, and then, death. Hypothermia can occur in a matter of minutes in water just a few degrees above freezing, but even 50°F water is unbearably cold.

To make things worse, panic can set in when the paddler is faced with a long swim through rapids. Heat loss occurs much more quickly than believed. A drop in body temperature to 96°F makes swimming and pulling yourself to safety almost impossible, and tragically, the harder you struggle, the more heat your body loses. Body temperatures below 90°F lead to unconsciousness, and a further drop to about 87°F usually results in death. (But this same lowering of the body temperature slows metabolism and delays brain death in cases of drowning, therefore heroic rescue efforts have a higher chance of success.)

Paddlers subjected to spray and wetting from waves splashing into an open boat are in almost as much danger of hypothermia as a paddler completely immersed after a spill. The combination of cold air and water drains the body of precious heat at an alarming rate although it is the wetness that causes the major losses since water conducts heat away from the body twenty times faster than air. Clothes lose their insulating properties quickly when immersed in water, and skin temperatures will rapidly drop to within a few degrees of the water temperature. The body, hard pressed to conserve heat, will then reduce blood circulation to the extremities. This reduction in blood flowing to arms and legs makes movement and heavy work next to impossible. Muscular activity increases heat loss because blood forced to the extremities is quickly cooled by the cold water. It's a vicious, deadly cycle.

The best safeguards against cold weather hazards are: recognizing the symptoms of hypothermia, preventing exposure to cold by wearing proper clothing (wool and waterproof outerwear or wet suits), understanding and respecting cold weather, knowing how the body gains, loses, and conserves body heat, and knowing how to treat hypothermia when it is detected. Actually, cold weather deaths may be attributed to a number of factors: physical exhaustion, *inadequate food intake, dehydration of the body,* and psychological elements such as fear, panic, and despair. Factors such as body fat, the metabolism rate of an individual, and skin thickness are variables in a particular person's reaction and endurance when immersed in cold water. Since the rate of metabolism is actually the rate at which the body produces heat from "burning" fats, carbohydrates, and proteins, one person may have a higher tolerance for cold weather than another. Stored fatty tissues also help the body resist a lowering of its core temperature. Shivering is "involuntary exercise"—the body is calling on its energy resources to produce heat. Proper food intake and sufficient water to prevent dehydration are important in any cold weather strenuous exercise, especially paddling.

The key to successfully bringing someone out of hypothermia is understanding that their body must receive heat from an *external source.* In a field situation, strip off all wet clothes and get the victim into a sleeping bag with another person. Skin-to-skin transfer of body heat is by far the best method of getting the body's temperature up. By all means don't let the victim go to sleep, and feed him or her warm liquids but not alcohol, which is a depressant. Build a campfire if possible. Mouth-to-mouth resuscitation or external cardiac massage may be necessary in extreme cases when breathing has stopped, but remember that a person in the grips of hypothermia has a significantly reduced metabolic rate, so the timing of artificial respiration should correspond to the victim's slowed breathing.

Photo courtesy of *Brown's Guide to Georgia.*

Southern Georgia "blackwater" stream.

Alligators

Alligators populate southern Georgia in healthy numbers. According to Ron Odom, Senior State Biologist for Endangered Wildlife, gators can be found along almost any stream south of a line running from east to west through Macon. While incidents involving alligators and sportsmen or boaters are exceedingly rare, the potential for confrontation and injury exists.

Although alligators are found throughout southern Georgia, they become more numerous the farther south one travels; there are particular concentrations southwest of Albany and in the vicinity of the Okefenokee Swamp (Satilla, Suwanee, and St. Marys rivers). Generally nonaggressive and retiring in encounters with humans, gators can sometimes be rather unpredictable. Alligator attacks are not completely unknown, but wildlife experts speculate that these arise from some confusion on the part of the beast as to just what it is attacking. Since it is well documented that confused alligators neither wreak less damage nor appear any more apologetic than unconfused alligators, the obvious lesson is to preclude confusion. With this in mind, a few simple "do's" and "don'ts" should suffice to keep a paddler safe from less than lucid crocodilians.

1. First and foremost, give the alligators, wherever they are found, a wide berth. A large gator can render incredible damage with its tail alone. Observe them from a safe distance.
2. Never feed alligators; they have difficulty discerning where the food ends and the feeder begins. (This is probably not a problem except in the Okefenokee where some gators have become accustomed to humans).
3. Never disturb an alligator's nest (it seems ridiculous to have to tell somebody this). Females with nests are fearless in protecting their eggs and often display remarkably aggressive behavior. If they are guarding their nests, they will hiss and thrash about and will try to maintain a position between you and the nest. If, however, you somehow stumble on a nest

with the mother momentarily absent, watch out! When she returns (and it won't be long), she will charge. Bear in mind also that gators are surprisingly fast on land as well as in the water.

4. Do not swim at night. Gators are night feeders.
5. Do not clean fish in camp or leave fish heads or other remains in an area where humans will be.
6. Do not leave children unattended.
7. Do not make sounds like a female alligator in heat.

Legal Rights of Landowners

Landowners' rights to prohibit tresspassing on their land along streams, if they so desire, is guaranteed; therefore, access to rivers must be secured at highway rights-of-way or on publicly owned land if permission to cross privately owned land cannot be secured. In granting you access to a river, landowners are extending a privilege to you such as they extend to hunters who stop by their doors and seek permission to shoot doves in their cornfields. Don't betray landowners' trust if they give you permission to camp or launch canoes or kayaks from their riverbanks. Always pick up your litter, close any gates you open, and respect planted fields. Tenure of land, landholding, and the right to do with it what you want, is serious business to some landowners. Many farmers do not subscribe to the concept of "land stewardship." They do not feel any responsibility towards the paddling community, and in some cases might even resent people driving hundreds of miles for the pleasure of floating down a river.

On the other hand, it may be that the landowner you seek permission from is intrigued with paddling and will be quite friendly and approachable. Value this friendship and don't give cause for denying access at some time in the future. Remember also that your conduct and courtesy (or lack thereof) shape a landowner's opinion of paddlers in general. Discourteous behavior by a single individual can easily result in a landowner cutting off access to all. A positive approach is the best approach; take up the slack when you encounter evidence that others have been careless or irresponsible. Allow a few extra minutes to share the virtues of your sport with the landowner if it seems welcome. Pick up and carry out garbage and refuse you find along the stream or where paddlers park. Beware of sensitive issues such as changing clothes in view of others.

Paddlers are trespassing when they portage, camp, or even stop for a lunch break. If you are approached by a landowner when tresspassing, by all means be cordial and understanding and explain what you're doing (making a lunch stop or portage). Never knowingly camp on private land without permission. If you do encounter a perturbed landowner, don't panic. Keep cool and be respectful.

Ecological Considerations

Presenting a set of ecological guidelines for all paddlers sounds like preaching, but with the number of people using our creeks and rivers today, it is indeed a valid point. Many of the streams listed in this guide flow through national parks and forests, state-owned forests and wildlife management areas, and privately owned lands that in some cases are superior in quality and aesthetics to lands under public ownership. It is the paddling community's responsibility to uphold the integrity of these lands and their rivers by exercising ecologically sound guidelines. Litter, fire scars, pollution from human excrement, and the cutting of live trees is unsightly and affects the land in a way that threatens to ruin the outdoor experience for everyone.

Paddlers should pack out everything they packed in: all paper litter and such nonbiodegradable items as cartons, foil, plastic jugs, and cans. Help keep our waterways clean for those who follow. If you are canoe camping, leave your campsite in better shape than you found it. If you must build a fire, build it at an established site, and when you leave, dismantle rock fireplaces, thoroughly drown all flames and hot coals, and scatter the ashes. Never cut live trees for firewood (in addition to destroying a part of the environment, they don't burn well). Dump all dishwater in the woods away from watercourses, and emulate the cat, bury all excrement.

Chapter 2

Stream Dynamics

Understanding Hydrology

Understanding hydrology—how rivers are formed and how they affect man's activities—is at the very heart of paddling. To aid the paddler, here is a brief discussion of the effects on paddling of seasonal variations of rainfall, water temperatures, volume, velocity, gradient, and stream morphology.

The most basic concept about water that all paddlers must understand is the hydrologic (water) cycle, which moves water from the earth to the atmosphere and back again. Several things happen to water that falls to the earth: it becomes surface runoff that drains directly into rivers or their tributaries, or it is retained by the soil and used by plants, or it may be returned directly to the atmosphere through evaporation, or else it becomes ground water by filtering down through subsoil and layers of rock.

Local soil conditions have a great deal to do with streamflow as do plant life, terrain slope, ground cover, and air temperature. In summer, during the peak growing season, water is used more readily by plants, and higher air temperatures encourage increased evaporation. The fall and winter low-water periods are caused by decreased precipitation, although since the ground is frozen and plant use of water is for the most part halted, abnormally high amounts of rain, or water from melting snow, can cause flash floods because surface runoff is high—there's no place for the water to go but into creeks and rivers. Though surface runoff is first to reach the river, it is ground water that keeps many larger streams flowing during rainless periods. Drought can lower the water table drastically. Soil erosion is related to surface runoff—hilly land in intensive agricultural use is a prime target for loss of topsoil and flashflooding.

The Water Cycle

The water on and around the earth moves in a never-ending cycle from the atmosphere to the land and back to the atmosphere again. Atmospheric moisture flows constantly over Georgia, and the amount that falls on the state now is much the same as it was when only the Indians worried about dried-up springs and floods in their villages.

Beginning the cycle with the oceans, which cover some 75 percent of the earth's surface, the movement of the water follows these steps:

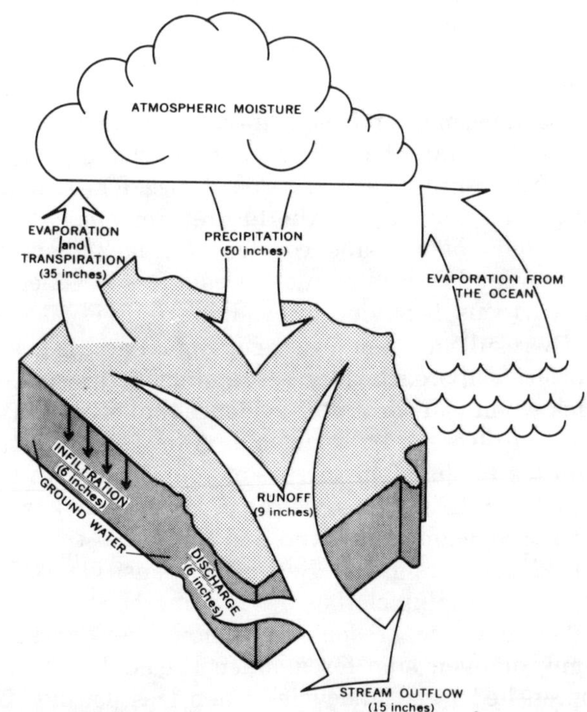

SOURCE: *Water Resources Investigations in Georgia, 1974.* U.S. Dept. of Interior Geological Survey.

Figure 1: Water Cycle in Georgia

1. Water from the surface of the oceans (and from the lands between) evaporates into the atmosphere as vapor. This water vapor rises and moves with the winds.
2. Eventually, either over the ocean or over the land, this moisture is condensed by various processes and falls back to the earth as precipitation. Some falls on the ocean; some falls on the land where it becomes of particular concern to man.
3. Of the rain, snow, sleet, or hail that falls on the land, some runs off over the land, some soaks down into the ground to replenish the great ground-water reservoir, some is taken up by the roots of plants and is transpired as water vapor, and some is again evaporated directly into the atmosphere.
4. The water that flows over the land or soaks down to become ground water feeds the streams that eventually flow back into the oceans, completing the cycle.

The key steps in this great circulation of the earth's moisture are evaporation, precipitation, transpiration, and streamflow. All occur constantly and simultaneously over the earth. Over Georgia and its river basins the quantities in any part of the cycle vary widely from day to day or from season to season. Precipitation may be excessive or may stop entirely for days or weeks. Evaporation and transpiration demands are lower in winter and higher in July and August. Streamflow depends on the interrelation of these processes.

Rainfall and Weather in Georgia

Rainfall in Georgia averages about 50 inches a year, but it is not uniformly distributed by season or location. The Augusta area annually receives about 43 inches while a small area in the mountains of northeastern Georgia receives nearly twice that amount. Most of Georgia's rainfall comes from warm, moist, air masses formed over the Gulf of Mexico. Lesser amounts of rainfall come from air masses that form over the Atlantic Ocean. The average annual rainfall decreases with distance from the Atlantic Ocean and the Gulf of Mexico up to the Fall Line. The Fall Line is the discernible geologic break between the hard rock strata of the Piedmont and the more easily eroded rock of the Coastal Plain. This line, which roughly parallels the eastern seaboard, is marked by steep cliffs, waterfalls, and rapids. North of the Fall Line average rainfall increases because the moist air is forced to rise thus precipitating moisture as it passes over the ridges and mountains.

In addition to the above, there are also seasonal variations in rainfall. More rain falls in winter,

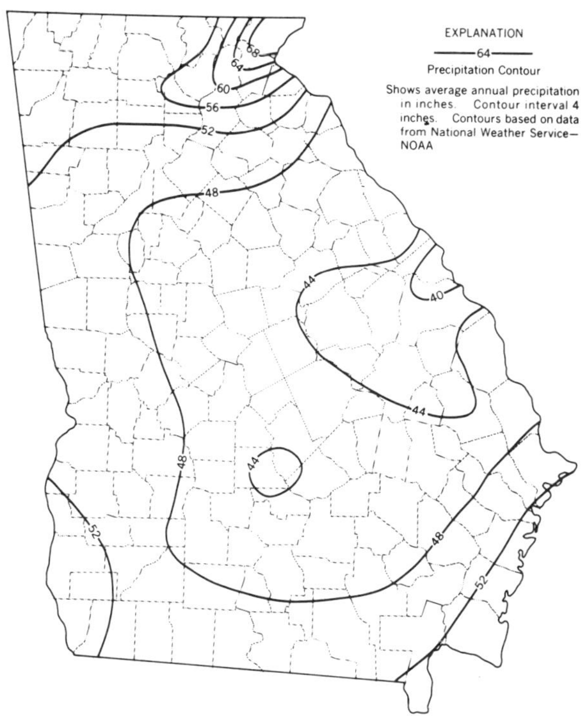

SOURCE: *Water Resources Investigations in Georgia, 1974.* U.S. Dept. of Interior Geological Survey.

Figure 2: Average Annual Precipitation

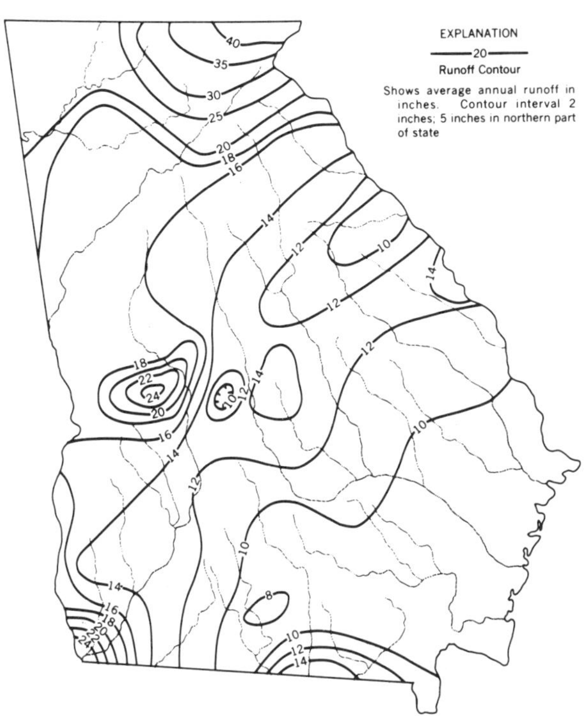

SOURCE: *Water Resources Investigations in Georgia, 1974.* U.S. Dept. of Interior Geological Survey.

Figure 3: Average Annual Runoff

early spring, and midsummer than in May or June or in the usually dry months of October and November.

Water Temperature

Water temperature is another important factor to be considered by paddlers because of the obvious dangers of encountering cold water when you're not prepared for it.

Surface water temperatures tend to follow air temperatures. Generally, the shallower the stream or reservoir, the closer the water temperature will be to the air temperature. Streams show a wide variation in temperature throughout the years, ranging from a low of 32°F in winter to a high of about 90°F on some days in July, August, and early September. Streams also show a daily variation: the smaller the stream, the greater the variations, with the least variation occurring in large rivers. The Flint River may change only one or two degrees in a day while changes in a small stream can be almost equal to the range in the day's air temperature.

Coal-burning steam plants and industrial plants may influence the water temperature in some rivers through thermal discharges. Usually, the added heat is lost within twenty miles downstream from the entry point, but this heat loss depends on the amount of water used, the temperature of the waste water, the size of the stream, the air temperature, and other factors.

Stream Evolution and Morphology

Often, when teaching canoeing or paddling socially, someone will fix an inquisitive stare at a large boulder in midstream and ask, "How in the blazes did that thing get in the middle of the river?" The frequency of being asked this and similar questions about the river has prompted us to include in this book a brief look at river dynamics.

Basically river dynamics represent the relationship between geology and hydraulics, or, expressed differently, what effect flowing water has on the land surface, and, conversely, how the land surface modifies the flow of water.

To begin at a rather obvious point, we all know that water flows downhill, moving from a higher elevation to a lower elevation and ultimately flowing into the sea. Contrary to what many people believe, however, the water on its downhill journey does not flow as smoothly as we sometimes imagine the water in our home plumbing flows. Instead, to varying degrees depending on the geology, it has to pound and fight every inch of the way. Squeezed around obstructions, ricocheted from rock to rock, and funneled from side to side, almost any river's course is tortuous at best. This is because the land was there first and is very reluctant to surrender its domain to the moving water, and therefore it does so very slowly and grudgingly. In other words, the water must literally carve out a place in the land through which to flow. It accomplishes this through erosion.

There are three main types of moving-water erosion; downward erosion, lateral erosion, and headward erosion. All three represent the wearing away of the land by the water. *Downward erosion* is at work continuously on all rivers and can be loosely defined as moving water wearing away the bottom of the river, eroding the geological strata that compose the river bottom, and descending deeper and deeper down into the ground. A graphic example of downward erosion in its purest form is a river that runs through a vertical-walled canyon or gorge. Here the density of the rock forming the

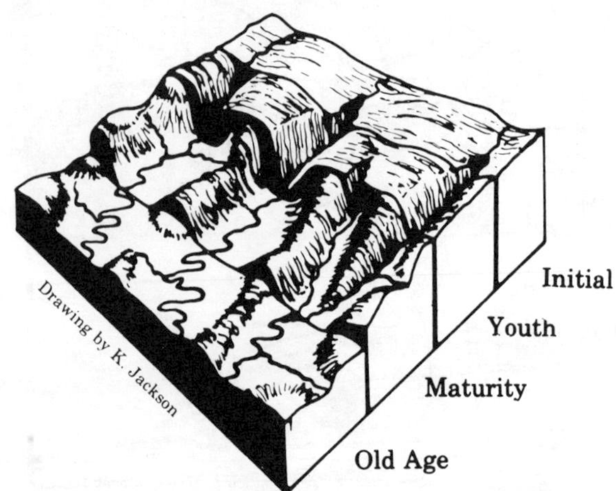

Figure 4: Stages of Erosion, Evolution of a Landscape

Figure 5: Headward Erosion: Waterfalls

canyon walls has limited erosion to the side and left most of the work for downward erosion. Down and down the river cuts without proprotional expansion of its width. A gorge or canyon is formed this way. (see Figure 4.)

Most of the time, however, two and usually three kinds of erosion are working simultaneously. When the water, through downward erosion, for example, cuts into the bottom of the river, it encounters geological substrata of varying density and composition. A layer of clay might overlay a shelf of sandstone, under which may be granite or limestone. Since the water is moving downhill at an angle, the flowing water at the top of a mountain might be working against a completely different type of geological substratum than the water halfway down or at the foot of the mountain. Thus, to carve its channel, the water has to work harder in some spots than in others.

Where current crosses a seam marking the boundary between geological substrata of differing resistance to erosion, an interesting phenomenon occurs. Imagine that upstream of this seam the water has been flowing over sandstone, which is worn away by the erosive action of the current at a rather slow rate. As the current crosses the seam, it encounters limestone, which erodes much faster. Downward erosion wears through the limestone relatively quickly while the sandstone on top remains little changed over the same period of time. The result is a waterfall (see Figure 5). It may only be a foot high or it may be 100 feet high, depending on the thickness of the layer eaten away. The process is complete when the less resistant substratum is eroded and the water again encounters sandstone or another equally resistant formation. The evolution of a waterfall by downward erosion is similar to covering your wooden porch stairs with snow and then smoothing the snow so that from top to bottom the stairs resemble a nice snowy hill in the park, with the normal shape of the stairs being hidden. Wood (the stairs) and snow can both be eaten away by water. Obviously though, the water will melt the snow much faster than it will rot the wood. Thus, if a tiny stream of water is launched downhill from the top of the stairs, it will melt through the snow quickly, not stopping until it reaches the more resistant wood on the next stair down. This is how erosion forms a waterfall in nature.

Once a waterfall has formed, regardless of its size, headward erosion comes into play. *Headward erosion* is the wearing away of the base of the waterfall. This action erodes the substrata in an upstream direction toward the headwaters or source of the stream, thus it is called headward erosion. Water falling over the edge of the waterfall lands below with substantial force. As it hits the surface of the water under the falls, it causes a depression in the surface that water from downstream rushes to fill in. This is a hydraulic, or what paddlers call a souse hole. Continuing through the surface water, the falling current hits the bottom of the stream. Some of the water is disbursed in an explosive manner, some deflected downstream, and some drawn back to the top where it is recirculated to refill the depression made by yet more falling current. A great deal

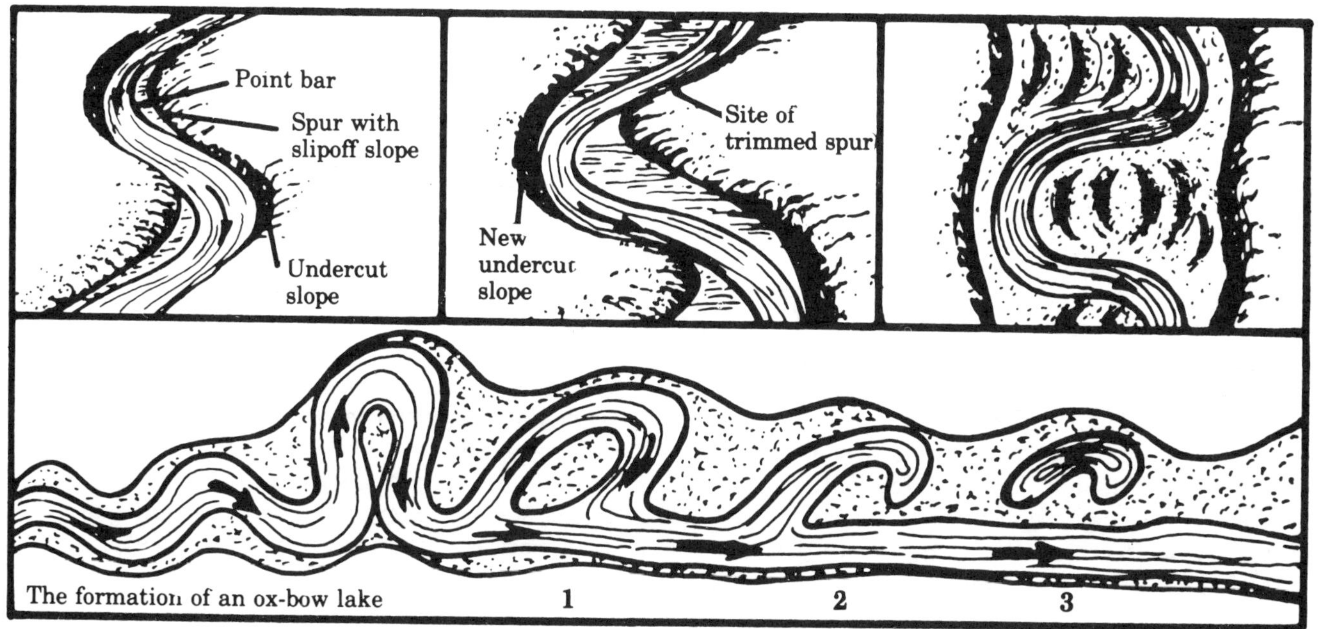

Drawing by K. Jackson

Figure 6: Meanders and Oxbow Lakes

of energy is expended in this process and the ensuing cyclical turbulence, which combines with bits of rock to make an abrasive mixture, carves slowly away at the rock base of the falls. If the falls are small, the turbulence may simply serve to smooth out the drop, turning a vertical drop into a slanting drop. If the falls are large, the base of the falls may be eroded, leaving the top of the falls substantially intact but precariously unsupported. After a period of time the overhang thus created will surrender to gravity and fall into the river. And that is one way that huge boulders happen to arrive in the middle of the river. Naturally the process is ongoing, and the altered facade of the waterfall is immediately attacked by the currents.

Lateral erosion is the wearing away of the sides of the river by the moving current. While occurring continuously on most rivers to a limited degree, lateral erosion is much more a function of volume and velocity (collectively known as discharge and expressed in cubic feet per seconds, cfs) than either downward or headward erosion. In other words, as more water is added to a river (beyond that simply required to cover its bottom), the increase in the volume and the speed of the current cause significant additional lateral erosion while headward and downward erosion remain comparatively constant. Thus, as a river swells with spring rain, the amount of water in the river increases. Since water is noncompressible, the current rises on the banks and through lateral erosion tries to enlarge the river bed laterally to accommodate the extra volume. Effects of this activity can be observed every year following seasonal rains. Even small streams can widen their beds substantially by eroding large chunks of the banks and carrying them downstream. Boulders and trees in the river are often the result of lateral erosion undercutting the bank.

Through a combination of downward erosion, lateral erosion, and meandering, running water can carve broad valleys between mountains and deep canyons through solid rock. Downward and lateral erosion act on the terrain to determine the morphology (depth, width, shape, and course) of a river. Headward erosion serves to smooth out the rough spots that remain.

Curves in a river are formed much as waterfalls are formed; i.e., the water will follow the path of least resistance and its path will twist and turn as it is diverted by resistant substrata. Rivers constantly change and do not continue indefinitely in their courses once they are formed. Water is continuously seeking to decrease the energy required to move from the source to the mouth. This is the essence of all erosion.

As we have observed, headward erosion works upstream to smooth out the waterfalls and rapids. Lateral erosion works to make more room for increased volume, and downward erosion deepens the bed and levels obstructions and irregularities. When a river is young (in the geological sense), it cuts downward and is diverted into sharp turns by differing resistance from underlying rock layers. As a stream matures, it carves a valley, sinks even closer to sea level, and leaves behind, in many instances, a succession of terraces marking previous valley floors.

Moving water erodes the outside of river bends and deposits much of the eroded matter on the inside of the turn, thereby forming a sand or gravel bar. Jagged turns are changed to sweeping bends. The results in more mature streams is a meander, or the formation of a series of horseshoe-shaped and geometrically predictable loops in the river (see Figure 6). A series of such undulating loops markedly widens the valley floor. Often, as time passes, the current erodes the neck of a loop and creates an island in midstream and eliminates a curve in the river; this is called a meander by-pass or cut-off island.

In the theoretically mature stream, the bottom is smooth and undisturbed by obstructing boulders, rapids, or falls. Straight stretches in the river give way to serpentine meanders, and the water flows at a very moderate rate of descent from the source to the sea. Of course, there are no perfect examples of a mature stream, although rivers such as the Ohio and the Mississippi tend to approach the mature end of the spectrum. A stream exhibiting a high gradient and frequent rapids and sharp turns is described as a young stream in the evolutional sense of the word (stream maturity having more to do with the evolutional development of a stream than with actual age; see Figure 4).

All streams carry a load that consists of all the particles, large and small, that are a result of the multiple forms of erosion we discussed. The load, then, is solid matter transported by the current. Rocky streams at high altitudes carry the smallest loads. Their banks and bottoms are more resistant to erosion and their tributary drainages are usually small. Scarcity of load is evident in the clarity of the water. Rivers such as the Mississippi and Ohio carry enormous loads collected from numerous tributaries as well as from their own banks and bottoms. Water in these and in similarly large rivers is almost always dark and murky with sediment. Since it takes a lot of energy to move a load, many rivers transport conspicuous (readily visible) loads only during rainy periods when they are high, fast, and powerful. When the high waters abate, there is insufficient energy to continue to transport the large load that then, for the most part, settles as silt or alluvium on the bottom of the stream.

Understanding stream dynamics gives any boater an added advantage in working successfully with the river. Knowledge of stream evolution and morphology tells a paddler where to find the strongest current and deepest channel, where rapids and falls are most likely to occur, and what to expect from a given river if the discharge increases or decreases. But more, understanding the river's evolution and continuing development contributes immeasurably to the paddler's aesthetic experience and allows for a communion and harmony with the river that otherwise might be superficial.

Volume, Velocity and Gradient

Being able to recognize potential river hazards depends on a practical knowledge of river hydrology—why the water flows the way it does. Since river channels vary greatly in depth and width and the composition of stream beds and their gradients also enter into the river's character, these major components of streamflow bear explanation.

Discharge is the volume of water moving past a given point of the river at any one time. The river current, or velocity, is commonly expressed as the speed of water movement in feet per seconds (fps), and stage is the river's height in feet based on an arbitrary measurement gauge. These terms are interrelated; increased water levels mean increased volume and velocity.

Another factor in assessing stream difficulty is gradient, which is expressed in feet per mile (ft/mi). As gradient increases, so does velocity. The streams profiled in this book have gradients that range from about one foot per mile to an astounding 200 feet per mile. The gradient in any stream or section of a stream changes with the landforms, the geology of the basin. If a river flows over rock or soil with varying resistance to erosion, ledges, waterfalls, and rapids sometimes form and dramatically affect gradient.

Velocity is also affected by the width and depth of the stream bed. Rapids form where streams are shallow and swift. Large obstructions in shallow streams of high velocity cause severe rapids. Within a given channel there are likely to be rapids with different levels of difficulty. The current on straight sections of river is usually fastest in the middle. The depth of water in river bends is determined by flow rates and soil types; water tends to cut away the land and form deep holes on the outside of bends where the current is the swiftest.

Savannah River Wildlife Refuge.

Photo courtesy of *Brown's Guide to Georgia.*

Chapter 3

Georgia's Land and Water

Physiographic Regions of Georgia

To understand and appreciate the varied and beautiful waterways of Georgia, it is necessary to understand something of the geology and topography of the state. Water shaped Georgia into its present physical form by attacking, eroding and dissolving the land for millions of years. Everytime it rains a little more of Georgia is carried away to the sea as grains of sand or dissolved salts. The rock shapes resulting from this continual action of water make possible the division of the state into five major physiographic provinces or regions. (See Figure 7.)

Distinguishing these provinces are differences in rock strata. Some rocks lie flat, one on top of the other like the pages in a book. Other rocks are folded, while still others are broken, cracked, and without apparent layering. Each of these rock types reacts differently to the action of water.

Georgia has been subjected to the unheavals of the earth time after time in recent millenia. Oceans sweeping across the state have eroded the land in one place and built it up in others. In northwestern Georgia, the Cumberland Plateau region and the Valley and Ridge region are characterized by parallel valleys and ridges that are underlain by Paleozoic sedimentary rocks, some of which lie nearly flat and some are much folded. The Blue Ridge region is a mountainous area underlain by very hard crystalline rocks. The Piedmont, adjacent to the south, is a hilly rolling area where the ridgetops have a uniform level and slope southward. It is underlain by the same crystalline rocks as the Blue Ridge region. The Coastal Plain, stretching south from the Piedmont to Florida and the sea, is nearly flat everywhere and is underlain by thick beds of sand and limestone that were deposited in an ocean whose shoreline was north of Macon. The streams of the more mountainous sections of the state are found in a companion book, *Northern Georgia Canoeing: A Canoeing and Kayaking Guide to the Streams of the Cumberland Plateau, Blue Ridge Mountains and Eastern Piedmont.*

Climatic conditions are similar in all parts of Georgia although northern Georgia is slightly cooler and wetter than southern Georgia. Geology, topography, and stream channel development, however, vary significantly from region to region.

Piedmont Region

The Piedmont region is the most densely populated part of the state. About 66 percent of Georgia's population inhabits this region, which contains 31 percent of the state's area. The Piedmont was primarily an agricultural region for two centuries. In the last half century, however, the textile industry has expanded, and in recent years a completely diversified industrial expansion has taken place.

The Piedmont is underlain by the same crystalline rocks as the Blue Ridge, but it lacks the high relief of the Blue Ridge Mountain region. Instead it is an area of rolling plain broken occasionally by narrow stream valleys and prominent hills. The soil cover in the Piedmont is not as thick or as capable of slowing runoff as that of the Blue Ridge.

The Piedmont region includes parts of several drainages. The Savannah, Ogeechee, Ocmulgee, and Oconee rivers drain into the Atlantic Ocean while the Flint and Chattahoochee drain into the Gulf of Mexico. Throughout most of the region the main streams flow southeastward, the direction of the general slope of the upland, and cross the underlying rock structure at right angles. In the northwestern section of the Piedmont, the Chattahoochee and some streams in the Mobile basin tend to parallel the direction of the rock strata. Rivers there generally have moderate slopes interrupted by occasional rapids and falls and flow in well-defined channels within comparatively narrow valleys.

The ridges between the major drainage systems of the Piedmont are broad and rather sinuous and have the region's primary cities, highways, railroads, and farmlands concentrated on top of them. Towns were established on the ridges along the old wagon trails and railroads because the ridges were well-drained routes that required a minimum number of bridges and were free of the danger of floods.

Rainfall along the northern Piedmont, the area of highest elevation, averages more than 50 inches annually. To the south and east the rainfall is less. The Augusta area receives less than any other part of the state, a little more than 42 inches annually.

Coastal Plain Region

Over sixty percent of Georgia lies in the Coastal Plain, with the population concentrated along the Fall Line (where the Piedmont descends to the Coastal Plain) in the cities of Augusta, Macon, and Columbus, and in the coastal city of Savannah.

Because of the great difference in the runoff characteristics of the Coastal Plains streams, hydrologists differentiate between the upper Coastal Plain and the lower Coastal Plain. Streams in the upper Coastal Plain have relatively uniform flows and high volume because of small storm runoff and large groundwater inflow. The very small streams commonly have very little runoff because the permeable soil absorbs rainwater rapidly and the channels are not entrenched deeply enough to intercept much groundwater flow. The average annual runoff of the larger streams ranges from 12 to 28 inches. The streams are generally sluggish and flow in deep meandering, low-banked, tree-choked channels bordered by wide, swampy, densely wooded valleys.

The lower Coastal Plain generally has the least runoff of any part of Georgia, averaging from 9 to 14 inches annually. The streams wander in wide, swampy, heavily wooded valleys separated by very wide and very low, flat ridges. Swamp vegetation consumes large quantities of water and evaporation loss is high.

Cretaceous sand aquifers, a blanket of sand and gravel, begin at the Fall Line and thicken to the south. Rainfall filters into this sand blanket and recharges the sand aquifer with water. When the stream levels are high, water moves from the streams into the sands. When the stream levels are low, water feeds back from the sands into the streams.

In the southwestern area of the upper Coastal Plain, near Albany, limestone–sand aquifers give rise to lime sinks, caves, underground rivers, and artesian wells. These features are formed by the solvent action of water on limestone. When the limestone is dissolved, caverns and interconnected channels are left below the surface. If the cavern roof collapses, sink holes are created.

Streams originating in the Coastal Plain generally carry very little sediment. Running over sand and sandy clay, their waters flow clear and sparkling, colored a reddish tea color by tannic acid derived from decaying vegetation. Streams crossing the Coastal Plain that originate in the Piedmont or in the Blue Ridge transport heavy loads of sediment.

The annual rainfall in the Coastal Plain averages from 45 to 52 inches, draining slowly over the flat terrain, with the part that does not sink into the ground quickly evaporated or consumed by vegetation.

Water and Rivers in Georgia

Georgia receives approximately 50 inches of rainfall each year, primarily in the winter and early spring. Due to the varied topography of the state, the mean annual precipitation varies from place to place and ranges from a maximum of 68 inches to a minimum of 40 inches.

Of the state's mean annual average rainfall of 50 inches, only 9 to 24 inches (depending on the part of the state) becomes a part of the surface or groundwater system. The remaining inches return to the atmosphere by evaporation or transpiration.

Since the greater part of the rainfall occurs during the winter when plant life is dormant, the soil must store moisture for plant use during the periods of minimum rainfall. However, the capacity of the soil to retain moisture varies considerably over the state. A soil of one type can receive more rainfall than another but can experience drought conditions quicker because of its inability to hold moisture.

Several of the chief surface-water systems in Georgia are dam controlled. The smaller tributaries of these great systems are not regulated. Their flow varies greatly from year to year, from month to month, and from day to day. Average streamflow in a wet year may be five or ten times that in a dry year, but flow in a wet month may be several thousand times that in a dry month, and the flow during the instant of flood peak may be tens of hundreds of thousands times greater than the minimum daily flow. The low flow dependability of the streams of the state varies according to their geographic location.

Georgia Streamflow

The amount of water that finds its way into the stream channels of Georgia is on the average less than half of the rain that falls on the state. Streamflow is residual water that is left over after the heavy demands of evaporation and transpiration have been met.

Streamflow is made up basically of two runoff components. These are direct runoff, or the water that flows over the ground or just under the surface during and immediately after a rainstorm, and ground-water storage that comes out in seeps and springs for days and weeks after the rain. Direct runoff supplies most of the volume of streamflow in flood periods. Ground-water runoff feeds the streams in the periods between rains.

The proportion of total streamflow that comes from direct runoff or ground-water runoff varies among streams, depending on such watershed features as elevation of the land and the density and type of vegetation.

The Major Drainages of Georgia*

Georgia, the largest state east of the Mississippi River, encompasses nearly sixty thousand square miles and has ten major river basins. It is estimated that there are over 20,000 miles of streams in Georgia. All of Georgia's rivers flow south except tributaries of the Tennessee River. The Coosa River and its tributaries in northwest Georgia represent the eastern headwaters of the Alabama River system and cross out of the state into Alabama. All other large drainages flow within Georgia though the Savannah has numerous South Carolina tributaries and the Chattachoochee has many Alabama tributaries. Two of Georgia's largest rivers, the Flint and the Chattahoochee, meet at Lake Seminole near the southwestern corner of the state to form the Apalachicola River, which runs through Florida to the Gulf of Mexico. These rivers, therefore, are considered part of the Apalachicola system.

Rivers of the Savannah, Altamaha, Apalachicola, and Ogeechee systems flow through two or more physiographic regions and their flow characteristics change to reflect regional differences in rainfall, runoff, topography, and rock structure.

The Satilla flows entirely within the Georgia Coastal Plain while the Ochlockonee and Suwannee systems originate in the Coastal Plain and cross into Florida. In the far southeastern corner of Georgia the St. Marys River forms the Florida–Georgia boundary.

Flow from the Savannah, Ogeechee, Altamaha, Satilla, and St. Marys systems empties into the Atlantic Ocean while the Apalachicola (Flint and Chattahoochee), Ochlockonee, Alabama (Coosa), and Suwannee drain into the Gulf of Mexico.

The Savannah, Altamaha, Ogeechee, Alabama, and Apalachicola systems carry large sediment loads and are therefore considered to be "alluvial rivers." Distinguished from these rivers are those drainages that originate on the Coastal Plain. The Coastal Plain drainages run over sandy beds and transport very little suspended sediment. Their water is characteristically colored red from the tannic acid released by tree roots and decaying vegetation. Because the red water appears glossy and black in direct sunlight, these streams are known as "blackwater rivers."

The Altamaha is the largest river lying wholly within Georgia's boundaries. Originating in the Piedmont, flowing across the Coastal Plain and entering the Atlantic near St. Simons Island, the Altamaha drains 14,200 square miles. The longest river in Georgia is the Chattahoochee, which runs 436 miles from source to mouth. The Chattahoochee's 8,770 square mile drainage area includes part of southeastern Alabama and lies in three physiographic regions, the Blue Ridge, the Piedmont, and the Coastal Plain.

Of the four major systems that cross the Piedmont into the Coastal Plain, only the Ogeechee remains free flowing. All of the others (Apalachicola, Savannah, Altamaha) are punctuated to varying degrees with dams, lakes, and other navigational and flood control projects.

Alabama–Coosa River Basin of Alabama and Georgia

The upper reaches of the Coosa and Tallapoosa rivers drain about 5,350 square miles in northwestern Georgia. This area is a part of the extensive Alabama–Coosa river basin, which extends about 320 miles from southeastern Tennessee and northwestern Georgia diagonally across Alabama to the southwestern corner of that state.

The Coosa River is formed by the junction of the Oostanaula and Etowah rivers at Rome. Their headwaters, which rise in the Blue Ridge Mountains, include the Conasauga, Coosawattee, Cartecay, and Ellijay rivers, all scenic mountain streams flowing through steep, narrow, forested valleys among high, rounded mountains. The Oostanaula River is 47 miles long and has a relatively flat slope. The Etowah River is 150 miles long. Rising in the Blue Ridge Mountains, the Etowah falls steeply for about 60 miles, then more moderately for the remaining distance to its junction with the Oostanaula. From its beginning at Rome, the Coosa River flows westward though a wide valley between high ridges for about 30 miles before reaching the Alabama line. This part of the Coosa River passes through the old Corps of Enginners' Mayos Bar Pool

---

*Much of the information in this section was derived from *Water Resources Development in Georgia*, South Altantic Division, U.S. Army Corps of Engineers.

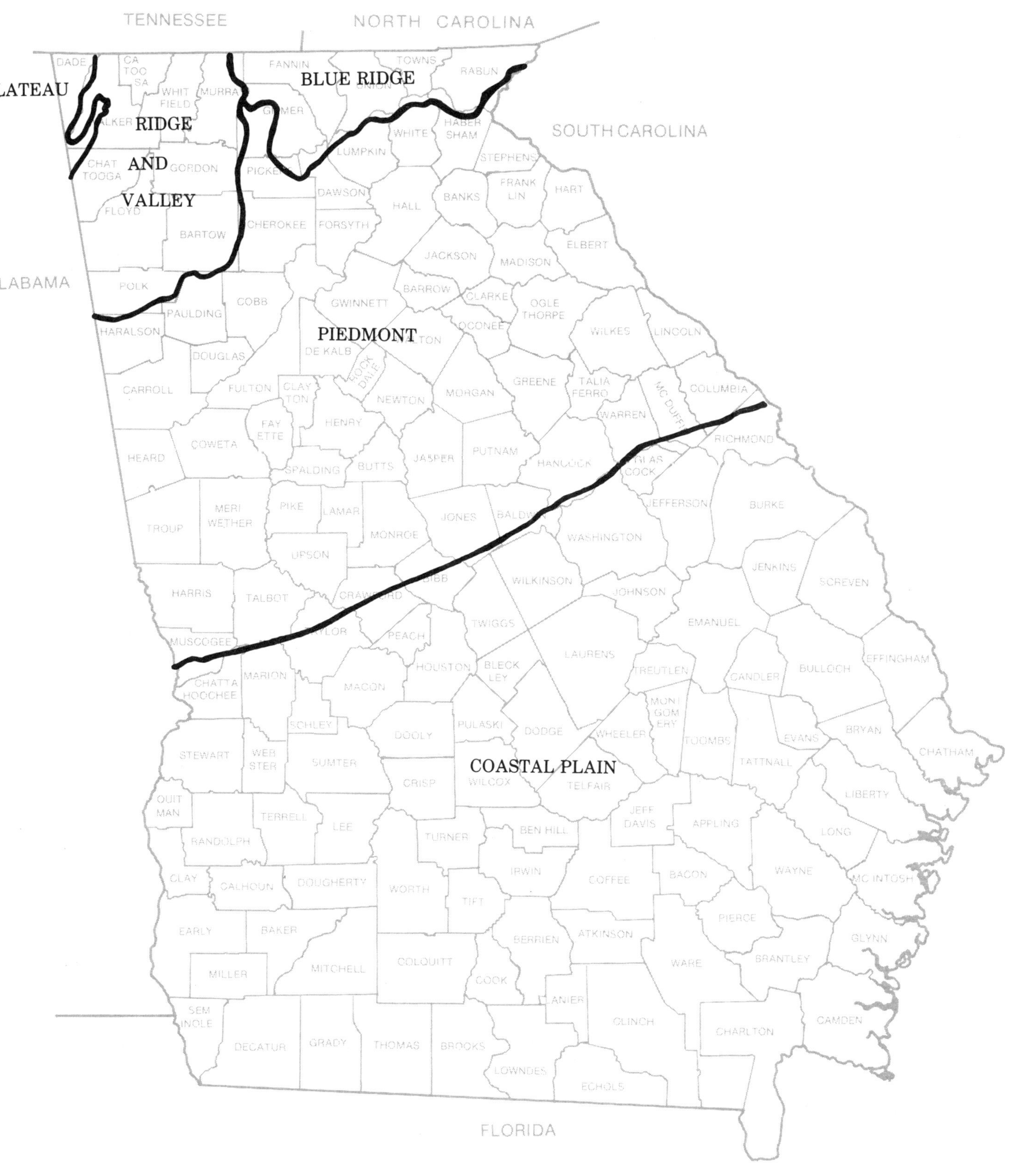

Figure 7: Physiographic Regions of Georgia

SOURCE: *Water Quality Monitoring Data for Georgia Streams, 1977.* Georgia Department of Natural Resources, Environmental Protection Division. Drawing by K. Jackson.

and the Alabama Power Company's Weiss Lake. The Coosa River and its headwaters drain about 4,630 square miles in Georgia.

The Tallapoosa River begins about 40 miles west of Atlanta and flows southwestward through hilly terrain for about 45 miles in Georgia before entering Alabama. It drains about 720 square miles in Georgia.

Rainfall is plentiful in the basin, and generalized storms periodically inundate bottom lands along the principal streams in Georgia. Streamflows, if controlled, would be adequate for foreseeable water supply needs along the larger streams. Unfortunately, pollution is a problem near large population centers.

Agriculture is a major factor in the economy of the area, but, as a result of rapid industrial development, manufacturing has become an integral part of the economy. Major industries produce textiles, machine parts, and wood and food products. Manufacturing is centered mainly in Rome, but it is also scattered in smaller urban areas throughout the region.

Apalachicola–Chattahoochee–Flint River Basin of Florida, Georgia and Alabama

The Apalachicola–Chattahoochee—Flint River system drains an area of 19,600 square miles, of which 8,770 square miles lies along the Chattahoochee River arm, 8,460 square miles lie along the Flint River arm, and the remaining 2,370 square miles lie along the Apalachicola River below the confluence of the Chattahoochee and Flint rivers. Beginning in northeastern Georgia, this basin extends for 385 miles to the Gulf of Mexico. It covers most of northern and western Georgia, an area of about 14,400 square miles, and extends into southeastern Alabama and northwestern Florida. The largest Georgia cities in the basin are Atlanta, Albany, Bainbridge, and Columbus.

The main stem of the system is the Apalachicola River, which flows southward across northwestern Florida from the vicinity of the Georgia line to the Gulf, a distance of about 108 miles. The Apalachicola is formed by the junction of the Chattahoochee and Flint rivers in the southwestern corner of Georgia.

The Chattahoochee River flows 120 miles southwestward from the Blue Ridge Mountains in northeastern Georgia near the western tip of South Carolina. It then flows southward for 200 miles, forming the boundary between Georgia and Alabama and between Georgia and a small portion of Florida.

The Flint River flows south in a wide eastward arc from the southeastern edge of Atlanta for 349 miles to its junction with the Chattahoochee River.

The topography of the Apalachicola–Chattahoochee–Flint river basin varies widely; elevations range from 4500 feet above mean sea level to sea level. In Georgia, the land is low, rolling, clay hills and sandy bottoms along the lower Chattahoochee River and broad, often swampy, flatlands along the lower Flint River that extend to the Fall Line, which is the transition zone between the Coastal Plain and the upland plateau of the central part of the state. Both rivers fall about 375 feet in this transition zone. Practically all the fall on the Chattahoochee River has been developed for power generation by a series of privately owned dams betwen West Point and Columbus. The upper reaches of the Flint River and about 200 miles of the Chattahoochee River above the Fall Line flow through a plateau characterized by red hills somewhat steeper than those of the Coastal Plain. The uppermost reaches of the Chattahoochee River watershed extend into the Blue Ridge Mountains, where rugged, densely wooded knobs, rising to as much as 4,500 feet above sea level, are not uncommon.

The climate in the basin is generally mild and humid. Rainfall is usually greater in the upper and lower areas than in the center. Major flood-producing storms usually occur in the winter or spring and last for several days. Floods in the upper basin tend to be sudden because of the hilly terrain and high runoff rates, while floods in the lower basin tend to rise more slowly and last longer because of the flatter land and more moderate slope of the streams.

The long growing season, abundant rainfall, and productive soils have made agriculture a major component of the basin's economy. However, the trend is toward fewer farms and larger farm units. Principal sources of farm income are poultry and poultry products in the region above Atlanta, and field crops, nuts and fruits in the upper Coastal Plain. Although forest products are important throughout the basin, they are of primary importantance only in the lower reaches.

Altamaha River Basin

All 14,200 square miles of the Altamaha River basin are in the state of Georgia. The basin is 260 miles long, has a minimum width of about six miles at the lower end, a miximum width of about eighty miles, and an average width of fifty-five miles.

The headwaters of the river rise in the Piedmont along the base of the Chattahoochee Ridge between Atlanta and a point ten miles north-northeast of Gainesville. The two principle tributaries, the Ocmulgee and Oconee rivers, unite to form the Altamaha River. The confluence of these streams is known locally as The Forks near Hazlehurst.

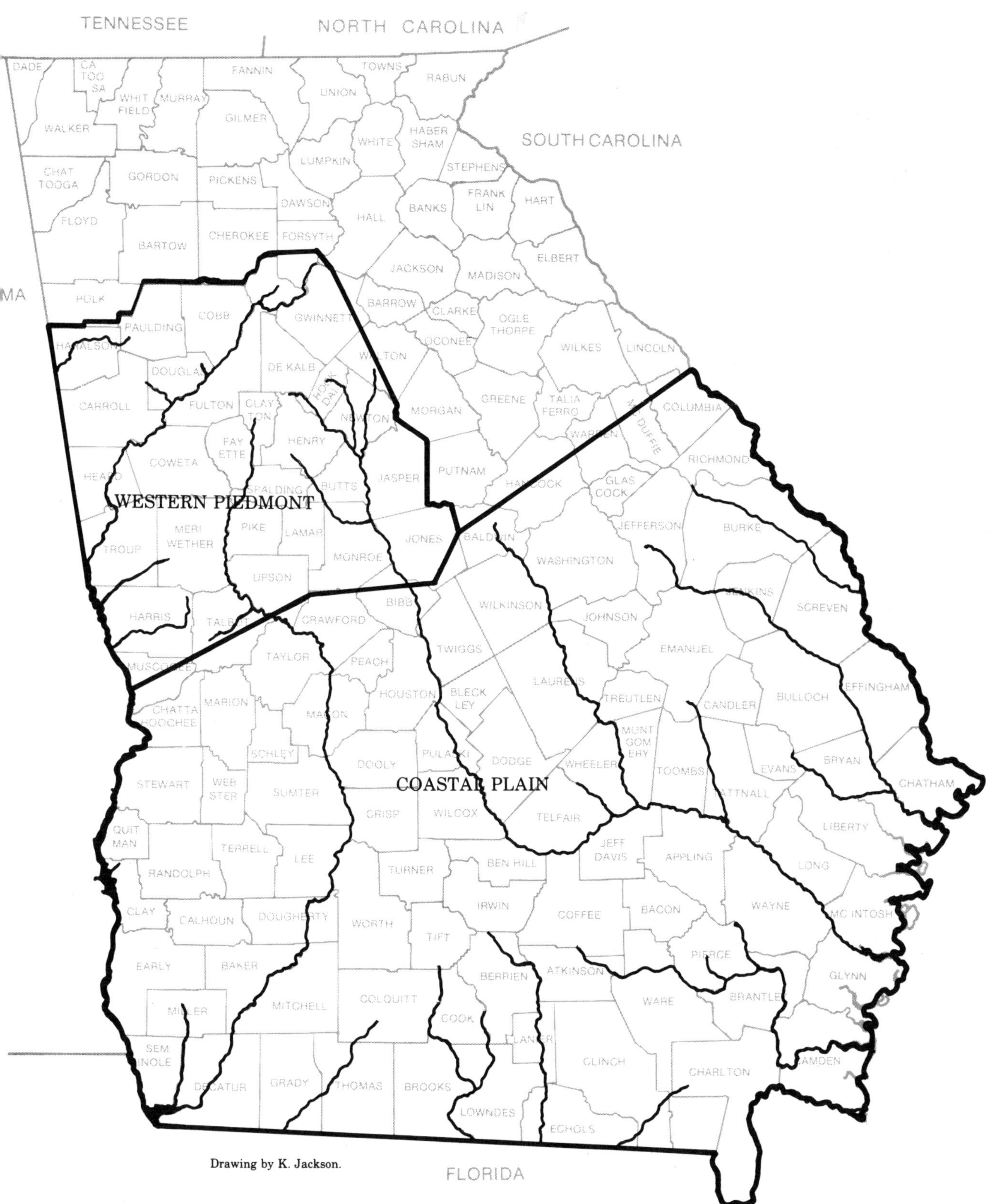

Drawing by K. Jackson.

Figure 8: Canoeing Divisions

The Altamaha River system has its headwaters and about 5,800 square miles of its drainage area in the central uplands of Georgia. The remaining 8,400 square miles of drainage area, which include that of the lower Ocmulgee, lower Oconee, and the Altamaha proper, lie in the Coastal Plain.

The headwaters of the Ocmulgee River are in the vicinity of Altanta at an elevation of about 1,000 feet above mean sea level (m.s.l.). The South and Yellow rivers join to form the Ocmulgee at a location within Jackson Lake, a reservoir with normal elevation 530 feet m.s.l. formed by the Lloyd Shoals Dam at about elevation 530 feet m.s.l. The Ocmulgee River flows in a generally narrow valley over rocky shoals about 43 miles and falls steeply to Macon, Georgia, where the river enters the Coastal Plain and the slope becomes gentle. The floodplain widens greatly below Macon and becomes a wooded swamp up to three miles wide in places.

The headwaters of the Oconee River rise at the base of the Chattahoochee Ridge. The North Oconee and Middle Oconee rivers join to form the Oconee River about six miles south of Athens. The Apalachee River enters the Oconee from the northeast at Carey. The Little River of Putnam County enters the Oconee at Lake Sinclair, a reservoir with normal elevation 340 feet m.s.l. that is formed by the Furman Shoals Dam of the Georgia Power Company just above Milledgeville. In this reach the Oconee has the characteristic rocky stream bed, shoals and pools of upland or mountain streams. The river valley is narrow and bordered by high hills. This portion of the Altamaha River basin is described in a companion book, *Northern Georgia Canoeing: A Canoeing and Kayaking Guide to the Streams of the Cumberland Plateau, Blue Ridge Mountains and Eastern Piedmont*. The lower Altamaha River basin is described in this book.

Below Milledgeville the Oconee River is very crooked, flows in a floodplain up to 4.5 miles wide, and is similar to the Ocmulgee River south of Macon. The materials in the banks of the low-water channel are also similar to those of the Ocmulgee. Rock shoals are numerous between river miles 73 and 105. A few rock outcrops are found in the stream bed below this reach and in the vicinity of Milledgeville.

From the junction of the Oconee and Ocmulgee Rivers, the Altamaha River flows through a broad, relatively flat floodplain to the Atlantic. The floodplain is typical of meandering, alluvial streams. It consists of swamps, hardwood forests, and sandy ridges.

At a point 22.8 miles above the mouth, the river divides into two branches, the Altamaha and the South Altamaha. These branches reunite and again subdivide into three mainstreams: Altamaha River, which empties into Altamaha Sound; South Altamaha River, which empties into Buttermilk Sound; and Darien River, which empties into Doboy Sound. These three delta streams are 1,000 to 2,000 feet wide. Tidal effects extend up the Altamaha River to about mile 39.

The Atlantic Intracoastal Waterway extends from Trenton, New Jersey, to Fort Pierce, Florida, at a depth of twelve feet, from Fort Pierce to Miami at a depth of ten feet; and from Miami to Key West at a depth of seven feet. The waterway traverses Buttermilk Sound at the mouth of the Altamaha River.

Ogeechee River Basin

The Ogeechee River basin lies in eastern Georgia and includes the drainage of the Ogeechee River and its tributaries and areas between the Savannah and Altamaha basins that drain directly into the Atlantic Ocean. It is wedge-shaped, 170 miles in length, and about 45 miles wide at its base along the Atlantic coast.

The basin area totals 5,535 square miles. The land area totals 5,436 square miles, and 99 square miles are in large water bodies. The land area includes small water bodies such as farm ponds, small reservoirs, and stream basins less than one mile in width, which cover about 43 square miles. There are twenty-one counties within or partly within the basin.

A chain of islands bordering the Atlantic Ocean coastline so impressed the first Spanish explorers that they named them the Golden Isles, and of these, Wassaw Island, Ossabaw Island, St. Catherines Island, Blackbeard Island, and Sapelo Island are included in the Ogeechee basin.

Maximum elevations of about 650 feet above mean sea level occur near Union Point in the Piedmont province. This area constitutes about 5 percent of the basin area and is rather steeply rolling.

The upper Coastal Plain extends some 90 miles to the southeast and includes about 57 percent of the basin area. This area ranges from gently rolling to nearly level and has well-drained sandy soils and many small diversified farms.

The lower Coastal Plain, making up about 38 percent of the basin area, is nearly flat. Mixed pine and hardwood forests cover much of the land, giving way to swamp conditions in the lower lying areas. At the extreme seaward end of the lower Coastal Plain, land and water form an irregular and intricate pattern in which estuaries, sloughs, lagoons, mudflats, brackish water, and fringing islands all play an important role.

The Ogeechee River, about 245 miles long, flows

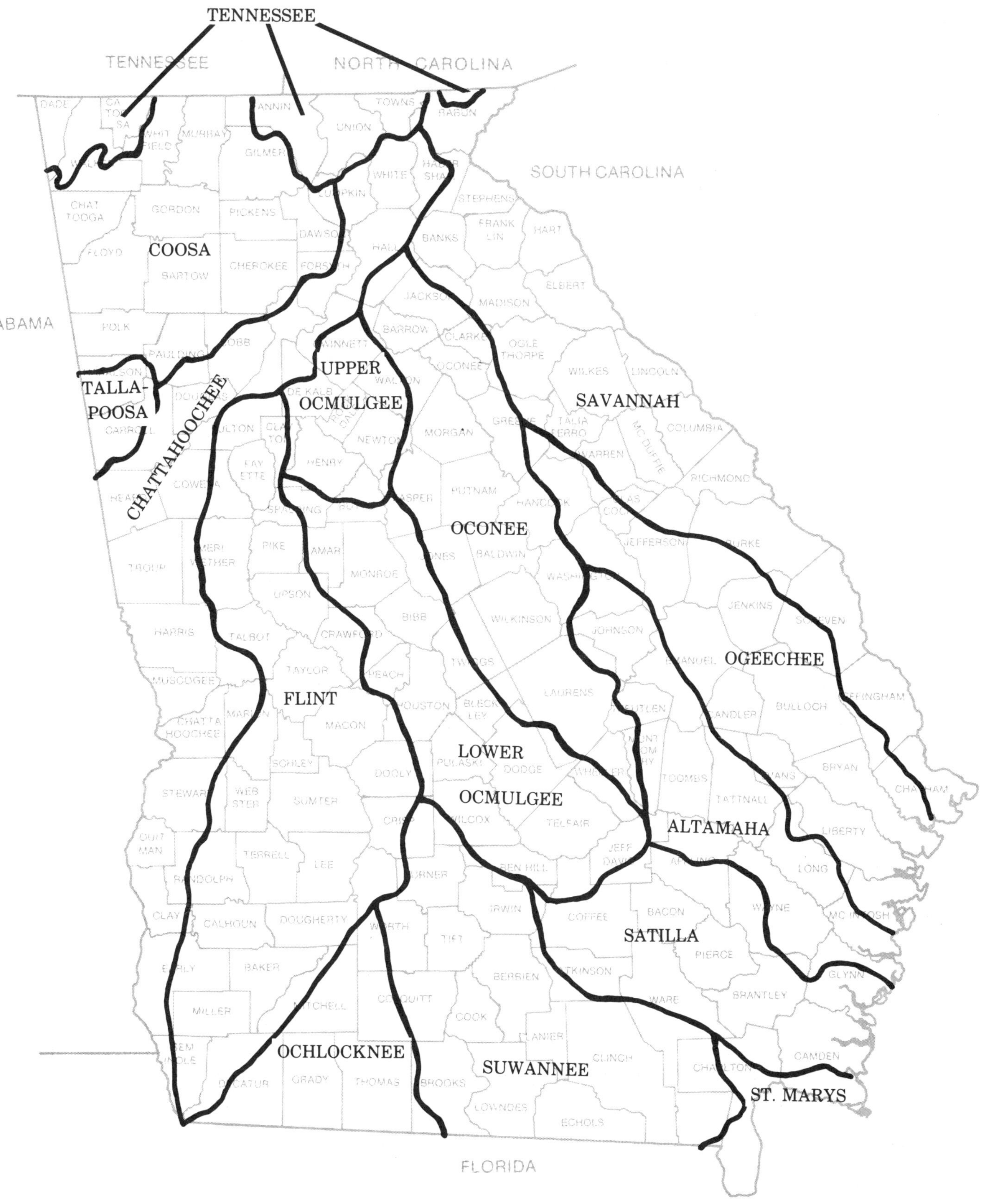

Figure 9: River Basins of Georgia

SOURCE: *Water Quality Monitoring Data for Georgia Streams, 1977.* Georgia Department of Natural Resources, Environmental Protection Division. Drawing by K. Jackson.

the length of the basin and empties into Ossabaw Sound 15 miles south of Savannah, Georgia. Its principal tributary, the Canoochee River, originates in the upper Coastal Plain southwest of the Ogeechee River and for most of its 85 miles flows parallel to the Ogeechee. The Canoochee River joins the Ogeechee River about 35 miles above its mouth.

The basin has long, warm summers and short, mild winters. Snowfall is extremely rare. The mild climate has important agricultural implications as it permits three to five hay cuttings each year and a second crop of legumes or grain sorghum after the first harvest of small grain in early summer. Livestock require little, if any, winter housing and are able to graze nine to twelve months of the year.

The average yearly rainfall over the basin ranges from 45 inches in the upper basin to 52 inches along the coast. The wettest months are June through September. The runoff from the basin averages about 11 inches annually, or 3 million acre-feet.

The basin usually has an ample suppy of surface and ground water of good quality. Except for the area that drains directly into the Atlantic Ocean, the Ogeechee River and its tributaries drain nearly the entire basin. There are no large storage reservoirs, hydroelectric plants, or major stream diversions in the basin. The many small lakes, reservoirs and ponds have little effect on the streamflow.

Tidal effects extend upstream to just above the junction of the Canoochee and Ogeechee rivers. The saltwater wedge extends nearly as far, depending on the flow of the stream.

Savannah River Basin of Georgia and South Carolina

The Savannah River basin has a surface area of 10,577 square miles, of which 4,581 square miles are in western South Carolina, 5,821 square miles in Georgia, and 175 square miles in southwestern North Carolina.

The headwaters of the Savannah River are on the high forested slopes of the Blue Ridge Mountains in North Carolina, South Carolina, and Georgia. The Tallulah and Chattooga rivers, which form the Tugaloo River on the Georgia–South Carolina state line, and the Whitewater and Toxaway rivers, which form Keowee River in South Carolina, start in the mountains of North Carolina. Keowee River and Twelve Mile Creek join near Clemson, South Carolina, to form the Seneca River. The two principal headwater streams, the Seneca and Tugaloo rivers, join near Hartwell, Georgia, to form the Savannah River.

From this point, the Savannah flows about 300 miles south-southeastward to discharge into the Atlantic Ocean near Savannah, Georgia. Its major downstream tributaries include the Broad River in Georgia, the two Little rivers in Georgia and South Carolina, Brier Creek in Georgia, and Stevens Creek in South Carolina.

The topography of the basin descends from an elevation of 5,500 feet at the headwaters of the Tallulah River, to about 1,000 feet in the rolling and hilly Piedmont, to around 200 feet at Augusta, Georgia, to the gently rolling then nearly flat Coastal Plain from Augusta to the Atlantic Ocean. In the mountains, the summers are moderately cool, and the winters are cold. In the Piedmont and the Coastal Plain, the summers are warm and the winters are mild. The average annual rainfall in the basin is about 53 inches. Snow cover is rare except in the mountains.

Runoff averages about 15 inches annually for the entire drainage area. Runoff at Augusta, Georgia, averages about 19 inches, compared with the United States average of 8 inches. The total streamflow varies considerably from year to year. In addition, there is also great variation within a year. Streams in the basin are typically high in the winter and early spring. During the summer and warm weather, flows recede and remain low through autumn.

The Savannah basin is predominantly forested. The wildlife resources of the basin are many and varied. Most of the land supports game animals. Small game is found principally on agricultural lands, while wild ducks and geese are found in the swamps and marshes.

Industry has settled along the Savannah River at Augusta, Georgia, where there is an inland port, and Savannah, Georgia, where there is a deep-draft harbor.

Ochlockonee–Aucilla River Basins

The upper portions of the Ochlokonee and Aucilla river basins form a triangular area in southwestern Georgia with its apex in Worth County. The area covers about 1,500 square miles and includes parts of seven counties. The principal city is Thomasville.

The Georgia portions of the basins lie entirely in the lower Coastal Plain and are characterized by rolling terrain with broad ridges and gentle slopes. The principal land uses are forestry, general farming, and livestock production.

The Ochlockonee and Aucilla rivers both originate in Georgia and flow generally south through Florida to the Gulf of Mexico. For the most part, the Georgia portions of the streams and their tributaries are sluggish and flow in low-banked, tree-choked meandering channels.

Aucilla River Basin. The Aucilla River originates in Thomas County, Georgia, ten miles northeast of

Thomasville. It drains about 800 square miles as it flows south across south-central Georgia and northwestern Florida to the Gulf. The headwaters are at an elevation of 250 feet above mean sea level. The channel meanders listlessly through a flat area of dense brush. The water goes underground at several places along its course, and at the lower end of the river it flows through a wide marsh. The principal tributary is the crystal-clear Wacissa River.

Ochlockonee River Basin (Georgia and Florida). The Ochlockonee River is about 190 miles long and originates in Worth County, Georgia, at an elevation of 420 feet above mean sea level and flows south and southwest past Thomasville, Georgia, and Tallahassee, Florida, into Lake Talquin. From the lake, it flows in a westerly semicircle to enter the Gulf in an easterly direction through Ochlockonee Bay. The watershed totals about 2,677 square miles. Principal tributaries of the Ochlockonee River are the Little Ochlockonee River, Tired Creek, Little River, Telogia Creek, and Crooked River.

Suwannee River Basin

There are 11,020 square miles in the Suwannee River basin; they are equally divided between south-central Georgia and north-central Florida. Valdosta, Georgia, is the largest city in the basin.

North of the Georgia–Florida state line, in the western part of the basin, are the low, rolling hills of the Georgia portion of the lower Coastal Plain. This area, which is drained by the Alapaha and Withlacoochee rivers, rises gradually from an elevation of about 120 feet at the state line to about 460 feet along the northern divide. Slopes here are generally steeper than in the other parts of the basin. Diversified agriculture is carried on throughout the area.

Okefenokee Swamp lies on the eastern side of the basin. It is fed by several small streams and totals about 1,000 square miles. The Suwannee River drains about 800 square miles of the swamp, and the St. Marys River drains the remainder. The swamp varies in elevation from 100 to 120 feet above mean sea level in the lower Coastal Plain. A low dam, or sill, on the Suwannee River at the swamp outlet controls the water level in most of the swamp to about elevation 115.

Extending from the Florida state line and Okefenokee Swamp flatlands southward to the Gulf of Mexico is the area, largely in the lower Coastal Plain, drained by the Suwannee and Santa Fe rivers. It is characterized generally by less relief, lower elevations, and fewer tributary streams than the rolling lands of Georgia.

The Suwannee and its three large tributaries, the Alapaha, Withlacoochee, and Santa Fe rivers, are similar. Their channels are 15 to 30 feet deep and often cut through the shallow earth overburden well into limestone. The narrow valleys are usually wooded and contain marshes or cypress sloughs. The rises from the valleys to the upland are low but abrupt.

Numerous channels converge at the southwest corner of Okefenokee Swamp near Fargo, Georgia, to form the Suwannee River. It flows south 45 miles to White Springs and then forms a wide loop toward the west, picking up, in turn, its principal tributaries, the Alapaha, Withlacoochee, and Santa Fe rivers. Continuing on southward, the Suwannee empties into the Gulf of Mexico.

The Alapaha River rises in the northernmost part of the basin near elevation 460 and flows generally south-southeastward about 134 miles to its confluence with the Suwannee River some seven miles upstream from Ellaville, Florida.

Tributaries of the Withlacoochee River rise at about elevation 450 along the basin divide southwest of the Alapaha River headwaters. The main Withlacoochee River rises near Tifton, Georgia, and flows south-southeast 86 miles to join the Suwannee River at Ellaville.

The Okefenokee or "Land of the Trembling Earth" was so named by the Seminole Indians because of the unstable floating peat islands. The swamp is one of the largest freshwater swamplands in the United States and by far the most significant inland body of water in the Suwannee basin. About two-thirds of the swamp, including 331,000 acres in Suwannee basin, has been set aside as a wildlife refuge administered by state and federal agencies for wildlife preservation, recreation use, and to maintain its unique beauty and environment. Short stretches of tidal marsh along the Gulf of Mexico adjacent to the river mouth are its only direct exposure to saltwater.

The Suwannee basin encompasses some 7 million acres in a thinly populated area. More than two-thirds of the basin is forested. More than half of the forest is pine, and one-fourth is bottomland hardwoods. Pure upland hardwoods mixed with occasional pines are scattered throughout the basin. About 119,000 acres of the basin forest land are in the Osceola National Forest northeast of Lake City, Florida.

The Suwannee basin has a generous supply of good quality water from both ground water and surface sources.

Satilla–St. Marys River Basin

Satilla River basin lies entirely within the state of Georgia. It is bounded on the north by the Altamaha River basin, on the west by the Suwannee River basin, and on the south by the Okefenokee Swamp and St. Marys River basin.

The Satilla River rises in Ben Hill and Coffee counties at an elevation of about 350 feet. It flows generally east-southeast about 260 river miles and empties into the Atlantic Ocean through St. Andrew Sound. The two principal tributaries of the Satilla River are the Alabaha and the Little Satilla rivers. The Alabaha River's headwaters rise in Jeff Davis County at about elevation 235 and flow generally southeast to join the Satilla at river mile 140. The Little Satilla River headwaters rise in Jeff Davis and Appling counties at about elevation 250 and flow generally southeast to join the Satilla at river mile 107.

The drainage area of the Satilla River covers about 3,530 square miles, of which the principal tributaries, the Little Satilla and Alabaha rivers drain about 829 square miles and 474 square miles, respectively.

At its mouth, the Satilla River is about 1.5 miles wide. It gradually narrows to one-fourth mile in width at mile 7. Between mile 46 and the Seaboard Coast Line railroad crossing at Waycross, Georgia, (mile 166) the river is a winding stream with an average width of about 150 feet.

The Atlantic Intracoastal Waterway passes through St. Andrew Sound near the entrance to the Satilla River. The waterway has a depth of 12 feet and widths of 90 feet in land cuts and narrow streams and 150 feet in open waters. There is an alternate and more protected route of this waterway with a depth of 7 feet at mean low water. The alternate route enters the Satilla River from the north through Dover Creek and leaves the river to the south through Todds Creek.

In the lower reaches of the river it is bordered by a salt marsh that has a maximum width of about three miles. In the upper reaches the river is bordered by swamps, except where touched by bluffs that sometimes reach a height of 50 feet above the river. Above Waycross, the topography is somewhat rolling, the banks are high, and the tributaries are generally well defined. Both the river and tributaries are generally well defined, but both can run through swamplands sometimes as much as one mile wide. Between Waycross and the sea the watershed is covered mostly with timber lands. The high sandy flats are covered with pine, and the lower areas by cypress, gum, and hardwoods. Above Waycross, the land not covered by swamps has a growth of pine, blackjack oak, and some hardwood.

The St. Marys River basin is located in southeastern Georgia and northeastern Florida. It is bounded on the north by the Satilla River basin, on the west and south by the Suwannee River basin, and on the south and east by the Nassau and St. Johns river basins. The area of the watershed is approximately 1,500 square miles.

The St. Marys River originates in the Okefenokee Swamp in Charlton and Ware counties, Georgia, at an elevation between 110 and 120 feet. It flows circuitously eastward about 125 river miles, forming part of the boundary between Georgia and Florida, and empties into the Atlantic Ocean through Cumberland Sound. There are no major tributaries. Minor tributaries are the Middle Prong, Cedar Creek, South Prong, Spanish Creek, Little St. Marys River, and North River.

The St. Marys River is about 1,200 feet wide at St. Marys, Georgia, 600 feet wide at Crandall, Florida, and gradually decreases to 125 feet in width at the head of navigation at Traders Hill, Georgia. Beyond this point, to the headwaters, the river is a winding stream with an average width of about 100 feet.

The economic development of the basin is based largely on the harvesting and processing of timber products. Commercial activities within the basin that are associated with this include the operation of sawmills, planing mills and plywood mills, the cutting and treating of poles and posts, the production of pulpwood, and the production of naval stores. Other commercial activities are the manufacture of cigars and shoes, the production of poultry and livestock, and the growing of grain for feed used locally.

Water Quality in Georgia

Georgia is unique in the type of streams that flow in the state. They include small cold mountain brooks that support native and introduced trout (many of these streams are described in a companion book, *Northern Georgia Canoeing: A Canoeing and Kayaking Guide to the Streams of the Cumberland Plateau, Blue Ridge Mountains and Eastern Piedmont),* larger more turbid streams of the Piedmont, large "black water" streams of the upper and lower Coastal Plain, and short rivers that are influenced by tides for their entire length. Some of the streams of the Coastal Plain of Georgia (including the great Okefenokee Swamp) possess water quality in their natural states that is characterized by low pH, low dissolved oxygen, high color, and very low flows in the late summer and autumn. This natural water extends into some estuarine regions where very low dissolved oxygen concentrations may also occur in the summer and autumn.

No major streams in Georgia are grossly polluted for their entire lengths.

The Atlanta metropolitan area is responsible, through industrial and domestic wastewater and urban runoff, for gross pollution of the Chattahoochee, Flint, and South rivers immediately downstream of Atlanta. Atlanta wastewater adversely influence the water chemistry and organisms of the Flint River to the Flat Shoals region, the South River to and including Jackson Lake, and the Chattahoochee River to West Point. Farther downstream, the city of Columbus and other smaller communities in Alabama degrade the Chattahoochee River, primarily by fecal coliform bacteria in domestic wastes. Many dams on this stream create a hazardous environment for the fauna downstream of the impoundments. Apart from the Atlanta area, the Flint River is noticeably degraded only below the Cordele and Albany (Lake Blackshear) regions. The Flint River in the Bainbridge region is discussed as a portion of Lake Seminole.

The Ocmulgee River is degraded immediately below the Macon area by thermal, industrial, and domestic wastewater. Wastewater from Athens is detectable in the Oconee River; however, recovery occurs a short distance downstream. The Ocmulgee and Oconee rivers become the great Altamaha River downstream from their confluence. The Altamaha River has excellent quality water.

Streams of far lower flow rates drain the southern and southeastern portion of the state. These streams have localized pollution problems, as follows, and recover within a short distance: Withlacoochee River (near Valdosta), Ochlocknee River (near Thomasville and Moultrie), and Satilla River (near Waycross).

The Ogeechee River is one of Georgia's most undisturbed and natural streams. No significant wastewater problems exist. The next major stream to the northeast, the Savannah River, however, is highly developed for navigation (to Augusta). Many impoundments adversely alter the stream as a habitat for aquatic life. Municipalities and industries near Augusta, Georgia, and North Augusta, South Carolina, moderately degrade the steam by contributing large amounts of organic wastewater. Outstanding pollution problems include high fecal coliform bacterial densities and high densities of nuisance periphyton, organisms that live attached to underwater surfaces. In no region, however, can the freshwater portions of the stream be termed grossly polluted.

Of Georgia's many reservoirs, only one, Jackson Lake, is totally eutrophic ("dying"). Seven others,

Table 5: Estimated Natural Water Quality Levels

Estimated Natural Trend Monitoring Index Range	Location
90–100	Savannah River (above Augusta)
	Coosawattee River
	Etowah River
	Chattahoochee River (above West Point)
85–95	Oostanaula River
	Coosa River
	Tallapoosa River
	Chattahoochee River (below West Point)
	South River
	Yellow River
	Savannah River (below Augusta)
	Alcovy River
	Oconee River
	Flint River (above Culloden)
	Conasauga River
80–90	Ogeechee River
	Ocmulgee River
	Altamaha River
	Flint River (below Culloden)
	Chattooga River (Coosa Basin)
75–85	Satilla River
70–80	Suwannee River
	Withlacoochee River
	Ochlockonee River
70–90	Estuarine Waters

Allatoona, Sinclair, Walter F. George, Sidney Lanier, Blackshear, High Falls, and Seminole have localized problems usually involving of one or two embayments, e.g., Lake Seminole has had a nuisance algal problem and high fecal coliform densities downstream from discharges of untreated wastewater from Bainbridge. The new Bainbridge wastewater treatment facility will improve water quality conditions in the upper part of Lake Seminole.

Georgia's coast is the pride of the state and a national treasure. It consists largely of *Spartina* marshes that are responsible for a thriving shrimp fishery. Only two major wastewater sources, the Savannah and Brunswick regions, degrade streams, the Savannah and Turtle rivers, respectively. In the St. Marys area, residual wastewater from a large paper mill degrades the North River, a short tidal stream.

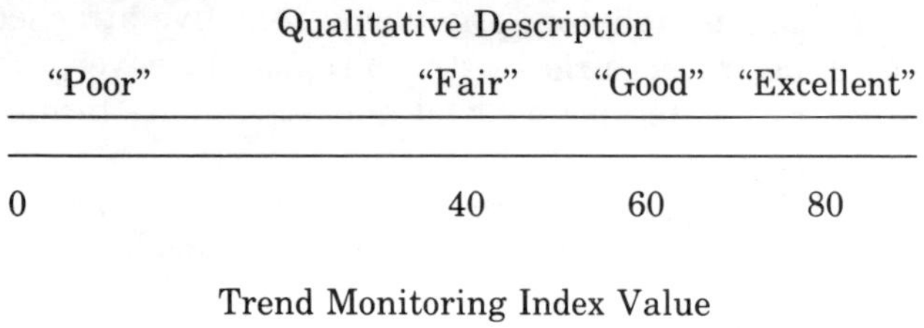

Qualitative Description

"Poor"	"Fair"	"Good"	"Excellent"
0	40	60	80

Trend Monitoring Index Value

Figure 10: The Water Quality Index Scale

In summary, other streams and reaches of streams, apart from some small tributaries, have no serious wastewater problems. Of the many thousands of miles of streams in the state, only 500 miles have serious water quality problems and water quality standards that are being violated. These areas are basically downstream of publicly owned sewage systems. In the near future, it is expected that sections where violations occur will be substantially reduced.

Monitoring Trends in Georgia's Waters

The Georgia Environmental Protection Division operates a trend monitoring network in the streams, lakes, and estuaries of the ten river basins of the state. The trend monitoring network was established in 1967 and has been periodically expanded since that time to the 1977 total of 124 stations from which water samples are collected and analyzed on a routine basis. Most stations are sampled once every three months where specific site conditions do not require more frequent sampling. Each sample collected is analyzed for chemical and fecal coliform bacterial content. Physical properties of the water are also measured.

The Trend Monitoring Index

Due to the complex nature of water quality evaluation and the large number of different parameters routinely used to evaluate water quality, it is helpful to define quality in simple terms that can be understood by everyone. To meet this need, a trend monitoring index is used to compare relative water quality trends throughout the state on a common basis. The trend monitoring index combines eight important physical, chemical, and microbiological measures of water quality in a single number. The index, adapted from a similar index developed by the National Sanitation Foundation, is not intended as a replacement for detailed scientific examination of water quality data, but as a means with which the division provides information on water quality to those without technical training. The trend monitoring index can range from 0 to 100 (see Figure 10), with higher numbers indicating better water quality conditions. The eight items included in the trend monitoring index are:

- Dissolved Oxygen
- Fecal Coliform Bacteria
- pH
- Biochemical Oxygen Demand
- Ammonia
- Nitrite plus Nitrate
- Phosphorus
- Turbidity

For each monitoring station, the trend monitoring index is computed for each sample collected throughout the year. The lowest and highest observed values for the index during the year represent the index range and the annual median index is that value for which one half of the observed index values are higher and the other half of the observed index values are lower. A larger annual index range is indicative of large variations in water quality conditions during the year while a small range indicates stable conditions. Long-term water quality trends are evaluated by comparisons of the annual median index values over several years of record at the same sampling location.

The trend monitoring index has been reported for seven years at selected trend monitoring stations in Georgia, although at some of those the index has been computed for as many as nine years.

The quality of all waters is changing with time as all streams experience seasonal changes according to natural weather patterns. In general, water quality is lowest when temperatures are high and streamflows are low as a result of minimal rainfall. Streams that are influenced by man's activities are subject to additional changes in water quality that are superimposed on the natural quality variations. Man-made influences on quality include runoff from farm lands and developed areas, the discharge of municipal and industrial wastewater, and the operation of stream impoundments.

Natural water quality limits also vary from one physiographic region to another in Georgia. For example, streams of southern Georgia can exhibit natural pH values as low as 4 and dissolved oxygen concentrations as low as 3.5 milligrams

Although most streams are influenced by man's activities, it is possible to estimate the probable natural limits for water quality at most locations on the basis of a detailed interpretation of available data. Table 5 shows that natural trend monitoring index values can range from 70 to 100 in Georgia. Although single values for the index have been found to run as high as 100, it is unlikely that any stream, natural or otherwise, could have a yearly median index greater than 95.

Water quality in 95 percent of Georgia's 20,000 miles of streams is in the good or excellent range and meets the federal "fishable, swimmable" requirements. Additionally, there are other near-natural streams that marginally meet the "fishable, swimmable" standard where growth and development in the future, without precaution, might trigger a decline in water quality.

Where the trend monitoring index was in the fair or poor range, the problems could usually be related to municipal or industrial wastewater discharges. However, non-point sources of pollution, such as urban area runoff, can reduce the index to the fair, or even poor, range for limited periods of time.

Note: Much of the information contained herein was provided by the Environmental Protection Division, Georgia Department of Natural Resources.

Southern Georgia "blackwater" stream.

Photo courtesy of *Brown's Guide to Georgia.*

The Streams of Southern Georgia

Yellow River.

Photo courtesy of *Brown's Guide to Georgia.*

Chapter 4

Streams of the Western Piedmont

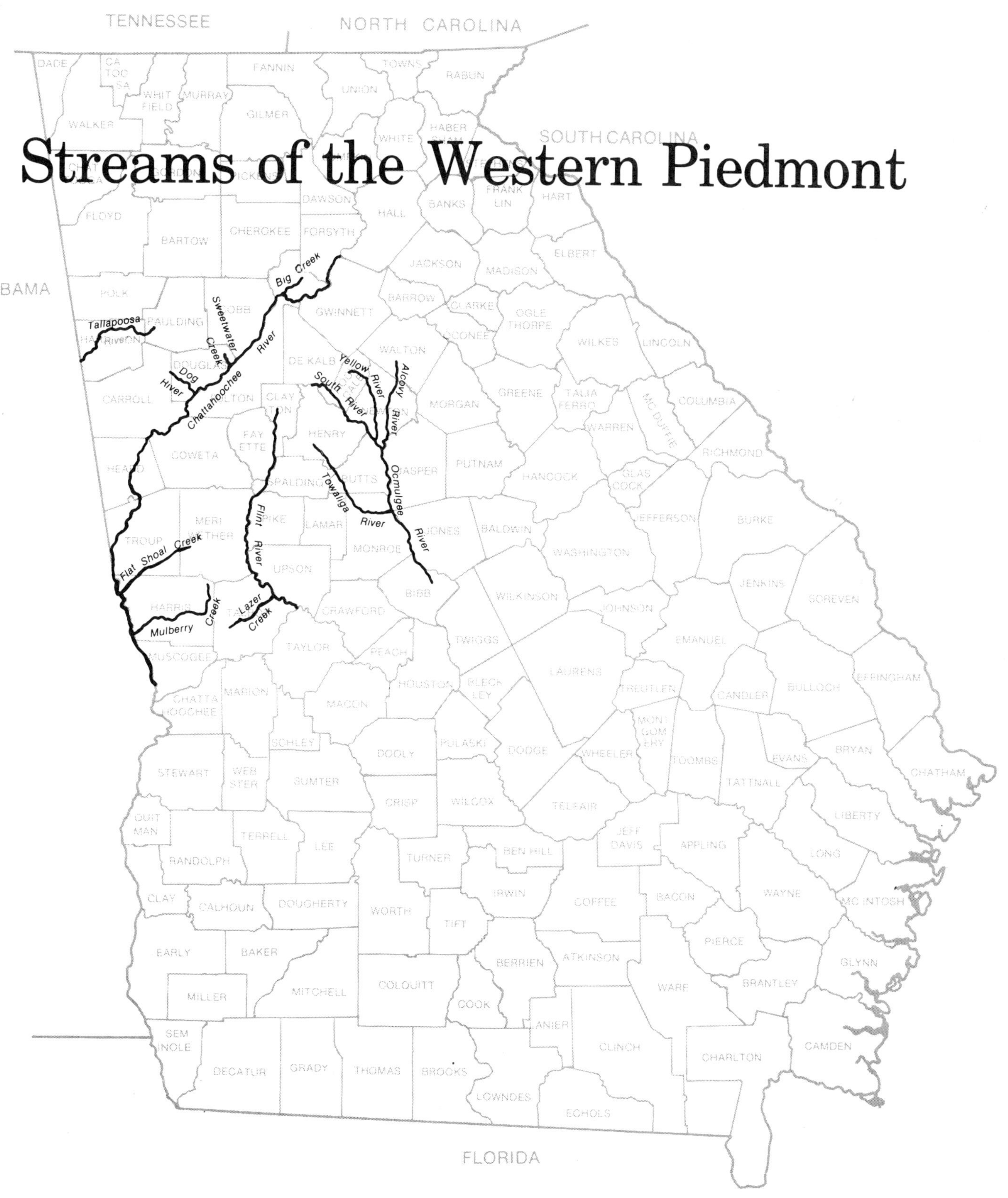

Alcovy River

A Piedmont stream rich in beauty and diverse in flora and wildlife, the Alcovy is born in Gwinnett County near Lawrenceville and flows south draining Walton and Newton counties before emptying into Jackson Lake. One of the main tributaries of the Ocmulgee River, the Alcovy is runnable downstream of the US 278 bridge east of Covington from November to early July in years of average rainfall. Below the US 278 crossing the Alcovy meanders through a wooded lowland swamp terrain with by-pass islands and oxbow lakes supporting large stands of tupelo gum.

Passing under the Central of Georgia railroad bridge, the river emerges from the watery lowlands and continues in a well-defined channel with red clay banks of three to six feet sloping at an angle of 45 to 90 degrees. The surrounding terrain remains wooded but is drier than it was upstream. Common tree varieties in the floodplain forests include sweet gum, swamp chestnut, oak, red ash, red maple, dogwood, possum haw, willow oak, and overcup oak. Along the banks, river birch, sugarberry, sycamore, and green ash predominate.

Downstream from the Henderson Mill Road the Alcovy begins to drop at a greater rate. One short series of ledges punctuates the run a mile below the mouth of Long Branch Creek. Farther downstream the Alcovy remains calm until just upstream of the Newton Factory bridge. Here the Alcovy begins a series of Class III (IV) rapids, narrows, and ledges that culminate below the bridge in a rock garden that is followed by a six-foot plunge into the lake pool. This thousand-yard section varies in difficulty and intensity according to water level and should be scouted. The surrounding terrain continues to be well forested and attractive.

The river's width varies from 25 to 40 feet at the GA 213 bridge, to an average of 45 to 65 feet for most of its runnable length, and then expands to 280 feet in spots as the Alcovy crashes down White and Factory shoals. Dangers, other than the rapids mentioned, are limited primarily to deadfalls. The current on the Alcovy is generally moderate and the water color is usually a murky brown indicative of the high concentration of dissolved clays. Access is good throughout.

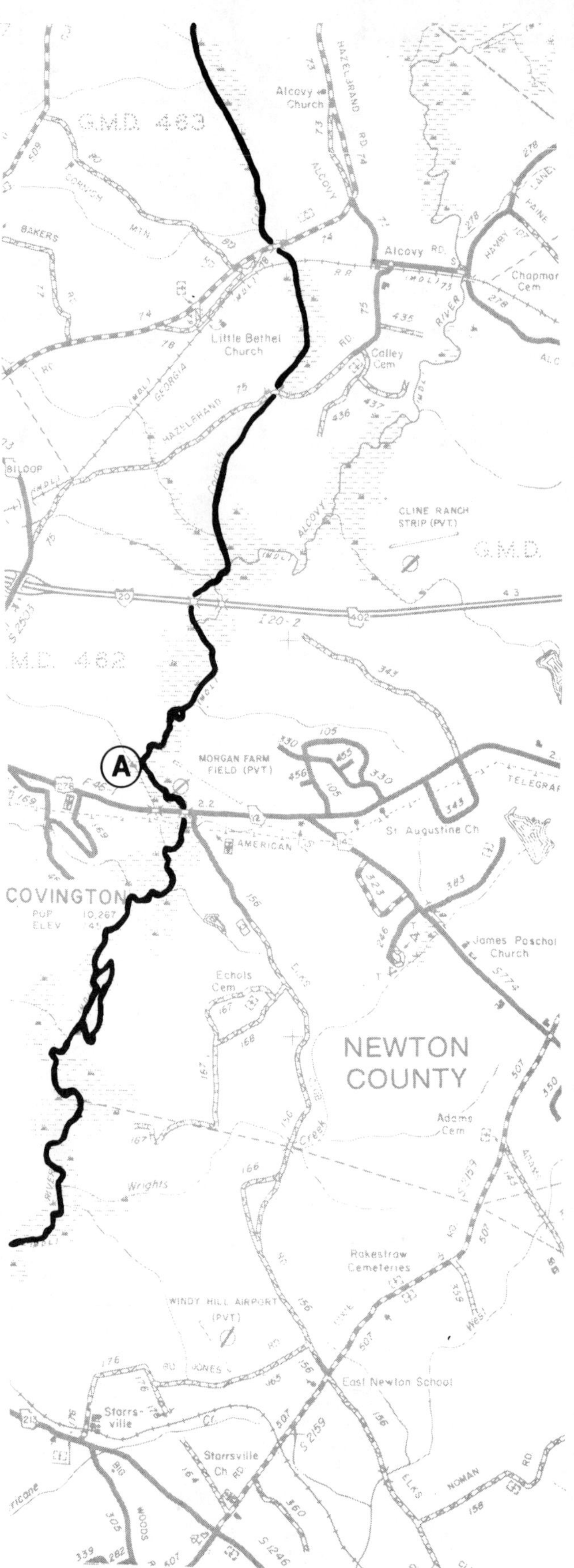

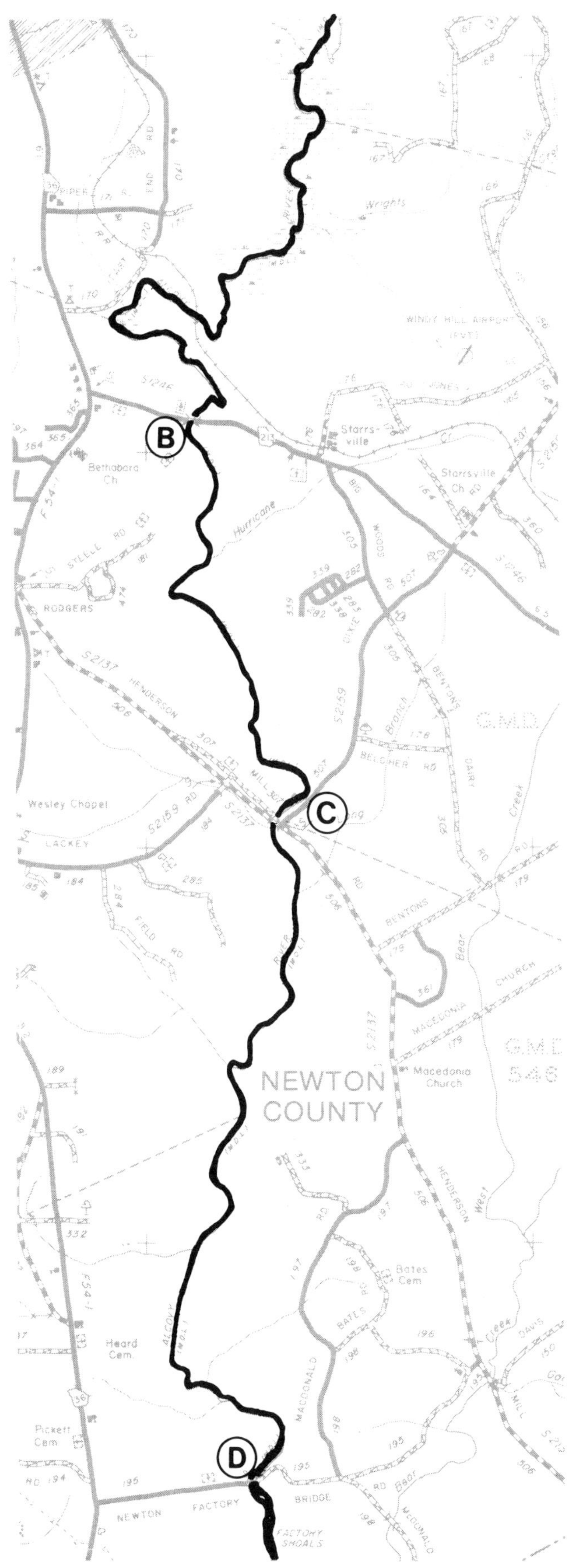

Section: Covington to Lake Jackson

Counties: Newton

Suitable For: Cruising

Appropriate For: Intermediates, advanced

Months Runnable: Late November through June

Interest Highlights: Scenery, wildlife, whitewater, local culture and industry
Scenery: Pretty to pretty in spots

Difficulty: International Scale I-III
Numerical Points 14

Average Width: 45-65 ft.
Velocity: Moderate to fast
Gradient: 6.14 ft./mi.

Runnable Water Level: Minimum 170 cfs
(Covington gauge) Maximum Up to flood stage

Hazards: Deadfalls, difficult rapids, large hole at bottom of Factory Shoals
Scouting: White and Factory shoals

Portages: White and Factory shoals, if situation warrants

Rescue Index: Accessible to accessible but difficult

Mean Water Temperature (°F)

Jan	41	Feb	43	Mar	48	Apr	56	May	65	Jun	73
Jul	75	Aug	73	Sep	69	Oct	61	Nov	52	Dec	43

Source of Additional Information: Walton Game and Fish Office (404) 557-2227

Access Point	Access Code
A	1357
B	1367
C	1357
D	1357
E	1357

Access Key
1 Paved Road
2 Unpaved Road
3 Short Carry
4 Long Carry
5 Easy Grade
6 Steep Incline
7 Clear Trail
8 Brush and Trees
9 Launching Fee Charged
10 Private Property, Need Permission
11 No Access, Reference Only

USGS Quads: Covington, Stewart

ACCESS POINTS	RIVER MILES	SHUTTLE MILES
A-B	6.1	8
B-C	3.2	3.5
C-D	5.1	5
D-E	4	5

Section: Covington to Lake Jackson

Counties: Newton

Suitable For: Cruising

Appropriate For: Intermediates, advanced

Months Runnable: Late November through June

Interest Highlights: Scenery, wildlife, whitewater, local culture and industry
Scenery: Pretty to pretty in spots

Difficulty: International Scale I-III
Numerical Points 14

Average Width: 45-65 ft.
Velocity: Moderate to fast
Gradient: 6.14 ft./mi.

Runnable Water Level: Minimum 170 cfs
(Covington gauge) Maximum Up to flood stage

Hazards: Deadfalls, difficult rapids, large hole at bottom of Factory Shoals
Scouting: White and Factory shoals

Portages: White and Factory shoals, if situation warrants

Rescue Index: Accessible to accessible but difficult

Mean Water Temperature (°F)

Jan 41	Feb 43	Mar 48	Apr 56	May 65	Jun 73
Jul 75	Aug 73	Sep 69	Oct 61	Nov 52	Dec 43

Source of Additional Information: Walton Game and Fish Office (404) 557-2227

Access Point	Access Code
A	1357
B	1367
C	1357
D	1357
E	1357

Access Key
1 Paved Road
2 Unpaved Road
3 Short Carry
4 Long Carry
5 Easy Grade
6 Steep Incline
7 Clear Trail
8 Brush and Trees
9 Launching Fee Charged
10 Private Property, Need Permission
11 No Access, Reference Only

Alcovy River.

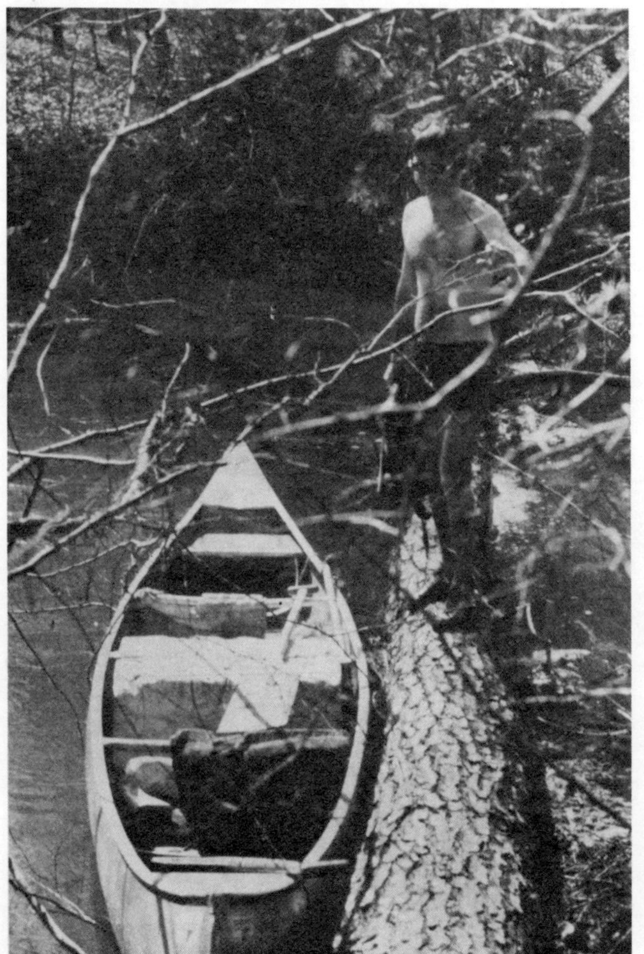

Photo courtesy of *Brown's Guide to Georgia.*

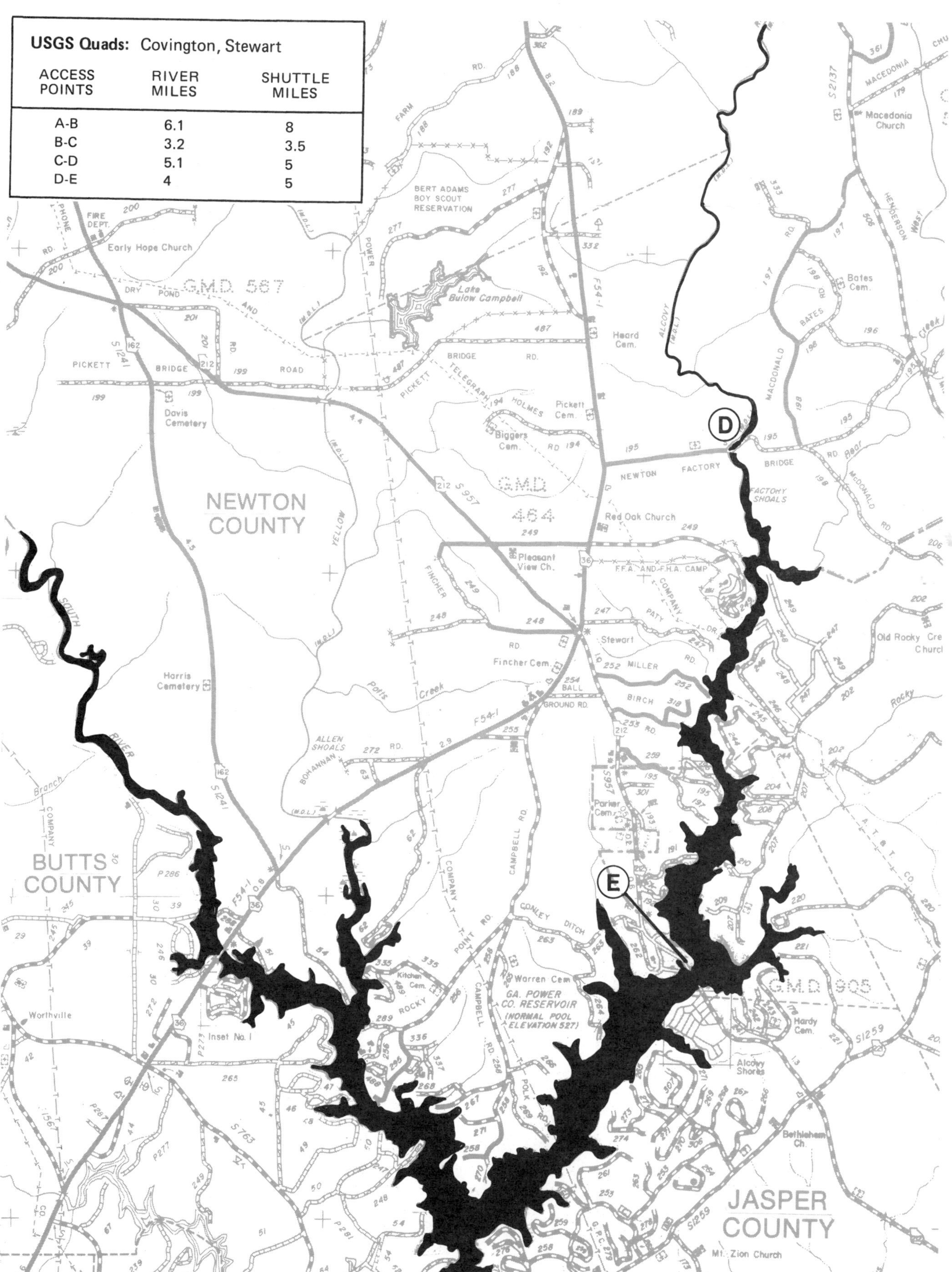

USGS Quads: Covington, Stewart

ACCESS POINTS	RIVER MILES	SHUTTLE MILES
A-B	6.1	8
B-C	3.2	3.5
C-D	5.1	5
D-E	4	5

Yellow River

The Yellow River originates in DeKalb County near Stone Mountain and flows south draining portions of the Piedmont counties of Rockdale and Newton before entering the backwaters of Jackson Lake. Running between well-defined banks of two to eight feet in height that are composed of red clay, the Yellow follows a general course of moderate straight sections followed by tight turns. The surrounding floodplain is forested with hickories, oaks, red maple, ash, sweet gum, and pine, and it is higher and drier than the comparable Alcovy River floodplain fifteen miles east. Birch, sycamore, ash, and willow trees line the banks. Though signs of habitation are common, and though the Yellow flows along or through several large settlements, the wilderness atmosphere of this section of the Piedmont remains largely intact. Wildlife is common and the flora is luxurious and diverse. Runnable downstream of the Irwin Bridge Road north of Conyers, the Yellow generally flows flat and easy.

Below the GA 20 bridge at Conyers is a dam that must be portaged. This is followed by a series of Class II, borderline Class III, rapids. Continuing downstream the Yellow resumes its tranquil demeanor and only occasional deadfalls pose a hazard to navigation. Two miles below I-20 and above the Brown bridge west of Covington, a pipeline crosses the river. This spot is dangerous at most water levels and should be portaged.

At the GA 81 bridge in Porterdale a rather long portage is required around a dam. At the foot of the dam is a series of Class II rapids that cannot be run except in higher water. The portage trail, from the riverside corner of a small parking lot on the southwest side of the GA 81 bridge, can be somewhat difficult to find. From Porterdale to the lake the Alcovy runs flat with a few intermittent Class I riffles and very small shoals. The river corridor remains wooded and serene in spite of frequent signs of habitation. Once again deadfalls constitute the major hazard to navigation. The river's width averages 45 to 70 feet and the current is moderate. The water is high in sediment and ranges in color from light to greenish brown most of the year. Access is good throughout.

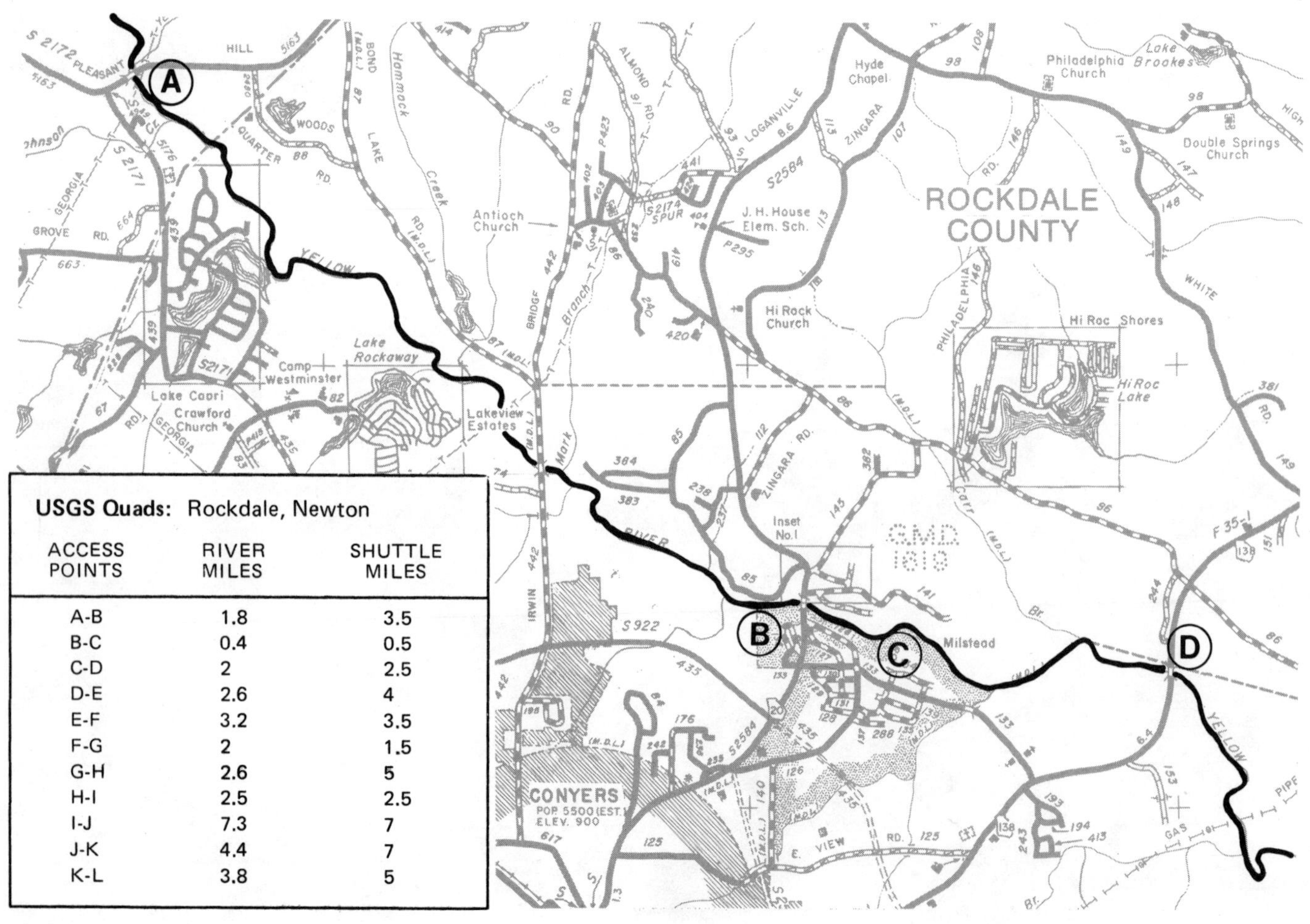

USGS Quads: Rockdale, Newton

ACCESS POINTS	RIVER MILES	SHUTTLE MILES
A-B	1.8	3.5
B-C	0.4	0.5
C-D	2	2.5
D-E	2.6	4
E-F	3.2	3.5
F-G	2	1.5
G-H	2.6	5
H-I	2.5	2.5
I-J	7.3	7
J-K	4.4	7
K-L	3.8	5

Section: North of Conyers to Jackson Lake

Counties: Rockdale, Newton

Suitable For: Cruising

Appropriate For: Practiced beginners, intermediates, advanced

Months Runnable: November through mid-July

Interest Highlights: Scenery, wildlife, local culture and industry

Scenery: Pretty in spots to beautiful in spots

Difficulty: International Scale I-II (III)
Numerical Points 11

Average Width: 45-70 ft.

Gradient: Moderate

Velocity: 5.6 ft./mi. (7.8 ft./mi., C-F)

Runnable Water Level: Minimum 175
(Covington gauge) Maximum Up to flood stage

Hazards: Deadfalls, dams, pipe crossing

Scouting: None required

Portages: Dam at Milstead; pipe crossing below access point G; dam at Porterdale

Rescue Index: Accessible to accessible but difficult

Mean Water Temperature (°F)

Jan 41	Feb 43	Mar 48	Apr 57	May 66	Jun 72
Jul 75	Aug 73	Sep 68	Oct 60	Nov 51	Dec 43

Source of Additional Information: Walton Game and Fish Office (404) 557-2227

Access Point	Access Code
A	1357
B	1357
C	1367
D	1357
E	1357
F	1367
G	2357
H	1367
I	1467
J	2357

Access Key

1 Paved Road
2 Unpaved Road
3 Short Carry
4 Long Carry
5 Easy Grade
6 Steep Incline
7 Clear Trail
8 Brush and Trees
9 Launching Fee Charged
10 Private Property, Need Permission
11 No Access, Reference Only

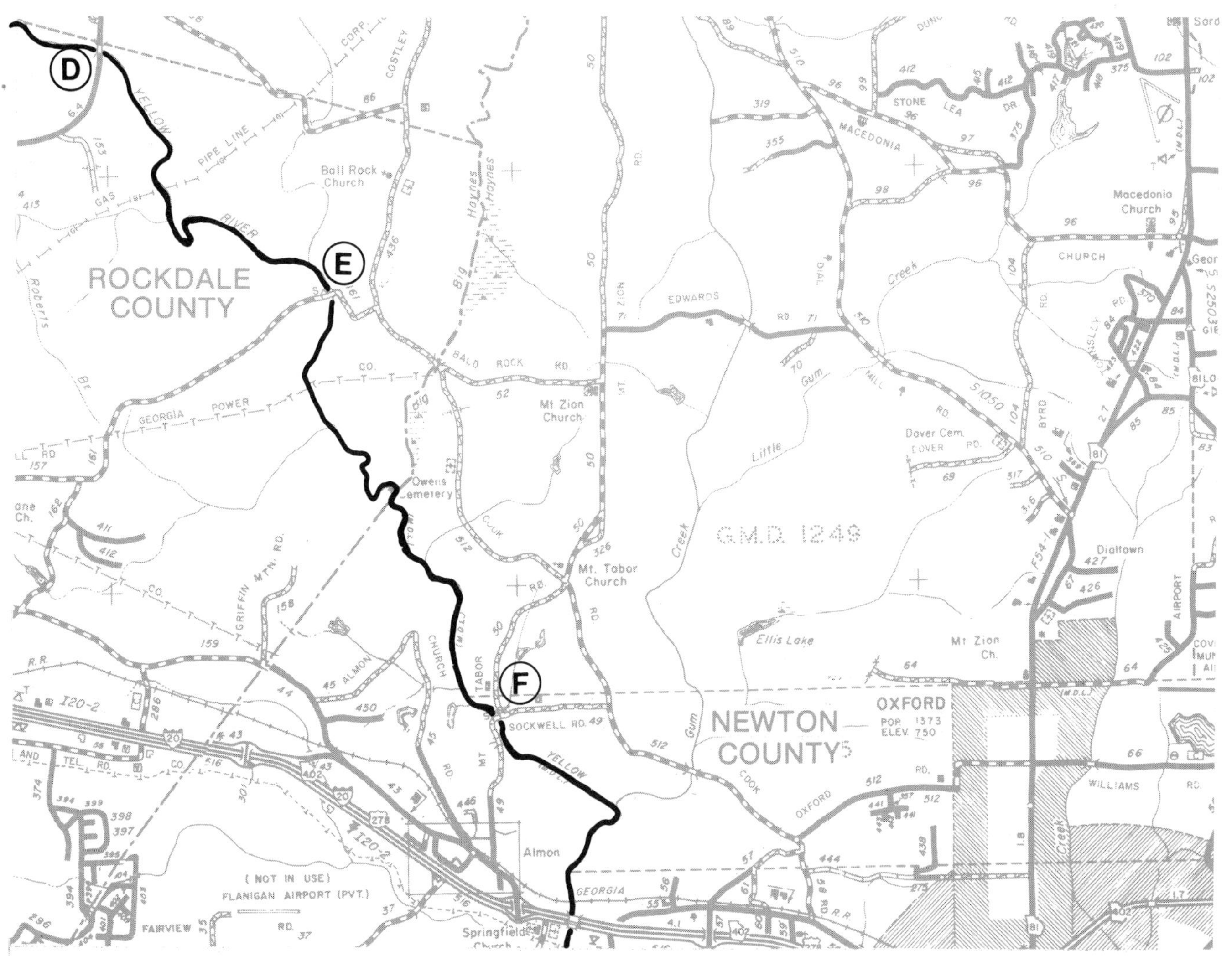

Yellow River—*Continued*

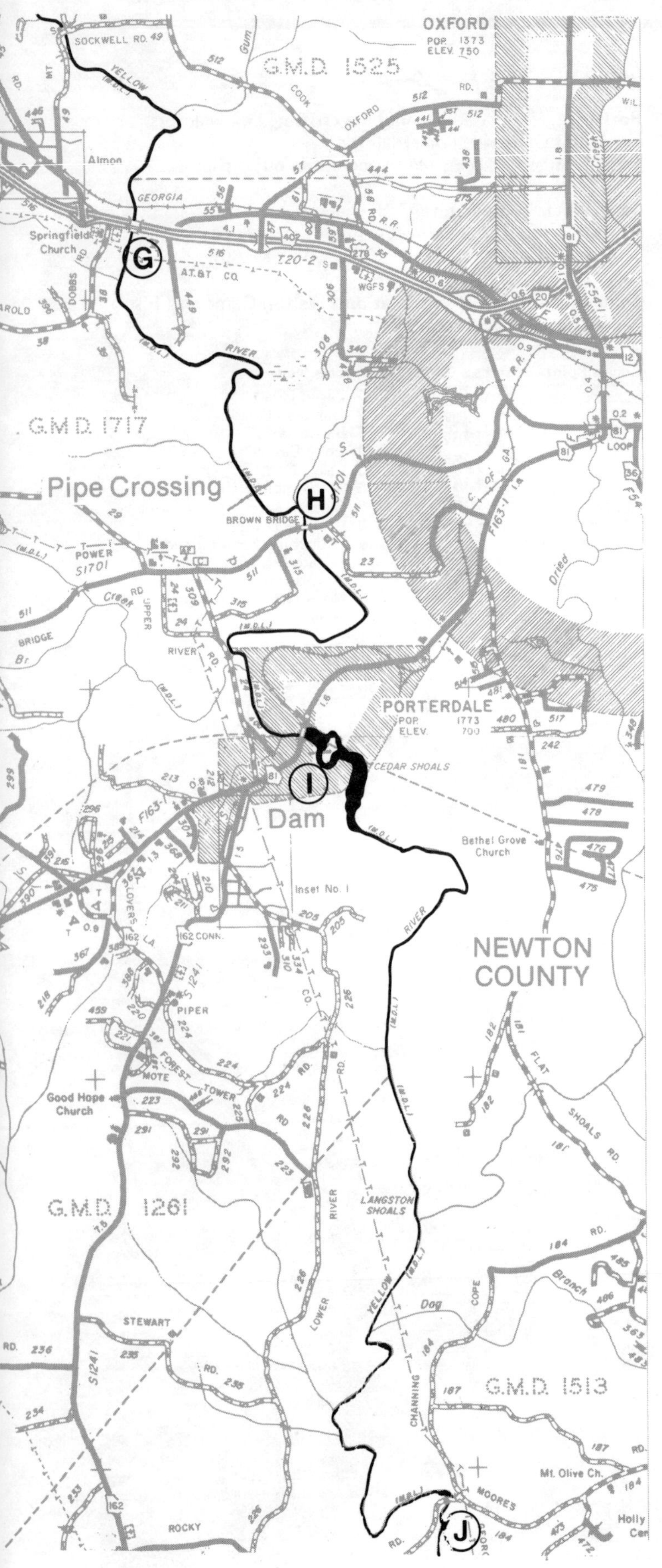

Section: North of Conyers to Jackson Lake

Counties: Rockdale, Newton

Suitable For: Cruising

Appropriate For: Practiced beginners, intermediates, advanced

Months Runnable: November through mid-July

Interest Highlights: Scenery, wildlife, local culture and industry

Scenery: Pretty in spots to beautiful in spots

Difficulty: International Scale I-II (III)
Numerical Points 11

Average Width: 45-70 ft.
Gradient: Moderate
Velocity: 5.6 ft./mi. (7.8 ft./mi., C-F)

Runnable Water Level: (Covington gauge) Minimum 175
Maximum Up to flood stage

Hazards: Deadfalls, dams, pipe crossing

Scouting: None required

Portages: Dam at Milstead; pipe crossing below access point G; dam at Porterdale

Rescue Index: Accessible to accessible but difficult

Mean Water Temperature (°F)

Jan 41	Feb 43	Mar 48	Apr 57	May 66	Jun 72
Jul 75	Aug 73	Sep 68	Oct 60	Nov 51	Dec 43

Source of Additional Information: Walton Game and Fish Office (404) 557-2227

Access Point	Access Code	Access Key
A	1357	1 Paved Road
B	1357	2 Unpaved Road
C	1367	3 Short Carry
D	1357	4 Long Carry
E	1357	5 Easy Grade
F	1367	6 Steep Incline
G	2357	7 Clear Trail
H	1367	8 Brush and Trees
I	1467	9 Launching Fee Charged
J	2357	10 Private Property, Need Permission
		11 No Access, Reference Only

Photo courtesy of *Brown's Guide to Georgia.*

Yellow River.

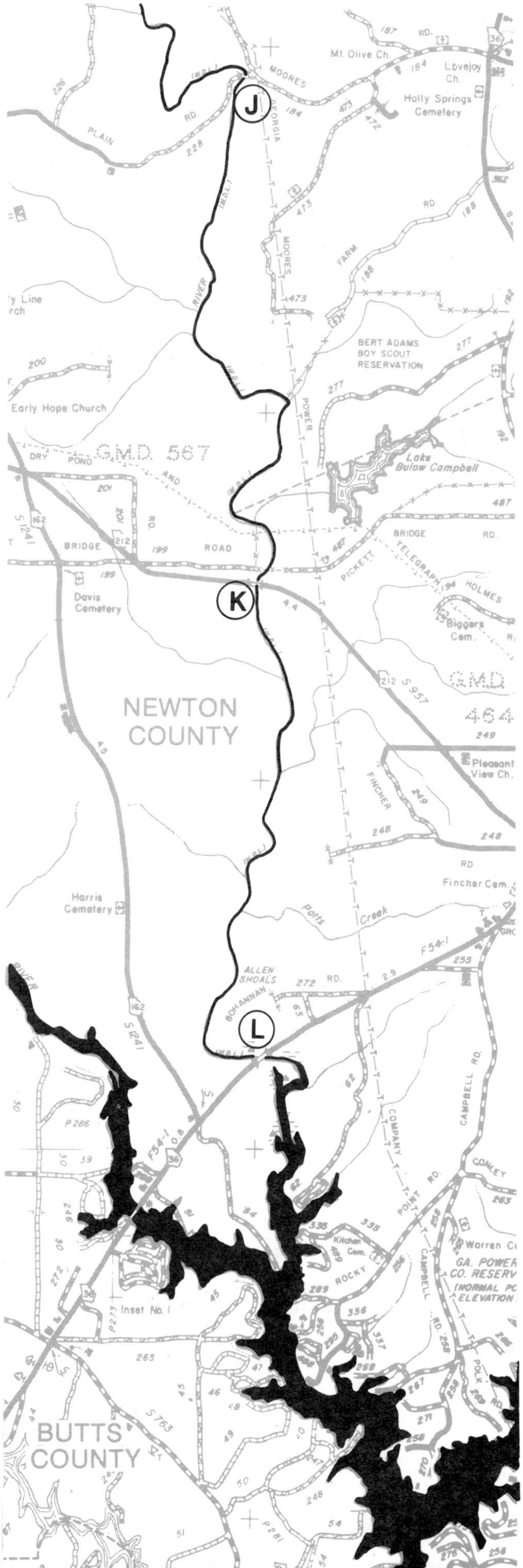

USGS Quads: Rockdale, Newton

ACCESS POINTS	RIVER MILES	SHUTTLE MILES
A-B	1.8	3.5
B-C	0.4	0.5
C-D	2	2.5
D-E	2.6	4
E-F	3.2	3.5
F-G	2	1.5
G-H	2.6	5
H-I	2.5	2.5
I-J	7.3	7
J-K	4.4	7
K-L	3.8	5

South River

The South River rolls out of the southeastern suburbs of Atlanta and flows across the bottom of DeKalb County into Rockdale County and thence along the Henry–Newton county line to empty into Jackson Lake. Runnable downstream of GA 155 December through May, and below GA 20 all year, the South River is partially fed by the Atlanta water system.

Tree-covered and intimate below GA 155, the South tumbles playfully over sandbars and intermittent Class I+ shoals and small rapids down to the Klondike Road bridge. Midway in this section is a low-water bridge that can be dangerous at certain water levels. Below the Klondike Road bridge the river crashes through a series of narrows 150 yards in length and ends with a Class III section that starts on the right and runs left with a four-foot drop and big hole extending from the right to the middle of the stream at the bottom. Smaller rapids and shoals, not exceeding Class II in difficulty, persist to the vicinity of the GA 138 bridge. From the GA 138 bridge to beyond the GA 20 highway crossing, the channel is frequently obstructed by deadfalls.

Below the GA 20 bridge are some short Class II shoals followed by a flatwater stretch extending down into the pool of the Snapping Shoals Dam. The dam can be portaged on the right. Below the dam Snapping Shoals provide several hundred yards of Class I+ and Class II entertainment. From here to the lake the South River is generally incapable of more than a good ripple from time to time and never again exceeds Class I in difficulty.

Surrounding terrain is interesting and varied all along the runnable section of the South. Running in a narrow wooded valley above GA 20, the river skirts some exposed bluffs and winds along the base of several tall, gumdrop-shaped hills that include the famed Stone Mountain. In Rockdale County the valley broadens slightly with typical Piedmont bottomland forests cradling the stream. As the South approaches the lake in Newton County, the floodplain becomes increasingly wet and swampy, giving rise to a gum-dominated flora.

The course of the South is convoluted and serpentine in the upper section, but it straightens to some degree downstream of the Butler bridge crossing in Newton County. The current is moderate to swift in the upper sections and moderate to slow below Snapping Shoals; banks are of clay and sand and generally range from three to seven feet in height; water color is usually murky green to brown depending on the amount of sediment in solution. Evidence of habitation and development are common along the South River but do not generally occur in sufficient concentration to spoil the wilderness beauty of the stream. Access is adequate to good throughout.

Section: GA 155 bridge to Jackson Lake

Counties: Dekalb, Rockdale, Henry, Newton

Suitable For: Cruising

Appropriate For: Practiced beginners, intermediates, advanced
Months Runnable: GA 155-GA 20; December through April; below GA 20, all
Interest Highlights: Scenery, whitewater, local culture and industry
Scenery: Pretty to beautiful in spots[1]

Difficulty: International Scale I-III
Numerical Points 13

Average Width: 70-100 ft.
Gradient: Moderate
Velocity: 4.58 ft./mi.

Runnable Water Level: Minimum 400 cfs
(Butler Bridge gauge) Maximum Up to flood stage

Hazards: Large hydraulics, low bridges, dams, deadfalls

Scouting: At rapids and shoals as situation warrants

Portages: Low water bridge on Klondike Rd., dam at Snapping Shoals
Rescue Index: Accessible to accessible but difficult

Mean Water Temperature (°F)

Jan 41	Feb 42	Mar 47	Apr 56	May 66	Jun 72
Jul 76	Aug 73	Sep 69	Oct 60	Nov 51	Dec 43

Source of Additional Information: Walton Game and Fish Office (404) 557-2227

Access Point	Access Code
A	1357
B	2357
C	13679
D	1367
E	2357
F	1368
G	2368
H	1357
I	1357
J	2368
K	2357
L	1367

Access Key
1 Paved Road
2 Unpaved Road
3 Short Carry
4 Long Carry
5 Easy Grade
6 Steep Incline
7 Clear Trail
8 Brush and Trees
9 Launching Fee Charged
10 Private Property, Need Permission
11 No Access, Reference Only

[1]Sewage from Atlanta makes this river unpleasant in summer

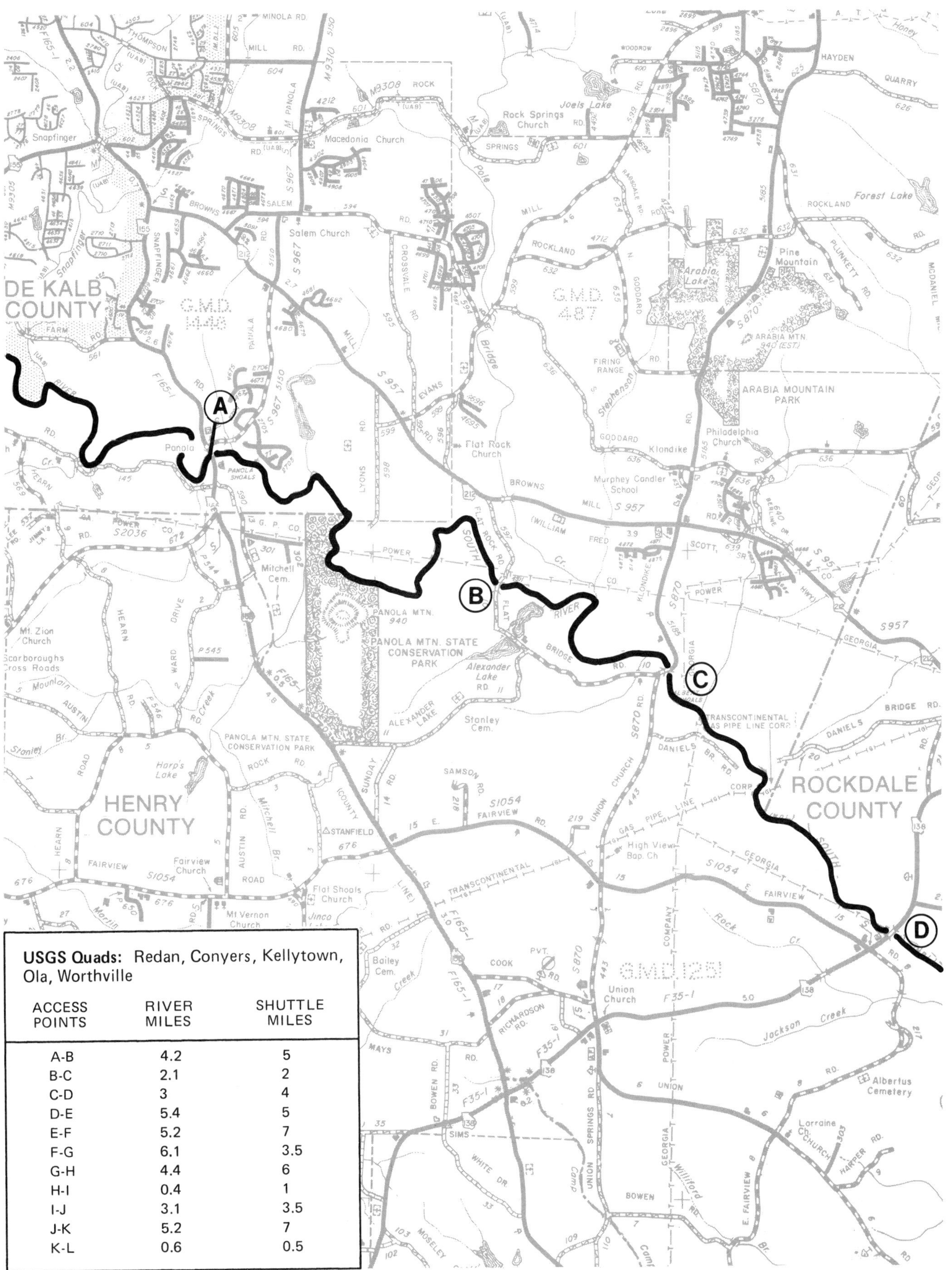

USGS Quads: Redan, Conyers, Kellytown, Ola, Worthville

ACCESS POINTS	RIVER MILES	SHUTTLE MILES
A-B	4.2	5
B-C	2.1	2
C-D	3	4
D-E	5.4	5
E-F	5.2	7
F-G	6.1	3.5
G-H	4.4	6
H-I	0.4	1
I-J	3.1	3.5
J-K	5.2	7
K-L	0.6	0.5

South River—*Continued*

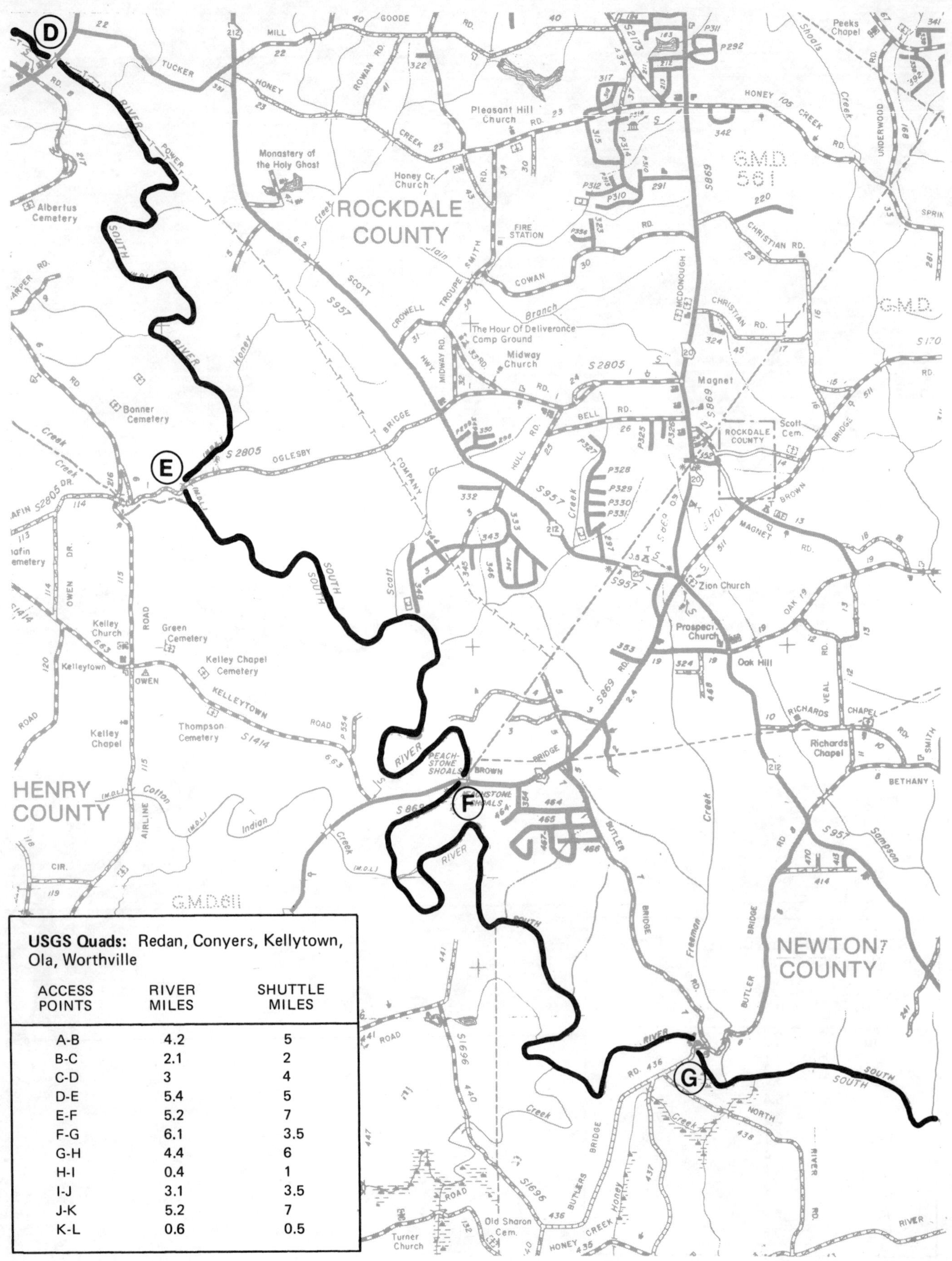

USGS Quads: Redan, Conyers, Kellytown, Ola, Worthville

ACCESS POINTS	RIVER MILES	SHUTTLE MILES
A-B	4.2	5
B-C	2.1	2
C-D	3	4
D-E	5.4	5
E-F	5.2	7
F-G	6.1	3.5
G-H	4.4	6
H-I	0.4	1
I-J	3.1	3.5
J-K	5.2	7
K-L	0.6	0.5

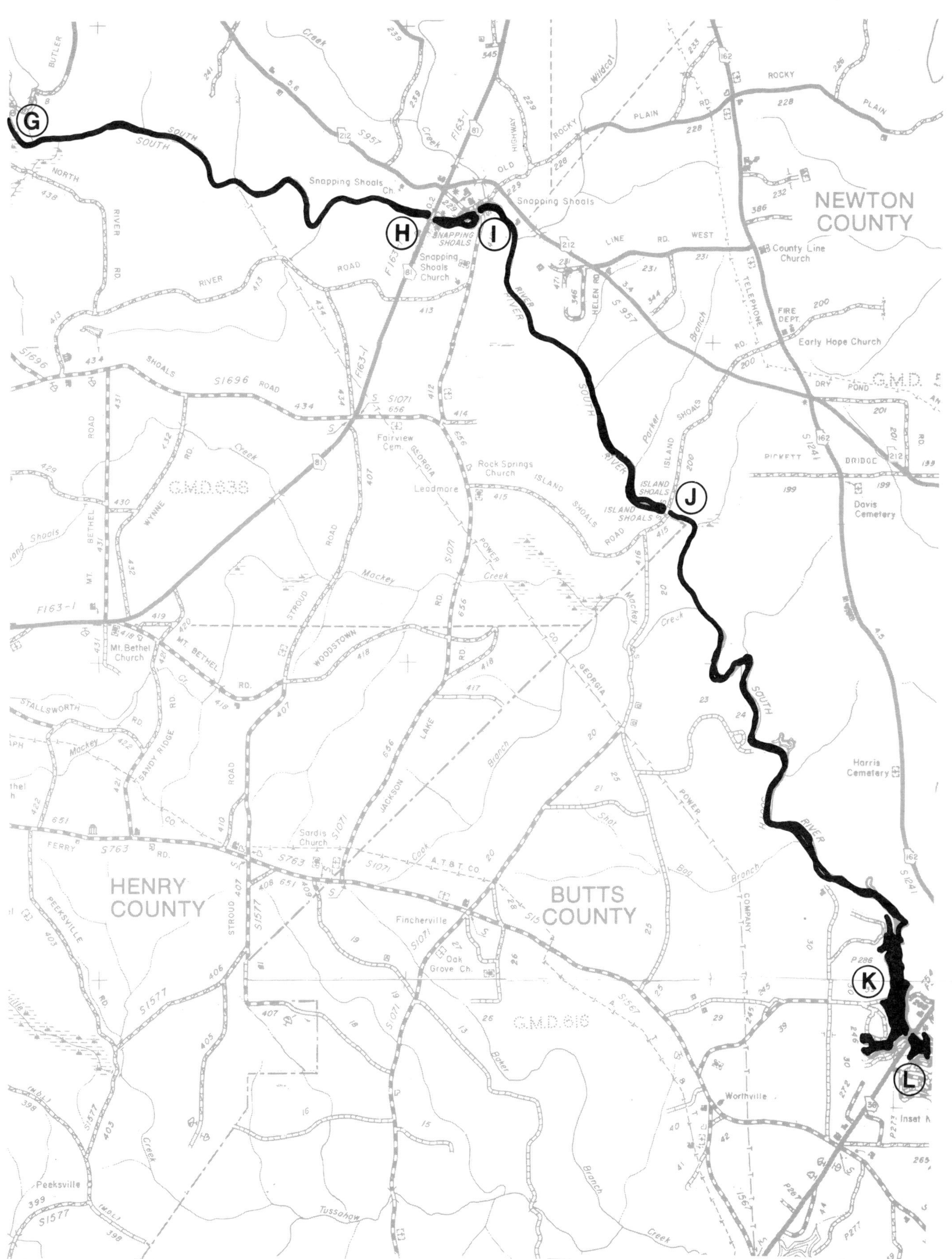
NEWTON COUNTY
HENRY COUNTY
BUTTS COUNTY
Snapping Shoals
Snapping Shoals Church
Fairview Cem.
Rock Springs Church
Leadmore
Island Shoals
Early Hope Church
County Line Church
Davis Cemetery
Harris Cemetery
Mt. Bethel Church
Sardis Church
Fincherville
Oak Grove Ch.
Worthville
Peeksville
SOUTH RIVER
G
H
I
J
K
L

Towaliga River

The Towaliga begins and ends in the central Piedmont flowing south out of Henry County and draining portions of Butts and Monroe counties before emptying into the Ocmulgee above Juliette. Runnable below High Falls in Monroe County from late November to May, the Towaliga is a pleasant and scenic stream with good access. Below spectacular High Falls the Towaliga broadens to 300 feet with large ledges and boulder rapids continuing for several hundred feet beyond the bottom of the falls. A trail along the left bank provides a number of possible put-ins, depending on which, if any, of the rapids beyond the bottom of the falls the paddler is willing to tackle. These rapids are technical in low water, but due to the width of the stream, they exhibit numerous sneak routes at higher levels. In any event they would not exceed Class III in difficulty.

Following this short but challenging wide section, the Towaliga narrows first to 80 feet and then shortly to its average width of 45 to 60 feet. From here to the GA 42 bridge the river is at its best with delightful, bouncy Class II rapids and ledges interspersed with pools and completely overhung by white oak, sweet gum, red maple, hickory, sycamore, and beech. The river banks are of brownish red clay bordered in the upper reaches by rocks, and they average four to six feet in height with varying degrees of slope. The current is moderate to swift and usually runs brown with a high concentration of sediment. Dangers in this section, other than the rapids mentioned, are limited to deadfalls.

Below the GA 42 bridge the Towaliga flattens out and runs with only an occasional riffle between well-defined clay banks of five to ten feet. Deadfalls are numerous in this lower section all the way to the juction with the Ocmulgee, and these are particularly dangerous in high water.

Throughout the runnable sections described, the Towaliga snakes a winding path through an intimate forested valley. Hills rise sharply from the streamside during the first five miles below High Falls and then recede gradually as a corridor of cultivated land encroaches on the river just upstream of the GA 42 bridge. Below the GA 42 crossing the river slips back into the forest, but the valley remains slightly broadened. On the banks, catalpa, ash, and birch become more common, and the river continues to be well shaded.

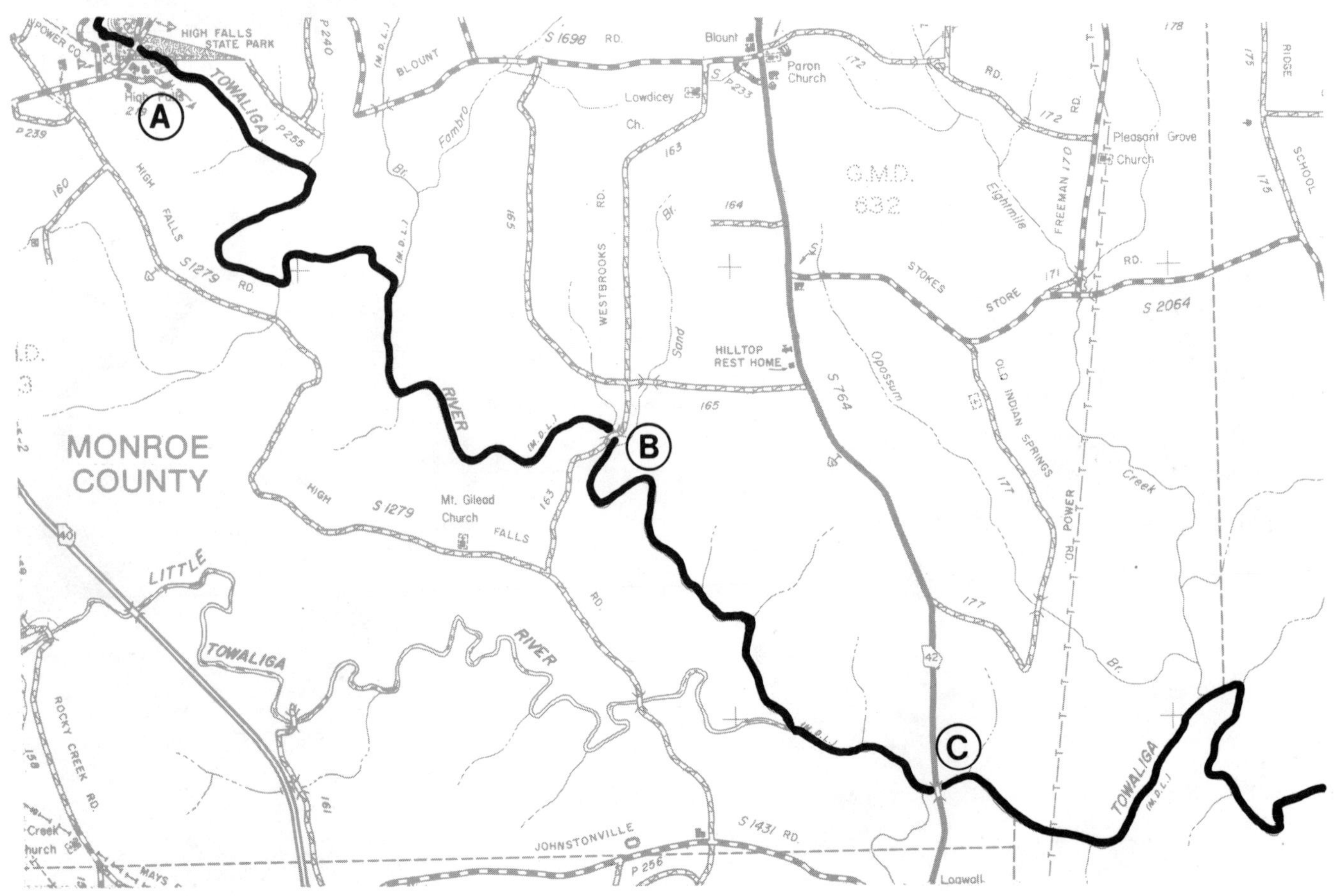

Section: High Falls to Ocmulgee River

Counties: Monroe

Suitable For: Cruising, camping

Appropriate For: Beginners, intermediates, advanced

Months Runnable: Late November to May and after heavy rains

Interest Highlights: Scenery, wildlife, whitewater, geology

Scenery: Beautiful in spots to beautiful

Difficulty: International Scale I-III
Numerical Points 9

Average Width: 45-60 ft.
Gradient: Moderate to fast
Velocity: 6.65 ft./mi.

Runnable Water Level: Minimum Unknown
Maximum Up to flood stage

Hazards: Deadfalls, rapids

Scouting: At rapids as situation requires

Portages: Around deadfalls

Rescue Index: Accessible to accessible but difficult

Mean Water Temperature (°F)

Jan 42	Feb 44	Mar 48	Apr 57	May 66	Jun 73
Jul 75	Aug 73	Sep 68	Oct 60	Nov 51	Dec 45

Source of Additional Information: Macon Game and Fish Office (912) 744-3228

Access Point	Access Code
A	1357
B	1357
C	1357
D	1357
E	1357
F[1]	1357

Access Key
1 Paved Road
2 Unpaved Road
3 Short Carry
4 Long Carry
5 Easy Grade
6 Steep Incline
7 Clear Trail
8 Brush and Trees
9 Launching Fee Charged
10 Private Property, Need Permission
11 No Access, Reference Only

[1]On the Ocmulgee River

USGS Quads: High Falls, Indian Springs, Forsyth, Berner, East Juliette

ACCESS POINTS	RIVER MILES	SHUTTLE MILES
A-B	5.2	6
B-C	3.3	4
C-D	5.5	8.5
D-E	7.8	6
E-F	4	2.5

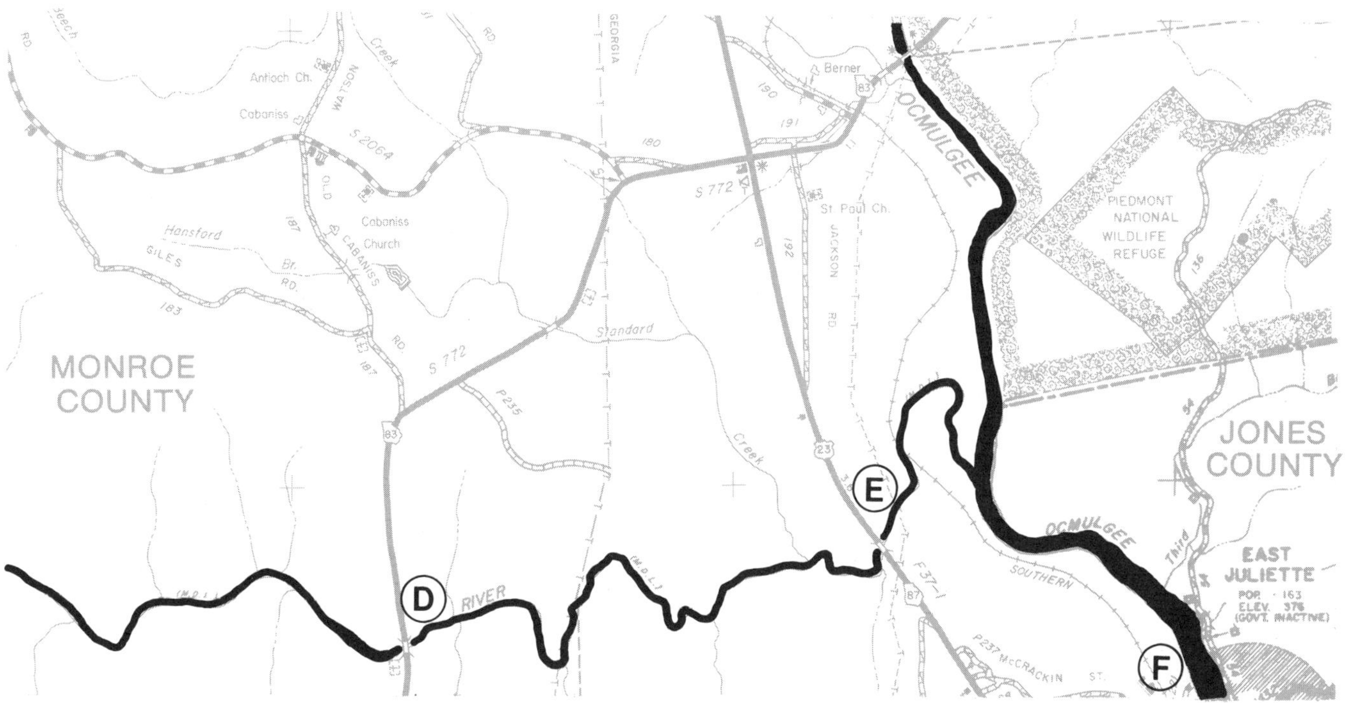

Ocmulgee River

The Ocmulgee is born at the confluence of the Alcovy and South rivers in the backwaters of Jackson Lake in Butts and Jasper counties. Flowing southeast below Lloyd Shoals Dam through the Piedmont, the Ocmulgee winds through steep to rolling hills and narrow valleys flanked by a wooded corridor of pine, sweet gum, hickory, willow, red maple, white oak, black oak, and beech. Rock outcroppings occasionally grace the riverside as the stream runs within well-defined red clay banks of six to fourteen feet in height, which are sharply inclined at 60 to 90 degrees. Scrub vegetation is thick with a diverse flora of ferns, vines, and shrubs. The Ocmulgee carries a high concentration of sediment and therefore appears muddy most of the year. Its course in the Piedmont from Lloyd Shoals Dam to Macon tends towards broad gentle curves and moderate to long straightaways followed by an occasional sharp bend.

Paddling downstream from Lloyd Shoals Dam there are intermittent Class II and borderline Class III shoals and ledges down to the backwaters of John Birch Dam from near the mouth of Big Sandy Creek. The greatest concentration of whitewater occurs about one mile below the GA 16 bridge and persists in a semicontinuous fashion for a mile and a half. For the following five miles to the backwater of the dam, shoals occur approximately every one-third to one-half mile but are generally an easy Class II. At Juliette, a quarter-mile portage on the left around the Birch Dam is required.

Below the dam the shoals resume at half-mile intervals and continue, seldom exceeding easy Class II, all the way to Arkwright. This is a particularly pristine section of the Ocmulgee, running along the western boundary of the Piedmont National Wildlife Refuge. The large Arkwright Power Plant signals the approach of the end of whitewater on the Ocmulgee and the departure of the river from the Piedmont. Below Arkwright the Ocmulgee rejoins civilization as it flows through Macon's industrial suburbs and downtown. On the east side of Macon the valley broadens and confining hills taper and level off marking the Ocmulgee's descent into the Coastal Plain. The remaining portion of the river is described in the next chapter.

The Ocmulgee is runnable from Jackson Lake to Macon all year subject to releases at the Lloyd Shoals Dam. Dangers include shoals, the dam at Juliette, as mentioned, and the likelihood of hypothermia in cooler weather following capsize, due to the low temperature of the water released at the Lloyd Shoals Dam. Islands are common throughout the Piedmont, and though thickly forested, they're suitable for canoe camping. The river's width in the Piedmont varies from 90 to 120 feet in the upper stretches to 260 feet at some shoals and pools above the shoals.

Section: Lloyd Shoals Dam to Macon

Counties: Jasper, Butts, Monroe, Jones, Bibb

Suitable For: Cruising, camping

Appropriate For: Practiced beginners, intermediates, advanced paddlers
Months Runnable: All when dam is releasing

Interest Highlights: Scenery, wildlife, local culture and industry
Scenery: Beautiful in spots to beautiful

Difficulty: International Scale I-II (III)
Numerical Points 12

Average Width: 90-120 ft.
Gradient: Moderate
Velocity: 3.87 ft./mi.

Runnable Water Level: Minimum Not applicable
Maximum Up to flood stage

Hazards: Dams, shoals, cold water

Scouting: At shoals and rapids

Portages: Dam at Juliette

Rescue Index: Accessible but difficult

Mean Water Temperature (°F)

Jan 46	Feb 48	Mar 52	Apr 61	May 71	Jun 79
Jul 83	Aug 82	Sep 76	Oct 65	Nov 59	Dec 51

Source of Additional Information: Macon Game and Fish Office (912) 744-3228

Access Point	Access Code
A	1367
B	1367
C	2357
D	2357
E	1357
F	1357
G	1367
H	1357
I	1357

Access Key
1 Paved Road
2 Unpaved Road
3 Short Carry
4 Long Carry
5 Easy Grade
6 Steep Incline
7 Clear Trail
8 Brush and Trees
9 Launching Fee Charged
10 Private Property, Need Permission
11 No Access, Reference Only

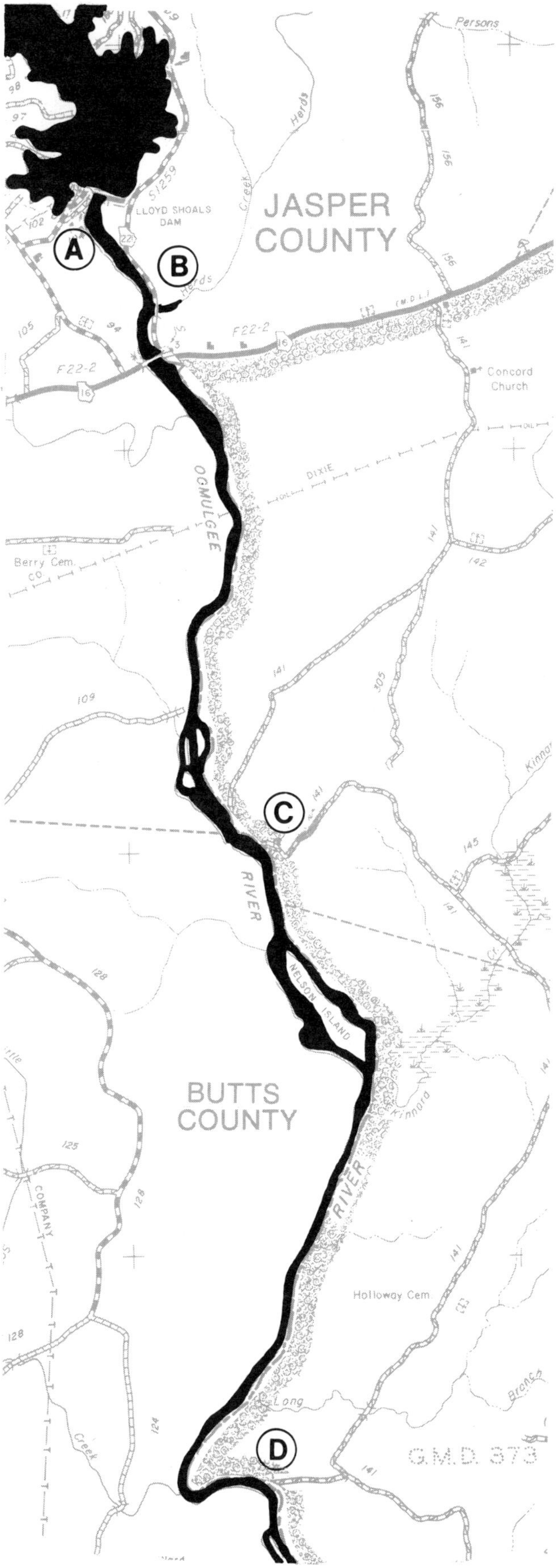

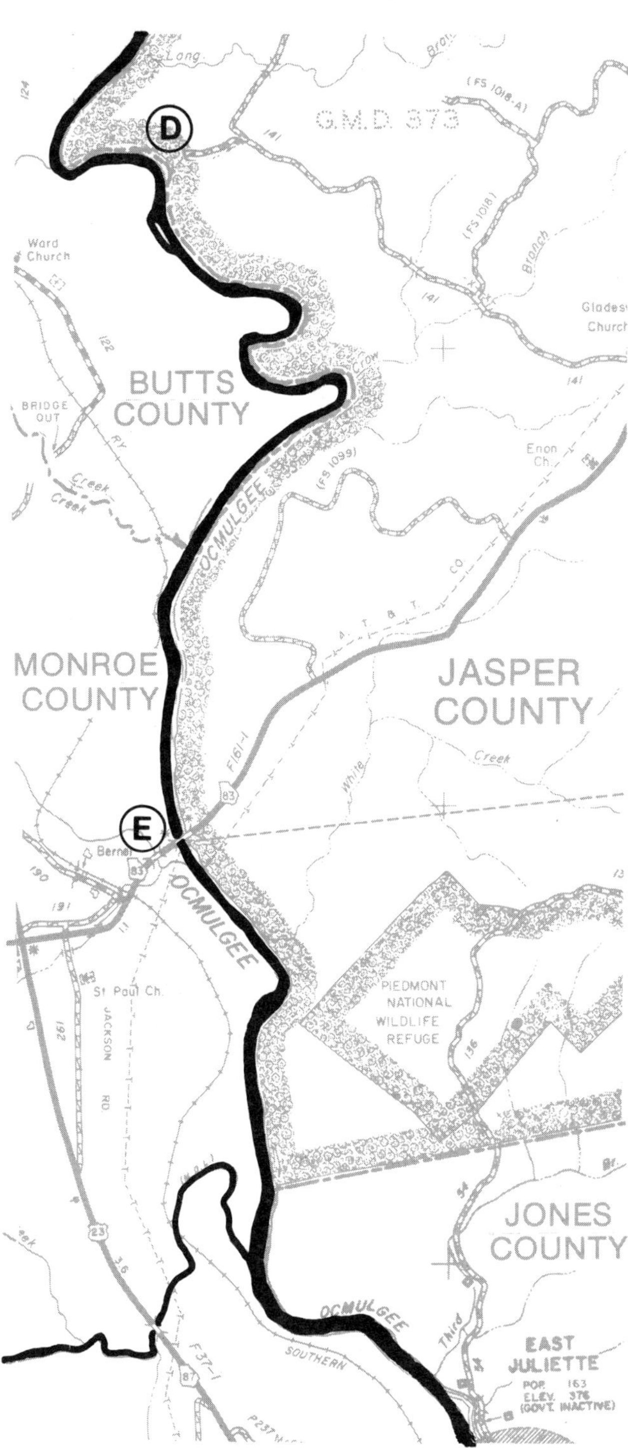

USGS Quads: Lloyd Shoals Dam, Berner, East Juliette

ACCESS POINTS	RIVER MILES	SHUTTLE MILES
A-B	0.8	0.5
B-C	4.8	6.5
C-D	5.3	3.8
D-E	5	7
E-F	4.5	6

Ocmulgee River—*Continued*

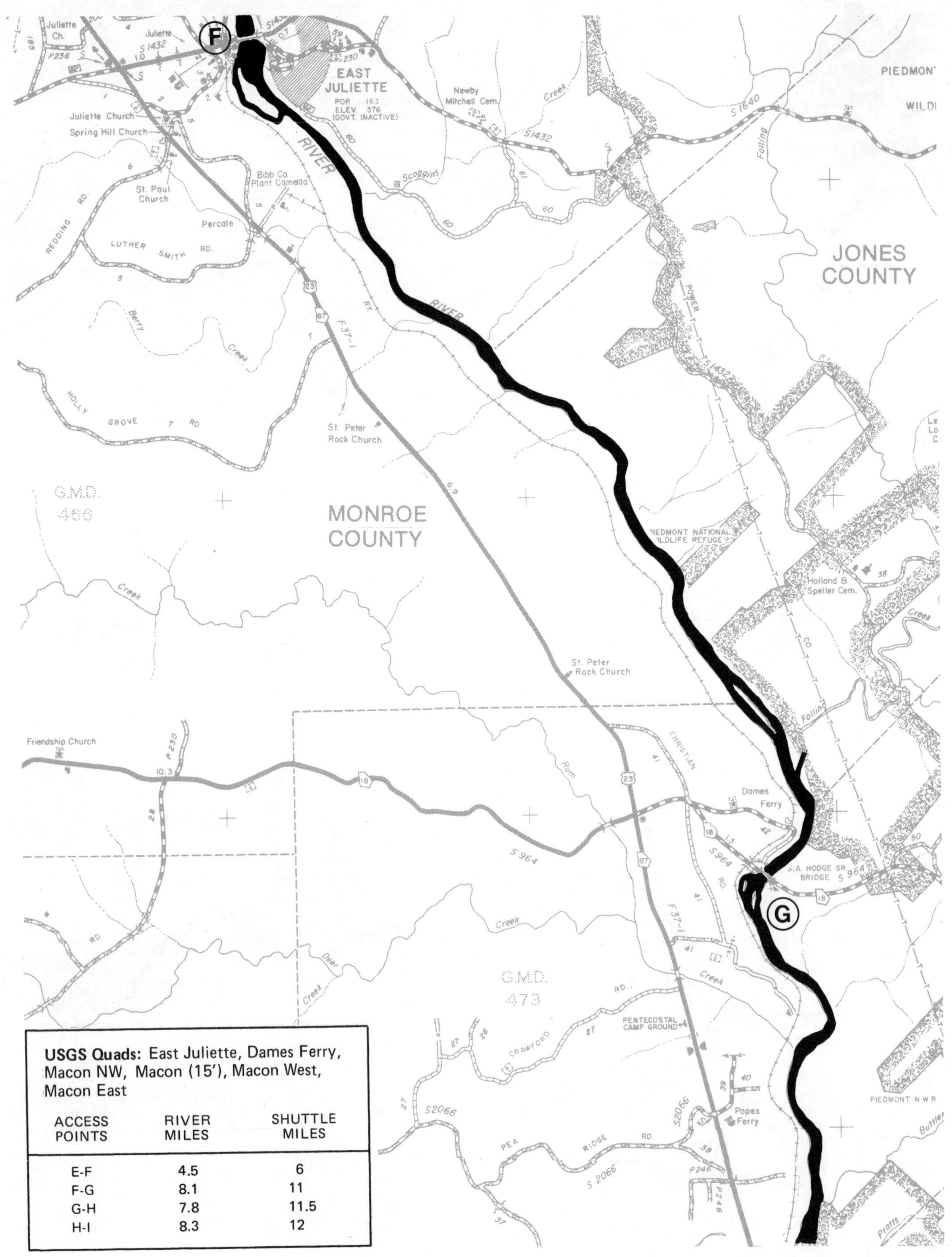

USGS Quads: East Juliette, Dames Ferry, Macon NW, Macon (15′), Macon West, Macon East

ACCESS POINTS	RIVER MILES	SHUTTLE MILES
E-F	4.5	6
F-G	8.1	11
G-H	7.8	11.5
H-I	8.3	12

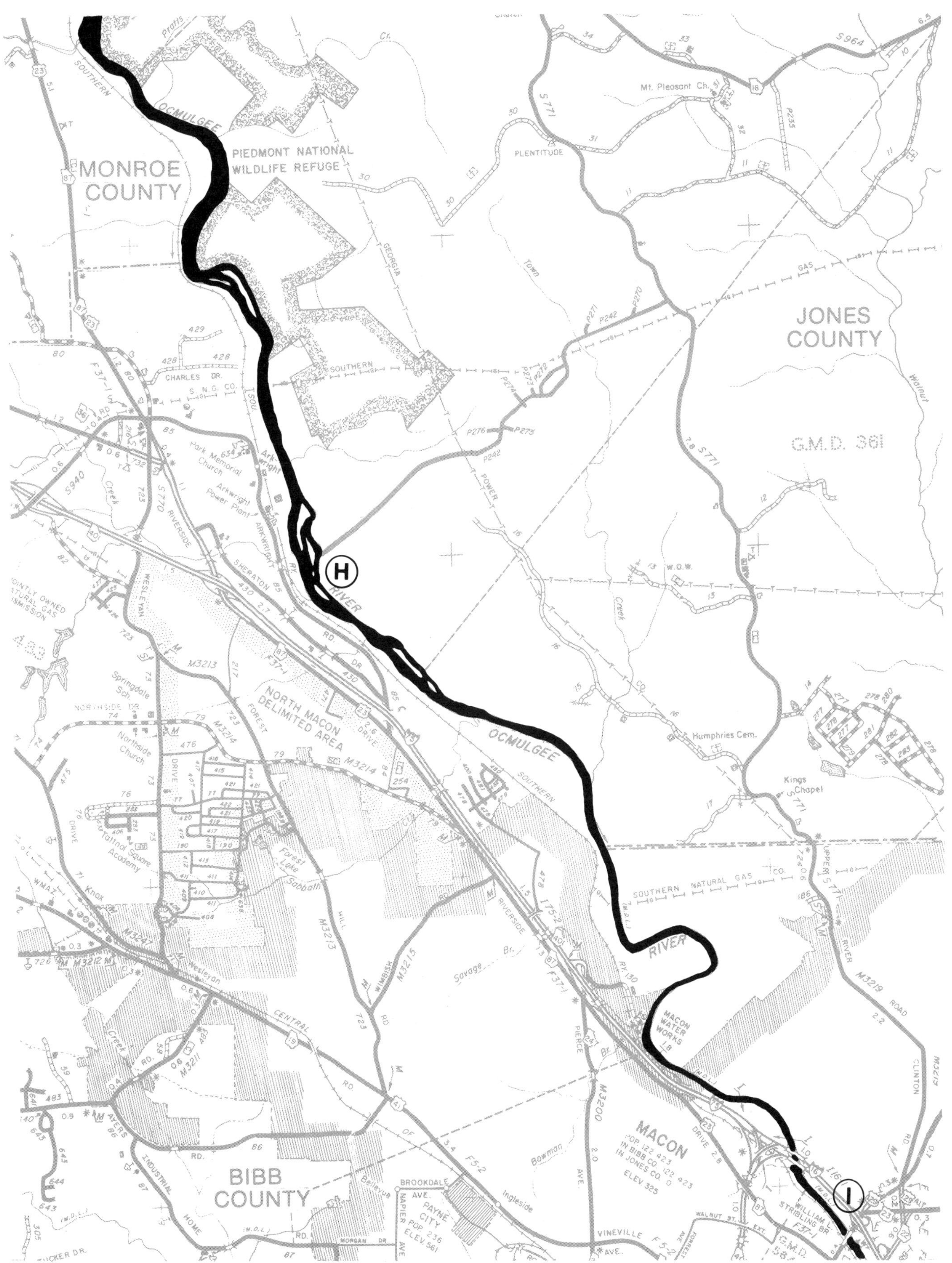

MONROE COUNTY
PIEDMONT NATIONAL WILDLIFE REFUGE
OCMULGEE
JONES COUNTY
G.M.D. 361
Mt. Pleasant Ch.
PLENTITUDE
Park Memorial Church
Arkwright Power Plant
NORTH MACON DELIMITED AREA
Springdale Sch.
Northside Church
Tattnall Square Academy
OCMULGEE
RIVER
Humphries Cem.
Kings Chapel
SOUTHERN NATURAL GAS CO.
MACON WATER WORKS
MACON
POP. 122,423
IN BIBB CO. 122,423
IN JONES CO. 0
ELEV. 325
BIBB COUNTY
PAYNE CITY
POP. 236
ELEV. 561
WILLIAM L. STRIBLING BR.

Lazer Creek

Lazer Creek flows northeastward and drains Talbot County in the western-central part of the state. Its headwaters are on Pine Mountain, and it drains into the Flint River just below Hightower Shoals, near Thomaston. Talbot County is ninety-three percent forested, and Lazer Creek is virtually undisturbed wilderness, thickly overgrown, and only now and then displays signs of man. The hills rise to 200 feet over the water in some sections, surprisingly mountainous territory for this part of the state. The stream bed is predominantly sandy and rocky. Quartzite ledges cross the stream, which causes precipitous drops and exciting shoals of Class II and III difficulty.

Narrow and intimate at the beginning of its canoeable length, Lazer Creek becomes 80 yards or more wide toward its mouth. The Flint, on which this section ends, is 150 or more yards wide. Hazards consist of the shoals themselves, which should be scouted, and the occasional hornets' nests hanging from overhead branches. Lazer Creek is remarkably free of deadfalls and strainers.

Section: Hendricks Rd. to Po Biddy Rd.

Counties: Talbot, Upson

Suitable For: Cruising

Appropriate For: Intermediate and advanced paddlers

Months Runnable: November through April and after heavy rains

Interest Highlights: Wildlife, geology, whitewater

Scenery: Beautiful

Difficulty: International Scale II (III)
Numerical Points 11

Average Width: 60-80 ft.
Gradient: Moderate to swift
Velocity: 7.9 ft./mi.

Runnable Water Level: (GA 36 bridge at Flint River) Minimum 8.5 ft. Maximum 11 ft.

Hazards: Rapids, hornets' nests

Scouting: At shoals

Portages: At shoals, as necessary

Rescue Index: Remote to accessible but difficult

Mean Water Temperature (°F)

Jan 48	Feb 50	Mar 58	Apr 68	May 74	Jun 76
Jul 80	Aug 78	Sep 74	Oct 69	Nov 62	Dec 54

Source of Additional Information: Cordele Game and Fish Office (912) 273-8945

Access Point	Access Code
A	1367
N[1]	2357

Access Key
1 Paved Road
2 Unpaved Road
3 Short Carry
4 Long Carry
5 Easy Grade
6 Steep Incline
7 Clear Trail
8 Brush and Trees
9 Launching Fee Charged
10 Private Property, Need Permission
11 No Access, Reference Only

[1]On the Flint River

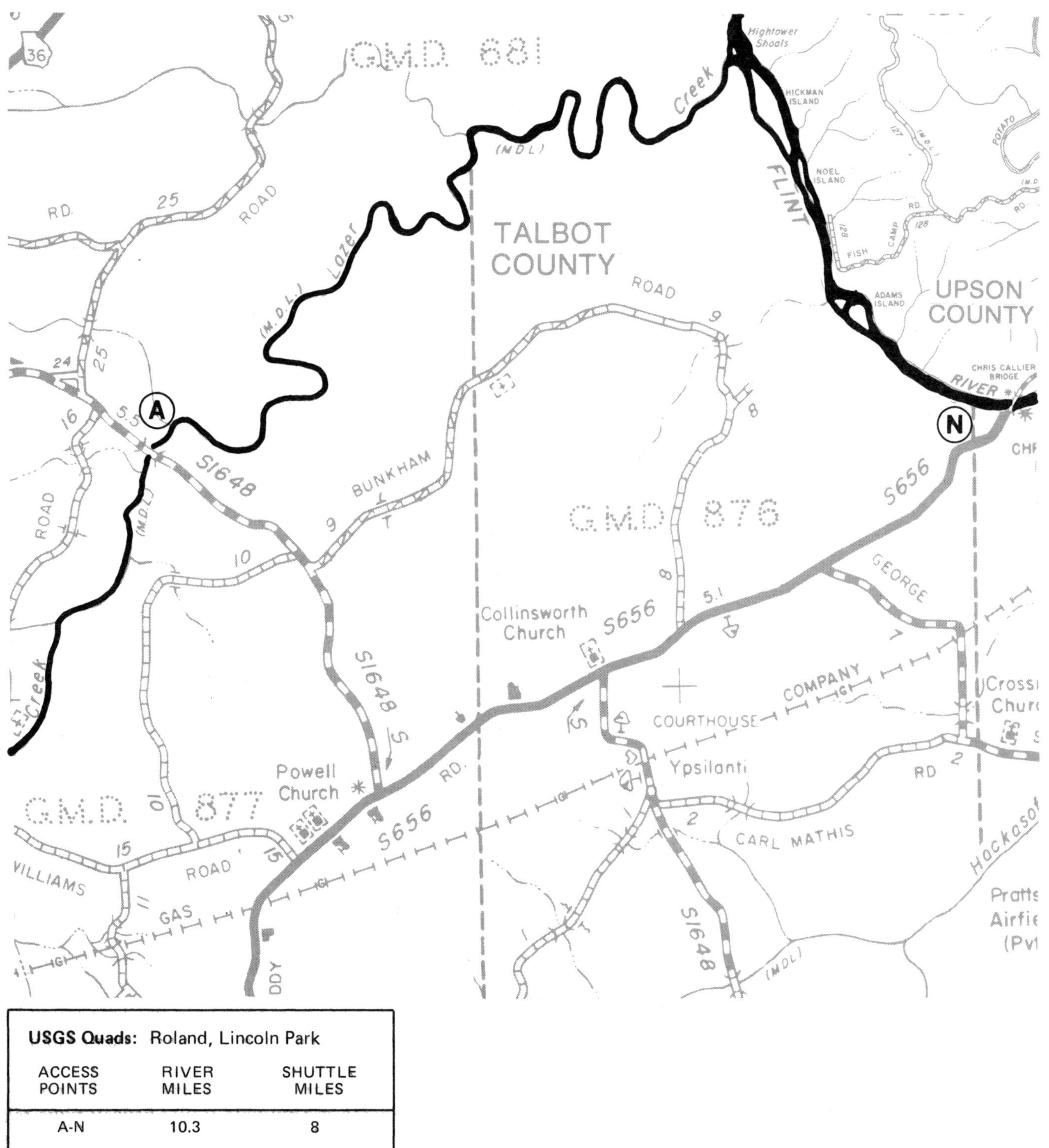

USGS Quads: Roland, Lincoln Park

ACCESS POINTS	RIVER MILES	SHUTTLE MILES
A-N	10.3	8

Flint River

The Flint is one of Georgia's longest rivers. It originates near Forest Park south of Atlanta and drains portions of twenty-seven counties and approximately 8,500 square miles as it journeys southwest to join the Chattahoochee River at Lake Seminole on the Georgia–Florida border. In terms of wilderness beauty, spectacular vistas, and varied terrain, the Flint is rivaled by no other large Georgia river. In the Piedmont alone the Flint alternately flows broad and narrow, beneath pine covered bluffs and at the foot of high rock walls, through winding bottomland swamp, past cities and towns, and between fertile cultivated plateaus. In the Coastal Plain (described in the next chapter) the Flint meanders through alternating pine forests and swamp and reclaimed crop and pasture land.

The Flint is runnable all year but is subject to sudden flashflooding during the winter and spring, particularly in the Piedmont. Late summer and fall are favorite paddling times that offer clearer water and exposed sandbars for camping. Though a passage can be forced in the headwaters sections, epidemic numbers of deadfalls (largely the result of beavers) restrict paddling upstream of Woolsey in Fayette County.

Heading downstream from the Hampton Road bridge east of Woolsey, Class I riffles and small ledges combine with more deadfalls to keep paddlers awake. The stream winds continuously and is well insulated in a canopy of willow, ash, birch, and silver maple. One-half mile below the crossing of GA 92 is a dam that must be portaged. Beyond the GA 16 bridge west of Griffin deadfalls completely block the stream in several places and must be carried around. Not until the Flint passes beneath the GA 362 bridge east of Alvaton does the channel become generally clear of obstructions.

Below GA 362 the river becomes slightly less curving and broadens from 45 to 65 feet in width, on the average. Bottom lands to either side of the stream are inundated and swampy. Continuing on, small shoals persist at approximately half-mile intervals, with each shoal being only 30 to 40 feet in length, and the river widens midway through Pike County to about 90 feet. An agricultural plain encroaches on the stream's wooded corridor but never robs the Flint of its remote atmosphere. Passing beneath the David Knott bridge west of Concord, old bridge pilings obstruct the stream by sometimes catching driftwood and debris and forming strainers. Below the pilings is a shoal of larger size and complexity than the others upstream. Extending several hundred yards, this Class II (borderline Class III) stretch is basically a matter of route selection with several alternatives available.

No further shoals of significance interrupt the tranquil flow of the Flint until downstream of the GA 18 bridge. Here the terrain alters dramatically with the river expanding to over 250 feet and descending a long series of ledges while steep wooded hills and small mountains converge to form an intimate and spectacular valley. Tall bluffs alternate with steep, sloping, forested hills and exposed rock walls and ledges. Pine Mountain looms majestically on both sides of the stream as the Flint passes along the Upson–Meriwether county line.

Section: Woolsey to Molena

Counties: Fayette, Spalding, Pike, Meriwether

Suitable For: Cruising

Appropriate For: Beginners, intermediates, advanced

Months Runnable: December to May; all year sometimes

Interest Highlights: Scenery, wildlife, whitewater

Scenery: Beautiful in spots

Difficulty: International Scale I-II (III)
Numerical Points 8

Average Width: 45-65 ft.
Velocity: Moderate
Gradient: 2.60 ft./mi.

Runnable Water Level: Minimum 150 cfs
(Griffin gauge) Maximum Up to flood stage

Hazards: Strainers, deadfalls, flashflooding, dams

Scouting: At shoals

Portages: Dam below GA 92 and around deadfalls

Rescue Index: Accessible but difficult

Mean Water Temperature (°F)

Jan 42	Feb 44	Mar 50	Apr 59	May 69	Jun 75
Jul 78	Aug 76	Sep 69	Oct 60	Nov 52	Dec 45

Source of Additional Information: Cordele Game and Fish Office (912) 273-8945

Access Point	Access Code
A	1358
B	1358
C	2367
D	2357
E	1357
F	2358
G	1367
H	1368
I	1357
J	1458

Access Key
1 Paved Road
2 Unpaved Road
3 Short Carry
4 Long Carry
5 Easy Grade
6 Steep Incline
7 Clear Trail
8 Brush and Trees
9 Launching Fee Charged
10 Private Property, Need Permission
11 No Access, Reference Only

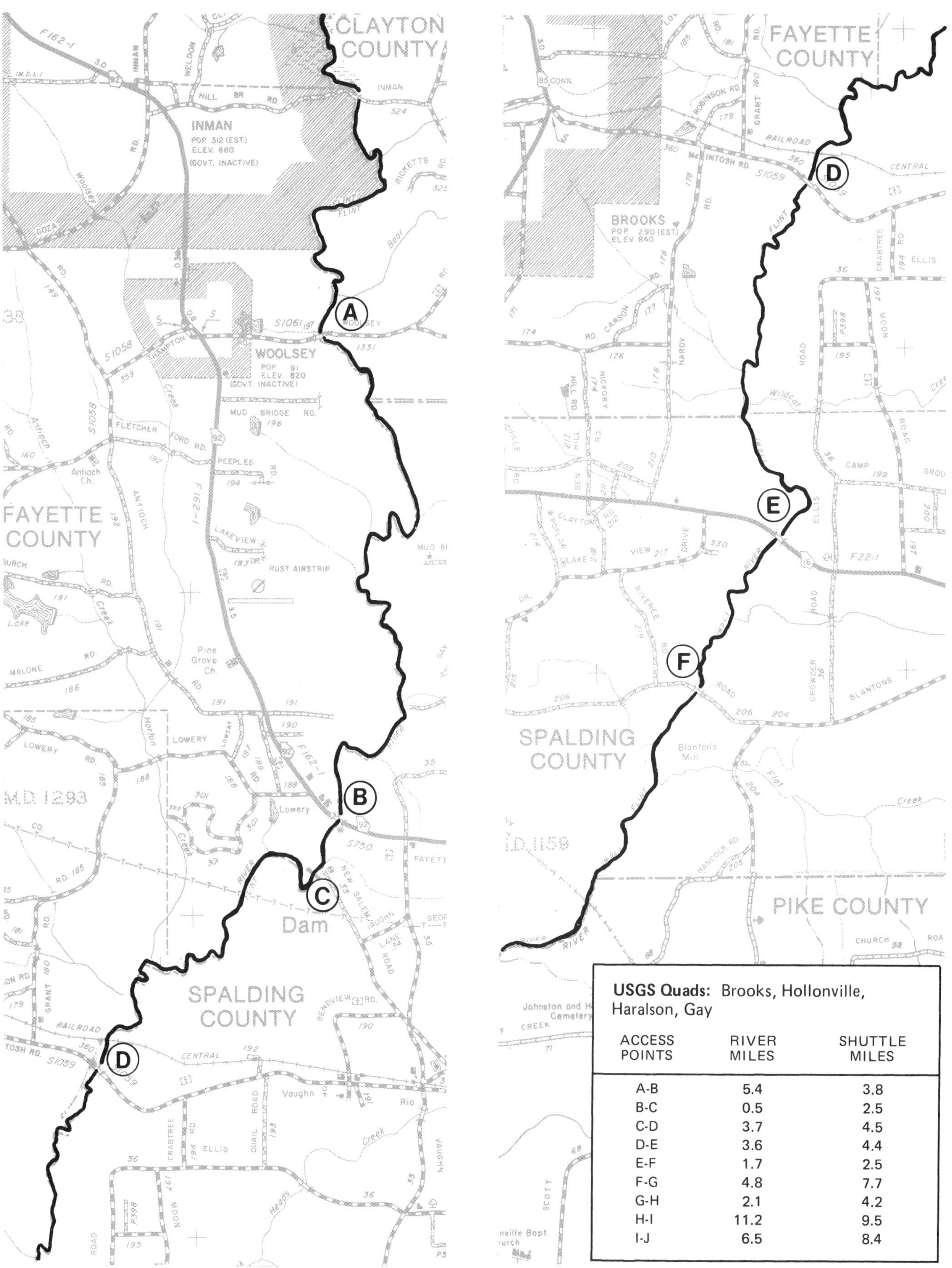

USGS Quads: Brooks, Hollonville, Haralson, Gay

ACCESS POINTS	RIVER MILES	SHUTTLE MILES
A-B	5.4	3.8
B-C	0.5	2.5
C-D	3.7	4.5
D-E	3.6	4.4
E-F	1.7	2.5
F-G	4.8	7.7
G-H	2.1	4.2
H-I	11.2	9.5
I-J	6.5	8.4

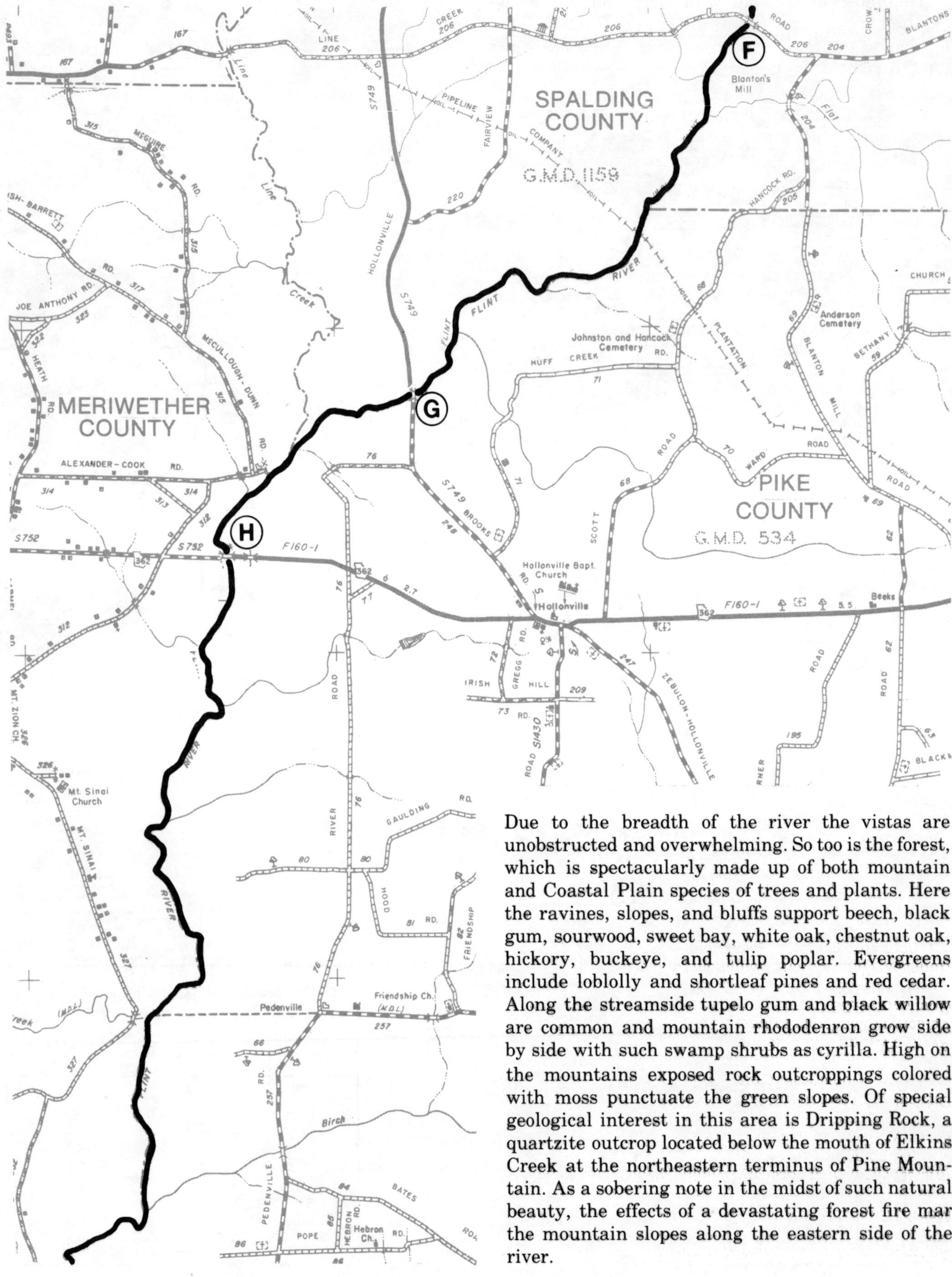

Due to the breadth of the river the vistas are unobstructed and overwhelming. So too is the forest, which is spectacularly made up of both mountain and Coastal Plain species of trees and plants. Here the ravines, slopes, and bluffs support beech, black gum, sourwood, sweet bay, white oak, chestnut oak, hickory, buckeye, and tulip poplar. Evergreens include loblolly and shortleaf pines and red cedar. Along the streamside tupelo gum and black willow are common and mountain rhododenron grow side by side with such swamp shrubs as cyrilla. High on the mountains exposed rock outcroppings colored with moss punctuate the green slopes. Of special geological interest in this area is Dripping Rock, a quartzite outcrop located below the mouth of Elkins Creek at the northeastern terminus of Pine Mountain. As a sobering note in the midst of such natural beauty, the effects of a devastating forest fire mar the mountain slopes along the eastern side of the river.

The most formidable whitewater on the Flint occurs between Spewrell Bluff and the Chris Callier bridge on the Po Biddy Road. Below Spewrell Bluff to the GA 36 bridge, shoals remain easy Class II although they tend to be more continuous than upstream. In low water the current pools above each ledge. In high water, however, the current is appreciably faster and precipitates the formation of some respectable holes.

Approximately one-half mile beyond the GA 36 bridge lies Yellow Jacket Shoals. At low water this borderline Class III is technical with a couple of big drops and some hidden boat-eating rocks. Since this rapid defies a "straight through" approach, paddlers attempting Yellow Jacket Shoals should possess skill in water reading, eddy turns, and ferrying. Those not wishing to run can line down. At higher levels the eddies disappear and the rapid becomes more intense. Fortunately, however, alternate routes become more numerous. Below Yellow Jacket Shoals a series of islands divide the channel and create occasional narrows as the Flint passes around them. Shoals persist through the island section but occur less frequently and never exceed Class II. Surrounding terrain remains mountainous, remote, and spectacular.

Downstream of Po Biddy Road the rugged, steep slopes begin to recede and taper, filing down to an agricultural plateau by the time the river reaches the US 80 bridge. The gradient diminishes in this section and shoals are smaller and occur less often. Passing an island midway between US 80 and GA 137, the last significant shoal is encountered as the river winds between high banks surrounded by cultivated table land. The river narrows to 85 to 110 feet and flows flat and calm with sandbars appearing on the inside of turns at low water. This marks the Flint's departure from the Piedmont and its arrival onto the Coastal Plain. The Coastal Plain section is found in the next chapter.

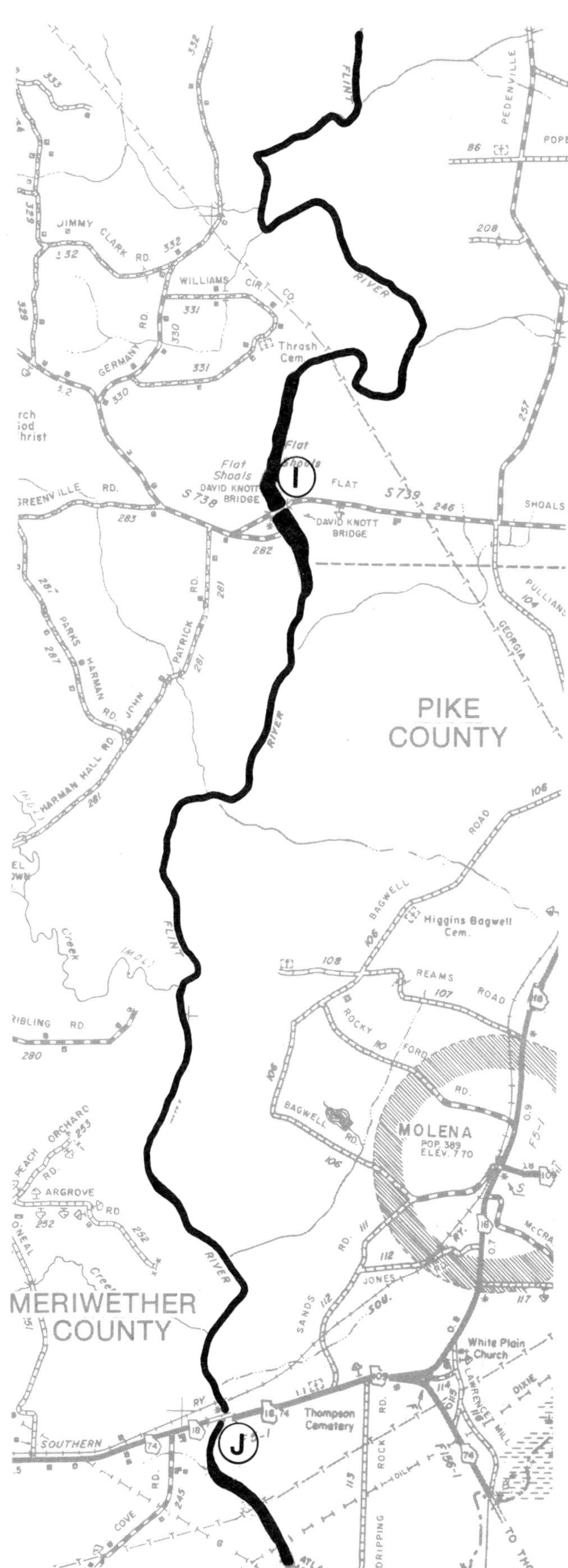

USGS Quads: Brooks, Hollonville, Haralson, Gay

ACCESS POINTS	RIVER MILES	SHUTTLE MILES
A-B	5.4	3.8
B-C	0.5	2.5
C-D	3.7	4.5
D-E	3.6	4.4
E-F	1.7	2.5
F-G	4.8	7.7
G-H	2.1	4.2
H-I	11.2	9.5
I-J	6.5	8.4

Flint River—*Continued*

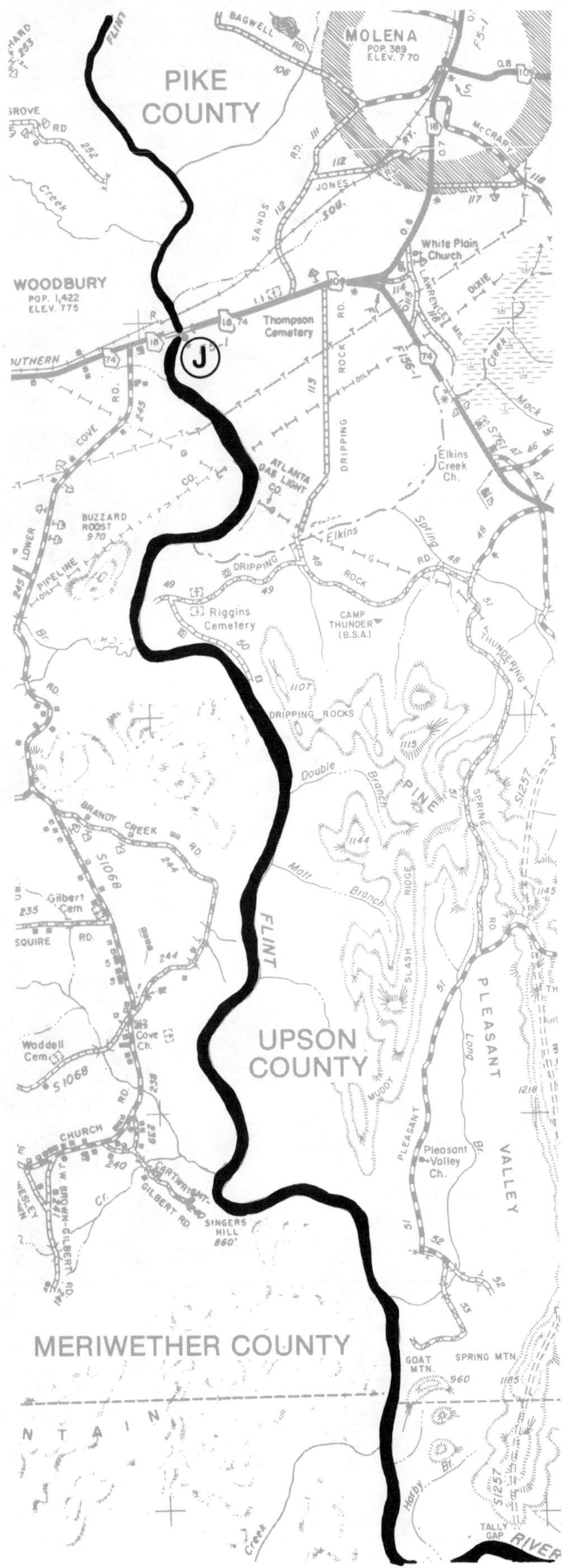

Section: Molena to US 80 bridge

Counties: Pike, Meriwether, Upson, Talbot, Taylor

Suitable For: Cruising, camping

Appropriate For: Intermediates, advanced paddlers

Months Runnable: All

Interest Highlights: Scenery, wildlife, whitewater, geology (Dripping Rock)
Scenery: Exceptionally beautiful

Difficulty: International Scale II (III)
Numerical Points 11

Average Width: 200-250 ft.
Velocity: Moderate to fast
Gradient: 8.39 ft./mi.

Runnable Water Level: Minimum 300 cfs
(Thomaston gauge) Maximum Up to flood stage

Hazards: Flashflooding, long rapids, excessive width, difficulty of rescue from water
Scouting: At shoals and rapids

Portages: At shoals and rapids as needed

Rescue Index: Remote to accessible but difficult

Mean Water Temperature (°F)

Jan	45	Feb	47	Mar	54	Apr	63	May	73	Jun	80
Jul	82	Aug	80	Sep	74	Oct	64	Nov	54	Dec	48

Source of Additional Information: Cordele Game and Fish Office (912) 273-8945

Access Point	Access Code
J	1458
K	1357
L	1357
M	2357
N	1357
O	1357

Access Key
1 Paved Road
2 Unpaved Road
3 Short Carry
4 Long Carry
5 Easy Grade
6 Steep Incline
7 Clear Trail
8 Brush and Trees
9 Launching Fee Charged
10 Private Property, Need Permission
11 No Access, Reference Only

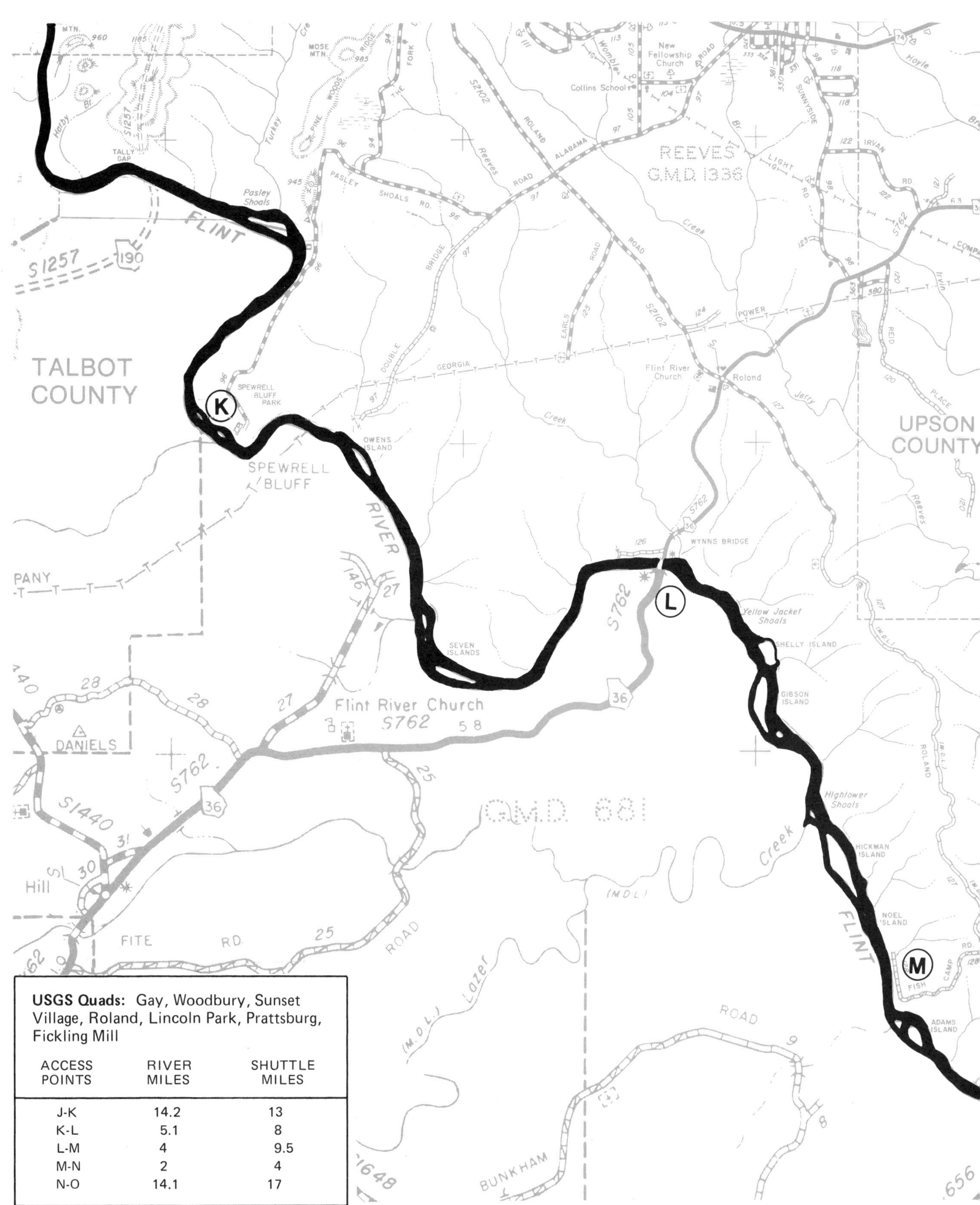

USGS Quads: Gay, Woodbury, Sunset Village, Roland, Lincoln Park, Prattsburg, Fickling Mill

ACCESS POINTS	RIVER MILES	SHUTTLE MILES
J-K	14.2	13
K-L	5.1	8
L-M	4	9.5
M-N	2	4
N-O	14.1	17

Flint River—*Continued*

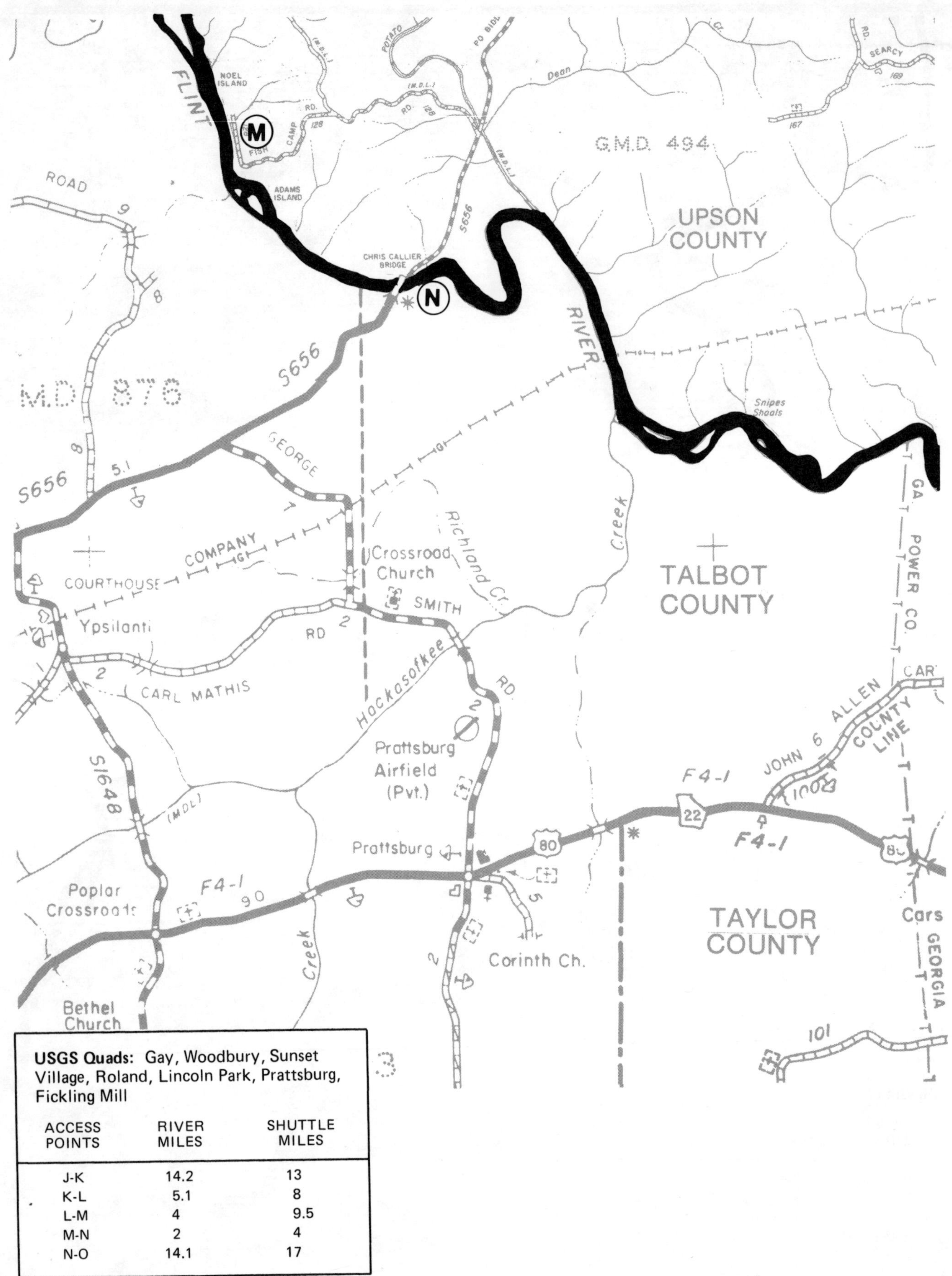

USGS Quads: Gay, Woodbury, Sunset Village, Roland, Lincoln Park, Prattsburg, Fickling Mill

ACCESS POINTS	RIVER MILES	SHUTTLE MILES
J-K	14.2	13
K-L	5.1	8
L-M	4	9.5
M-N	2	4
N-O	14.1	17

Section: Molena to US 80 bridge

Counties: Pike, Meriwether, Upson, Talbot, Taylor

Suitable For: Cruising, camping

Appropriate For: Intermediates, advanced paddlers

Months Runnable: All

Interest Highlights: Scenery, wildlife, whitewater, geology (Dripping Rock)

Scenery: Exceptionally beautiful

Difficulty: International Scale II (III)
Numerical Points 11

Average Width: 200-250 ft.
Velocity: Moderate to fast
Gradient: 8.39 ft./mi.

Runnable Water Level: Minimum 300 cfs
(Thomaston gauge) Maximum Up to flood stage

Hazards: Flashflooding, long rapids, excessive width, difficulty of rescue from water

Scouting: At shoals and rapids

Portages: At shoals and rapids as needed

Rescue Index: Remote to accessible but difficult

Mean Water Temperature (°F)

Jan 45	Feb 47	Mar 54	Apr 63	May 73	Jun 80
Jul 82	Aug 80	Sep 74	Oct 64	Nov 54	Dec 48

Source of Additional Information: Cordele Game and Fish Office (912) 273-8945

Access Point	Access Code
J	1458
K	1357
L	1357
M	2357
N	1357
O	1357

Access Key
1 Paved Road
2 Unpaved Road
3 Short Carry
4 Long Carry
5 Easy Grade
6 Steep Incline
7 Clear Trail
8 Brush and Trees
9 Launching Fee Charged
10 Private Property, Need Permission
11 No Access, Reference Only

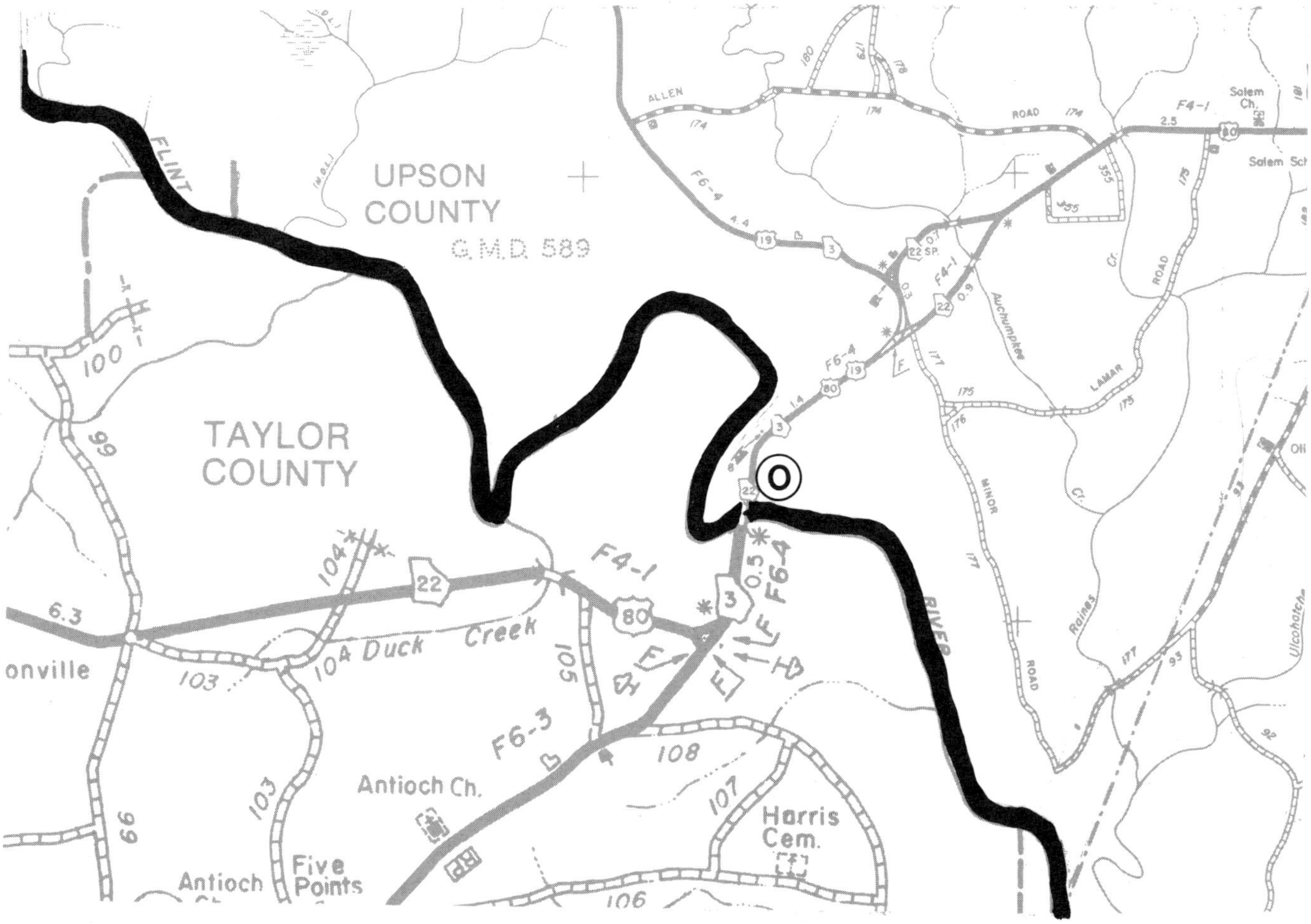

Big Creek

Big Creek is a tributary of the Chattahoochee River on the northern outskirts of Atlanta. It passes through the residential fringes of Roswell and thus is no stranger to development. Houses overlook its banks in several sections, and aqueducts feeding water to Roswell cross over the stream occasionally. The oldest development on the creek is a scenic wonder—a thirty-foot-high stone dam (and mandatory portage) that was part of the textile mill complex built in 1838.

Big Creek is narrow, slow, and intimate as it flows between brush-covered banks for most of its length, but there are rapids below the dam that are technical at any time and hazardous in high water. Though runnable all year, these shoals may be low in the summer. Normally Class II, when the water is up they approach Class III in difficulty. There is no gauge on Big Creek, but the stream can be scouted by entering the road at the mill site. Though aqueducts present more of an esthetic blight than a danger, be careful when approaching them at higher water levels.

Section: Oxbo Rd. to Chattahoochee Nature Center on the Chattahoochee River
Counties: Fulton

Suitable For: Cruising

Appropriate For: Beginners, intermediates, advanced

Months Runnable: November through July; all during wet years
Interest Highlights: Local culture and industry; Roswell Mill
Scenery: Pleasant, but marred by man's intrusions

Difficulty: International Scale II (III)
Numerical Points 12

Average Width: 45-60 ft.
Gradient: Slow to moderate
Velocity: 3.5 ft./mi.

Runnable Water Level: (Alpharetta gauge) Minimum 55 cfs
Maximum 250 cfs, open; up to flood stage, decked

Hazards: Overhead aqueducts, 30-ft. dam

Scouting: Ledge on left side of stream 100 yds. below dam, in high water
Portages: Around right side of Roswell Mill Dam

Rescue Index: Accessible

Mean Water Temperature (°F)

Jan 43	Feb 44	Mar 49	Apr 56	May 63	Jun 69
Jul 71	Aug 68	Sep 66	Oct 59	Nov 51	Dec 46

Source of Additional Information: Macon Game and Fish Office (912) 744-3228

Access Point	Access Code
A[1]	1368
B	1357

Access Key
1 Paved Road
2 Unpaved Road
3 Short Carry
4 Long Carry
5 Easy Grade
6 Steep Incline
7 Clear Trail
8 Brush and Trees
9 Launching Fee Charged
10 Private Property, Need Permission
11 No Access, Reference Only

[1] At path down steep bank below small, green, cinderblock substation

Sweetwater Creek.

Photo courtesy of *Brown's Guide to Georgia.*

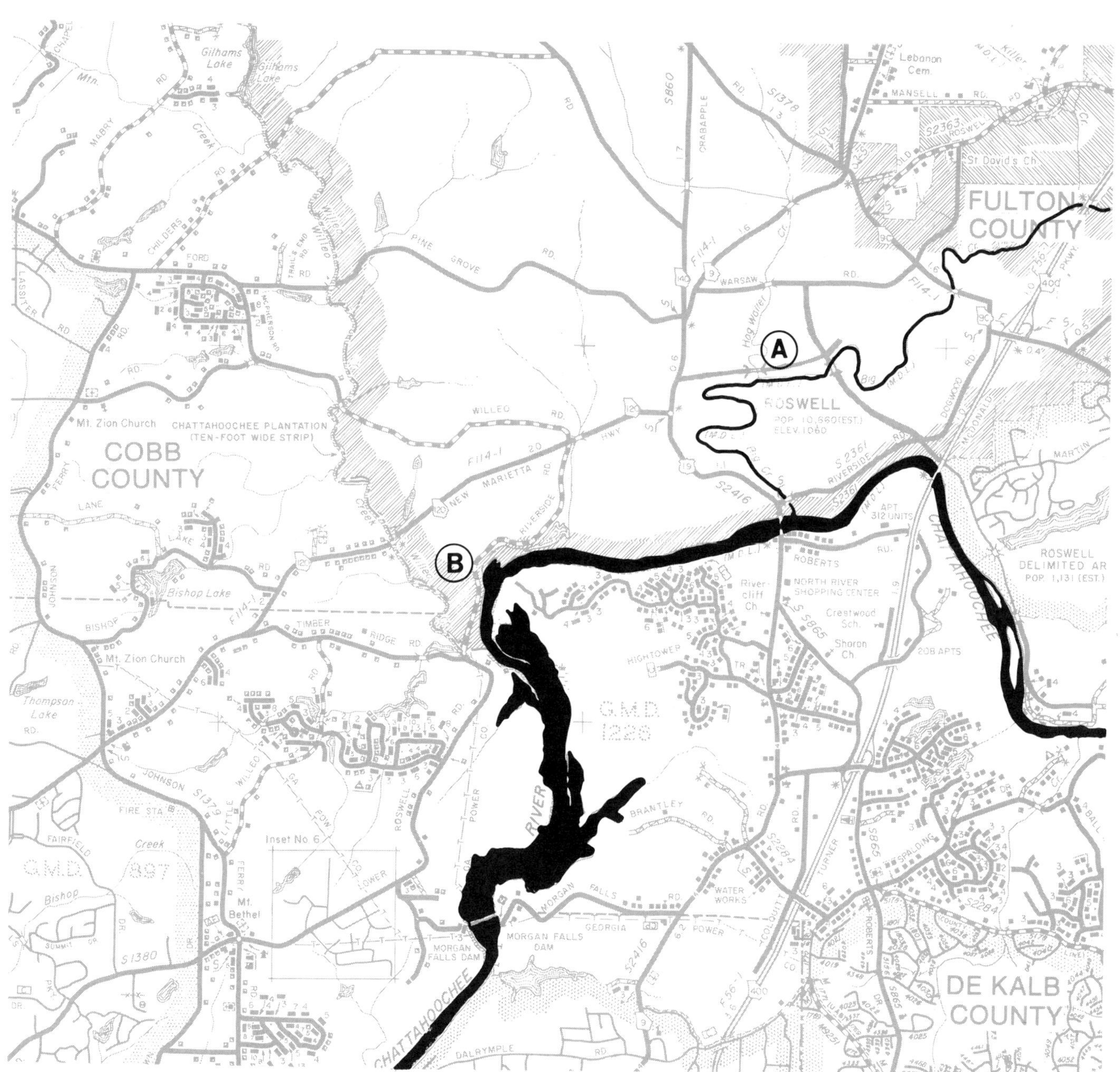

USGS Quads: Roswell, Mountain Park		
ACCESS POINTS	RIVER MILES	SHUTTLE MILES
A-B	2.85	2.8

Sweetwater Creek

Sweetwater Creek is a shady, scenic little stream that drains the corner of Douglas County southwest of Atlanta before emptying into the Chattahoochee River. Known primarily to Atlanta area boaters, the creek varies markedly from section to section. Runnable most of the year downstream of Blairs Bridge Road, Sweetwater Creek meanders serenely south between four-foot banks of varying steepness until it passes under the Douglas Hill Road bridge. Here, as the creek traverses the Brevard Fault Zone, serenity turns to mayhem as the creek crashes over six-foot ledges and churns through complex rock gardens. This intense bump and grind continues for almost three miles before the Sweetwater spends its fury and reverts to its former easy-going personality. In the several remaining miles downstream to its mouth, the creek flows through often narrow channels between sandy banks with many deadfalls obstructing the stream, but there are no more rapids.

Like many streams close to Atlanta, Sweetwater Creek is grossly polluted. Even so, the creek is often beautiful and worthwhile to paddle. The level of difficulty, in the whitewater section, is Class II and III, with Old Factory Shoals (one-half mile below the Douglas Hill Road bridge) approaching Class IV at some water levels. At higher water levels, low-hanging limbs pose an added danger.

Section: Blairs Bridge Rd. to Lower River Rd.

Counties: Douglas

Suitable For: Cruising

Appropriate For: Intermediate and advanced paddlers

Months Runnable: All except during dry spells

Interest Highlights: Whitewater

Scenery: Pretty

Difficulty: International Scale II-III (IV)
Numerical Points 17

Average Width: 80-120 ft.
Gradient: Moderate
Velocity: 21.7 ft./mi.

Runnable Water Level: Minimum 1.6 ft.
(I-20 bridge gauge) Maximum 2.3 ft., open; 3.0 ft., decked

Hazards: Rapids, deadfalls, low limbs at higher water

Scouting: Old Factory Shoals and other rapids, as needed

Portages: Ledges at Old Factory Shoals (either side)

Rescue Index: Accessible

Mean Water Temperature (°F)

Jan 42	Feb 43	Mar 48	Apr 57	May 68	Jun 75
Jul 79	Aug 77	Sep 73	Oct 63	Nov 54	Dec 47

Source of Additional Information: Sweetwater Creek State Park (404) 944-1700

Access Point	Access Code
A	2357
B	1457

Access Key
1 Paved Road
2 Unpaved Road
3 Short Carry
4 Long Carry
5 Easy Grade
6 Steep Incline
7 Clear Trail
8 Brush and Trees
9 Launching Fee Charged
10 Private Property, Need Permission
11 No Access, Reference Only

USGS Quads: Mableton, Austell, Ben Hill, Campbellton

ACCESS POINTS	RIVER MILES	SHUTTLE MILES
A-B	6.5	6

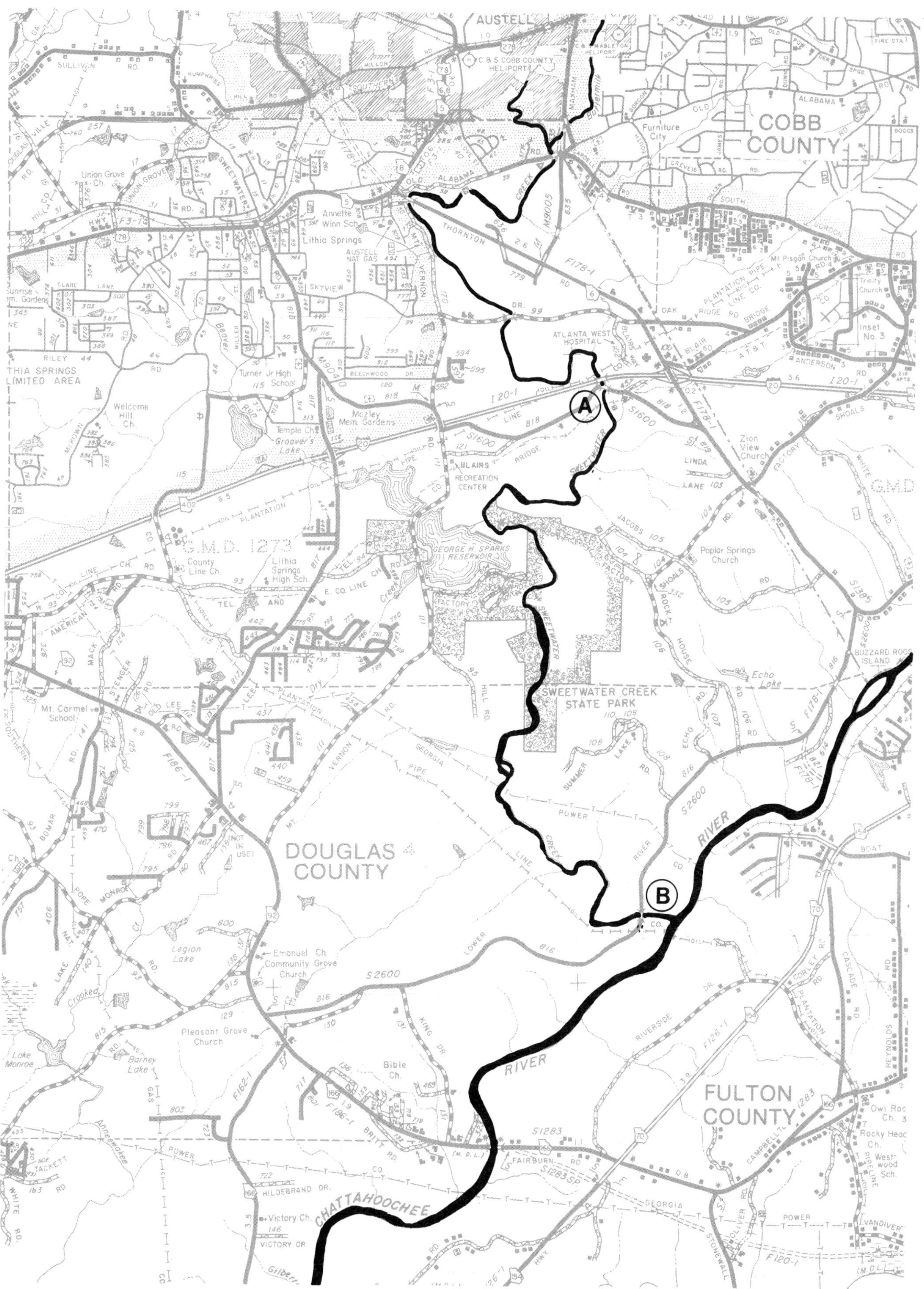

AUSTELL
COBB
COUNTY
DOUGLAS
COUNTY
FULTON
COUNTY
SWEETWATER CREEK
STATE PARK
GEORGE H. SPARKS
RESERVOIR
Lithia Springs
Furniture City
ATLANTA WEST HOSPITAL
CHATTAHOOCHEE
RIVER
A
B

Dog River

The Dog River is a scrambling, pounding, high-water stream firing off the Piedmont hills of Douglas County and descending into the Chattahoochee River. Runnable only after heavy rains, the Dog is a serious Class III (IV) whitewater run complete with big waves, heavy-duty holes, and more than a few hair-raising vertical drops.

From the Post Road bridge to the Banks Mill Road the Dog bounces over intermittent small ledges separated by short pools. Approaching the GA 5 bridge the difficulty of the run increases as ledges become larger and more numerous. Just downstream of the GA 5 crossing is where the Dog begins to bite. Large ledges, tricky converging currents, and nasty holes form continuous Class III (IV) whitewater action as the river winds through a mile and a half long reverse-S. The confluence of Flyblow Creek on the right signals the end of the S and the transition to more tranquil water a quarter mile downstream. Here ledges first become small then scarce as the Dog trots under the GA 166 bridge and drifts on down to the Chattahoochee.

Lined with hardwoods along its well-defined banks, the Dog is surrounded for the most part by woodland and farms. Paddlers should be on their best behavior since local landowners are somewhat sensitive to outsiders using the stream.

Though tempting because of its easy proximity to Atlanta, the Dog is definitely not a river to trifle with. When it's runnable at all it's pushy, technical in spots, and demanding. Occasional deadfalls add to the danger. Scouting, portaging, and rescue are difficult. Those attempting the Dog should be experienced with Class III whitewater and should make every effort to accompany someone who knows the run.

The scenery is pleasant when you have time to notice it, and access is good.

Section: Post Road bridge to Chattahoochee River

Counties: Douglas

Suitable For: Cruising

Appropriate For: Intermediates, advanced paddlers

Months Runnable: January through March and after heavy rains

Interest Highlights: Scenery, wildlife, whitewater

Scenery: Beautiful

Difficulty: International Scale II-III (IV)
Numerical Points 21

Average Width: 35-45 ft.
Velocity: Fast
Gradient: 16.8 ft./mi.

Runnable Water Level: Minimum 260 cfs
Maximum 450 cfs

Hazards: Deadfalls, difficult rapids, keeper hydraulics

Scouting: Rapids, as necessary

Portages: Rapids, as necessary

Rescue Index: Accessible to accessible but difficult

Mean Water Temperature (°F)

Jan 48	Feb 51	Mar 56	Apr 61	May 68	Jun 73
Jul 75	Aug 74	Sep 69	Oct 61	Nov 56	Dec 51

Source of Additional Information: Macon Game and Fish Office (912) 744-3228; High Country Outfitters (404) 955-1866

Access Point	Access Code
A	1468
B	2367
C	(11)
D	2357
E	1367
AA[1]	1357

Access Key
1 Paved Road
2 Unpaved Road
3 Short Carry
4 Long Carry
5 Easy Grade
6 Steep Incline
7 Clear Trail
8 Brush and Trees
9 Launching Fee Charged
10 Private Property, Need Permission
11 No Access, Reference Only

[1]On the Chattahoochee River

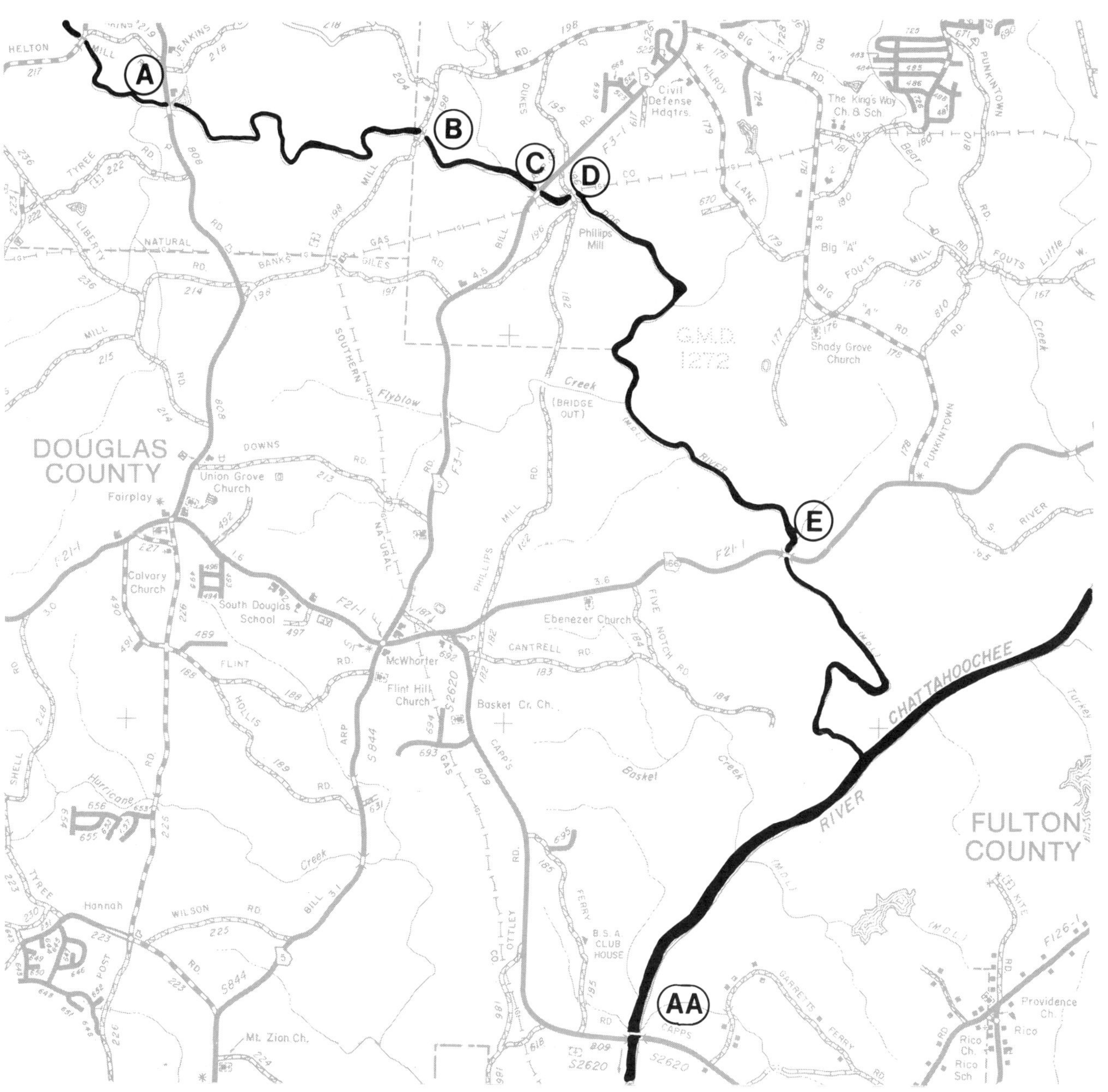

USGS Quads: Winston, Rico		
ACCESS POINTS	RIVER MILES	SHUTTLE MILES
A-B	2.7	2.5
B-C	0.9	2.2
C-D	0.2	0.5
D-E	3.5	5.5
E-AA	4.6	6.3

Flat Shoal Creek

Flat Shoal Creek, a tributary of the Chattahoochee, flows southwestward draining portions of Troup and Harris counties in the west-central part of the state. Paralleled by I-85, it is one of the most easily visited streams in the Piedmont. Though runnable below the US 27 bridge, logjams punctuate the stream in the upper sections. Downstream the channel is clearer, but access is a major problem, since very few take-outs are available. Described here is a relatively painless five-mile run from GA 18 to GA 103, flowing through four miles of pleasantly forested flat water followed by a half mile of delightful Class II+ shoals. In these shoals there are no big drops, but the ledges follow one another almost without interruption. The going here is frequently technical and requires good water reading ability and quick thinking. In low water expect to get stuck a few times. In high water beginners may be in for a long tumbling swim. Scout or portage from the right bank as water levels require.

Flat Shoal Creek runs between steep, sandy clay banks averaging four to six feet in height. Surrounding terrain consists of oak–hickory forest with a plentiful sprinkling of loblolly pines on rocky points. An intimate stream except at the broader shoals, Flat Shoals Creek is shady and inviting. Flora, in addition to the above, consists of a dazzling spring display of spider lilies bordering the shoals and a bumper crop of poison ivy, especially at the put-in.

The level of difficulty is Class I and II with the shoals, as mentioned, and deadfalls are the primary hazards to navigation.

Section: GA 18 to GA 103

Counties: Troup, Harris

Suitable For: Cruising

Appropriate For: Intermediate and advanced paddlers

Months Runnable: November through June

Interest Highlights: Scenery, whitewater

Scenery: Pretty

Difficulty: International Scale I-II+
Numerical Points 10

Average Width: 60-70 ft.
Velocity: Moderate
Gradient: 5 ft./mi. (40 ft./mi. at shoals)

Runnable Water Level: Minimum No gauge
Maximum Up to flood stage

Hazards: Deadfalls, long rapids, poison ivy at put-in

Scouting: Shoals from right bank

Portages: None required

Rescue Index: Accessible

Mean Water Temperature (°F)

Jan 48	Feb 50	Mar 59	Apr 71	May 74	Jun 77
Jul 79	Aug 78	Sep 72	Oct 66	Nov 59	Dec 52

Source of Additional Information: Macon Game and Fish Office (912) 744-3228

Access Point	Access Code
A	1357
B	1467

Access Key

1 Paved Road
2 Unpaved Road
3 Short Carry
4 Long Carry
5 Easy Grade
6 Steep Incline
7 Clear Trail
8 Brush and Trees
9 Launching Fee Charged
10 Private Property, Need Permission
11 No Access, Reference Only

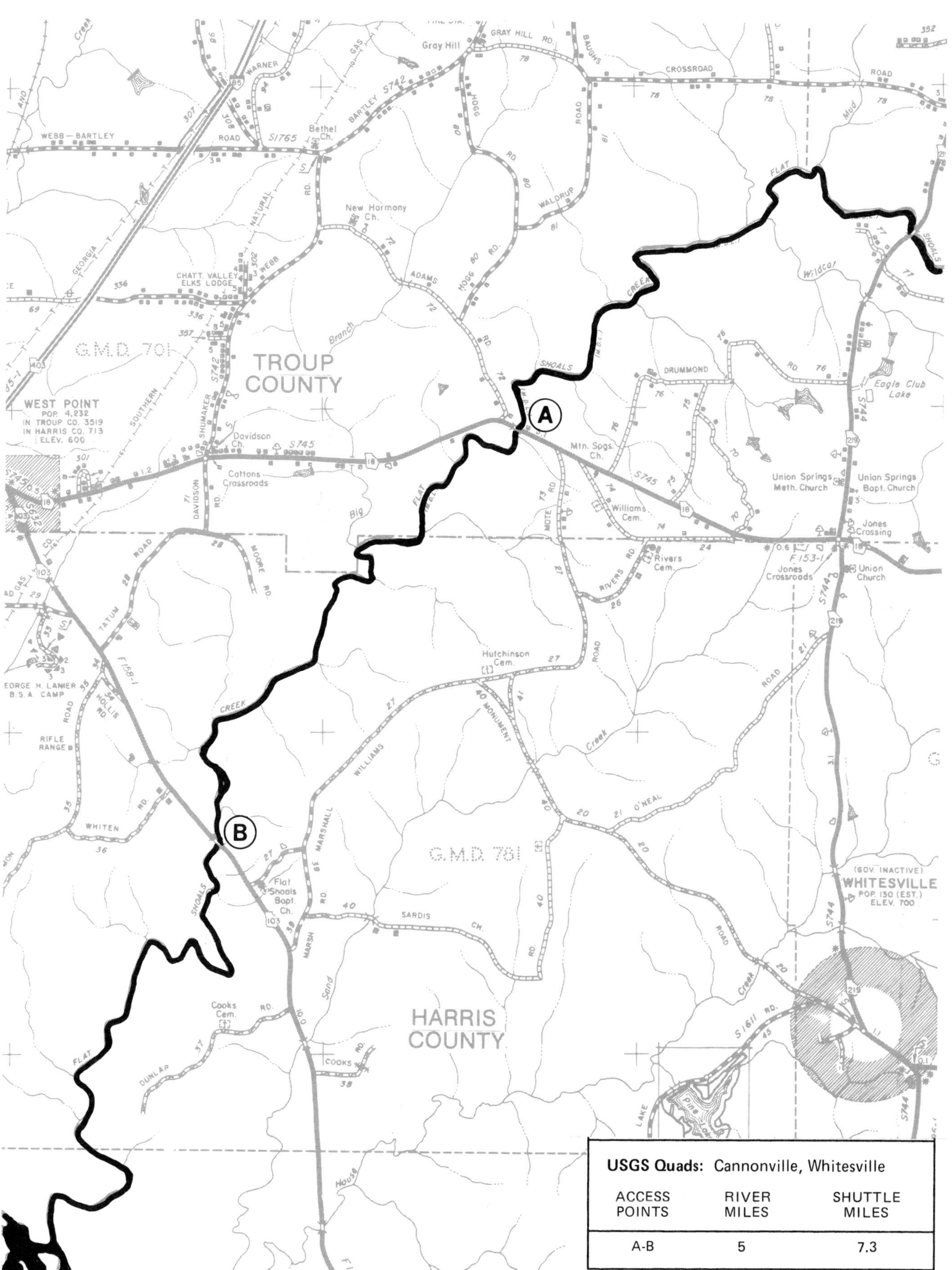

USGS Quads: Cannonville, Whitesville

ACCESS POINTS	RIVER MILES	SHUTTLE MILES
A-B	5	7.3

Mulberry Creek

Mulberry Creek flows east off Pine Mountain and empties into the Chattahoochee River twenty miles north of Columbus. A wilderness stream except for intersecting roads and a dam near US 27, it is virtually undisturbed by man. For most of its course it is a placid, shaded stream with high banks covered with mulberry and mountain laurel. At High Shoals, however, it makes an unexpected drop over a four-foot rock ledge. Below the last take-out there is a torturous and impassable forty-foot falls. This is a major hazard and should be avoided at all costs. Another danger is the Kingsboro Dam above US 27. Portage on the left. A half mile above the dam a yellow cable stretched across the stream signals the approach of the dam. The cable itself presents a dangerous obstruction at higher water levels.

USGS Quads: Cataula, Mulberry Grove, Bartletts Ferry Dam

ACCESS POINTS	RIVER MILES	SHUTTLE MILES
A-B	3.3	4.7
B-C	4.3	4.6
C-D	3.0	6.5
D-E	5.5	7.2
E-F	4.0	5.8

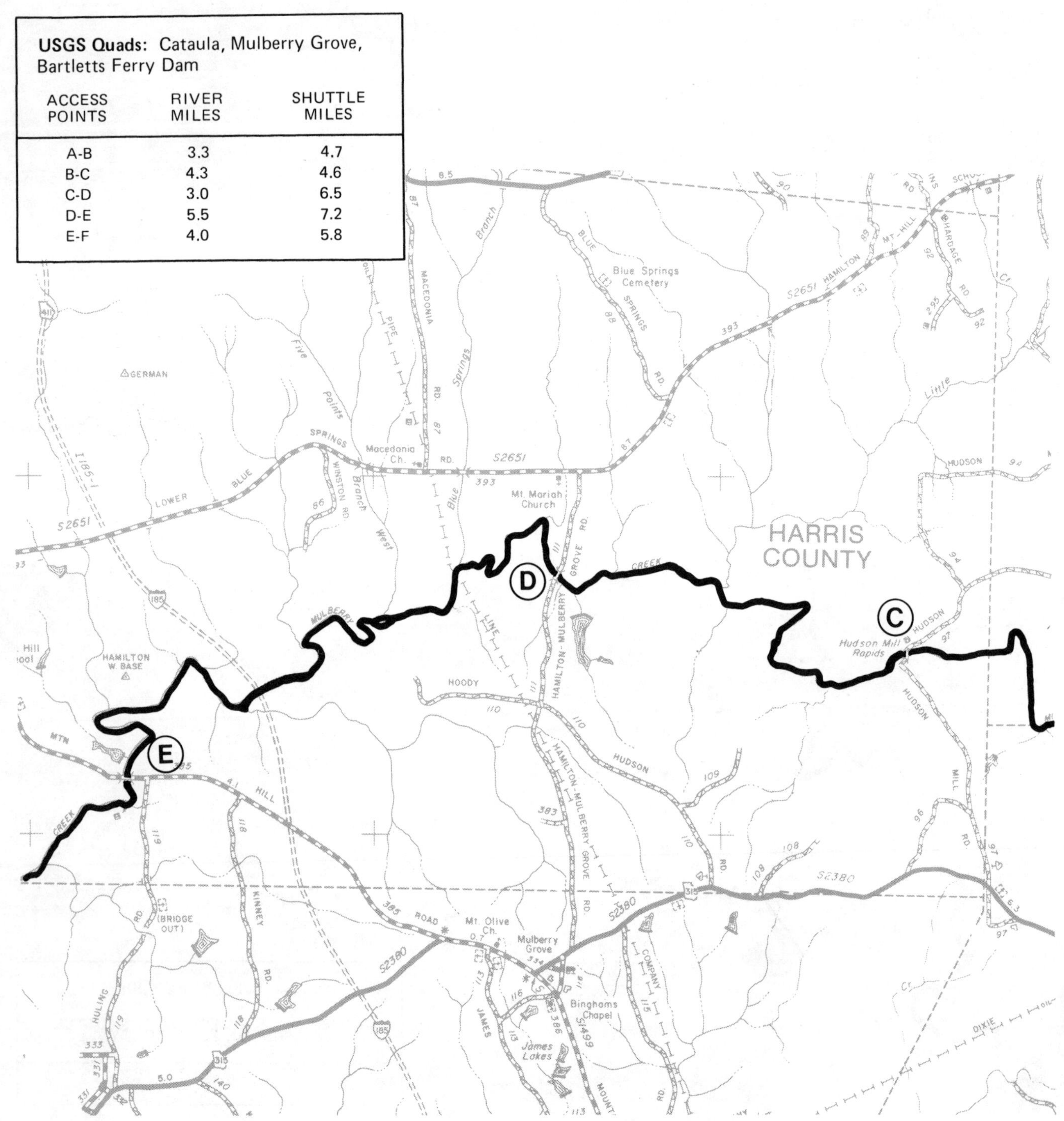

Section: Winfree Rd. to GA 103

Counties: Harris

Suitable For: Cruising

Appropriate For: Beginners and intermediates

Months Runnable: All except during dry spells

Interest Highlights: Scenery, wildlife, whitewater at High Shoals

Scenery: Pretty

Difficulty: International Scale I-II
Numerical Points 8

Average Width: 45-70 ft.
Gradient: Moderate
Velocity: 8.9 ft./mi.

Runnable Water Level: Minimum No gauge
Maximum Up to flood stage

Hazards: Strainers, deadfalls, dams

Scouting: At High Shoals

Portages: Difficult portage at mill dam near GA 27 bridge. Portage to left to avoid mill dam; lining canoe through shoals below dam may be necessary. Good portage route over center rocks at High Shoals.

Rescue Index: Accessible but difficult

Mean Water Temperature (°F)

Jan	47	Feb	50	Mar	59	Apr	70	May	72	Jun	77
Jul	79	Aug	77	Sep	72	Oct	66	Nov	60	Dec	52

Source of Additional Information: Macon Game and Fish Office (912) 744-3228

Access Point	Access Code
A	2367
B	1468
C	2367
D	1367
E	1358
F	1457

Access Key
1 Paved Road
2 Unpaved Road
3 Short Carry
4 Long Carry
5 Easy Grade
6 Steep Incline
7 Clear Trail
8 Brush and Trees
9 Launching Fee Charged
10 Private Property, Need Permission
11 No Access, Reference Only

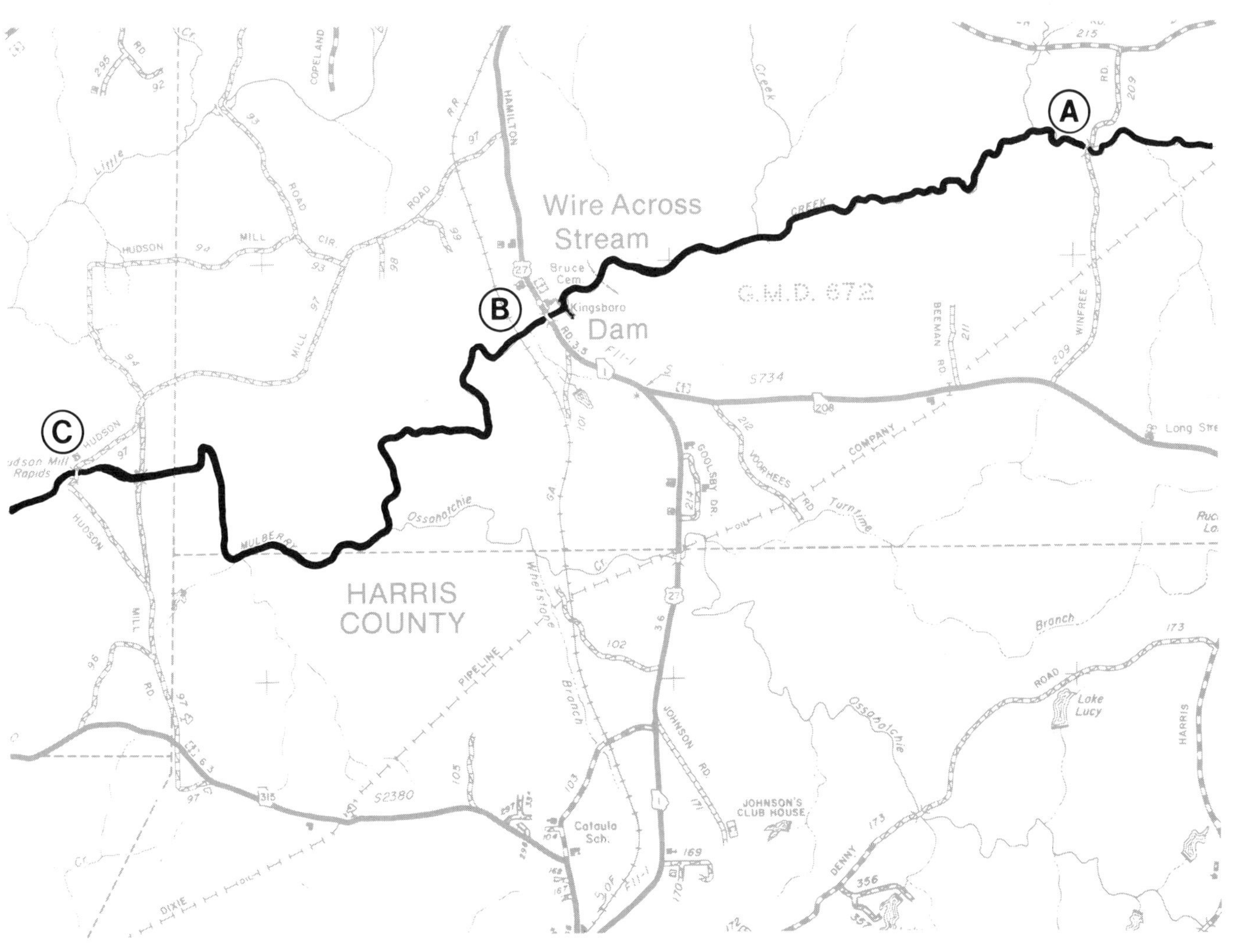

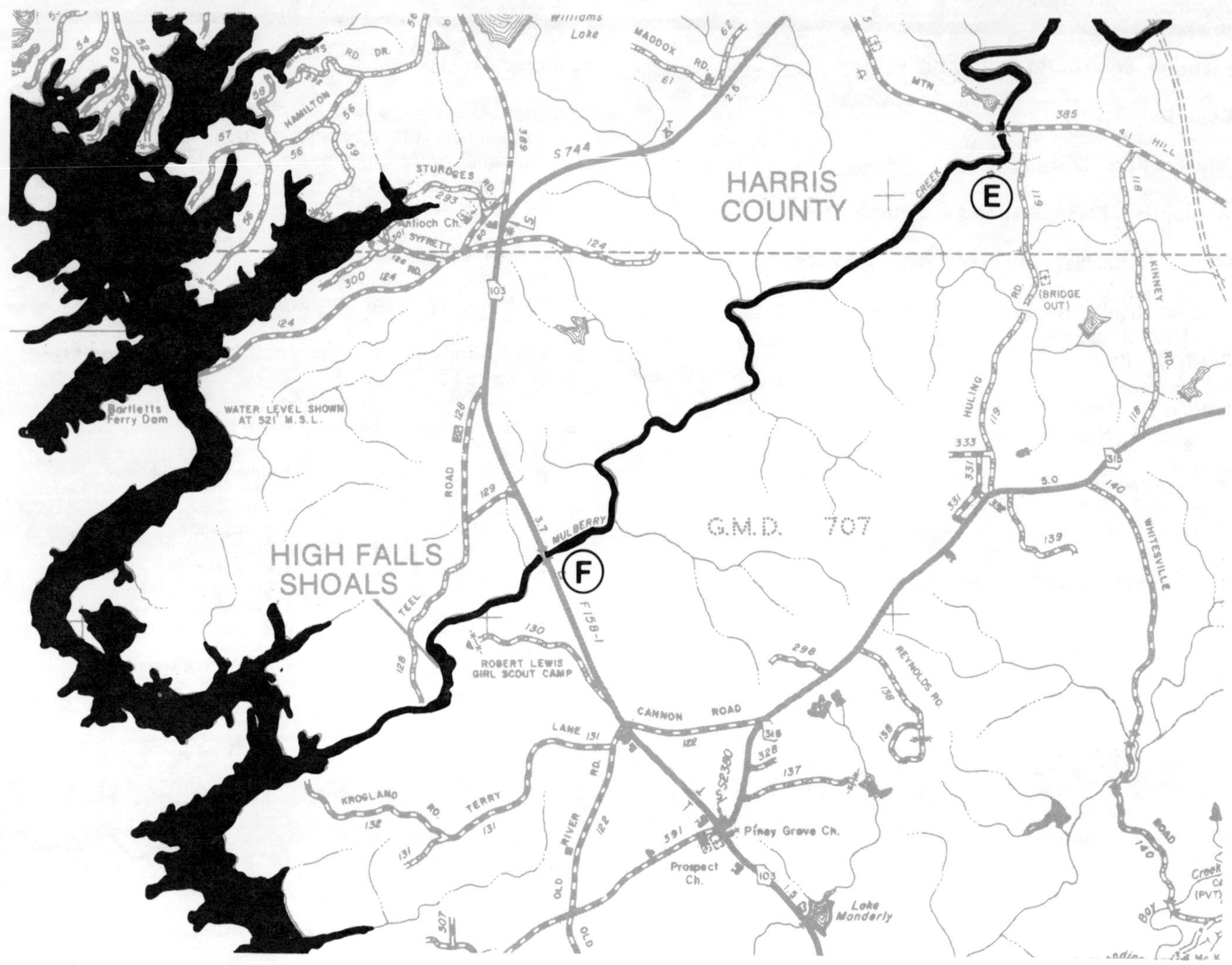

USGS Quads: Cataula, Mulberry Grove, Bartletts Ferry Dam

ACCESS POINTS	RIVER MILES	SHUTTLE MILES
A-B	3.3	4.7
B-C	4.3	4.6
C-D	3.0	6.5
D-E	5.5	7.2
E-F	4.0	5.8

Flint River.

Photo courtesy of *Brown's Guide to Georgia.*

Chattahoochee River

The Chattahoochee River is one of the major rivers draining the State of Georgia, and its remarkable diversity is an accurate reflection of Georgia's topography. It is navigable by canoe or kayak from the dramatic mountain headwaters to the Florida border, where it becomes the Apalachicola, and remains navigable to the Gulf of Mexico. In this book the river below Buford Dam of Lake Sidney Lanier is described. Here, in Chapter 5, the river as it flows through the western Piedmont is presented. In Chapter 6 is the Coastal Plain portion of the river. The sections above Lake Lanier are found in a companion book, *Northern Georgia Canoeing: A Canoeing and Kayaking Guide to the Streams of the Cumberland Plateau, Blue Ridge Mountains and Eastern Piedmont.*

Below Buford Dam, on the border between Forsyth and Gwinnett counties, the Chattahoochee River flows between clay banks of six to ten feet as it winds throught the Piedmont enroute to Atlanta. Tree-lined and pleasant, the river averages 120 feet in width and flows with a moderate current. Water is clear with a greenish cast in this stretch most of the year. Small ripples and occasional tiny shoals keep the paddling interesting. Two miles below the GA 141 bridge on the northeastern outskirts of Atlanta the backwaters of the Morgan Falls Dam are encountered. Though the water is slack, passage through this wealthy suburban residential area is nonetheless interesting since some of Atlanta's finest residential architecture is nestled among the hills and bluffs that border the river.

Downstream of the Morgan Falls Dam the parade of homes continues for about four more miles. A half mile below the I-285 crossing, two stairstep shoals of low Class II difficulty keep paddlers awake. Moving along, small shoals persist until one and one-half miles below Paces Ferry Road where there are two partial dams. Both can be run without danger. A clear downstream V marks the route through the first, while the second should be run on the far right. Below the partial dams the river enters a congested industrial corridor complete with factories, junkyards, freight sidings, and just about anything and everything else you can think of. Access is very limited throughout this section down to the mouth of Sweetwater Creek in Douglas County.

Downstream of Atlanta the Chattahoochee runs within tree-lined banks with alternating agricultural table land and forest cradling the stream. The course of the Chattahoochee tends toward long, straight sections followed by broad, looping bends. Shoals are intermittent and usually consist of small ledges that are straightforward and rarely exceed Class I+ in difficulty. An exception is Bush Head

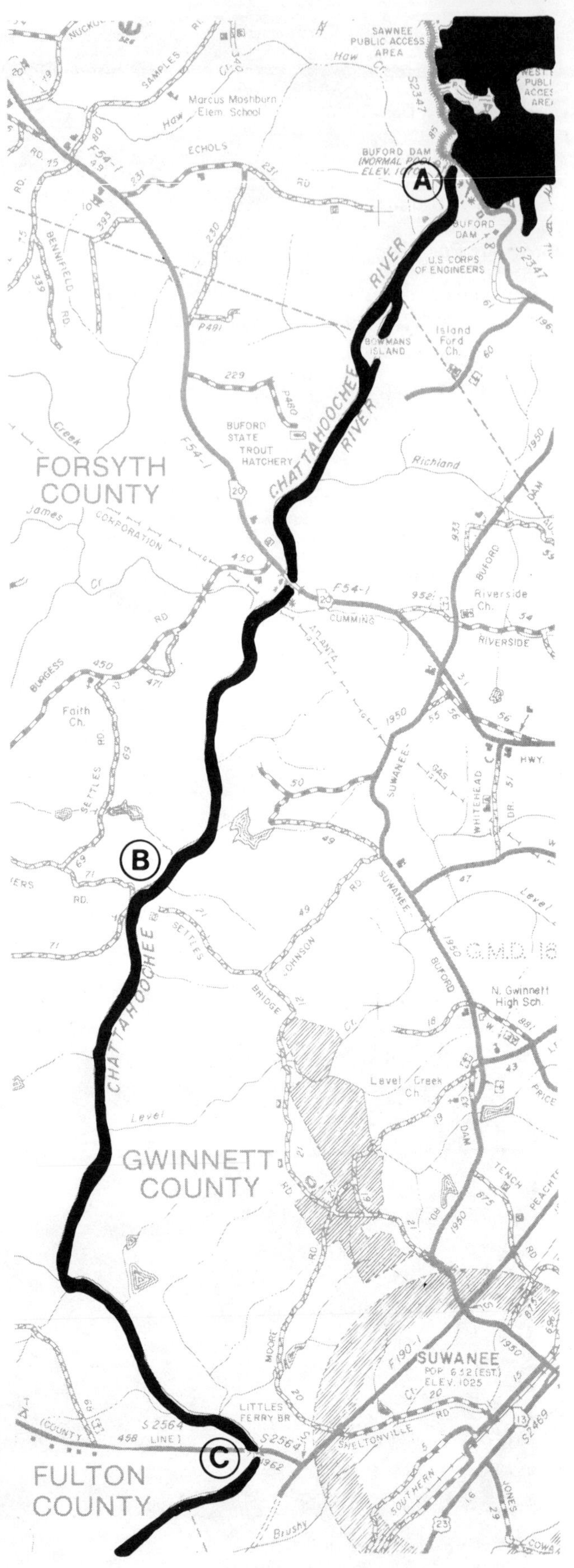

Section: Buford Dam to Morgan Falls Dam

Counties: Forsythe, Gwinnett, Fulton

Suitable For: Cruising

Appropriate For: Beginners, intermediates, advanced

Months Runnable: All when Buford Dam is releasing

Interest Highlights: Scenery, wildlife, local culture and industry

Scenery: Pretty in spots to beautiful in spots

Difficulty: International Scale I (II)
Numerical Points 6

Average Width: 120 ft.
Velocity: Moderate
Gradient: 2.32 ft./mi.

Runnable Water Level: Minimum Not applicable
Maximum Up to flood stage

Hazards: Cold water

Scouting: None

Portages: None

Rescue Index: Accessible

Mean Water Temperature (°F)

Jan	47	Feb	46	Mar	47	Apr	50	May	54	Jun	56
Jul	58	Aug	58	Sep	57	Oct	54	Nov	51	Dec	49

Source of Additional Information: High Country Outfitters (404) 955-1866

Access Point	Access Code
A	1357
B	2367
C	1367
D	2368
E	1357
F	1357
G	(11)
H	1357
I	1357
J	1357
K[1]	1357

Access Key
1 Paved Road
2 Unpaved Road
3 Short Carry
4 Long Carry
5 Easy Grade
6 Steep Incline
7 Clear Trail
8 Brush and Trees
9 Launching Fee Charged
10 Private Property, Need Permission
11 No Access, Reference Only

[1] Above Morgan Falls Dam

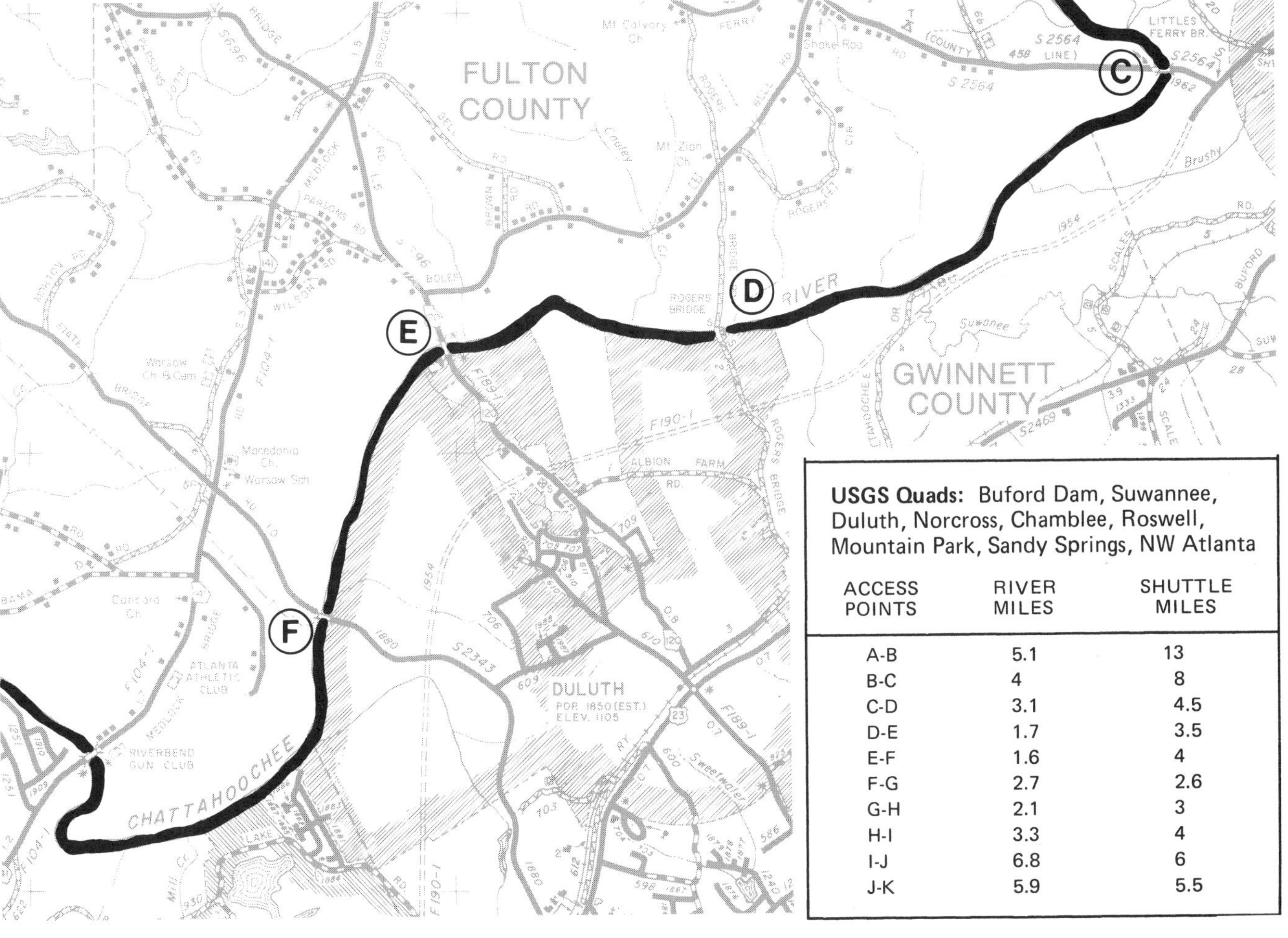

USGS Quads: Buford Dam, Suwannee, Duluth, Norcross, Chamblee, Roswell, Mountain Park, Sandy Springs, NW Atlanta

ACCESS POINTS	RIVER MILES	SHUTTLE MILES
A-B	5.1	13
B-C	4	8
C-D	3.1	4.5
D-E	1.7	3.5
E-F	1.6	4
F-G	2.7	2.6
G-H	2.1	3
H-I	3.3	4
I-J	6.8	6
J-K	5.9	5.5

Shoals, a legitimate Class II section about three miles upstream of Franklin in Heard County. The best route here is to go to the right around the large island at the top of the shoals and then to move to the middle of the stream at the downstream base of the island to run the lower shoals. Daniel Shoals, farther downstream, is borderline Class II and should present no difficulty. Below Daniel Shoals is the city of Franklin and the lake pool of West Point Lake.

Released at West Point Dam, the Chattahoochee moves from one impoundment to another all the way to Columbus, where four dams within a three-mile section of river provide an ironic finale for this dammed, power-plant infested, and damned section of the Chattahoochee. Slack water, dull scenery, and an abundance of portages combine to make a paddle trip suitable only for bad dreams.

The Chattahoochee through the Piedmont from Buford Dam to Franklin (industrial Atlanta excepted), however, is pleasant paddling. Modest bluffs and some exposed rock combine with a young forest dominated by pignut hickory, river birch, tulip poplar, sassafras, water oak, black walnut, box elder, and loblolly pine that approach and retreat from the river's edge. Undergrowth consists of honeysuckle, various asters, Christmas fern, trumpet creeper, and river cane. Between Franklin and Columbus (where the river is passed from dam to dam) banks diminish in height marking the river's transition from the Piedmont to the Coastal Plain. The section below Columbus is found in the next chapter.

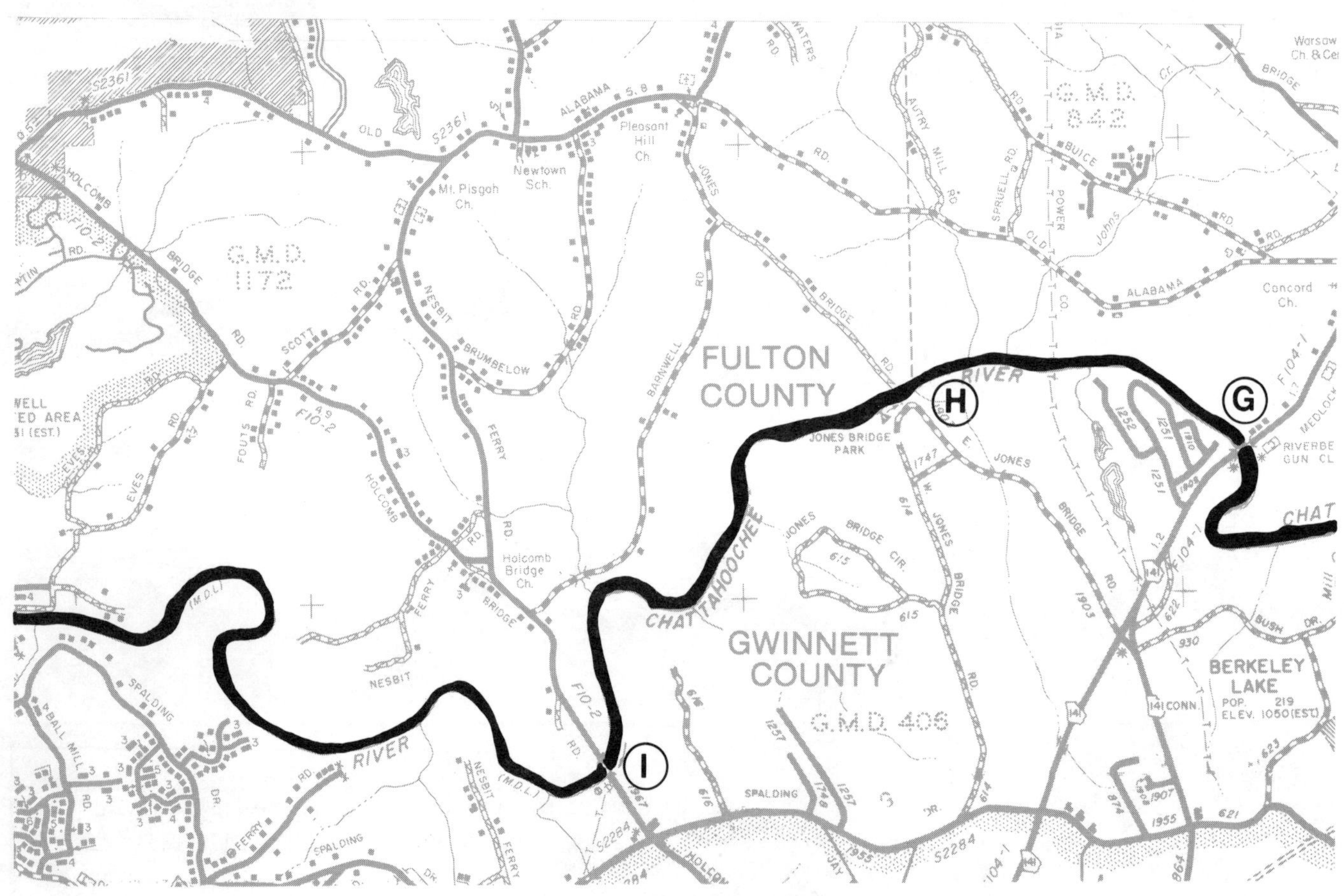

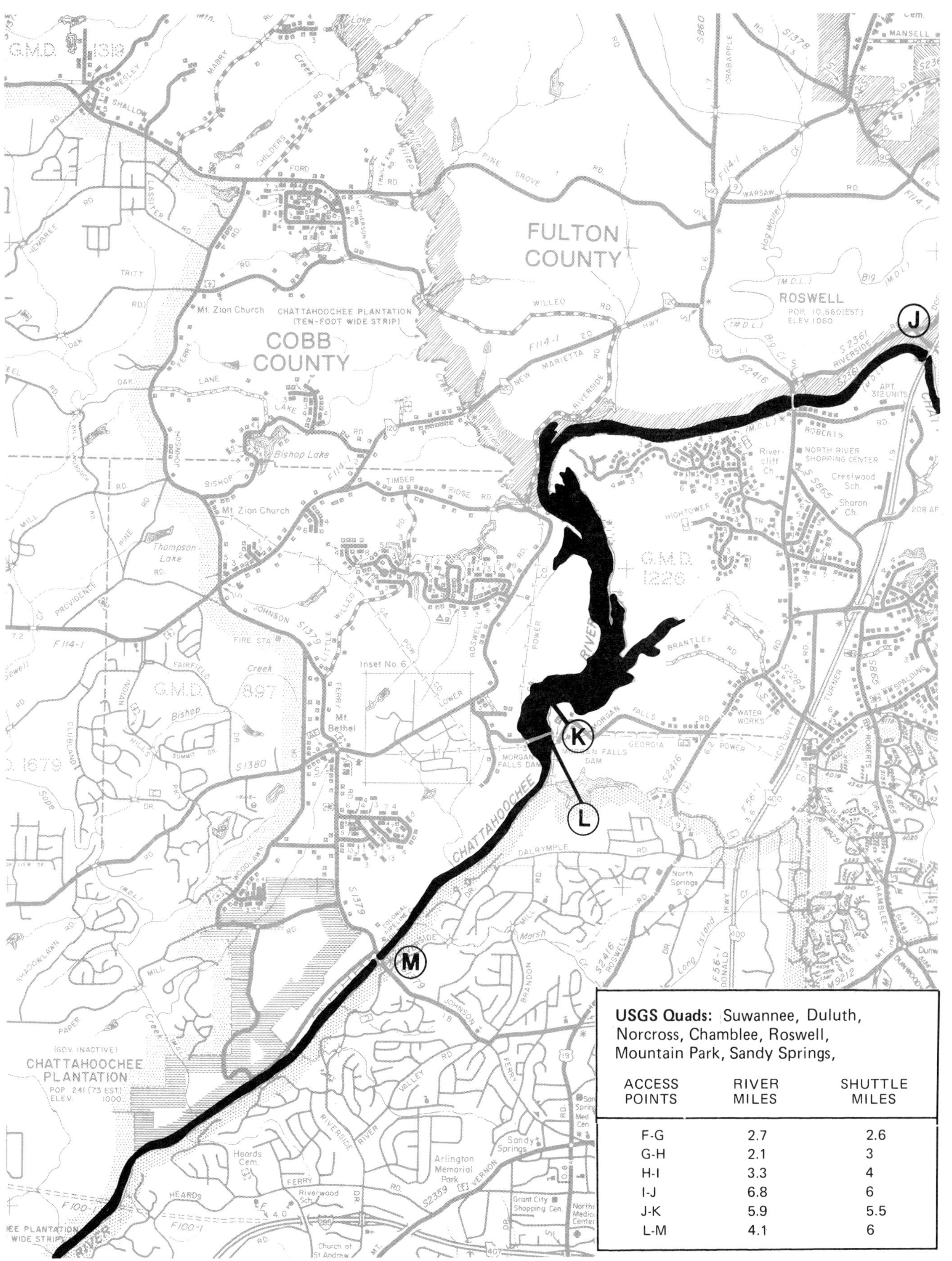

USGS Quads: Suwannee, Duluth, Norcross, Chamblee, Roswell, Mountain Park, Sandy Springs,

ACCESS POINTS	RIVER MILES	SHUTTLE MILES
F-G	2.7	2.6
G-H	2.1	3
H-I	3.3	4
I-J	6.8	6
J-K	5.9	5.5
L-M	4.1	6

Section: Morgan Falls Dam to Sweetwater Creek

Counties: Fulton, Cobb, Douglas

Suitable For: Cruising

Appropriate For: Practiced beginners, intermediates, advanced

Months Runnable: All when Buford Dam is releasing

Interest Highlights: Scenery, local culture and industry

Scenery: Pleasant to pretty

Difficulty: International Scale I-II
Numerical Points 8

Average Width: 120-140 ft.
Velocity: Moderate
Gradient: 2.88 ft./mi.

Runnable Water Level: Minimum Not applicable
Maximum Up to flood stage

Hazards: Partial dams

Scouting: Partial dams below Paces Ferry Rd.

Portages: Partial dams below Paces Ferry Rd., as necessary

Rescue Index: Accessible to accessible but difficult

Mean Water Temperature (°F)

Jan 44	Feb 44	Mar 46	Apr 51	May 56	Jun 60
Jul 63	Aug 63	Sep 61	Oct 54	Nov 50	Dec 47

Source of Additional Information: High Country Outfitters (404) 955-1866

Access Point	Access Code
L[1]	1357
M	1357
N	(11)
O	(11)
P	13579
Q	13579
R	(11)
S	(11)
T	(11)
U	1357
V	(11)
W[2]	1357

Access Key
1 Paved Road
2 Unpaved Road
3 Short Carry
4 Long Carry
5 Easy Grade
6 Steep Incline
7 Clear Trail
8 Brush and Trees
9 Launching Fee Charged
10 Private Property, Need Permission
11 No Access, Reference Only

[1]Below Morgan Falls Dam
[2]On Sweetwater Creek

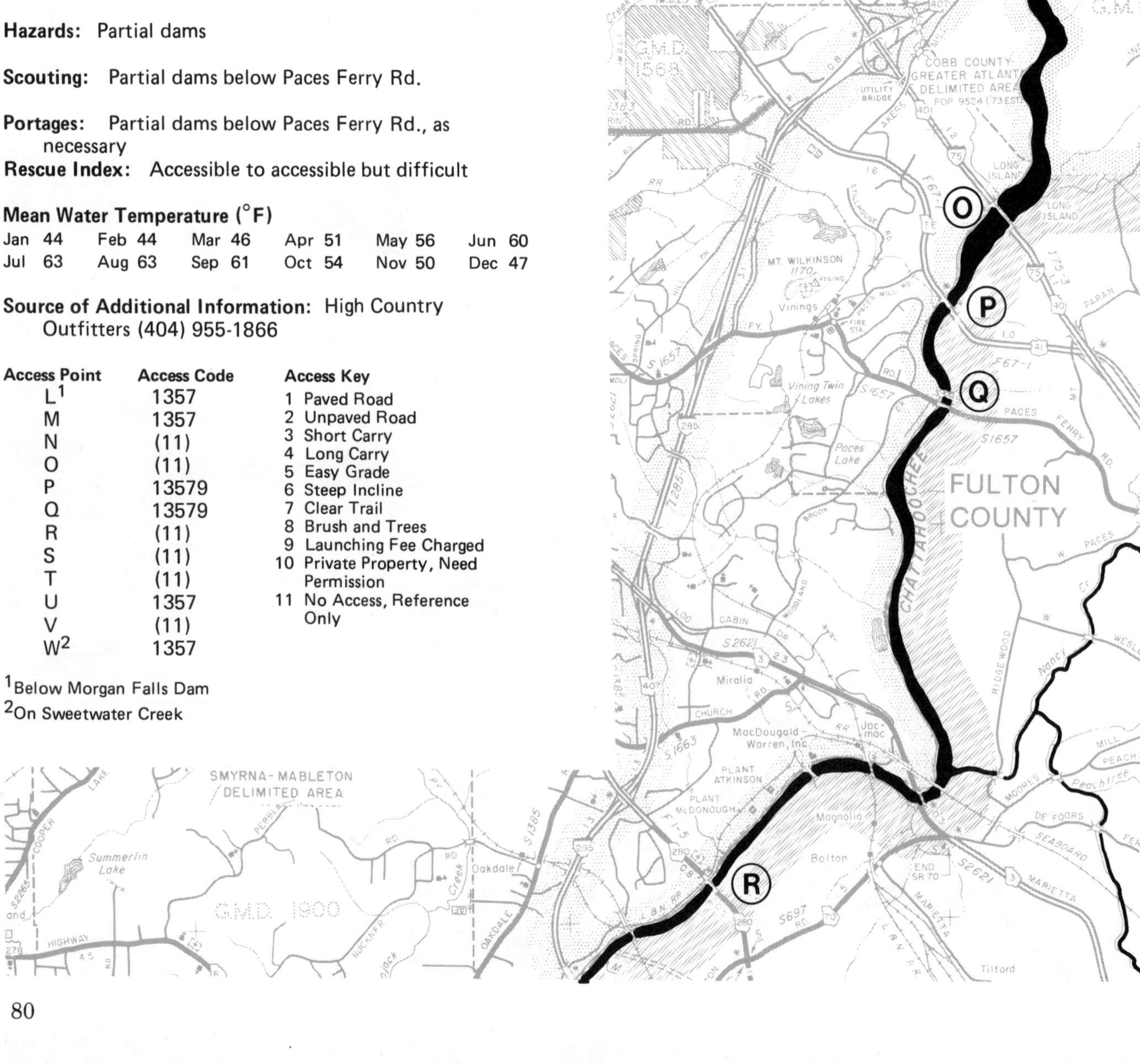

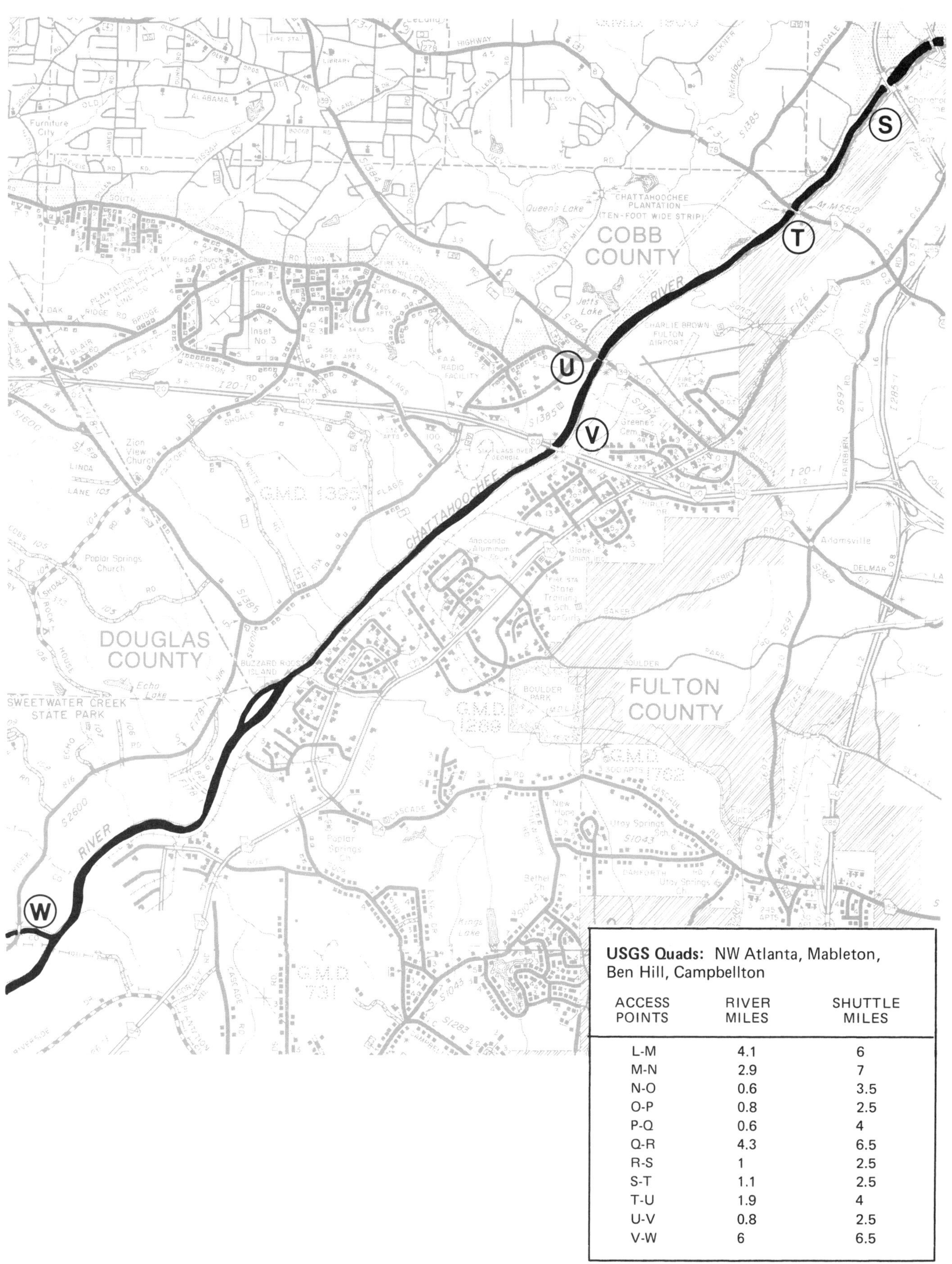

USGS Quads: NW Atlanta, Mableton, Ben Hill, Campbellton

ACCESS POINTS	RIVER MILES	SHUTTLE MILES
L-M	4.1	6
M-N	2.9	7
N-O	0.6	3.5
O-P	0.8	2.5
P-Q	0.6	4
Q-R	4.3	6.5
R-S	1	2.5
S-T	1.1	2.5
T-U	1.9	4
U-V	0.8	2.5
V-W	6	6.5

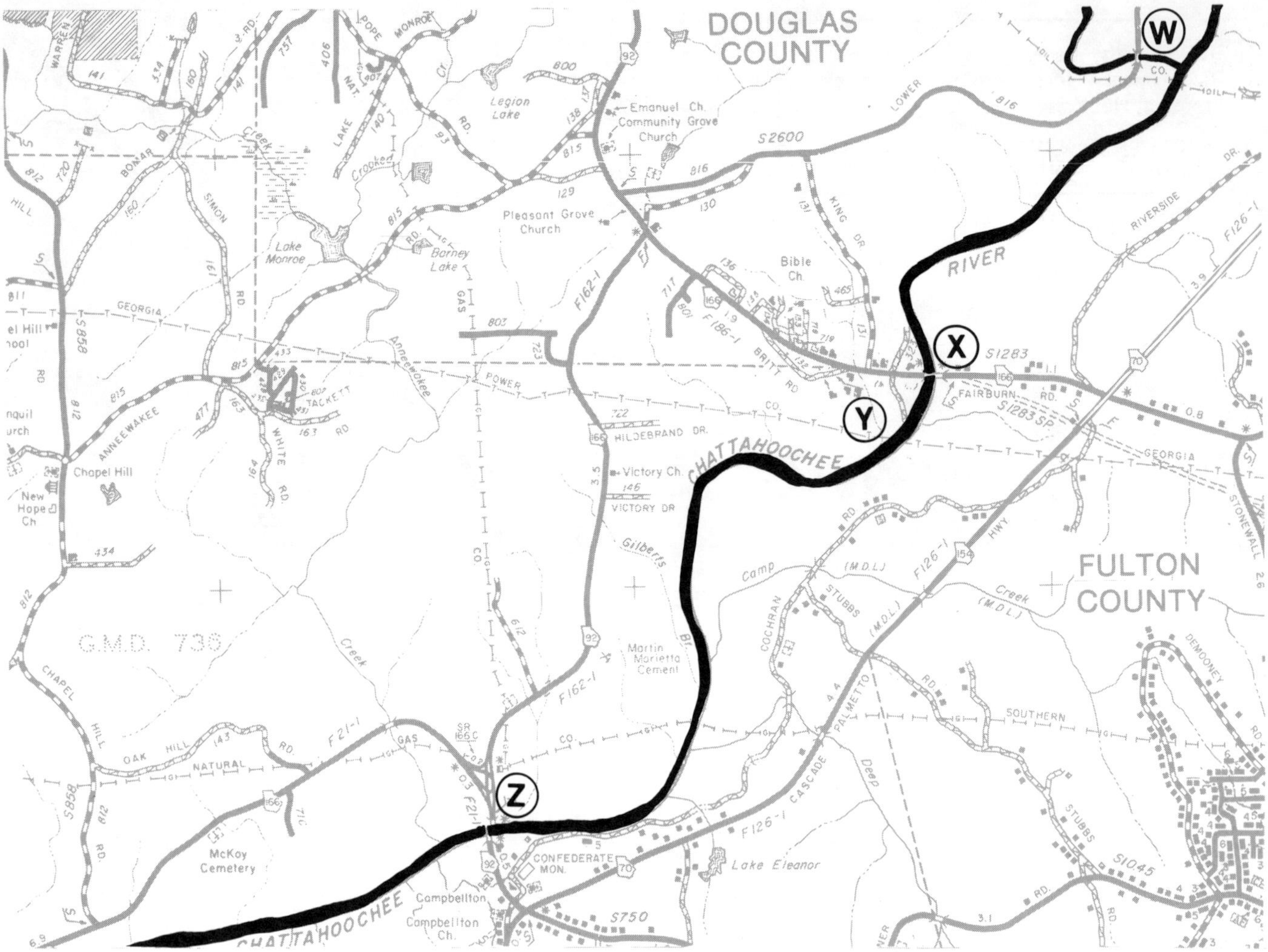

Chattahoochee River—*Continued*

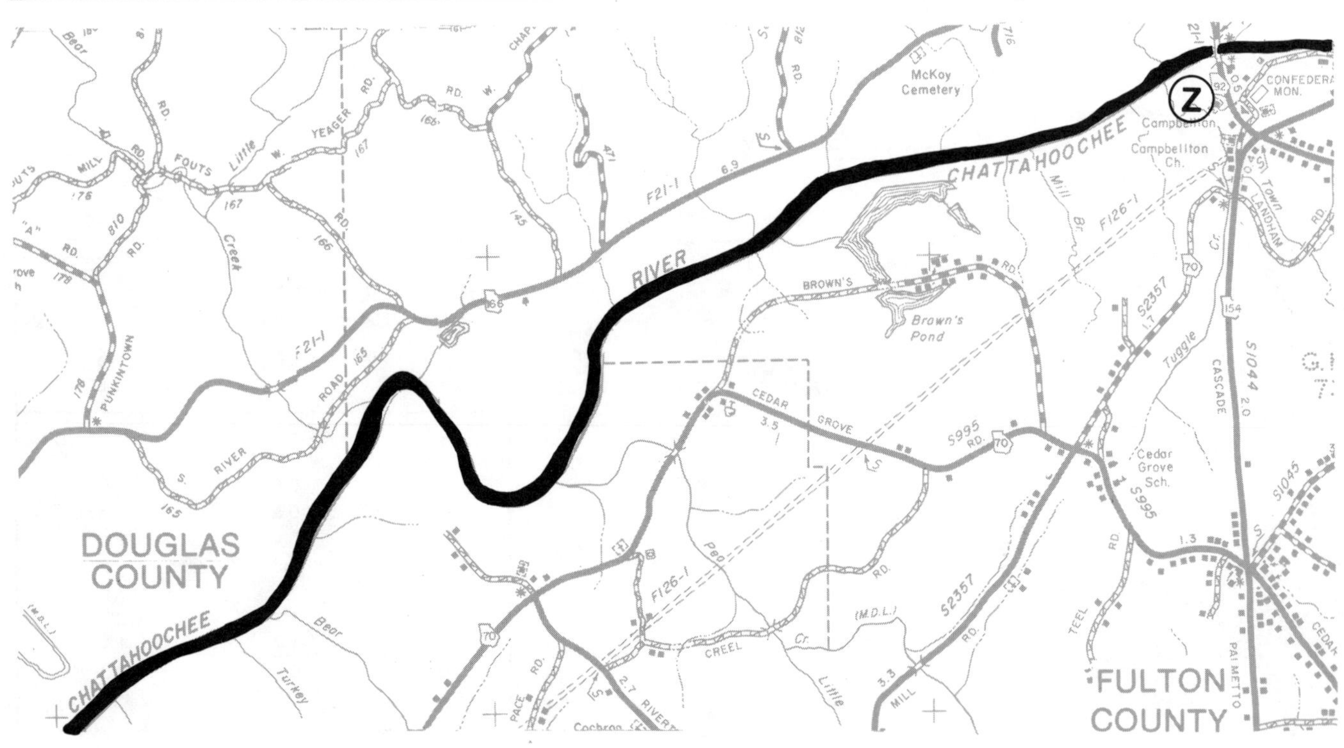

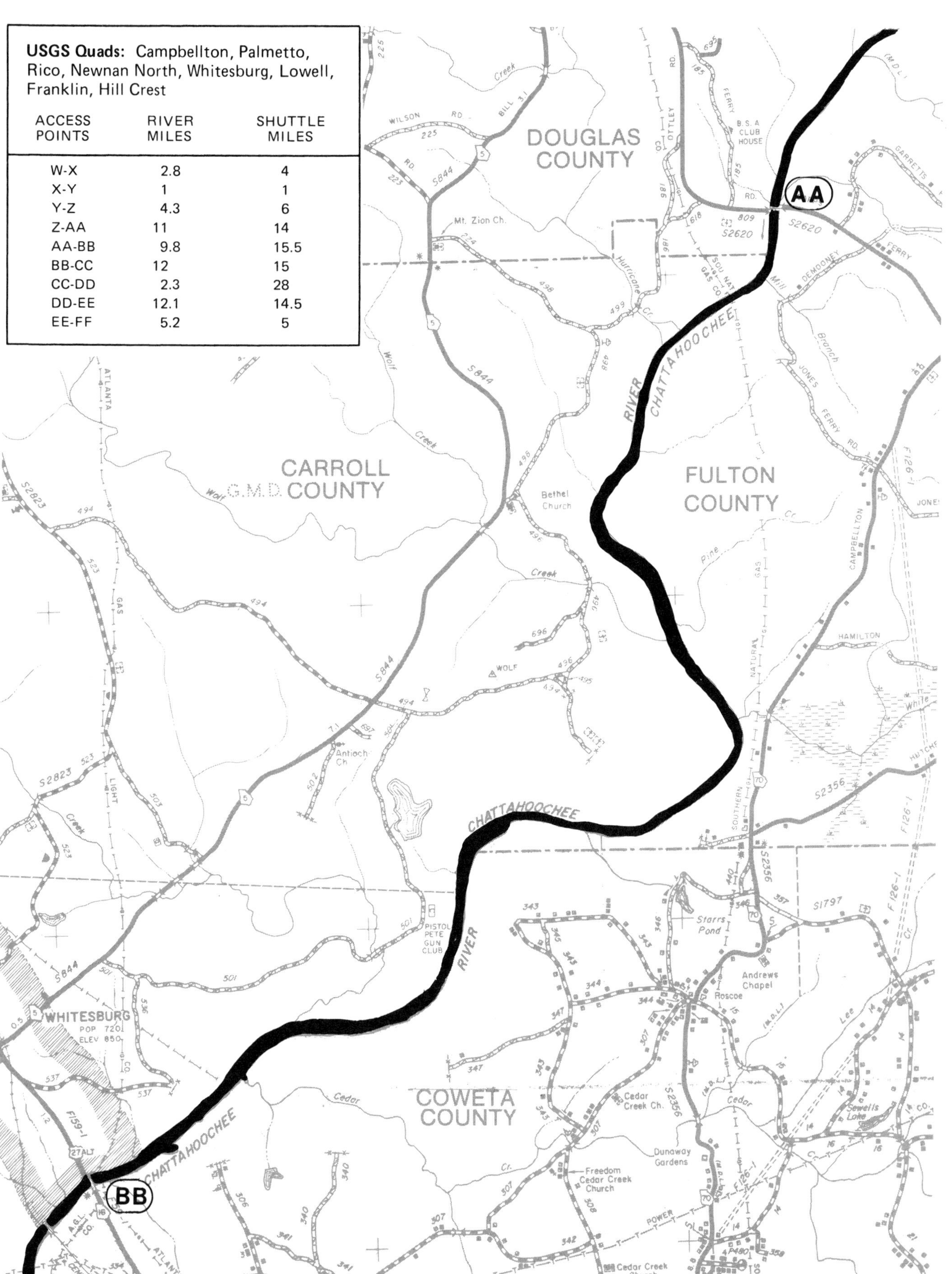

USGS Quads: Campbellton, Palmetto, Rico, Newnan North, Whitesburg, Lowell, Franklin, Hill Crest

ACCESS POINTS	RIVER MILES	SHUTTLE MILES
W-X	2.8	4
X-Y	1	1
Y-Z	4.3	6
Z-AA	11	14
AA-BB	9.8	15.5
BB-CC	12	15
CC-DD	2.3	28
DD-EE	12.1	14.5
EE-FF	5.2	5

Chattahoochee River—*Continued*

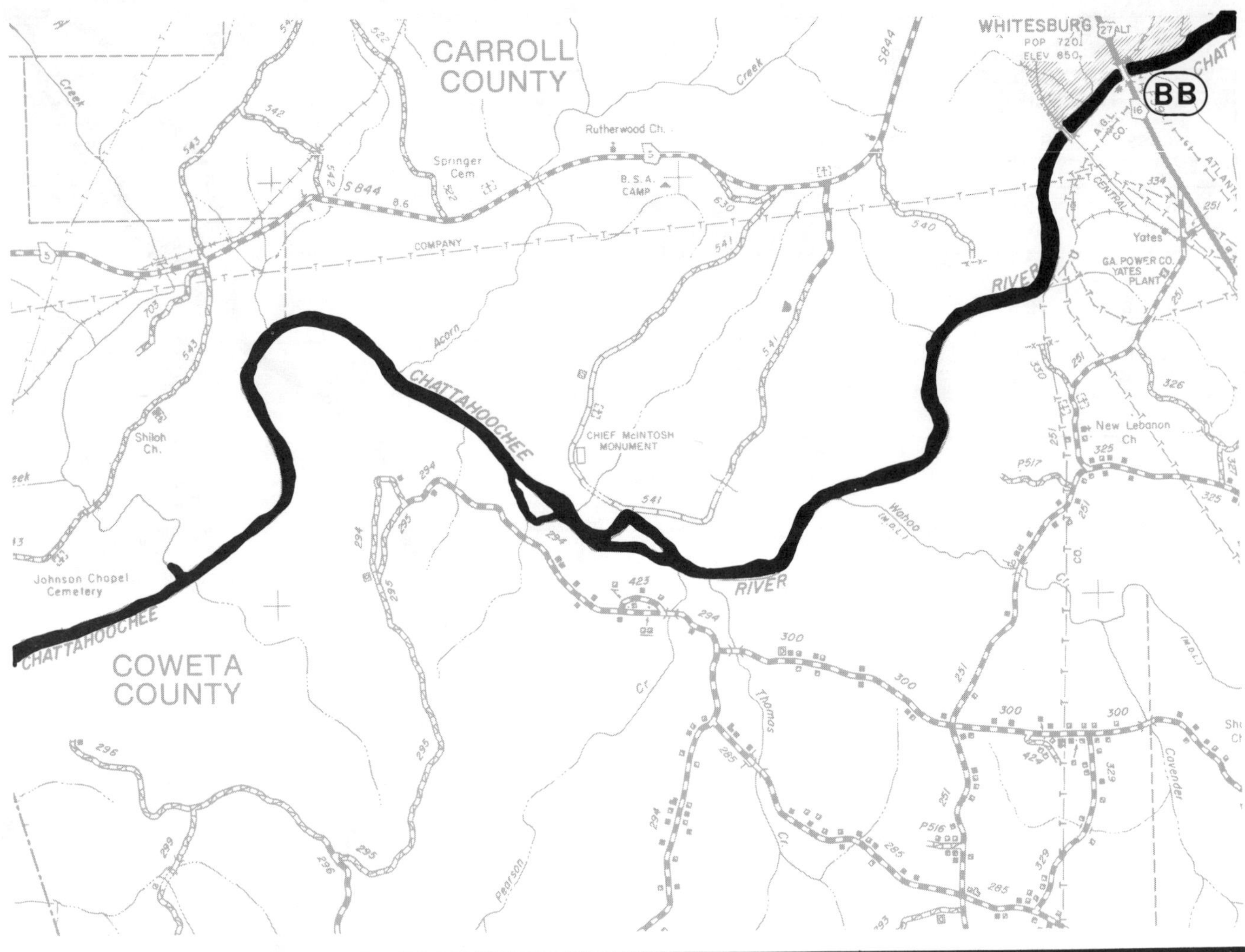

Section: Sweetwater Creek to West Point Lake

Counties: Fulton, Cobb, Douglas, Carroll, Coweta, Heard

Suitable For: Cruising, camping

Appropriate For: Practiced beginners, intermediates, advanced

Months Runnable: All when Buford Dam is releasing

Interest Highlights: Scenery, wildlife, mild whitewater, local culture and industry

Scenery: Pretty to beautiful in spots

Difficulty: International Scale I-II
Numerical Points 8

Average Width: 125-145 ft.
Velocity: Moderate
Gradient: 1.66 ft./mi.

Runnable Water Level: Minimum Not applicable
Maximum Up to flood stage

Hazards: Mild rapids

Scouting: None required

Portages: None required

Rescue Index: Accessible but difficult

Mean Water Temperature (°F)

Jan 49	Feb 50	Mar 55	Apr 62	May 69	Jun 74
Jul 76	Aug 74	Sep 70	Oct 62	Nov 56	Dec 50

Source of Additional Information: High Country Outfitters (404) 955-1866

Access Point	Access Code
W[1]	1357
X	(11)
Y	2357
Z	1367
AA	1357
BB	1367
CC	1357
DD	2357
EE	1357
FF[2]	1357

Access Key
1 Paved Road
2 Unpaved Road
3 Short Carry
4 Long Carry
5 Easy Grade
6 Steep Incline
7 Clear Trail
8 Brush and Trees
9 Launching Fee Charged
10 Private Property, Need Permission
11 No Access, Reference Only

[1] On Sweetwater Creek
[2] FF-GG is a series of lakes. Access point GG is below Columbus

CC
DD
EE
FF
CHATTAHOOCHEE
RIVER
HEARD COUNTY
CENTRALHATCHEE
POP. 186
FRANKLIN
POP. 749
ELEV. 700
Bush Head Shoals
Daniel Shoals
Ebenezer Church
Yellow Dirt
GA. POWER CO. PLANT
Friendship Cem.
Hollingsworth Cem.
Hardegree Cem.
Yellow Dirt Ch. & Cem.
Simms Cem.
Faver Cem.
Jackson Cem.
McWaters Cem.
Pine Grove Cem.
Harmony Ch.
Owensby Cem.
Summerlin Pullen Cem.
G.M.D. 779
Red Bone Creek
Centralhatchee Creek
Zachry Creek
Harris Creek
WEST

Tallapoosa River

The Tallapoosa River originates in Carroll County, cuts across a corner of Paulding County, and traverses the breadth of Haralson County. It enters Alabama just west of the town of Tallapoosa.

Few canoeists frequent the Tallapoosa. Bridge access points are often choked with vegetation along the banks, making boat launching difficult. Once the boats are in the water, the river offers seclusion and serene beauty. Rolling hills stretch in all directions, but dense streamside flora and high banks usually block the view.

The rains of winter and infrequent summer deluges give the Tallapoosa sufficient volume for boating at GA 120 (access point A) in Paulding County. Most seasons of the year boaters will be forced to launch well into Haralson County at access points J or K. Access point K is on GA 1, north of Buchanan, and is easy to locate.

The only hazards to navigation are deadfalls and strainers. Shoals are minor and infrequent. The average gradient is five feet per mile.

USGS Quads: Draketown, Rockmar South, Buchanan

ACCESS POINTS	RIVER MILES	SHUTTLE MILES
A-B	0.4	1.5
B-C	1.71	1.25
C-D	1.15	3.0
D-E	1.9	3.5
E-F	1.0	1.5
F-G	1.0	2.0
G-H	3.1	2.75
H-I	3.3	7.5
I-J	1.6	2.0
J-K	4.5	7.5

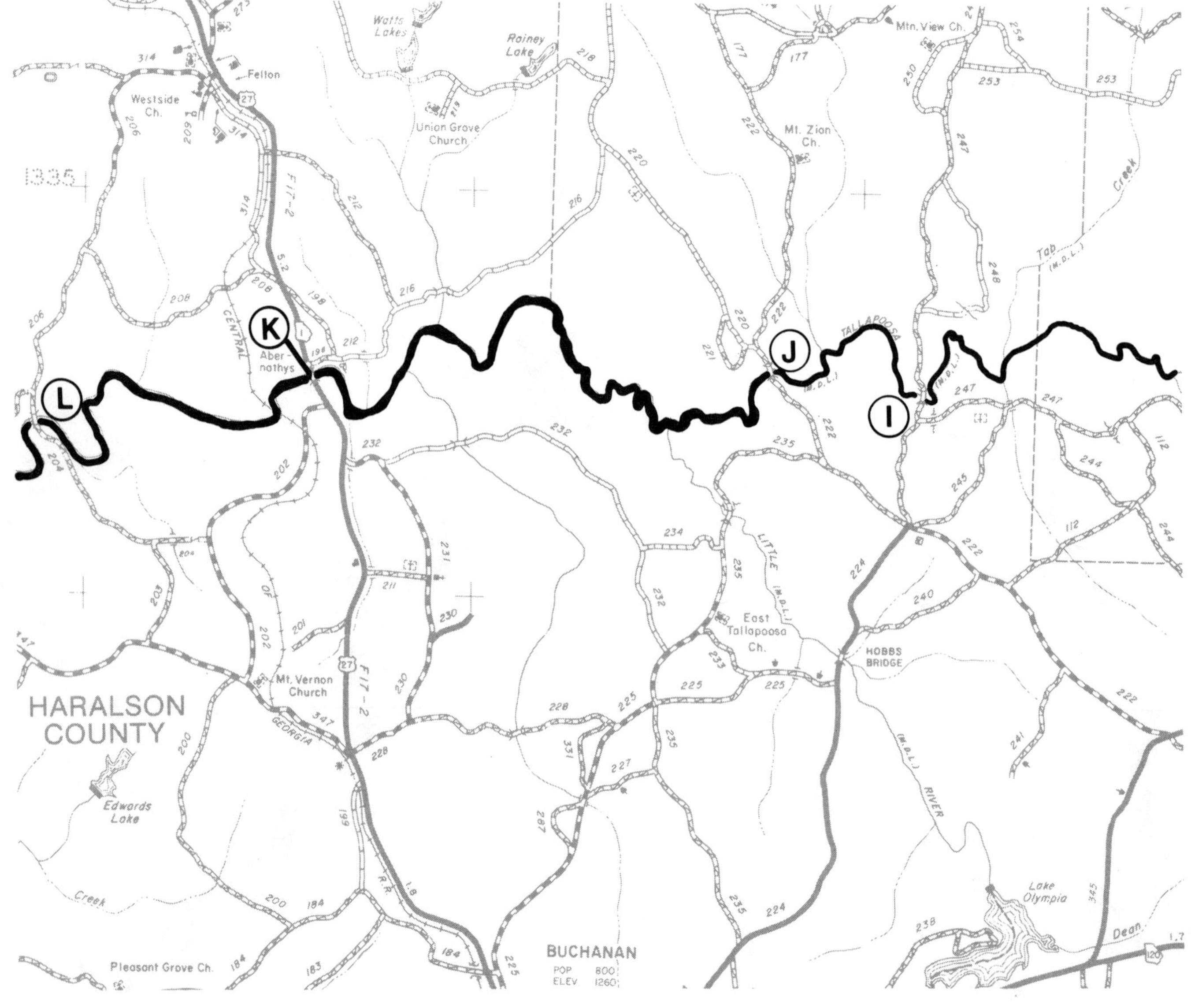

Section: GA 120 to GA 1

Counties: Paulding, Haralson

Suitable For: Cruising, camping

Appropriate For: Families, beginners, intermediates, advanced

Months Runnable: All except during dry spells

Interest Highlights: Scenery, wildlife

Scenery: Pretty

Difficulty: International Scale I
Numerical Points 6

Average Width: 15-40 ft.
Gradient: Slack to slow
Velocity: 5 ft./mi.

Runnable Water Level: Minimum 5 ft.
(Tallapoosa gauge) Maximum 18 ft.

Hazards: Strainers, deadfalls

Scouting: None required

Portages: Around and over deadfalls on upper section

Rescue Index: Accessible to accessible but difficult

Mean Water Temperature (°F)

Jan 42	Feb 45	Mar 49	Apr 56	May 64	Jun 71
Jul 76	Aug 74	Sep 69	Oct 61	Nov 52	Dec 44

Source of Additional Information: Haralson County Sheriff Dept. (404) 646-8911

Access Point	Access Code
A	1358
B	2358
C	2358
D	2358
E	2357
F	2358
G	1358
H	1358
I	2358
J	2358
K	1357

Access Key
1 Paved Road
2 Unpaved Road
3 Short Carry
4 Long Carry
5 Easy Grade
6 Steep Incline
7 Clear Trail
8 Brush and Trees
9 Launching Fee Charged
10 Private Property, Need Permission
11 No Access, Reference Only

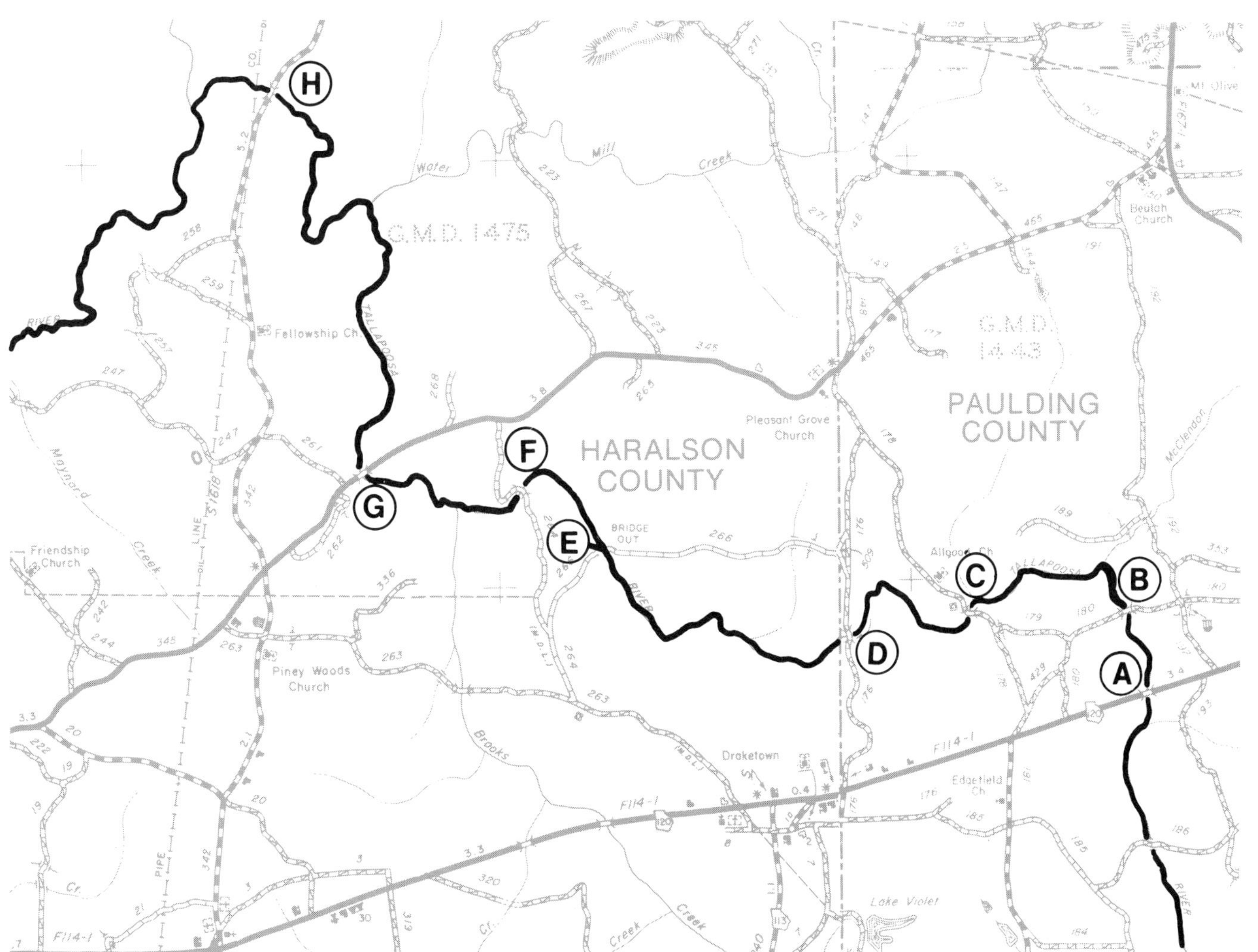

Tallapoosa River—*Continued*

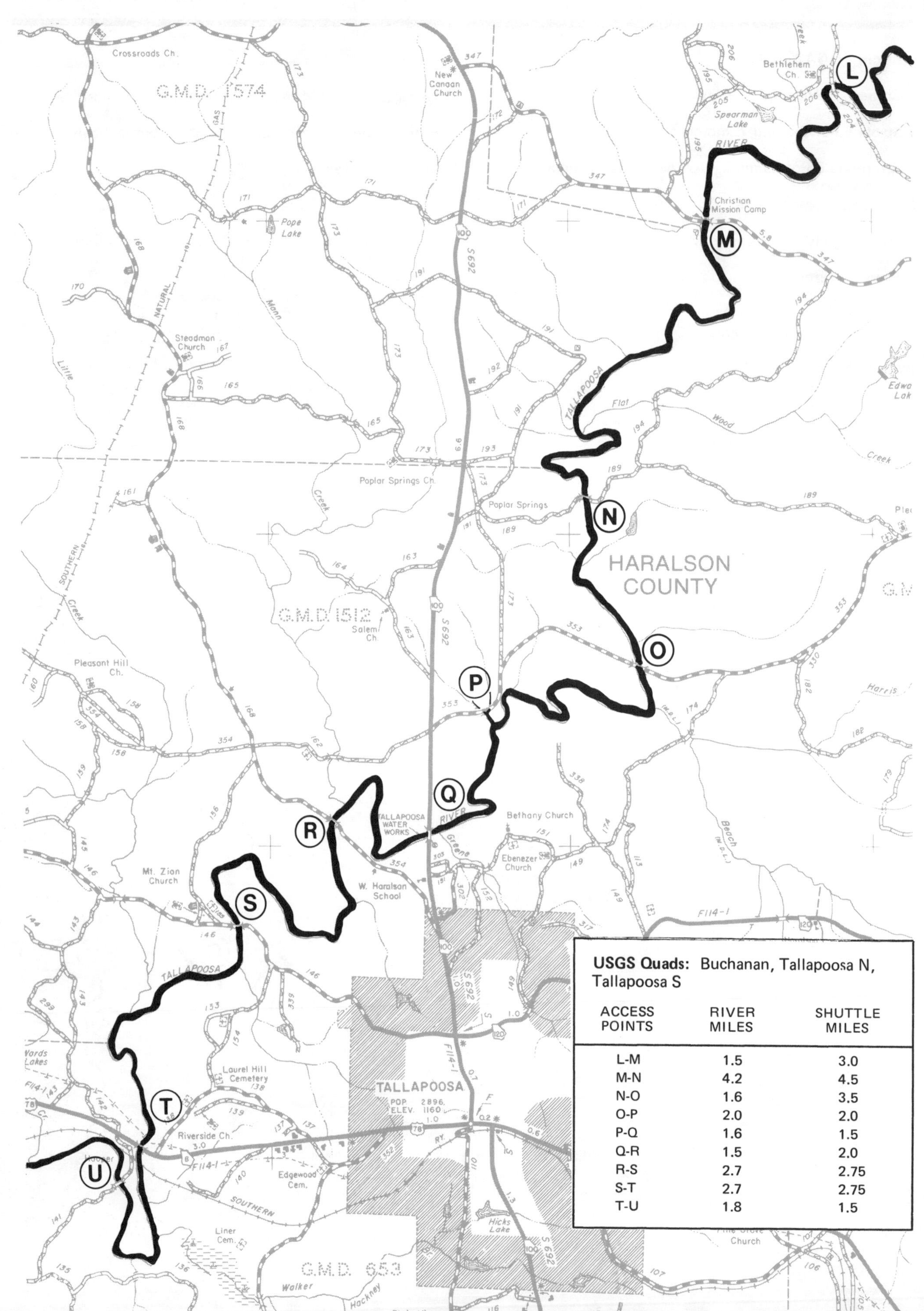

USGS Quads: Buchanan, Tallapoosa N, Tallapoosa S

ACCESS POINTS	RIVER MILES	SHUTTLE MILES
L-M	1.5	3.0
M-N	4.2	4.5
N-O	1.6	3.5
O-P	2.0	2.0
P-Q	1.6	1.5
Q-R	1.5	2.0
R-S	2.7	2.75
S-T	2.7	2.75
T-U	1.8	1.5

Section: GA 1 to Alabama state line

Counties: Haralson

Suitable For: Cruising, camping

Appropriate For: Families, beginners, intermediates, advanced

Months Runnable: All

Interest Highlights: Scenery, wildlife

Scenery: Pretty

Difficulty: International Scale I
Numerical Points 6

Average Width: 15-40 ft.
Gradient: Slack to slow
Velocity: 4.9 ft./mi.

Runnable Water Level: Minimum 5 ft.
(Tallapoosa gauge) Maximum 18 ft.

Hazards: Strainers, deadfalls

Scouting: None required

Portages: None required

Rescue Index: Accessible to accessible but difficult

Mean Water Temperature (°F)

Jan 42	Feb 45	Mar 49	Apr 56	May 64	Jun 71
Jul 76	Aug 74	Sep 69	Oct 61	Nov 52	Dec 44

Source of Additional Information: Haralson County Sheriff Dept. (404) 646-8911

Access Point	Access Code
L	2357
M	1357
N	2357
O	1357
P	1358
Q	1357
R	1357
S	1357
T	1357
U	2357

Access Key
1 Paved Road
2 Unpaved Road
3 Short Carry
4 Long Carry
5 Easy Grade
6 Steep Incline
7 Clear Trail
8 Brush and Trees
9 Launching Fee Charged
10 Private Property, Need Permission
11 No Access, Reference Only

Photo courtesy of *Brown's Guide to Georgia.*

Tallapoosa River.

Southern Georgia "blackwater" stream.

Photo courtesy of *Brown's Guide to Georgia.*

Chapter 5

Streams of the Coastal Plain

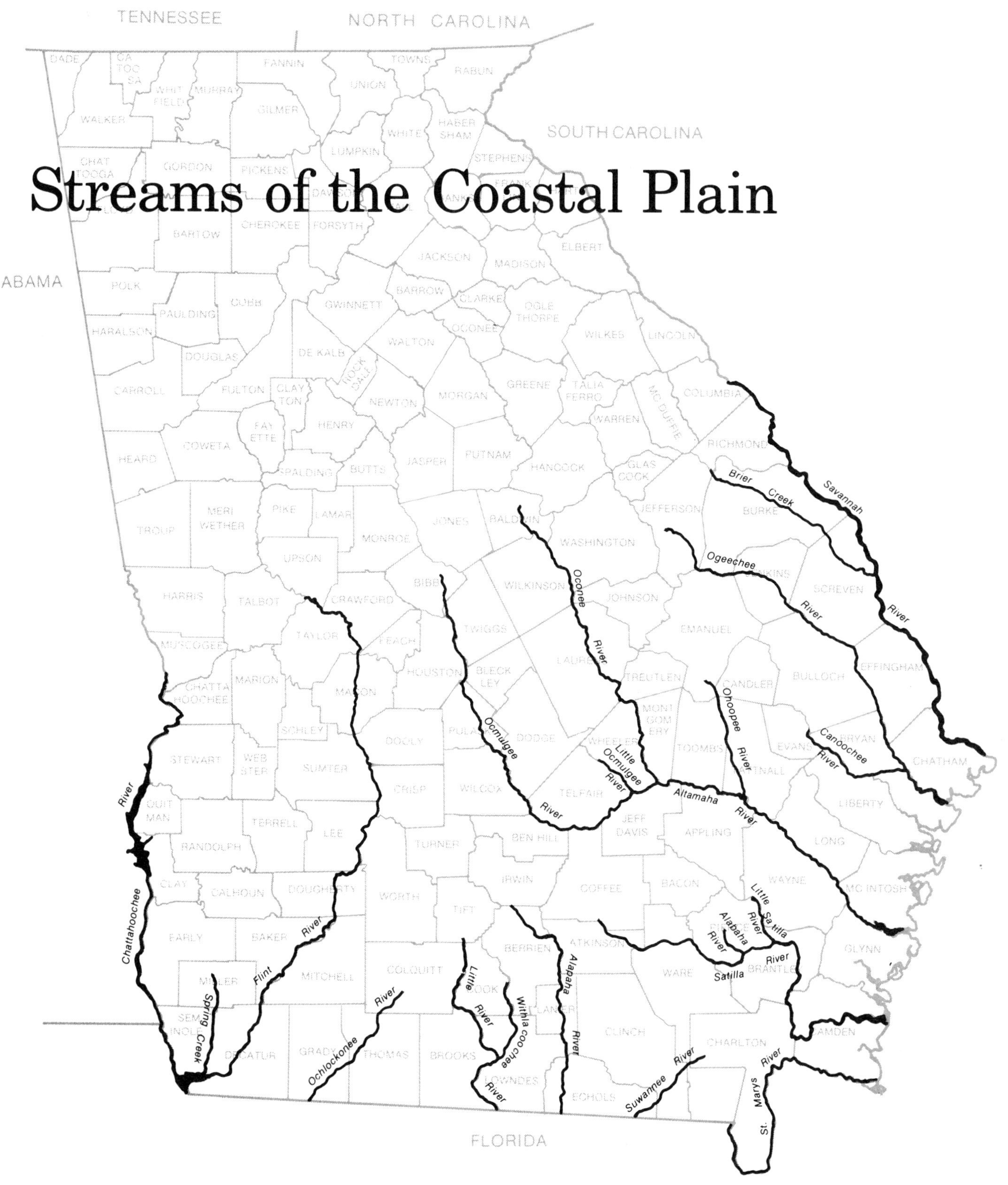

Brier Creek

Brier Creek originates in McDuffie and Warren counties near the Fall Line that separates the Piedmont from the Coastal Plain, and flows southeast draining portions of Richmond, Jefferson, Burke and Screven counties before emptying into the Savannah River east of Sylvania. An intimate stream of primeval beauty, Brier Creek flows between thickly vegetated, red clay banks of two to four feet in height that have an average slope of 50 degrees. Runnable except during dry weather downstream of the GA 56 bridge, Brier Creek averages 30 to 50 feet in width in the upper sections and widens to 60 to 85 feet near its mouth. The current on Brier Creek is generally slow as it flows a comparatively straight course beneath a luxurious canopy of bald cypress, sycamore, willow, and sweet gum. Graceful Spanish moss mysteriously drapes trees at streamside, which adds to the primitive atmosphere. Surrounding terrain consists of a wooded corridor with pine dominating the low, barely rolling swells beyond the river banks. As the creek approaches its mouth in Screven County, this high ground gives way to lowland swamp and bogs. Hazards to navigation consist primarily of deadfalls and level of difficulty is Class I throughout. Access is generally good.

USGS Quads: McBean, Idlewood, Alexander

ACCESS POINTS	RIVER MILES	SHUTTLE MILES
A-B	8.3	8.5
B-C	11.7	11
C-D	3.7	4.3

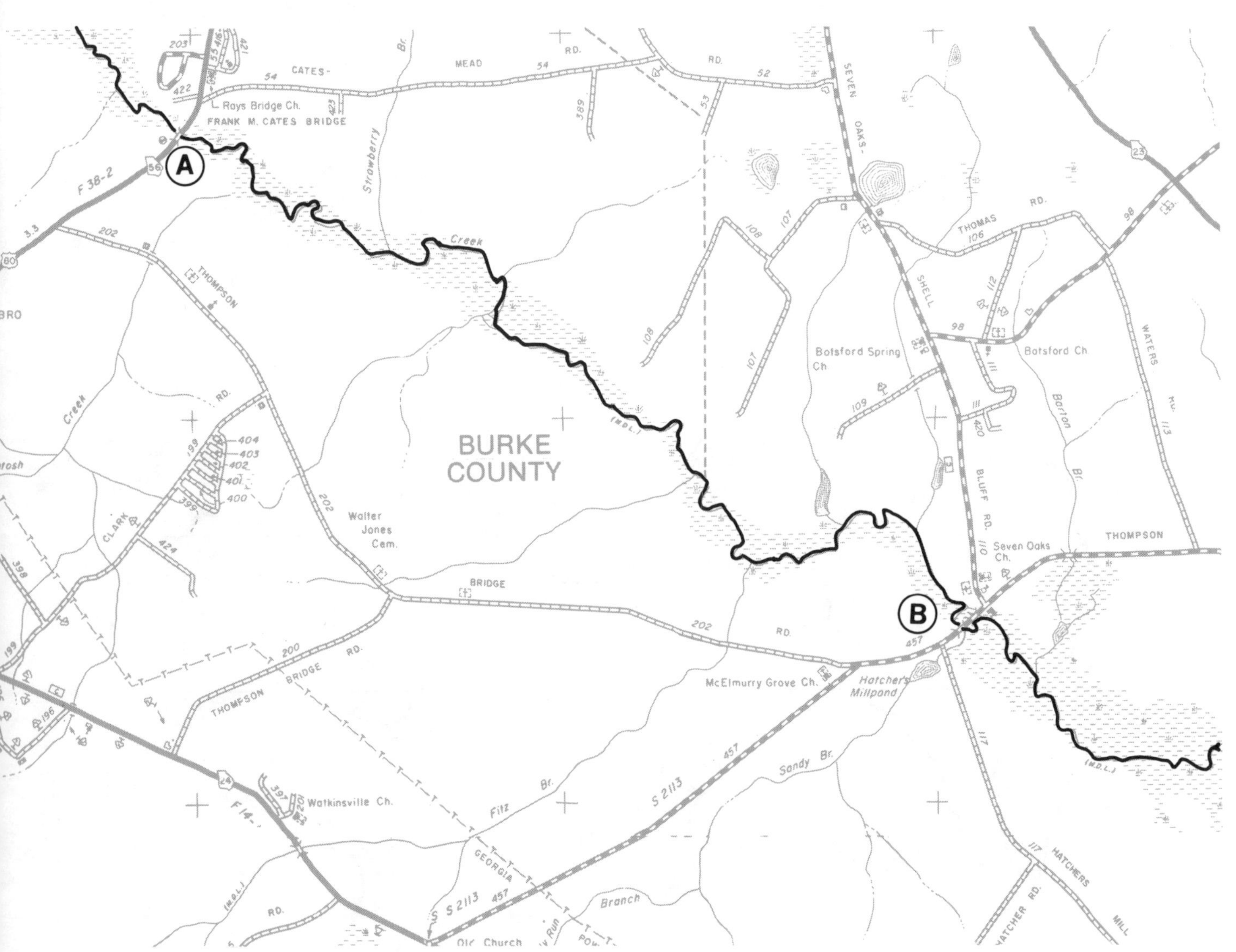

Section: GA 56 bridge to Savannah River

Counties: Burke, Screven

Suitable For: Cruising

Appropriate For: Beginners, intermediates, advanced

Months Runnable: November through mid-July

Interest Highlights: Scenery, wildlife

Scenery: Beautiful in spots

Difficulty: International Scale I
Numerical Points 5

Average Width: 40-55 ft.
Velocity: Slow to moderate
Gradient: 2.47 ft./mi.

Runnable Water Level: Minimum 180 cfs
(Waynesboro gauge) Maximum Up to flood stage

Hazards: Strainers, deadfalls

Scouting: None required

Portages: Around deadfalls

Rescue Index: Remote to accessible but difficult

Mean Water Temperature (°F)

Jan 47	Feb 49	Mar 56	Apr 62	May 68	Jun 74
Jul 77	Aug 75	Sep 70	Oct 62	Nov 55	Dec 50

Source of Additional Information: Metter Game and Fish Office (912) 685-2145

Access Point	Access Code
A	1357
B	1357
C	1358

Access Key
1 Paved Road
2 Unpaved Road
3 Short Carry
4 Long Carry
5 Easy Grade
6 Steep Incline
7 Clear Trail
8 Brush and Trees
9 Launching Fee Charged
10 Private Property, Need Permission
11 No Access, Reference Only

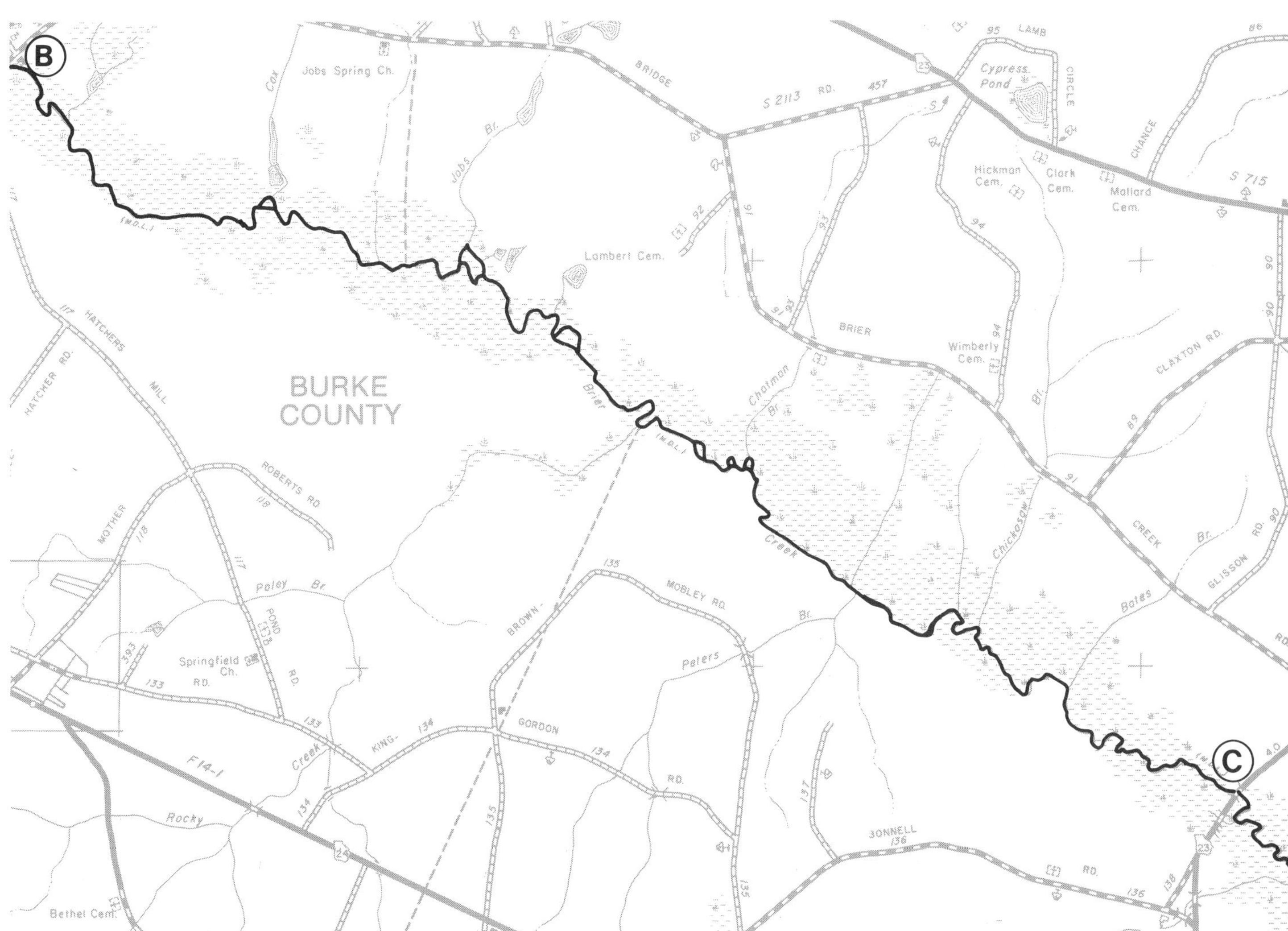

Brier Creek—*Continued*

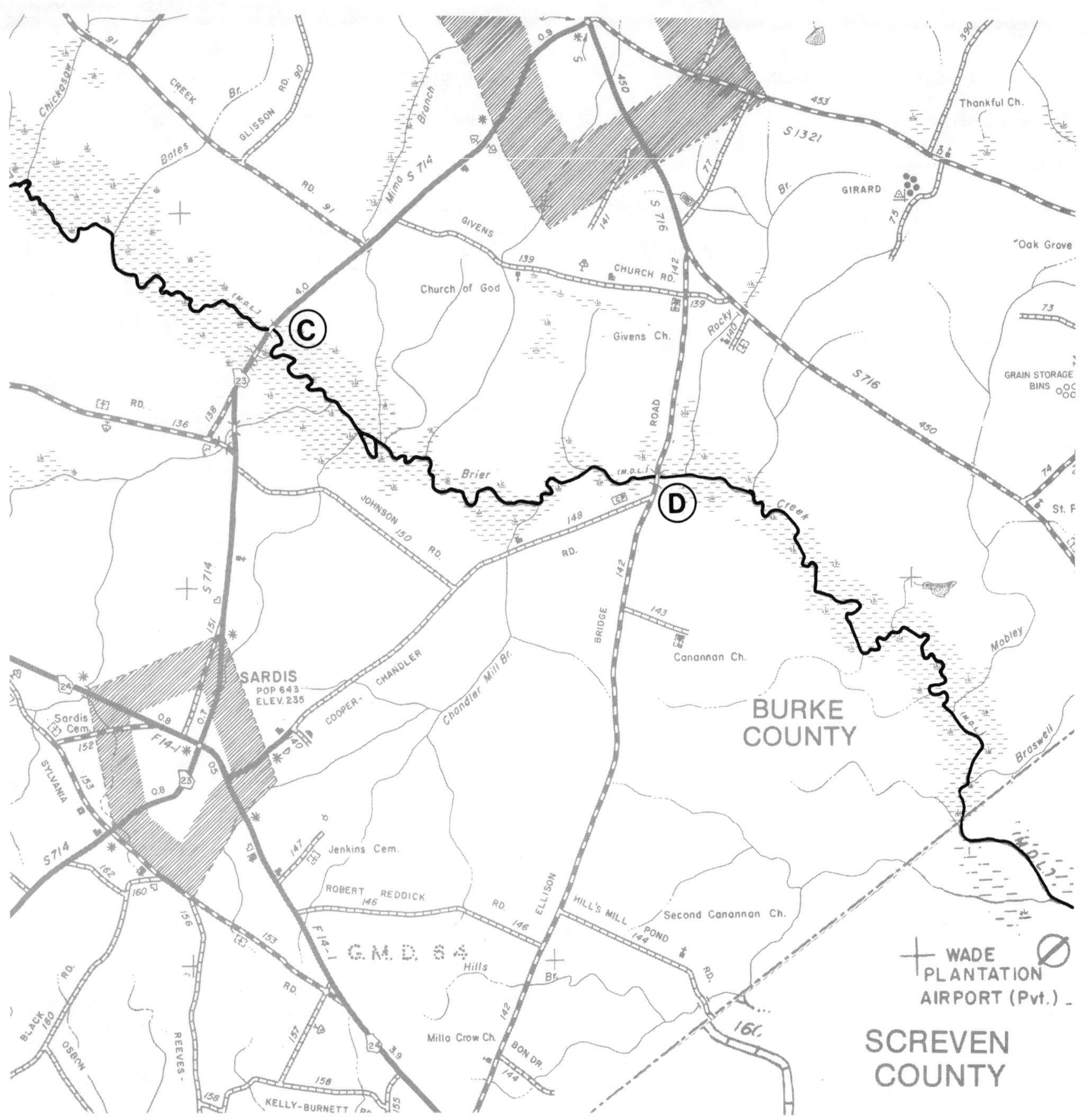

USGS Quads: Alexander, Hilltonia		
ACCESS POINTS	RIVER MILES	SHUTTLE MILES
B-C	11.7	11
C-D	3.7	4.3
D-E	7.2	8.5
E-F	5	6
F-G	3	5.3
G-H	10.5	11.5

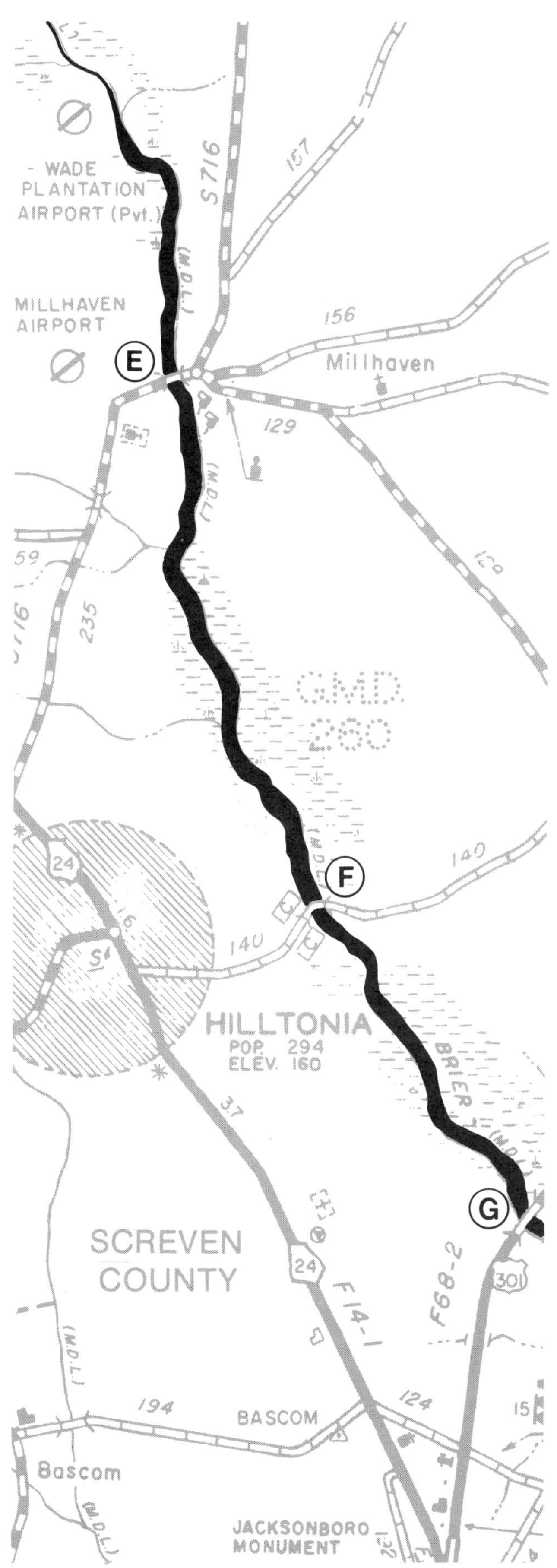

Section: GA 56 bridge to Savannah River

Counties: Burke, Screven

Suitable For: Cruising

Appropriate For: Beginners, intermediates, advanced

Months Runnable: November through mid-July

Interest Highlights: Scenery, wildlife

Scenery: Beautiful in spots

Difficulty: International Scale I
Numerical Points 5

Average Width: 40-55 ft.
Velocity: Slow to moderate
Gradient: 2.47 ft./mi.

Runnable Water Level: (Waynesboro gauge) Minimum 180 cfs; Maximum Up to flood stage

Hazards: Strainers, deadfalls

Scouting: None required

Portages: Around deadfalls

Rescue Index: Remote to accessible but difficult

Mean Water Temperature (°F)

Jan 47	Feb 49	Mar 56	Apr 62	May 68	Jun 74
Jul 77	Aug 75	Sep 70	Oct 62	Nov 55	Dec 50

Source of Additional Information: Metter Game and Fish Office (912) 685-2145

Access Point	Access Code
C	1358
D	1357
E	1358
F	2357
G	1357

Access Key
1 Paved Road
2 Unpaved Road
3 Short Carry
4 Long Carry
5 Easy Grade
6 Steep Incline
7 Clear Trail
8 Brush and Trees
9 Launching Fee Charged
10 Private Property, Need Permission
11 No Access, Reference Only

Brier Creek—*Continued*

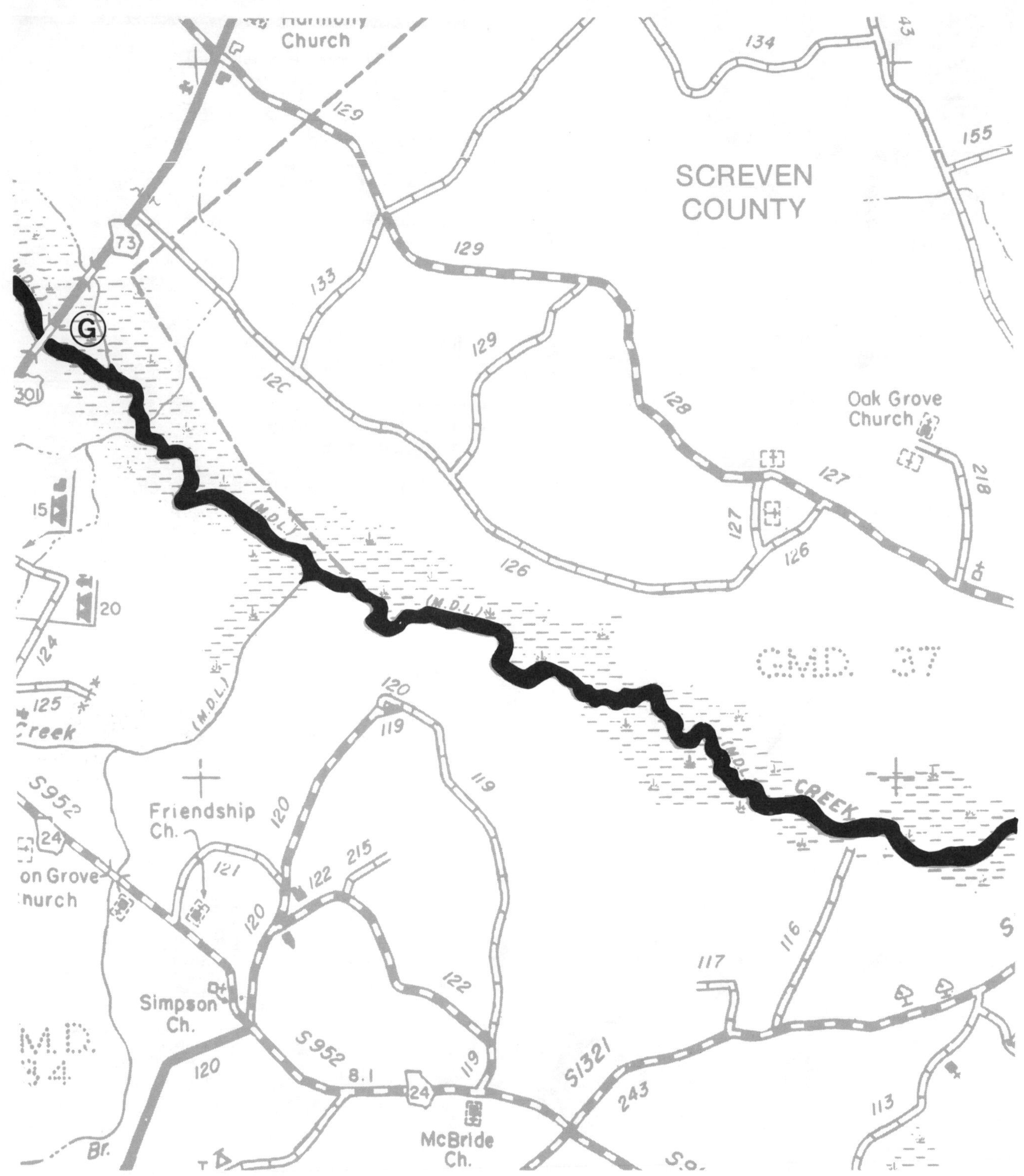

USGS Quads: Hilltonia, Peeples		
ACCESS POINTS	RIVER MILES	SHUTTLE MILES
G-H	10.5	11.5
H-V	27	17

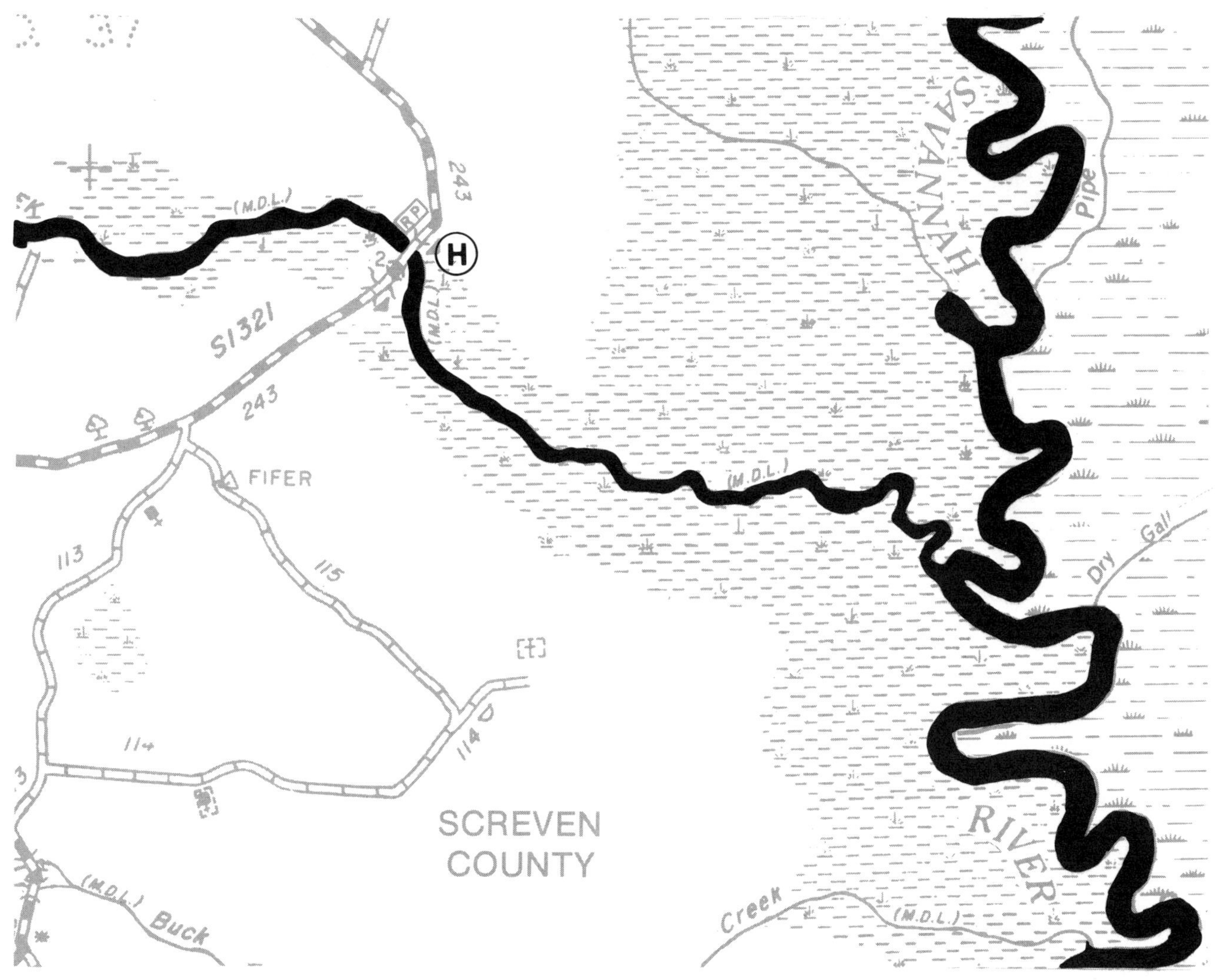

Section: GA 56 bridge to Savannah River

Counties: Burke, Screven

Suitable For: Cruising

Appropriate For: Beginners, intermediates, advanced

Months Runnable: November through mid-July

Interest Highlights: Scenery, wildlife

Scenery: Beautiful in spots

Difficulty: International Scale I
Numerical Points 5

Average Width: 40-55 ft.
Velocity: Slow to moderate
Gradient: 2.47 ft./mi.

Runnable Water Level: Minimum 180 cfs
(Waynesboro gauge) Maximum Up to flood stage

Hazards: Strainers, deadfalls

Scouting: None required

Portages: Around deadfalls

Rescue Index: Remote to accessible but difficult

Mean Water Temperature (°F)

Jan 47	Feb 49	Mar 56	Apr 62	May 68	Jun 74
Jul 77	Aug 75	Sep 70	Oct 62	Nov 55	Dec 50

Source of Additional Information: Metter Game and Fish Office (912) 685-2145

Access Point	Access Code
G	1357
H	1357
V[1]	2357

[1]On the Savannah River

Access Key
1 Paved Road
2 Unpaved Road
3 Short Carry
4 Long Carry
5 Easy Grade
6 Steep Incline
7 Clear Trail
8 Brush and Trees
9 Launching Fee Charged
10 Private Property, Need Permission
11 No Access, Reference Only

Savannah River

One of Georgia's longest and largest rivers, the Savannah originates in Hart County in northestern Georgia at the confluence of the Seneca and Tugaloo rivers. Flowing southeast, the Savannah travels approximately three hundred miles and drains an area of 10,600 square miles before emptying into the Atlantic Ocean near the City of Savannah.

The journey of the Savannah from source to mouth is a study of contrasts. It originates clear, cool, and free-flowing in the mountains of the Blue Ridge. However, the Savannah's mountain tributaries are dammed and impounded many times before even reaching the Savannah. The Savannah itself comes into being, not as a surging, vibrant stream, but as a still mass of backwater in the Hartwell Reservoir, into which the Savannah's parent tributaries, the Tugaloo and the Seneca, empty.

Released below Hartwell Dam, the Savannah is never again clear or freeflowing. As it traverses the Piedmont it flows reddish to light brown and transports a massive suspension of sediment and silt. Its flow is regulated by a series of impoundments throughout the Piedmont, so there is less than thirty miles of free-flowing river between the Clark Hill Dam and Augusta. (Because of its distance from the last access point on the Savannah at the head of Clark Hill Reservoir and its proximity to Augusta, this section of the river is included with the Coastal Plain section although, technically, it is still an eastern Piedmont stream until it crosses the Fall Line.)

Below Augusta, as the Savannah sweeps across the Coastal Plain towards the sea, the river is left more or less to its own devices and no subsequent dams or impoundments are encountered.

For paddlers the Savannah has its good points and bad. On the negative side the water is usually not aesthetically pleasing. In the Piedmont (Hartwell Dam to Augusta) the flow is frequently disrupted by lakes and dams. On the positive side, there is plenty of that funny-looking water since upstream dams and hydroelectric plants must release sufficient water daily to support navigation in the Coastal Plain. Further, except in the environs of large cities, and at two or three isolated industrial sites, the river corridor is surprisingly isolated and pristine and is rich in flora and fauna. Islands in the Piedmont and meander by-passes (islands formed when a meander loop is cut off) in the Coastal Plain provide opportunity for canoe camping.

Clark Hill Dam to Augusta

Below Clark Hill Dam, the Savannah averages 350 feet in width and runs through deep, well-defined, sandy clay banks for approximately six miles before entering the backwaters of the Stevens Creek Dam. Banks are four to eight feet high and treelined. The level of difficulty is Class I with very little in the way of hazards to navigation. Since Clark Hill Dam is responsible for ensuring adequate water for navigation on the lower Savannah, releases are more uniform and predictable than at Hartwell. The minimum discharge from Clark Hill is 5,800 cfs and the maximum is approximately 30,000 cfs. Runnable levels are therefore assured all year.

Three miles below the GA 28 bridge is the Stevens Creek Dam followed shortly downstream by a

---

Section: Clark Hill Dam to southeastern Augusta

Counties: Columbia, Richmond

Suitable For: Cruising, camping

Appropriate For: Families, beginners, intermediates, advanced
Months Runnable: All

Interest Highlights: Scenery, wildlife, local culture and industry
Scenery: Pretty in spots to pretty

Difficulty: International Scale I
Numerical Points 5

Average Width: 350 ft.
Gradient: Moderate
Velocity: 3.02 ft./mi.

Runnable Water Level: Minimum Not applicable
Maximum Not applicable

Hazards: Dams, powerboat traffic

Scouting: None

Portages: Stevens Creek Dam, Augusta Canal Dam

Rescue Index: Accessible to accessible but difficult

Mean Water Temperature (°F)

Jan 48	Feb 46	Mar 50	Apr 56	May 60	Jun 68
Jul 72	Aug 73	Sep 71	Oct 64	Nov 58	Dec 50

Source of Additional Information: Thomson Game and Fish Office (404) 595-4211

Access Point	Access Code
A	1357
B	1357
C	1367
D	1367
E	(11)
F	1357

Access Key
1 Paved Road
2 Unpaved Road
3 Short Carry
4 Long Carry
5 Easy Grade
6 Steep Incline
7 Clear Trail
8 Brush and Trees
9 Launching Fee Charged
10 Private Property, Need Permission
11 No Access, Reference Only

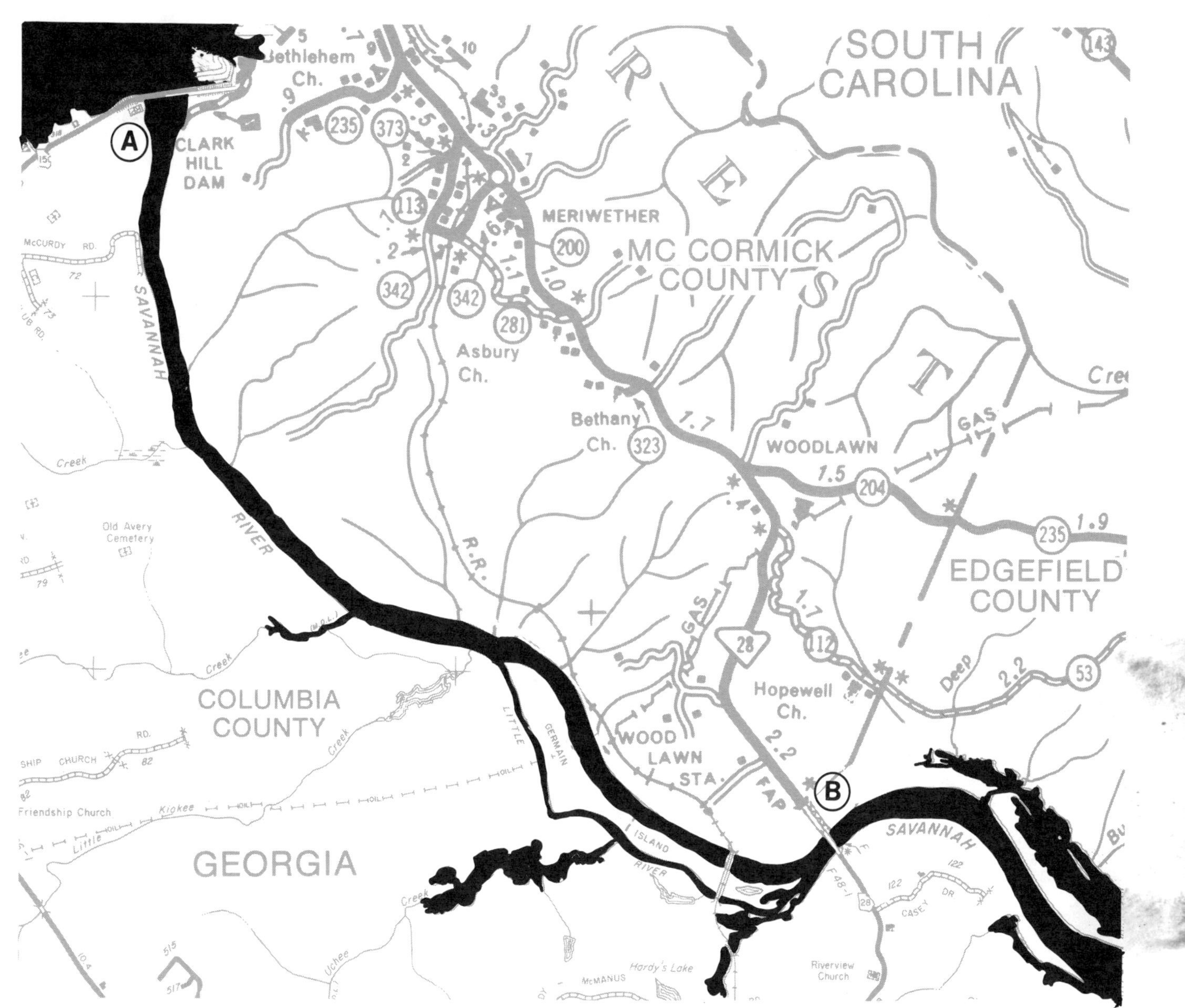

navigation dam with locks. Both of these must either be portaged or locked through. Immediately following the navigation lock and dam the Savannah broadens and shoals appear again and run intermittently until the river narrows and winds to the left before passing the city of Augusta. It is at this point that the Savannah emerges from its wooded corridor into a heavily populated and industrialized area. Flowing first past the levees of downtown Augusta and then through the heavy industry and junkyards on Augusta's southeast river bank, the Savannah leaves the Piedmont behind and begins to change character as it plods irrevocably towards the Atlantic Ocean. River access in the Augusta area is rare at bridge crossings and is better sought at private and public boat ramps.

(*Continued on page 102*)

USGS Quads: Clarks Hill, Evans, Martinez, N. Augusta, Augusta East

ACCESS POINTS	RIVER MILES	SHUTTLE MILES
A-B	7.3	20.5
B-C	5.1	6
C-D	1	2.3
D-E	1	5.5
E-F	5.7	9

Savannah River—*Continued*

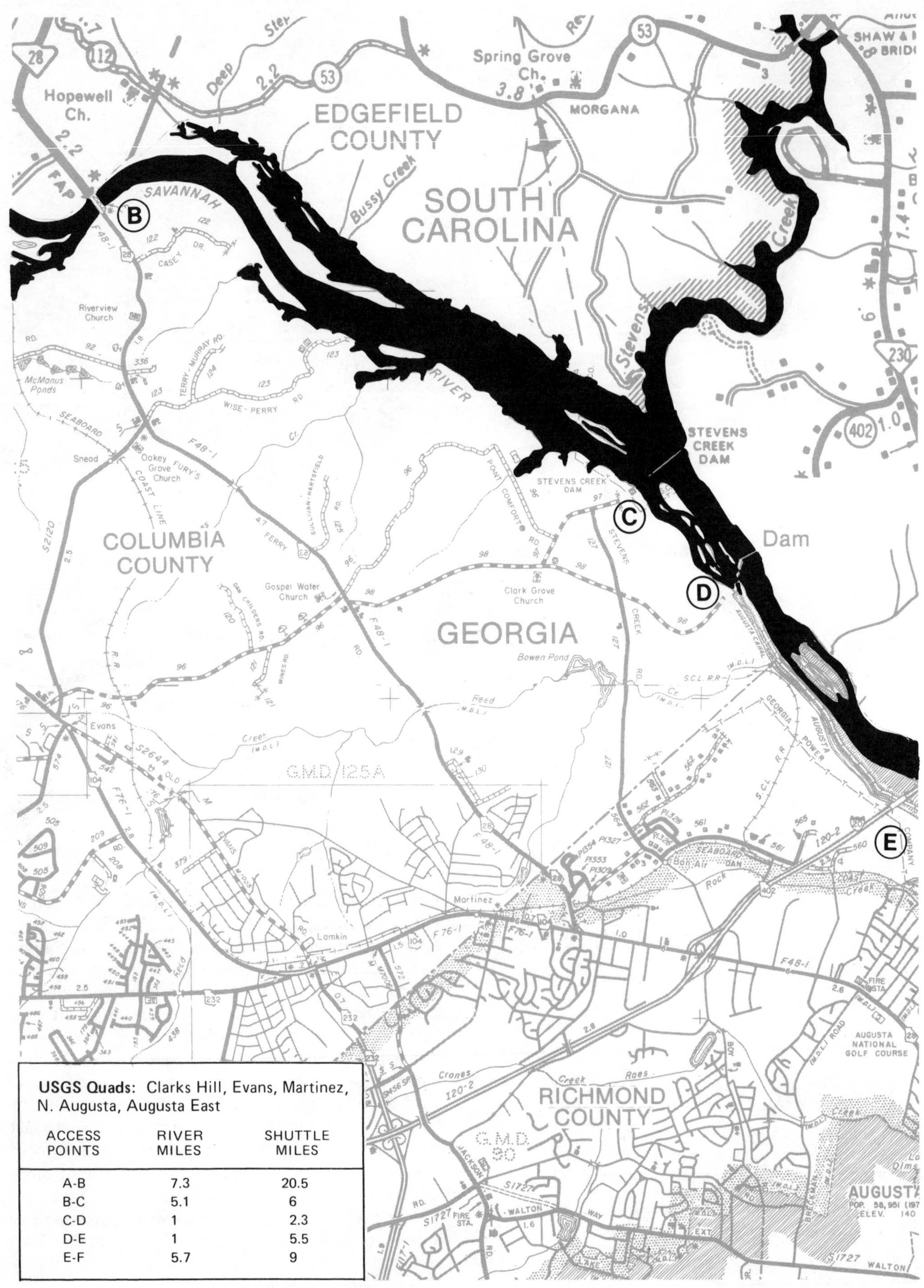

USGS Quads: Clarks Hill, Evans, Martinez, N. Augusta, Augusta East

ACCESS POINTS	RIVER MILES	SHUTTLE MILES
A-B	7.3	20.5
B-C	5.1	6
C-D	1	2.3
D-E	1	5.5
E-F	5.7	9

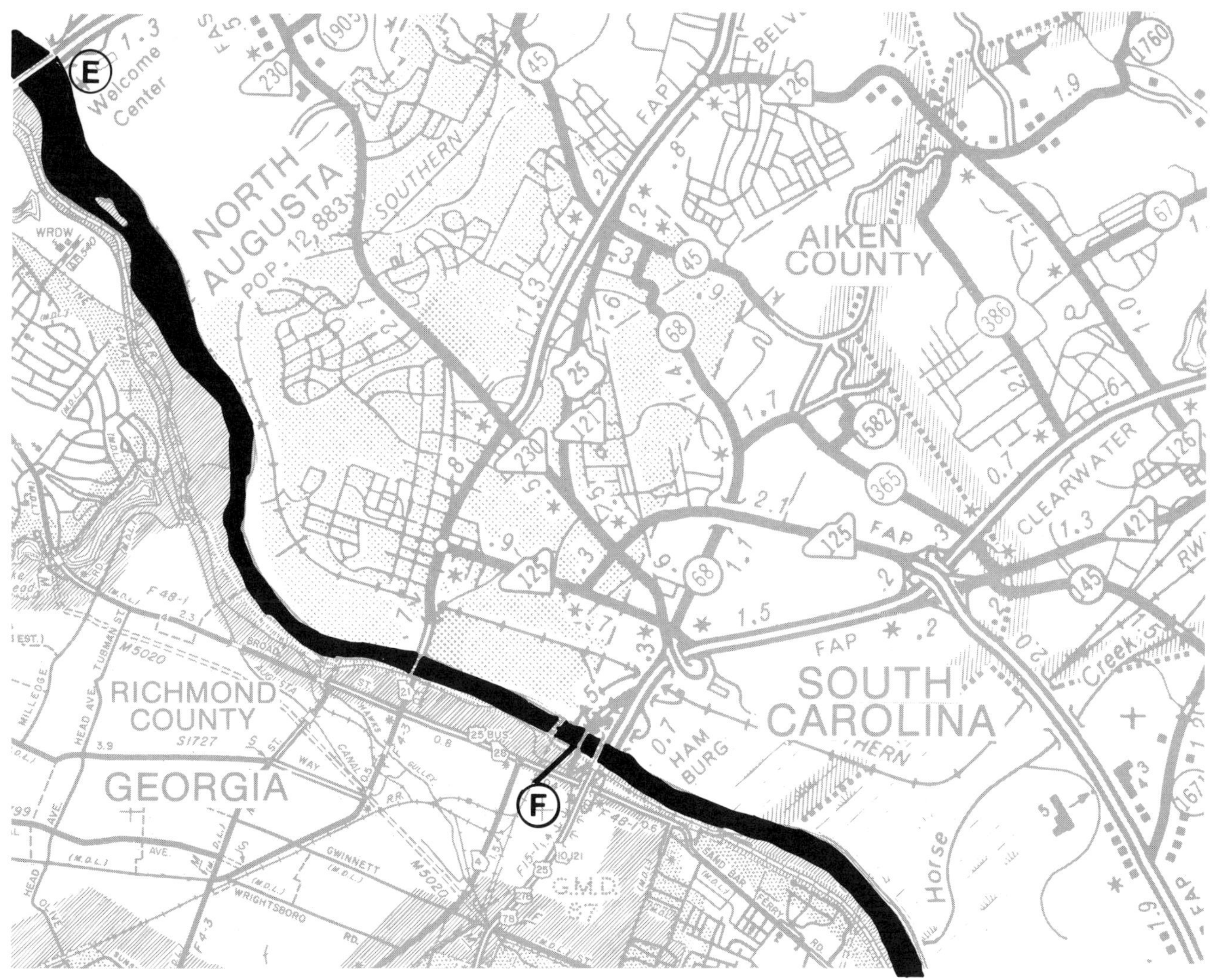

Section: Clark Hill Dam to southeastern Augusta

Counties: Columbia, Richmond

Suitable For: Cruising, camping

Appropriate For: Families, beginners, intermediates, advanced
Months Runnable: All

Interest Highlights: Scenery, wildlife, local culture and industry
Scenery: Pretty in spots to pretty

Difficulty: International Scale I
Numerical Points 5

Average Width: 350 ft.
Gradient: Moderate
Velocity: 3.02 ft./mi.

Runnable Water Level: Minimum Not applicable
Maximum Not applicable

Hazards: Dams, powerboat traffic

Scouting: None

Portages: Stevens Creek Dam, Augusta Canal Dam

Rescue Index: Accessible to accessible but difficult

Mean Water Temperature (°F)

Jan 48	Feb 46	Mar 50	Apr 56	May 60	Jun 68
Jul 72	Aug 73	Sep 71	Oct 64	Nov 58	Dec 50

Source of Additional Information: Thomson Game and Fish Office (404) 595-4211

Access Point	Access Code
A	1357
B	1357
C	1367
D	1367
E	(11)
F	1357

Access Key
1 Paved Road
2 Unpaved Road
3 Short Carry
4 Long Carry
5 Easy Grade
6 Steep Incline
7 Clear Trail
8 Brush and Trees
9 Launching Fee Charged
10 Private Property, Need Permission
11 No Access, Reference Only

Augusta to Savannah

Below Augusta, in Richmond County, the character of the Savannah changes markedly as it bids farewell to the rolling hills of the Piedmont and enters the agricultural flats and bottom lands of the Coastal Plain. Here the river deepens and constricts to an average 250 to 300 feet and flows beneath well-defined, sandy clay banks of two to six feet. Where the Savannah was shallow and turbulent upstream, it is now deep and calm. Islands are smaller and much less common, and the straight sections of the Piedmont have given way to broad meanders and horseshoe loops complete with lowland swamp and oxbow lakes. While a forest corridor continues to cradle the river, it frequently yields to lowland swamp on the far side of the river's natural levee. Nevertheless, the streamside forest remains diverse and beautiful. Dominant along the Savannah in the Coastal Plain are bald cypress, tupelo, overcup oak, water hickory, green ash, and swamp black gum with understory vegetation consisting of swamp privet, swamp dogwood, and swamp palm. Frequently encountered inhabitants of the Savannah along the Coastal Plain include the marsh rabbit, muskrat, several species of bat, mink, opossum, raccoon, gray squirrel, bobcat, long-tailed weasel, red fox, striped skunk, whitetailed deer, beaver and river otter. Reptiles and amphibians are numerous and include several species of rattlesnake as well as the southern copperhead, and the eastern cottonmouth. The many species of birds are plentiful.

Paddling is enjoyable and the setting pristine and remote with the exception of several isolated riverside power plants and industries. Hazards to navigation are limited to power traffic (which is far from overwhelming) and to a dam eight miles south of Augusta that must be portaged. Islands created by meander loop cut-offs and the river's bank provide adequate opportunities for canoe camping although the streamside vegetation is luxurious and thick. The level of difficulty is Class I throughout. Access is good in Richmond and Burke counties but somewhat limited in Screven and Effingham counties.

(Continued on page 113)

Section: Southeastern Augusta to US 301 bridge

Counties: Richmond, Burke, Screven

Suitable For: Cruising, camping

Appropriate For: Families, beginners, intermediates, advanced

Months Runnable: All

Interest Highlights: Scenery, wildlife, local culture and industry

Scenery: Beautiful in spots

Difficulty: International Scale I
Numerical Points 4

Average Width: 250-300 ft.
Gradient: Moderate
Velocity: 0.74 ft./mi.

Runnable Water Level: Minimum Not applicable
Maximum Not applicable

Hazards: Dams, powerboat traffic

Scouting: None

Portages: Corps of Engineers dam at access point H

Rescue Index: Accessible but difficult to remote

Mean Water Temperature (°F)

Jan 48	Feb 48	Mar 51	Apr 56	May 60	Jun 69
Jul 73	Aug 72	Sep 70	Oct 64	Nov 59	Dec 51

Source of Additional Information: Thomson Game and Fish Office (404) 595-4211

Access Point	Access Code
F	1357
G	1357
H	1357
I	1357
J	1357
K	2357
L	2357
M	2357
N	1357

Access Key
1 Paved Road
2 Unpaved Road
3 Short Carry
4 Long Carry
5 Easy Grade
6 Steep Incline
7 Clear Trail
8 Brush and Trees
9 Launching Fee Charged
10 Private Property, Need Permission
11 No Access, Reference Only

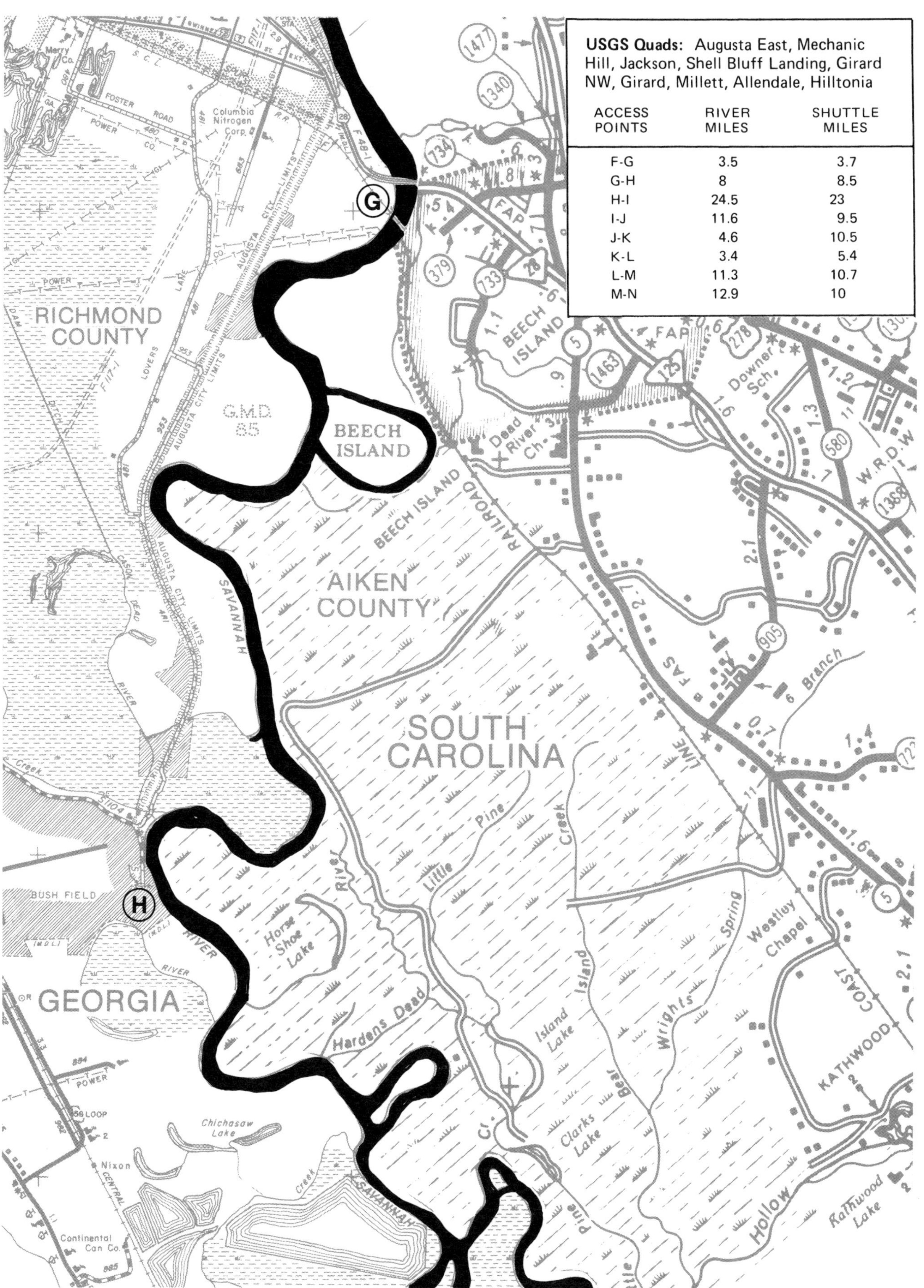

USGS Quads: Augusta East, Mechanic Hill, Jackson, Shell Bluff Landing, Girard NW, Girard, Millett, Allendale, Hilltonia

ACCESS POINTS	RIVER MILES	SHUTTLE MILES
F-G	3.5	3.7
G-H	8	8.5
H-I	24.5	23
I-J	11.6	9.5
J-K	4.6	10.5
K-L	3.4	5.4
L-M	11.3	10.7
M-N	12.9	10

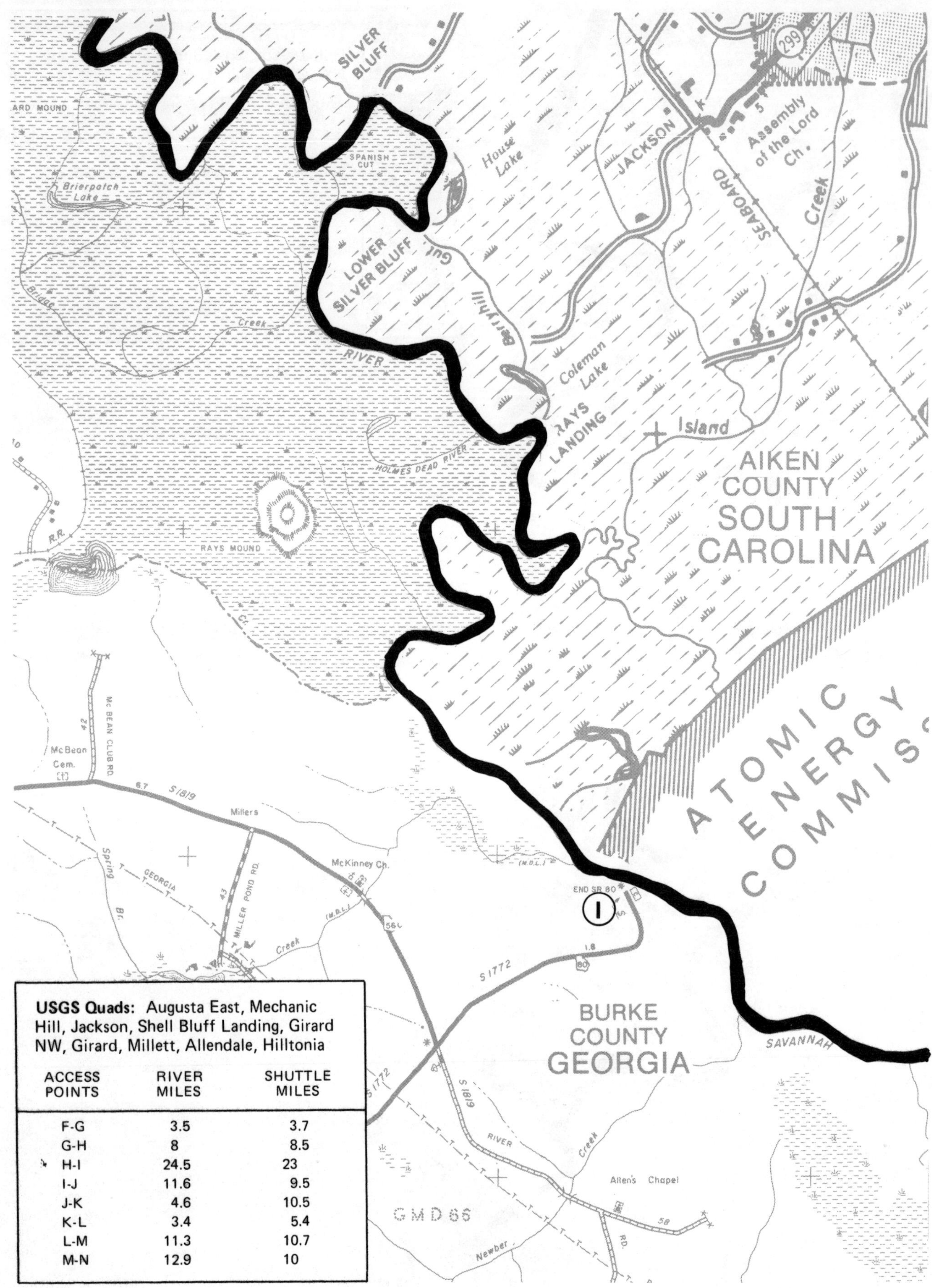

USGS Quads: Augusta East, Mechanic Hill, Jackson, Shell Bluff Landing, Girard NW, Girard, Millett, Allendale, Hilltonia

ACCESS POINTS	RIVER MILES	SHUTTLE MILES
F-G	3.5	3.7
G-H	8	8.5
H-I	24.5	23
I-J	11.6	9.5
J-K	4.6	10.5
K-L	3.4	5.4
L-M	11.3	10.7
M-N	12.9	10

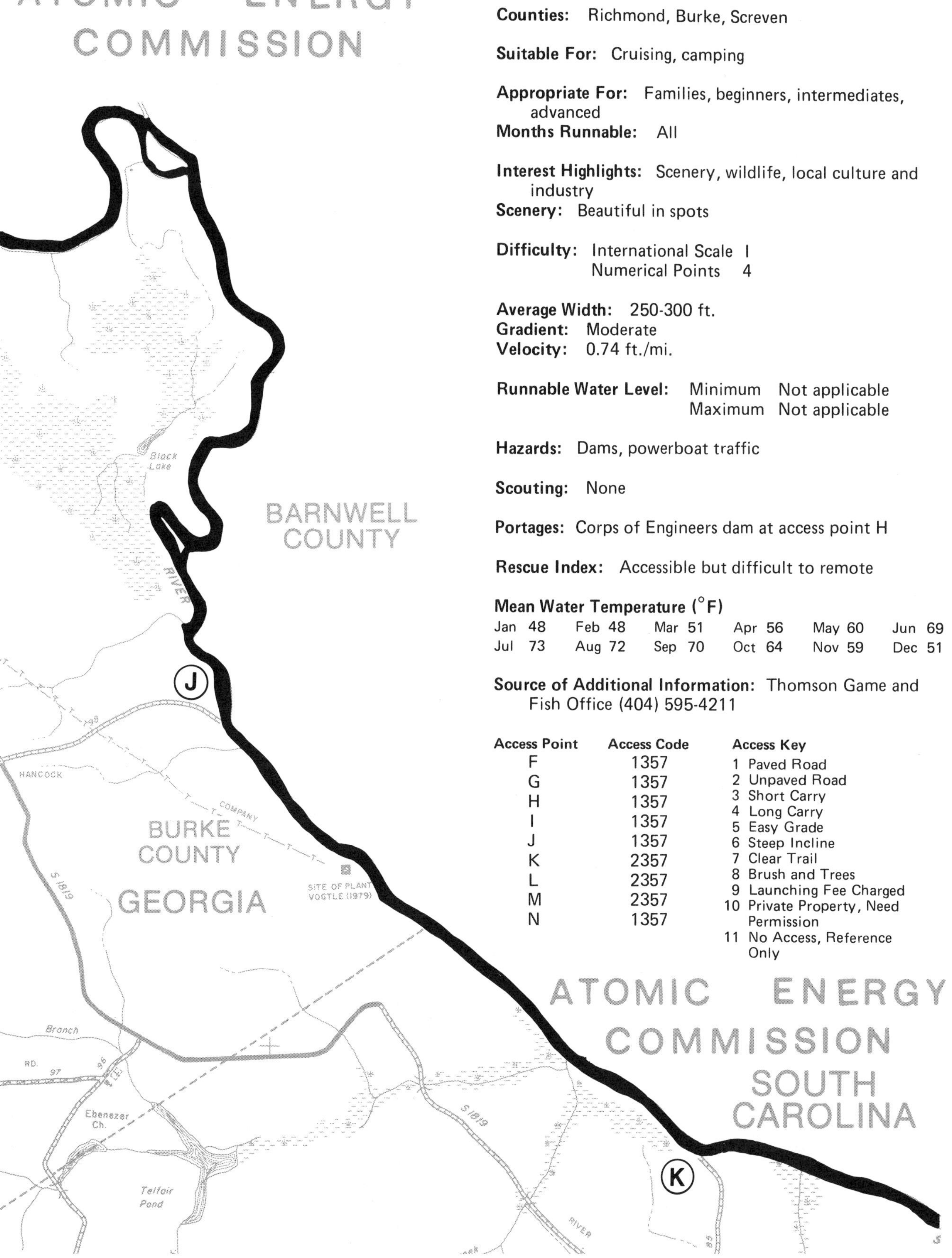

Section: Southeastern Augusta to US 301 bridge

Counties: Richmond, Burke, Screven

Suitable For: Cruising, camping

Appropriate For: Families, beginners, intermediates, advanced
Months Runnable: All

Interest Highlights: Scenery, wildlife, local culture and industry
Scenery: Beautiful in spots

Difficulty: International Scale I
Numerical Points 4

Average Width: 250-300 ft.
Gradient: Moderate
Velocity: 0.74 ft./mi.

Runnable Water Level: Minimum Not applicable
Maximum Not applicable

Hazards: Dams, powerboat traffic

Scouting: None

Portages: Corps of Engineers dam at access point H

Rescue Index: Accessible but difficult to remote

Mean Water Temperature (°F)

Jan 48	Feb 48	Mar 51	Apr 56	May 60	Jun 69
Jul 73	Aug 72	Sep 70	Oct 64	Nov 59	Dec 51

Source of Additional Information: Thomson Game and Fish Office (404) 595-4211

Access Point	Access Code
F	1357
G	1357
H	1357
I	1357
J	1357
K	2357
L	2357
M	2357
N	1357

Access Key
1 Paved Road
2 Unpaved Road
3 Short Carry
4 Long Carry
5 Easy Grade
6 Steep Incline
7 Clear Trail
8 Brush and Trees
9 Launching Fee Charged
10 Private Property, Need Permission
11 No Access, Reference Only

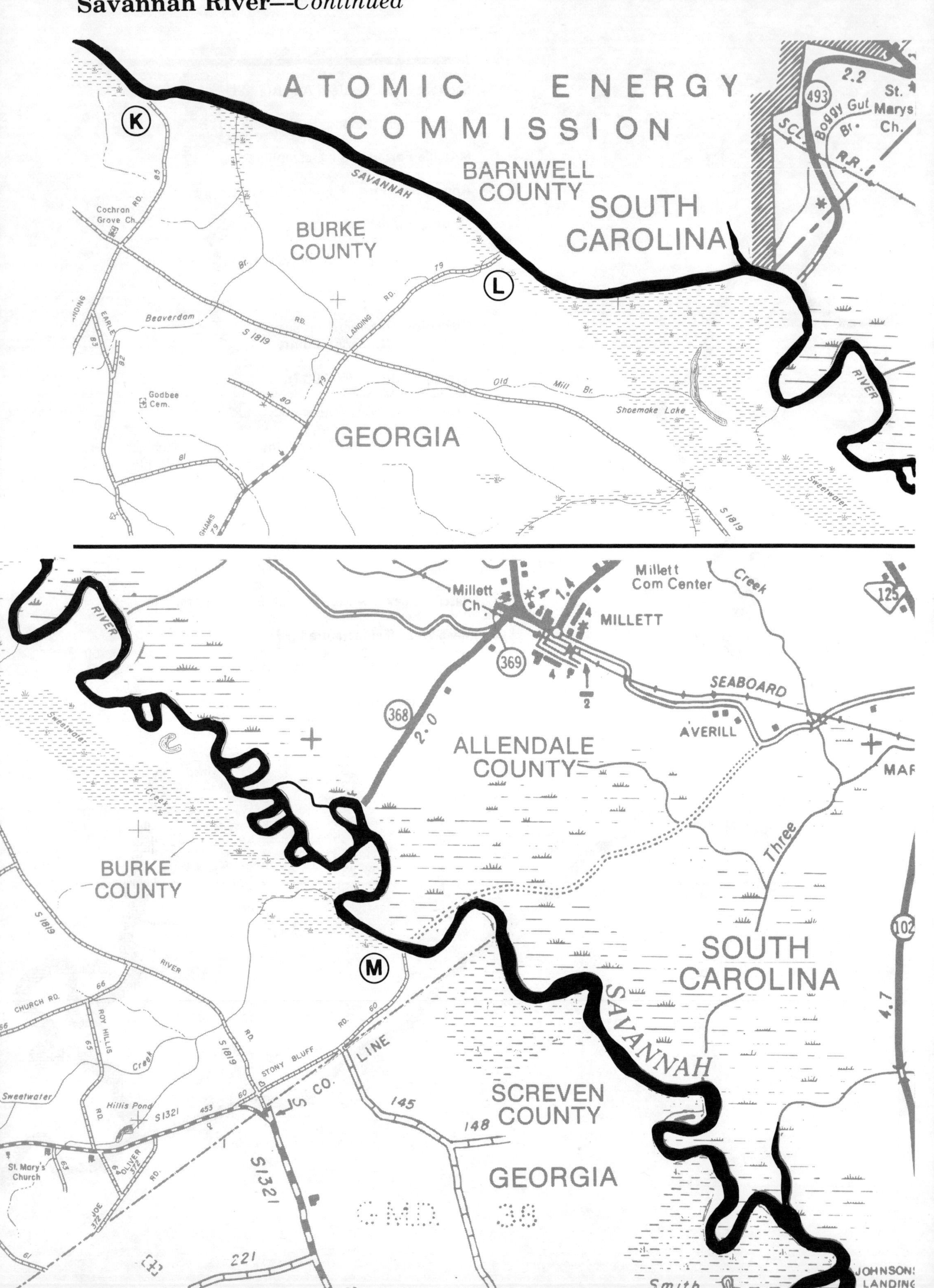

ATOMIC ENERGY COMMISSION
BARNWELL COUNTY
SOUTH CAROLINA
BURKE COUNTY
GEORGIA
SAVANNAH
K
L
Cochran Grove Ch.
Beaverdam
Godbee Cem.
Old Mill Br.
Shoemake Lake
Boggy Gut Br.
St. Marys Ch.
SCL R.R.
493
2.2
S 1819
LANDING RD.
EARLE
Millett Ch.
MILLETT
Millett Com Center
Creek
SEABOARD
AVERILL
ALLENDALE COUNTY
369
368
125
102
2.0
1.4
4.7
RIVER
Sweetwater
Creek
Three
M
SOUTH CAROLINA
SAVANNAH
SCREVEN COUNTY
GEORGIA
BURKE COUNTY
CHURCH RD.
ROY HILLIS RD.
STONY BLUFF RD.
S CO. LINE
Hillis Pond
S1321
St. Mary's Church
JOE
OLIVER
G.M.D. 38
145
148
221
JOHNSONS LANDING
Smith

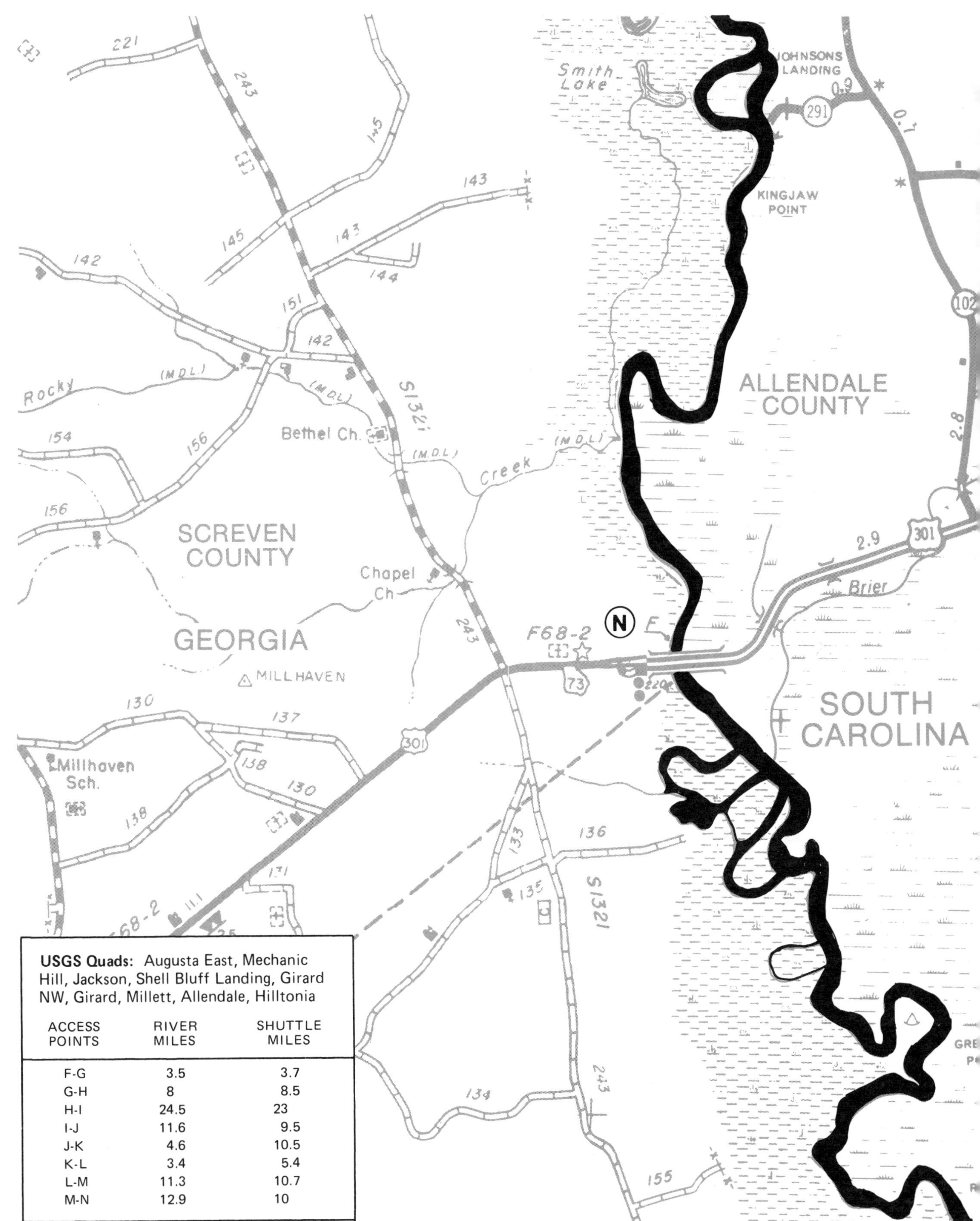

USGS Quads: Augusta East, Mechanic Hill, Jackson, Shell Bluff Landing, Girard NW, Girard, Millett, Allendale, Hilltonia

ACCESS POINTS	RIVER MILES	SHUTTLE MILES
F-G	3.5	3.7
G-H	8	8.5
H-I	24.5	23
I-J	11.6	9.5
J-K	4.6	10.5
K-L	3.4	5.4
L-M	11.3	10.7
M-N	12.9	10

To N
RED BLUFF POINT
SOUTH CAROLINA
Gaul
King
HAMPTON COUNTY
Blue Lake
FAS
60
RIVER
BOAT RAMP
Creek
41
St. Matthews Ch.
SCREVEN COUNTY
Pipe
(M.D.L.)
Dry
Gall
GEORGIA
Creek
(M.D.L.)
To O
SOUTH CAROLINA
Bridge
Creek
Three
Pike
Neufrıl Pond
SCREVEN COUNTY
SAVANNAH
GEORGIA
BLUE SPRINGS MEM. PARK
79
HAMPTON COUNTY
O
(M.D.L.)
RIVER

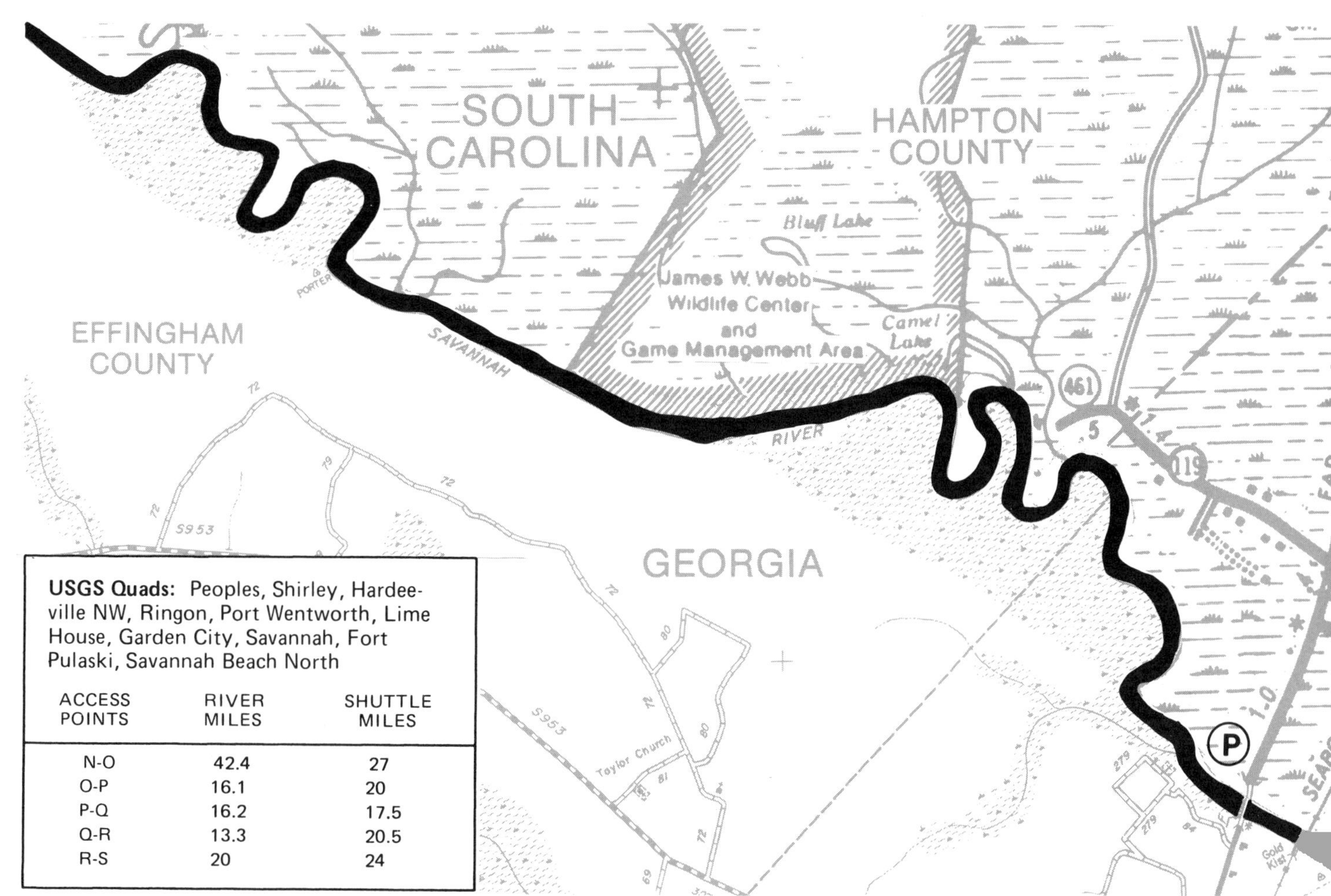

USGS Quads: Peoples, Shirley, Hardeeville NW, Ringon, Port Wentworth, Lime House, Garden City, Savannah, Fort Pulaski, Savannah Beach North

ACCESS POINTS	RIVER MILES	SHUTTLE MILES
N-O	42.4	27
O-P	16.1	20
P-Q	16.2	17.5
Q-R	13.3	20.5
R-S	20	24

Section: US 301 bridge to Fort Pulaski

Counties: Screven, Chatham

Suitable For: Cruising, camping

Appropriate For: Families, beginners, intermediates, advanced

Months Runnable: All

Interest Highlights: Scenery, wildlife, local culture and industry, Savannah and Ft. Pulaski history

Scenery: Pretty to beautiful in spots

Difficulty: International Scale I
Numerical Points 4

Average Width: 350-600 ft.
Gradient: Slow to moderate
Velocity: 0.57 ft./mi.

Runnable Water Level: Minimum Not applicable
Maximum Not applicable

Hazards: Powerboat traffic, tidal currents

Scouting: None

Portages: None

Rescue Index: Accessible to accessible but difficult

Mean Water Temperature (°F)

Jan 47	Feb 48	Mar 52	Apr 60	May 68	Jun 74
Jul 77	Aug 76	Sep 70	Oct 64	Nov 56	Dec 50

Source of Additional Information: Metter Fish and Game Office (912) 685-2145

Access Point	Access Code
N	1357
O	2357
P	1457
Q	1357
R	1357
S	1357

Access Key
1 Paved Road
2 Unpaved Road
3 Short Carry
4 Long Carry
5 Easy Grade
6 Steep Incline
7 Clear Trail
8 Brush and Trees
9 Launching Fee Charged
10 Private Property, Need Permission
11 No Access, Reference Only

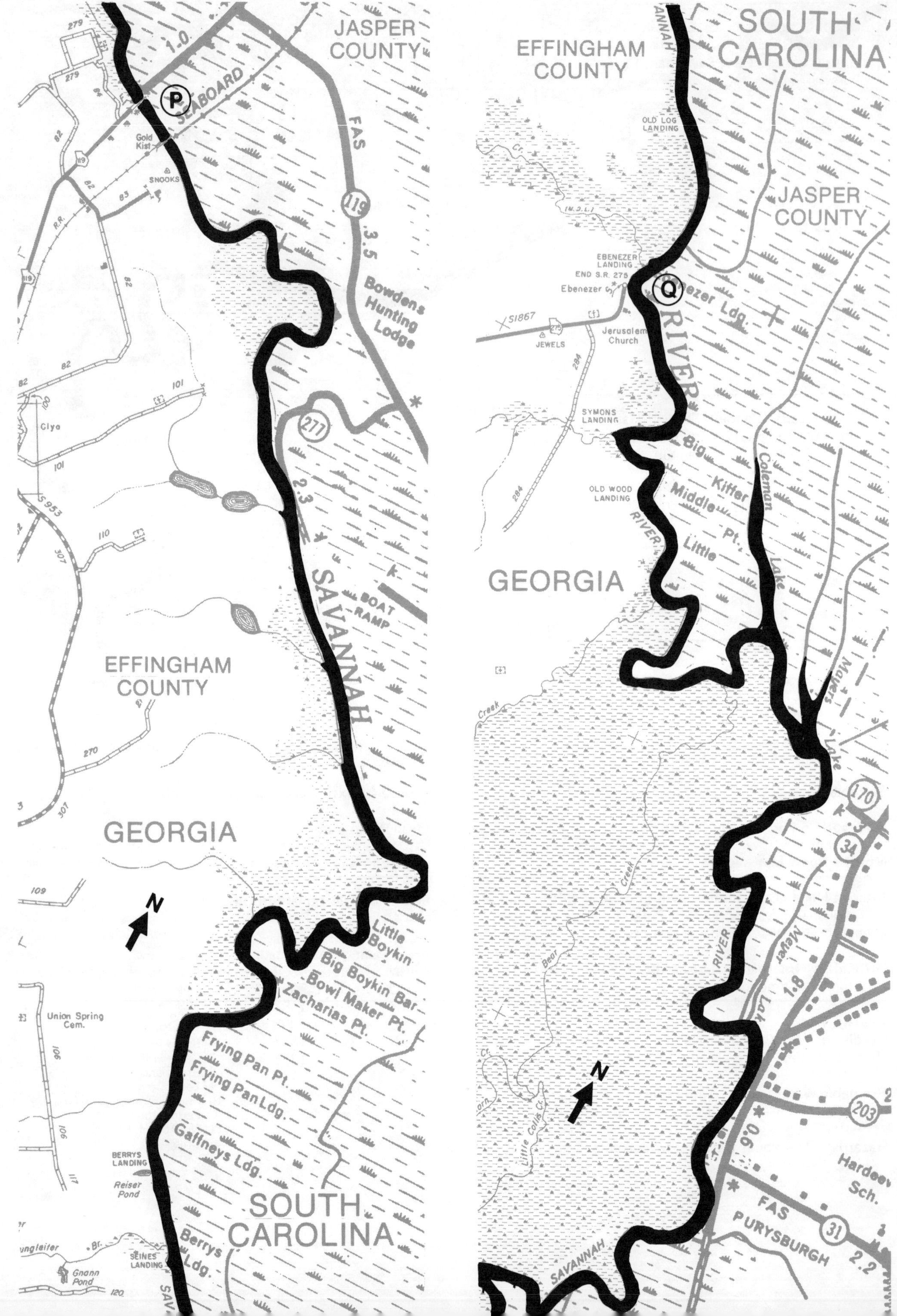
JASPER COUNTY
SEABOARD
Gold Kist
SNOOKS
FAS
119
3.5
Bowdens Hunting Lodge
277
Clyo
2.3
SAVANNAH
BOAT RAMP
EFFINGHAM COUNTY
GEORGIA
N
Little Boykin
Big Boykin Bar
Bowl Maker Pt.
Zacharias Pt.
Union Spring Cem.
Frying Pan Pt.
Frying Pan Ldg.
Gaffneys Ldg.
BERRYS LANDING
Reiser Pond
SOUTH CAROLINA
Berrys Ldg.
SEINES LANDING
Gnann Pond
EFFINGHAM COUNTY
SOUTH CAROLINA
OLD LOG LANDING
JASPER COUNTY
EBENEZER LANDING
END S.R. 275
Ebenezer
Ebenezer Ldg.
Jerusalem Church
JEWELS
RIVER
SYMONS LANDING
Big
Kiffer
Middle
Pt.
Little
OLD WOOD LANDING
GEORGIA
Coleman Lake
Mayers Lake
170
34
RIVER
Meyer Lake
1.8
203
0.6
Hardeeville Sch.
FAS
31
PURYSBURGH
2.2
SAVANNAH
N

USGS Quads: Peoples, Shirley, Hardeeville NW, Ringon, Port Wentworth, Lime House, Garden City, Savannah, Fort Pulaski, Savannah Beach North

ACCESS POINTS	RIVER MILES	SHUTTLE MILES
N-O	42.4	27
O-P	16.1	20
P-Q	16.2	17.5
Q-R	13.3	20.5
R-S	20	24

Section: US 301 bridge to Fort Pulaski

Counties: Screven, Chatham

Suitable For: Cruising, camping

Appropriate For: Families, beginners, intermediates, advanced

Months Runnable: All

Interest Highlights: Scenery, wildlife, local culture and industry, Savannah and Ft. Pulaski history

Scenery: Pretty to beautiful in spots

Difficulty: International Scale I
Numerical Points 4

Average Width: 350-600 ft.
Gradient: Slow to moderate
Velocity: 0.57 ft./mi.

Runnable Water Level: Minimum Not applicable
Maximum Not applicable

Hazards: Powerboat traffic, tidal currents

Scouting: None

Portages: None

Rescue Index: Accessible to accessible but difficult

Mean Water Temperature (°F)

Jan 47	Feb 48	Mar 52	Apr 60	May 68	Jun 74
Jul 77	Aug 76	Sep 70	Oct 64	Nov 56	Dec 50

Source of Additional Information: Metter Fish and Game Office (912) 685-2145

Access Point	Access Code
N	1357
O	2357
P	1457
Q	1357
R	1357
S	1357

Access Key
1 Paved Road
2 Unpaved Road
3 Short Carry
4 Long Carry
5 Easy Grade
6 Steep Incline
7 Clear Trail
8 Brush and Trees
9 Launching Fee Charged
10 Private Property, Need Permission
11 No Access, Reference Only

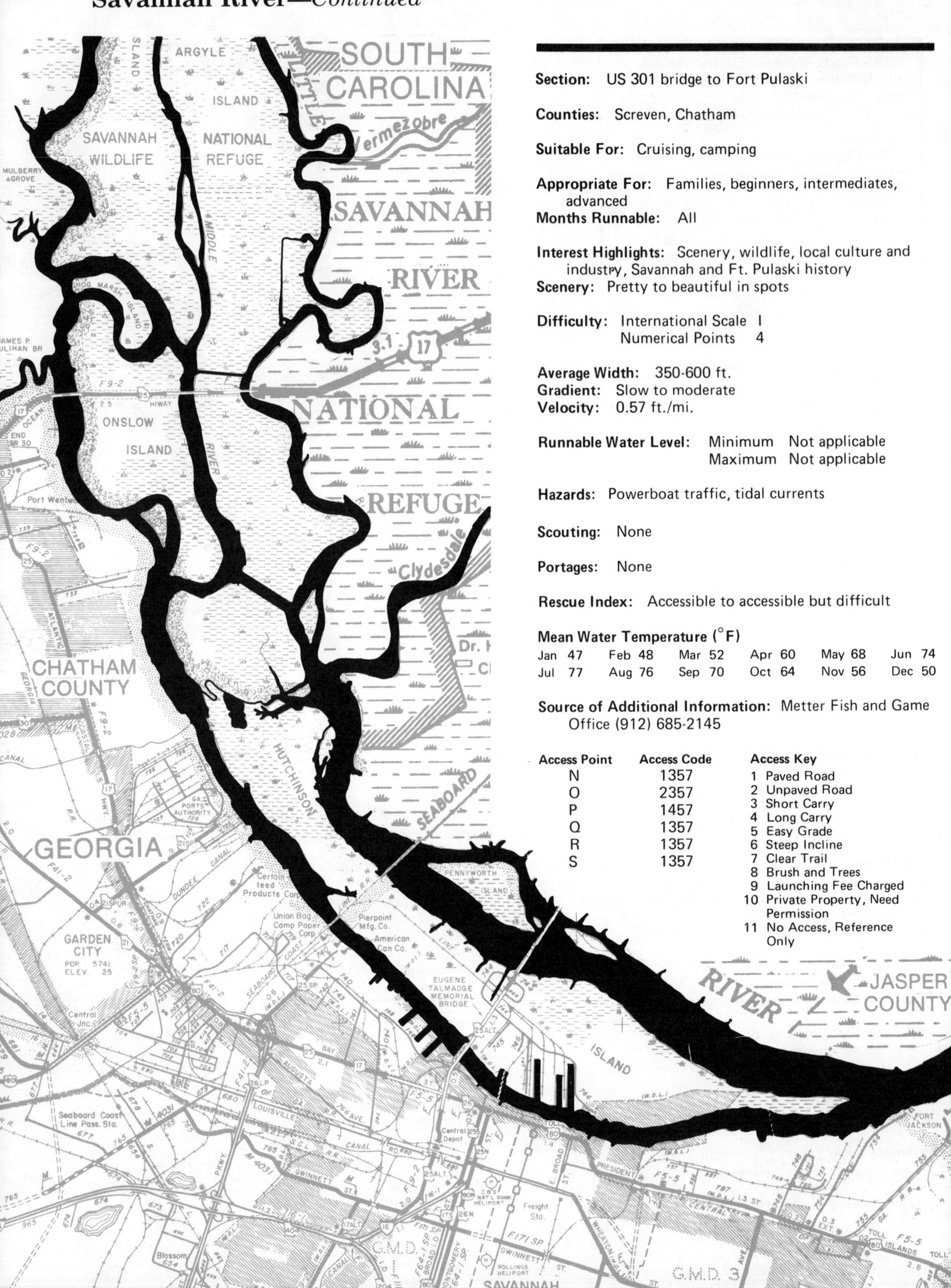

Section: US 301 bridge to Fort Pulaski

Counties: Screven, Chatham

Suitable For: Cruising, camping

Appropriate For: Families, beginners, intermediates, advanced

Months Runnable: All

Interest Highlights: Scenery, wildlife, local culture and industry, Savannah and Ft. Pulaski history

Scenery: Pretty to beautiful in spots

Difficulty: International Scale I
Numerical Points 4

Average Width: 350-600 ft.
Gradient: Slow to moderate
Velocity: 0.57 ft./mi.

Runnable Water Level: Minimum Not applicable
Maximum Not applicable

Hazards: Powerboat traffic, tidal currents

Scouting: None

Portages: None

Rescue Index: Accessible to accessible but difficult

Mean Water Temperature (°F)

Jan 47	Feb 48	Mar 52	Apr 60	May 68	Jun 74
Jul 77	Aug 76	Sep 70	Oct 64	Nov 56	Dec 50

Source of Additional Information: Metter Fish and Game Office (912) 685-2145

Access Point	Access Code
N	1357
O	2357
P	1457
Q	1357
R	1357
S	1357

Access Key
1 Paved Road
2 Unpaved Road
3 Short Carry
4 Long Carry
5 Easy Grade
6 Steep Incline
7 Clear Trail
8 Brush and Trees
9 Launching Fee Charged
10 Private Property, Need Permission
11 No Access, Reference Only

City of Savannah to Fort Pulaski

After passing beneath I-95, the Savannah enters the Savannah National Wildlife Refuge. Formerly the site of many fine plantations and extensive rice cultivation, the rice pools have been allowed to revert to grassy marsh and now serve as the wintering grounds for waterfowl. Here begins a series of alternate cuts, canals, and river passages that branch off the main Savannah channel and parallel it to the east, return to the main channel at the southern end of the wildlife refuge, and immediately fork again around Hutchinson Island. Beyond doubt, several days pleasant paddling can be had while exploring the wildlife refuge.

Moving south beyond the refuge the paddler's choice is to paddle through Savannah city and port or to bypass the harbor on the less trafficked Back River. While the Savannah waterfront is not without historical, industrial, and cultural interest, it is nevertheless somewhat dangerous due to the busy maritime traffic. Our advice: See Savannah harbor from the deck of a sightseeing boat.

As the Back River rejoins the Savannah on the southeastern edge of the city, the river slips again into the tidal marsh. Continuing downstream, the Savannah is divided by Elba and Long islands at the southern end of which is historic Fort Pulaski and the last available take-out before the river empties into the Atlantic. Level of difficulty for this section is Class I with powerboat traffic being the principal hazard to navigation. At the end of the run in the tidal marsh, varied opportunities for side trips of two hours to two months are available via the Wilmington and Tybee rivers, which join the South Channel of the Savannah opposite Elba Island. Paddlers interested in exploring the lower Savannah or any of its connecting waterways should remember to consider the ebb and flow of the tide when planning the trip.

Canoochee River

The Canoochee River originates in central Emanuel County and flows southeastward draining Chandler County and portions of Evans, Bulloch, Bryan, and Liberty counties before emptying into the Ogeechee north of Richmond Hill. Pristine and secluded, and rich in wildlife and vegetation, the Canoochee is a delightful paddling stream. Characterized by its sparkling burgundy-colored water and white banks and sandbars, the river can be run most of the year, except in dry periods, downstream of the US 280 bridge. Its banks are three to seven feet in height, average 45 degrees in slope, and are lined with black gum, sweet gum, swamp palm, cypress, willow, and swamp white oak. Adjacent floodplains range from unusually wide to virtually nonexistent (in the latter case pine forests penetrate almost to the river's edge). Stream width varies from 40 to 60 feet in the upper reaches (US 280 to GA 119), where the Canoochee is well shaded, to an alternating pattern of broad sections and narrows for most of the remainder of its length. Here the Canoochee constricts to 50 feet or less for several hundred feet and then broadens to 140 feet or more. Near its mouth at the Ogeechee, the Canoochee reaches a width approaching 185 to 210 feet.

Current on the upper and middle Canoochee is moderate while current near the mouth is modified by the ebb and flow of the tide. The level of difficulty is Class I throughout with deadfalls in the upper section and powerboat traffic in the lower section being the only hazards to navigation. Sandbars and well-defined banks provide suitable sites for canoe camping. Since, however, the Canoochee flows through Fort Stewart army base, permission to camp should be obtained prior to departure. Access is good.

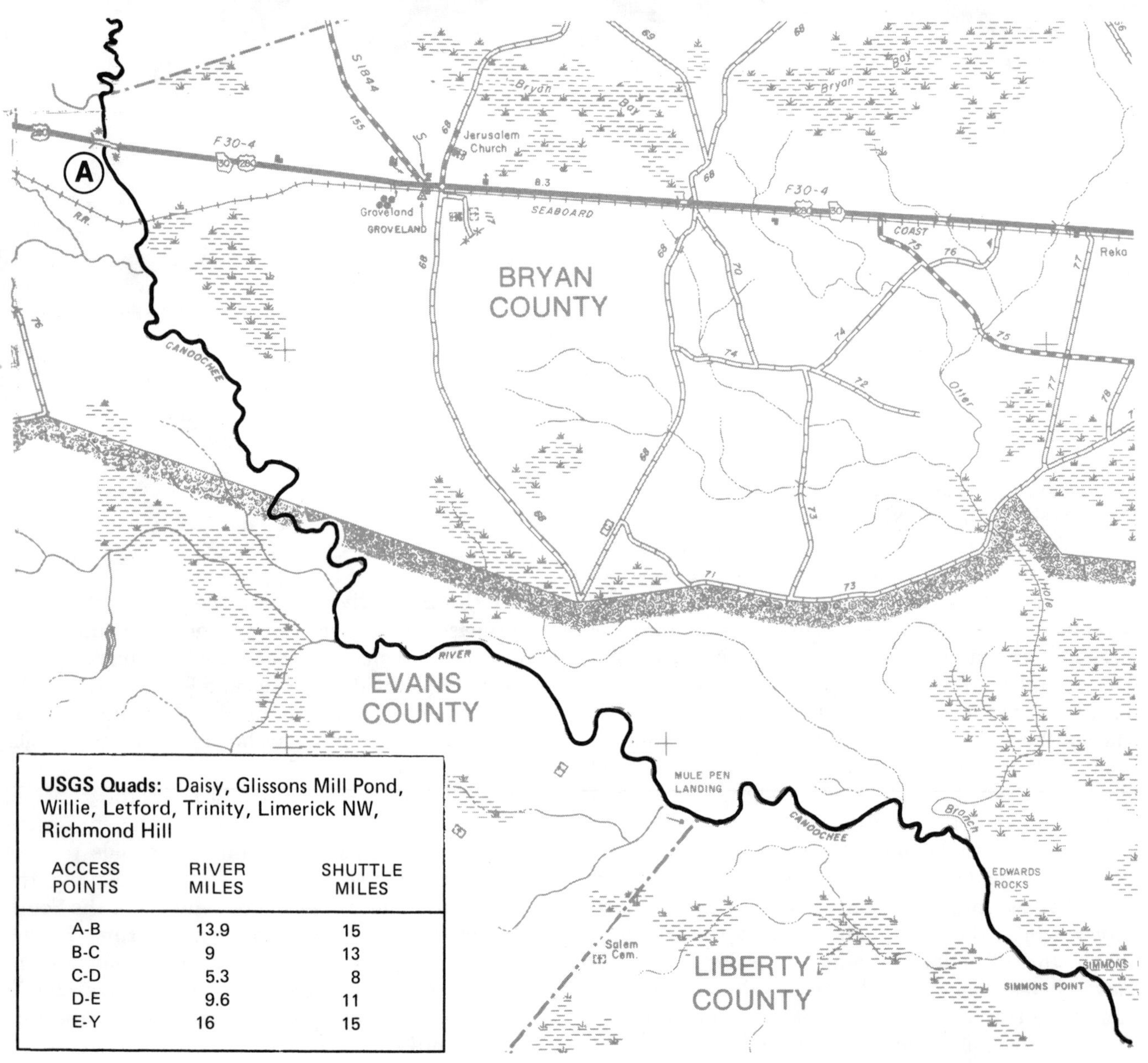

USGS Quads: Daisy, Glissons Mill Pond, Willie, Letford, Trinity, Limerick NW, Richmond Hill

ACCESS POINTS	RIVER MILES	SHUTTLE MILES
A-B	13.9	15
B-C	9	13
C-D	5.3	8
D-E	9.6	11
E-Y	16	15

Section: US 280 bridge to Ogeechee River

Counties: Bryan

Suitable For: Cruising, camping

Appropriate For: Families, beginners, intermediates, advanced

Months Runnable: Late December to August

Interest Highlights: Scenery, wildlife, Ft. Stewart military base

Scenery: Beautiful

Difficulty: International Scale I
Numerical Points 4

Average Width: 70-150 ft.
Velocity: Slow to moderate
Gradient: 1.12 ft./mi.

Runnable Water Level: Minimum 190 cfs
(Clarkton gauge) Maximum Up to high flood stage

Hazards: Deadfalls in upper sections, powerboats in lower sections

Scouting: Permission to pass through Fort Stewart

Portages: None required

Rescue Index: Accessible but difficult

Mean Water Temperature (°F)

Jan 49	Feb 51	Mar 56	Apr 64	May 71	Jun 77
Jul 79	Aug 78	Sep 74	Oct 65	Nov 58	Dec 52

Source of Additional Information: Demeries Creek Game and Fish Office (912) 727-2111

Access Point	Access Code
A	2357
B	13579
C	23679
D	23579
E	23579
Y[1]	1357

Access Key
1 Paved Road
2 Unpaved Road
3 Short Carry
4 Long Carry
5 Easy Grade
6 Steep Incline
7 Clear Trail
8 Brush and Trees
9 Launching Fee Charged
10 Private Property, Need Permission
11 No Access, Reference Only

[1]On the Ogeechee River

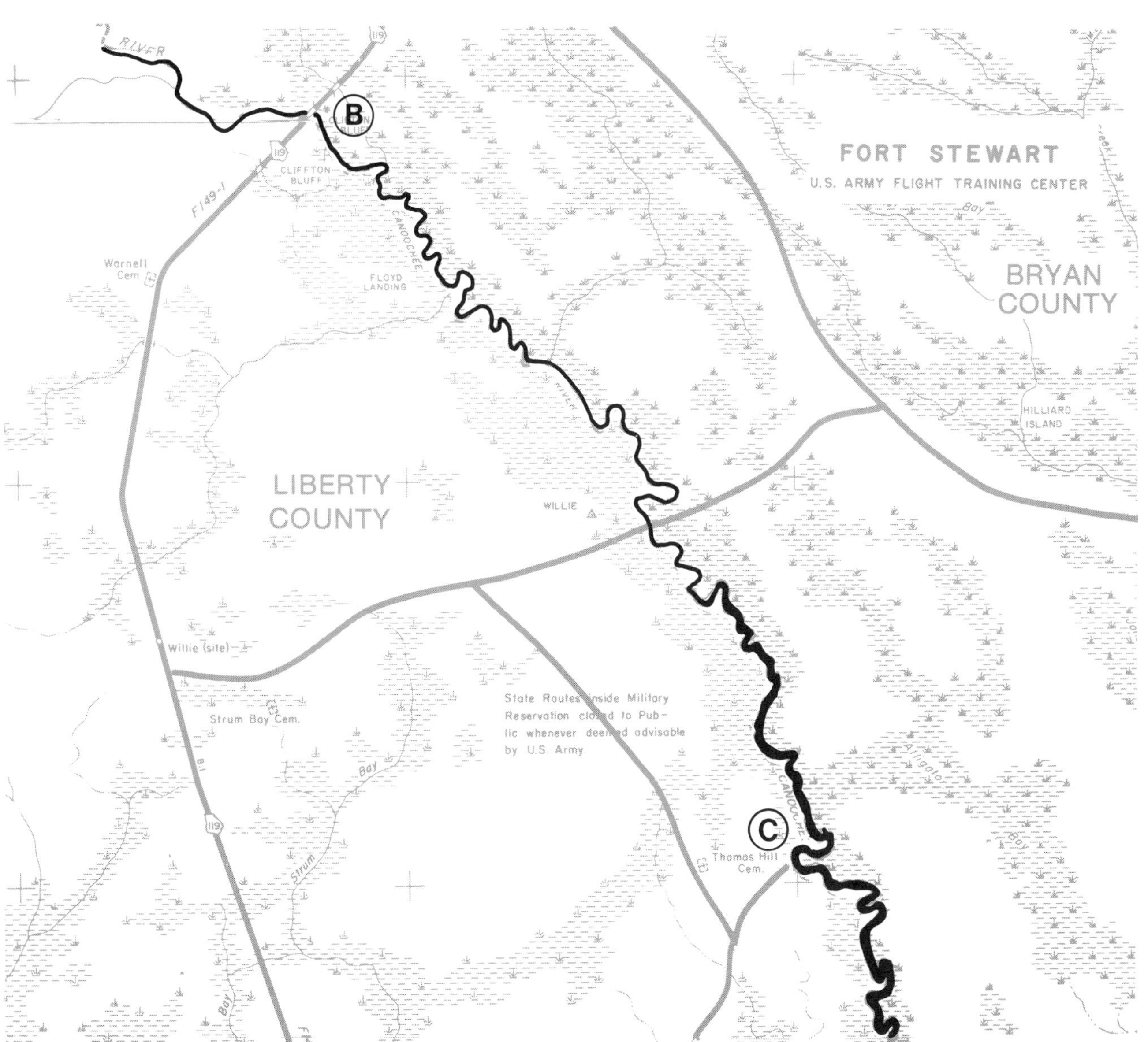

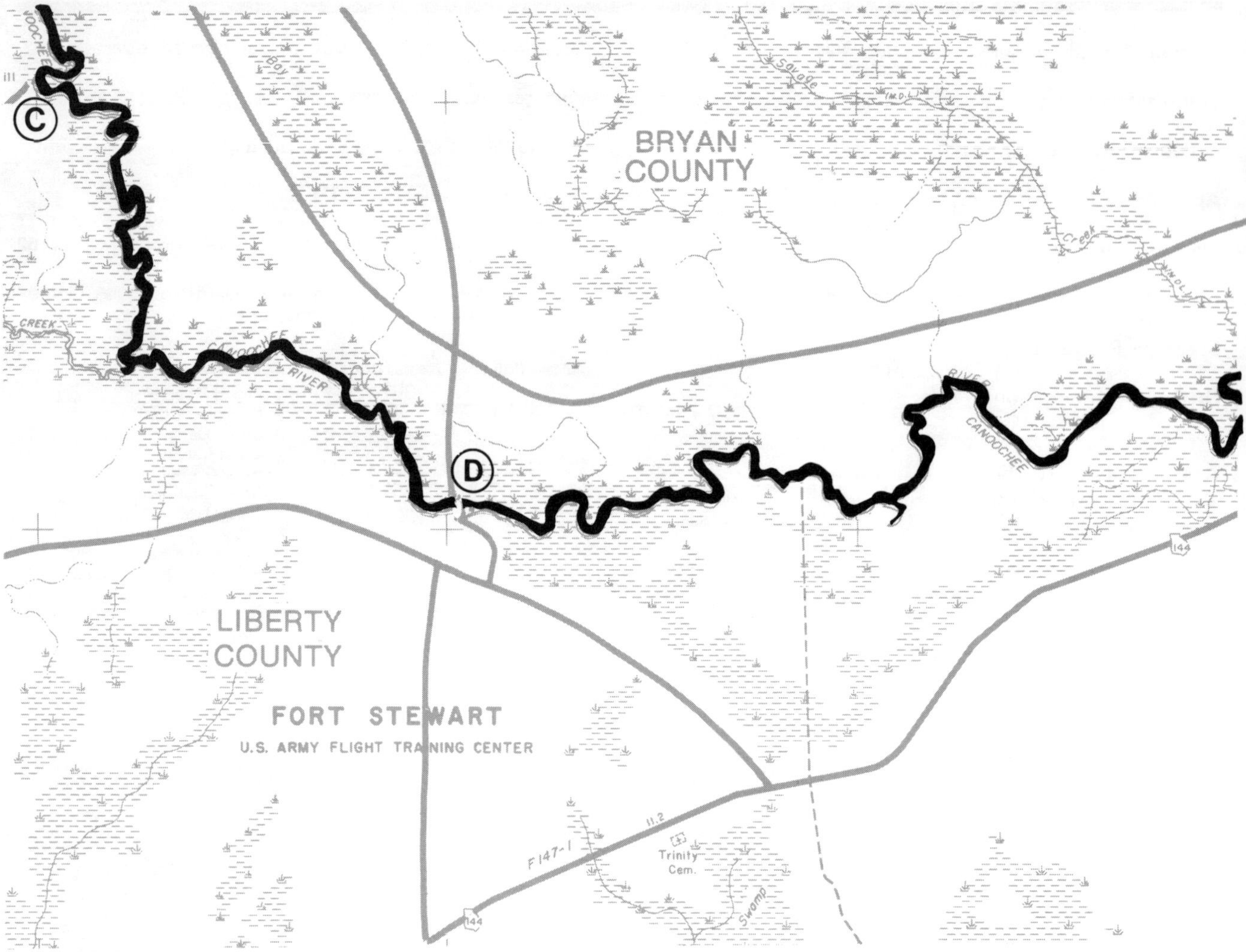

Canoochee River—*Continued*

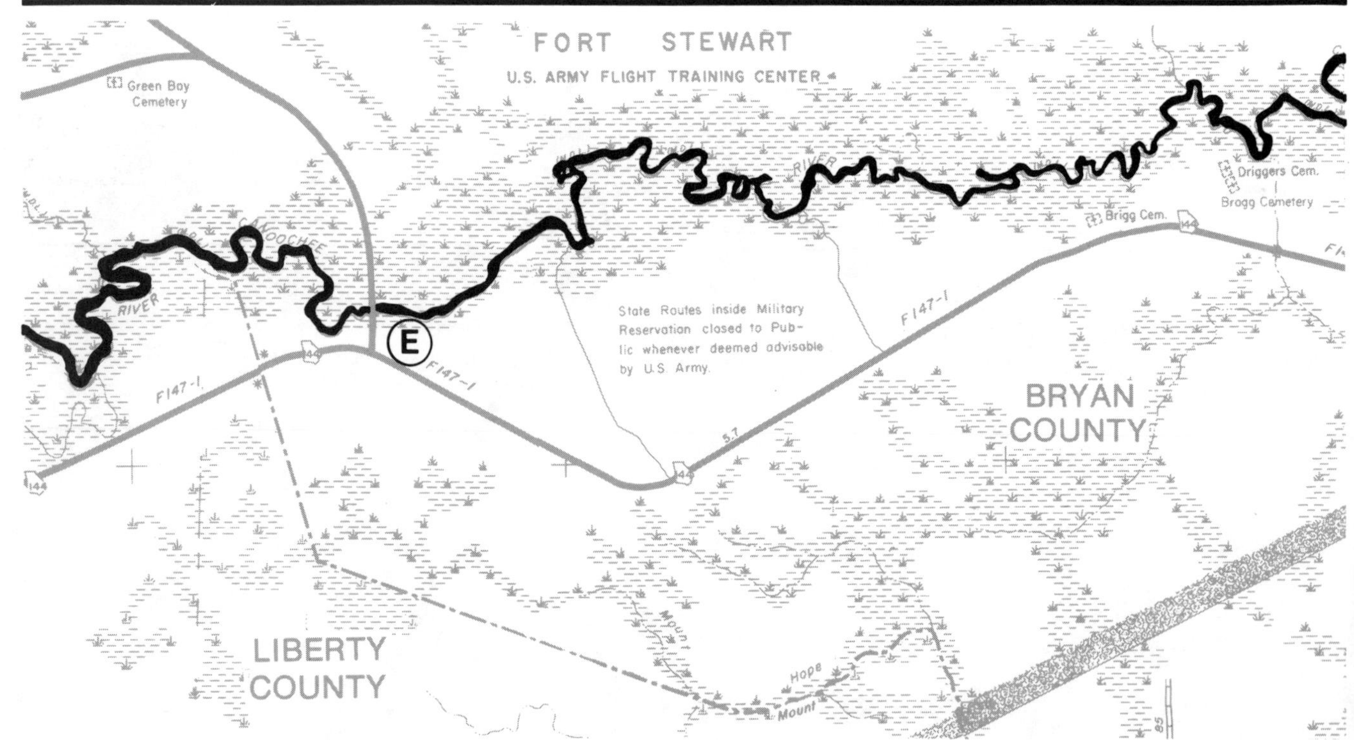

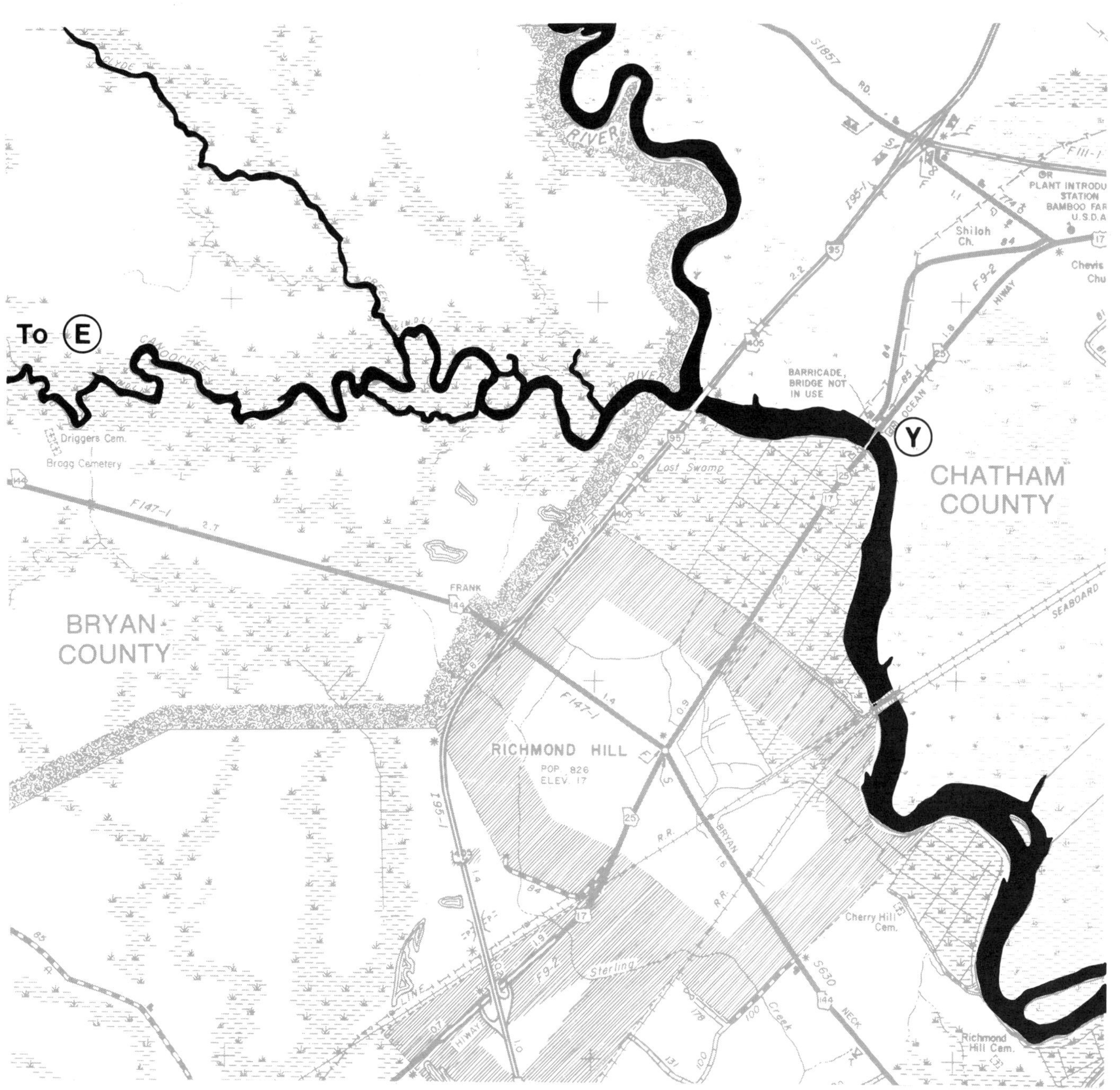

USGS Quads: Daisy, Glissons Mill Pond, Willie, Letford, Trinity, Limerick NW, Richmond Hill

ACCESS POINTS	RIVER MILES	SHUTTLE MILES
A-B	13.9	15
B-C	9	13
C-D	5.3	8
D-E	9.6	11
E-Y	16	15

Ogeechee River

The Ogeechee River originates in eastern Greene County where it is partially spring fed. Running shallow and rocky as it drains the Piedmont counties of Warren and Hancock, the Ogeechee crosses over the Fall Line as it passes through Washington and Glascock counties. Having reached the Coastal Plain, the Ogeechee exhibits characteristics typical of both Coastal Plain blackwater and Coastal Plain alluvial streams. In a blackwater stream, the water is colored a weak-tea red caused by tannic acid stain from tree roots and decaying vegetation. However, unlike the typical blackwater stream, the Ogeechee flows between clay banks averaging two to four feet in height and varying in slope. At times the stream is deep and well channeled with bluffs occasionally rising from streamside. At other times the Ogeechee passes through broad expanses of lowland swamp.

Above Louisville countless deadfalls and a dependence on seasonal rain for additional flow preclude good paddling conditions. Intimate, serene, and beautiful, the Ogeechee becomes runnable downstream of the US 1 bridge crossing south of Louisville. Here the river is 35 to 50 feet in width and almost completely shaded by sycamore, willow, sweet gum, and cypress laden with moss. The current is slow, in keeping with the tranquil, lazy atmosphere.

For the most part, the Ogeechee runs in the center of a heavily forested lowland swamp as it moves southeastward through Jefferson, Burke, and Emmanuel counties. The course of the river is meandering and convoluted with numerous horseshoe bends, oxbow lakes, and small meander islands. Beyond the lowland swamp the terrain rises gradually to a plateau about twenty feet above the swamp floor. The setting is primitive in the extreme with a swamp or woodland corridor ranging for a mile or more to either side of the river.

In Jenkins County south of Millen, Buckhead Creek enters the Ogeechee. Buckhead Creek is largely fed by Magnolia Springs, a vibrant, cold, clear, and extremely prolific spring located off US 25 north of Millen. A worthwhile side exploration can be had by putting in at Magnolia Springs State Park and paddling to Buckhead Creek and thence to the Ogeechee.

Below Millen the swamp expands and contracts as the Ogeechee flows past one of the tall (65 feet) sand and clay bluffs that give the stream a special identity. These bluffs, and many others more modest in size, occur intermittently almost all the way to the tidewater section below the Seaboard Coast Line railroad crossing east of Richmond Hill, and they offer the best canoe camping sites on the Ogeechee.

Continuing through Screven and Burke counties, bluffs continue to approach the river and swamp, then suddenly recede to leave vast primeval gardens of backwater sloughs and thickly forested watery lowland.

As the Ogeechee passes the GA 24 bridge, the river widens and the channel becomes more well defined. Moving into Bryan and southern Effingham counties, small islands suitable for canoe camping become more prevalent. Just downstream from GA 204 the Ogeechee separates into multiple channels

(Continued on page 123)

Section: Louisville to Scarboro

Counties: Jefferson, Burke, Emanuel, Jenkins

Suitable For: Cruising, camping

Appropriate For: Families, beginners, intermediates, advanced

Months Runnable: All

Interest Highlights: Scenery, wildlife

Scenery: Pretty to beautiful

Difficulty: International Scale I
Numerical Points 6

Average Width: 45-65 ft.
Gradient: Slow to moderate
Velocity: 1.69 ft./mi.

Runnable Water Level: (Eden gauge) Minimum 500 cfs; Maximum Up to high flood stage

Hazards: Deadfalls

Scouting: None required

Portages: None required

Rescue Index: Accessible but difficult

Mean Water Temperature (°F)

Jan 46	Feb 47	Mar 51	Apr 66	May 68	Jun 74
Jul 77	Aug 75	Sep 71	Oct 64	Nov 56	Dec 50

Source of Additional Information: Metter Game and Fish Office (912) 685-2145

Access Point	Access Code
A	1357
B	1357
C	2357
D	1357
E	2357
F	1357
G	1357
H	2357
I	1357
J	2357

Access Key
1 Paved Road
2 Unpaved Road
3 Short Carry
4 Long Carry
5 Easy Grade
6 Steep Incline
7 Clear Trail
8 Brush and Trees
9 Launching Fee Charged
10 Private Property, Need Permission
11 No Access, Reference Only

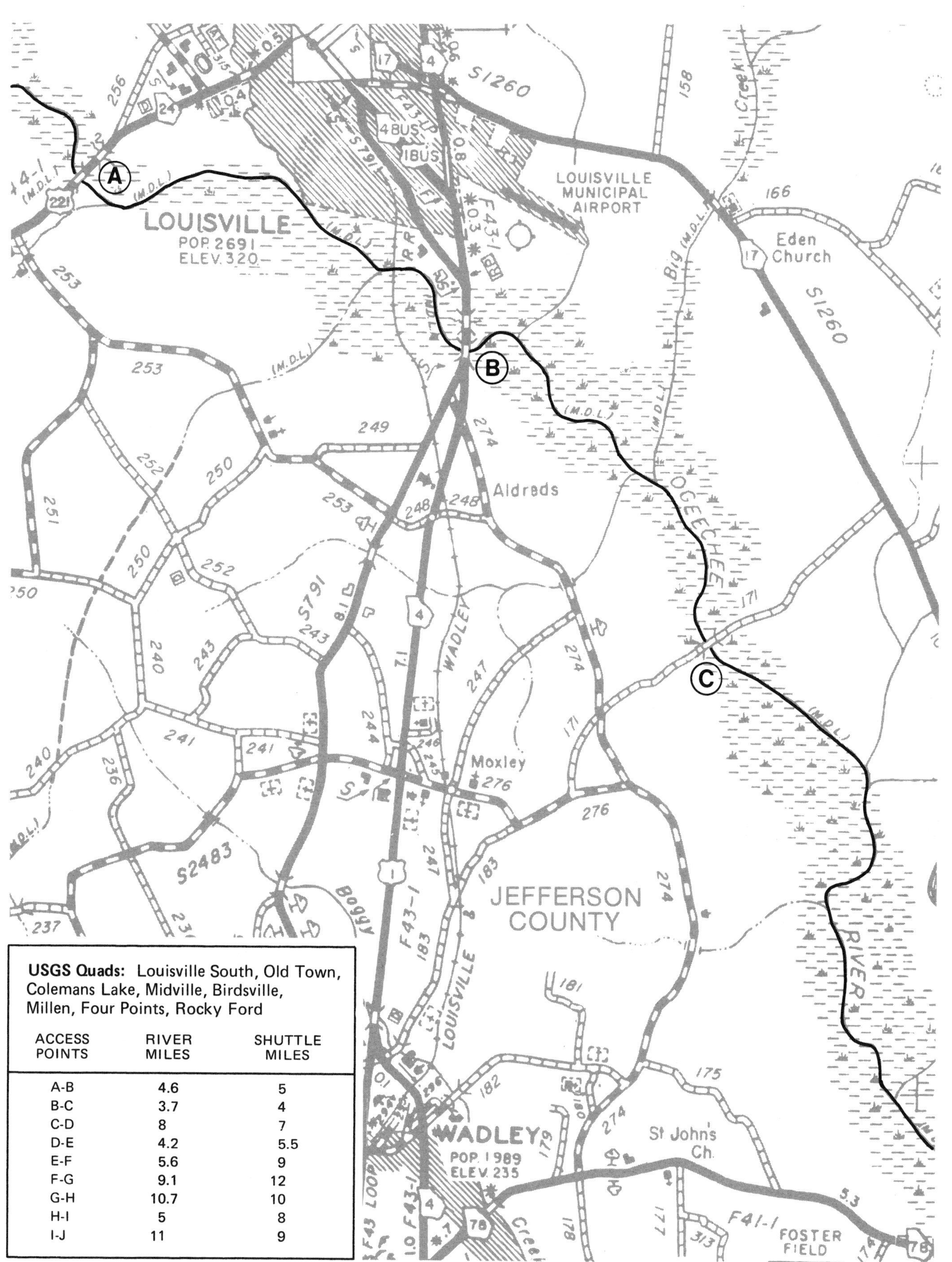

USGS Quads: Louisville South, Old Town, Colemans Lake, Midville, Birdsville, Millen, Four Points, Rocky Ford

ACCESS POINTS	RIVER MILES	SHUTTLE MILES
A-B	4.6	5
B-C	3.7	4
C-D	8	7
D-E	4.2	5.5
E-F	5.6	9
F-G	9.1	12
G-H	10.7	10
H-I	5	8
I-J	11	9

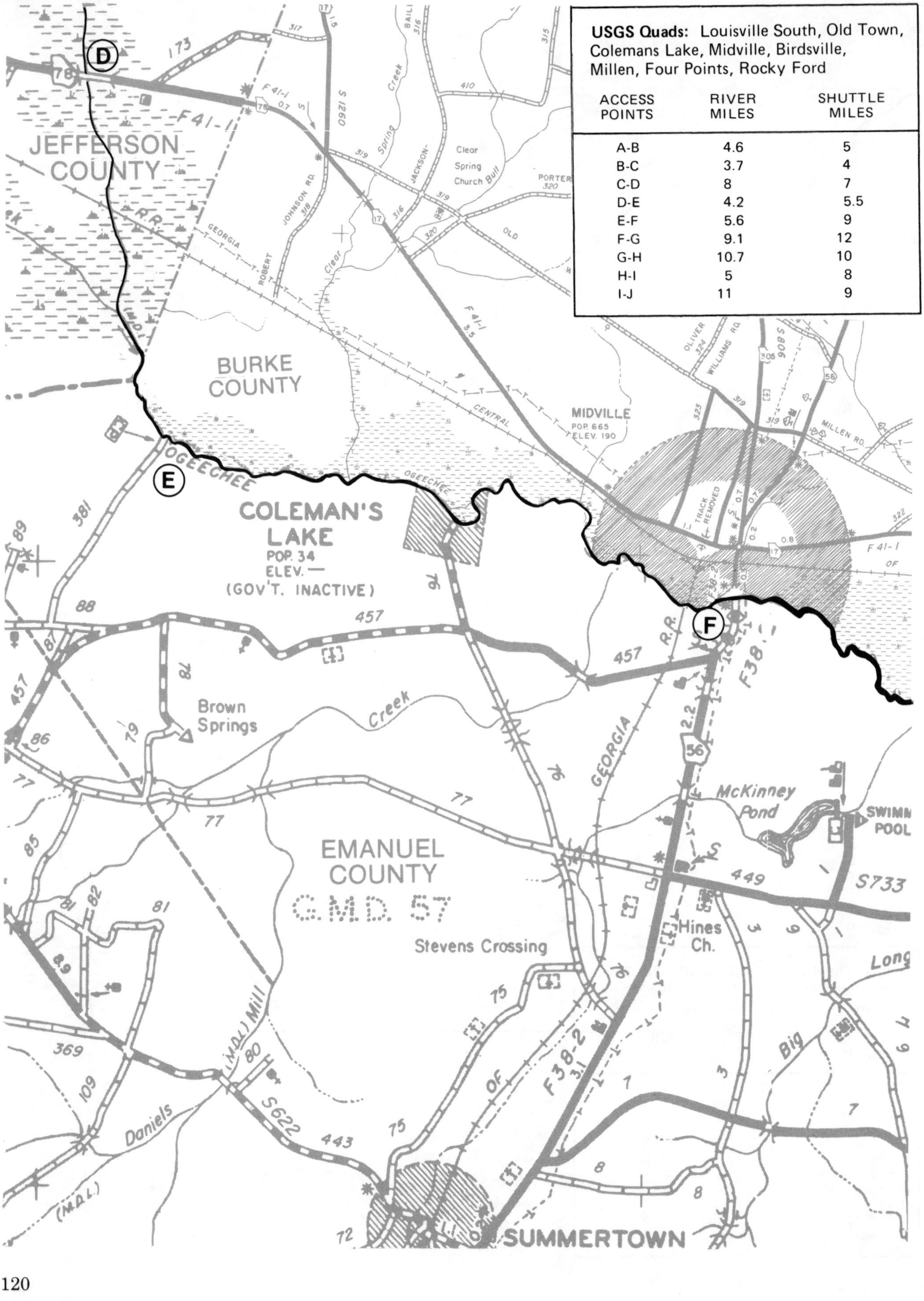

Ogeechee River—*Continued*

USGS Quads: Louisville South, Old Town, Colemans Lake, Midville, Birdsville, Millen, Four Points, Rocky Ford

ACCESS POINTS	RIVER MILES	SHUTTLE MILES
A-B	4.6	5
B-C	3.7	4
C-D	8	7
D-E	4.2	5.5
E-F	5.6	9
F-G	9.1	12
G-H	10.7	10
H-I	5	8
I-J	11	9

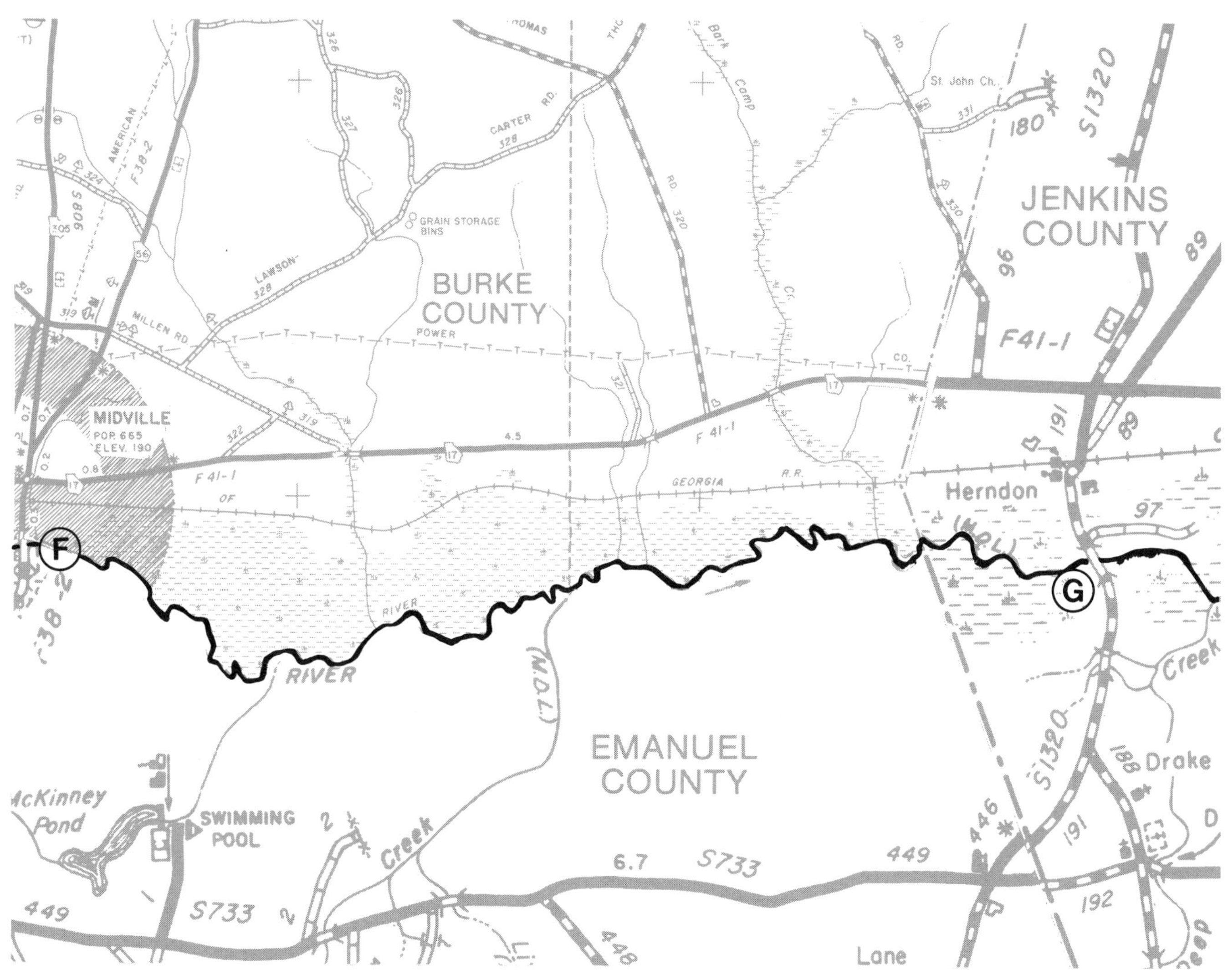

Section: Louisville to Scarboro

Counties: Jefferson, Burke, Emanuel, Jenkins

Suitable For: Cruising, camping

Appropriate For: Families, beginners, intermediates, advanced

Months Runnable: All

Interest Highlights: Scenery, wildlife

Scenery: Pretty to beautiful

Difficulty: International Scale I
Numerical Points 6

Average Width: 45-65 ft.
Gradient: Slow to moderate
Velocity: 1.69 ft./mi.

Runnable Water Level: Minimum 500 cfs
(Eden gauge) Maximum Up to high flood stage

Hazards: Deadfalls

Scouting: None required

Portages: None required

Rescue Index: Accessible but difficult

Mean Water Temperature (°F)

Jan 46	Feb 47	Mar 51	Apr 66	May 68	Jun 74
Jul 77	Aug 75	Sep 71	Oct 64	Nov 56	Dec 50

Source of Additional Information: Metter Game and Fish Office (912) 685-2145

Access Point	Access Code
A	1357
B	1357
C	2357
D	1357
E	2357
F	1357
G	1357
H	2357
I	1357
J	2357

Access Key
1 Paved Road
2 Unpaved Road
3 Short Carry
4 Long Carry
5 Easy Grade
6 Steep Incline
7 Clear Trail
8 Brush and Trees
9 Launching Fee Charged
10 Private Property, Need Permission
11 No Access, Reference Only

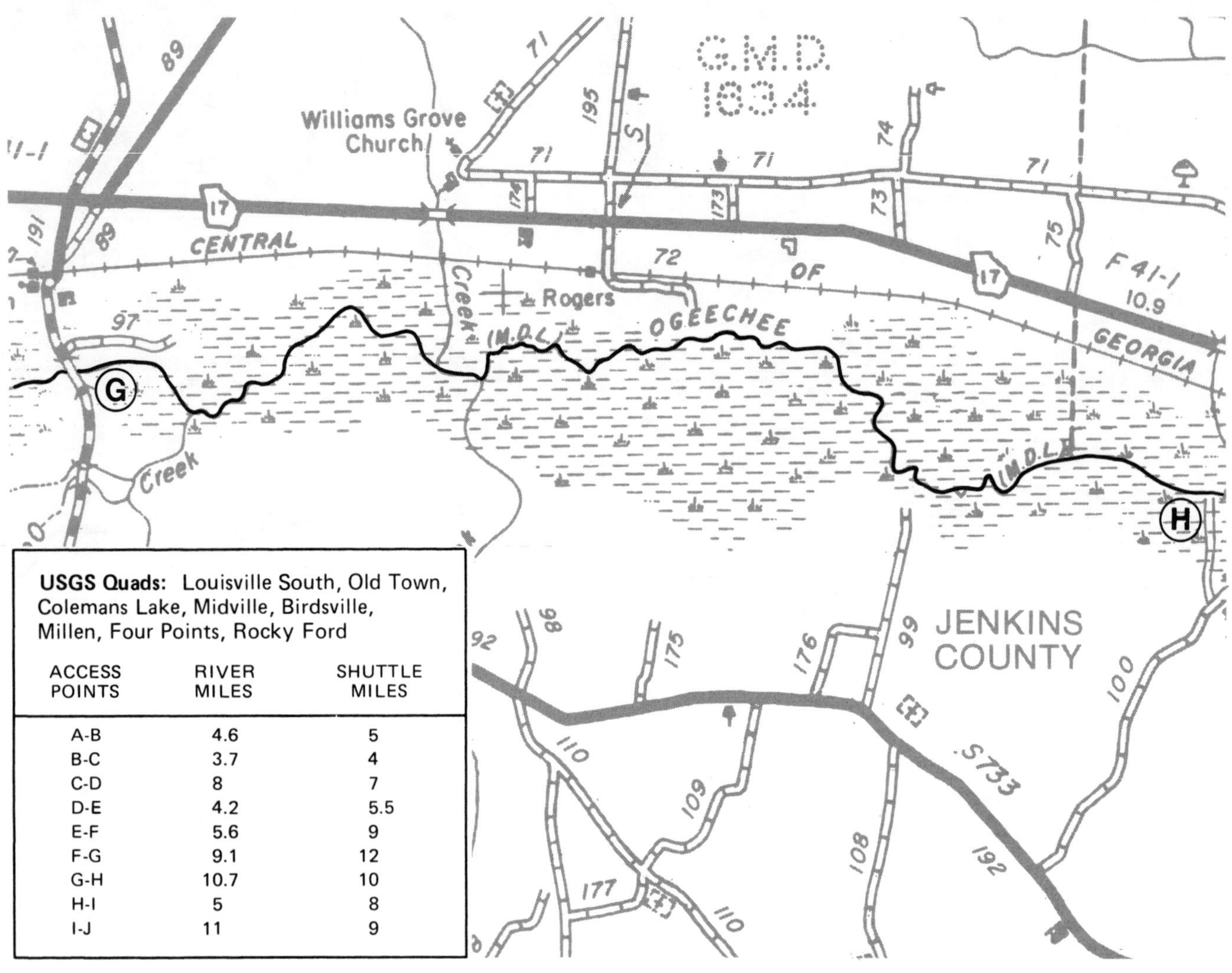

USGS Quads: Louisville South, Old Town, Colemans Lake, Midville, Birdsville, Millen, Four Points, Rocky Ford

ACCESS POINTS	RIVER MILES	SHUTTLE MILES
A-B	4.6	5
B-C	3.7	4
C-D	8	7
D-E	4.2	5.5
E-F	5.6	9
F-G	9.1	12
G-H	10.7	10
H-I	5	8
I-J	11	9

Section: Louisville to Scarboro

Counties: Jefferson, Burke, Emanuel, Jenkins

Suitable For: Cruising, camping

Appropriate For: Families, beginners, intermediates, advanced

Months Runnable: All

Interest Highlights: Scenery, wildlife

Scenery: Pretty to beautiful

Difficulty: International Scale I
Numerical Points 6

Average Width: 45-65 ft.
Gradient: Slow to moderate
Velocity: 1.69 ft./mi.

Runnable Water Level: Minimum 500 cfs
(Eden gauge) Maximum Up to high flood stage

Hazards: Deadfalls

Scouting: None required

Portages: None required

Rescue Index: Accessible but difficult

Mean Water Temperature (°F)

Jan 46	Feb 47	Mar 51	Apr 66	May 68	Jun 74
Jul 77	Aug 75	Sep 71	Oct 64	Nov 56	Dec 50

Source of Additional Information: Metter Game and Fish Office (912) 685-2145

Access Point	Access Code
A	1357
B	1357
C	2357
D	1357
E	2357
F	1357
G	1357
H	2357
I	1357
J	2357

Access Key
1 Paved Road
2 Unpaved Road
3 Short Carry
4 Long Carry
5 Easy Grade
6 Steep Incline
7 Clear Trail
8 Brush and Trees
9 Launching Fee Charged
10 Private Property, Need Permission
11 No Access, Reference Only

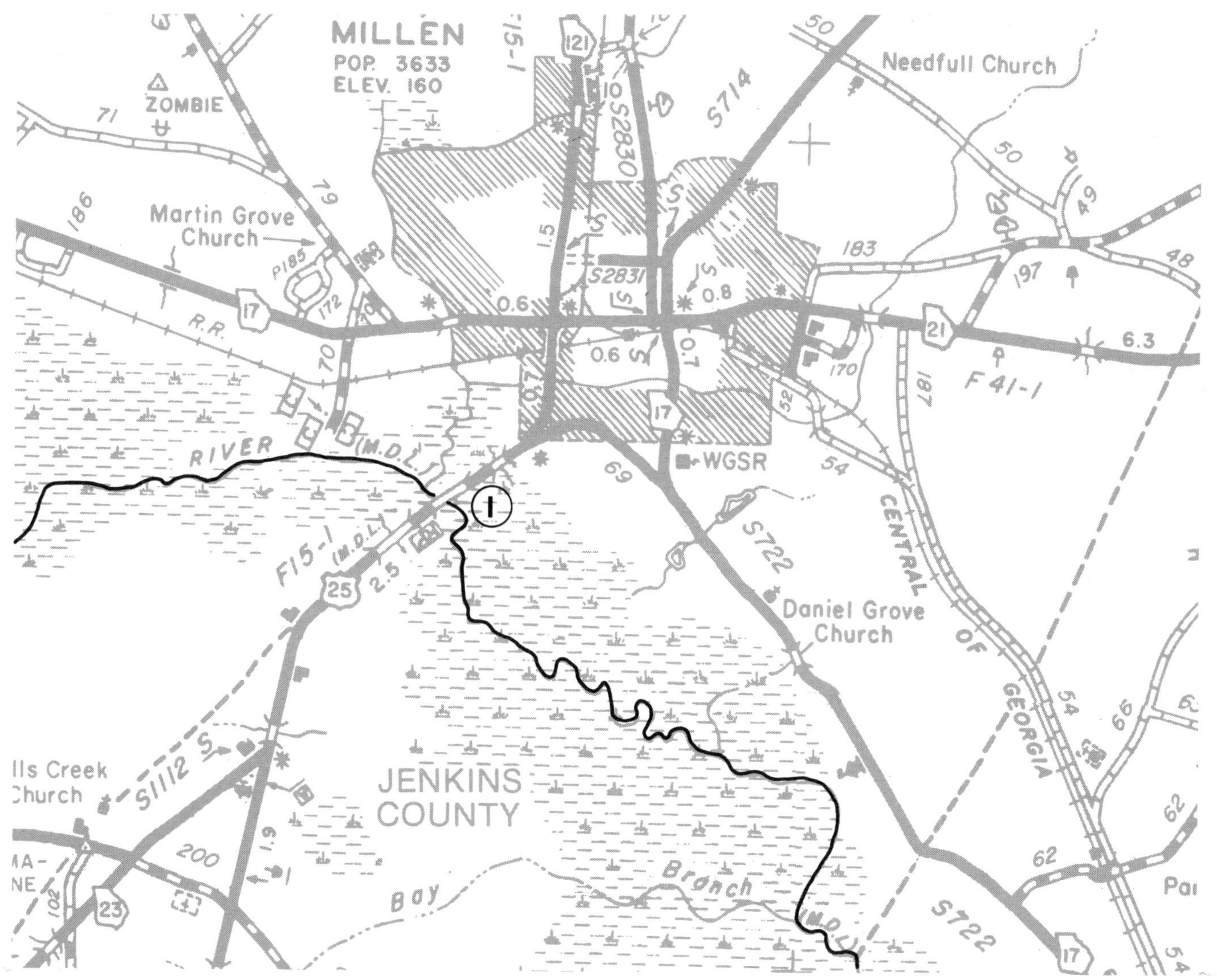

40 to 55 feet in width, which are all runnable. These rejoin and split a second time before coming together to stay. As the Ogeechee approaches and runs along the eastern boundary of Fort Stewart in Bryan County, the woodland swamp corridor widens to several miles and presents countless opportunities for side explorations. Just upstream of the Ogeechee's main tributary, the Canoochee River, the Ogeechee enters the tidewater zone. From this area downstream the banks and confining low-ridge plateaus bordering the swamp corridor begin to recede and flatten into a vast grassy marsh resembling a giant rice paddy. This topography persists all the way to Ossabaw Sound where the Ogeechee joins the Little Ogeechee and the Vernon River before emptying into the Atlantic Ocean. While the tidal marsh is unique in its flora, in its diverse fish and bird fauna, and in its labyrinthine creeks that carve graceful swaths through the marsh grasses, the marsh is extremely inaccessible. Paddle trips must begin upriver, proceed down into the marshes, and then return to the point of embarkation or to an access point up one of the other streams emptying into the sound. Careful attention must be given the tides in the planning of such trips, and paddlers should be completely self-sufficient in their equipment and preparation since dry land is often nonexistent.

From beginning to end the Ogeechee is of Class I difficulty with occasional deadfalls, especially above Millen, being the primary hazards to navigation. High-water conditions, when they occur, facilitate exploration of adjacent sloughs and swamps but also increase the possibility of getting lost. Paddlers anticipating off-river explorations should carry a compass and topographical maps and know how to use them. Powerboat traffic is not uncommon below the mouth of the Canoochee, and this constitutes an additional hazard.

(Continued on page 127)

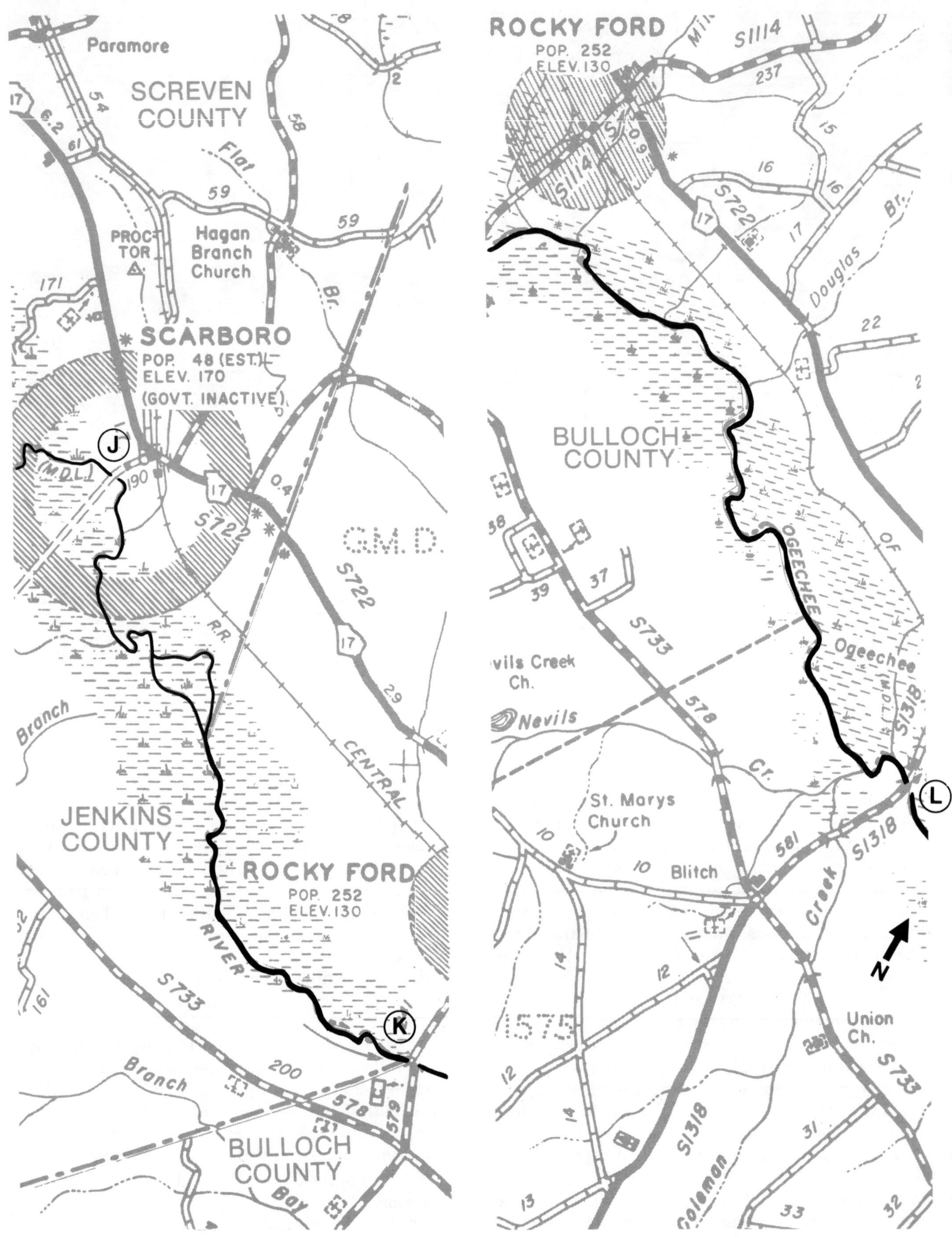
Paramore
SCREVEN COUNTY
Flat
59
Hagan Branch Church
PROCTOR
171
SCARBORO
POP. 48 (EST.)
ELEV. 170
(GOVT. INACTIVE)
J
(M.D.L.)
190
17
S722
0.4
G.M.D.
RR
29
CENTRAL
Branch
JENKINS COUNTY
ROCKY FORD
POP. 252
ELEV. 130
RIVER
K
S733
161
Branch
200
578
579
BULLOCH COUNTY
Bay
ROCKY FORD
POP. 252
ELEV. 130
S1114
237
16
S722
17
Douglas Br.
22
BULLOCH COUNTY
58
37
39
S733
OGEECHEE
Ogeechee
S1318
Nevils Creek Ch.
Nevils
578
Cr.
St. Marys Church
L
10
Blitch
581
Creek
S1318
12
14
1575
Union Ch.
S733
S1318
31
Coleman
13
33
32
N

Section: Scarboro to GA 24 bridge

Counties: Jenkins, Screven, Bulloch, Effingham

Suitable For: Cruising, camping

Appropriate For: Families, beginners, intermediates, advanced

Months Runnable: All

Interest Highlights: Scenery, wildlife

Scenery: Beautiful

Difficulty: International Scale I
Numerical Points 4

Average Width: 70-100 ft.
Gradient: Slow to moderate
Velocity: 1.47 ft./mi.

Runnable Water Level: Minimum Not applicable
Maximum Up to flood stage

Hazards: None

Scouting: None required

Portages: None

Rescue Index: Accessible but difficult

Mean Water Temperature (°F)

Jan	46	Feb	48	Mar	52	Apr	67	May	69	Jun	75
Jul	79	Aug	76	Sep	71	Oct	64	Nov	56	Dec	51

Source of Additional Information: Metter Game and Fish Office (912) 685-2145

Access Point	Access Code
J	2357
K	1357
L	1357
M	1357
N	2357
O	1357

Access Key
1 Paved Road
2 Unpaved Road
3 Short Carry
4 Long Carry
5 Easy Grade
6 Steep Incline
7 Clear Trail
8 Brush and Trees
9 Launching Fee Charged
10 Private Property, Need Permission
11 No Access, Reference Only

USGS Quads: Rocky Ford, Hopeulikit, Dover, Rocky Ford (15′), Oliver (15′), Brooklet (15′)

ACCESS POINTS	RIVER MILES	SHUTTLE MILES
J-K	6.5	9
K-L	7	8
L-M	6.2	7
M-N	6.2	7
N-O	9	10

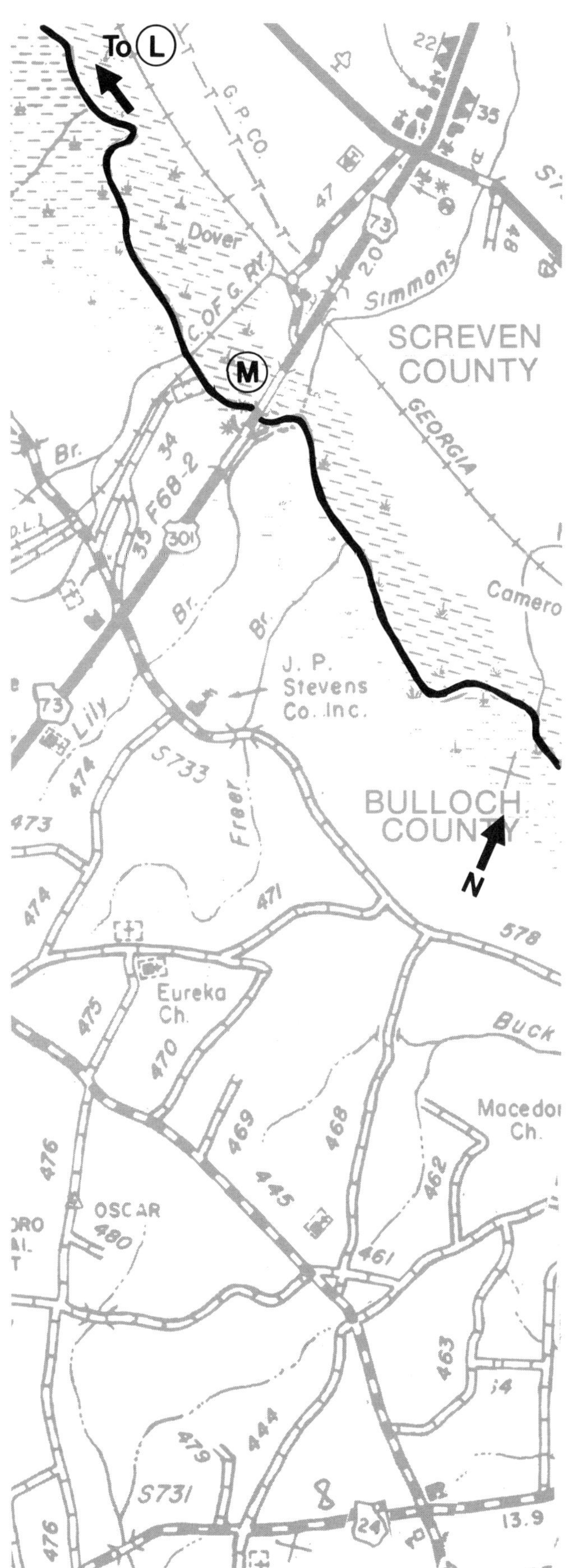

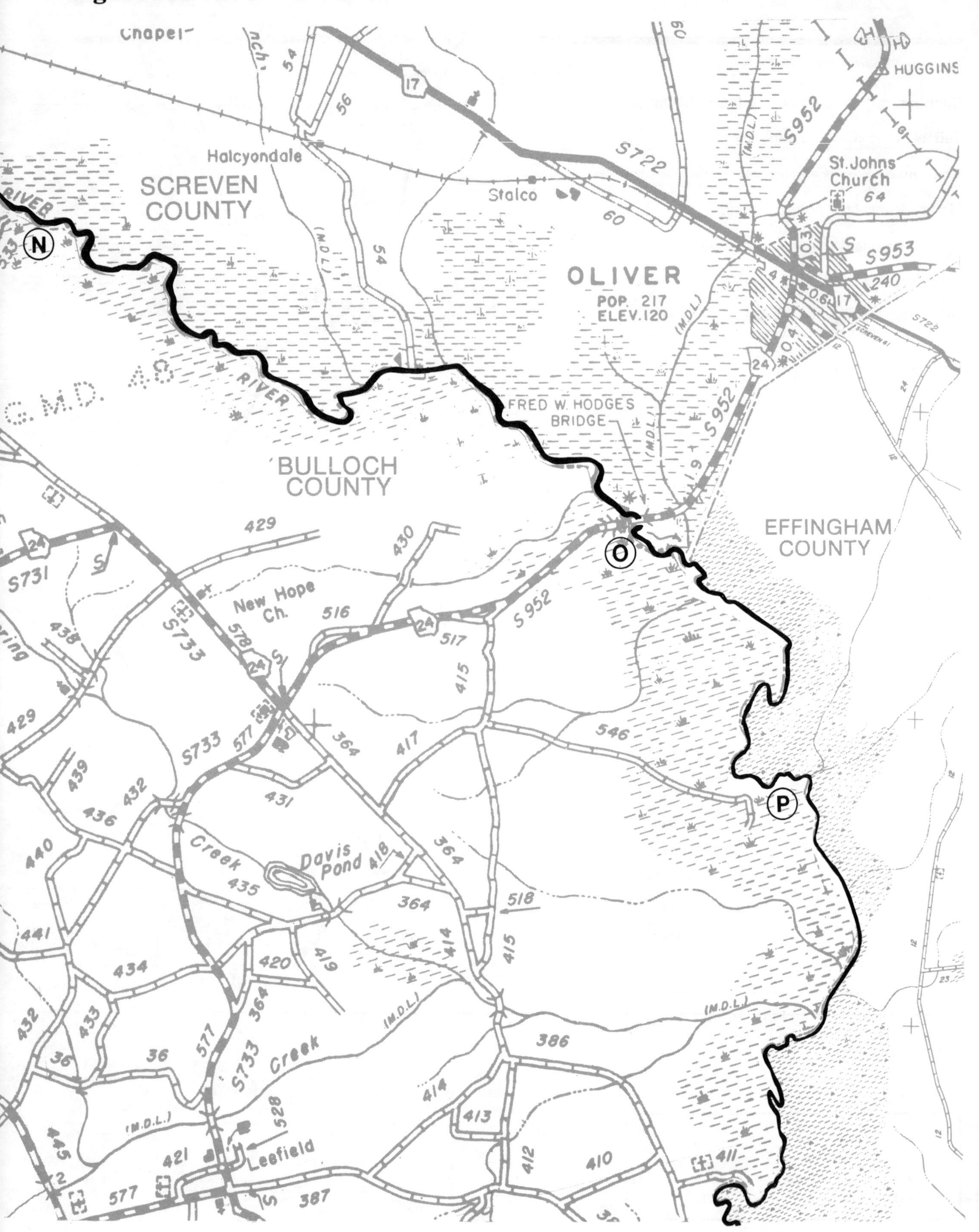
SCREVEN
COUNTY
Halcyondale
Stalco
OLIVER
POP. 217
ELEV. 120
St. Johns
Church
HUGGINS
FRED W. HODGES
BRIDGE
BULLOCH
COUNTY
EFFINGHAM
COUNTY
G.M.D. 48
RIVER
New Hope
Ch.
Davis
Pond
Creek
Creek
Leefield

Access is adequate all along the Ogeechee except in the tidal basin, as mentioned. The river's width varies from several hundred feet nearing the Ossabaw Sound to an average of 190 to 230 feet upstream to the Canoochee, narrowing to 110 feet in northern Effingham County, and 60 to 90 feet in the vicinity of Millen.

Current on the Ogeechee is sluggish to moderate throughout, and though no rapids are encountered, frequent meanders (bends) and trees growing in the stream keep the paddling lively and sharpen navigational skills. Scenery is excellent, flora and fauna are abundantly varied, and, except following heavy rains, the water is bright and clean.

USGS Quads: Rocky Ford, Hopeulikit, Dover, Rocky Ford (15′), Oliver (15′), Brooklet (15′)

ACCESS POINTS	RIVER MILES	SHUTTLE MILES
J-K	6.5	9
K-L	7	8
L-M	6.2	7
M-N	6.2	7
N-O	9	10

Section: Scarboro to GA 24 bridge

Counties: Jenkins, Screven, Bulloch, Effingham

Suitable For: Cruising, camping

Appropriate For: Families, beginners, intermediates, advanced

Months Runnable: All

Interest Highlights: Scenery, wildlife

Scenery: Beautiful

Difficulty: International Scale I
Numerical Points 4

Average Width: 70-100 ft.
Gradient: Slow to moderate
Velocity: 1.47 ft./mi.

Runnable Water Level: Minimum Not applicable
Maximum Up to flood stage

Hazards: None

Scouting: None required

Portages: None

Rescue Index: Accessible but difficult

Mean Water Temperature (°F)

Jan 46	Feb 48	Mar 52	Apr 67	May 69	Jun 75
Jul 79	Aug 76	Sep 71	Oct 64	Nov 56	Dec 51

Source of Additional Information: Metter Game and Fish Office (912) 685-2145

Access Point	Access Code
J	2357
K	1357
L	1357
M	1357
N	2357
O	1357

Access Key
1 Paved Road
2 Unpaved Road
3 Short Carry
4 Long Carry
5 Easy Grade
6 Steep Incline
7 Clear Trail
8 Brush and Trees
9 Launching Fee Charged
10 Private Property, Need Permission
11 No Access, Reference Only

Ogeechee River—*Continued*

Section: GA 24 bridge to Ossabaw Sound

Counties: Bulloch, Effingham, Bryan, Chatham

Suitable For: Cruising, camping

Appropriate For: Families, beginners, intermediates, advanced

Months Runnable: All

Interest Highlights: Scenery, wildlife

Scenery: Pretty to beautiful

Difficulty: International Scale I
Numerical Points 5

Average Width: 190-230 ft.
Gradient: Slow to moderate
Velocity: 0.88 ft./mi.

Runnable Water Level: Minimum Not applicable
Maximum Up to flood stage

Hazards: Powerboats, tides, getting lost in high water

Scouting: None

Portages: None

Rescue Index: Accessible but difficult

Mean Water Temperature (°F)

Jan 49	Feb 50	Mar 55	Apr 63	May 71	Jun 78
Jul 81	Aug 79	Sep 74	Oct 67	Nov 59	Dec 52

Source of Additional Information: Demeries Creek Game and Fish Office (912) 727-2111

Access Point	Access Code
Q	23579
R	23579
S	1357
T	1457
U	(11)

Access Key
1 Paved Road
2 Unpaved Road
3 Short Carry
4 Long Carry
5 Easy Grade
6 Steep Incline
7 Clear Trail
8 Brush and Trees
9 Launching Fee Charged
10 Private Property, Need Permission
11 No Access, Reference Only

USGS Quads: Egypt (15′), Eden, Meldrim SW, Meldrim SE, Richmond Hill, Burroughs, Isle of Hope, Raccoon Key

ACCESS POINTS	RIVER MILES	SHUTTLE MILES
Q-R	1.5	3
R-S	12	11.4
S-T	12	10
T-U	5.5	15

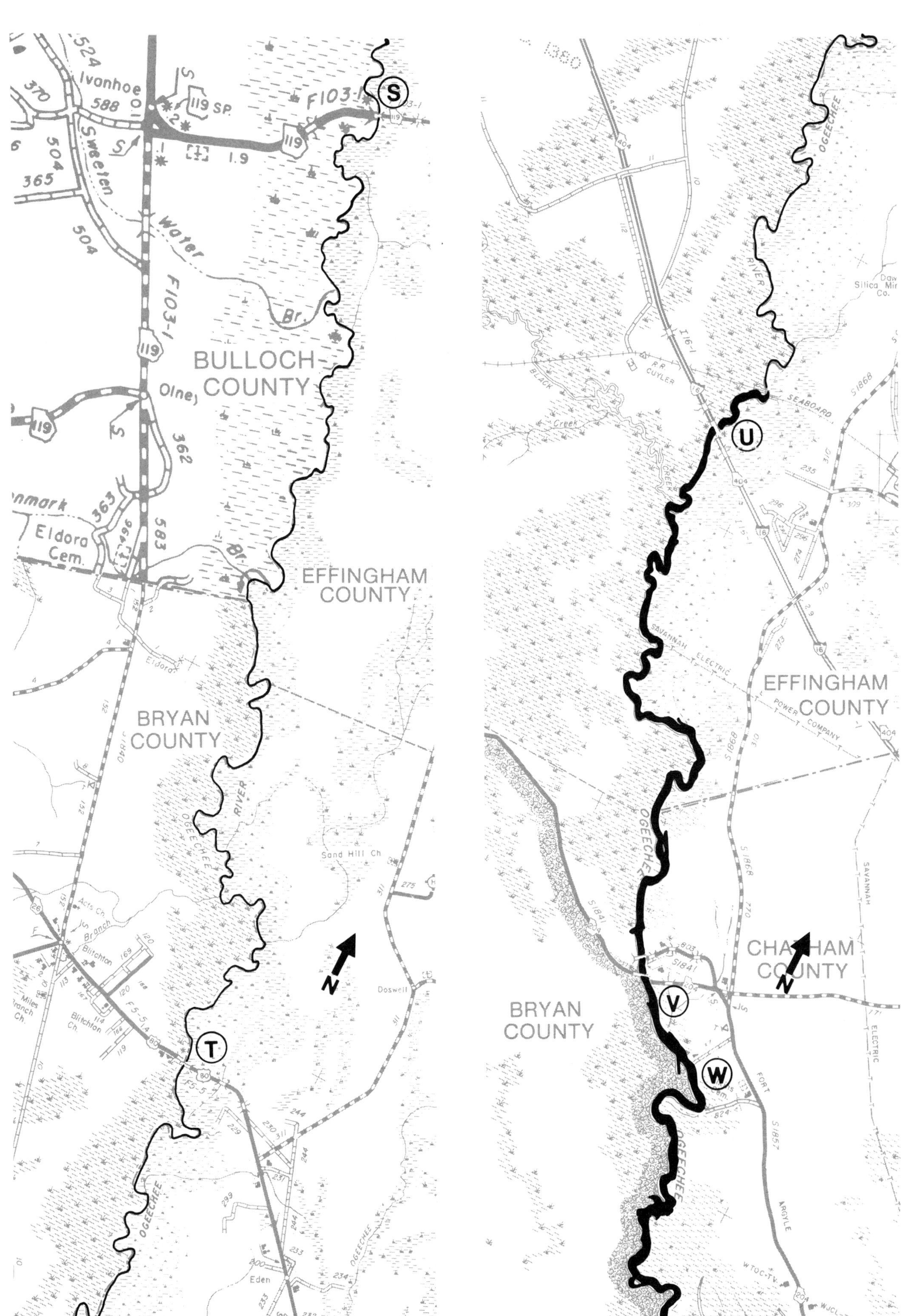

S
T
U
V
W
BULLOCH COUNTY
EFFINGHAM COUNTY
BRYAN COUNTY
CHATHAM COUNTY
Ivanhoe
Olney
Eldora Cem.
Sweeten Water Br.
OGEECHEE RIVER
Sand Hill Ch
Doswell
Eden
Blitchton
SAVANNAH ELECTRIC POWER COMPANY
SEABOARD
Black Creek
Daw Silica Min Co.
N

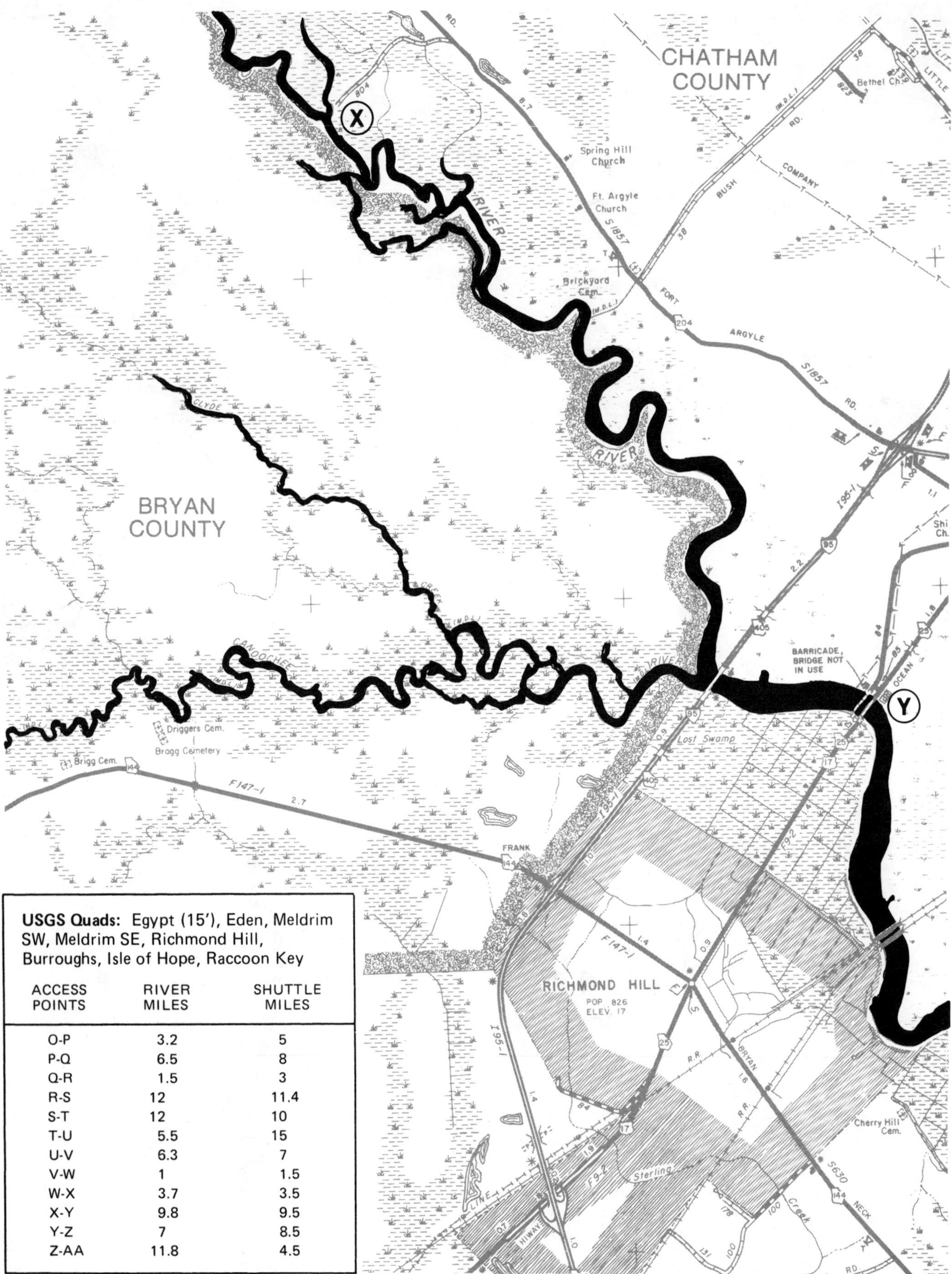

USGS Quads: Egypt (15′), Eden, Meldrim SW, Meldrim SE, Richmond Hill, Burroughs, Isle of Hope, Raccoon Key

ACCESS POINTS	RIVER MILES	SHUTTLE MILES
O-P	3.2	5
P-Q	6.5	8
Q-R	1.5	3
R-S	12	11.4
S-T	12	10
T-U	5.5	15
U-V	6.3	7
V-W	1	1.5
W-X	3.7	3.5
X-Y	9.8	9.5
Y-Z	7	8.5
Z-AA	11.8	4.5

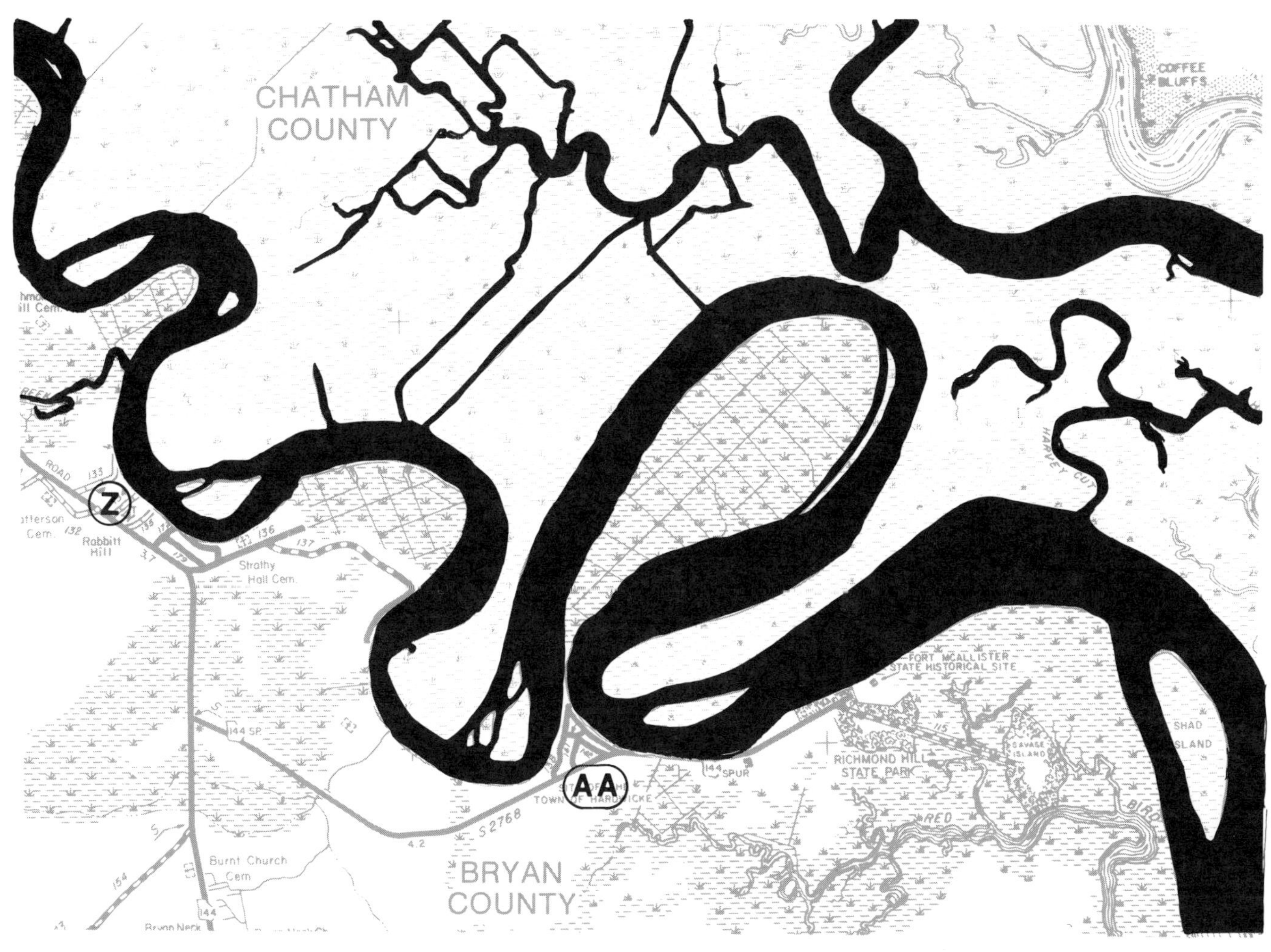

Section: GA 24 bridge to Ossabaw Sound

Counties: Bulloch, Effingham, Bryan, Chatham

Suitable For: Cruising, camping

Appropriate For: Families, beginners, intermediates, advanced

Months Runnable: All

Interest Highlights: Scenery, wildlife

Scenery: Pretty to beautiful

Difficulty: International Scale I
Numerical Points 5

Average Width: 190-230 ft.
Gradient: Slow to moderate
Velocity: 0.88 ft./mi.

Runnable Water Level: Minimum Not applicable
Maximum Up to flood stage

Hazards: Powerboats, tides, getting lost in high water

Scouting: None

Portages: None

Rescue Index: Accessible but difficult

Mean Water Temperature (°F)

Jan 49	Feb 50	Mar 55	Apr 63	May 71	Jun 78
Jul 81	Aug 79	Sep 74	Oct 67	Nov 59	Dec 52

Source of Additional Information: Demeries Creek Game and Fish Office (912) 727-2111

Access Point	Access Code
O	1357
P	2357
Q	23579
R	23579
S	1357
T	1457
U	(11)
V	1357
W	2357
X	2359
Y	1357
Z	2359
AA	1357

Access Key
1 Paved Road
2 Unpaved Road
3 Short Carry
4 Long Carry
5 Easy Grade
6 Steep Incline
7 Clear Trail
8 Brush and Trees
9 Launching Fee Charged
10 Private Property, Need Permission
11 No Access, Reference Only

Oconee River

The Oconee River, born in the eastern Piedmont in Hall County south of Lake Sidney Lanier, is technically still a Piedmont stream below Lake Sinclair; but because of its proximity to its Coastal Plain portion and its changed nature once it leaves Lake Sinclair, it has been included in this book. The portion of the river above Lake Sinclair is described in *Northern Georgia Canoeing: A Canoeing and Kayaking Guide to the Streams of the Cumberland Plateau, Blue Ridge Mountains and Eastern Piedmont.*

Below the Lake Sinclair Dam the Oconee slips sluggishly through what is left of Furman Shoals (Class I+) before being impounded once again, this time by a seven-foot dam in Milledgeville that reaches out from both sides of an island in midstream. Land on the island to carry around. Below Milledgeville, in Baldwin County, the Oconee River flows unobstructed in a winding, serpentine course through the Coastal Plain and drains portions of Baldwin, Washington, Wilkinson, Johnson, Laurens, Treutlen, Wheeler, and Montgomery counties before joining the Ocmulgee River south of Charlotteville to form the Altamaha River. A large river in the Coastal Plain, the Oconee broadens from 110 feet below Milledgeville to 250 to 280 feet at Dublin to almost 320 feet as it approaches its mouth at the Altamaha. Departing the populated and developed environs of Milledgeville, the river slips into a wooded lowland corridor and runs in broad bends and long straightaways for six miles before assuming the looping meander course that will typify its path the remainder of the way to the Altamaha.

As the Oconee loops through the Coastal Plain, sandbars suitable for camping become common on the insides of the bends and some oxbow lakes and meander by-pass islands appear. Surrounding the river is frequently flooded bottomland forest. Where the bottom land is flooded more than six months a year, bald cypress, tupelo gum, and swamp black gum predominate. In areas where the bottom land is inundated for six months or less, overcup oak and various water hickories combine with laurel and willow, oak, red maple, American elm, and green ash to form the lowland forest. On the bank, willow, cottonwood, river birch, some silver maple, sycamore, and bald cypress are common. Extremely remote, the forest bottomland swamp that surrounds the Oconee extends more than two miles in width above Dublin and expands below Dublin to a breadth approaching four miles. In Cow Hell Swamp north of Dublin, bald cypress grace the river in ever increasing numbers and algae-covered backwater sloughs and oxbow lakes teem with wildlife.

As the Oconee enters Dublin it flows through a well-defined channel below fifteen-foot banks before

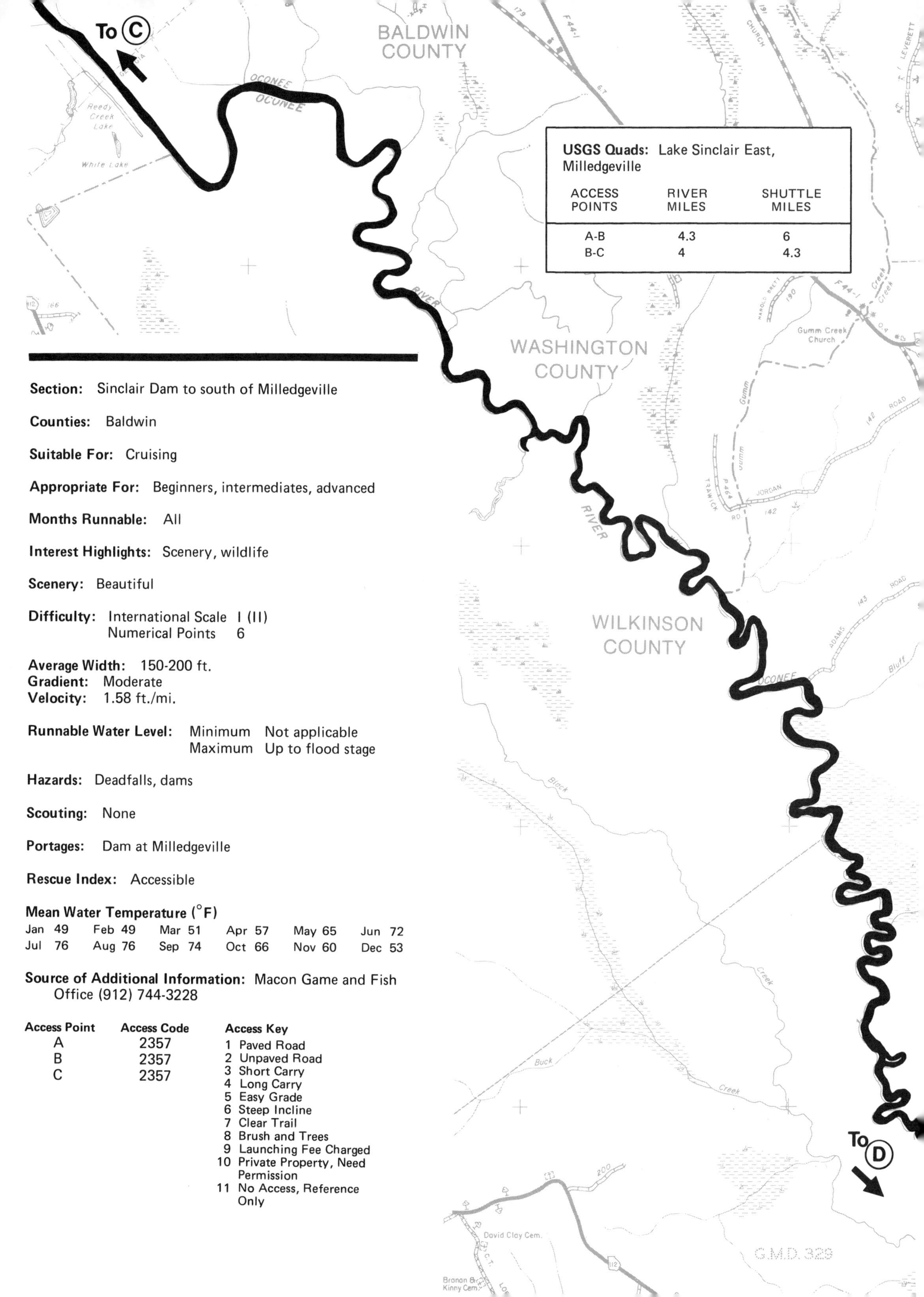

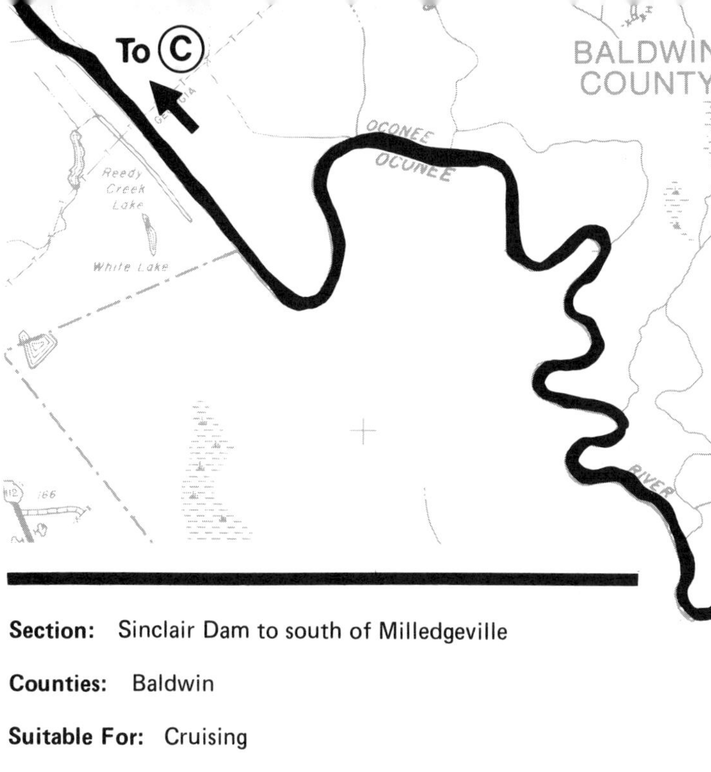

USGS Quads: Lake Sinclair East, Milledgeville

ACCESS POINTS	RIVER MILES	SHUTTLE MILES
A-B	4.3	6
B-C	4	4.3

Section: Sinclair Dam to south of Milledgeville

Counties: Baldwin

Suitable For: Cruising

Appropriate For: Beginners, intermediates, advanced

Months Runnable: All

Interest Highlights: Scenery, wildlife

Scenery: Beautiful

Difficulty: International Scale I (II)
Numerical Points 6

Average Width: 150-200 ft.
Gradient: Moderate
Velocity: 1.58 ft./mi.

Runnable Water Level: Minimum Not applicable
Maximum Up to flood stage

Hazards: Deadfalls, dams

Scouting: None

Portages: Dam at Milledgeville

Rescue Index: Accessible

Mean Water Temperature (°F)

Jan	49	Feb	49	Mar	51	Apr	57	May	65	Jun	72
Jul	76	Aug	76	Sep	74	Oct	66	Nov	60	Dec	53

Source of Additional Information: Macon Game and Fish Office (912) 744-3228

Access Point	Access Code
A	2357
B	2357
C	2357

Access Key
1 Paved Road
2 Unpaved Road
3 Short Carry
4 Long Carry
5 Easy Grade
6 Steep Incline
7 Clear Trail
8 Brush and Trees
9 Launching Fee Charged
10 Private Property, Need Permission
11 No Access, Reference Only

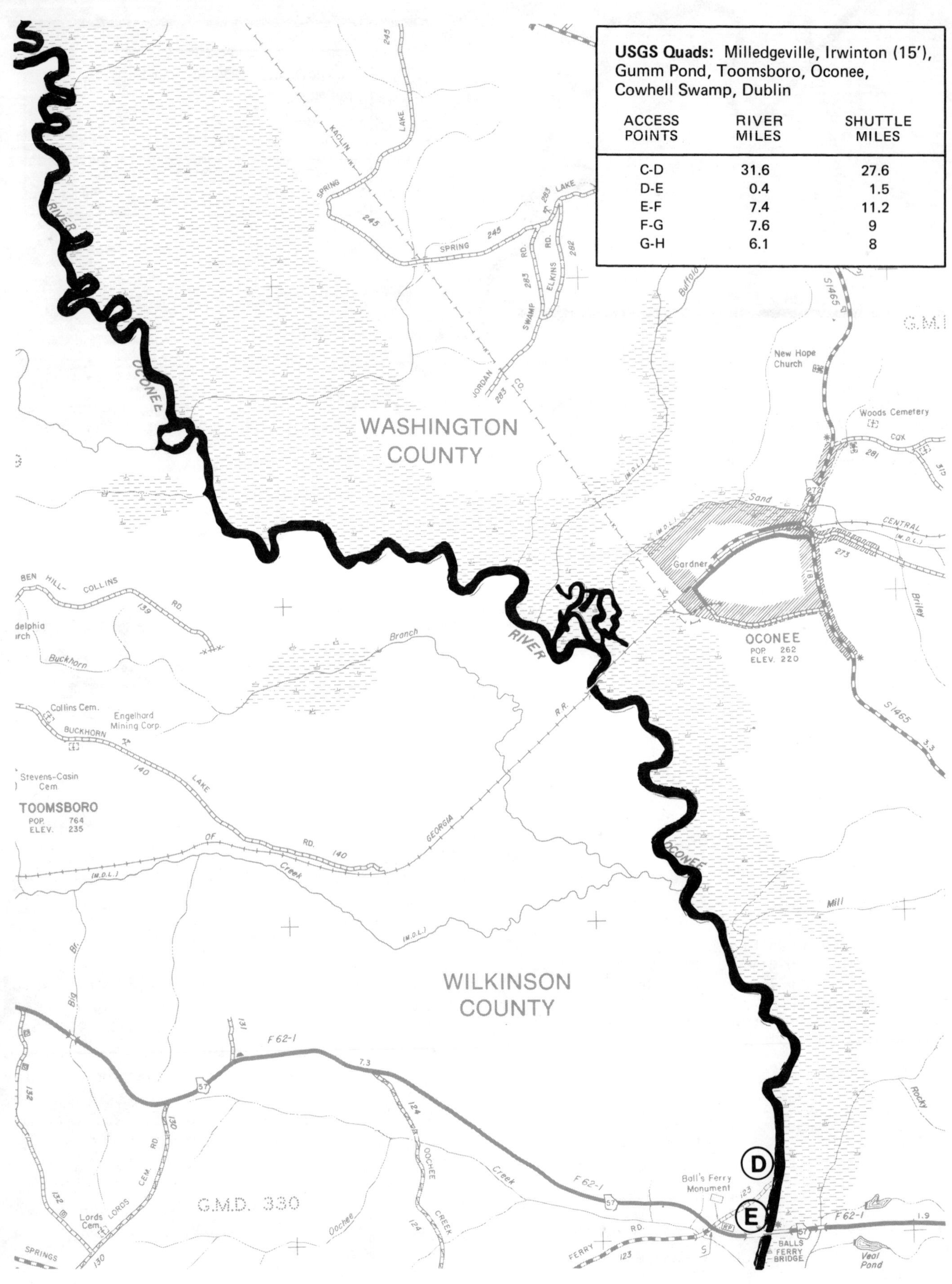

USGS Quads: Milledgeville, Irwinton (15′), Gumm Pond, Toomsboro, Oconee, Cowhell Swamp, Dublin

ACCESS POINTS	RIVER MILES	SHUTTLE MILES
C-D	31.6	27.6
D-E	0.4	1.5
E-F	7.4	11.2
F-G	7.6	9
G-H	6.1	8

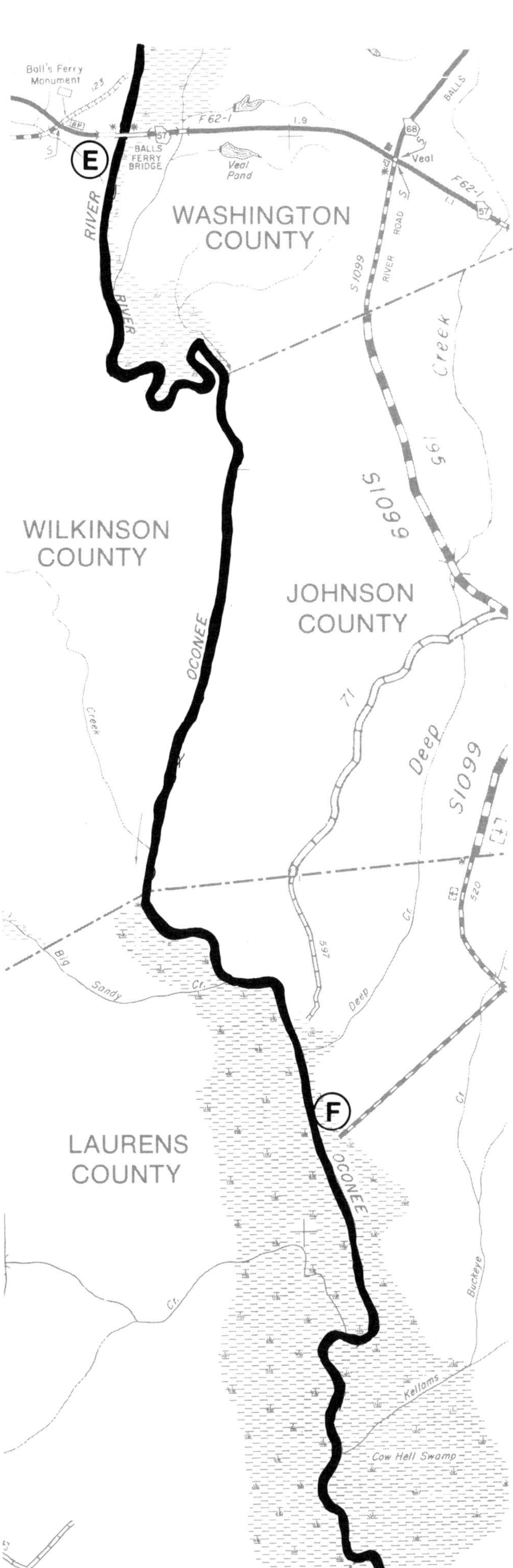

Section: South of Milledgeville to Dublin

Counties: Baldwin, Wilkinson, Washington, Johnson, Laurens

Suitable For: Cruising, camping

Appropriate For: Beginners, intermediates, advanced

Months Runnable: All

Interest Highlights: Scenery, wildlife

Scenery: Beautiful

Difficulty: International Scale I (II)
Numerical Points 6

Average Width: 250-280 ft.
Gradient: Moderate
Velocity: 1.58 ft./mi.

Runnable Water Level: Minimum Not applicable
Maximum Up to flood stage

Hazards: Deadfalls

Scouting: None

Portages: None

Rescue Index: Remote to accessible but difficult

Mean Water Temperature (°F)

Jan 49	Feb 49	Mar 51	Apr 57	May 65	Jun 72
Jul 76	Aug 76	Sep 74	Oct 66	Nov 60	Dec 53

Source of Additional Information: Macon Game and Fish Office (912) 744-3228

Access Point	Access Code
C	2357
D	2357
E	2357
F	2357
G	2357
H	23679

Access Key
1 Paved Road
2 Unpaved Road
3 Short Carry
4 Long Carry
5 Easy Grade
6 Steep Incline
7 Clear Trail
8 Brush and Trees
9 Launching Fee Charged
10 Private Property, Need Permission
11 No Access, Reference Only

slipping back into the lowlands and swamp on the southeast side of the town. From here to the Altamaha scenery remains similarly beautiful with little change other than the appearance of pine on the natural levee and on the perimeter of the swamp. The level of difficulty throughout is Class I with floating and stationary deadfalls being the only hazards to navigation. Current is slow and the water generally murky brown with sediment. Access points are few, especially between Dublin and Glenwood, thus limiting the lower Oconee for one day trips. The Oconee below Lake Sinclair is runnable all year.

Oconee River—*Continued*

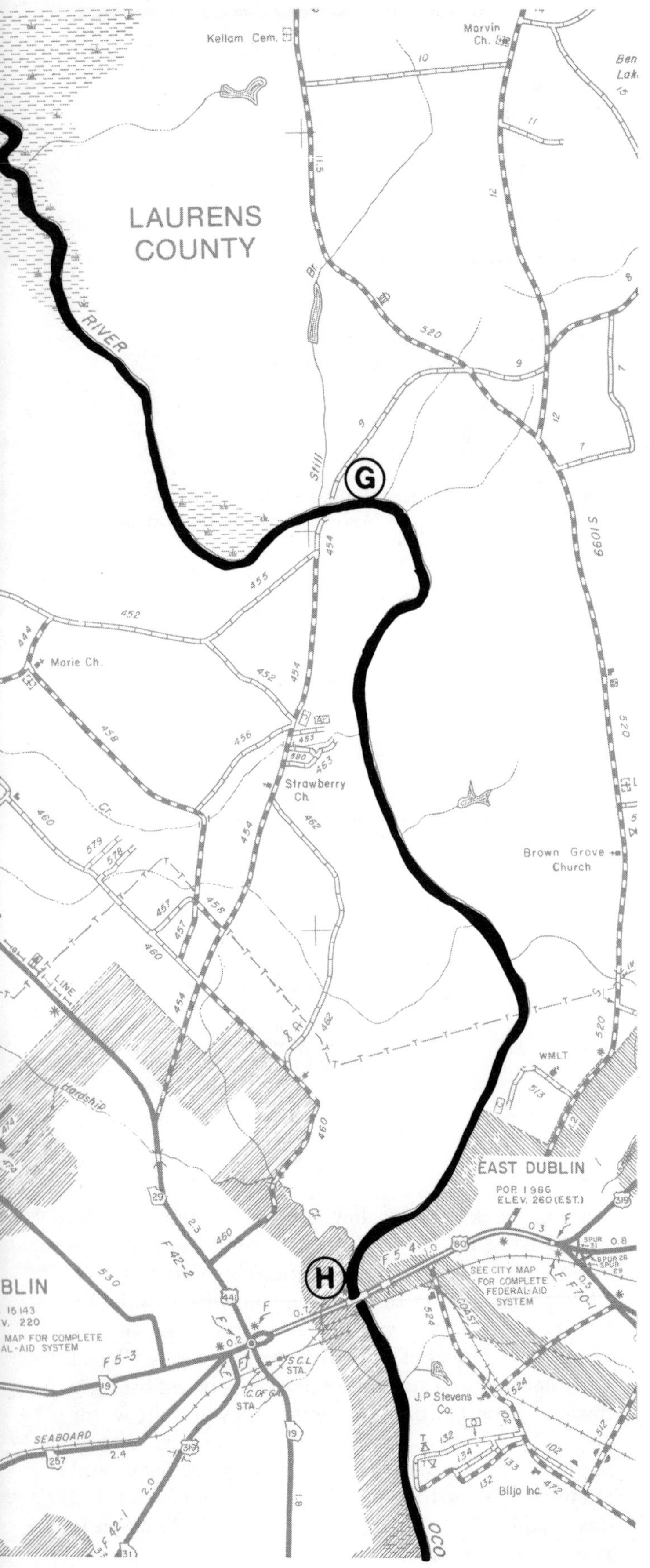

Section: Dublin to Altamaha River

Counties: Laurens, Treutlen, Wheeler, Montgomery

Suitable For: Cruising, camping

Appropriate For: Families, beginners, intermediates

Months Runnable: All

Interest Highlights: Scenery, wildlife

Scenery: Beautiful

Difficulty: International Scale I
Numerical Points 4

Average Width: 280-320 ft.
Gradient: Slow to moderate
Velocity: 1.01 ft./mi.

Runnable Water Level: Minimum Not applicable
Maximum Up to flood stage

Hazards: Deadfalls

Scouting: None

Portages: None

Rescue Index: Remote to accessible but difficult

Mean Water Temperature (°F)

Jan 49	Feb 51	Mar 53	Apr 61	May 69	Jun 77
Jul 81	Aug 80	Sep 76	Oct 69	Nov 60	Dec 53

Source of Additional Information: Metter Game and Fish Office (912) 685-2145

Access Point	Access Code
H	23679
I	2357
J	(11)
K	1357
L	1357
M	2357
A[1]	2357

Access Key
1 Paved Road
2 Unpaved Road
3 Short Carry
4 Long Carry
5 Easy Grade
6 Steep Incline
7 Clear Trail
8 Brush and Trees
9 Launching Fee Charged
10 Private Property, Need Permission
11 No Access, Reference Only

[1] On the Altamaha River

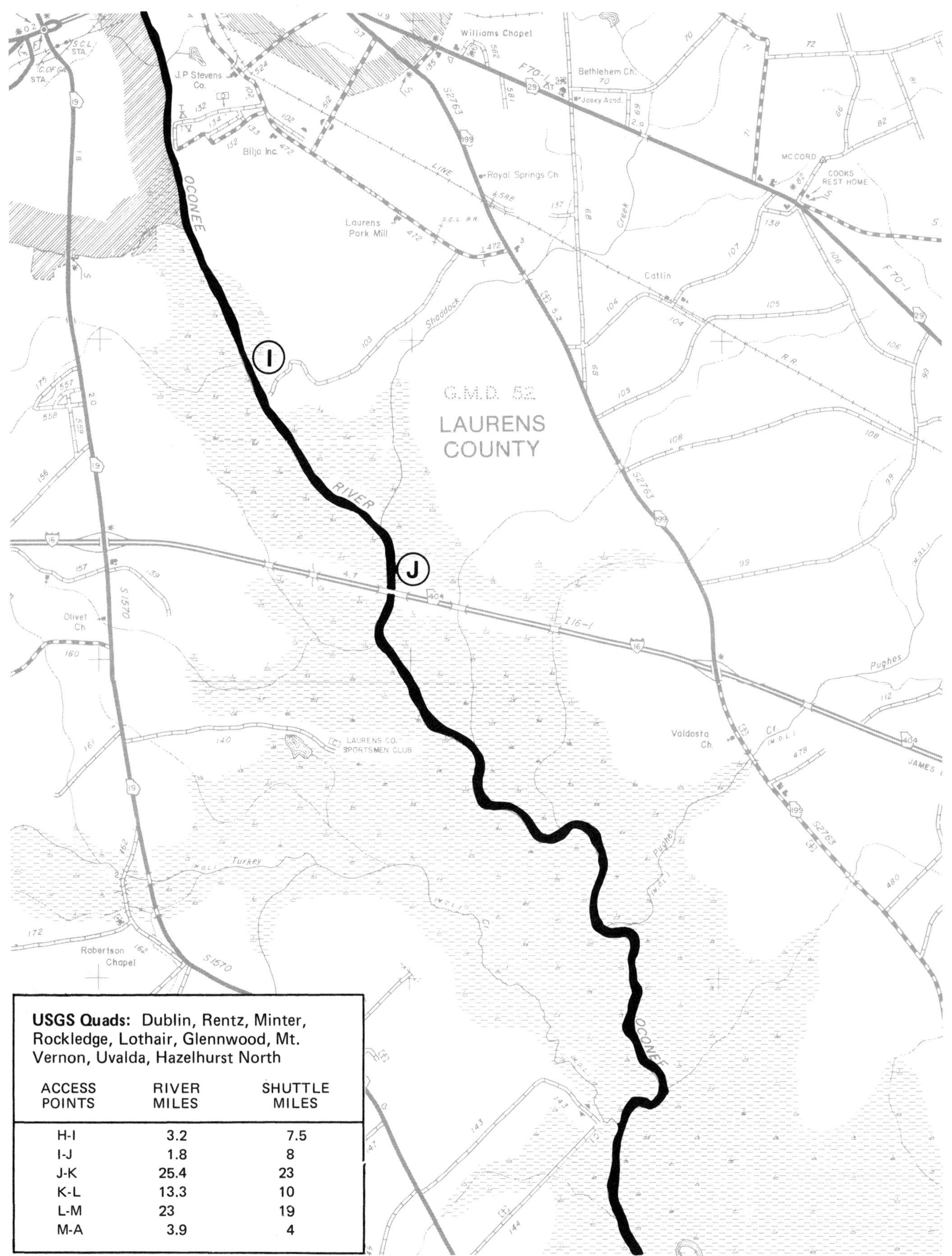

USGS Quads: Dublin, Rentz, Minter, Rockledge, Lothair, Glennwood, Mt. Vernon, Uvalda, Hazelhurst North

ACCESS POINTS	RIVER MILES	SHUTTLE MILES
H-I	3.2	7.5
I-J	1.8	8
J-K	25.4	23
K-L	13.3	10
L-M	23	19
M-A	3.9	4

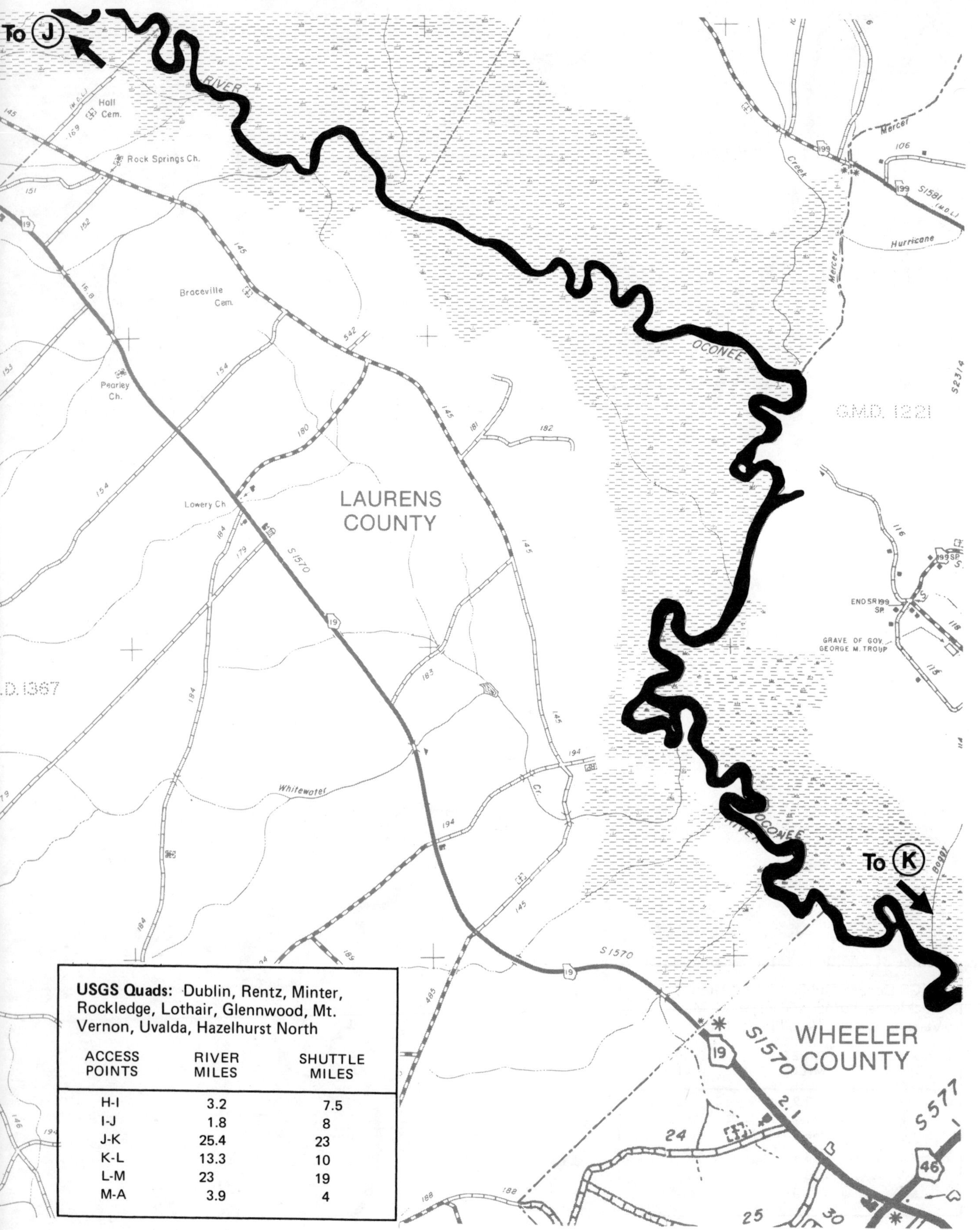

USGS Quads: Dublin, Rentz, Minter, Rockledge, Lothair, Glennwood, Mt. Vernon, Uvalda, Hazelhurst North

ACCESS POINTS	RIVER MILES	SHUTTLE MILES
H-I	3.2	7.5
I-J	1.8	8
J-K	25.4	23
K-L	13.3	10
L-M	23	19
M-A	3.9	4

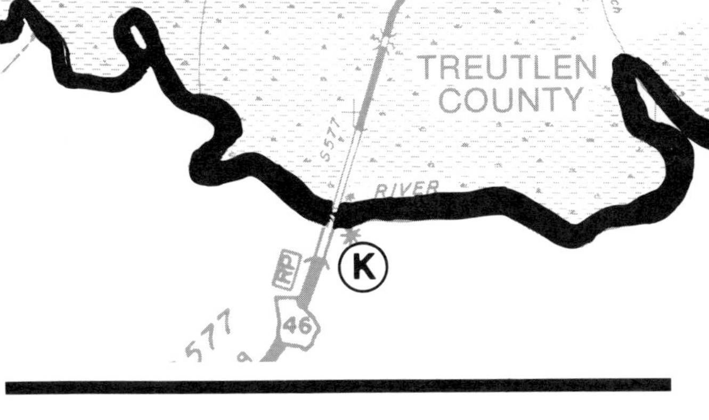

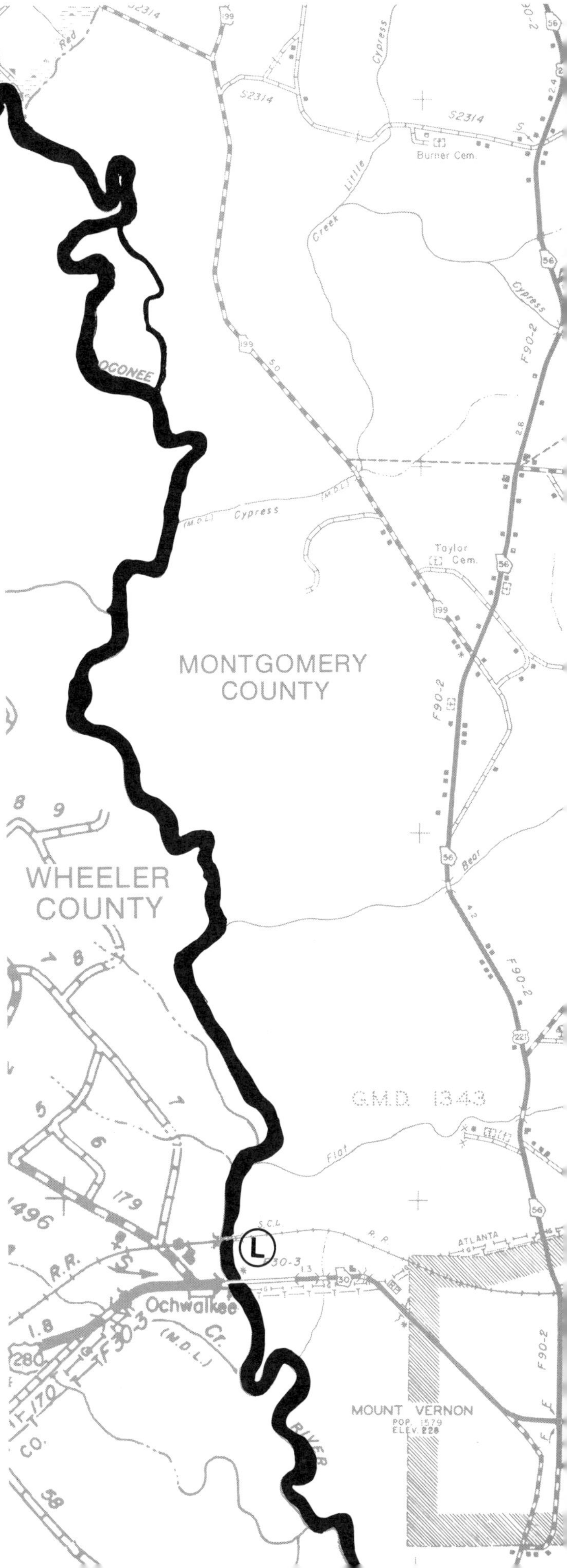

Section: Dublin to Altamaha River

Counties: Laurens, Treutlen, Wheeler, Montgomery

Suitable For: Cruising, camping

Appropriate For: Families, beginners, intermediates

Months Runnable: All

Interest Highlights: Scenery, wildlife

Scenery: Beautiful

Difficulty: International Scale I
Numerical Points 4

Average Width: 280-320 ft.
Gradient: Slow to moderate
Velocity: 1.01 ft./mi.

Runnable Water Level: Minimum Not applicable
Maximum Up to flood stage

Hazards: Deadfalls

Scouting: None

Portages: None

Rescue Index: Remote to accessible but difficult

Mean Water Temperature (°F)

Jan 49	Feb 51	Mar 53	Apr 61	May 69	Jun 77
Jul 81	Aug 80	Sep 76	Oct 69	Nov 60	Dec 53

Source of Additional Information: Metter Game and Fish Office (912) 685-2145

Access Point	Access Code
H	23679
I	2357
J	(11)
K	1357
L	1357
M	2357
A[1]	2357

Access Key
1 Paved Road
2 Unpaved Road
3 Short Carry
4 Long Carry
5 Easy Grade
6 Steep Incline
7 Clear Trail
8 Brush and Trees
9 Launching Fee Charged
10 Private Property, Need Permission
11 No Access, Reference Only

[1] On the Altamaha River

MONTGOMERY COUNTY

WHEELER COUNTY

OCONEE

RIVER

Ochwalkee Cr.

MOUNT VERNON

G.M.D. 1343

L

Oconee River—*Continued*

Section: Dublin to Altamaha River

Counties: Laurens, Treutlen, Wheeler, Montgomery

Suitable For: Cruising, camping

Appropriate For: Families, beginners, intermediates

Months Runnable: All

Interest Highlights: Scenery, wildlife

Scenery: Beautiful

Difficulty: International Scale I
Numerical Points 4

Average Width: 280-320 ft.
Gradient: Slow to moderate
Velocity: 1.01 ft./mi.

Runnable Water Level: Minimum Not applicable
Maximum Up to flood stage

Hazards: Deadfalls

Scouting: None

Portages: None

Rescue Index: Remote to accessible but difficult

Mean Water Temperature (°F)

Jan 49	Feb 51	Mar 53	Apr 61	May 69	Jun 77
Jul 81	Aug 80	Sep 76	Oct 69	Nov 60	Dec 53

Source of Additional Information: Metter Game and Fish Office (912) 685-2145

Access Point	Access Code
H	23679
I	2357
J	(11)
K	1357
L	1357
M	2357
A[1]	2357

[1]On the Altamaha River

Access Key
1 Paved Road
2 Unpaved Road
3 Short Carry
4 Long Carry
5 Easy Grade
6 Steep Incline
7 Clear Trail
8 Brush and Trees
9 Launching Fee Charged
10 Private Property, Need Permission
11 No Access, Reference Only

USGS Quads: Dublin, Rentz, Minter, Rockledge, Lothair, Glennwood, Mt. Vernon, Uvalda, Hazelhurst North

ACCESS POINTS	RIVER MILES	SHUTTLE MILES
H-I	3.2	7.5
I-J	1.8	8
J-K	25.4	23
K-L	13.3	10
L-M	23	19
M-A	3.9	4

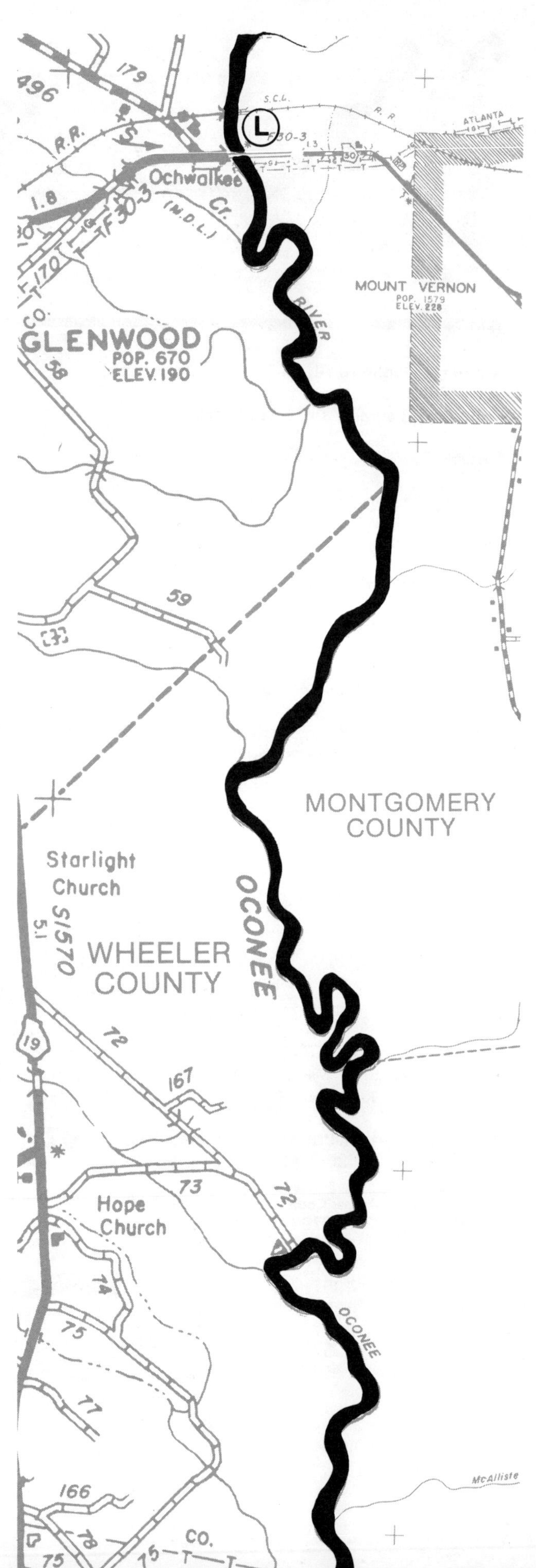

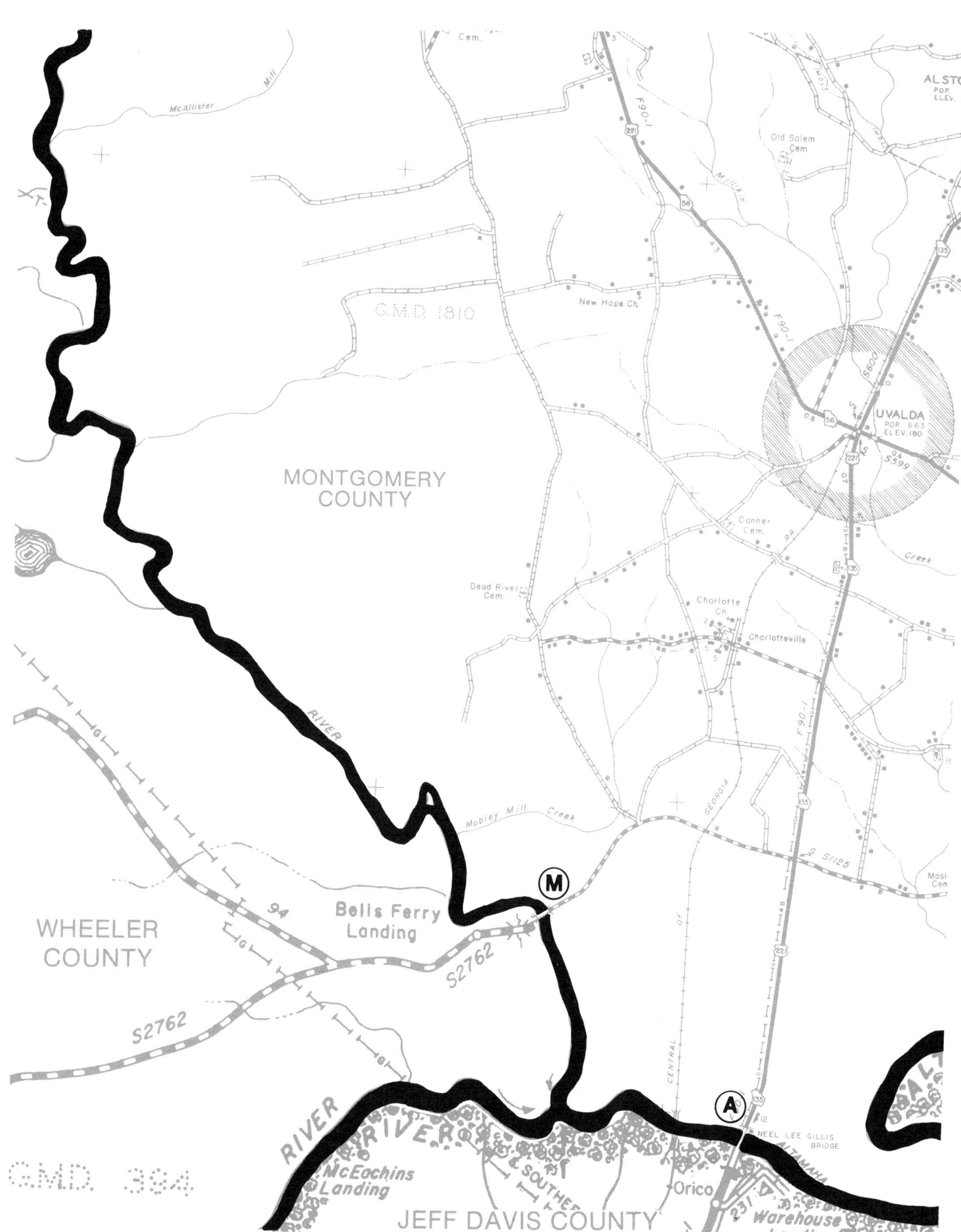
MONTGOMERY COUNTY
WHEELER COUNTY
JEFF DAVIS COUNTY
G.M.D. 1810
G.M.D. 394
UVALDA
POP. 663
ELEV. 180
ALSTON
Old Salem Cem.
New Hope Ch.
Conner Cem.
Dead River Cem.
Charlotte Ch.
Charlotteville
Mobley Mill Creek
McAllister
Bells Ferry Landing
RIVER
S2762
S1125
94
M
A
NEEL LEE GILLIS BRIDGE
McEachins Landing
Orico
Warehouse
CENTRAL OF GEORGIA
F90-I
221
135
56
S600
S599

Little Ocmulgee River

The Little Ocmulgee River originates in southern Twiggs County in central Georgia and flows southeastward draining portions of Bleckley, Dodge, Telfair, and Wheeler counties. A blackwater stream, the Little Ocmulgee has white sand banks two to five feet high with contrasting burgundy-red water. Runnable below the GA 134 bridge from December through mid-June in most years, the Little Ocmulgee is pleasant though frequent signs of habitation, including several small towns, essentially rob it of its wilderness atmosphere. Cypress and sweet gum dominate the banks along with some black gum, willow, and ash. The level of difficulty is Class I all the way to its mouth at the Ocmulgee below Lumber City. Hazards to navigation are limited to deadfalls. Current is moderate and access is good.

USGS Quads: Scotland, Jordan, Lumber City

ACCESS POINTS	RIVER MILES	SHUTTLE MILES
A-B	5.3	5.5
B-C	4.2	2

Brier Creek.

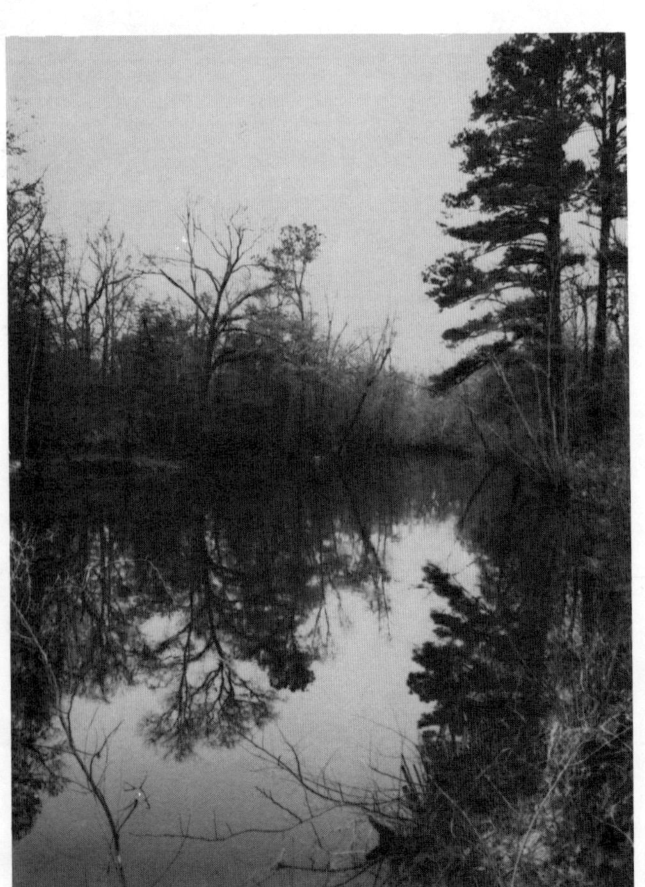

Photo courtesy of *Brown's Guide to Georgia.*

Section: Towns to Lumber City

Counties: Wheeler, Telfair

Suitable For: Cruising

Appropriate For: Families, beginners, intermediates, advanced

Months Runnable: December through June

Interest Highlights: Scenery, wildlife, local culture and industry

Scenery: Pretty to beautiful in spots

Difficulty: International Scale I
Numerical Points 5

Average Width: 30-45 ft.
Velocity: Slow to moderate
Gradient: 1.68 ft./mi.

Runnable Water Level: Minimum 125 cfs
Maximum Up to flood stage

Hazards: Deadfalls

Scouting: None required

Portages: Around deadfalls

Rescue Index: Accessible

Mean Water Temperature (°F)

Jan 49	Feb 51	Mar 57	Apr 65	May 75	Jun 80
Jul 83	Aug 82	Sep 77	Oct 69	Nov 60	Dec 52

Source of Additional Information: Cordele Game and Fish Office (912) 273-8945

Access Point	Access Code
A	1357
B	1357
C	1357

Access Key

1 Paved Road
2 Unpaved Road
3 Short Carry
4 Long Carry
5 Easy Grade
6 Steep Incline
7 Clear Trail
8 Brush and Trees
9 Launching Fee Charged
10 Private Property, Need Permission
11 No Access, Reference Only

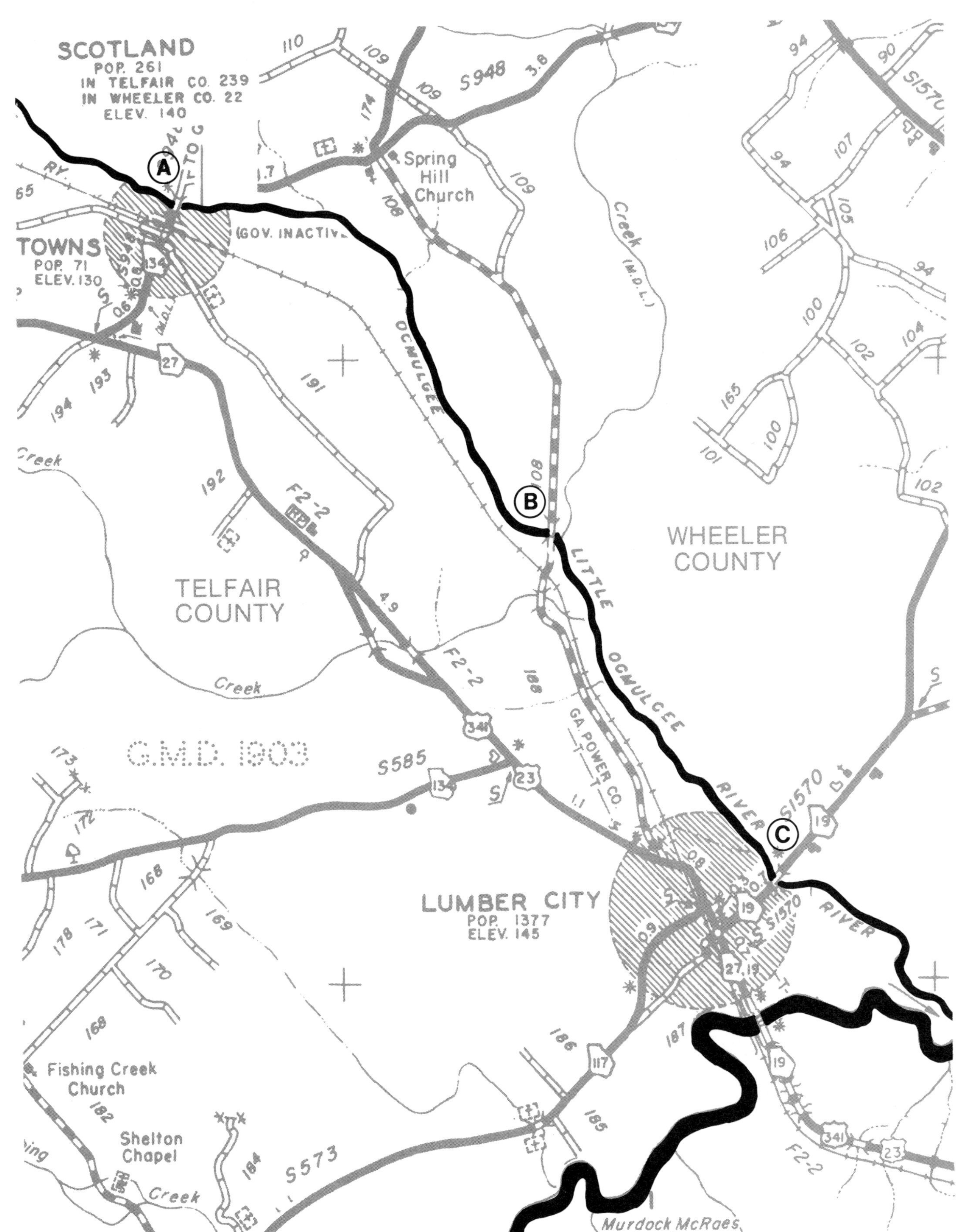
SCOTLAND
POP. 261
IN TELFAIR CO. 239
IN WHEELER CO. 22
ELEV. 140
TOWNS
POP. 71
ELEV. 130
Spring Hill Church
(GOV. INACTIVE
OCMULGEE
LITTLE OCMULGEE RIVER
WHEELER COUNTY
TELFAIR COUNTY
G.M.D. 1903
LUMBER CITY
POP. 1377
ELEV. 145
GA. POWER CO.
RIVER
Fishing Creek Church
Shelton Chapel
Murdock McRaes
Creek
A
B
C

Ocmulgee River

As the Ocmulgee slips out of Macon, away from the Piedmont (as described in the preceding chapter) and into the Coastal Plain, it assumes the characteristics of most alluvial Coastal Plain streams. Its course becomes convoluted and serpentine with horseshoe bends, meander by-pass islands, and some oxbow lakes. To either side of the river, bottom wetland forests envelope the Ocmulgee in a pristine wilderness corridor sometimes four miles across. Populated by water oak, overcup oak, cypress, sweet gum, red maple, tupelo gum, and swamp black gum, the bottomland forests are inundated with water much of the year. The river banks, composed of sandy clay and three to six feet in height, form a natural levee on which grow more cypress and gum along with birch, willow, and a variety of undergrowth. Current is moderate and the setting is generally wild and remote.

Moving south through Houston and Twiggs counties, the Ocmulgee flows by Warner Robbins Air Force Base and then past the Ocmulgee Wildlife Management Area on the east and, farther downstream, along the western boundary of the Oaky Woods Wildlife Management Area. In Pulaski County near Hawkinsville a fertile farm belt (reclaimed from the swamp) with immense cultivated fields replaces the wilderness corridor along the river. In Wilcox and Dodge counties swamp forest again prevails, and beige sandbars on the inside of turns and on the downstream side of islands become common as the Ocmulgee meanders south toward Abbeville. From Abbeville to the mouth of the Ocmulgee at its confluence with the Oconee, the riverside setting remains that of a wooded wilderness, though occasional cabins, boat landings, and powerboat traffic indicate frequent visitation by local outdoorsmen, fishermen, and hunters. River width in the Ocmulgee varies from 140 feet below Macon to about 350 feet as it approaches the mouth at the Altamaha. The level of difficulty is Class I throughout the section below Macon, with powerboat traffic being the primary hazard to navigation. The Ocmulgee is runnable below Macon all year and access is adequate. Wildlife is diverse and plentiful.

Section: Macon to Hawkinsville

Counties: Bibb, Twiggs, Houston, Bleckly, Pulaski

Suitable For: Cruising, camping

Appropriate For: Families, beginners, intermediates, advanced

Months Runnable: All

Interest Highlights: Scenery, wildlife, local culture and industry

Scenery: Beautiful in spots to beautiful

Difficulty: International Scale I
Numerical Points 4

Average Width: 180-230 ft.
Gradient: Slow to moderate
Velocity: 1.33 ft./mi.

Runnable Water Level: Minimum Not applicable
Maximum Up to flood stage

Hazards: Powerboats

Scouting: None

Portages: None

Rescue Index: Remote to accessible but difficult

Mean Water Temperature (°F)

Jan 47	Feb 49	Mar 52	Apr 61	May 72	Jun 80
Jul 83	Aug 82	Sep 77	Oct 66	Nov 60	Dec 52

Source of Additional Information: Macon Game and Fish Office (912) 744-3228

Access Point	Access Code
I	1357
J	1367
K	2367
L	2357
M	1357
N	2357
O	1357
P	1357
Q	2357

Access Key
1 Paved Road
2 Unpaved Road
3 Short Carry
4 Long Carry
5 Easy Grade
6 Steep Incline
7 Clear Trail
8 Brush and Trees
9 Launching Fee Charged
10 Private Property, Need Permission
11 No Access, Reference Only

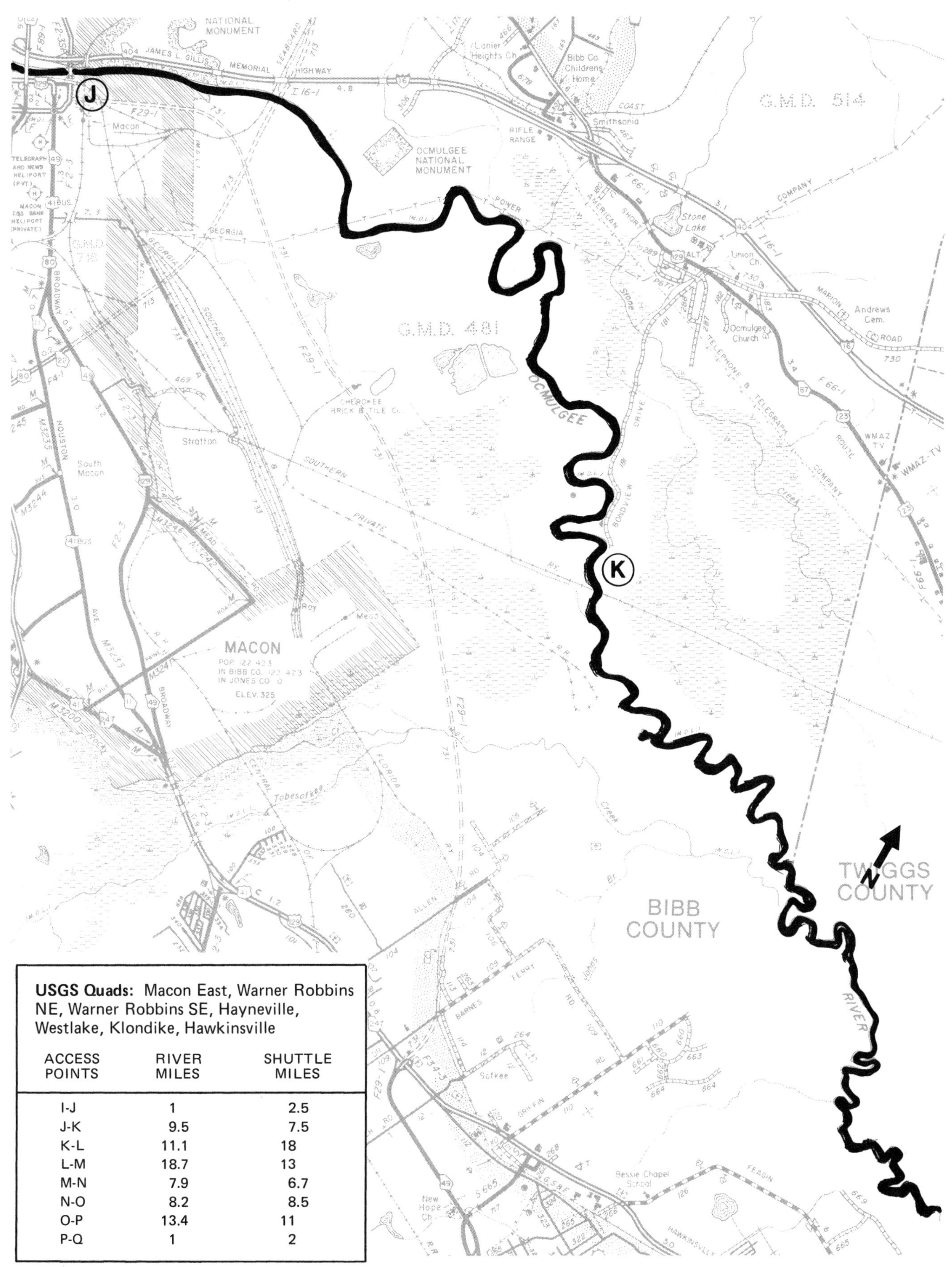

USGS Quads: Macon East, Warner Robbins NE, Warner Robbins SE, Hayneville, Westlake, Klondike, Hawkinsville

ACCESS POINTS	RIVER MILES	SHUTTLE MILES
I-J	1	2.5
J-K	9.5	7.5
K-L	11.1	18
L-M	18.7	13
M-N	7.9	6.7
N-O	8.2	8.5
O-P	13.4	11
P-Q	1	2

Ocmulgee River—*Continued*

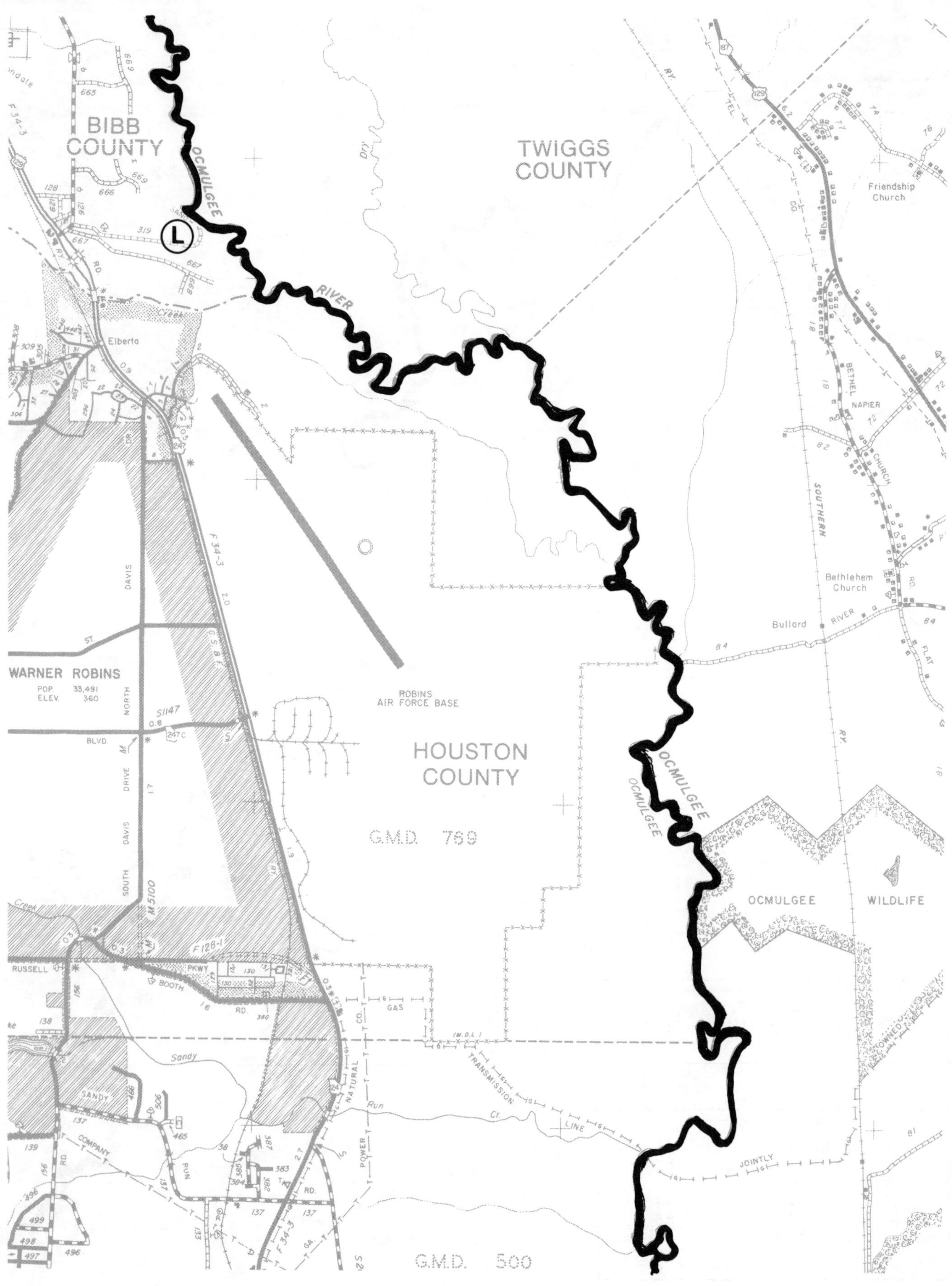

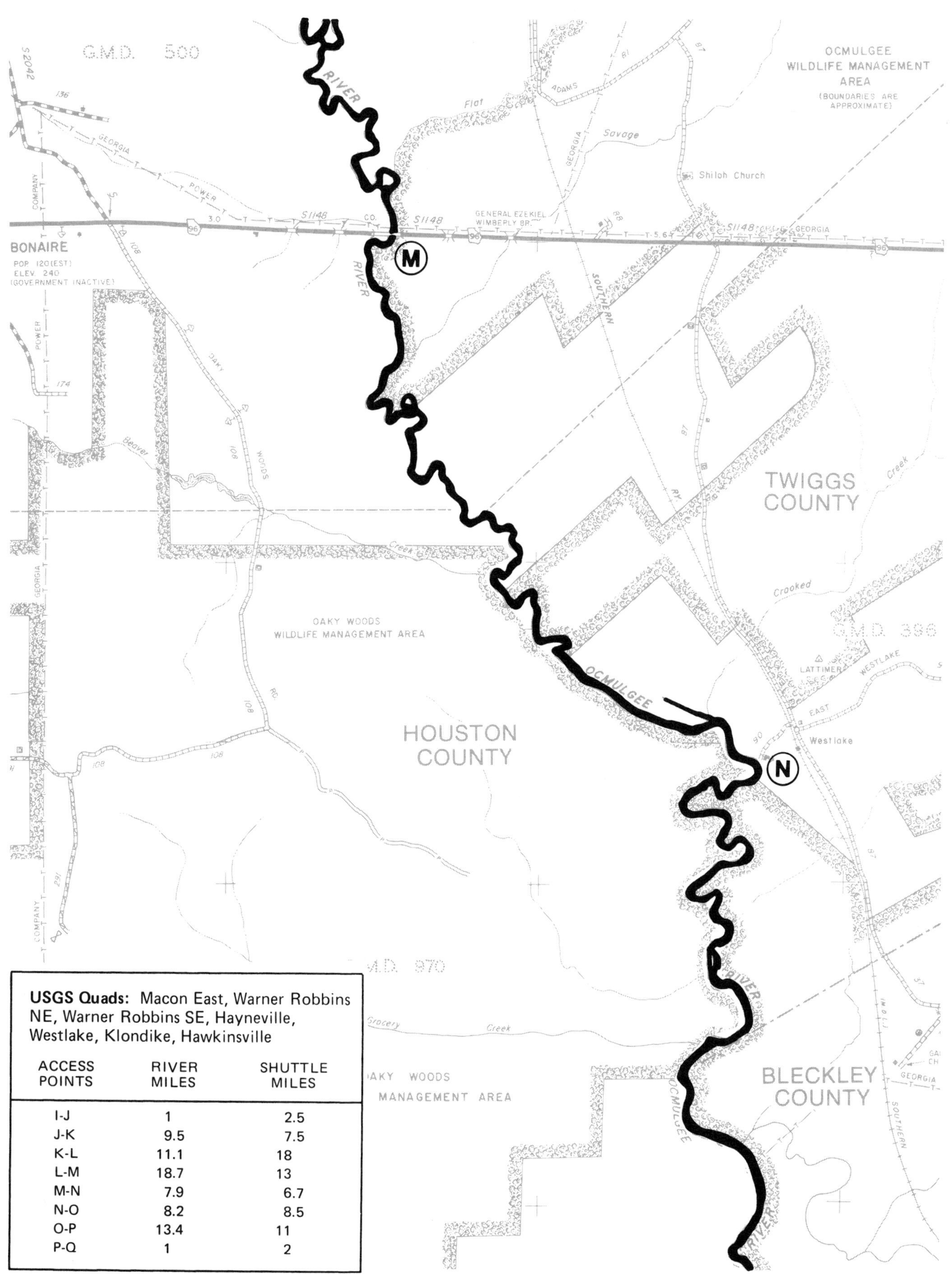

USGS Quads: Macon East, Warner Robbins NE, Warner Robbins SE, Hayneville, Westlake, Klondike, Hawkinsville

ACCESS POINTS	RIVER MILES	SHUTTLE MILES
I-J	1	2.5
J-K	9.5	7.5
K-L	11.1	18
L-M	18.7	13
M-N	7.9	6.7
N-O	8.2	8.5
O-P	13.4	11
P-Q	1	2

Ocmulgee River—*Continued*

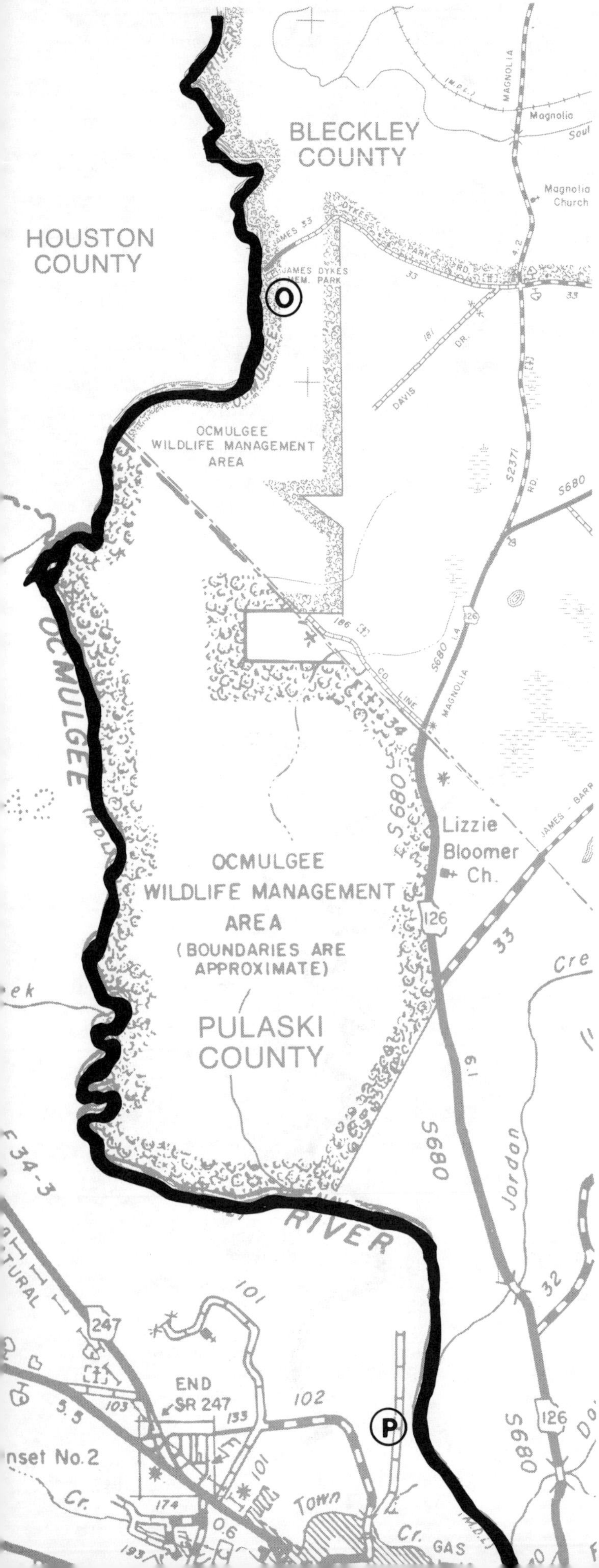

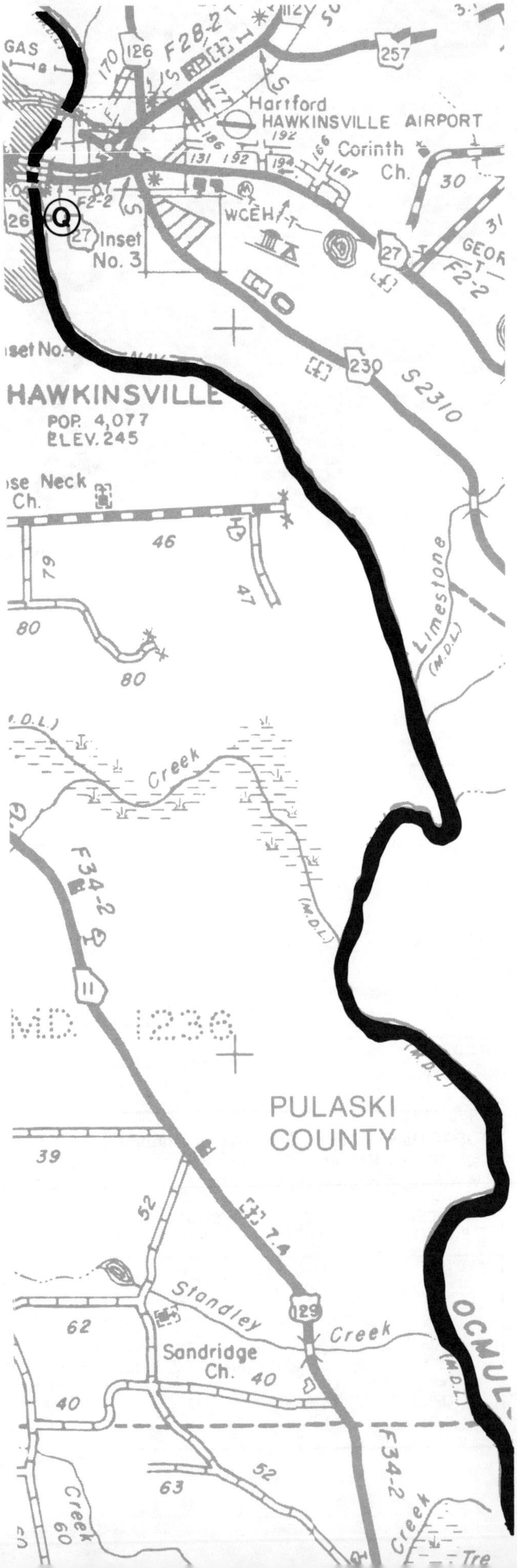

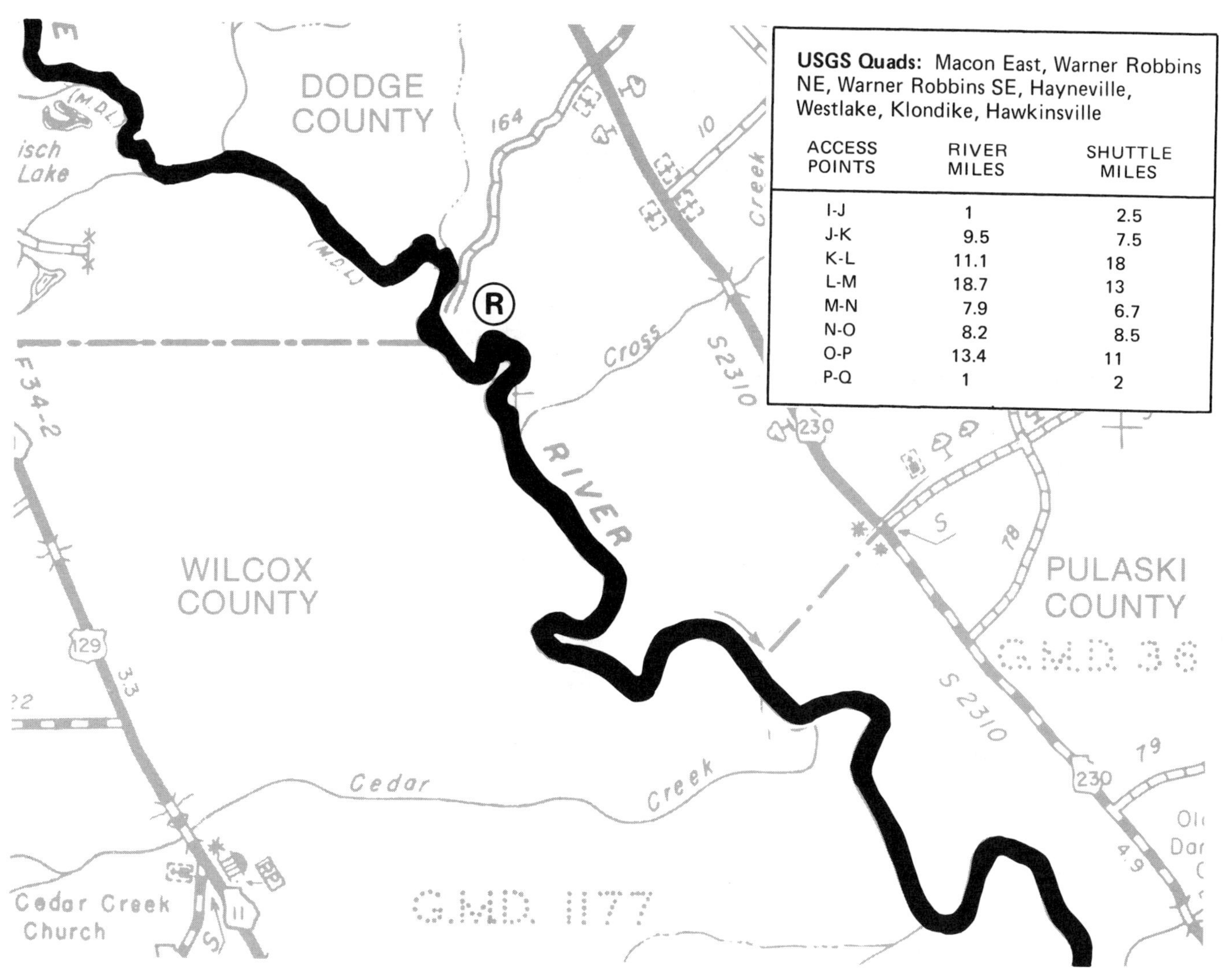

USGS Quads: Macon East, Warner Robbins NE, Warner Robbins SE, Hayneville, Westlake, Klondike, Hawkinsville

ACCESS POINTS	RIVER MILES	SHUTTLE MILES
I-J	1	2.5
J-K	9.5	7.5
K-L	11.1	18
L-M	18.7	13
M-N	7.9	6.7
N-O	8.2	8.5
O-P	13.4	11
P-Q	1	2

Section: Macon to Hawkinsville

Counties: Bibb, Twiggs, Houston, Bleckly, Pulaski

Suitable For: Cruising, camping

Appropriate For: Families, beginners, intermediates, advanced

Months Runnable: All

Interest Highlights: Scenery, wildlife, local culture and industry

Scenery: Beautiful in spots to beautiful

Difficulty: International Scale I
Numerical Points 4

Average Width: 180-230 ft.
Gradient: Slow to moderate
Velocity: 1.33 ft./mi.

Runnable Water Level: Minimum Not applicable
Maximum Up to flood stage

Hazards: Powerboats

Scouting: None

Portages: None

Rescue Index: Remote to accessible but difficult

Mean Water Temperature (°F)

Jan 47	Feb 49	Mar 52	Apr 61	May 72	Jun 80
Jul 83	Aug 82	Sep 77	Oct 66	Nov 60	Dec 52

Source of Additional Information: Macon Game and Fish Office (912) 744-3228

Access Point	Access Code
I	1357
J	1367
K	2367
L	2357
M	1357
N	2357
O	1357
P	1357
Q	2357

Access Key
1 Paved Road
2 Unpaved Road
3 Short Carry
4 Long Carry
5 Easy Grade
6 Steep Incline
7 Clear Trail
8 Brush and Trees
9 Launching Fee Charged
10 Private Property, Need Permission
11 No Access, Reference Only

Ocmulgee River—*Continued*

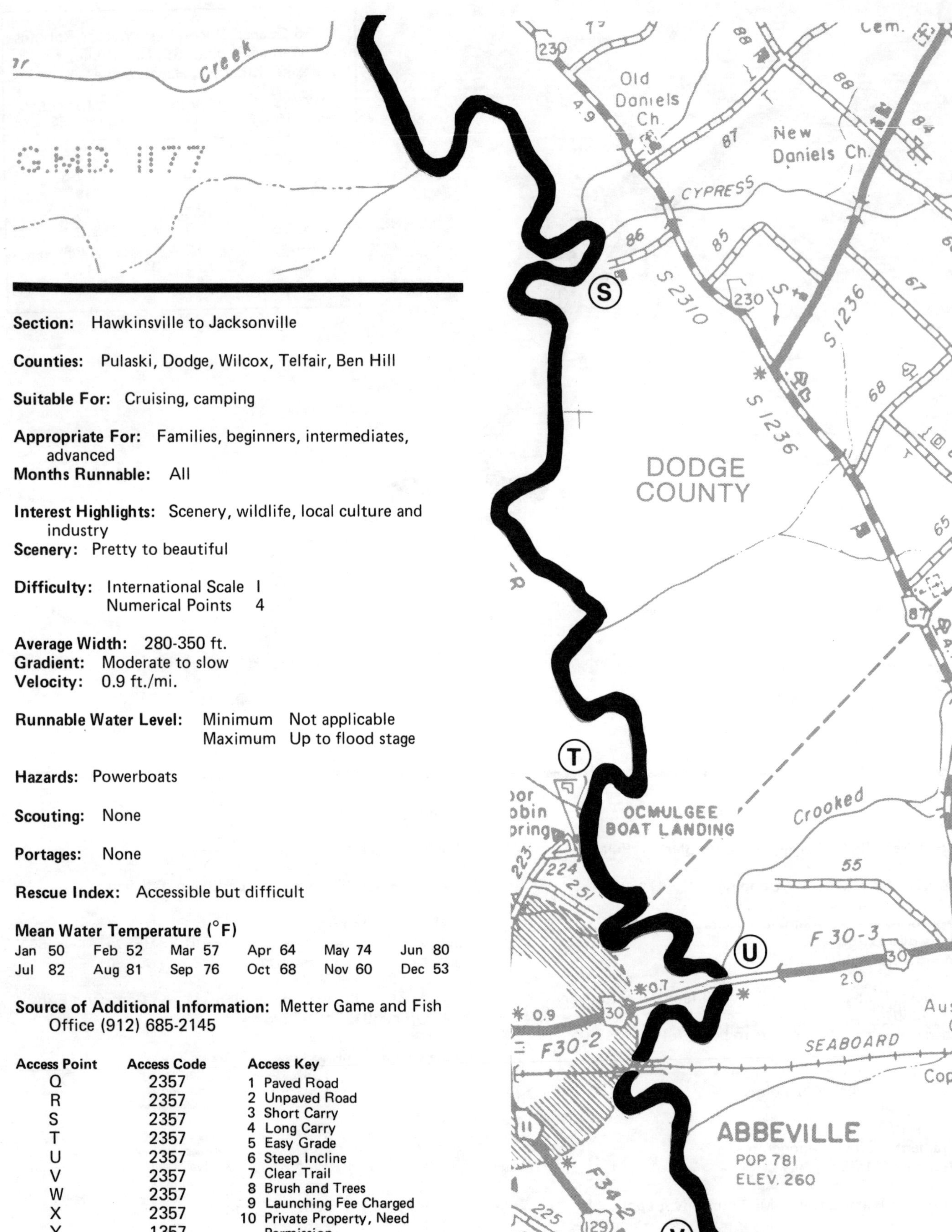

Section: Hawkinsville to Jacksonville

Counties: Pulaski, Dodge, Wilcox, Telfair, Ben Hill

Suitable For: Cruising, camping

Appropriate For: Families, beginners, intermediates, advanced
Months Runnable: All

Interest Highlights: Scenery, wildlife, local culture and industry
Scenery: Pretty to beautiful

Difficulty: International Scale I
Numerical Points 4

Average Width: 280-350 ft.
Gradient: Moderate to slow
Velocity: 0.9 ft./mi.

Runnable Water Level: Minimum Not applicable
Maximum Up to flood stage

Hazards: Powerboats

Scouting: None

Portages: None

Rescue Index: Accessible but difficult

Mean Water Temperature (°F)

Jan 50	Feb 52	Mar 57	Apr 64	May 74	Jun 80
Jul 82	Aug 81	Sep 76	Oct 68	Nov 60	Dec 53

Source of Additional Information: Metter Game and Fish Office (912) 685-2145

Access Point	Access Code
Q	2357
R	2357
S	2357
T	2357
U	2357
V	2357
W	2357
X	2357
Y	1357
Z	1357

Access Key
1 Paved Road
2 Unpaved Road
3 Short Carry
4 Long Carry
5 Easy Grade
6 Steep Incline
7 Clear Trail
8 Brush and Trees
9 Launching Fee Charged
10 Private Property, Need Permission
11 No Access, Reference Only

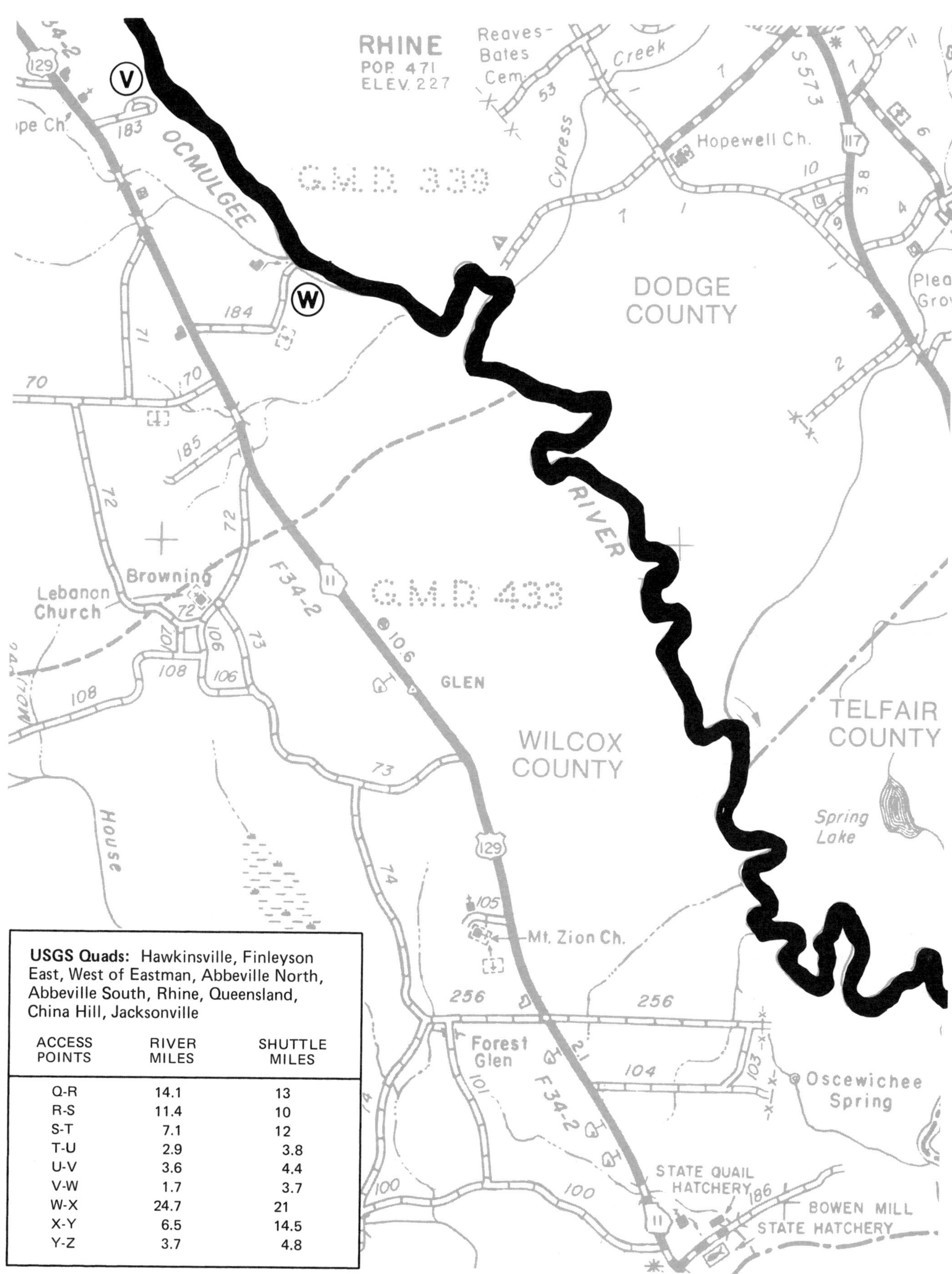

USGS Quads: Hawkinsville, Finleyson East, West of Eastman, Abbeville North, Abbeville South, Rhine, Queensland, China Hill, Jacksonville

ACCESS POINTS	RIVER MILES	SHUTTLE MILES
Q-R	14.1	13
R-S	11.4	10
S-T	7.1	12
T-U	2.9	3.8
U-V	3.6	4.4
V-W	1.7	3.7
W-X	24.7	21
X-Y	6.5	14.5
Y-Z	3.7	4.8

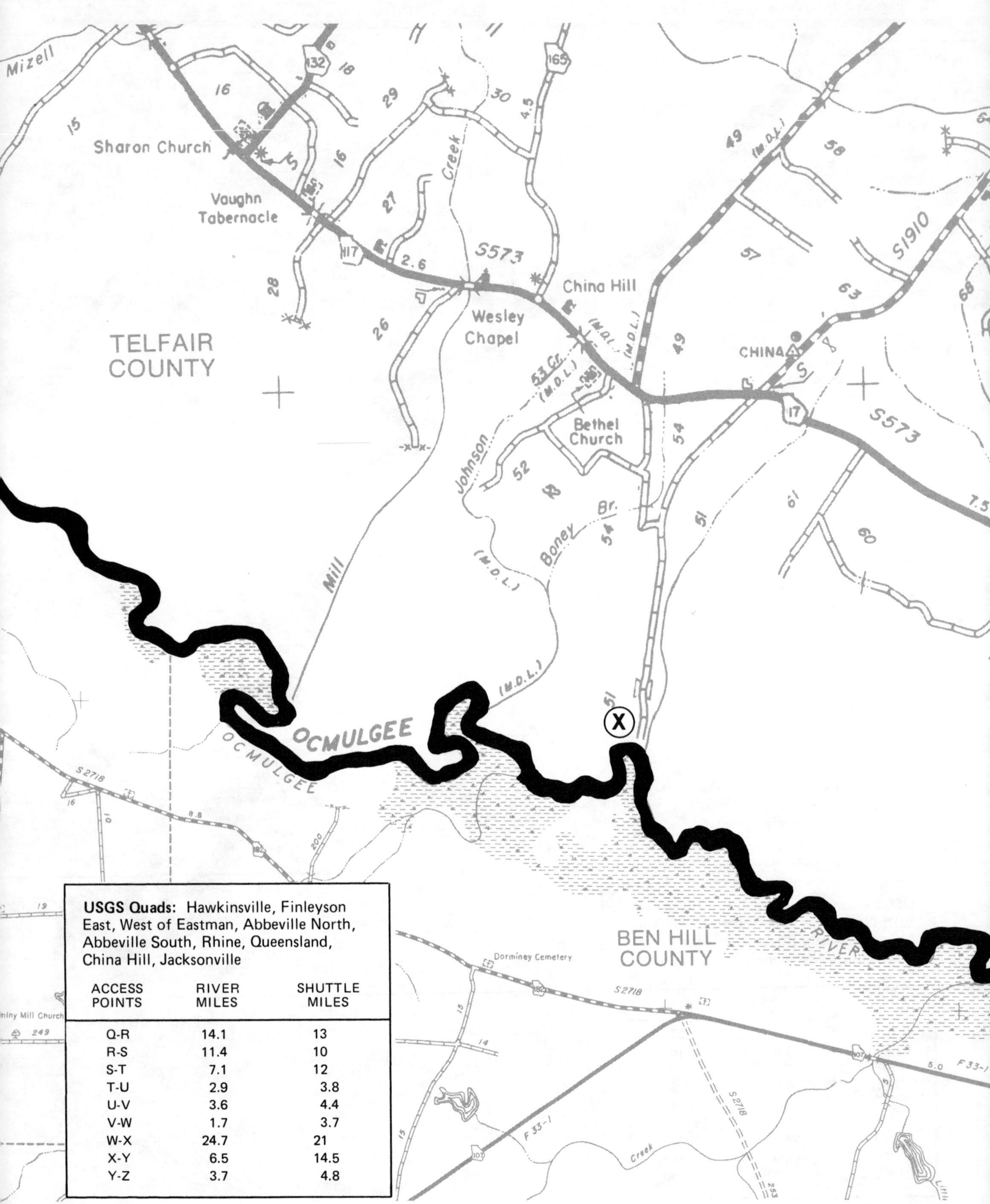

USGS Quads: Hawkinsville, Finleyson East, West of Eastman, Abbeville North, Abbeville South, Rhine, Queensland, China Hill, Jacksonville

ACCESS POINTS	RIVER MILES	SHUTTLE MILES
Q-R	14.1	13
R-S	11.4	10
S-T	7.1	12
T-U	2.9	3.8
U-V	3.6	4.4
V-W	1.7	3.7
W-X	24.7	21
X-Y	6.5	14.5
Y-Z	3.7	4.8

Section: Hawkinsville to Jacksonville

Counties: Pulaski, Dodge, Wilcox, Telfair, Ben Hill

Suitable For: Cruising, camping

Appropriate For: Families, beginners, intermediates, advanced

Months Runnable: All

Interest Highlights: Scenery, wildlife, local culture and industry

Scenery: Pretty to beautiful

Difficulty: International Scale I
Numerical Points 4

Average Width: 280-350 ft.
Gradient: Moderate to slow
Velocity: 0.9 ft./mi.

Runnable Water Level: Minimum Not applicable
Maximum Up to flood stage

Hazards: Powerboats

Scouting: None

Portages: None

Rescue Index: Accessible but difficult

Mean Water Temperature (°F)

Jan	50	Feb	52	Mar	57	Apr	64	May	74	Jun	80
Jul	82	Aug	81	Sep	76	Oct	68	Nov	60	Dec	53

Source of Additional Information: Metter Game and Fish Office (912) 685-2145

Access Point	Access Code
Q	2357
R	2357
S	2357
T	2357
U	2357
V	2357
W	2357
X	2357
Y	1357
Z	1357

Access Key
1 Paved Road
2 Unpaved Road
3 Short Carry
4 Long Carry
5 Easy Grade
6 Steep Incline
7 Clear Trail
8 Brush and Trees
9 Launching Fee Charged
10 Private Property, Need Permission
11 No Access, Reference Only

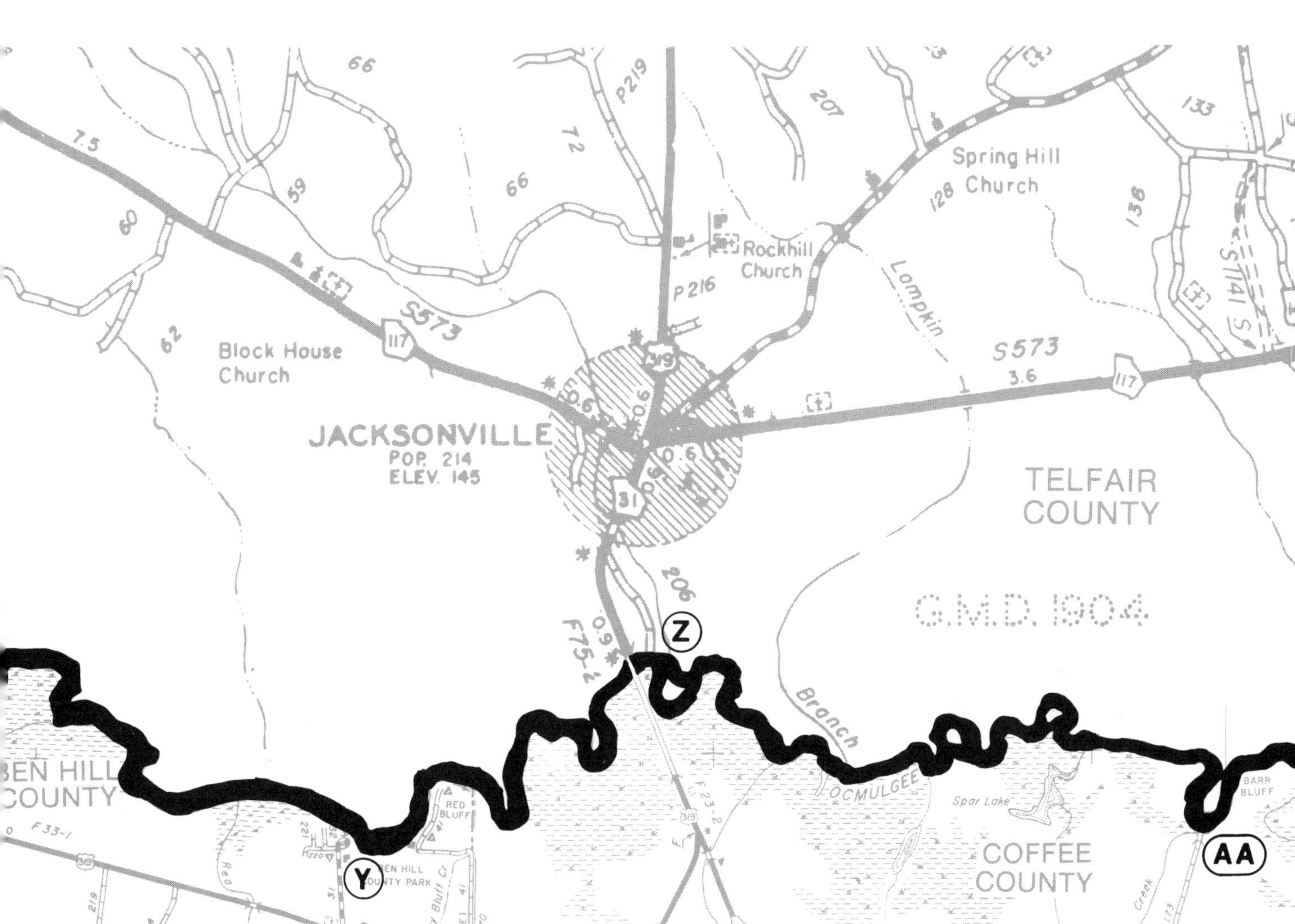

Ocmulgee River—*Continued*

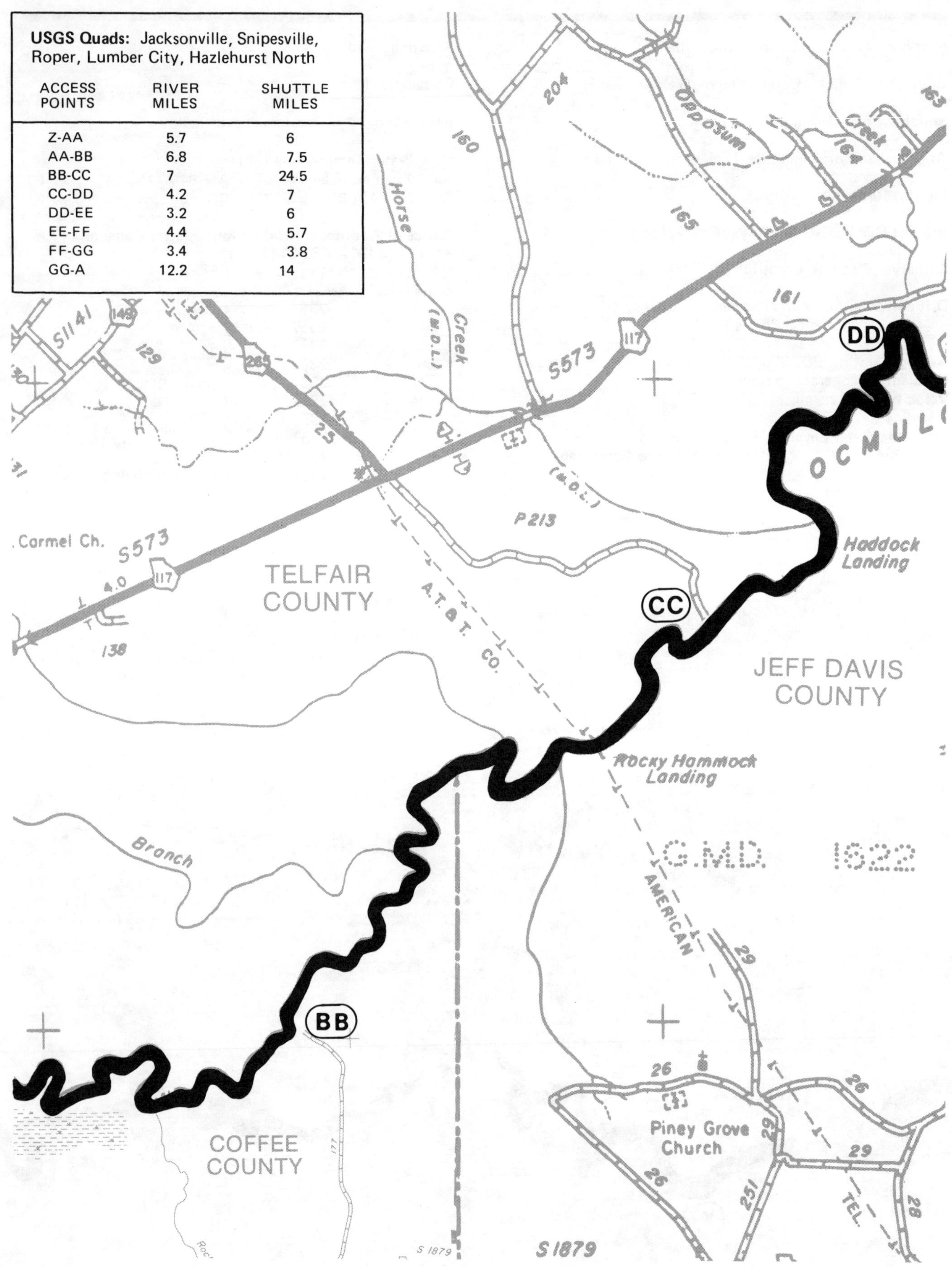

USGS Quads: Jacksonville, Snipesville, Roper, Lumber City, Hazlehurst North

ACCESS POINTS	RIVER MILES	SHUTTLE MILES
Z-AA	5.7	6
AA-BB	6.8	7.5
BB-CC	7	24.5
CC-DD	4.2	7
DD-EE	3.2	6
EE-FF	4.4	5.7
FF-GG	3.4	3.8
GG-A	12.2	14

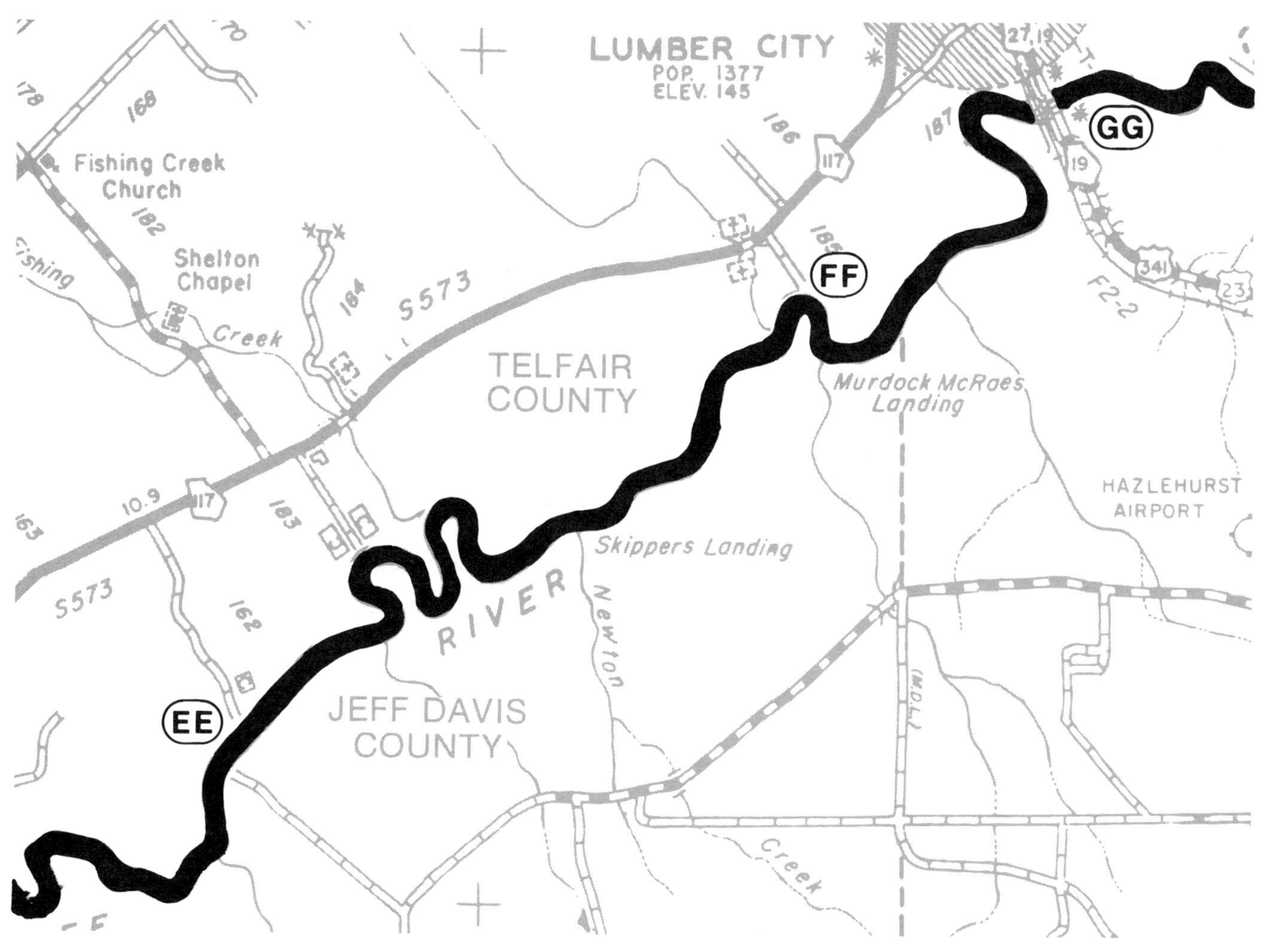

Section: Jacksonville to Altamaha River

Counties: Telfair, Ben Hill, Coffee, Jeff Davis, Wheeler, Montgomery
Suitable For: Cruising, camping

Appropriate For: Families, beginners, intermediates, advanced
Months Runnable: All

Interest Highlights: Scenery, wildlife, local culture and industry
Scenery: Pretty to beautiful

Difficulty: International Scale I
Numerical Points 4

Average Width: 280-350 ft.
Gradient: Moderate to slow
Velocity: 0.9 ft./mi.

Runnable Water Level: Minimum Not applicable
Maximum Up to flood stage

Hazards: Powerboats

Scouting: None

Portages: None

Rescue Index: Accessible but difficult

Mean Water Temperature (°F)

Jan 50	Feb 52	Mar 57	Apr 64	May 74	Jun 80
Jul 82	Aug 81	Sep 76	Oct 68	Nov 60	Dec 53

Source of Additional Information: Metter Game and Fish Office (912) 685-2145

Access Point	Access Code
Z	1357
AA	2357
BB	2357
CC	2357
DD	2357
EE	2357
FF	2357
GG	1357
A[1]	2357

Access Key
1 Paved Road
2 Unpaved Road
3 Short Carry
4 Long Carry
5 Easy Grade
6 Steep Incline
7 Clear Trail
8 Brush and Trees
9 Launching Fee Charged
10 Private Property, Need Permission
11 No Access, Reference Only

[1]On the Altamaha River

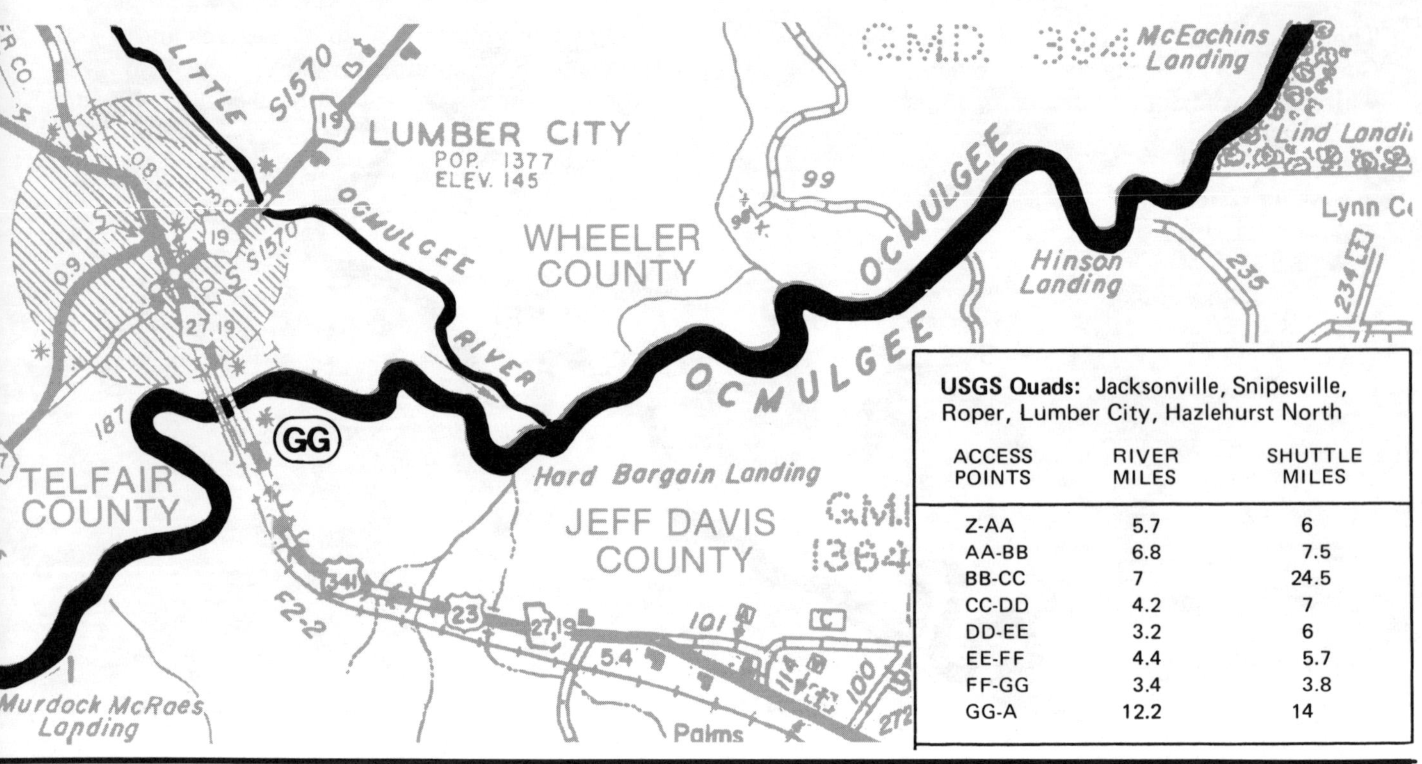

USGS Quads: Jacksonville, Snipesville, Roper, Lumber City, Hazlehurst North

ACCESS POINTS	RIVER MILES	SHUTTLE MILES
Z-AA	5.7	6
AA-BB	6.8	7.5
BB-CC	7	24.5
CC-DD	4.2	7
DD-EE	3.2	6
EE-FF	4.4	5.7
FF-GG	3.4	3.8
GG-A	12.2	14

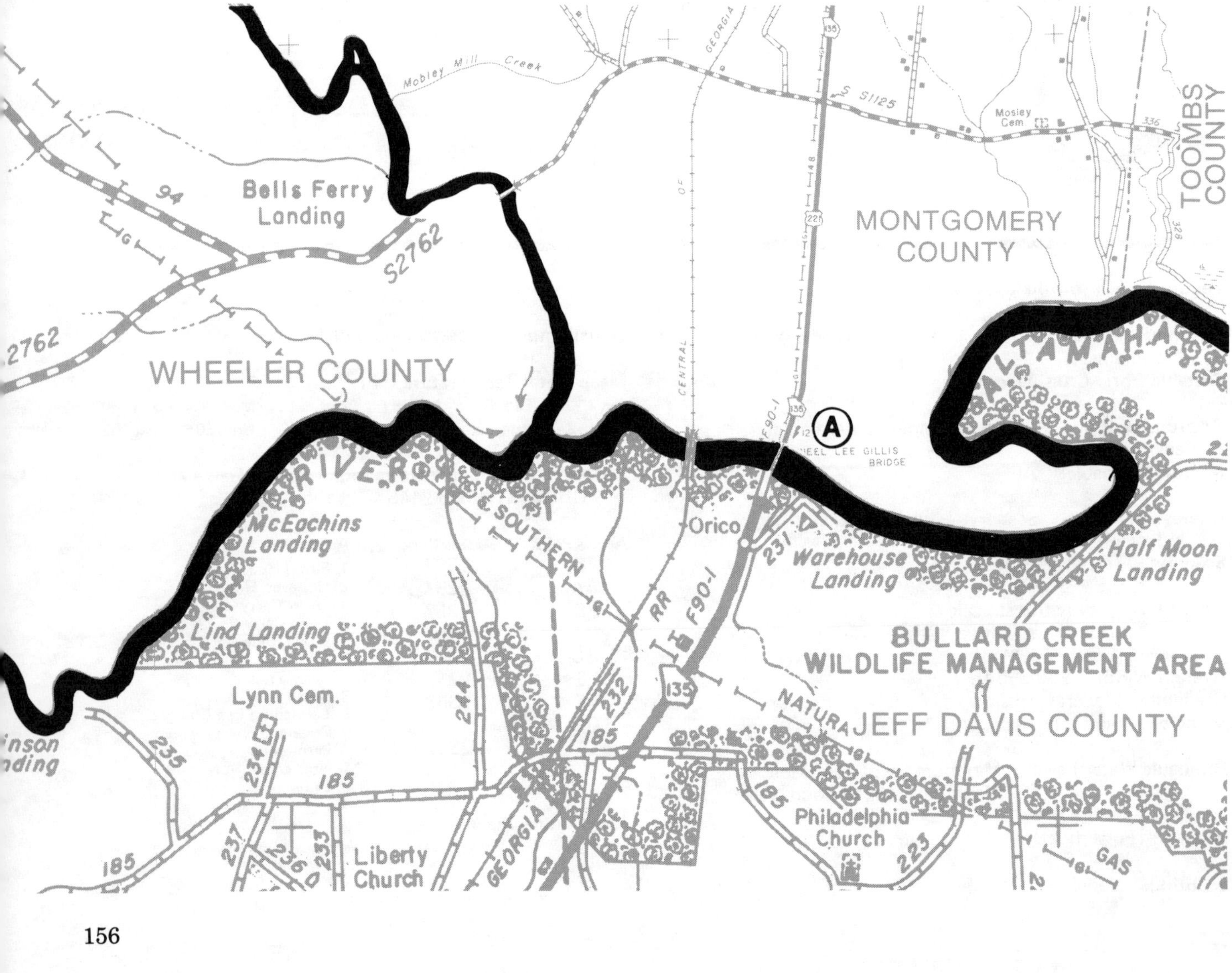

Ohoopee River

The Ohoopee River is born in southern Washington County, flows southeastward over sun-drenched white sand, and drains portions of Johnson, Emmanuel, Treutlen, Candler, Toombs, and Tattnall counties before emptying into the Altamaha east of Glenville. Runnable except during dry periods downstream of the US 1 bridge in Emmanuel County, the Ohoopee is one of the most exotic and beautiful streams in southern Georgia. A so-called blackwater river (the water is stained a burgundy red by tannic acid from the roots of trees and decaying vegetation), it runs clear and sparkling over the contrasting bottom and banks of white sand. A shading canopy of moss-draped bald cypress, willow, pond cypress, swamp black gum, Ogeechee lime, ash, red maple, water oak, and sweet bay combines with the Ohoopee's natural tranquility and remote, pristine setting to set it apart as a showplace of nature. Wildlife is varied and plentiful throughout the wide bottomland swamp corridor that cradles the Ohoopee along its serpentine course. Small islands, meander by-passes, and oxbows are not uncommon, particulary in the reaches below Swift Creek.

The stream's width ranges from 30 to 45 feet at the US 1 bridge, to 50 to 65 feet west of Collins, to 80 feet as it approaches the Altamaha. The current is moderate throughout, and the level of difficulty is Class I with sharp bends and trees growing in the stream to sharpen navigational skills and keep the paddling interesting. Hazards consist primarily of occasional deadfalls and a dam that must be portaged above the GA 56 bridge. Access is excellent and numerous white sandbars and beaches lend themselves to swimming, picnicking, and canoe camping. The banks are two to four feet in height, slope at approximately 30 to 45 degrees and are of white sand. Surrounding terrain is mixed lowland swamp forests rising gradually to a low upland plateau.

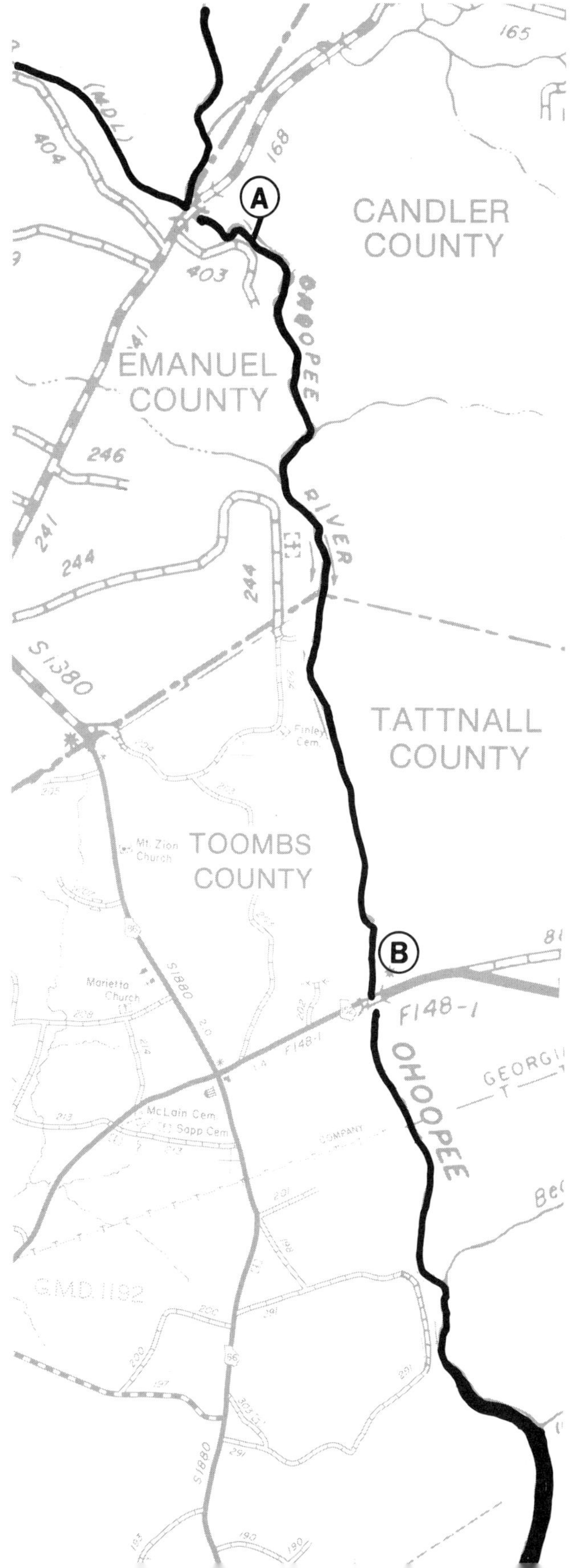

USGS Quads: Cobbtown, Ohoopee, Reidsville West, Altamaha, Tison, Altamaha SE

ACCESS POINTS	RIVER MILES	SHUTTLE MILES
A-B	6.1	12
B-C	8.6	11
C-D	4.5	6
D-E	3	12
E-F	1.2	2
F-G	1	7
G-H	3.2	3
H-I	4.5	6
I-J	5.3	5
J-K	4.8	7
K-F	8.4	10

Ohoopee River—*Continued*

Section: West of Metter to Altamaha River

Counties: Candler, Emanuel, Tatnall, Toombs

Suitable For: Cruising, camping

Appropriate For: Families, beginners, intermediates, advanced

Months Runnable: December through June

Interest Highlights: Scenery, wildlife

Scenery: Beautiful to exceptionally beautiful

Difficulty: International Scale I
Numerical Points 4

Average Width: 45-65 ft.
Gradient: Slow to moderate
Velocity: 1.48 ft./mi.

Runnable Water Level: Minimum 190 cfs
(Reidsville gauge) Maximum Up to high flood stage

Hazards: Deadfalls, dams, trees in stream

Scouting: None

Portages: Dam above GA 56

Rescue Index: Accessible but difficult

Mean Water Temperature (°F)

Jan 51	Feb 52	Mar 57	Apr 64	May 73	Jun 79
Jul 82	Aug 80	Sep 75	Oct 67	Nov 59	Dec 52

Source of Additional Information: Metter Game and Fish Office (912) 685-2145

Access Point	Access Code
A	1367
B	1357
C	1357
D	2357
E	1357
F	2357
G	1357
H	1357
I	1357
J	23579
K	1457
F[1]	1368

Access Key
1 Paved Road
2 Unpaved Road
3 Short Carry
4 Long Carry
5 Easy Grade
6 Steep Incline
7 Clear Trail
8 Brush and Trees
9 Launching Fee Charged
10 Private Property, Need Permission
11 No Access, Reference Only

[1]On the Altamaha River

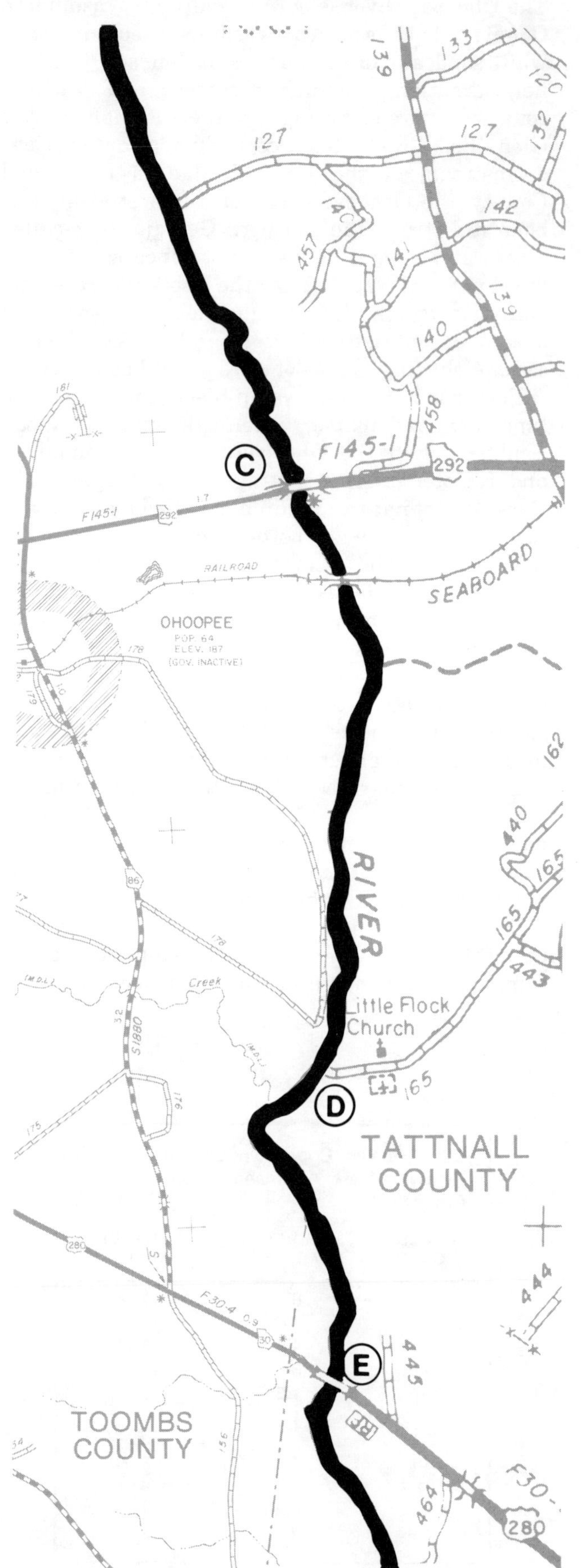

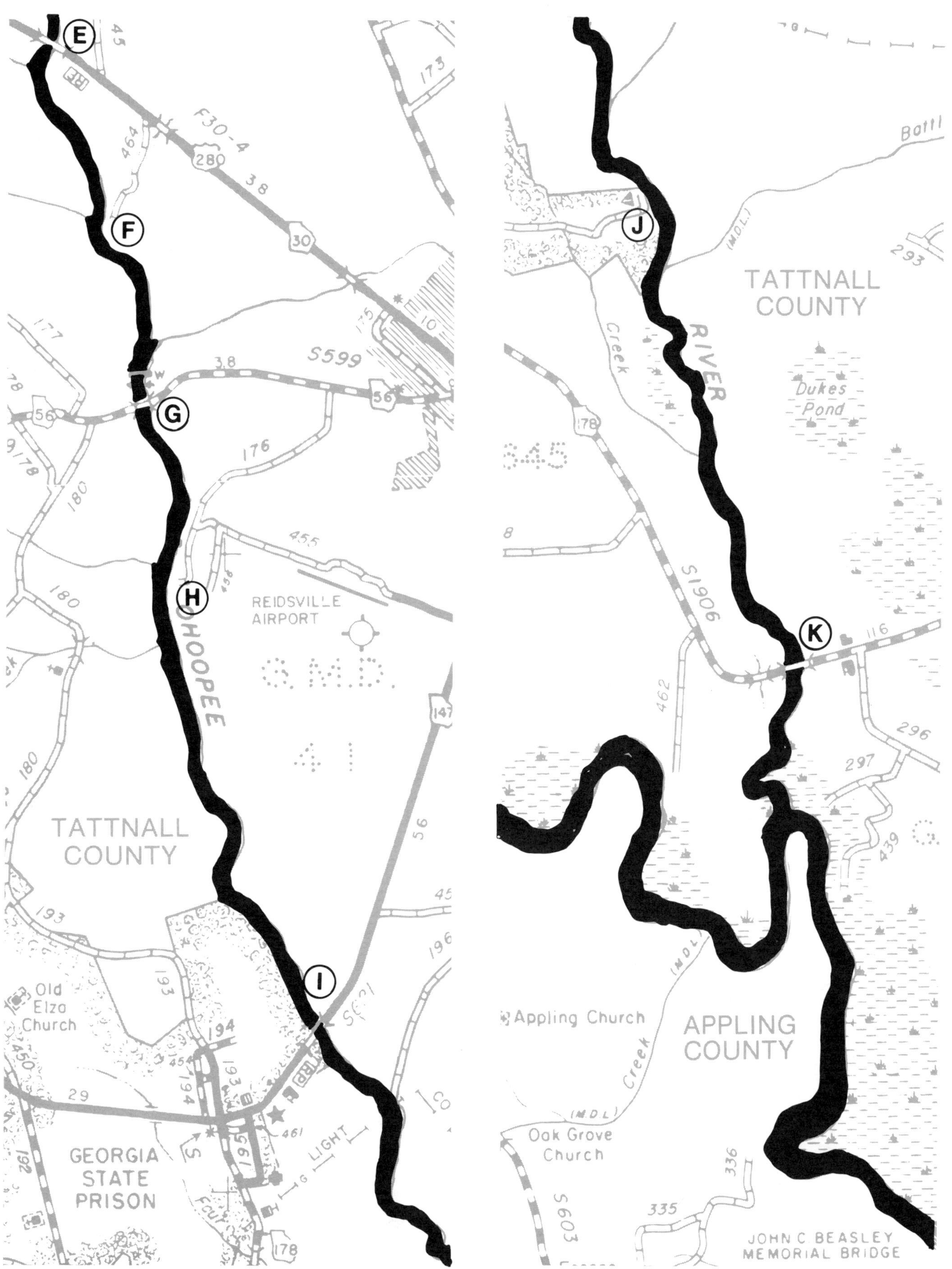
E
F
G
H
I
J
K
280
30
38
56
176
180
455
REIDSVILLE
AIRPORT
OHOOPEE
G.M.D.
TATTNALL
COUNTY
Old
Elzo
Church
GEORGIA
STATE
PRISON
LIGHT
RIVER
Creek
Dukes
Pond
S1906
116
296
297
439
Appling Church
APPLING
COUNTY
Oak Grove
Church
335
336
JOHN C BEASLEY
MEMORIAL BRIDGE

Altamaha River

The largest river flowing entirely within Georgia, the Altamaha originates high in the Piedmont in the headwaters of its parent streams, the Ocmulgee and the Oconee rivers. Running north to south, these two massive tributaries drain portions of forty counties before coming together north of Hazlehurst in Jeff Davis County to form the Altamaha. At the confluence, the Altamaha assumes a southeastward heading, drifting through the lower Coastal Plain to its mouth at the Atlantic Ocean near St. Simons Island. The length of the Altamaha from the mouth to its uppermost headwaters is more than four hundred miles. It drains a total of 14,400 square miles (5,800 square miles of the Piedmont and 8,600 square miles of the Coastal Plain).

The Altamaha below the confluence of the Ocmulgee and Oconee is a large, commercially navigable waterway that is continually attracting new development and industry to its banks. As with many large streams, canoeing appeal is somewhat limited. Industry and other commercial development at streamside is not overwhelming at present, but it exists in sufficient concentration to noticeably detract from the river's natural beauty. Powerboat traffic is heavy, although primarily of recreational use. The water quality is very good but is colored by heavy sedimentation. Finally, the Altamaha, because of its size, simply lacks the sense of intimacy that paddlers find so enjoyable on smaller streams.

Through most of its journey through the Coastal Plain, the river winds in great horseshoe arcs through a broad valley where bottomland swamp forest adjoins the stream on both sides. These forests, composed of overcup oak, water oak, cypress, sweet gum, water hickory, elm, ash, and red maple, are frequently bulldozed along the Altamaha to make room for commercial pine forests. Banks on the Altamaha are generally low, averaging three to five feet, and are sometimes buttressed by small "bluffs" or sand hills shaded by beautiful stands of live oak and mockernut hickory. The incline of the banks usually varies between 30 and 70 degrees. Vegetation on the bank consists of cypress, silver maple, willow, ash, and sweet gum, among others.

Sandbars and expansive natural beaches abound on the Altamaha at lower levels and are to be found on the inside of almost every turn and on the downstream side of many islands. Though completely exposed and unshaded, they provide excellent sites for camping, picnicking, or sunning. Below

(*Continued on page 162–163*)

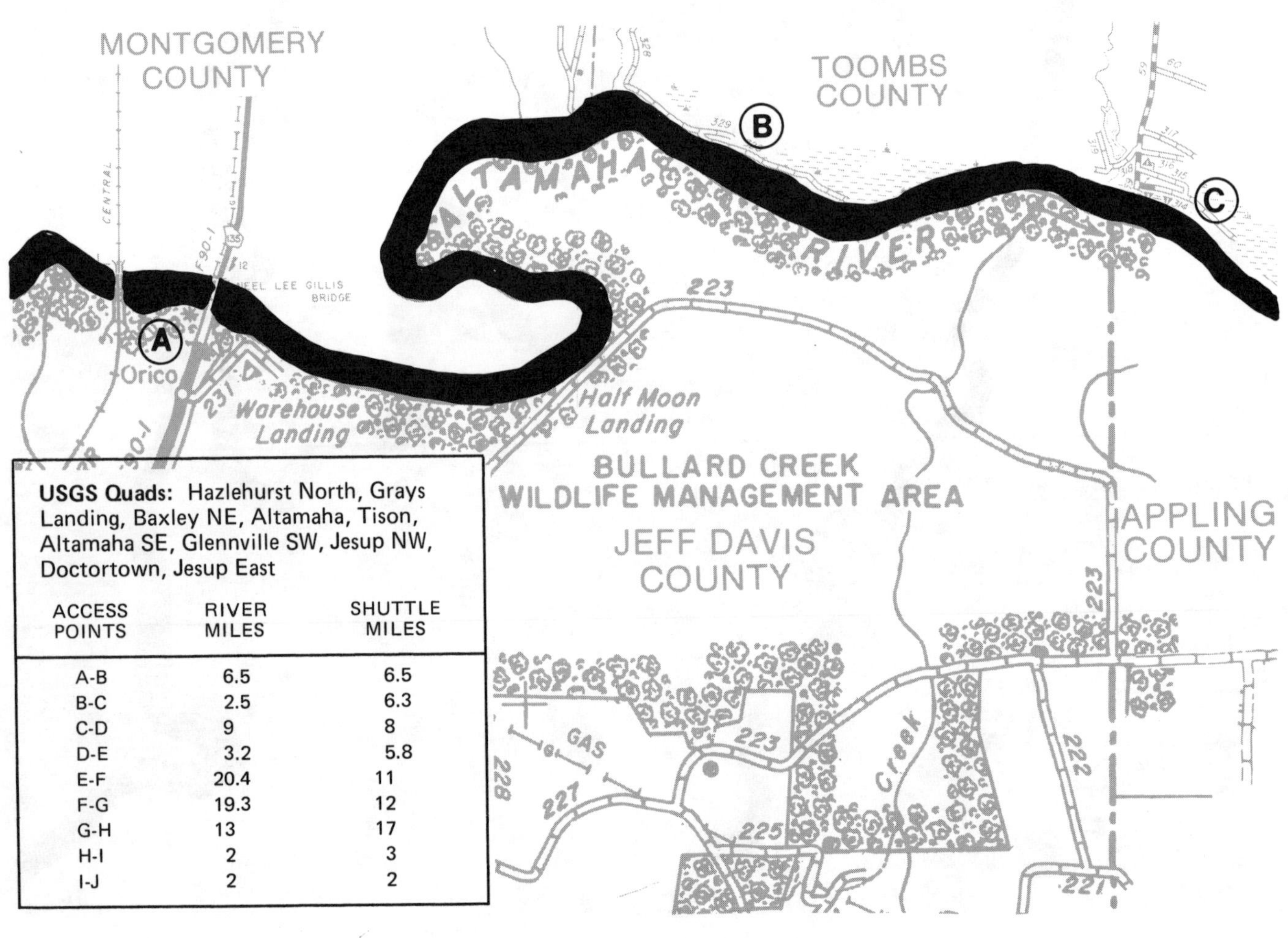

USGS Quads: Hazlehurst North, Grays Landing, Baxley NE, Altamaha, Tison, Altamaha SE, Glennville SW, Jesup NW, Doctortown, Jesup East

ACCESS POINTS	RIVER MILES	SHUTTLE MILES
A-B	6.5	6.5
B-C	2.5	6.3
C-D	9	8
D-E	3.2	5.8
E-F	20.4	11
F-G	19.3	12
G-H	13	17
H-I	2	3
I-J	2	2

Section: US 221 to Jesup

Counties: Wheeler, Montgomery, Jeff Davis, Toombs, Appling, Tattnall, Long, Wayne
Suitable For: Cruising, camping

Appropriate For: Families, beginners, intermediates, advanced
Months Runnable: All

Interest Highlights: Scenery, wildlife, local culture and industry
Scenery: Beautiful in spots

Difficulty: International Scale I
Numerical Points 4

Average Width: 450-510 ft.
Velocity: Slow to moderate
Gradient: 0.88 ft./mi.

Runnable Water Level: Minimum Not applicable
Maximum Up to high flood stage

Hazards: Powerboats

Scouting: None

Portages: None

Rescue Index: Accessible but difficult

Mean Water Temperature (°F)

Jan 50	Feb 51	Mar 55	Apr 64	May 73	Jun 81
Jul 85	Aug 84	Sep 80	Oct 69	Nov 61	Dec 53

Source of Additional Information: Brunswick Game and Fish Office (912) 264-7237

Access Point	Access Code
A	2357
B	2357
C	1357
D	2357
E	2357
F	1368
G	2357
H	1367
I	13579
J	1357

Access Key

1 Paved Road
2 Unpaved Road
3 Short Carry
4 Long Carry
5 Easy Grade
6 Steep Incline
7 Clear Trail
8 Brush and Trees
9 Launching Fee Charged
10 Private Property, Need Permission
11 No Access, Reference Only

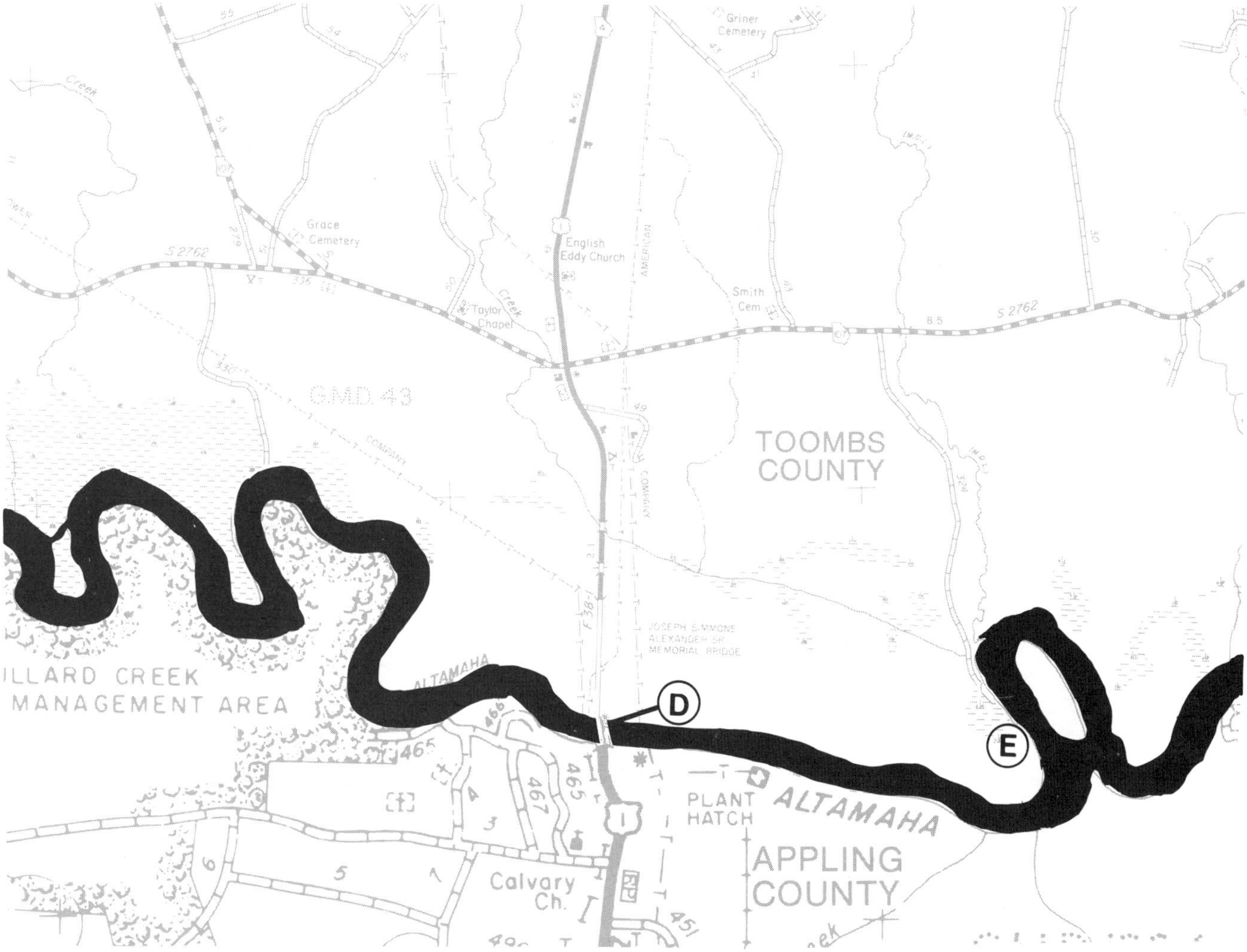

Altamaha River—*Continued*

USGS Quads: Hazlehurst North, Grays Landing, Baxley NE, Altamaha, Tison, Altamaha SE, Glennville SW, Jesup NW, Doctortown, Jesup East

ACCESS POINTS	RIVER MILES	SHUTTLE MILES
A-B	6.5	6.5
B-C	2.5	6.3
C-D	9	8
D-E	3.2	5.8
E-F	20.4	11
F-G	19.3	12
G-H	13	17
H-I	2	3
I-J	2	2

GA 121 islands become more numerous and there are dozens of feeder stream and sloughs, especially in Long and Wayne counties, that permit off-river explorations into the adjoining swamps. As the Altamaha moves south through McIntosh and Glynn counties the flora changes somewhat as tidal influence affects the streamside and swamp vegetation. Below the Seaboard Coast Line railroad bridge hardwoods are almost nonexistent. Cypress are larger than upstream, and sweet gum, tupelo gum and swamp black gum are plentiful. Shrubs consist of black willow, water elm, silky dogwood, alder, swamp privet, and swamp palm.

As the river nears the Atlantic Ocean a series of large islands splits the channel. These comprise several wildlife management areas. The surrounding terrain shifts from swamp forest to marshes where vast virgin gum and cypress swamps were destroyed in the early 1800s to convert the floodplain to rice plantations. In the refuges particularly, many of the old rice dikes are maintained to provide winter protection for waterfowl. Cypress and gum grow in small isolated stands in the marsh and are surrounded by a watery carpet of tall grasses. Throughout the marsh, small creeks, rivers, and sloughs cut labyrinthine paths and connect larger water courses. All of these are fascinating paddle trips and they abound with wildlife.

The level of difficulty on the Altamaha is Class I. Dangers consist primarily of powerboat traffic and getting lost in off-river explorations. The river's width varies from 350 feet at the confluence of the Ocmulgee and Oconee to 500 to 550 feet in Long and Wayne counties, and approaching 660 to 700 feet before splitting around the islands in lower McIntosh County. The current is moderate to slow. Access is adequate except in the delta area where intricate, confusing networks of waterways and access points located off the main river channels demand well-practiced map and compass skills. Good planning is essential for any trip into the delta and should take into account the ebb and flow of the tide.

Altamaha River delta at high tide. (See Page 274 for the same area at low tide.)

Photo courtesy of *Brown's Guide to Georgia.*

Section: US 221 to Jesup

Counties: Wheeler, Montgomery, Jeff Davis, Toombs, Appling, Tattnall, Long, Wayne

Suitable For: Cruising, camping

Appropriate For: Families, beginners, intermediates, advanced

Months Runnable: All

Interest Highlights: Scenery, wildlife, local culture and industry

Scenery: Beautiful in spots

Difficulty: International Scale I
Numerical Points 4

Average Width: 450-510 ft.

Velocity: Slow to moderate

Gradient: 0.88 ft./mi.

Runnable Water Level: Minimum Not applicable
Maximum Up to high flood stage

Hazards: Powerboats

Scouting: None

Portages: None

Rescue Index: Accessible but difficult

Mean Water Temperature (°F)

Jan	50	Feb	51	Mar	55	Apr	64	May	73	Jun	81
Jul	85	Aug	84	Sep	80	Oct	69	Nov	61	Dec	53

Source of Additional Information: Brunswick Game and Fish Office (912) 264-7237

Access Point	Access Code
A	2357
B	2357
C	1357
D	2357
E	2357
F	1368
G	2357
H	1367
I	13579
J	1357

Access Key

1 Paved Road
2 Unpaved Road
3 Short Carry
4 Long Carry
5 Easy Grade
6 Steep Incline
7 Clear Trail
8 Brush and Trees
9 Launching Fee Charged
10 Private Property, Need Permission
11 No Access, Reference Only

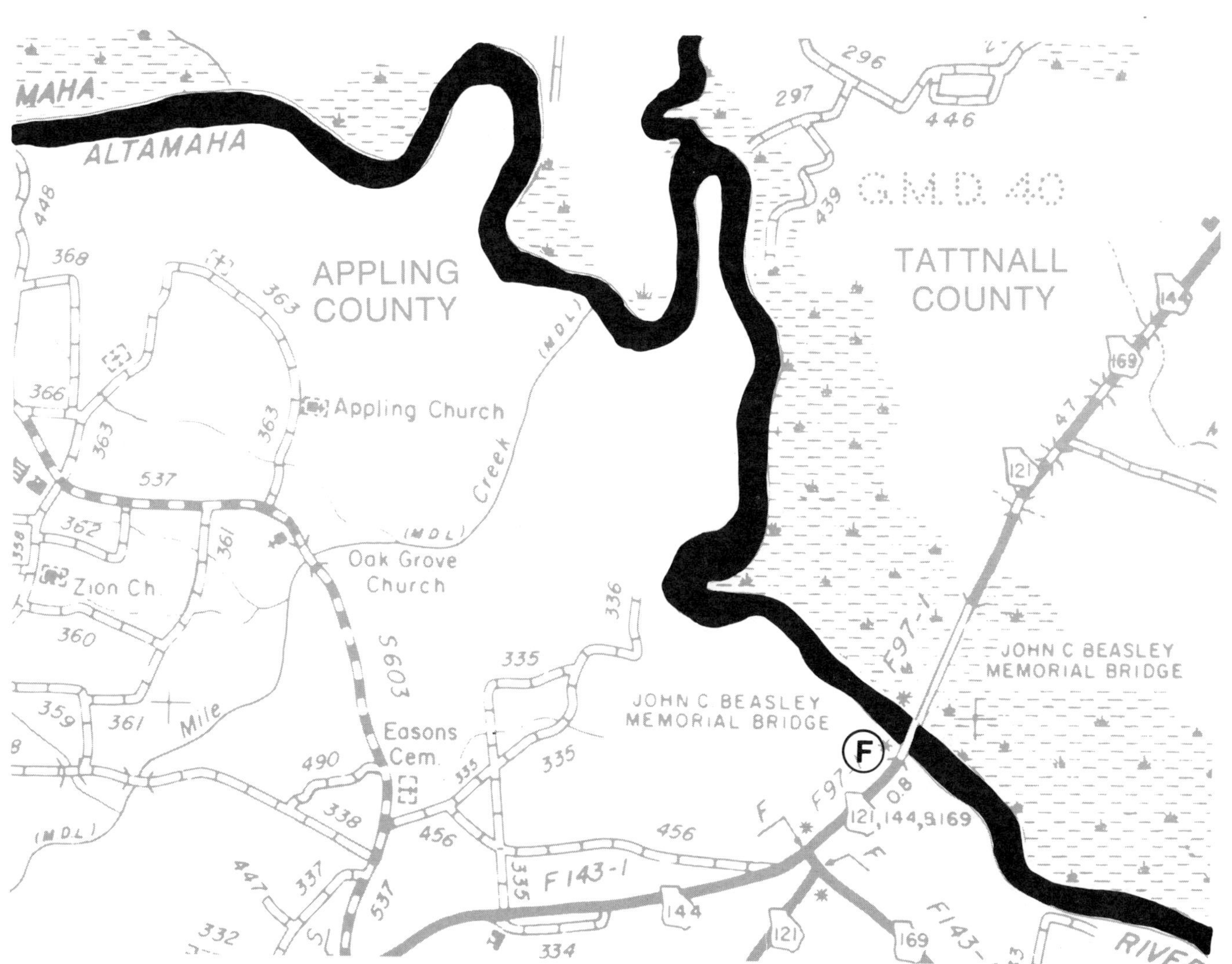

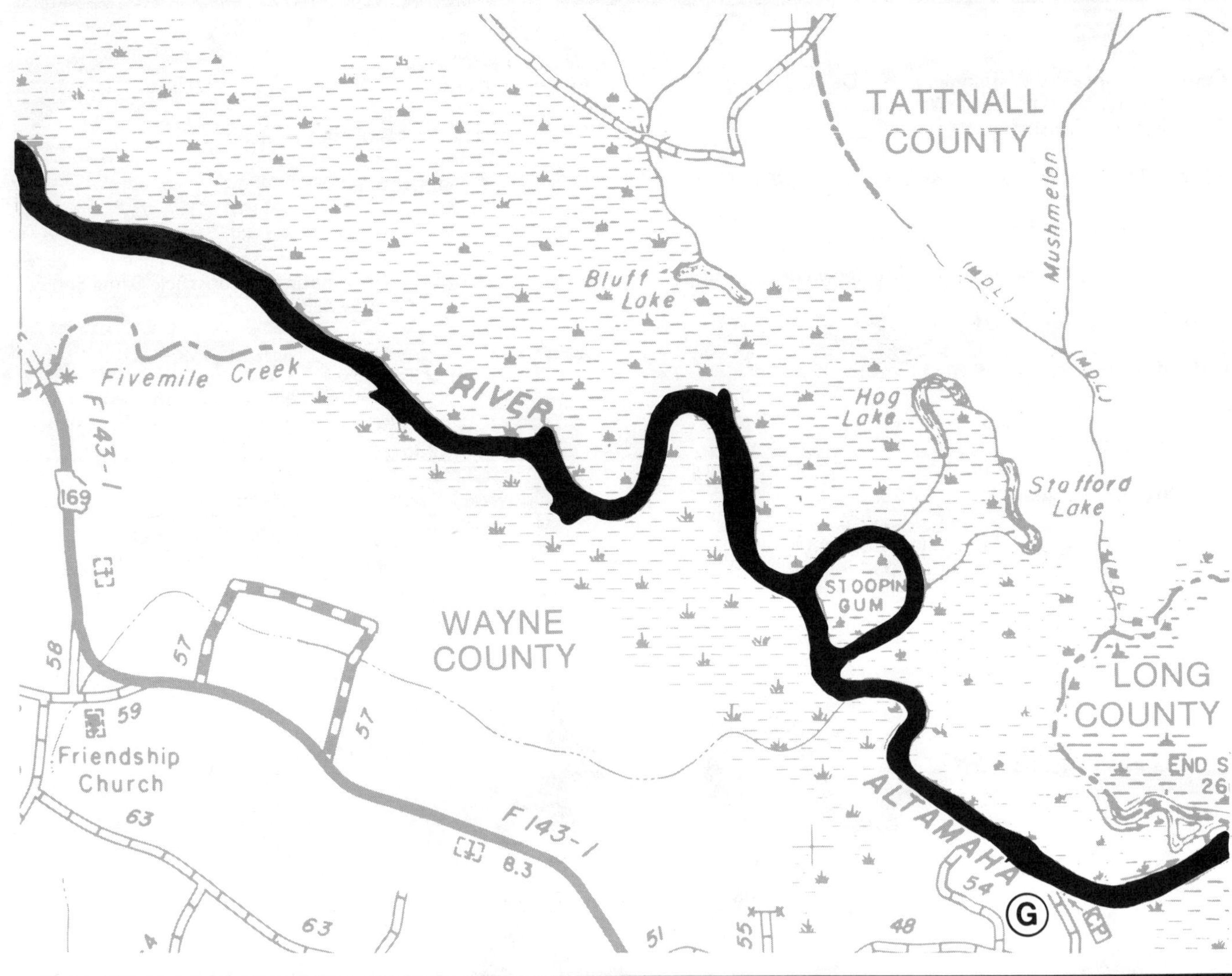

Section: US 221 to Jesup

Counties: Wheeler, Montgomery, Jeff Davis, Toombs, Appling, Tattnall, Long, Wayne
Suitable For: Cruising, camping

Appropriate For: Families, beginners, intermediates, advanced
Months Runnable: All

Interest Highlights: Scenery, wildlife, local culture and industry
Scenery: Beautiful in spots

Difficulty: International Scale I
Numerical Points 4

Average Width: 450-510 ft.
Velocity: Slow to moderate
Gradient: 0.88 ft./mi.

Runnable Water Level: Minimum Not applicable
Maximum Up to high flood stage

Hazards: Powerboats

Scouting: None

Portages: None

Rescue Index: Accessible but difficult

Mean Water Temperature (°F)

Jan 50	Feb 51	Mar 55	Apr 64	May 73	Jun 81
Jul 85	Aug 84	Sep 80	Oct 69	Nov 61	Dec 53

Source of Additional Information: Brunswick Game and Fish Office (912) 264-7237

Access Point	Access Code
A	2357
B	2357
C	1357
D	2357
E	2357
F	1368
G	2357
H	1367
I	13579
J	1357

Access Key
1 Paved Road
2 Unpaved Road
3 Short Carry
4 Long Carry
5 Easy Grade
6 Steep Incline
7 Clear Trail
8 Brush and Trees
9 Launching Fee Charged
10 Private Property, Need Permission
11 No Access, Reference Only

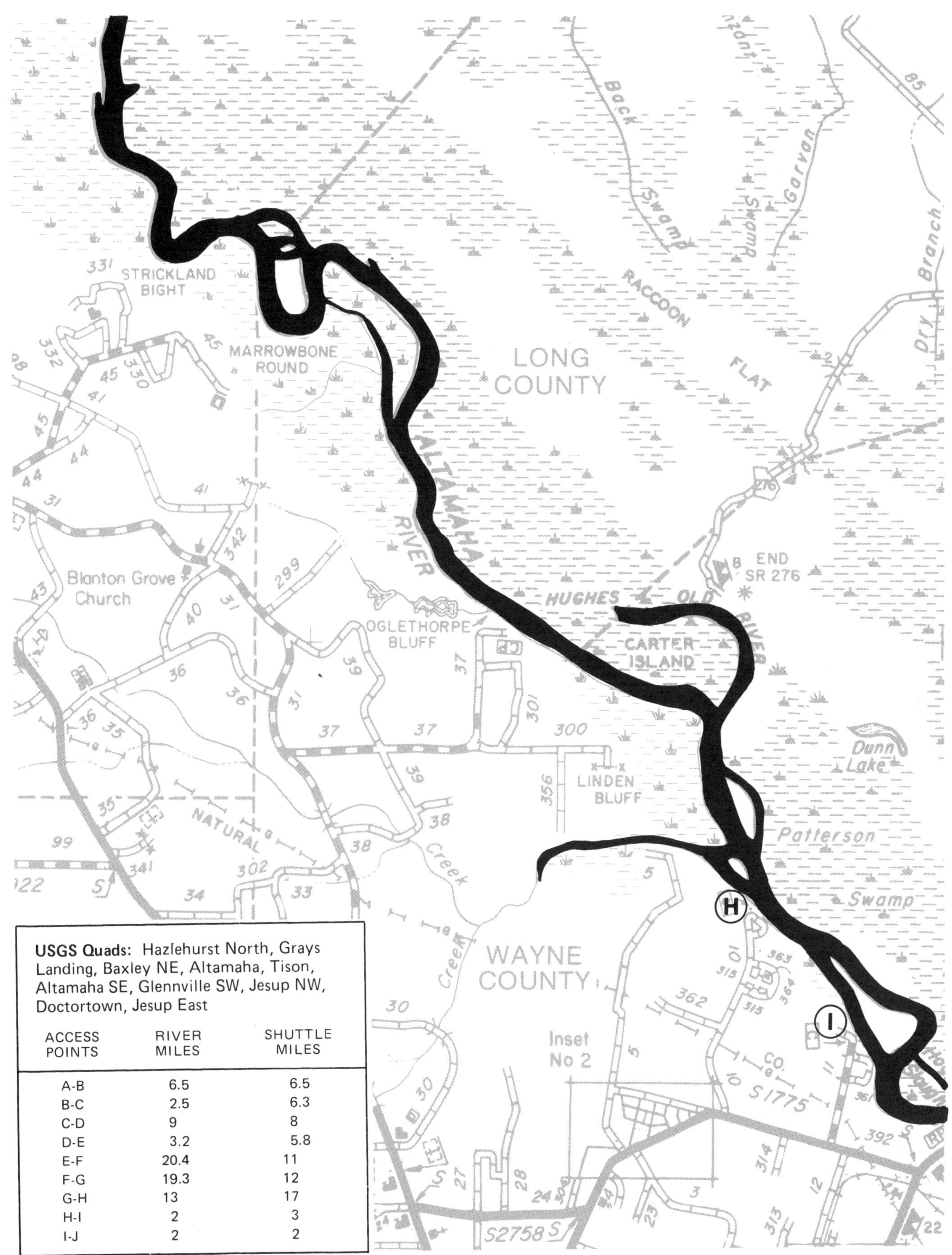

USGS Quads: Hazlehurst North, Grays Landing, Baxley NE, Altamaha, Tison, Altamaha SE, Glennville SW, Jesup NW, Doctortown, Jesup East

ACCESS POINTS	RIVER MILES	SHUTTLE MILES
A-B	6.5	6.5
B-C	2.5	6.3
C-D	9	8
D-E	3.2	5.8
E-F	20.4	11
F-G	19.3	12
G-H	13	17
H-I	2	3
I-J	2	2

Altamaha River—*Continued*

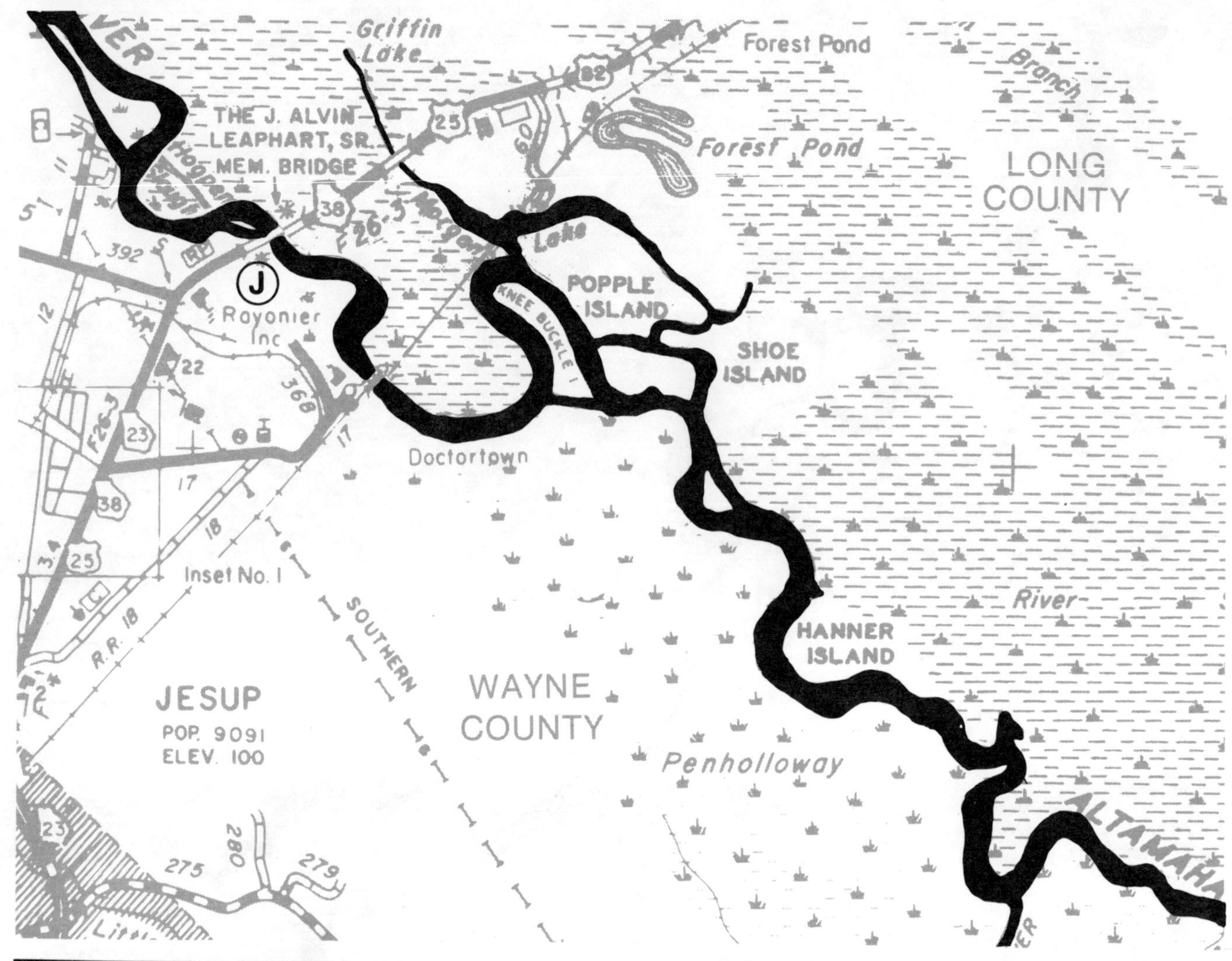

Section: Jesup to Altamaha Sound (Darien)

Counties: Wayne, Long, McIntosh, Glynn

Suitable For: Cruising, camping

Appropriate For: Families, beginners, intermediates, advanced

Months Runnable: All

Interest Highlights: Scenery, wildlife, local culture and industry

Scenery: Beautiful in spots

Difficulty: International Scale I
Numerical Points 4

Average Width: 510-610 ft.
Velocity: Slow to moderate
Gradient: 0.71 ft./mi.

Runnable Water Level: Minimum Not applicable
Maximum Up to high flood stage

Hazards: Powerboats, tidal effects, getting lost in surrounding swamps

Scouting: None

Portages: None

Rescue Index: Accessible but difficult

Mean Water Temperature (°F)

Jan 51	Feb 53	Mar 57	Apr 63	May 72	Jun 80
Jul 83	Aug 82	Sep 75	Oct 70	Nov 63	Dec 54

Source of Additional Information: Brunswick Game and Fish Office (912) 264-7237

Access Point	Access Code
J	1357
K	1357
L	2357

Access Key
1 Paved Road
2 Unpaved Road
3 Short Carry
4 Long Carry
5 Easy Grade
6 Steep Incline
7 Clear Trail
8 Brush and Trees
9 Launching Fee Charged
10 Private Property, Need Permission
11 No Access, Reference Only

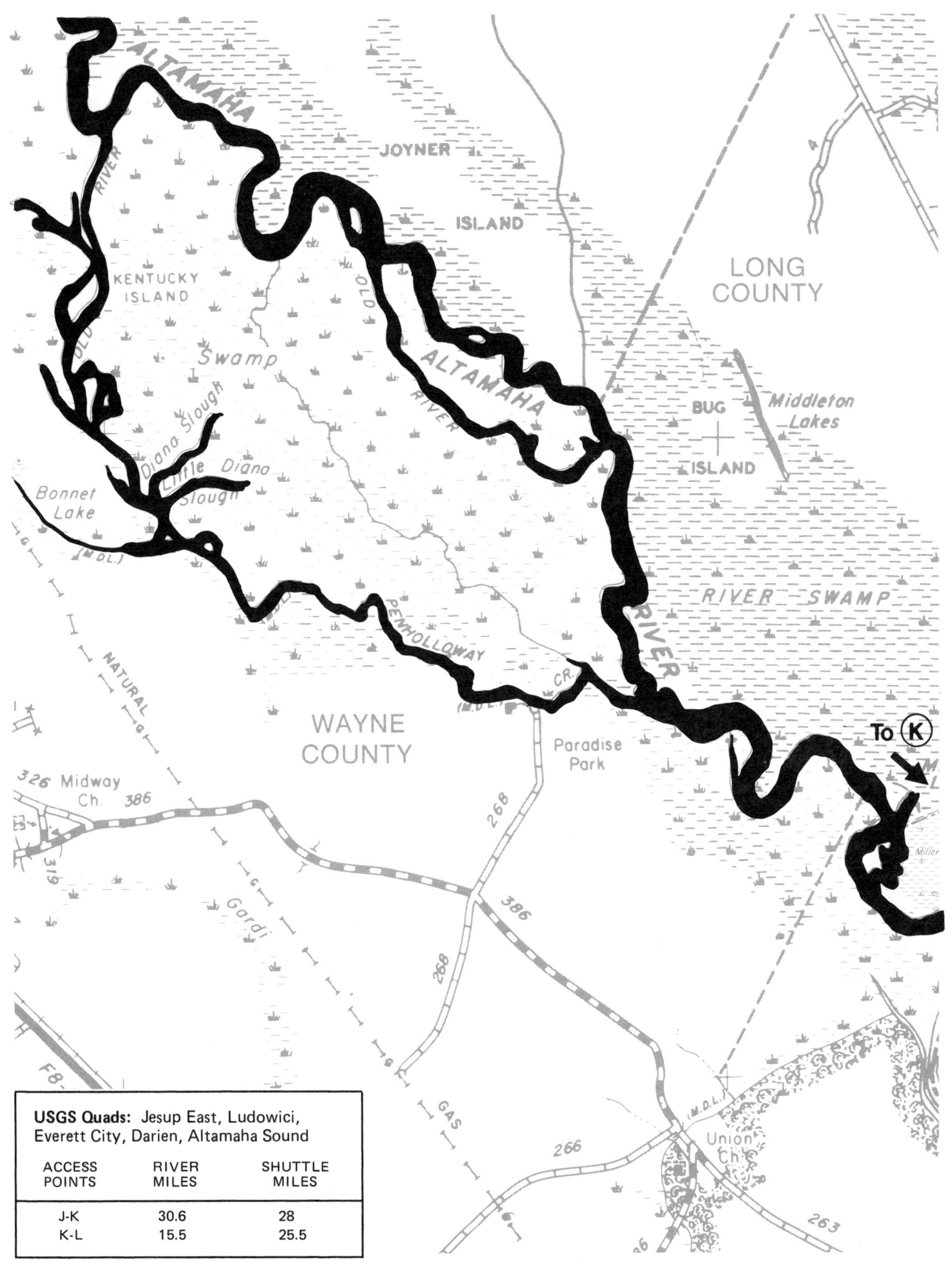

USGS Quads: Jesup East, Ludowici, Everett City, Darien, Altamaha Sound

ACCESS POINTS	RIVER MILES	SHUTTLE MILES
J-K	30.6	28
K-L	15.5	25.5

Altamaha River—*Continued*

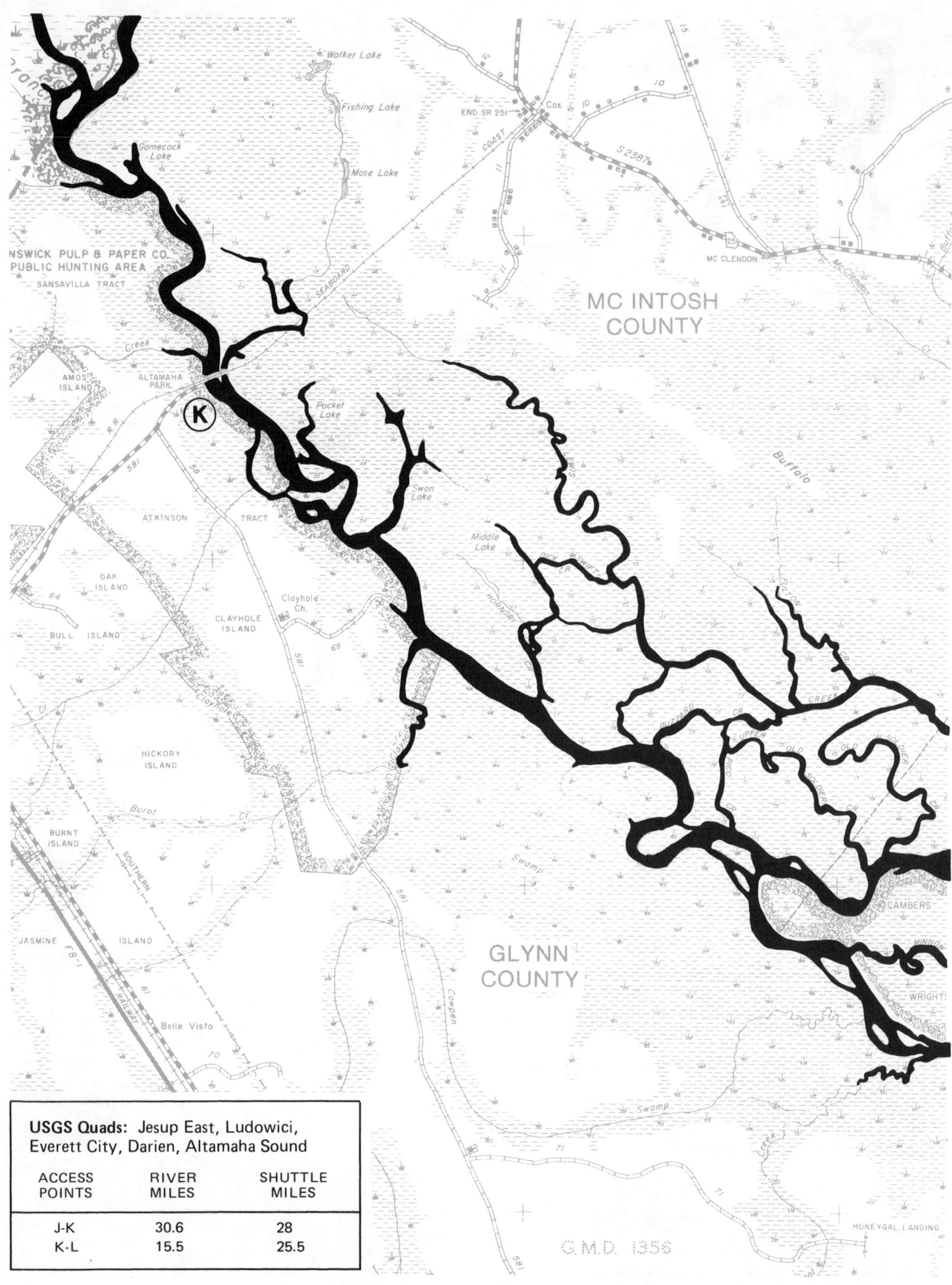

USGS Quads: Jesup East, Ludowici, Everett City, Darien, Altamaha Sound

ACCESS POINTS	RIVER MILES	SHUTTLE MILES
J-K	30.6	28
K-L	15.5	25.5

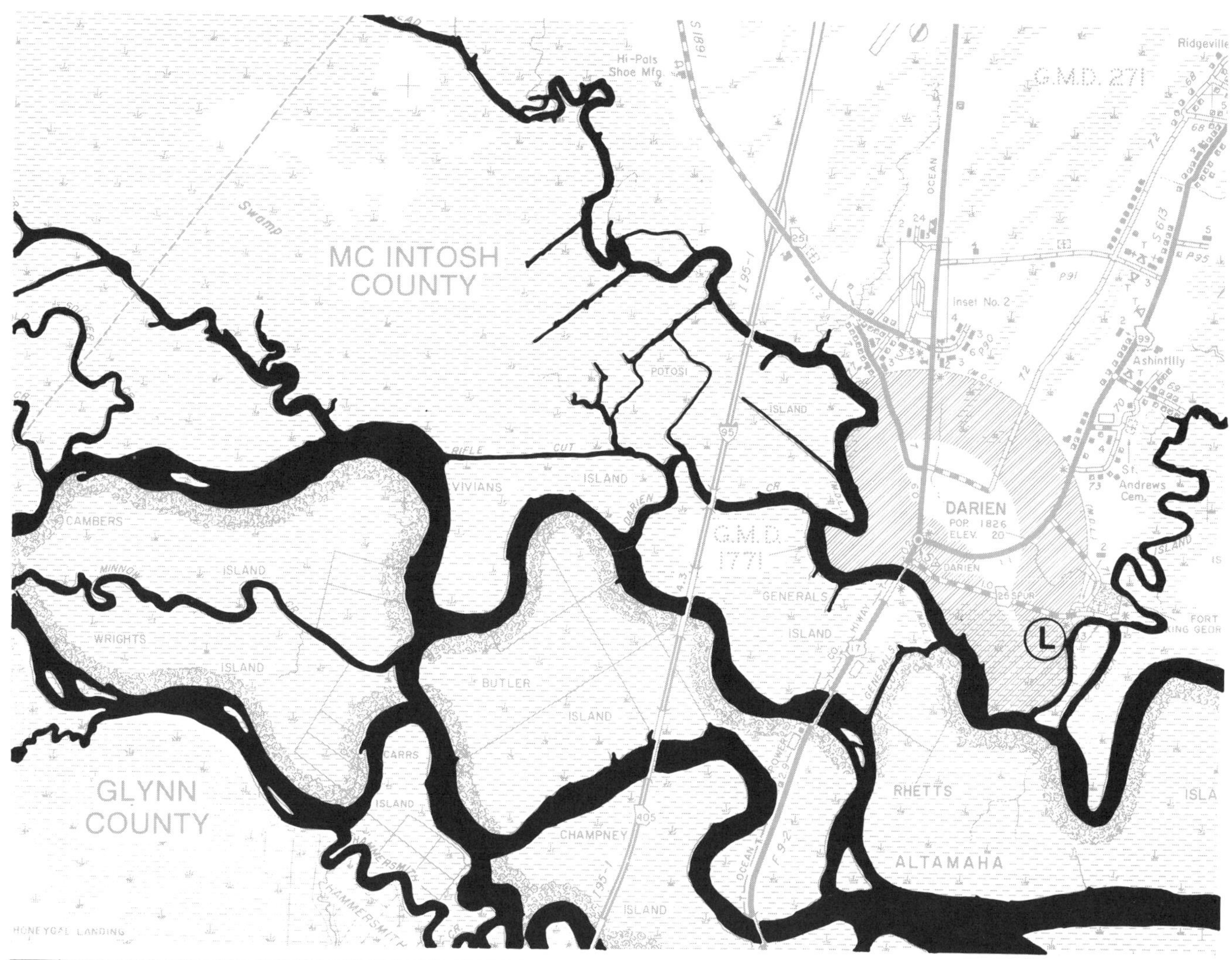

Section: Jesup to Altamaha Sound (Darien)

Counties: Wayne, Long, McIntosh, Glynn

Suitable For: Cruising, camping

Appropriate For: Families, beginners, intermediates, advanced
Months Runnable: All

Interest Highlights: Scenery, wildlife, local culture and industry
Scenery: Beautiful in spots

Difficulty: International Scale I
Numerical Points 4

Average Width: 510-610 ft.
Velocity: Slow to moderate
Gradient: 0.71 ft./mi.

Runnable Water Level: Minimum Not applicable
Maximum Up to high flood stage

Hazards: Powerboats, tidal effects, getting lost in surrounding swamps

Scouting: None

Portages: None

Rescue Index: Accessible but difficult

Mean Water Temperature (°F)

Jan 51	Feb 53	Mar 57	Apr 63	May 72	Jun 80
Jul 83	Aug 82	Sep 75	Oct 70	Nov 63	Dec 54

Source of Additional Information: Brunswick Game and Fish Office (912) 264-7237

Access Point	Access Code
J	1357
K	1357
L	2357

Access Key
1 Paved Road
2 Unpaved Road
3 Short Carry
4 Long Carry
5 Easy Grade
6 Steep Incline
7 Clear Trail
8 Brush and Trees
9 Launching Fee Charged
10 Private Property, Need Permission
11 No Access, Reference Only

Alabaha River

The Alabaha River originates in Jeff Davis County and flows southeastward through Bacon and Pierce counties before emptying into the Satilla River. A diminutive blackwater stream with a gum–cypress dominated floodplain, the Alabaha flows between banks of two to eight feet in height under a thick, tree canopy. Runnable below the GA 15 bridge except in the late summer and fall, the Alabaha is similar to the Satilla in flora, wildlife, and topography, but it is less convoluted in its course. The level of difficulty is Class I with a rare deadfall being the only hazard to navigation. Access is good and extended trips onto the Satilla are possible after reaching the mouth of the Alabaha. Like the Satilla, the Alabaha flows in a wooded swamp corridor sometimes penetrated by pine forests and agricultural development. The river's current is slow to moderate.

Clark Hill Dam, Savannah River.

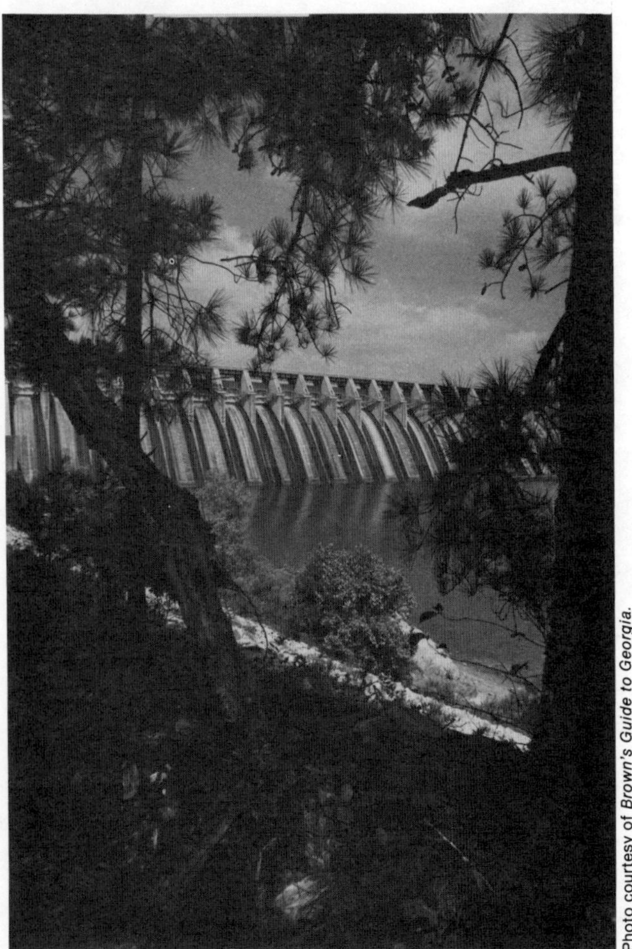

Photo courtesy of *Brown's Guide to Georgia.*

Section: North of Blackshear to Satilla River

Counties: Pierce

Suitable For: Cruising

Appropriate For: Families, beginners, intermediates, advanced

Months Runnable: November through mid-July

Interest Highlights: Scenery, wildlife

Scenery: Beautiful

Difficulty: International Scale I
Numerical Points 3

Average Width: 35-50 ft.
Velocity: Slow to moderate
Gradient: 1.77 ft./mi.

Runnable Water Level: Minimum 125 cfs
Maximum Up to flood stage

Hazards: Deadfalls

Scouting: None required

Portages: None required

Rescue Index: Accessible to accessible but difficult

Mean Water Temperature (°F)

Jan 52	Feb 53	Mar 57	Apr 66	May 74	Jun 80
Jul 82	Aug 80	Sep 76	Oct 68	Nov 60	Dec 54

Source of Additional Information: Waycross Game and Fish Office (912) 285-6093

Access Point	Access Code
A	1357
B	1357
C	2357
N[1]	2357

Access Key
1 Paved Road
2 Unpaved Road
3 Short Carry
4 Long Carry
5 Easy Grade
6 Steep Incline
7 Clear Trail
8 Brush and Trees
9 Launching Fee Charged
10 Private Property, Need Permission
11 No Access, Reference Only

[1]On the Satilla River

USGS Quads: Blackshear East

ACCESS POINTS	RIVER MILES	SHUTTLE MILES
A-B	2.9	4.5
B-C	4.8	4
C-N	3.6	4

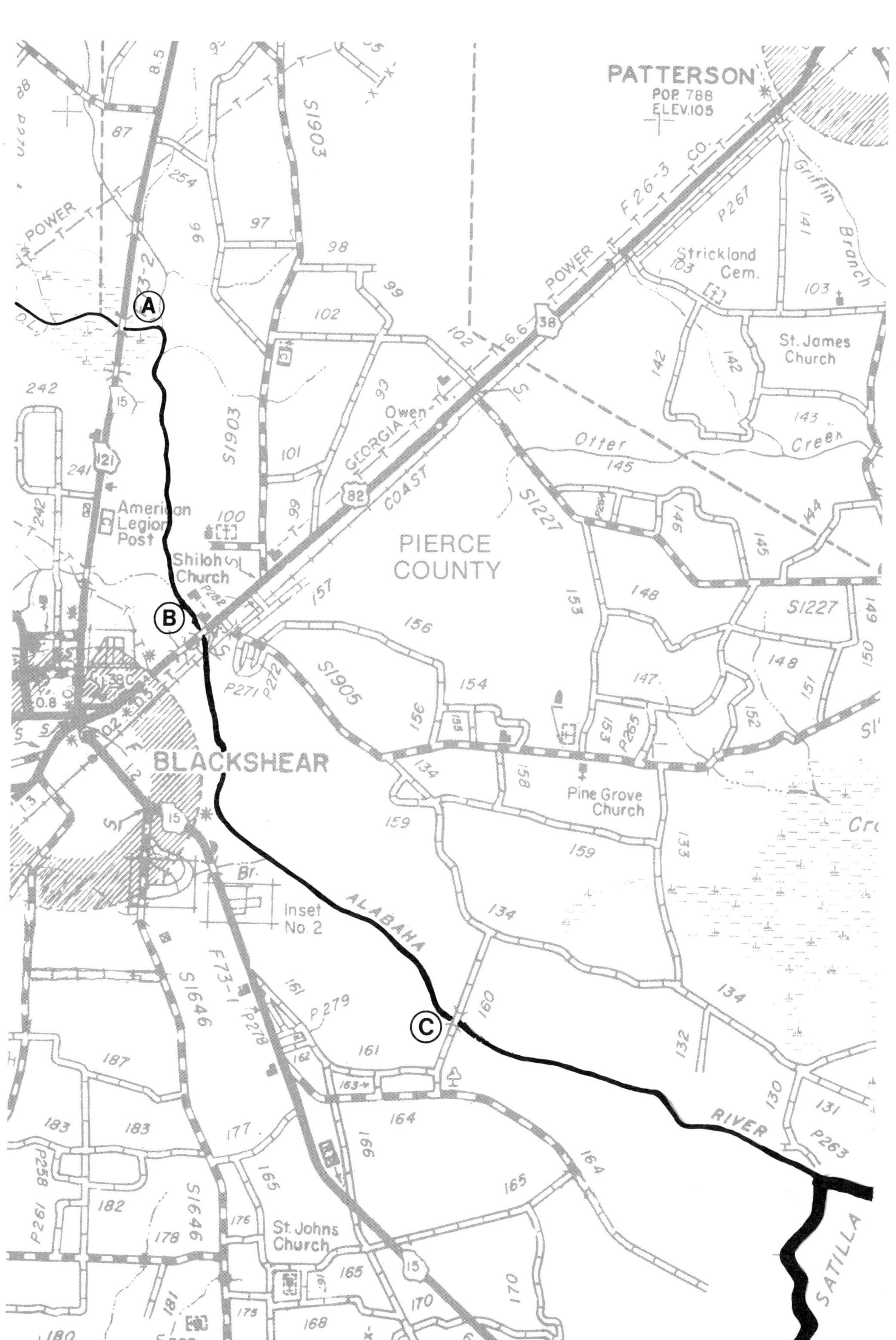

PATTERSON
POP. 788
ELEV. 105
Griffin Branch
Strickland Cem.
St. James Church
Otter Creek
POWER
GEORGIA COAST
Owen
PIERCE COUNTY
American Legion Post
Shiloh Church
BLACKSHEAR
Pine Grove Church
Inset No. 2
ALABAHA RIVER
St. Johns Church
Enon
SATILLA
A
B
C

Little Satilla River

The Little Satilla River is formed by the confluence of the Big Satilla Creek and Sweetwater Creek (of southeastern Georgia) and flows southeast along the eastern boundary of Pierce County before emptying into the Satilla River.

Runnable from the US 82 bridge to its mouth except in later summer and fall, the Little Satilla averages 45 to 75 feet in width and is confined on both sides by a thick, luxurious swamp forest of swamp black gum, sweet bay, pine, and cypress. Its banks are two to seven feet high and are composed of an off-white sandy clay. Throughout its runnable length the stream is shaded and the banks buffered with a thick undergrowth. Convoluted in its course, its current is slow to moderate and its water color brownish red. Wildlife, especially birds, abound and are easily observed by the quiet paddler. Generally remote and pristine, the river is nevertheless occasionally penetrated by agricultural development. Small bluffs grace the streamside from time to time and provide good highwater camping areas. Unlike the Satilla River, white sandbars are not to be found on the Little Satilla.

The level of difficulty is Class I throughout with occasional deadfalls being the only hazard to navigation. Areas of special interest include the Little Satilla Wildlife Management Area, which encompasses the stream between the US 82 and GA 32 bridge crossings. Access is good and trips on the Little Satilla can be extended beyond its mouth onto the Satilla River.

Section: East of Patterson to Satilla River

Counties: Pierce, Appling, Wayne, Brantley

Suitable For: Cruising, camping

Appropriate For: Families, beginners, intermediates, advanced
Months Runnable: November through mid-July

Interest Highlights: Scenery, wildlife, local culture and industry
Scenery: Beautiful

Difficulty: International Scale I
Numerical Points 4

Average Width: 50-65 ft.
Velocity: Slow to moderate
Gradient: 1.22 ft./mi.

Runnable Water Level: Minimum 190 cfs
Maximum Up to high flood stage

Hazards: Deadfalls

Scouting: None required

Portages: None required

Rescue Index: Accessible but difficult

Mean Water Temperature (°F)

Jan 52	Feb 54	Mar 58	Apr 66	May 74	Jun 79
Jul 82	Aug 80	Sep 75	Oct 67	Nov 60	Dec 54

Source of Additional Information: Waycross Game and Fish Office (912) 285-6093

Access Point	Access Code
A	1357
B	1457
C	2357
D	1357
R[1]	2357

Access Key
1 Paved Road
2 Unpaved Road
3 Short Carry
4 Long Carry
5 Easy Grade
6 Steep Incline
7 Clear Trail
8 Brush and Trees
9 Launching Fee Charged
10 Private Property, Need Permission
11 No Access, Reference Only

[1]On the Satilla River

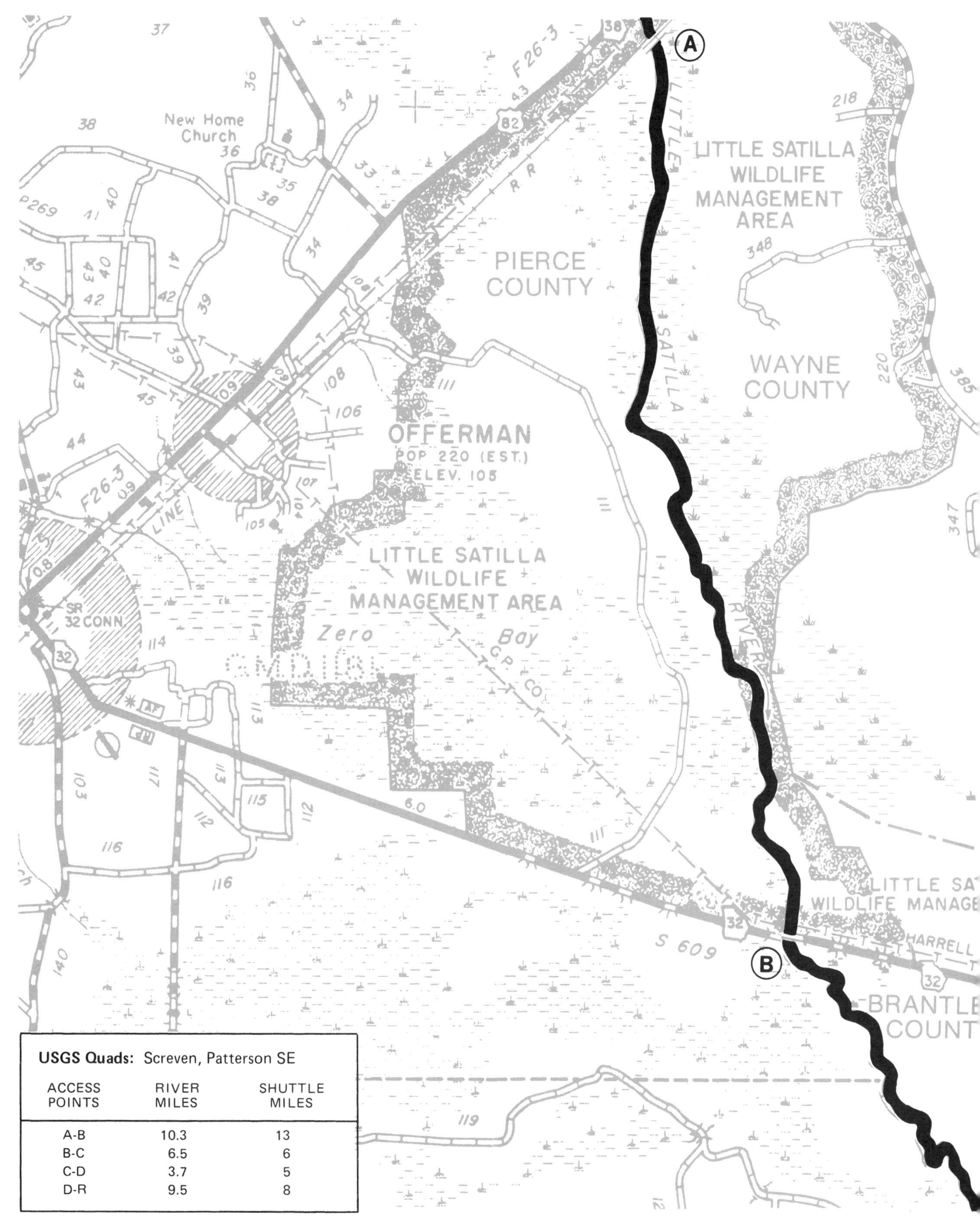

USGS Quads: Screven, Patterson SE

ACCESS POINTS	RIVER MILES	SHUTTLE MILES
A-B	10.3	13
B-C	6.5	6
C-D	3.7	5
D-R	9.5	8

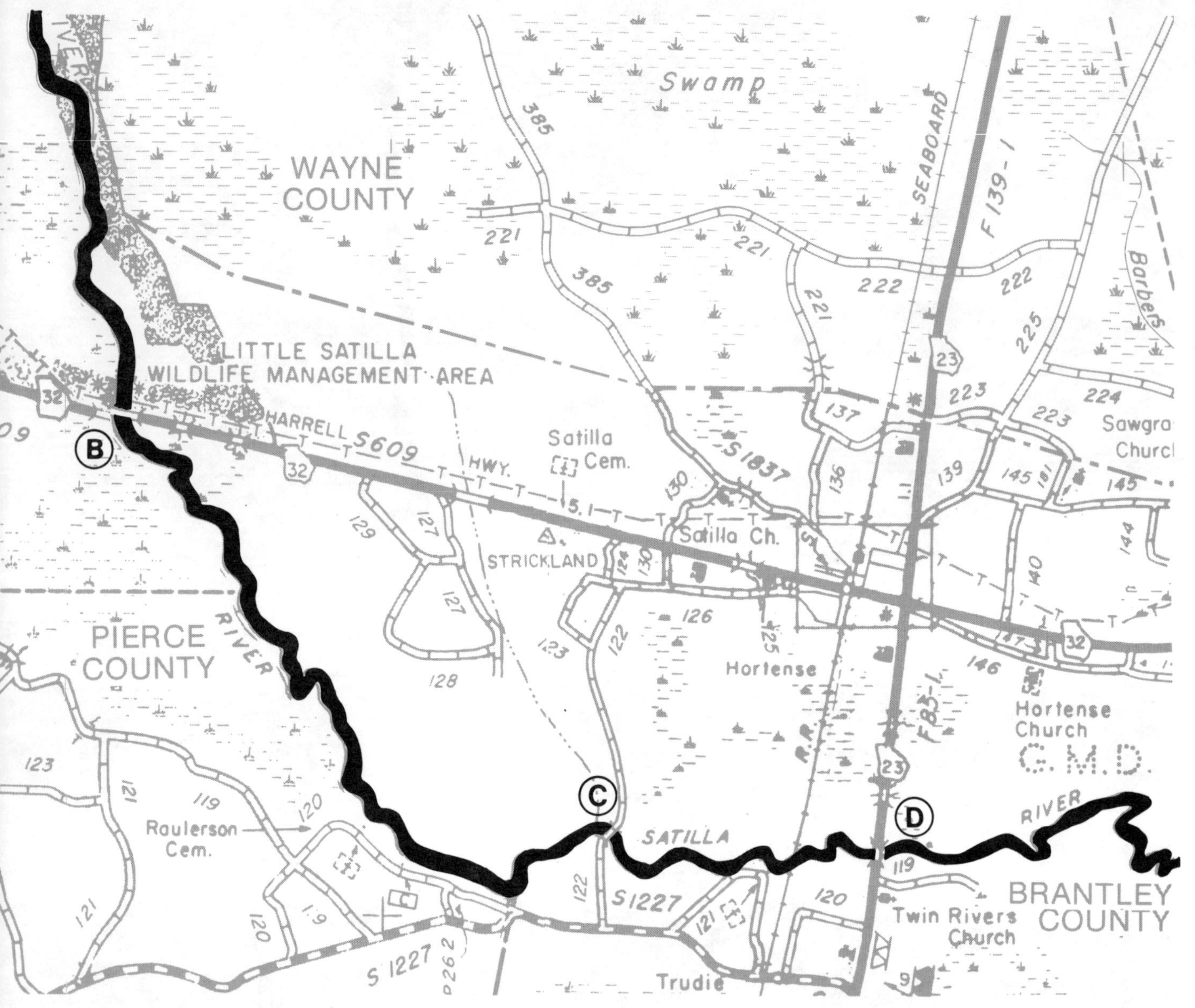
Swamp
WAYNE COUNTY
LITTLE SATILLA WILDLIFE MANAGEMENT AREA
HARRELL S609 HWY.
Satilla Cem.
STRICKLAND
Satilla Ch.
SEABOARD
PIERCE COUNTY
RIVER
Hortense
Hortense Church
G.M.D.
Sawgra
Church
Barbers
Raulerson Cem.
SATILLA
RIVER
BRANTLEY COUNTY
Twin Rivers Church
Trudie
B
C
D

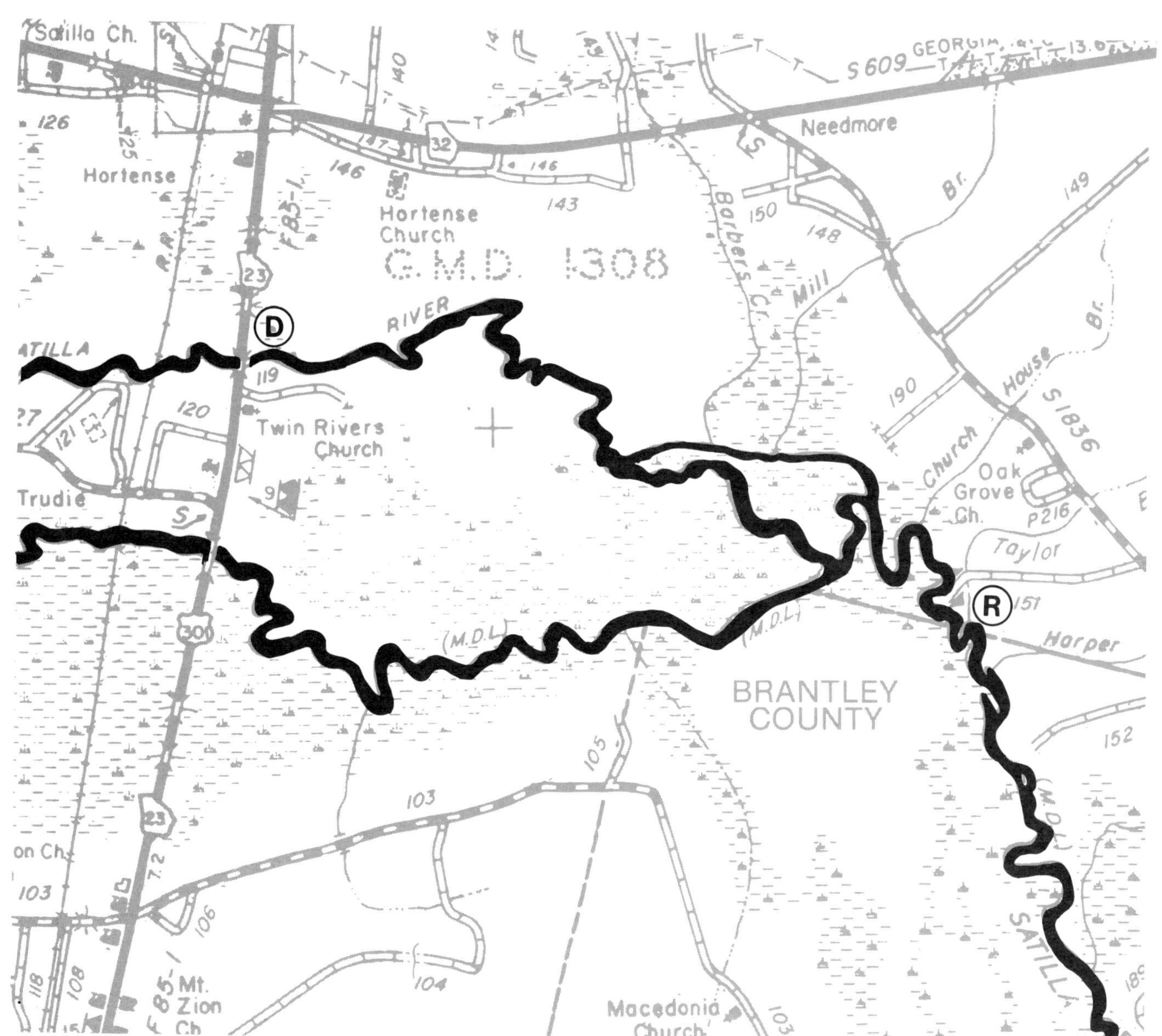

USGS Quads: Screven, Patterson SE

ACCESS POINTS	RIVER MILES	SHUTTLE MILES
A-B	10.3	13
B-C	6.5	6
C-D	3.7	5
D-R	9.5	8

Satilla River

The Satilla River is born on the south side of the Ocmulgee River divide in Ben Hill County and flows southeast passing just north of Waycross and the Okefenokee Swamp before looping south to its mouth at St. Andrew Sound where the Satilla empties into the Atlantic Ocean. On its journey to the sea, the Satilla drains portions of twelve Coastal Plain counties and forms the largest blackwater river system situated entirely in Georgia.

With waters stained a burgundy red by tannic acid from decaying vegetation, the Satilla winds between white sand banks one to eight feet high with sandy bluffs and the taller commercial pine forest plateau towering over the stream from time to time. Dignified and tranquil in its slow pace and remote beauty, the Satilla oozes along beneath an umbrella of pine, swamp black gum, water oak, laurel oak, sweet bay, and majestic cypress. Undergrowth is thick and luxurious with swamp cyrilla and azalea setting the river aflame with color in the early spring. Glistening white sandbars occupy the insides of turns and provide resting spots for the traveler while birds, animals, and reptiles hurry about their business in the swamp.

Although many acres have been reclaimed from the swamp for commercial pine planting, the river, cradled neatly by a wet bottomland forest corridor, remains pristine in appearance if not in fact. Since

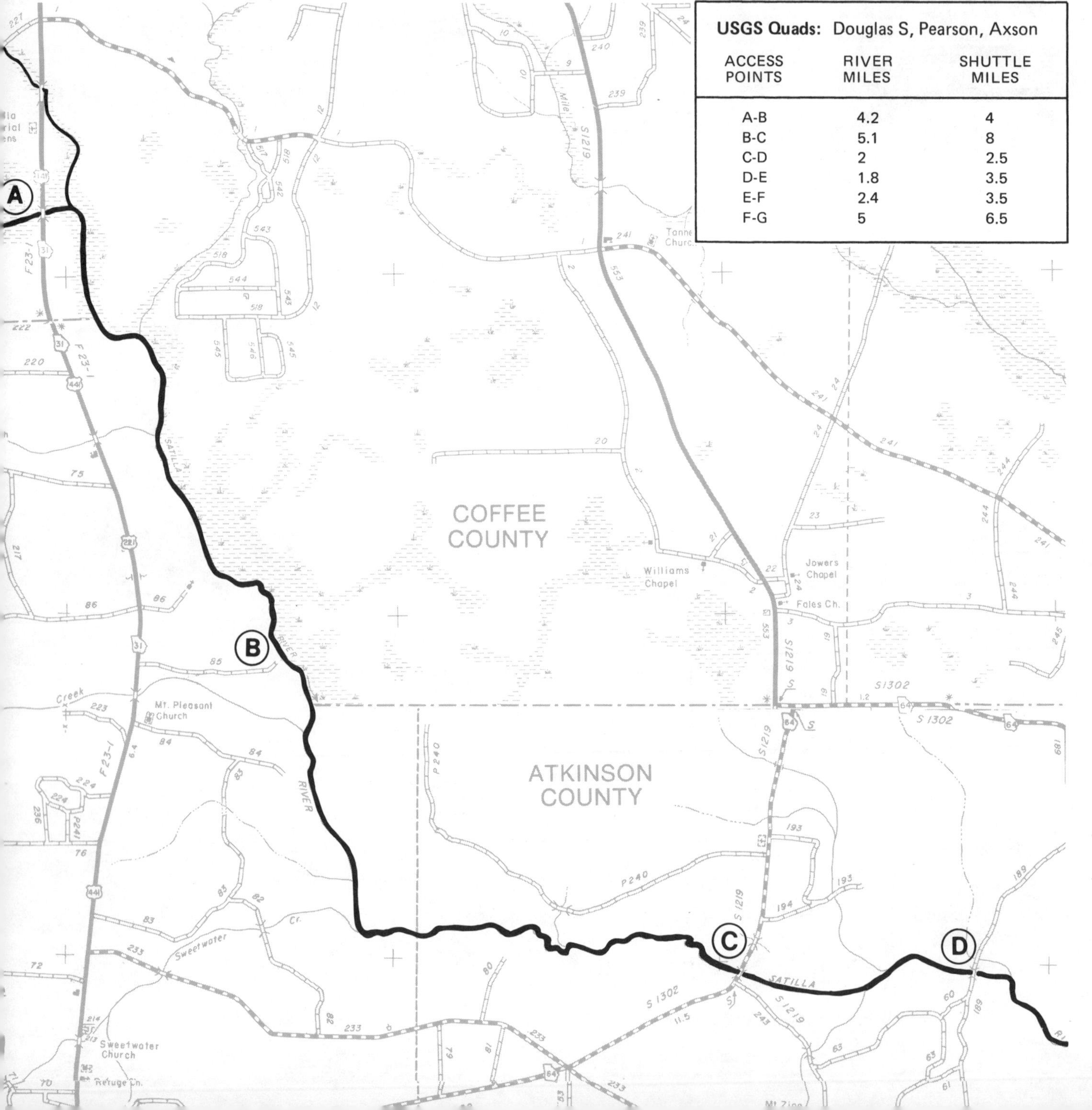

USGS Quads: Douglas S, Pearson, Axson

ACCESS POINTS	RIVER MILES	SHUTTLE MILES
A-B	4.2	4
B-C	5.1	8
C-D	2	2.5
D-E	1.8	3.5
E-F	2.4	3.5
F-G	5	6.5

Section: North of Pearson to Millwood

Counties: Coffee, Atkinson, Ware

Suitable For: Cruising, camping

Appropriate For: Families, beginners, intermediates, advanced

Months Runnable: Late November to early June

Interest Highlights: Scenery, wildlife

Scenery: Beautiful

Difficulty: International Scale I
Numerical Points 4

Average Width: 55-75 ft.
Gradient: Slow to moderate
Velocity: 1.60 ft./mi.

Runnable Water Level: (Waycross gauge) Minimum 530 cfs
Maximum Up to high flood stage

Hazards: Deadfalls

Scouting: None required

Portages: None required

Rescue Index: Accessible but difficult

Mean Water Temperature (°F)

Jan 51	Feb 54	Mar 59	Apr 67	May 75	Jun 82
Jul 84	Aug 82	Sep 77	Oct 68	Nov 60	Dec 53

Source of Additional Information: Waycross Game and Fish Office (912) 285-6093

Access Point	Access Code
A	1357
B	2357
C	1357
D	2357
E	2357
F	1367
G	2357

Access Key
1 Paved Road
2 Unpaved Road
3 Short Carry
4 Long Carry
5 Easy Grade
6 Steep Incline
7 Clear Trail
8 Brush and Trees
9 Launching Fee Charged
10 Private Property, Need Permission
11 No Access, Reference Only

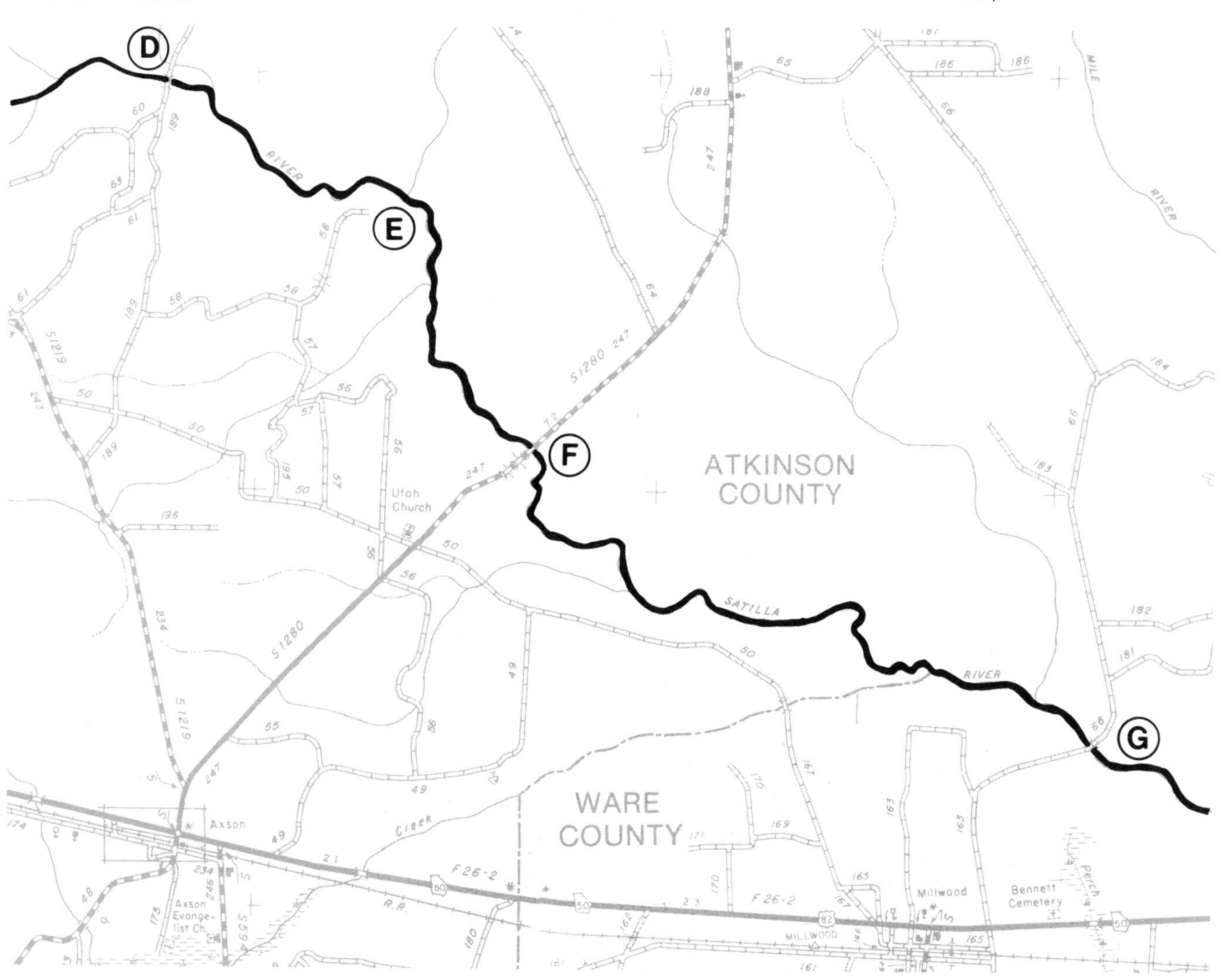

Satilla River—*Continued*

the area is favored by sportsmen, boat ramps are not uncommon and fishing camps are frequently encountered along the Satilla's course.

The Satilla is runnable below US 441 during the winter and spring and below the US 82 bridge east of Waycross most of the year. In Atkinson County the Satilla flows in a straighter course than in Ware County and below. Also, as the river enters Ware County, the characteristic white sandbars begin to materialize. Passing under the GA 158 bridge in Ware County, a rather barren strip of cultivated table land parallels the Satilla for about a mile before the stream again slips back into the wooded corridor. Throughout the environs of Waycross, open farm fields intrude on the privacy of the river. Below the GA 4 bridge the Satilla broadens to 55 to 80 feet and wriggles out from under its tree canopy to some extent. As the river flows along the Pierce–Brantley county line below the GA 121 bridge, local agriculture again becomes visible and the white sandbars become rare.

Below the mouth of the Little Satilla the white sandbars once again become prevalent, as do horseshoe loops, by-pass islands, and oxbow lakes, particularly where the river flows near Nahunta. The Satilla continues to broaden and reaches a width of 110 to 130 feet before passing into Camden County. Flowing along the Charlton–Camden county line, the wilderness hides any sign of civilization as immense woodland swamps settle in and the Satilla widens to 180–210 feet. Tall sandy bluffs offer high-ground camping above the GA 252 bridge, and the ruins of Burnt Fort, a pre-Revolutionary era bastion, make an interesting side trip. Below the GA 252 bridge tidal effects come into play with grassy marsh prairies alternating with bottom forest along the river channel, particularly below the mouth of Armstrong Creek. Below the US 17 bridge at Woodbine to the St. Andrew Sound, access is almost nonexistent and tidal currents tricky. Some sandy bluffs persist in this area but wet marshes, intricate networks of tidal creeks, and saltwater estuaries are the order of the day.

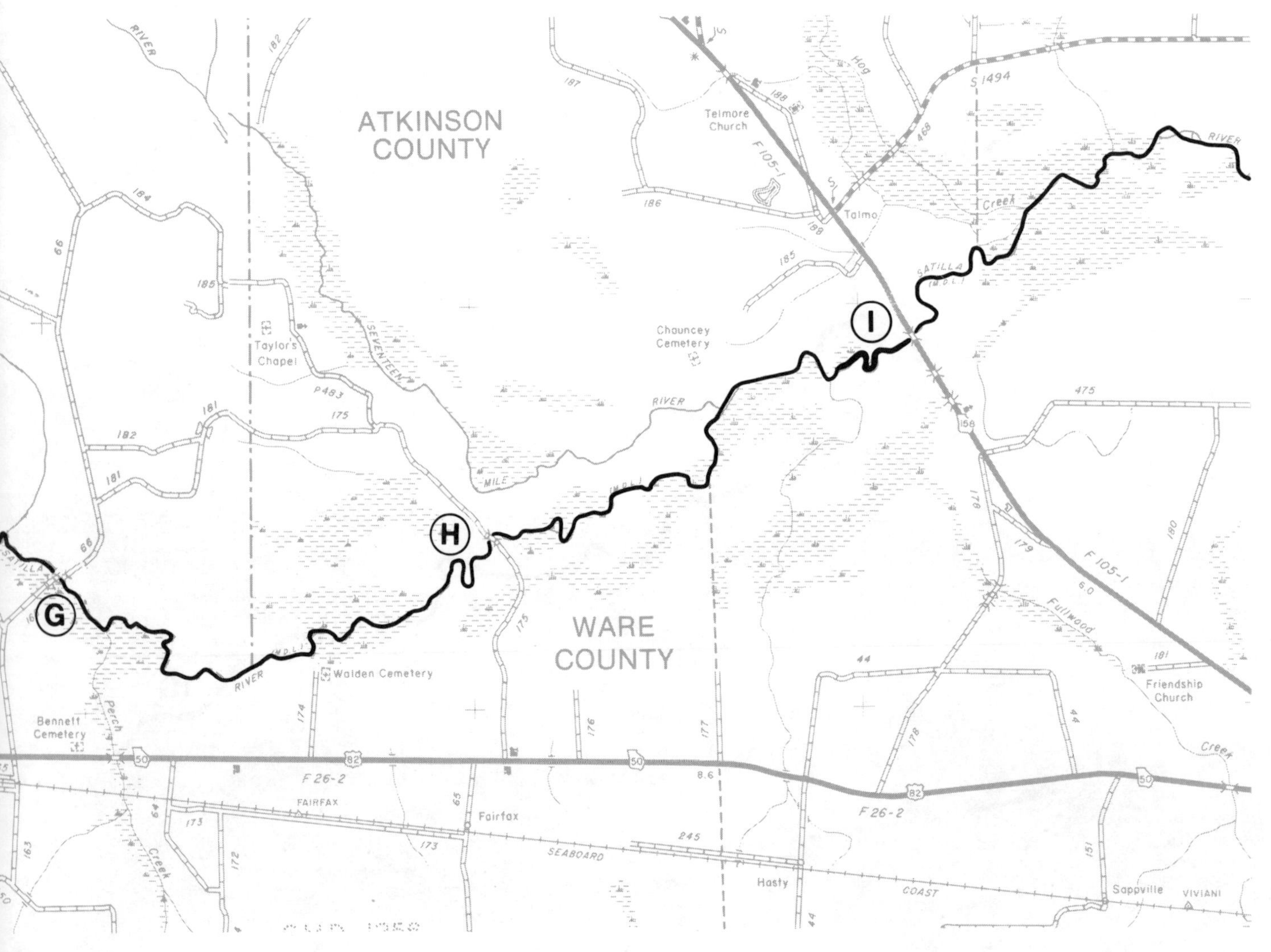

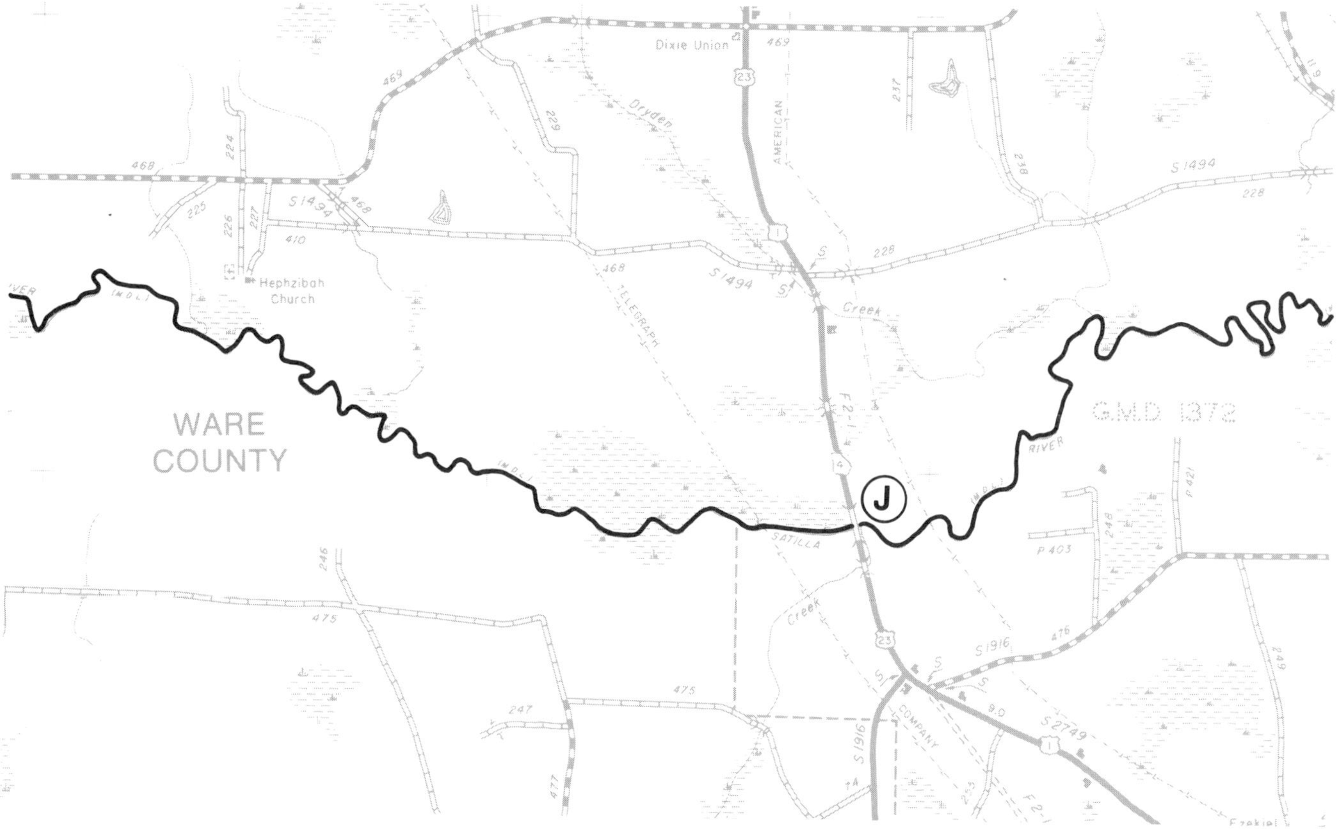

The Satilla is Class I in difficulty throughout and has a slow current. Occasional deadfalls above Waycross and tidal currents near St. Andrew Sound, along with some powerboat traffic in the lower reaches, pose the primary hazards to navigation. Though water levels fluctuate somewhat unpredictably, especially above Waycross, flashflooding is not considered a problem. Campsites, however, should be chosen on bluffs rather than sandbars in the winter and spring.

USGS Quads: Axson, Talmo, Dixie Union, Blackshear W, Waycross E

ACCESS POINTS	RIVER MILES	SHUTTLE MILES
G-H	4.4	6
H-I	4	7
I-J	5	9.5
J-K	11	5
K-L	8.2	9

Altamaha River.

Photo courtesy of *Brown's Guide to Georgia.*

Satilla River—*Continued*

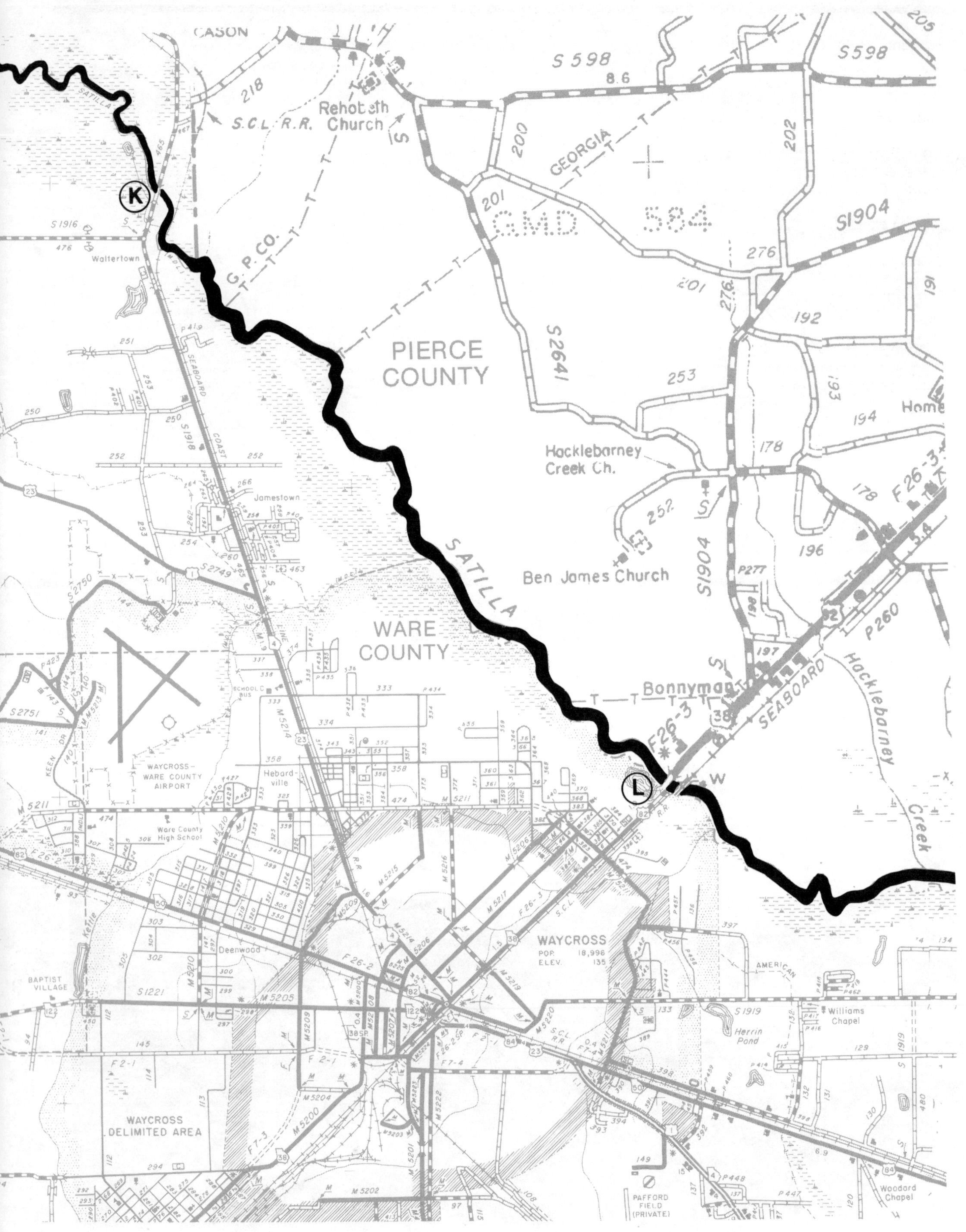

Section: Millwood to Waycross

Counties: Atkinson, Ware, Pierce

Suitable For: Cruising, camping

Appropriate For: Families, beginners, intermediates, advanced

Months Runnable: Late November to early June

Interest Highlights: Scenery, wildlife

Scenery: Beautiful

Difficulty: International Scale I
Numerical Points 4

Average Width: 70-100 ft.
Gradient: Slow to moderate
Velocity: 1.60 ft./mi.

Runnable Water Level: Minimum 530 cfs
(Waycross gauge) Maximum Up to high flood stage

Hazards: Deadfalls

Scouting: None required

Portages: None required

Rescue Index: Accessible but difficult

Mean Water Temperature (°F)

Jan 51	Feb 54	Mar 59	Apr 67	May 75	Jun 82
Jul 84	Aug 82	Sep 77	Oct 68	Nov 60	Dec 53

Source of Additional Information: Waycross Game and Fish Office (912) 285-6093

Access Point	Access Code
G	2357
H	1357
I	1357
J	1357
K	2357
L	1357

Access Key
1 Paved Road
2 Unpaved Road
3 Short Carry
4 Long Carry
5 Easy Grade
6 Steep Incline
7 Clear Trail
8 Brush and Trees
9 Launching Fee Charged
10 Private Property, Need Permission
11 No Access, Reference Only

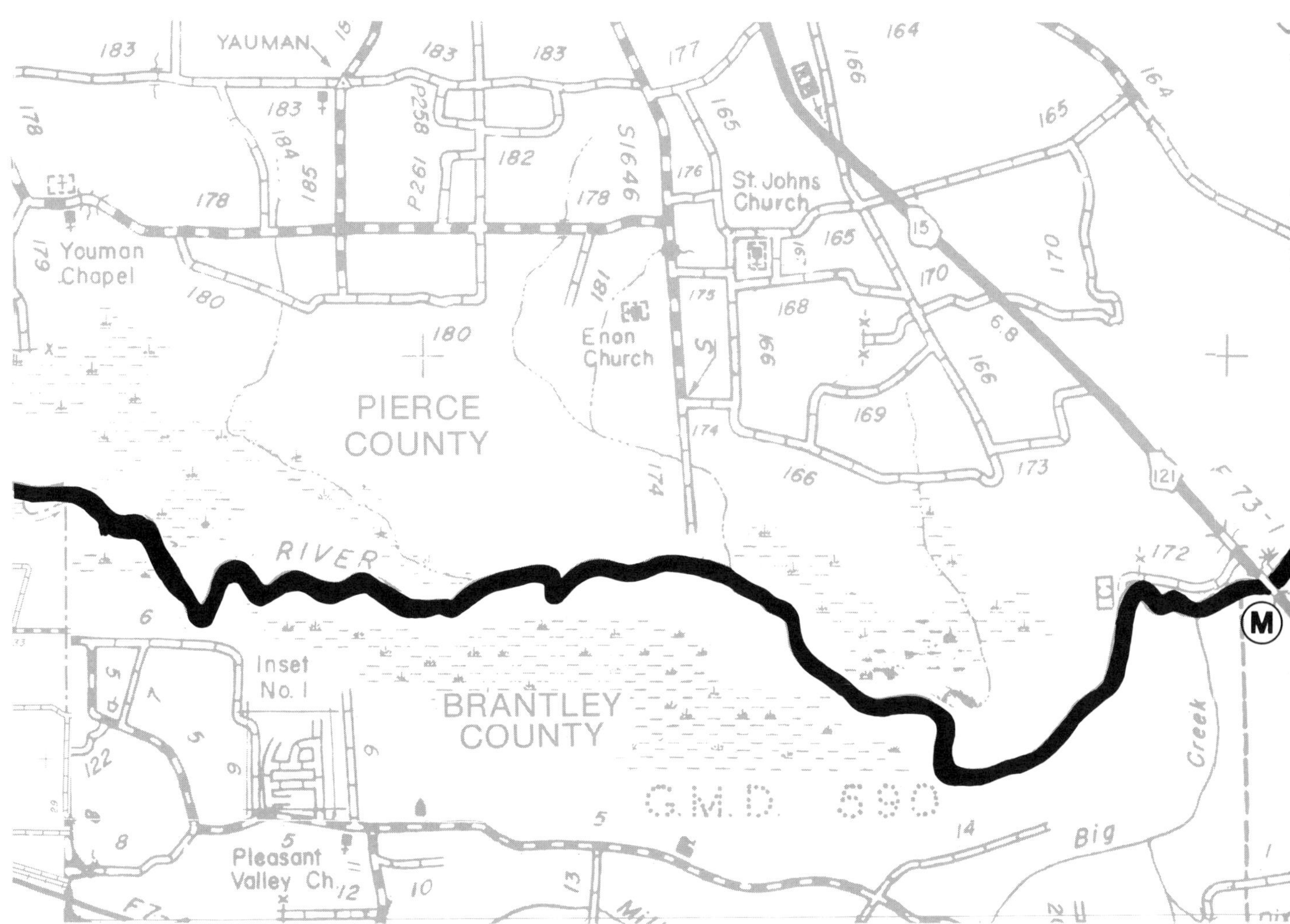

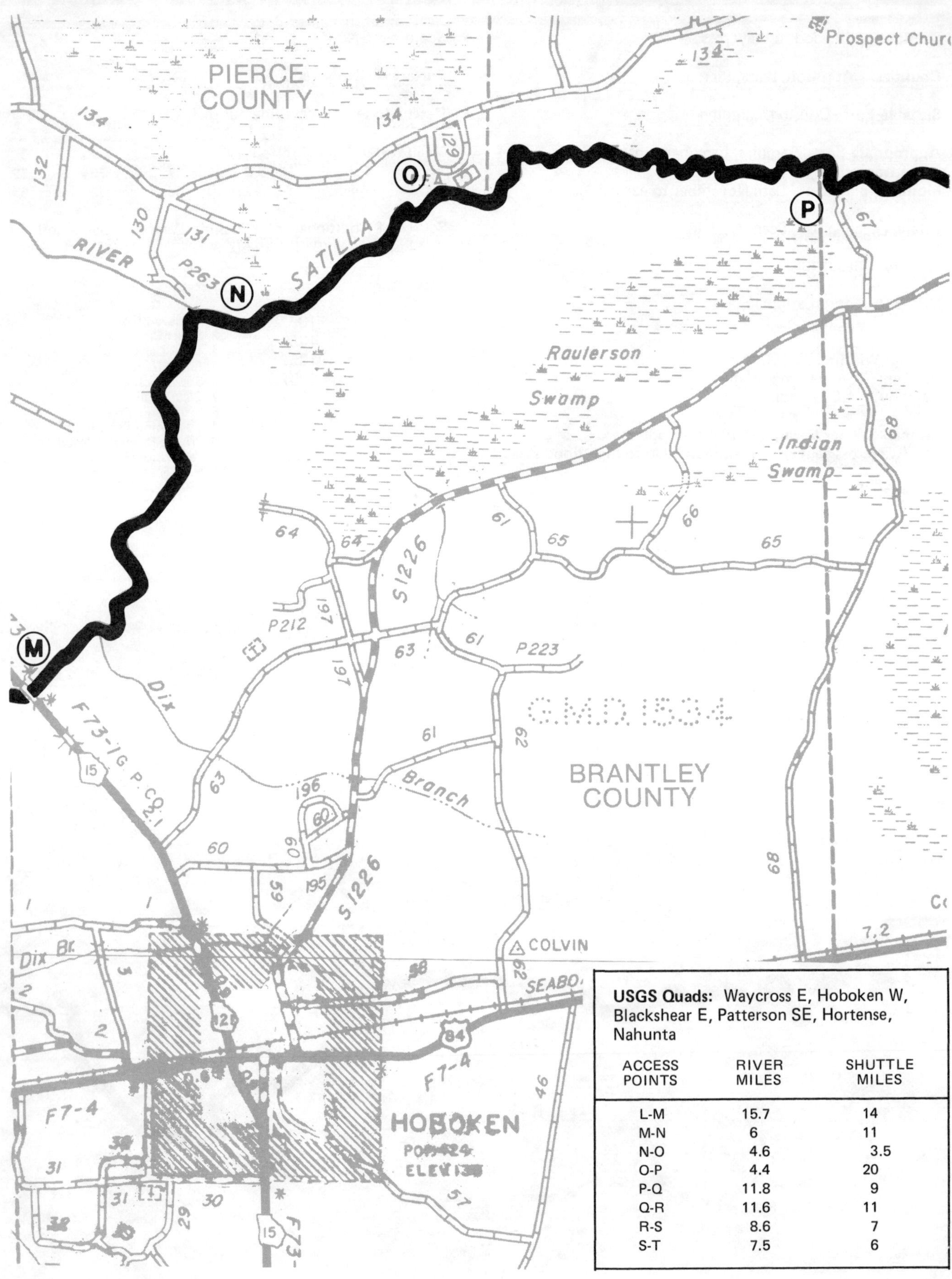

USGS Quads: Waycross E, Hoboken W, Blackshear E, Patterson SE, Hortense, Nahunta

ACCESS POINTS	RIVER MILES	SHUTTLE MILES
L-M	15.7	14
M-N	6	11
N-O	4.6	3.5
O-P	4.4	20
P-Q	11.8	9
Q-R	11.6	11
R-S	8.6	7
S-T	7.5	6

Section: Waycross to Nahunta

Counties: Ware, Pierce, Brantley

Suitable For: Cruising, camping

Appropriate For: Families, beginners, intermediates, advanced

Months Runnable: November to August; all during wet years

Interest Highlights: Scenery, wildlife

Scenery: Beautiful

Difficulty: International Scale I
Numerical Points 4

Average Width: 110-130 ft.
Gradient: Slow to moderate
Velocity: 0.60 ft./mi.

Runnable Water Level: Minimum 530 cfs
(Waycross gauge) Maximum Up to high flood stage

Hazards: Deadfalls

Scouting: None required

Portages: None required

Rescue Index: Accessible but difficult to remote

Mean Water Temperature (°F)

Jan 51	Feb 54	Mar 60	Apr 68	May 76	Jun 82
Jul 84	Aug 83	Sep 77	Oct 69	Nov 61	Dec 53

Source of Additional Information: Waycross Game and Fish Office (912) 285-6093

Access Point	Access Code
L	1357
M	1357
N	2357
O	23579
P	2357
Q	1357
R	2357
S	1357
T	2357

Access Key
1 Paved Road
2 Unpaved Road
3 Short Carry
4 Long Carry
5 Easy Grade
6 Steep Incline
7 Clear Trail
8 Brush and Trees
9 Launching Fee Charged
10 Private Property, Need Permission
11 No Access, Reference Only

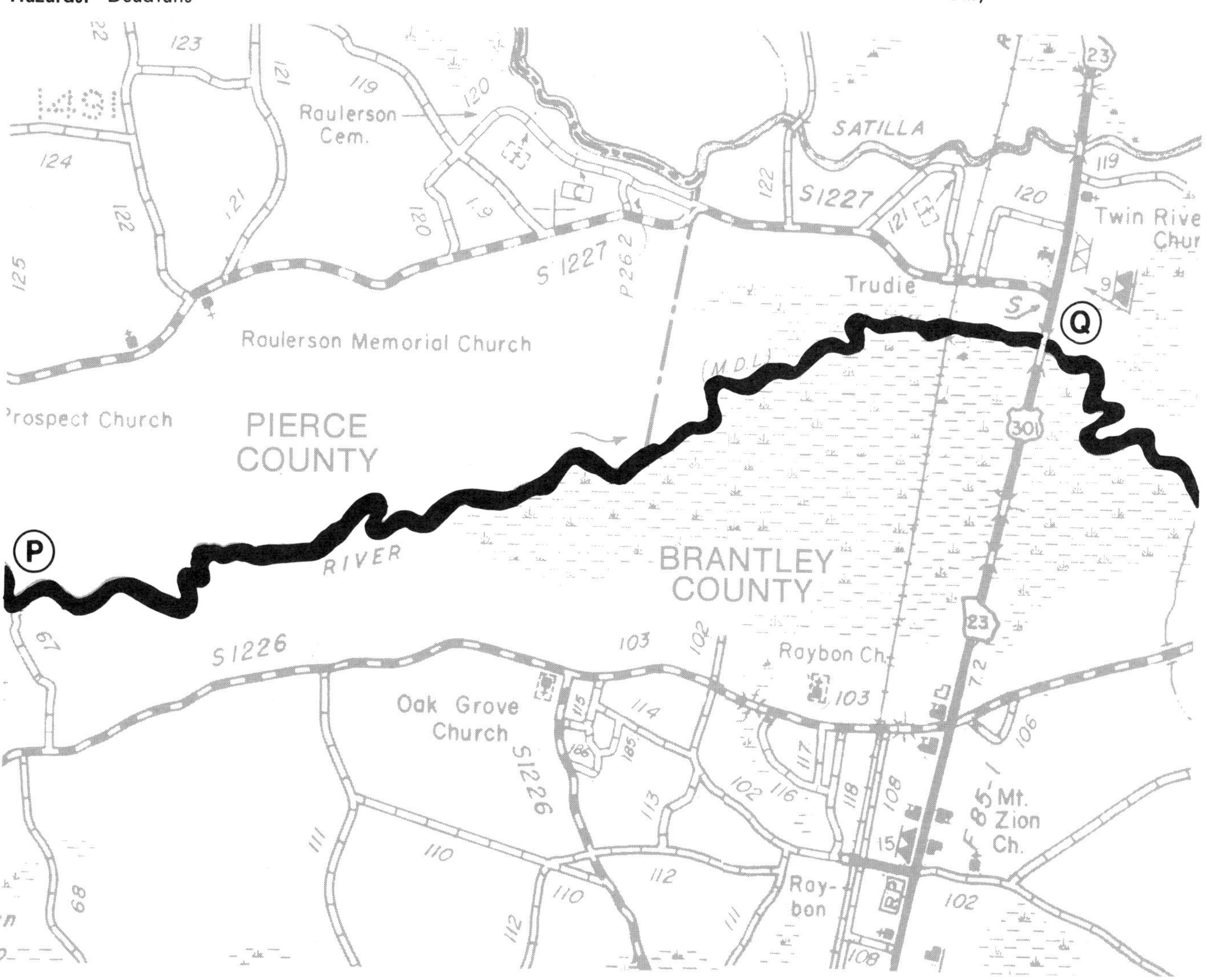

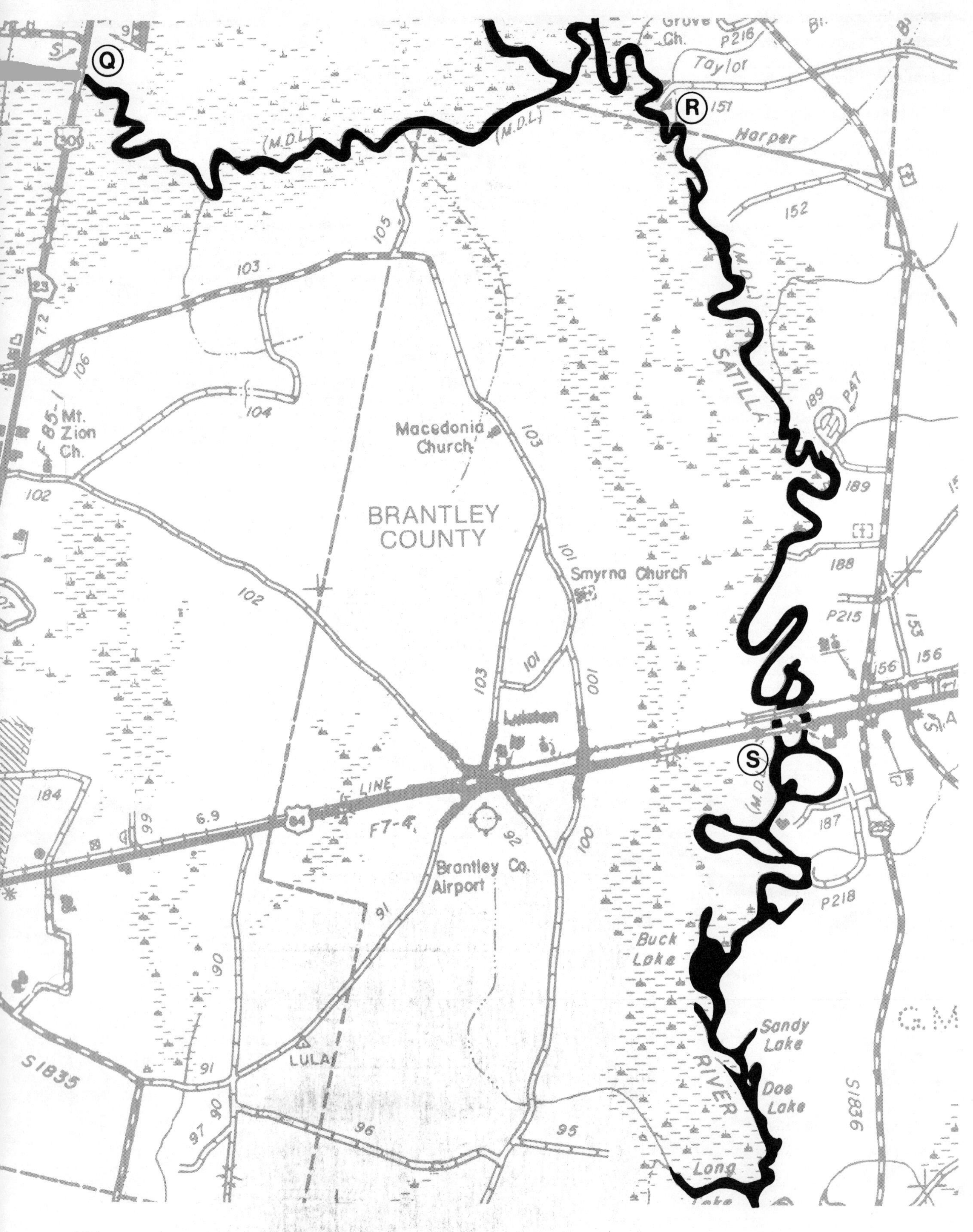
Q
R
S
Taylor
Harper
SATILLA
RIVER
Macedonia Church
BRANTLEY COUNTY
Smyrna Church
Mt. Zion Ch.
Brantley Co. Airport
LULA
Buck Lake
Sandy Lake
Doe Lake
Long
LINE

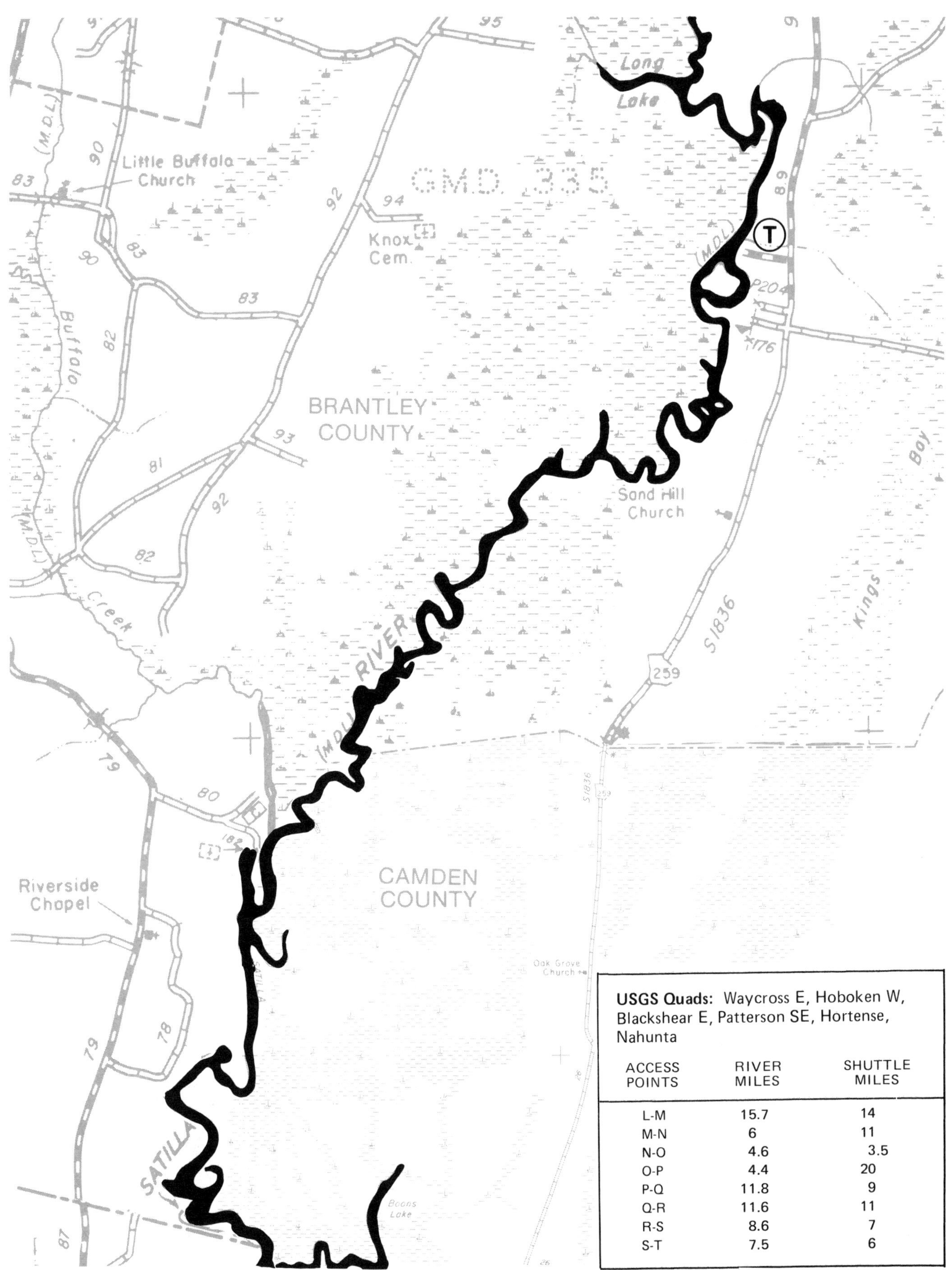

USGS Quads: Waycross E, Hoboken W, Blackshear E, Patterson SE, Hortense, Nahunta

ACCESS POINTS	RIVER MILES	SHUTTLE MILES
L-M	15.7	14
M-N	6	11
N-O	4.6	3.5
O-P	4.4	20
P-Q	11.8	9
Q-R	11.6	11
R-S	8.6	7
S-T	7.5	6

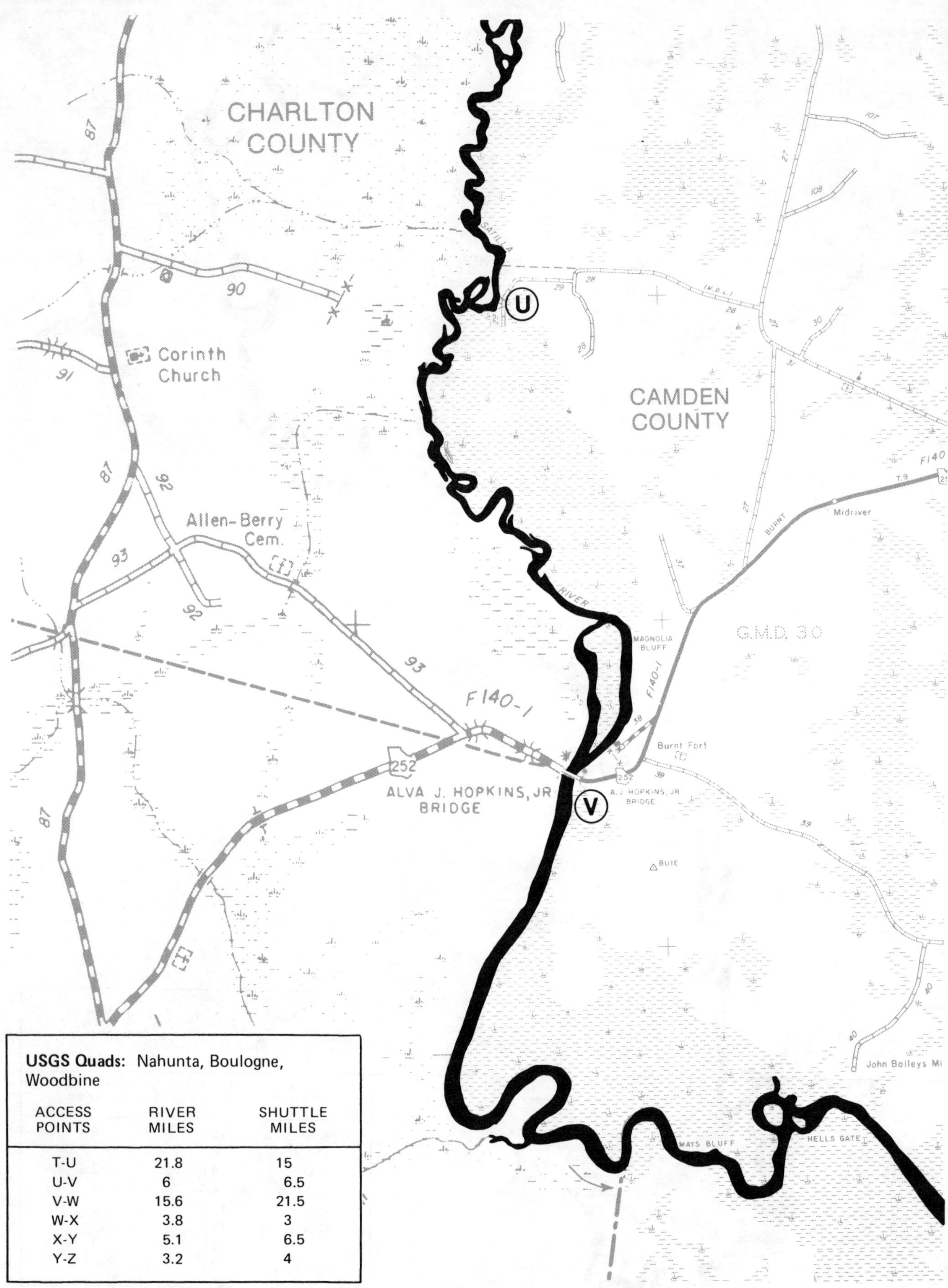

USGS Quads: Nahunta, Boulogne, Woodbine

ACCESS POINTS	RIVER MILES	SHUTTLE MILES
T-U	21.8	15
U-V	6	6.5
V-W	15.6	21.5
W-X	3.8	3
X-Y	5.1	6.5
Y-Z	3.2	4

Tarboro
Jerusalem
Midriver
Owens Ferry
Jefferson
G.M.D. 30
CAMDEN
COUNTY
Clarks
Bluff
Tom Baileys
Mill
Armstrong
Cr.
John Baileys Mill
Tompkins
HELLS GATE
MONFORT
ISLAND
BULLHEAD BLUFF
Rose
Creek
OLD NATIONAL HIGHWAY
X
W

Satilla River—*Continued*

Section: Nahunta to St. Andrew Sound

Counties: Brantley, Charlton, Camden

Suitable For: Cruising, camping

Appropriate For: Families, beginners, intermediates, advanced

Months Runnable: November to August; all during wet years

Interest Highlights: Scenery, wildlife, history (Burnt Fort)

Scenery: Beautiful

Difficulty: International Scale I
Numerical Points 4

Average Width: 180-210 ft.
Gradient: Slow to moderate
Velocity: 0.60 ft./mi.

Runnable Water Level: Minimum 530 cfs
(Waycross gauge) Maximum Up to high flood stage

Hazards: Deadfalls, tidal currents below GA 252, powerboats

Scouting: None required

Portages: None required

Rescue Index: Accessible but difficult to remote

Mean Water Temperature (°F)

Jan 51	Feb 54	Mar 60	Apr 68	May 76	Jun 82
Jul 84	Aug 83	Sep 77	Oct 69	Nov 61	Dec 53

Source of Additional Information: Waycross Game and Fish Office (912) 285-6093

Access Point	Access Code
T	2357
U	2357
V	1357
W	23689
X	23579
Y	1357
Z	1467

Access Key
1 Paved Road
2 Unpaved Road
3 Short Carry
4 Long Carry
5 Easy Grade
6 Steep Incline
7 Clear Trail
8 Brush and Trees
9 Launching Fee Charged
10 Private Property, Need Permission
11 No Access, Reference Only

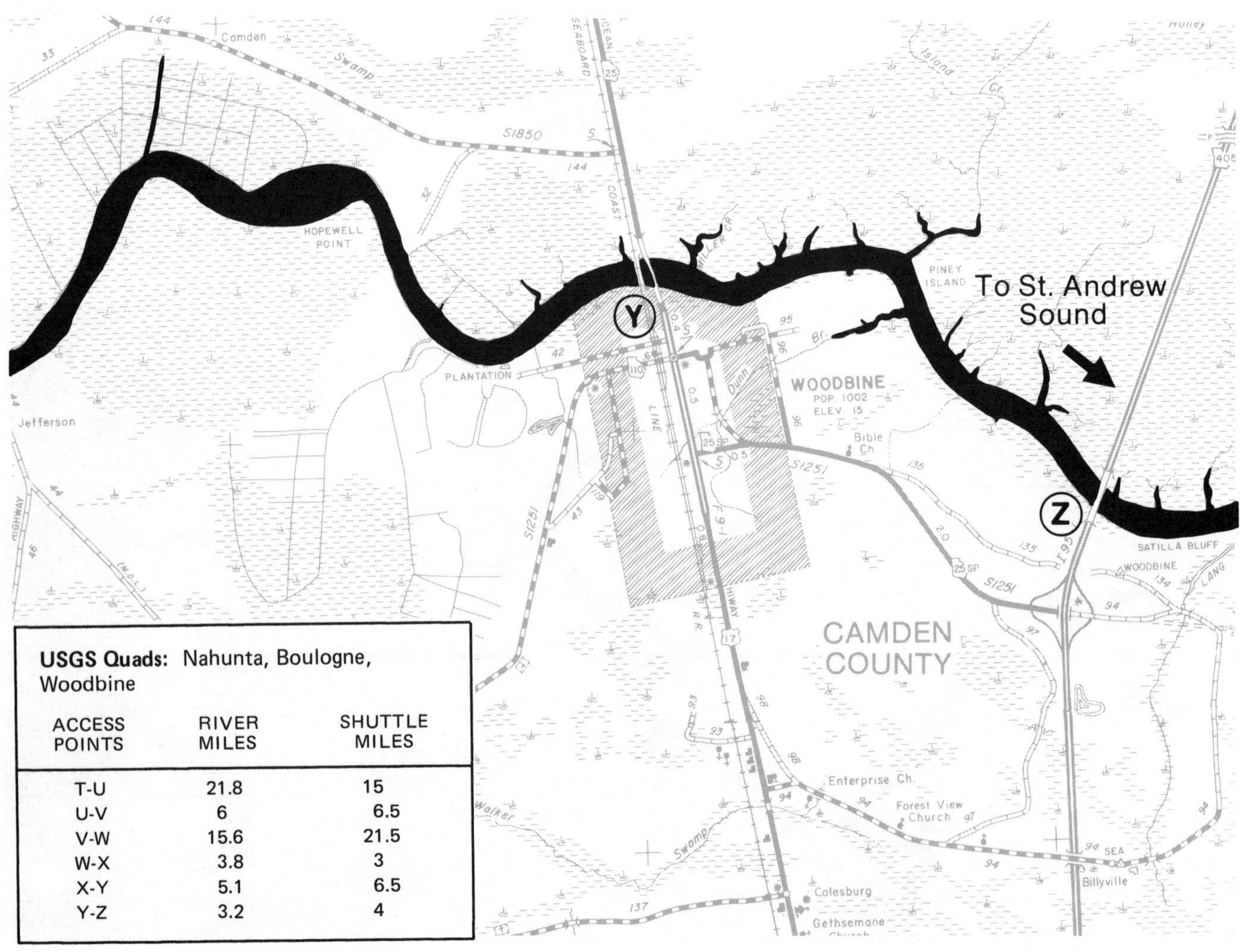

USGS Quads: Nahunta, Boulogne, Woodbine

ACCESS POINTS	RIVER MILES	SHUTTLE MILES
T-U	21.8	15
U-V	6	6.5
V-W	15.6	21.5
W-X	3.8	3
X-Y	5.1	6.5
Y-Z	3.2	4

Tidal marsh and grassland.

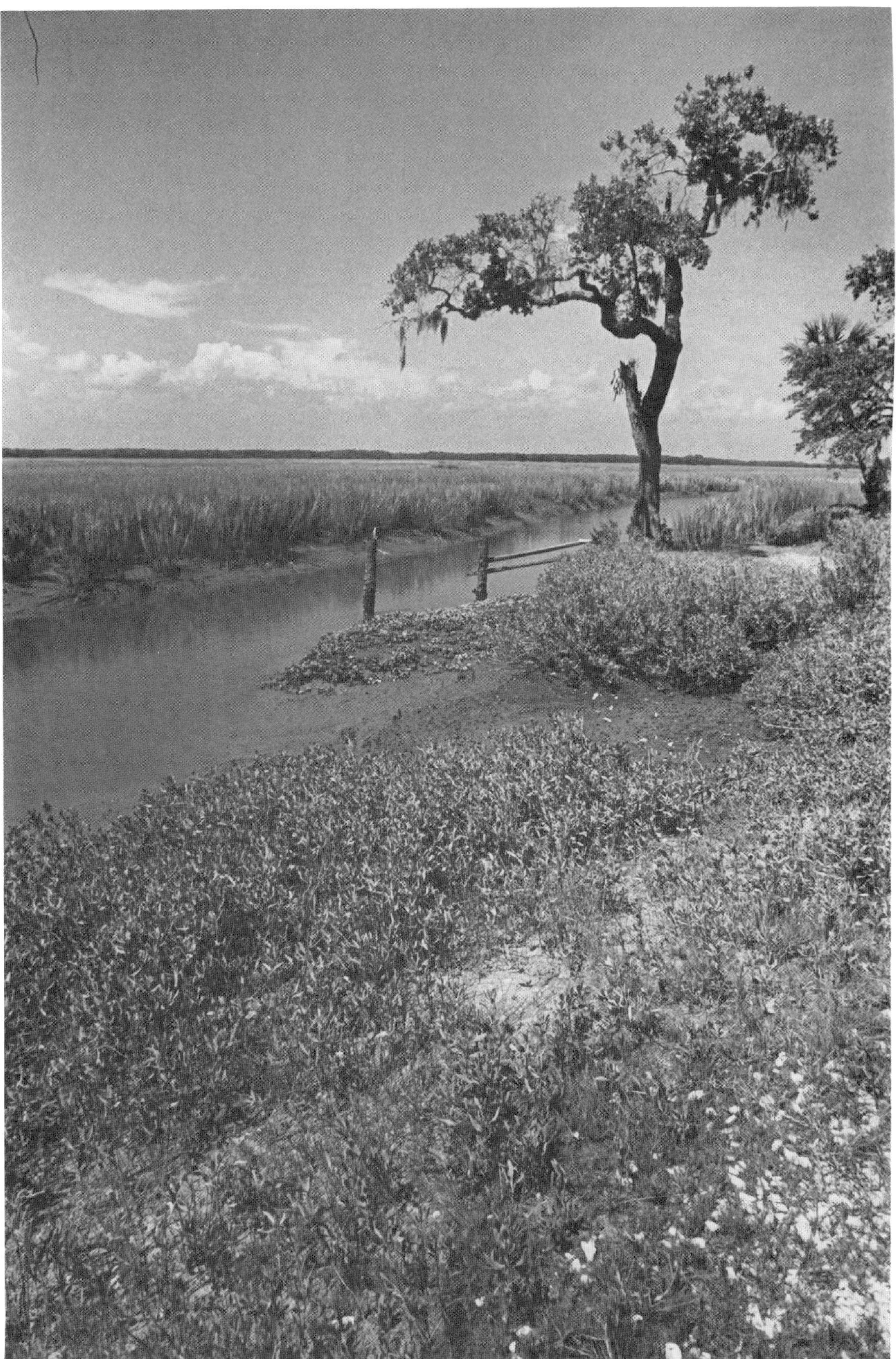

Photo courtesy of *Brown's Guide to Georgia*.

St. Marys River

The St. Marys River comes to life in two neighboring swamps. The North Prong of the St. Marys originates in Ware and Charlton counties (Georgia) in the southeastern bogs of the great Okefenokee Swamp and flows south along the Georgia–Florida state line. The Middle Prong of the St. Marys is born in similar circumstances in Pinhook Swamp in northern Baker County, Florida. Flowing east, the Middle Prong joins the North Prong to form the St. Marys River approximately two miles below the FL 120 bridge crossing.

A stream of beauty and distinction, the St. Marys can be run below the GA 94 bridge crossing on the North Prong. After the river emerges from the Okefenokee swamp under a dense gum–cypress canopy, trees in the channel become less prevalent by the time the river reaches the GA 94 bridge. Averaging 40 to 55 feet, the North Prong gradually settles into a more well-defined channel and becomes more exposed as it nears its confluence with the Middle Prong. Watery wooded swampland extends from both sides of the stream and swamp cyrilla and palmetto vegetate the banks.

When the Middle Prong joins the North Prong the river doubles in width and becomes immediately more winding. White sandbars begin to grace the insides of turns and provide sparkling contrast to the dark, burgundy-red water. Surrounding lowlands seem, on the average, a little drier and pine bluffs begin to intermittently extend to the river's edge.

Below the GA 121 bridge at the bottom of Charlton County the South Prong of the St. Marys enters the stream. This prong, rising completely out of Florida and flowing north, is much smaller than the Middle and North Prongs. In the vicinity of the mouth of the South Prong several small settlements appear along the St. Marys and intrude temporarily on its remote wilderness setting.

Swinging north, the St. Marys remains unspoiled for the most part. It widens slightly and entrenches itself in increasingly steeper banks. Bluffs and pine forests intermix with swamp flora and provide good high-water camp sites. Between St. George and Folkston its banks rise to more than seven feet and are often backed by sandy bluffs standing twenty feet or more above the river and are forested with a mixture of pine and tropical flora. The channel here is deep and well defined and powerboat traffic becomes common in the vicinity of Folkston.

The river's width below Folkston averages 90 to 120 feet but sometimes contracts as intervening bluffs create narrows. All along the St. Marys, sloughs and feeder creeks provide opportunities for side trips into the surrounding swamp corridor or between the approaching bluffs. This becomes more pronounced as the stream moves into Camden County, and marsh prairies indicate the entrance into the tidal zone. Amazingly, the St. Marys' high banks persist and, if anything, become more steeply inclined. Above the GA 25 bridge grassy marsh becomes prevalent on one side of the stream while gum and cypress remain dominant on the other. Below I-95 vast lime-colored grassy marshes combine with a complex network of tidal creeks and rivers and an occasional cypress hammock to turn the St. Marys into a tidewater garden. Banks decrease slightly in steepness but continue to form a natural levee between the stream and the surrounding marsh. Opportunities for side explorations remain excellent. The last access point before reaching Cumberland Sound and the Atlantic Ocean is the city boat ramp at St. Marys (township).

The level of difficulty is Class I throughout. Dangers consist of occasional deadfalls on the North Prong, powerboat traffic, and tricky tidal currents in the lower sections. The current is moderate to slow except where affected by tides (Camden County). Wildlife is diverse and abundant. Access is good. Rental canoes and shuttle service are available.

Section: Okefenokee Swamp to Folkston

Counties: Charlton, Camden (GA); Baker, Nassau (FL)

Suitable For: Cruising, camping

Appropriate For: Families, beginners, intermediates, advanced

Months Runnable: Late November to June

Interest Highlights: Scenery, wildlife

Scenery: Beautiful

Difficulty: International Scale I
Numerical Points 4

Average Width: 70-80 ft.
Gradient: Slow to moderate
Velocity: 1.31 ft./mi.

Runnable Water Level: Minimum 5.5 ft.
(Moniac gauge)[1] Maximum Up to high flood stage

Hazards: Deadfalls on the North Prong

Scouting: None

Portages: None

Rescue Index: Accessible but difficult

Mean Water Temperature (°F)

Jan 54	Feb 56	Mar 61	Apr 68	May 75	Jun 80
Jul 82	Aug 81	Sep 77	Oct 70	Nov 62	Dec 58

Source of Additional Information: Waycross Game and Fish Office (912) 285-6093; Canoe Outpost (904) 536-7929

Access Point	Access Code
A	1367
B	2368
C	1367
D	2367
E	2357
F	1357
G	2357
H	1357
I	2357
J	1357

Access Key
1 Paved Road
2 Unpaved Road
3 Short Carry
4 Long Carry
5 Easy Grade
6 Steep Incline
7 Clear Trail
8 Brush and Trees
9 Launching Fee Charged
10 Private Property, Need Permission
11 No Access, Reference Only

[1]GA 2/94 bridge

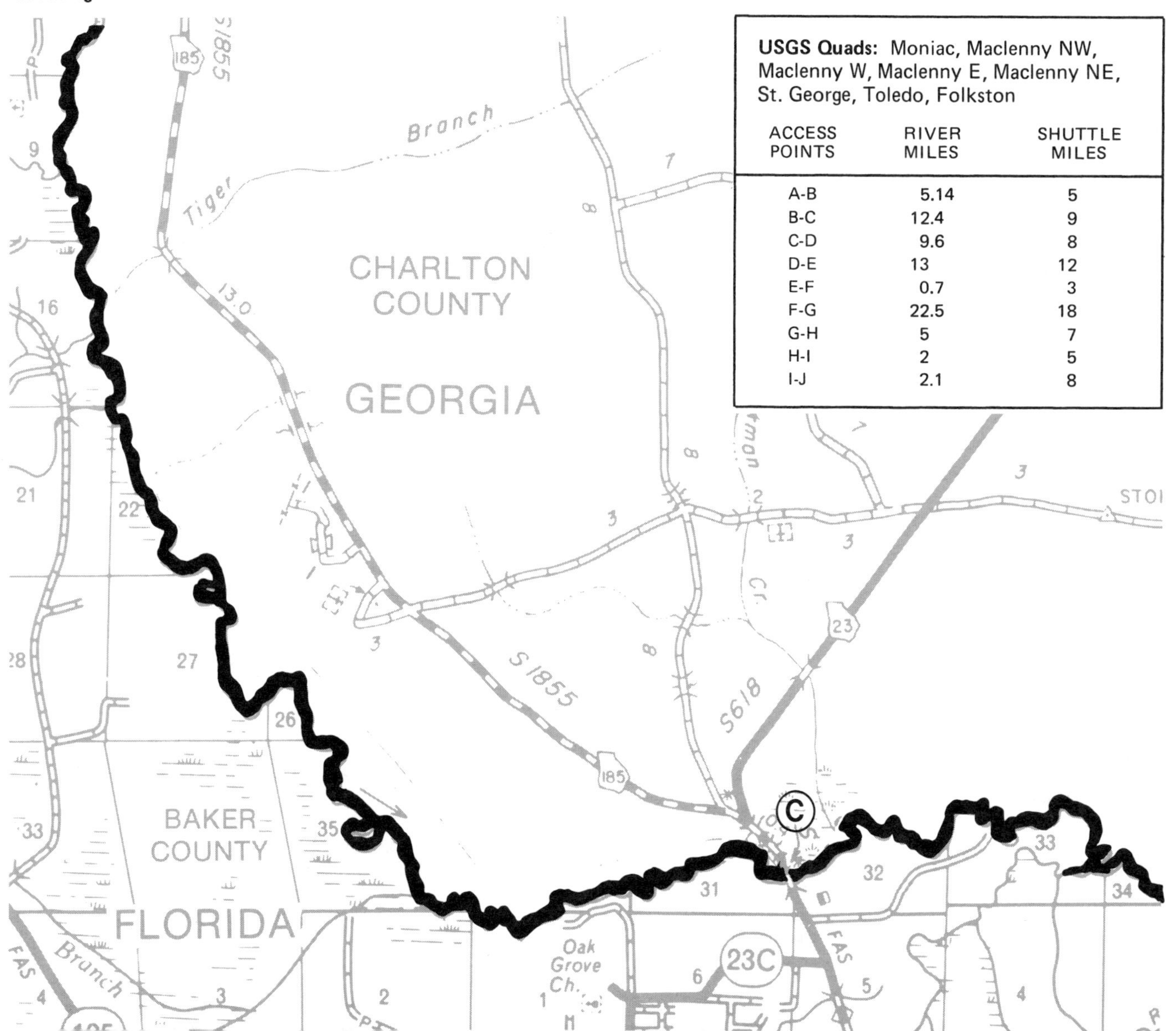

USGS Quads: Moniac, Maclenny NW, Maclenny W, Maclenny E, Maclenny NE, St. George, Toledo, Folkston

ACCESS POINTS	RIVER MILES	SHUTTLE MILES
A-B	5.14	5
B-C	12.4	9
C-D	9.6	8
D-E	13	12
E-F	0.7	3
F-G	22.5	18
G-H	5	7
H-I	2	5
I-J	2.1	8

St. Marys River—*Continued*

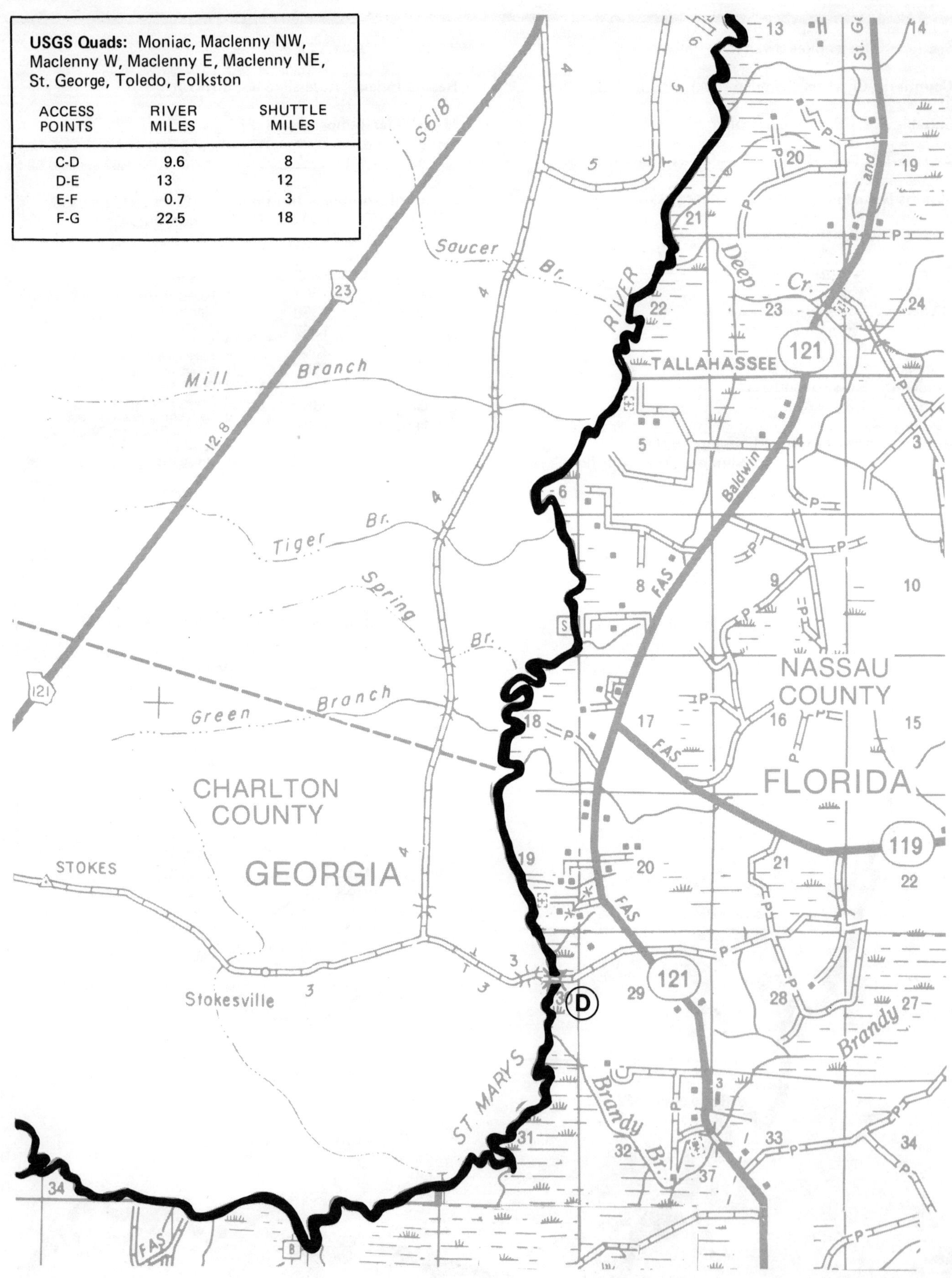

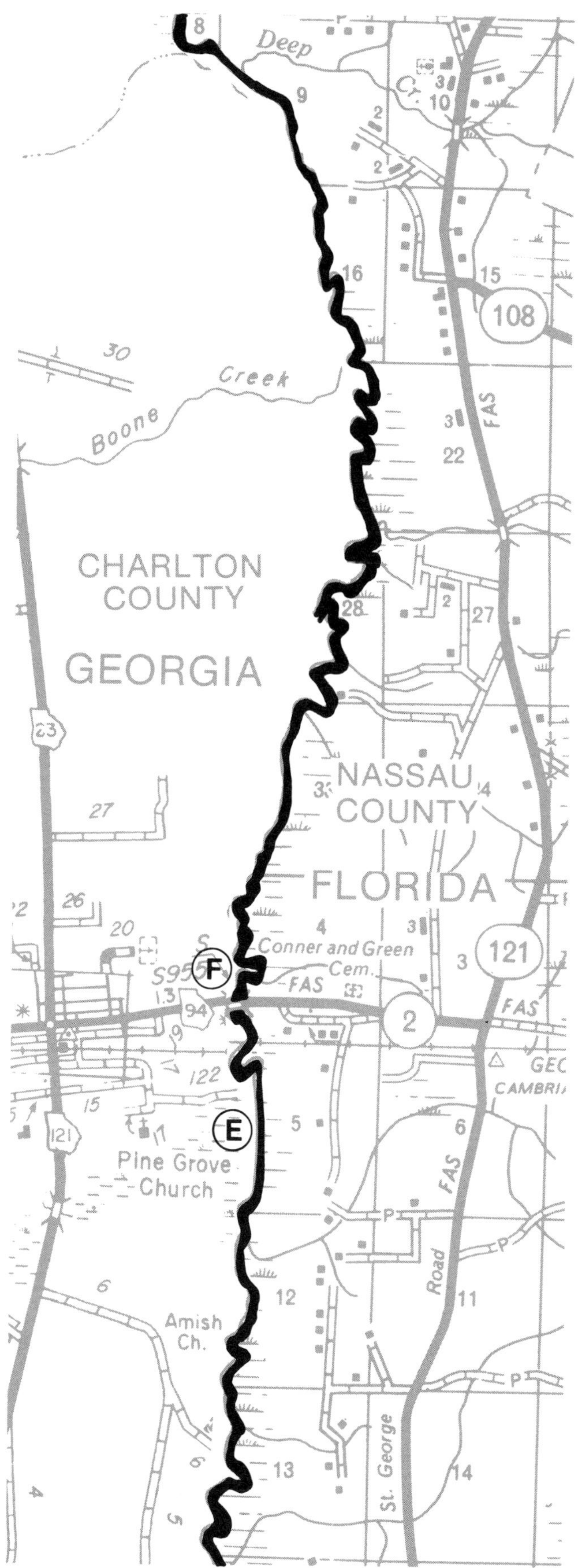

Section: Okefenokee Swamp to Folkston

Counties: Charlton, Camden (GA); Baker, Nassau (FL)

Suitable For: Cruising, camping

Appropriate For: Families, beginners, intermediates, advanced
Months Runnable: Late November to June

Interest Highlights: Scenery, wildlife

Scenery: Beautiful

Difficulty: International Scale I
Numerical Points 4

Average Width: 70-80 ft.
Gradient: Slow to moderate
Velocity: 1.31 ft./mi.

Runnable Water Level: Minimum 5.5 ft.
(Moniac gauge)[1] Maximum Up to high flood stage

Hazards: Deadfalls on the North Prong

Scouting: None

Portages: None

Rescue Index: Accessible but difficult

Mean Water Temperature (°F)

Jan 54	Feb 56	Mar 61	Apr 68	May 75	Jun 80
Jul 82	Aug 81	Sep 77	Oct 70	Nov 62	Dec 58

Source of Additional Information: Waycross Game and Fish Office (912) 285-6093; Canoe Outpost (904) 536-7929

Access Point	Access Code
A	1367
B	2368
C	1367
D	2367
E	2357
F	1357
G	2357
H	1357
I	2357
J	1357

Access Key
1 Paved Road
2 Unpaved Road
3 Short Carry
4 Long Carry
5 Easy Grade
6 Steep Incline
7 Clear Trail
8 Brush and Trees
9 Launching Fee Charged
10 Private Property, Need Permission
11 No Access, Reference Only

[1]GA 2/94 bridge

St. Marys River—*Continued*

Section: Okefenokee Swamp to Folkston

Counties: Charlton, Camden (GA); Baker, Nassau (FL)

Suitable For: Cruising, camping

Appropriate For: Families, beginners, intermediates, advanced

Months Runnable: Late November to June

Interest Highlights: Scenery, wildlife

Scenery: Beautiful

Difficulty: International Scale I
Numerical Points 4

Average Width: 70-80 ft.
Gradient: Slow to moderate
Velocity: 1.31 ft./mi.

Runnable Water Level: (Moniac gauge)[1] Minimum 5.5 ft.; Maximum Up to high flood stage

Hazards: Deadfalls on the North Prong

Scouting: None

Portages: None

Rescue Index: Accessible but difficult

Mean Water Temperature (°F)

Jan 54	Feb 56	Mar 61	Apr 68	May 75	Jun 80
Jul 82	Aug 81	Sep 77	Oct 70	Nov 62	Dec 58

Source of Additional Information: Waycross Game and Fish Office (912) 285-6093; Canoe Outpost (904) 536-7929

Access Point	Access Code
A	1367
B	2368
C	1367
D	2367
E	2357
F	1357
G	2357
H	1357
I	2357
J	1357

Access Key
1 Paved Road
2 Unpaved Road
3 Short Carry
4 Long Carry
5 Easy Grade
6 Steep Incline
7 Clear Trail
8 Brush and Trees
9 Launching Fee Charged
10 Private Property, Need Permission
11 No Access, Reference Only

[1]GA 2/94 bridge

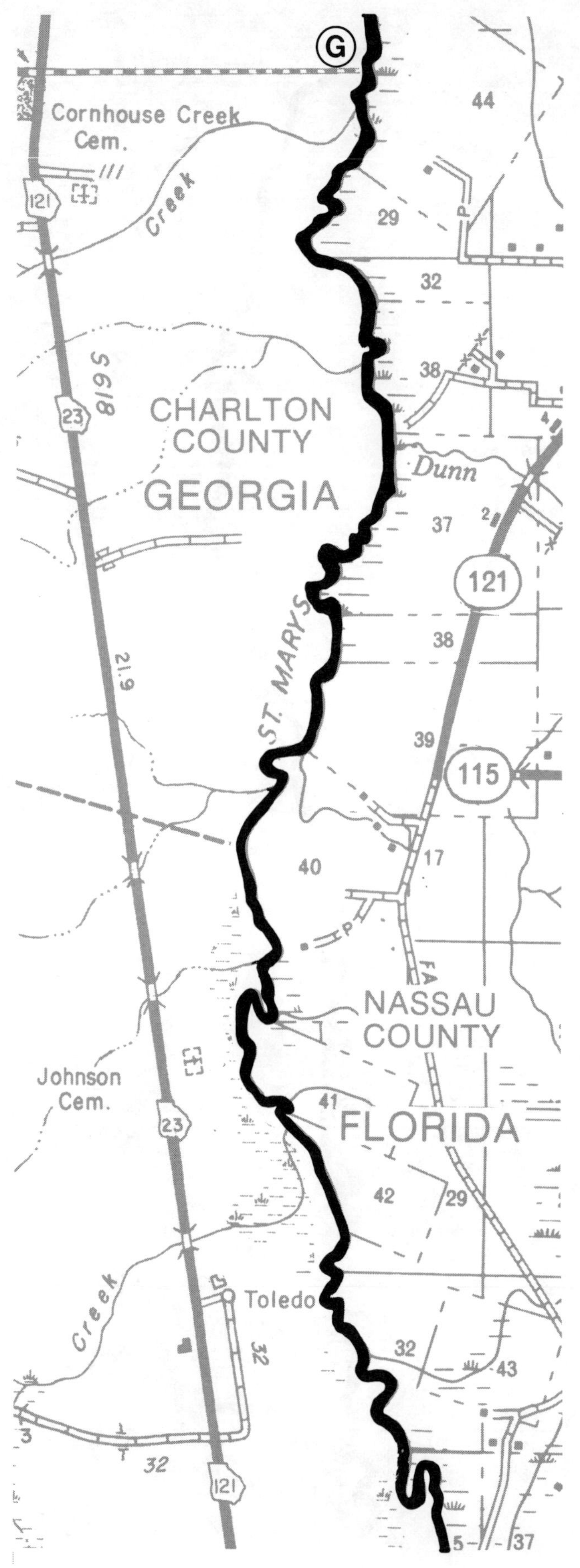

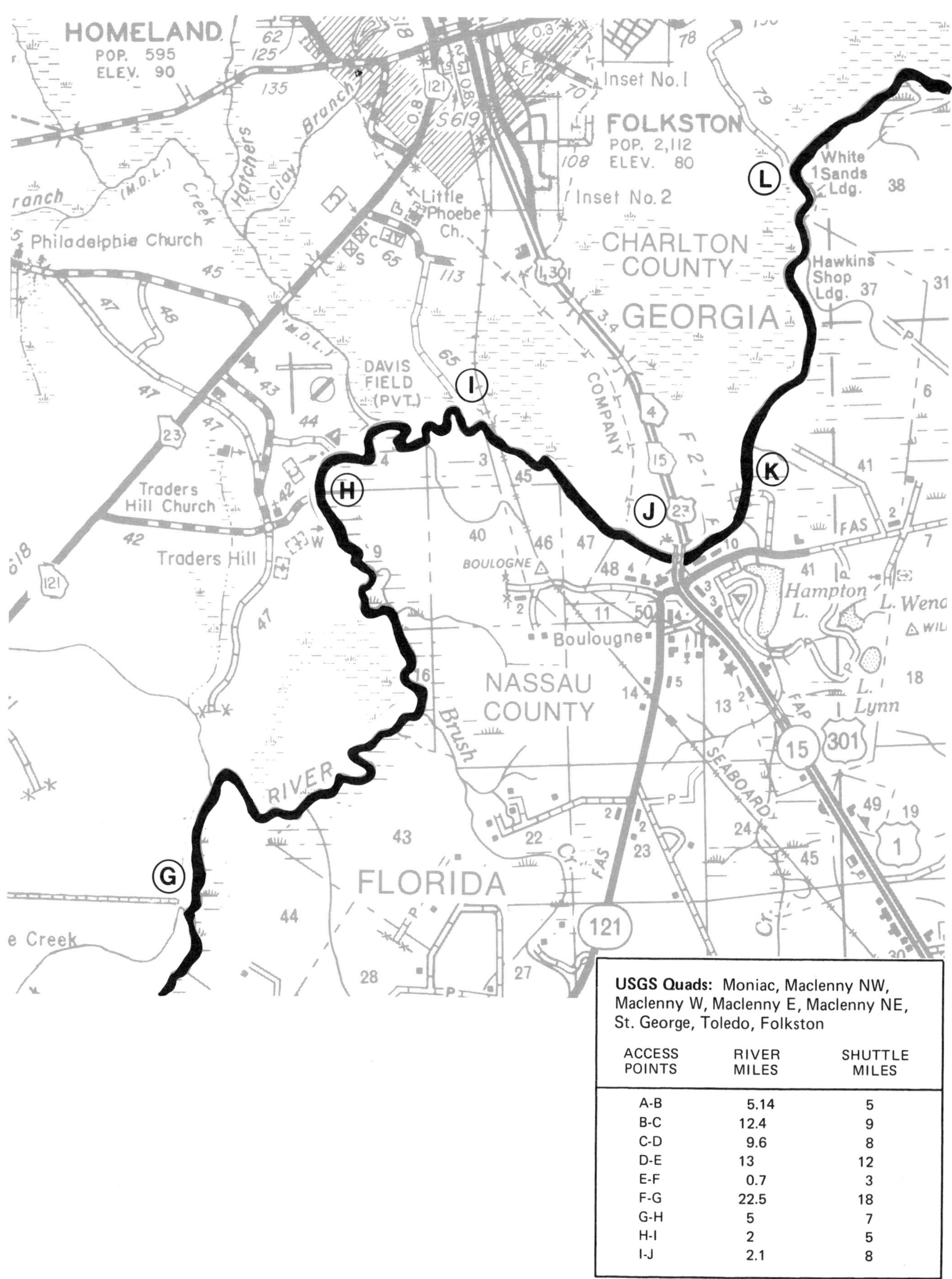

USGS Quads: Moniac, Maclenny NW, Maclenny W, Maclenny E, Maclenny NE, St. George, Toledo, Folkston

ACCESS POINTS	RIVER MILES	SHUTTLE MILES
A-B	5.14	5
B-C	12.4	9
C-D	9.6	8
D-E	13	12
E-F	0.7	3
F-G	22.5	18
G-H	5	7
H-I	2	5
I-J	2.1	8

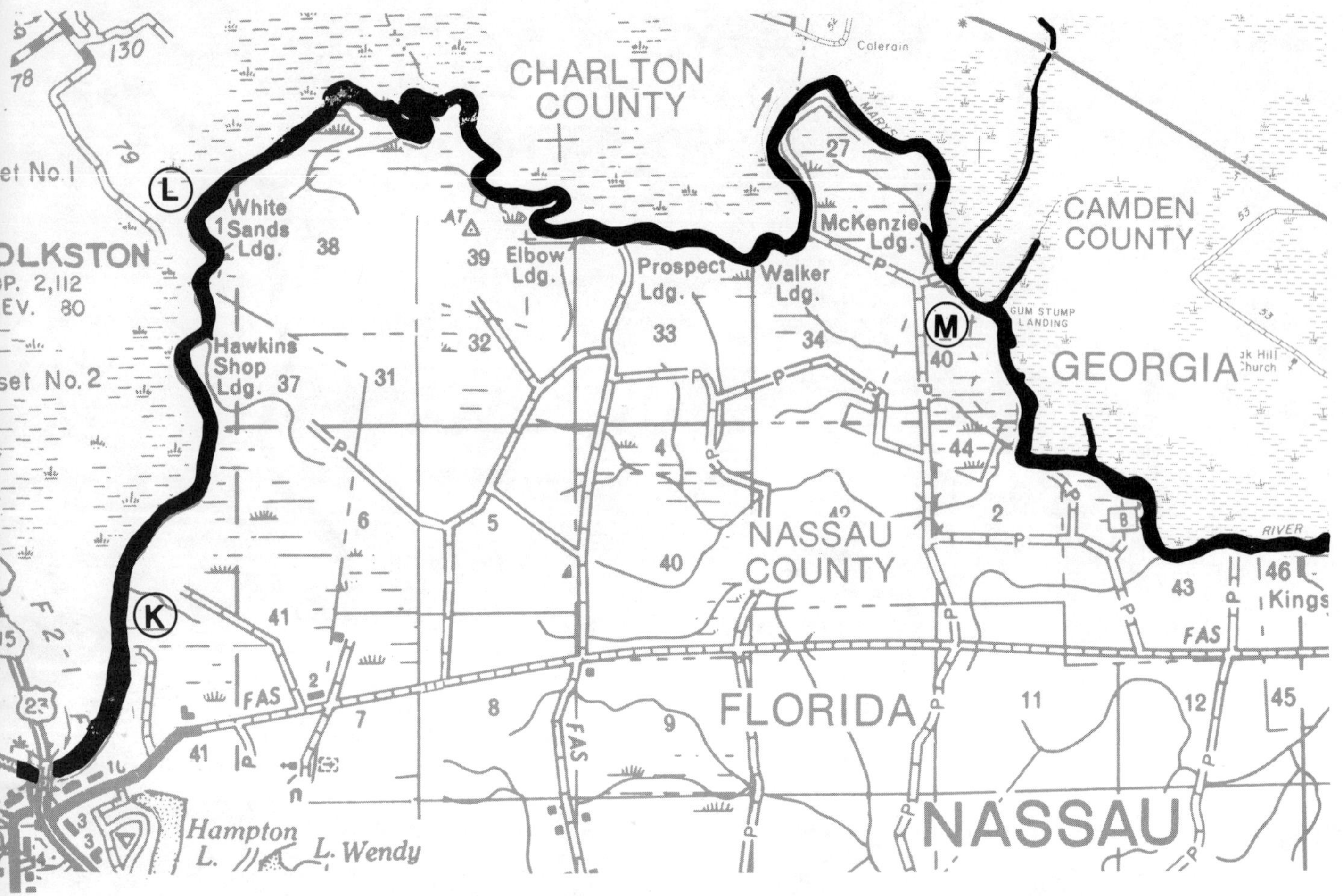

Section: Folkston to Cumberland Sound

Counties: Camden (GA); Baker, Nassau (FL)

Suitable For: Cruising, camping

Appropriate For: Families, beginners, intermediates, advanced

Months Runnable: All except during dry periods

Interest Highlights: Scenery, wildlife, local culture and industry

Scenery: Beautiful

Difficulty: International Scale I
Numerical Points 4

Average Width: 90-120 ft.
Gradient: Slow to moderate
Velocity: 0.11 ft./mi.

Runnable Water Level: Minimum 2 ft.
(MacClenny gauge)[1] Maximum Up to high flood stage

Hazards: Powerboat traffic, tidal effects in Camden Co.

Scouting: None

Portages: None

Rescue Index: Accessible but difficult

Mean Water Temperature (°F)

Jan 54	Feb 56	Mar 61	Apr 69	May 75	Jun 81
Jul 82	Aug 82	Sep 76	Oct 70	Nov 62	Dec 58

Source of Additional Information: Waycross Game and Fish Office (912) 285-6093; Canoe Outpost (904) 536-7929

Access Point	Access Code
J	1357
K	2357
L	2358
M	2368
N	13689
O	2367
P	23579
Q	2357
R	1357
S	2357
T	1357

Access Key
1 Paved Road
2 Unpaved Road
3 Short Carry
4 Long Carry
5 Easy Grade
6 Steep Incline
7 Clear Trail
8 Brush and Trees
9 Launching Fee Charged
10 Private Property, Need Permission
11 No Access, Reference Only

[1]In Florida, 1 mi. below confluence of North and South forks

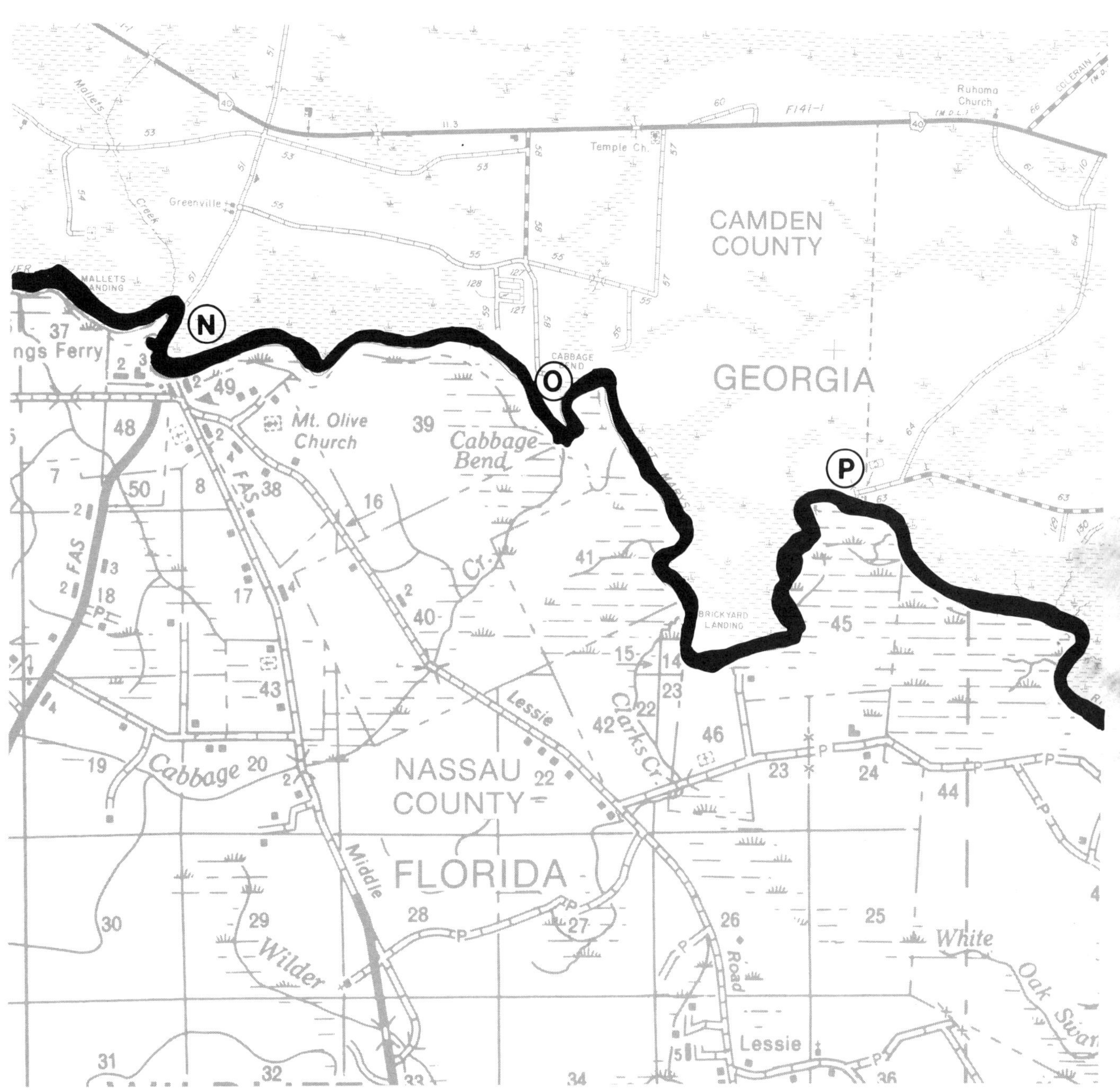

USGS Quads: Folkston, Boulogne, Kings Ferry, Kingsland, Gross, St. Marys

ACCESS POINTS	RIVER MILES	SHUTTLE MILES
J-K	0.8	3
K-L	2.8	10
L-M	7.6	18
M-N	4	10
N-O	3	3.5
O-P	5.2	8.5
P-Q	3.5	31
Q-R	3	24
R-S	5.6	6.3
S-T	11.2	9.5

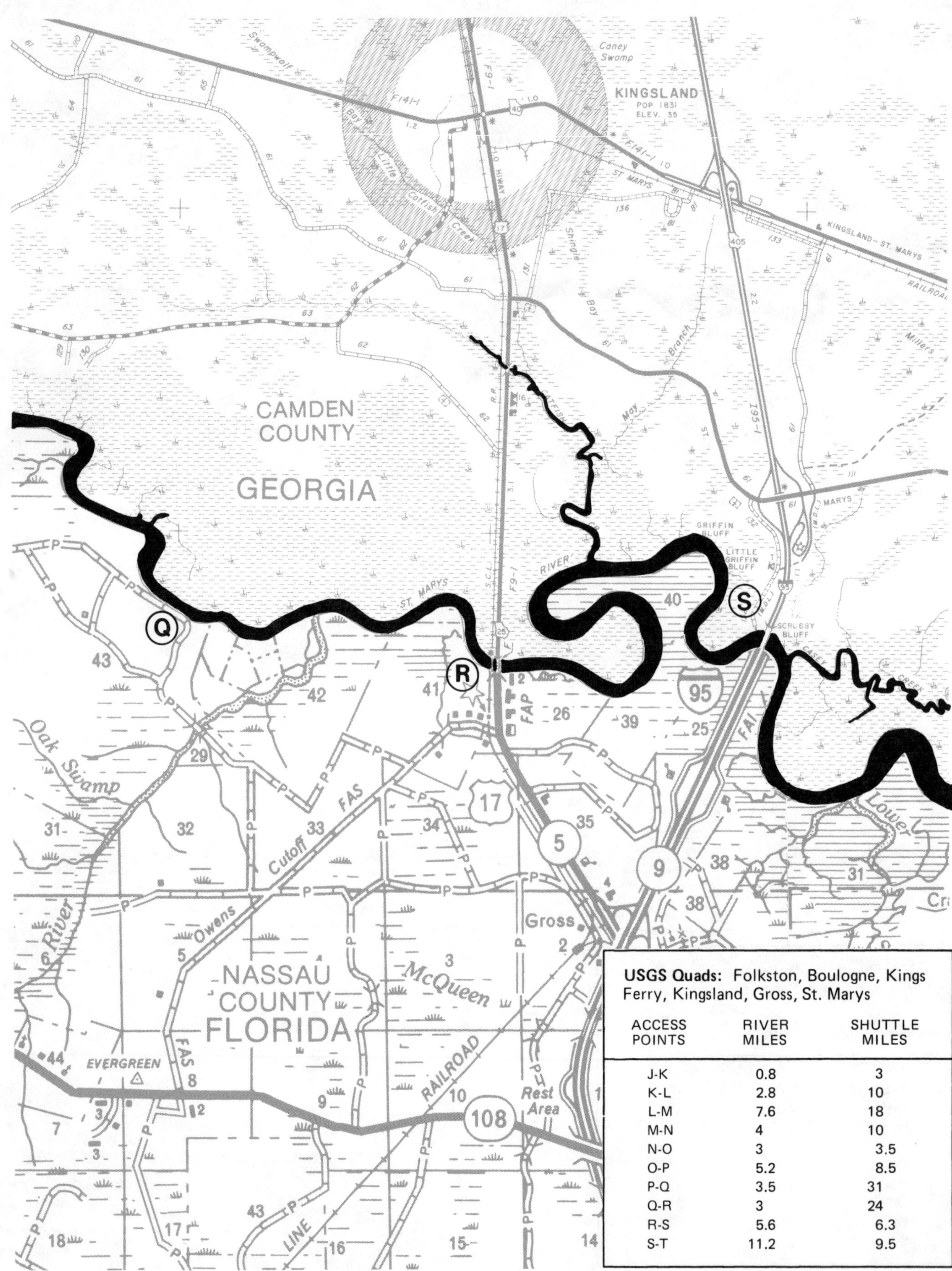

USGS Quads: Folkston, Boulogne, Kings Ferry, Kingsland, Gross, St. Marys

ACCESS POINTS	RIVER MILES	SHUTTLE MILES
J-K	0.8	3
K-L	2.8	10
L-M	7.6	18
M-N	4	10
N-O	3	3.5
O-P	5.2	8.5
P-Q	3.5	31
Q-R	3	24
R-S	5.6	6.3
S-T	11.2	9.5

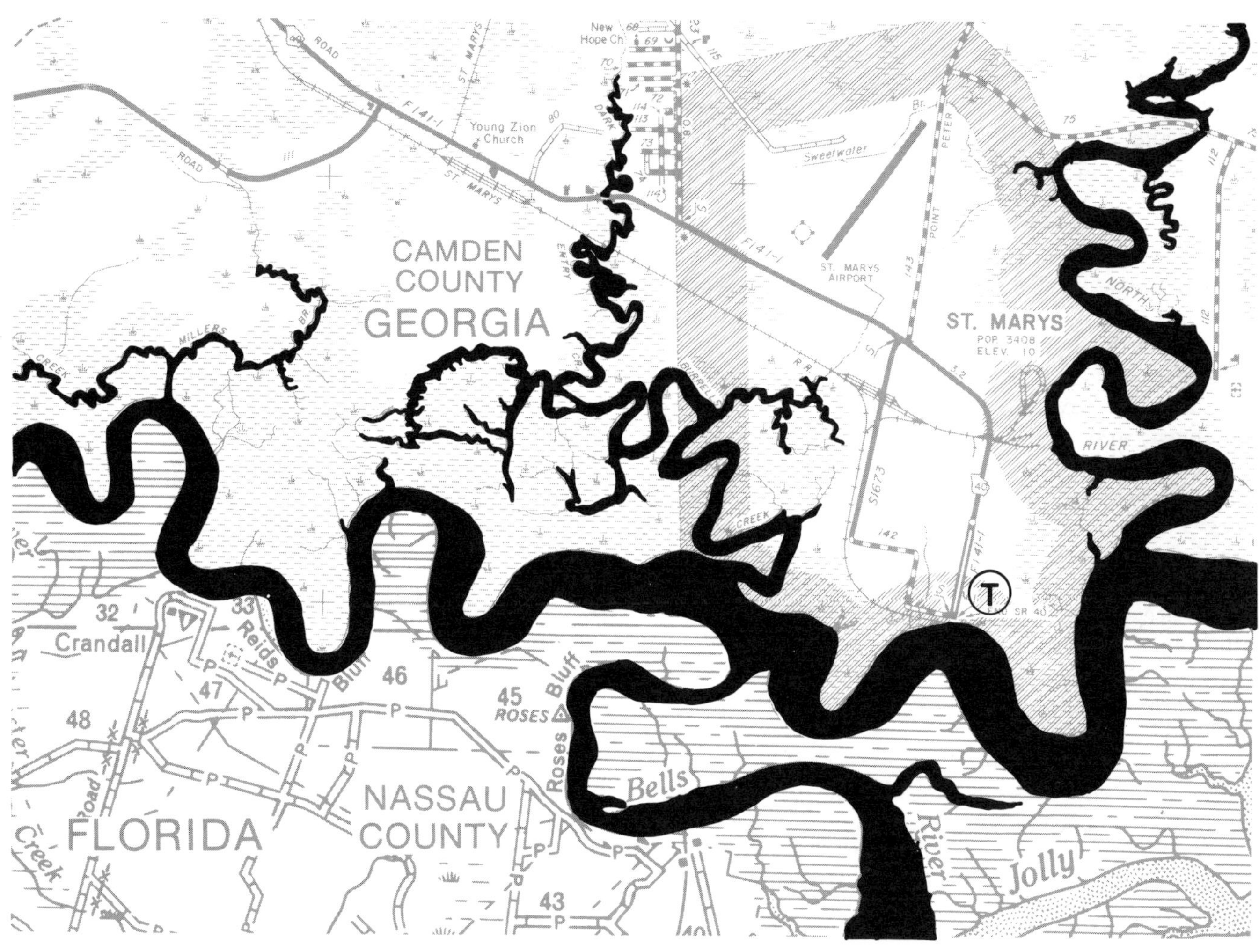

Section: Folkston to Cumberland Sound

Counties: Camden (GA); Baker, Nassau (FL)

Suitable For: Cruising, camping

Appropriate For: Families, beginners, intermediates, advanced

Months Runnable: All except during dry periods

Interest Highlights: Scenery, wildlife, local culture and industry

Scenery: Beautiful

Difficulty: International Scale I
Numerical Points 4

Average Width: 90-120 ft.

Gradient: Slow to moderate

Velocity: 0.11 ft./mi.

Runnable Water Level: Minimum 2 ft.
(MacClenny gauge)[1] Maximum Up to high flood stage

Hazards: Powerboat traffic, tidal effects in Camden Co.

Scouting: None

Portages: None

Rescue Index: Accessible but difficult

Mean Water Temperature (°F)

Jan 54	Feb 56	Mar 61	Apr 69	May 75	Jun 81
Jul 82	Aug 82	Sep 76	Oct 70	Nov 62	Dec 58

Source of Additional Information: Waycross Game and Fish Office (912) 285-6093; Canoe Outpost (904) 536-7929

Access Point	Access Code
J	1357
K	2357
L	2358
M	2368
N	13689
O	2367
P	23579
Q	2357
R	1357
S	2357
T	1357

Access Key
1 Paved Road
2 Unpaved Road
3 Short Carry
4 Long Carry
5 Easy Grade
6 Steep Incline
7 Clear Trail
8 Brush and Trees
9 Launching Fee Charged
10 Private Property, Need Permission
11 No Access, Reference Only

[1] In Florida, 1 mi. below confluence of North and South forks

Suwannee River

The celebrated Suwannee River originates deep in the bowels of the Okefenokee Swamp and flows southeast to drain small portions of Ware, Clinch, and Echols counties before escaping into Florida. Once safely across the border, the Suwannee heads southwest and eventually empties into the Gulf of Mexico.

There are few streams in American folklore and culture better known that the Suwannee, thanks to Stephen Foster. The mere mention of its name stirs fanciful visions of stately moss-draped cypress, sultry southern days, and a way of life long past. If the lifestyle has disappeared into history and imagination, the Suwannee remains, substantially unchanged, and available for any paddler to experience. No more beautiful than several dozen other southern Georgia rivers, the Suwannee is nevertheless a living legend in the most literal sense and therefore something special.

Only a small portion of the Suwannee flows within the state of its birth, a fact made much of by Florida tourism promoters. This section, however, is unique among all stretches of the river by virtue of the almost mystical aura conferred by the Okefenokee Swamp.

Deep in the middle of the swamp the Suwannee is born at the confluence of the East and Middle Forks of the Suwannee at the northern end of Billys Lake. Access is available at the nearby Stephen Foster (who else?) State Park. You will quickly find, however, that paddling within Okefenokee is heavily regulated (see the description of the Okefenokee Swamp in the next chapter). If you proceed downstream and out of the swamp, you will have to cross the sill, a man-made levee constructed to stablize the depth of water in the swamp. The portage is short and easy, but alas, a permit is required. If this sounds like the heavy hand of bureaucracy, remember that this regulation and several dozen more (like carrying all human waste out of the swamp) have preserved the pristine integrity of one of America's irreplaceable natural wonders.

Once across the sill, the Suwannee settles into shallow, white, sandy clay banks and flows southward through a watery floodplain forested with pond cypress, swamp black gum, sweet bay, swamp cyrilla, slash pine, magnolia, and palmetto. Since animals and birds do not need permits to cross the sill, the incredibly diverse fauna found in the Okefenokee can also be found along the upper Suwannee.

The water color is dark red, stained by tannic acid from decaying vegetation, and the current is slow. Below the sill to the GA 94 bridge crossing at Fargo, the river flows through several large midstream stands of cypress and gum, which at higher water require some heads-up navigation and present a nice opportunity to get lost in the surrounding inundated lowlands. While the flow of the main current is usually easy to follow, there are times when map, compass, and a little swamp luck are helpful. Access between the state park and Fargo is almost nonexistent except at a private fishing camp off GA 177 where permission to put-in should be obtained.

Below Fargo the Suwannee remains isolated in pristine, exotic wilderness and flows languidly along a shady, twisting course of moss-draped cypress. The first access point below Fargo is FL 6 just over the Sunshine State line. If you continue, you will notice that the banks are higher and more well defined and that numerous feeder streams enter the Suwannee. Farther downstream, Florida's largest rapid, Big Shoals, and the Stephen Foster (who else?) Memorial await you. Additional information concerning the Florida sections of the Suwannee can be obtained by writing: Florida Department of Natural Resources, Crown Building, Tallahassee, Florida 32304.

The Suwannee's level of difficulty is Class I throughout its Georgia course. The current is slow to moderate. Dangers to navigation are confined to deadfalls, and unfortunately, to a group of "good old boys" who get drunk at a park site near the GA 94 bridge crossing. Since campsites are rare above Fargo, paddlers should cross the sill with sufficient daylight remaining to make Fargo before dark. Canoe rentals and shuttle service are available in the area.

USGS Quads: Billys Island, The Pocket, Strange Island, Fargo, Needmore, Fargo SW

ACCESS POINTS	RIVER MILES	SHUTTLE MILES
A-B	17.1	20
B-C	3.1	3
C-D	20.4	13

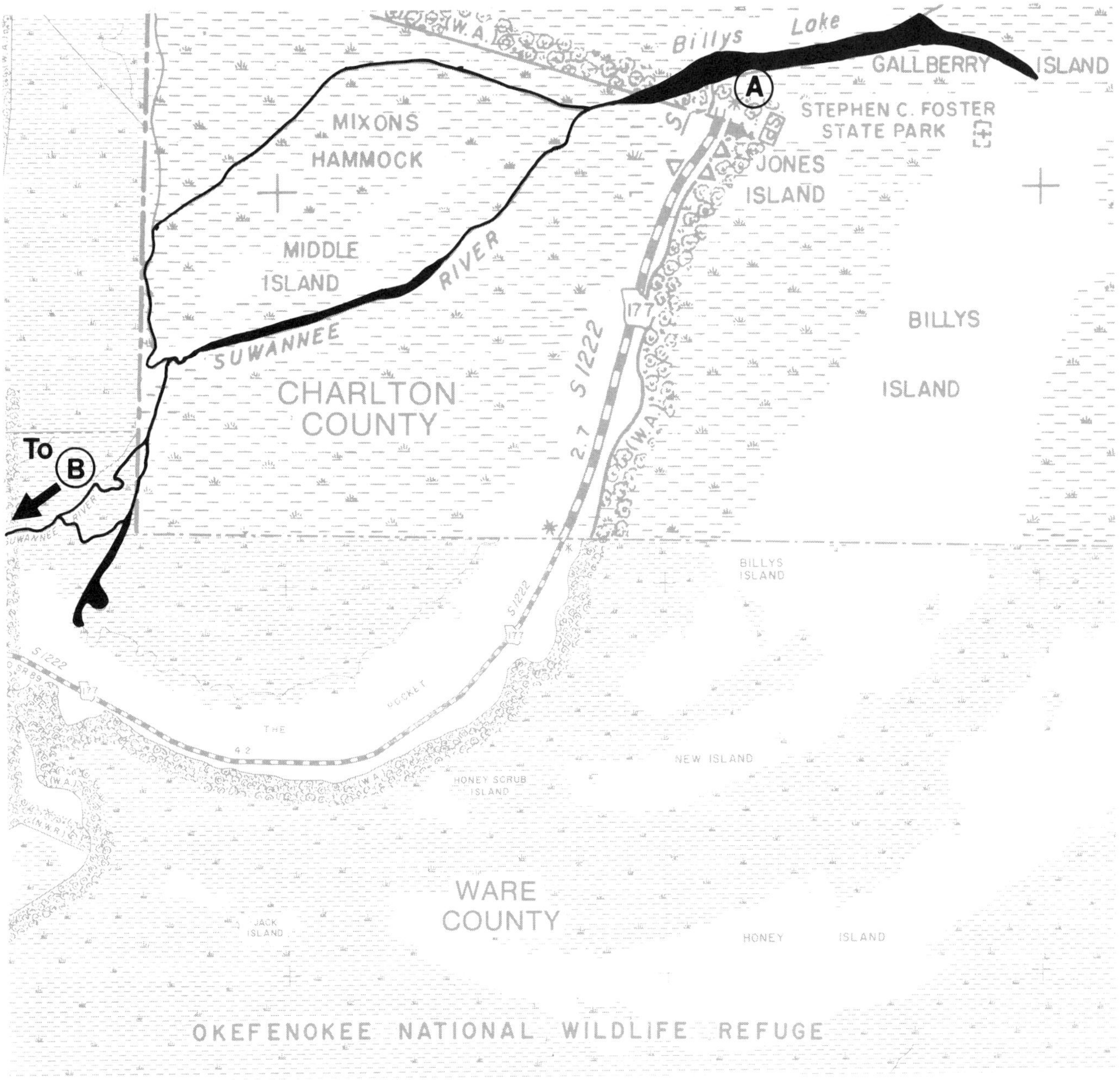

W. A.
Billys Lake
GALLBERRY ISLAND
A
STEPHEN C. FOSTER STATE PARK
MIXONS HAMMOCK
JONES ISLAND
MIDDLE ISLAND
SUWANNEE RIVER
177
S 1222
2.7
BILLYS ISLAND
CHARLTON COUNTY
To B
SUWANNEE RIVER
BILLYS ISLAND
S 1222
177
THE POCKET
NEW ISLAND
HONEY SCRUB ISLAND
WARE COUNTY
JACK ISLAND
HONEY ISLAND
OKEFENOKEE NATIONAL WILDLIFE REFUGE

Alapaha River.

Photo courtesy of *Brown's Guide to Georgia.*

Section: Okefenokee Swamp to FL 6

Counties: Charlton, Ware, Clinch, Echols

Suitable For: Cruising, camping

Appropriate For: Families, beginners, intermediates, advanced
Months Runnable: December through June

Interest Highlights: Scenery, wildlife, local culture and industry, history
Scenery: Beautiful

Difficulty: International Scale I
Numerical Points 5

Average Width: 40-65 ft.
Gradient: Slow to moderate
Velocity: 0.86 ft./mi.

Runnable Water Level: Minimum 240 cfs
Maximum Not applicable

Hazards: Deadfalls, locals drinking at GA 94 bridge, trees growing in stream

Scouting: None required

Portages: Suwanee Sill on edge of Okefenokee

Rescue Index: Accessible but difficult to remote

Mean Water Temperature (°F)

Jan 54	Feb 55	Mar 60	Apr 68	May 75	Jun 81
Jul 83	Aug 82	Sep 76	Oct 69	Nov 62	Dec 57

Source of Additional Information: Waycross Game and Fish Office (912) 285-6093, Canoe Outpost (904) 364-1683

Access Point	Access Code
A	1357
B	2357(10)
C	1357
D	1357

Access Key
1 Paved Road
2 Unpaved Road
3 Short Carry
4 Long Carry
5 Easy Grade
6 Steep Incline
7 Clear Trail
8 Brush and Trees
9 Launching Fee Charged
10 Private Property, Need Permission
11 No Access, Reference Only

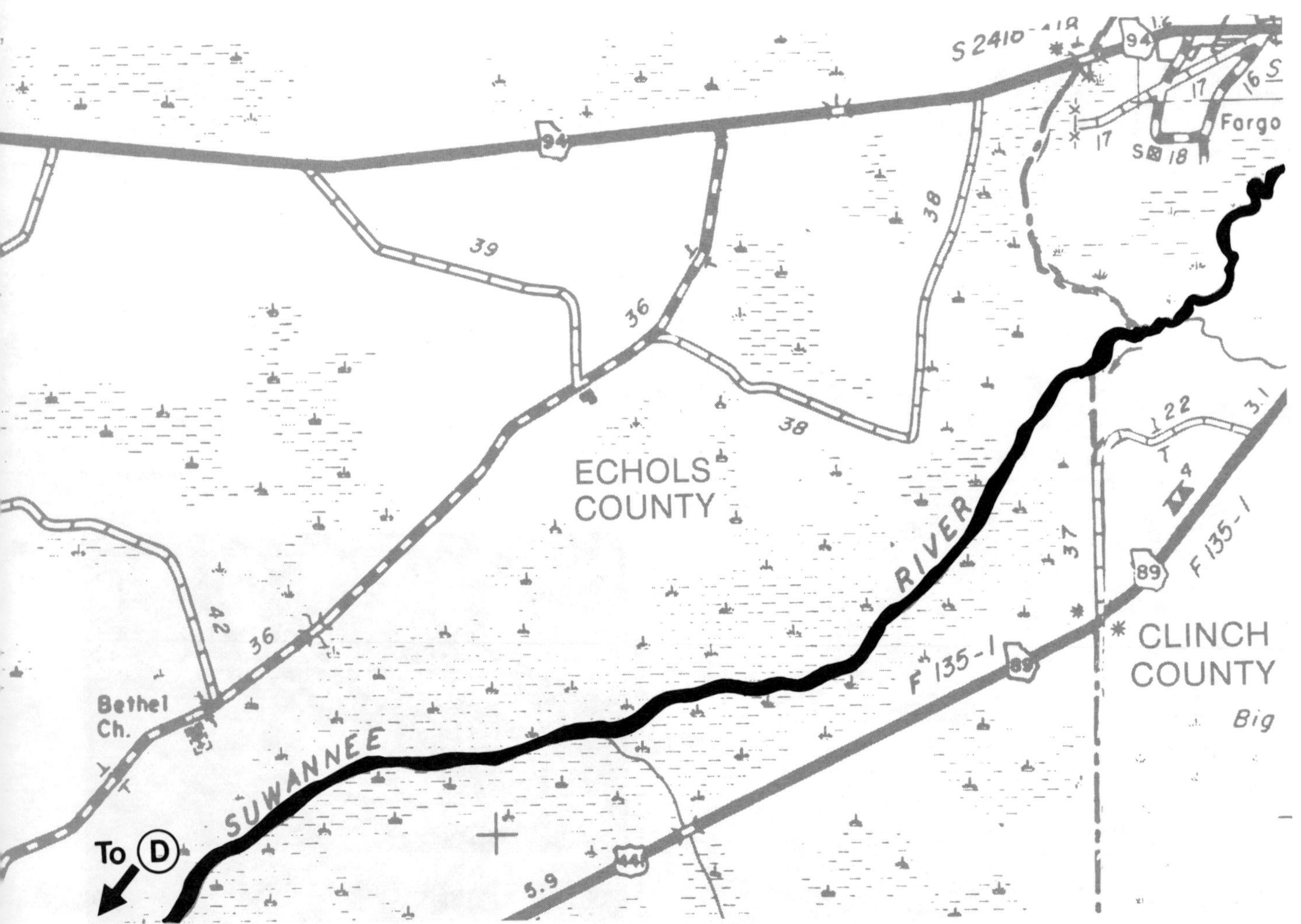

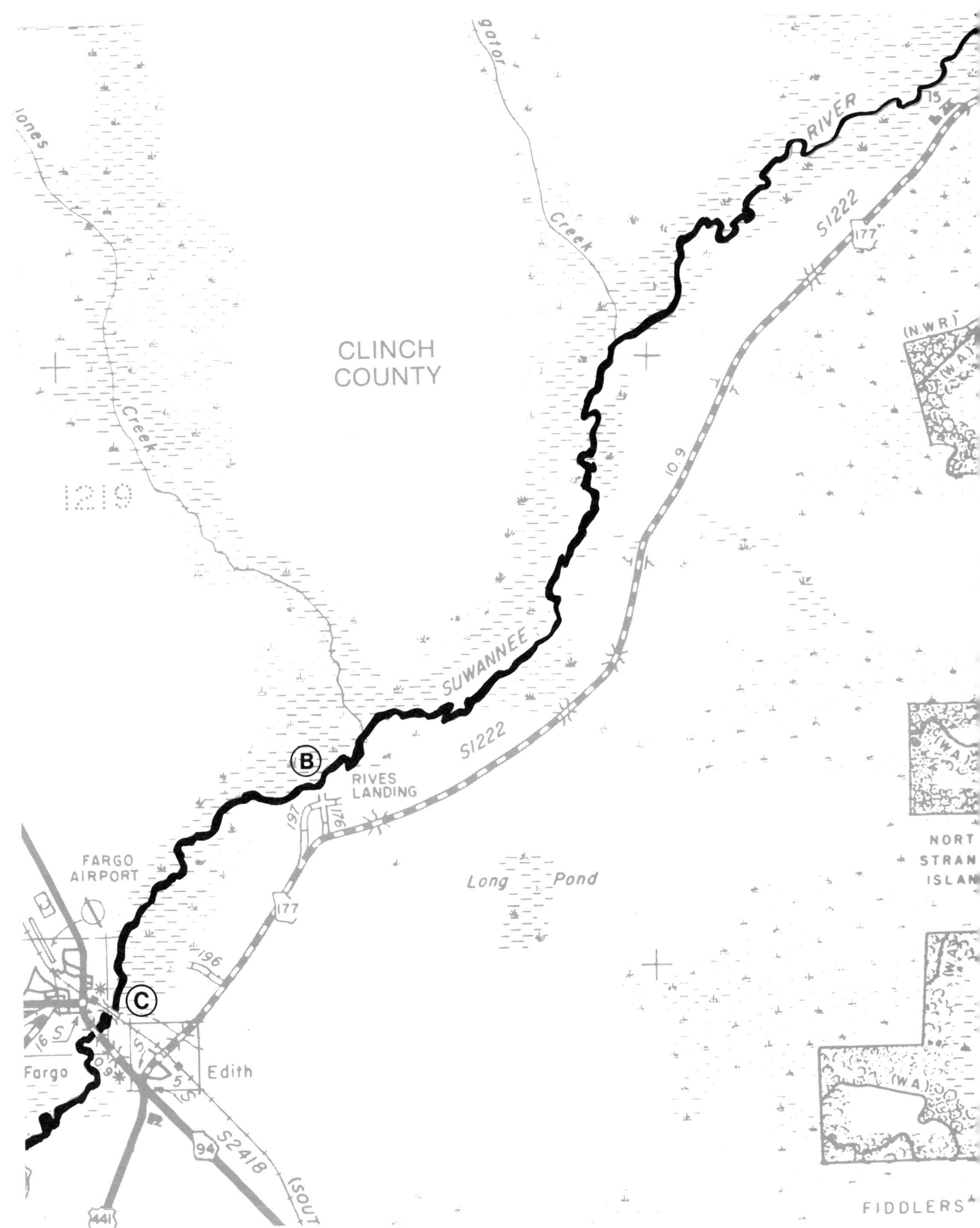
gator
Jones
Creek
RIVER
S1222
177
CLINCH
COUNTY
(N.W.R.)
(W.A.)
Creek
1219
10.9
SUWANNEE
S1222
B
RIVES
LANDING
197
176
NORT
STRAN
ISLAN
FARGO
AIRPORT
Long
Pond
177
196
C
16
Fargo
Edith
5
94
S2418
(SOUT
441
FIDDLERS

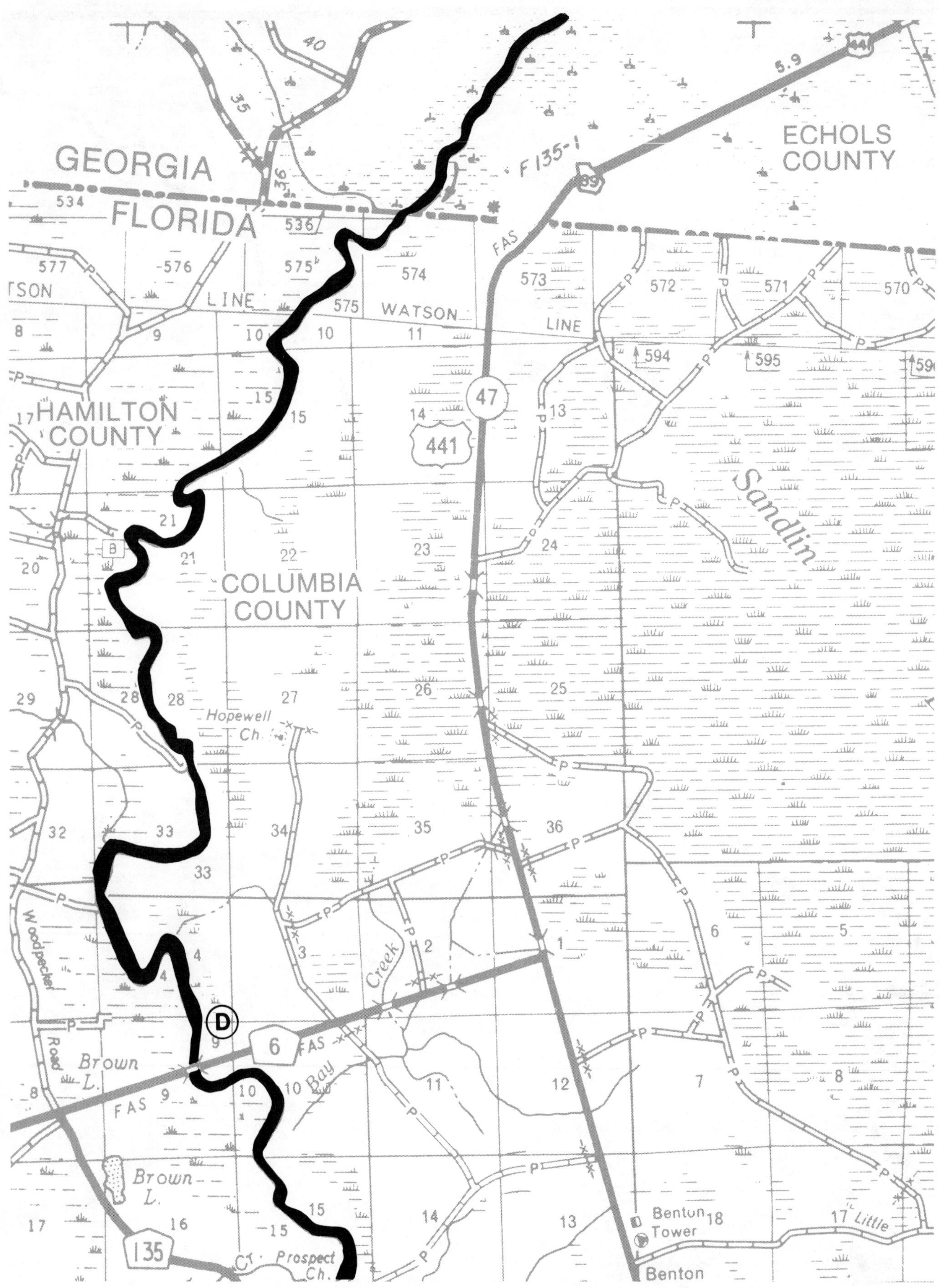

GEORGIA
FLORIDA
ECHOLS
COUNTY
HAMILTON
COUNTY
COLUMBIA
COUNTY
WATSON
LINE
Sandlin
Hopewell
Ch.
Woodpecker
Road
Brown
L.
Brown
L.
Bay
Creek
Benton
Tower
Benton
Prospect
Ch.
Little
441
47
6
135
FAS
F 135-1

Section: Okefenokee Swamp to FL 6

Counties: Charlton, Ware, Clinch, Echols

Suitable For: Cruising, camping

Appropriate For: Families, beginners, intermediates, advanced

Months Runnable: December through June

Interest Highlights: Scenery, wildlife, local culture and industry, history

Scenery: Beautiful

Difficulty: International Scale I
Numerical Points 5

Average Width: 40-65 ft.
Gradient: Slow to moderate
Velocity: 0.86 ft./mi.

Runnable Water Level: Minimum 240 cfs
Maximum Not applicable

Hazards: Deadfalls, locals drinking at GA 94 bridge, trees growing in stream

Scouting: None required

Portages: Suwanee Sill on edge of Okefenokee

Rescue Index: Accessible but difficult to remote

Mean Water Temperature (°F)

Jan 54	Feb 55	Mar 60	Apr 68	May 75	Jun 81
Jul 83	Aug 82	Sep 76	Oct 69	Nov 62	Dec 57

Source of Additional Information: Waycross Game and Fish Office (912) 285-6093, Canoe Outpost (904) 364-1683

Access Point	Access Code
A	1357
B	2357(10)
C	1357
D	1357

Access Key
1 Paved Road
2 Unpaved Road
3 Short Carry
4 Long Carry
5 Easy Grade
6 Steep Incline
7 Clear Trail
8 Brush and Trees
9 Launching Fee Charged
10 Private Property, Need Permission
11 No Access, Reference Only

USGS Quads: Billys Island, The Pocket, Strange Island, Fargo, Needmore, Fargo SW

ACCESS POINTS	RIVER MILES	SHUTTLE MILES
A-B	17.1	20
B-C	3.1	3
C-D	20.4	13

Alapaha River

One of Georgia's protected wild rivers, the Alapaha originates in western Ben Hill County and drains south across the Coastal Plain counties of Irwin, Tift, Berrien, Atkinson, Lanier, Lowndes, and Echols before crossing into Florida where it empties into the Suwannee.

Following a course of extreme and seemingly endless loops and tight turns, the Alapaha is runnable from late November through August below the US 82 bridge east of Alapaha. Junglelike in its remoteness and luxurious with exotic vegetation, the Alapaha winds through a swampy wonderland teeming with wildlife. Small shoals caused by an underlying limestone strata approach Class II in intensity and enliven the paddling. Trees, primarily sweet gum, cypress, and Australian pine grow profusely in the river channel where they stand over the dark brown water like proud sentinels. On the low, sandy clay banks, pine, water oak, laurel oak, sweet bay, birch, and an occasional live oak shade the dark waters from the sun.

At the US 82 bridge the Alapaha averages 20 to 35 feet in width and runs deep within its tree cover. On the eastern end of the Alapaha Wildlife Management Area the Alapaha's largest tributary, the Willacoochee, enters the stream and increases its size to about 45 to 60 feet. Moving into Lanier County, the Alapaha is slightly less curving as it flows in the center of a broad forested swamp corridor. White sandbars on the insides of bends provide excellent swimming or camping spots. After crossing beneath the Southern Railroad bridge the Alapaha again straightens slightly, and the white sandbars common upstream are no longer present. The stream width here averages 60 to 70 feet. Signs of habitation are rare along the Alapaha's course; only a few isolated cabins intrude on the stream's remote tranquility. From time to time sand bluffs up to ten feet high and populated with pine encroach on the bottom land. These make good camp sites during periods of higher water. The current is moderate on the Alapaha, and the level of difficulty is Class I except at infrequent shoals where borderline Class II difficulty prevails. Though the channel is remarkably clear of deadfalls, live trees growing in the stream do occasionally pose hazards to navigation. Access is good.

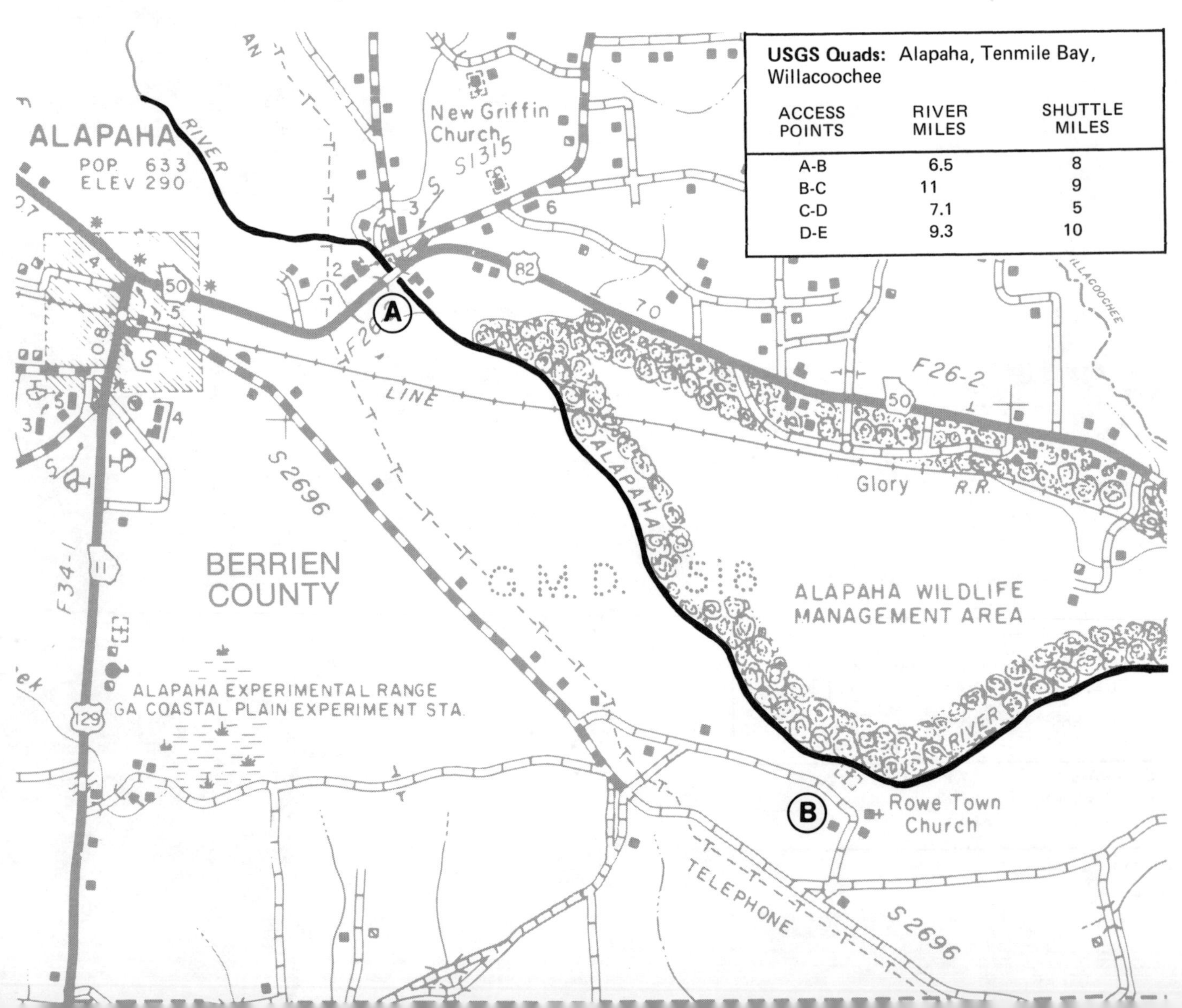
USGS Quads: Alapaha, Tenmile Bay, Willacoochee

ACCESS POINTS	RIVER MILES	SHUTTLE MILES
A-B	6.5	8
B-C	11	9
C-D	7.1	5
D-E	9.3	10

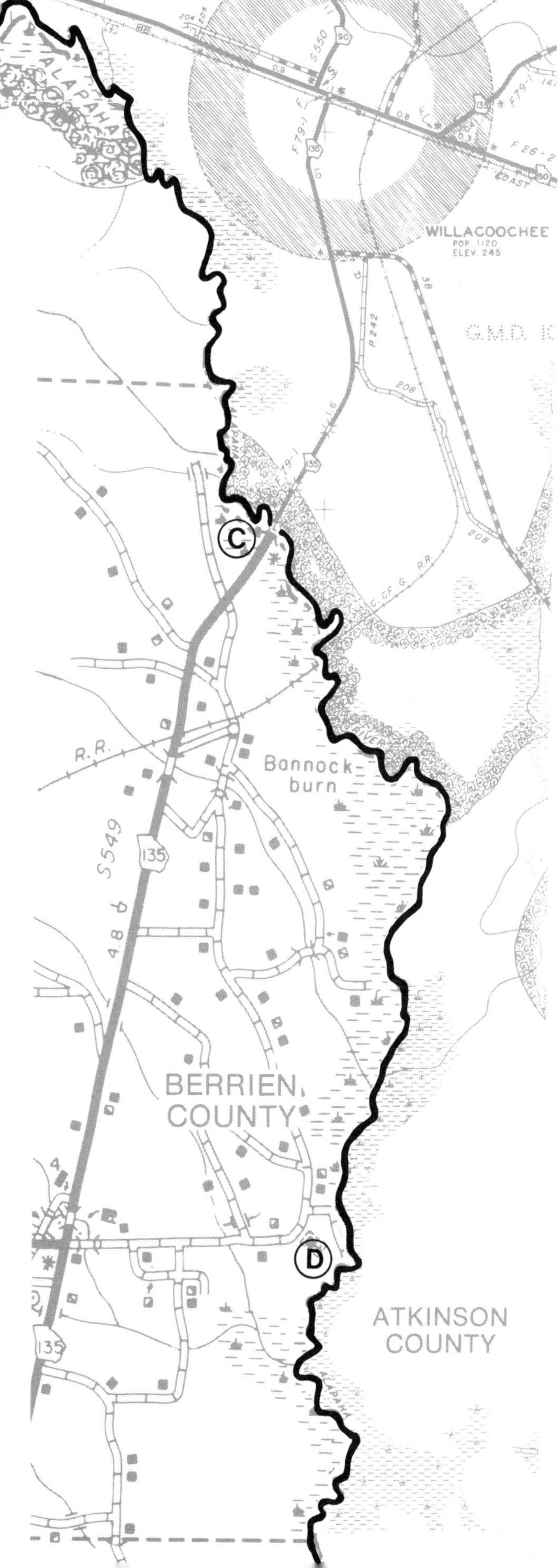

Section: Alapaha to FL 150

Counties: Berrien, Atkinson, Lanier, Lowndes, Echols

Suitable For: Cruising, camping

Appropriate For: Families, beginners, intermediates, advanced

Months Runnable: Late November through early October

Interest Highlights: Scenery, wildlife, limestone shoals geology

Scenery: Exceptionally beautiful

Difficulty: International Scale I (II)
Numerical Points 6

Average Width: 40-65 ft.
Velocity: Slow to moderate
Gradient: 1.56 ft./mi.

Runnable Water Level: Minimum 200 cfs
Maximum None

Hazards: Deadfalls, live trees growing in stream

Scouting: None required

Portages: None required

Rescue Index: Accessible but difficult to remote

Mean Water Temperature (°F)

Jan	52	Feb	55	Mar	60	Apr	66	May	74	Jun	80
Jul	83	Aug	81	Sep	77	Oct	69	Nov	61	Dec	55

Source of Additional Information: Waycross Game and Fish Office (912) 285-6093, Live Oak Canoe Outpost (904) 364-1683

Access Point	Access Code
A	1357
B	2357
C	1357
D	2357

Access Key

1 Paved Road
2 Unpaved Road
3 Short Carry
4 Long Carry
5 Easy Grade
6 Steep Incline
7 Clear Trail
8 Brush and Trees
9 Launching Fee Charged
10 Private Property, Need Permission
11 No Access, Reference Only

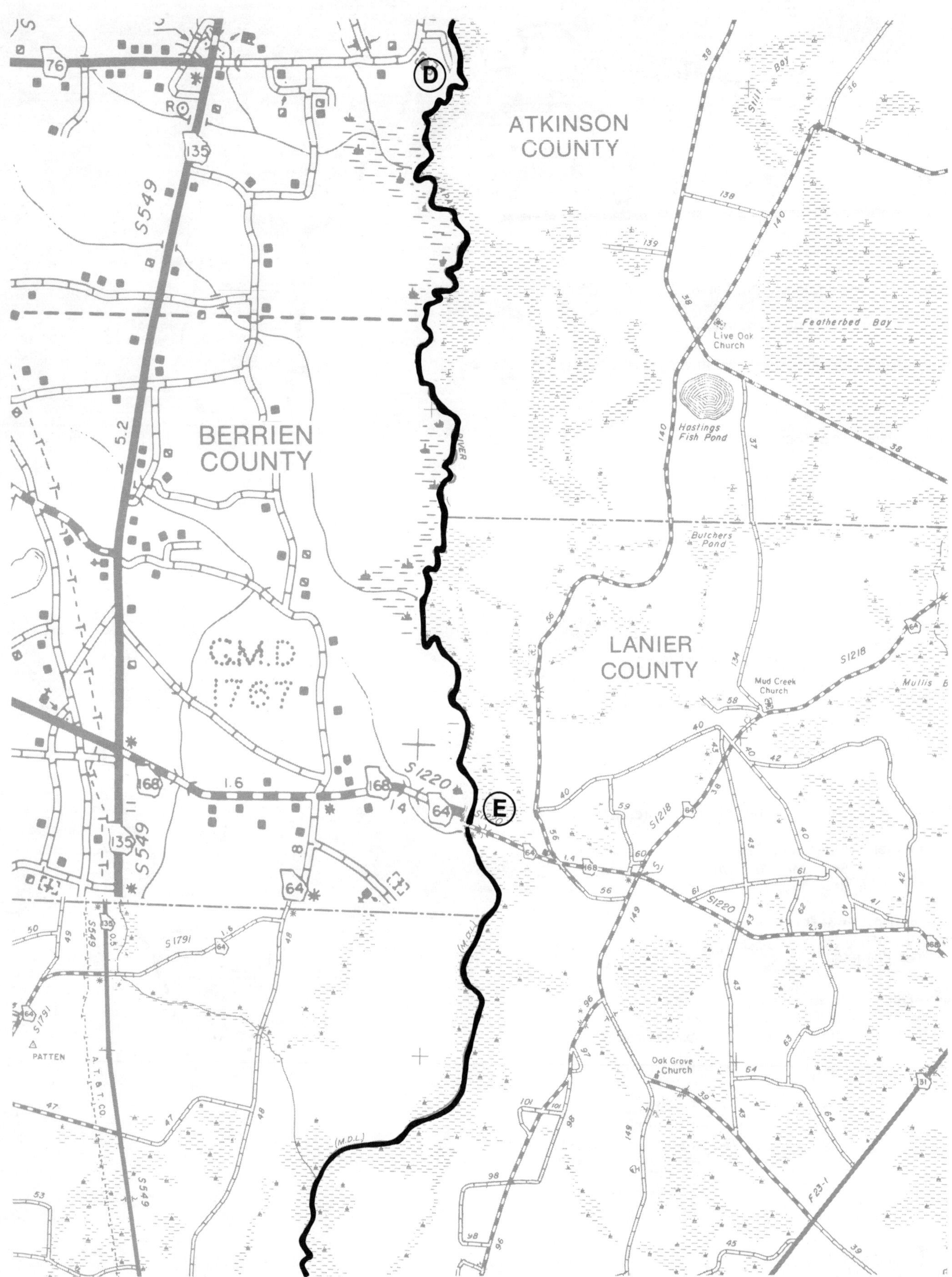
D
ATKINSON
COUNTY
BERRIEN
COUNTY
Featherbed Bay
Live Oak
Church
Hastings
Fish Pond
Butchers
Pond
G.M.D
1767
LANIER
COUNTY
Mud Creek
Church
E
PATTEN
A.T.&T. CO.
Oak Grove
Church
S549
S1220
S1218
S1791
F23-1
(M.D.L.)

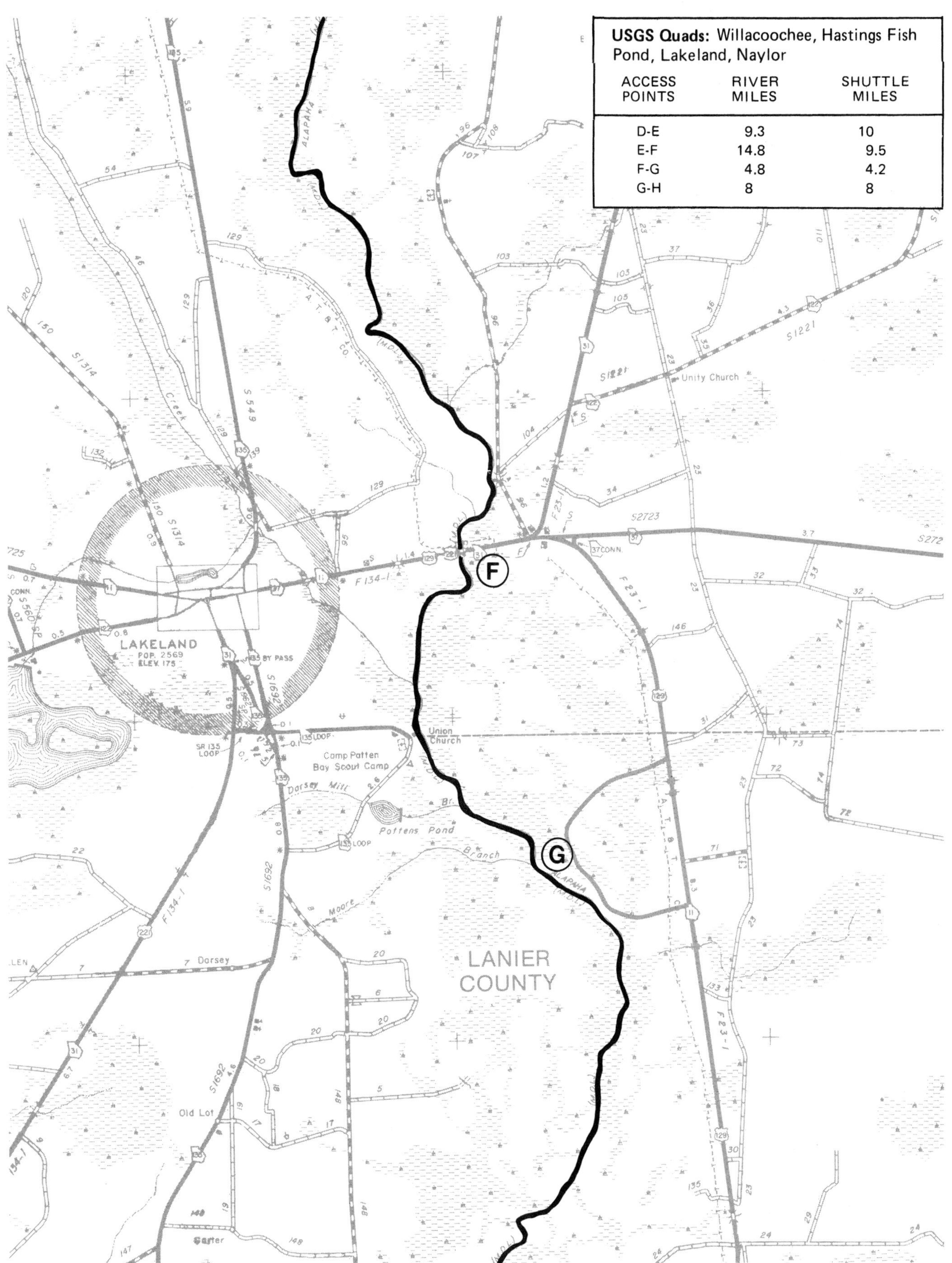

USGS Quads: Willacoochee, Hastings Fish Pond, Lakeland, Naylor

ACCESS POINTS	RIVER MILES	SHUTTLE MILES
D-E	9.3	10
E-F	14.8	9.5
F-G	4.8	4.2
G-H	8	8

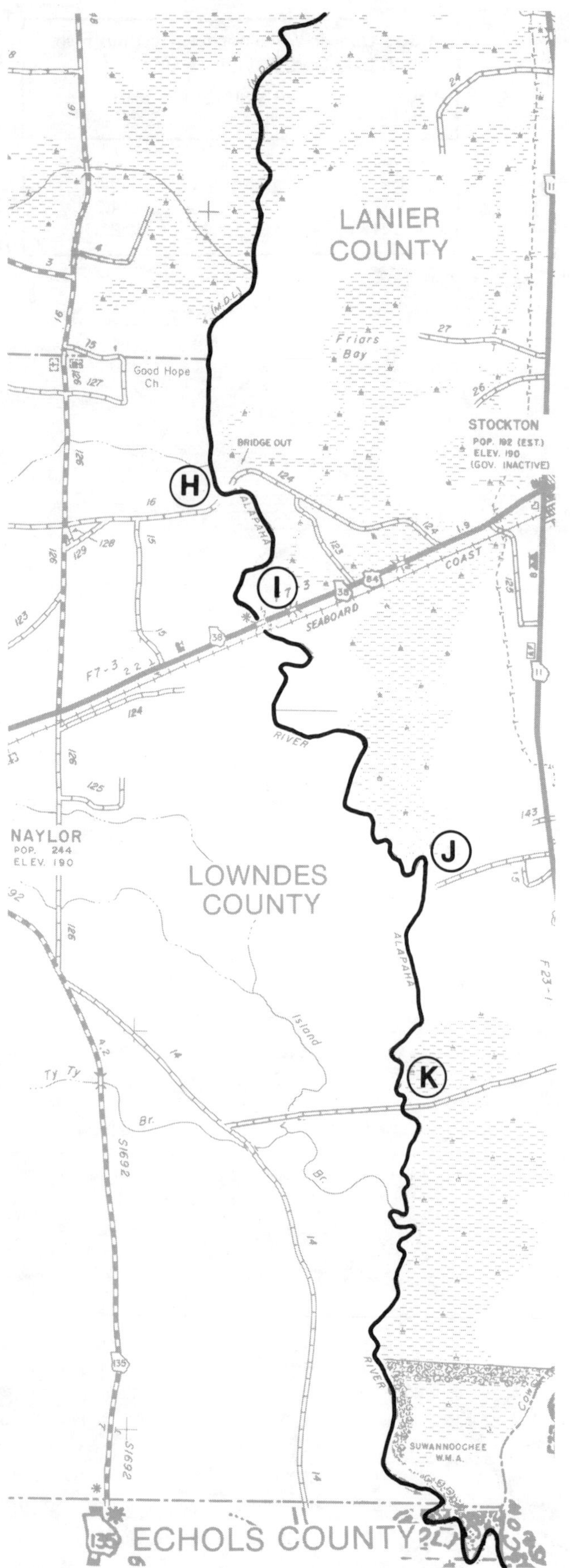

Section: Alapaha to FL 150

Counties: Berrien, Atkinson, Lanier, Lowndes, Echols

Suitable For: Cruising, camping

Appropriate For: Families, beginners, intermediates, advanced
Months Runnable: Late November through early October

Interest Highlights: Scenery, wildlife, limestone shoals geology
Scenery: Exceptionally beautiful

Difficulty: International Scale I (II)
Numerical Points 6

Average Width: 40-65 ft.
Velocity: Slow to moderate
Gradient: 1.56 ft./mi.

Runnable Water Level: Minimum 200 cfs
Maximum None

Hazards: Deadfalls, live trees growing in stream

Scouting: None required

Portages: None required

Rescue Index: Accessible but difficult to remote
Mean Wat
Mean Water Temperature (°F)

Jan 52	Feb 55	Mar 60	Apr 66	May 74	Jun 80
Jul 83	Aug 81	Sep 77	Oct 69	Nov 61	Dec 55

Source of Additional Information: Waycross Game and Fish Office (912) 285-6093, Live Oak Canoe Outpost (904) 364-1683

Access Point	Access Code
H	2357
I	2357
J	2357
K	2357
L	1357
M	1357
N	1367

Access Key
1 Paved Road
2 Unpaved Road
3 Short Carry
4 Long Carry
5 Easy Grade
6 Steep Incline
7 Clear Trail
8 Brush and Trees
9 Launching Fee Charged
10 Private Property, Need Permission
11 No Access, Reference Only

USGS Quads: Naylor, Howell, Statenville, Jennings

ACCESS POINTS	RIVER MILES	SHUTTLE MILES
G-H	8	8
H-I	1.1	1.5
I-J	3.3	4.5
J-K	1.9	3.5
K-L	5.3	5.5
L-M	13.7	10
M-N	9.4	12

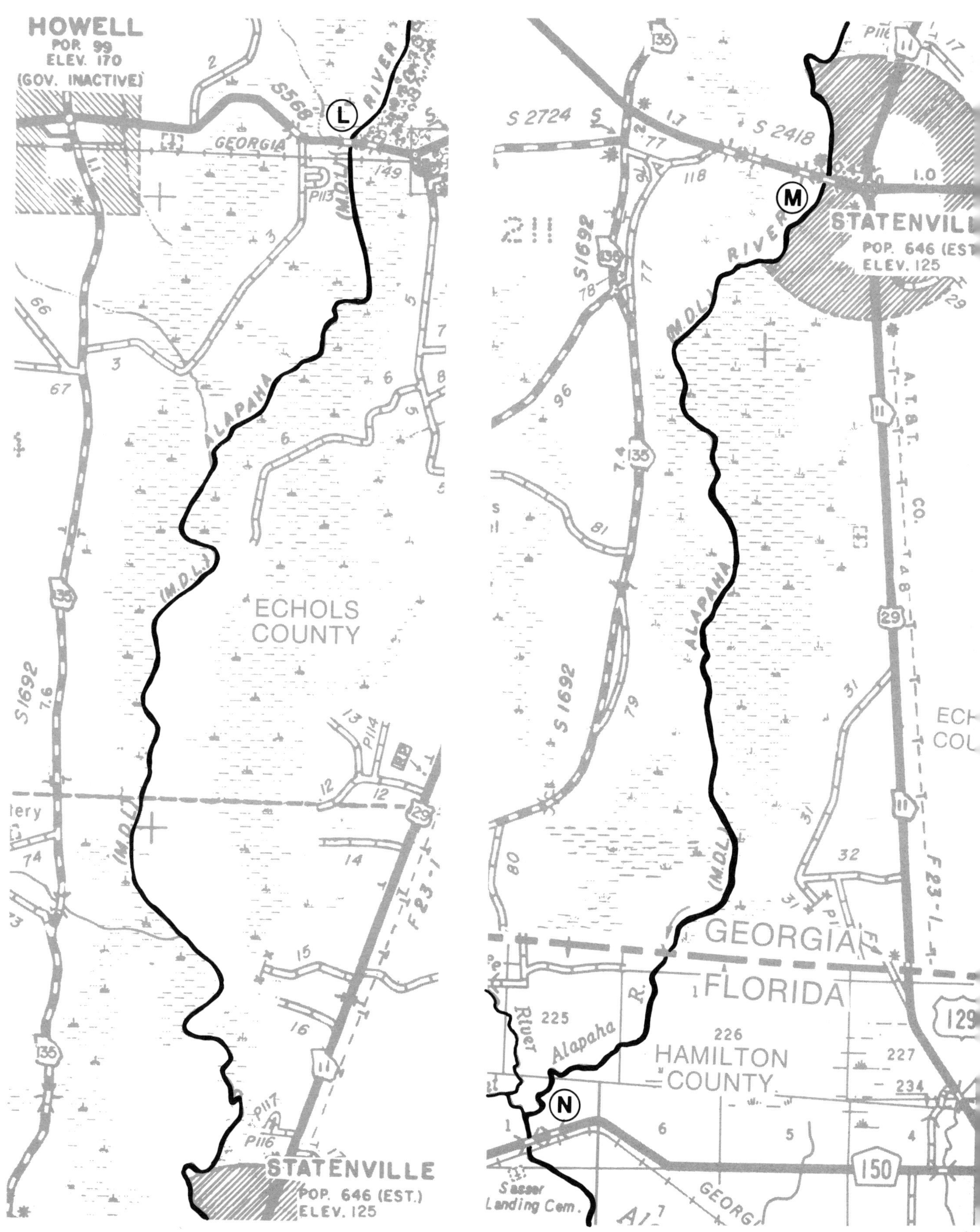

HOWELL
POP. 99
ELEV. 170
(GOV. INACTIVE)
S568
RIVER
GEORGIA
P113
(M.D.L.)
ALAPAHA
ECHOLS
COUNTY
S1692
STATENVILLE
POP. 646 (EST.)
ELEV. 125
F23-1
S 2724
S 2418
A.T.&T. CO.
GEORGIA
FLORIDA
River
Alapaha
R.
HAMILTON
COUNTY
Sasser
Landing Cem.

Little River of Southern Georgia

The Little River is born in Turner County west of Ashburn and flows southeast through Tift, Colquitt, Cook, Brooks, and Lowndes counties before merging with the Withlacoochee near Valdosta. A diminutive blackwater stream lacking a prominent floodplain, the Little is canopied with Ogeechee lime, water elm, and scattered cypress. Remote and enticing, the Little's acid-stained water bubbles playfully over small limestone ledges and between brilliantly contrasting white sandbars. Its banks are low and gently inclined, on the average, and are thick with Sebastian bush and deciduous holly.

Runnable below the Cool Springs bridge west of Lenox in Cook County in winter and spring, the Little is 25 to 30 feet in width and is frequently obstructed by deadfalls. Below the Ellington bridge west of Sparks the Little enters the backwaters of a beautiful swamp lake at the Reed Bingham State Park. A sort of Okefenokee in miniature with a variety of watery flora, this small lake is definitely worthy of exploration. Downstream of the dam at the lake's southern end, the Little continues in uninterrupted tranquility except for a short section below the GA 122 bridge where a number of small cabins line the stream. For the remainder of its journey to join the Withlacoochee, the Little never exceeds 50 feet in width and continues to hide bashfully beneath the canopy of its exotic flora.

The Little River's level of difficulty is Class I throughout but numerous deadfalls are a primary hazard to navigation. Woodland swamp surrounds the Little throughout its course, which is substantially less convoluted than that of similar blackwater streams in the Coastal Plain. The current is moderate to slow, and access is good. Trips on the Little can easily be combined with floats on the Withlacoochee.

Section: West of Lenox to Withlacoochee River

Counties: Colquitt, Cook, Brooks, Lowndes

Suitable For: Cruising, camping

Appropriate For: Families, beginners, intermediates, advanced

Months Runnable: Late November to June

Interest Highlights: Scenery, wildlife

Scenery: Beautiful

Difficulty: International Scale I
Numerical Points 5

Average Width: 30-40 ft.
Velocity: Slow to moderate
Gradient: 1.88 ft./mi.

Runnable Water Level: Minimum 150 cfs
Maximum Up to high flood stage

Hazards: Deadfalls

Scouting: None required

Portages: Dam at Reed Bingham State Park

Rescue Index: Accessible but difficult

Mean Water Temperature (°F)

Jan 52	Feb 54	Mar 60	Apr 65	May 75	Jun 80
Jul 82	Aug 81	Sep 78	Oct 68	Nov 61	Dec 55

Source of Additional Information: Waycross Game and Fish Office (912) 285-6093; Live Oak Canoe Outpost (904) 364-1683

Access Point	Access Code
A	2357
B	1357
C	1357
D	1357

Access Key
1 Paved Road
2 Unpaved Road
3 Short Carry
4 Long Carry
5 Easy Grade
6 Steep Incline
7 Clear Trail
8 Brush and Trees
9 Launching Fee Charged
10 Private Property, Need Permission
11 No Access, Reference Only

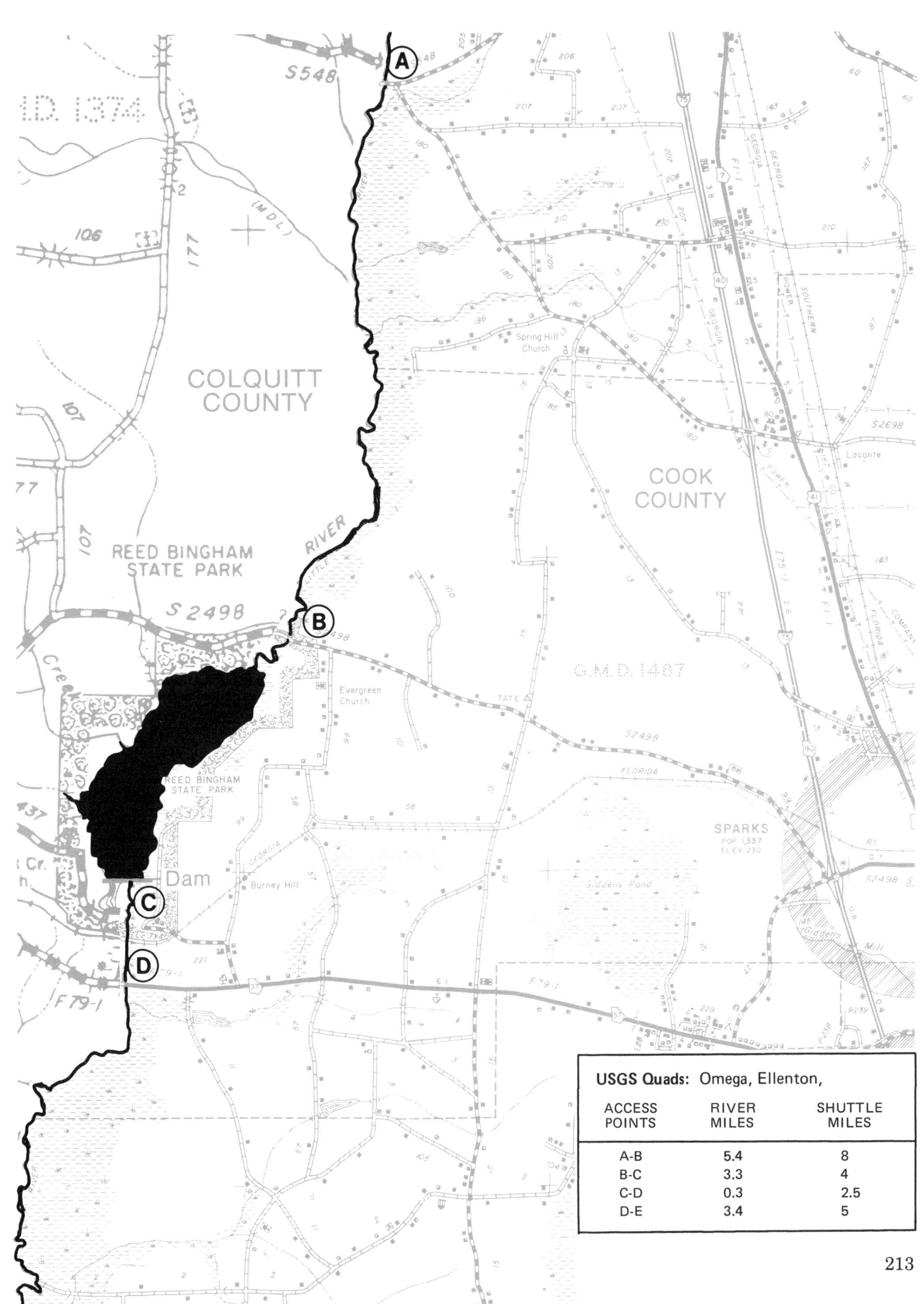

USGS Quads: Omega, Ellenton,

ACCESS POINTS	RIVER MILES	SHUTTLE MILES
A-B	5.4	8
B-C	3.3	4
C-D	0.3	2.5
D-E	3.4	5

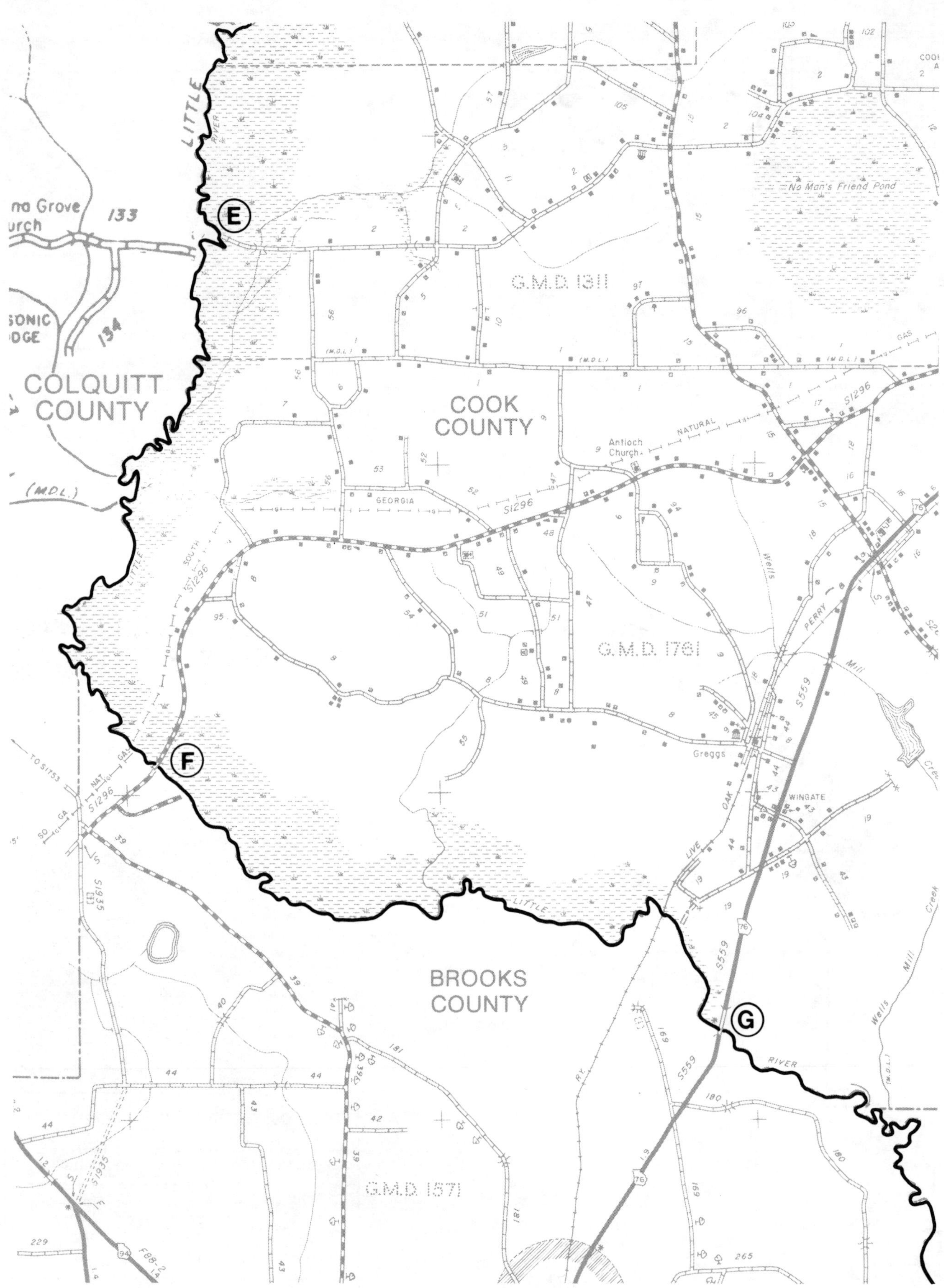
E
F
G
COLQUITT COUNTY
COOK COUNTY
BROOKS COUNTY
G.M.D. 1311
G.M.D. 1761
G.M.D. 1571
No Man's Friend Pond
Antioch Church
Greggs
WINGATE
LITTLE RIVER

Section: West of Lenox to Withlacoochee River

Counties: Colquitt, Cook, Brooks, Lowndes

Suitable For: Cruising, camping

Appropriate For: Families, beginners, intermediates, advanced

Months Runnable: Late November to June

Interest Highlights: Scenery, wildlife

Scenery: Beautiful

Difficulty: International Scale I
Numerical Points 5

Average Width: 30-40 ft.
Velocity: Slow to moderate
Gradient: 1.88 ft./mi.

Runnable Water Level: Minimum 150 cfs
Maximum Up to high flood stage

Hazards: Deadfalls

Scouting: None required

USGS Quads: Berlin East, Cecil, Hahira West, Hahira East, Valdosta

ACCESS POINTS	RIVER MILES	SHUTTLE MILES
D-E	3.4	5
E-F	6.8	5.2
F-G	6.4	8
G-H	5.2	6

Portages: Dam at Reed Bingham State Park

Rescue Index: Accessible but difficult

Mean Water Temperature (°F)

Jan 52	Feb 54	Mar 60	Apr 65	May 75	Jun 80
Jul 82	Aug 81	Sep 78	Oct 68	Nov 61	Dec 55

Source of Additional Information: Waycross Game and Fish Office (912) 285-6093; Live Oak Canoe Outpost (904) 364-1683

Access Point	Access Code
E	2357
F	1357
G	1357

Access Key
1 Paved Road
2 Unpaved Road
3 Short Carry
4 Long Carry
5 Easy Grade
6 Steep Incline
7 Clear Trail
8 Brush and Trees
9 Launching Fee Charged
10 Private Property, Need Permission
11 No Access, Reference Only

Southern Georgia "blackwater" stream.

Photo courtesy of *Brown's Guide to Georgia.*

Little River of Southern Georgia—*Continued*

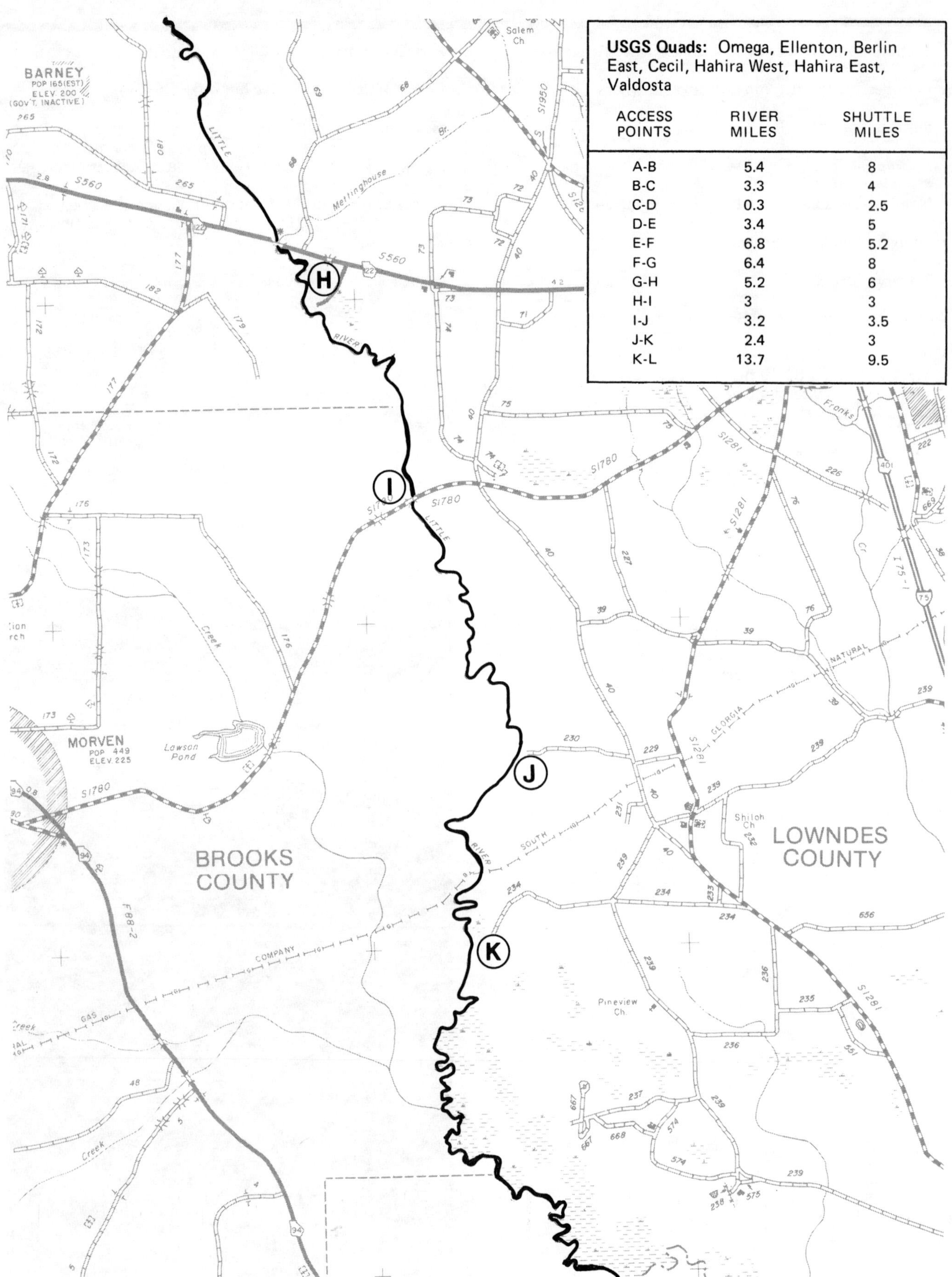

USGS Quads: Omega, Ellenton, Berlin East, Cecil, Hahira West, Hahira East, Valdosta

ACCESS POINTS	RIVER MILES	SHUTTLE MILES
A-B	5.4	8
B-C	3.3	4
C-D	0.3	2.5
D-E	3.4	5
E-F	6.8	5.2
F-G	6.4	8
G-H	5.2	6
H-I	3	3
I-J	3.2	3.5
J-K	2.4	3
K-L	13.7	9.5

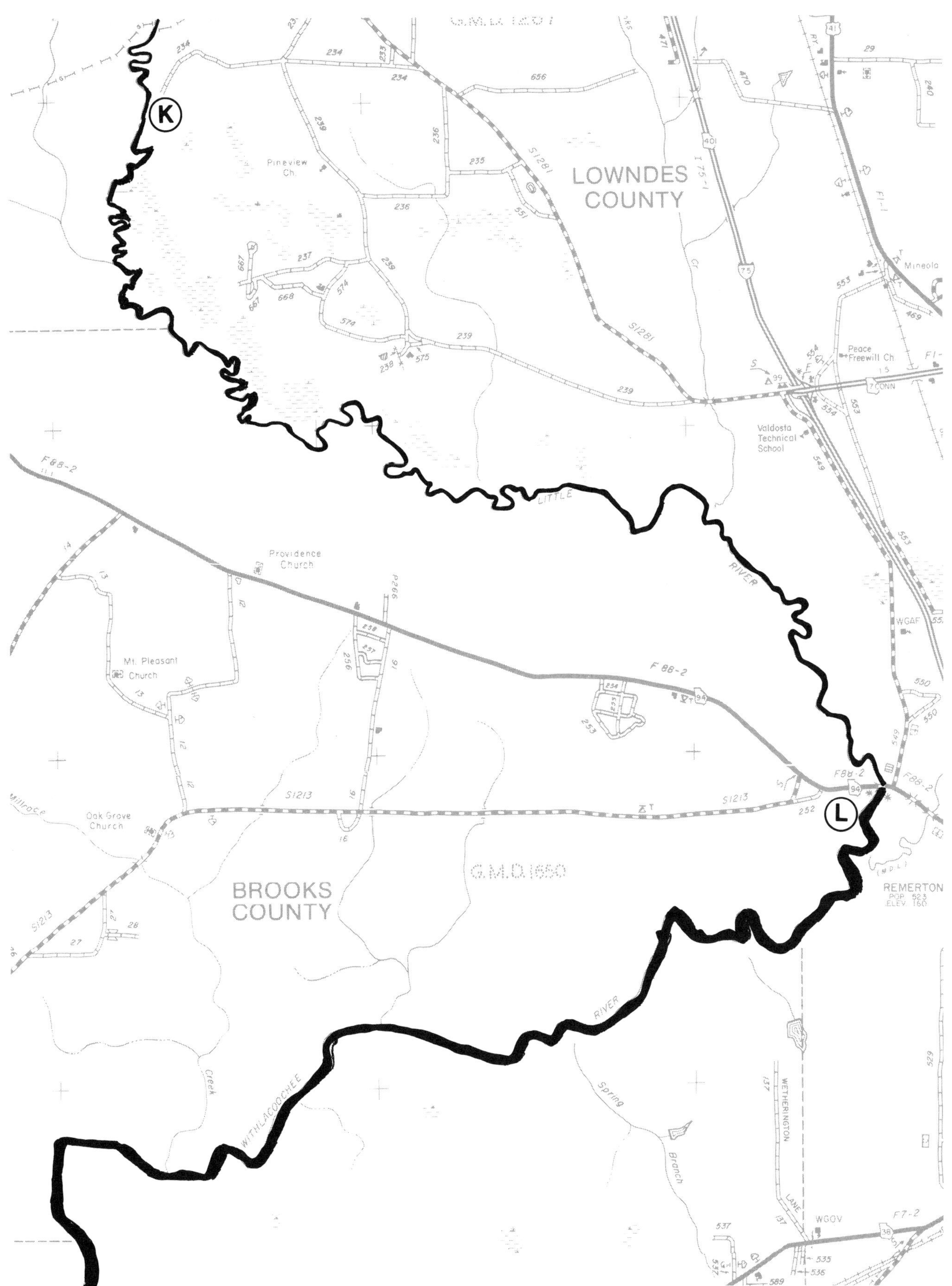
K
L
LOWNDES COUNTY
BROOKS COUNTY
Pineview Ch.
Providence Church
Mt. Pleasant Church
Oak Grove Church
LITTLE
RIVER
WITHLACOOCHEE
RIVER
Creek
Spring
Branch
Mineola
Peace Freewill Ch
Valdosta Technical School
REMERTON
POP. 523
ELEV. 160
WETHERINGTON
LANE
WGAF
WGOV
G.M.D.1650
F88-2
S1213
S1281
Millrace

Withlacoochee River

One of Georgia's truly beautiful scenic streams, the Withlacoochee flows entirely within the Coastal Plain. Originating in Tift and Berrien counties, it flows south along the Cook County line into Lowndes County where it is joined by its largest tributary, (ironically) the Little River. Continuing south in a broad loop, the Withlacoochee passes quietly into Florida where it empties into the Suwannee. Though only the Georgia portion of the Withlacoochee is described, the Florida section is equally beautiful and fully worthy of exploration.

Runnable from GA 37 to the confluence with the Little during the winter and spring, and below the confluence of the Little River from late November to early August, the Withlacoochee flows through a thickly wooded swamp corridor bordered by cultivated table land and commercial pine forests. Its banks are two to four feet in height and are sandy clay. The water is a clear, burgundy red color, which contrasts strikingly with the white sand banks and often appears glossy black where the channel is deep.

Intimate, shaded, and mysterious in its beauty, the Withlacoochee is one of the few Coastal Plain streams in which limestone ledges form small shoals. Occuring primarily in the Lowndes–Brooks counties segment of the stream, these shoals rarely surpass Class I + in difficulty, but they enliven the paddling nonetheless. A second distinctive feature of the Withlacoochee is white sandbars on the insides of bends which are perfect for swimming or camping.

Both the Withlacoochee and the Little inundate their narrow floodplains for long periods of time giving rise to bottom forests of swamp black gum and cypress. Cypress and gum grow in the stream as well as on the banks where they are joined by Ogeechee lime, water elm, water oak, laurel oak, and sweet bay. Scrub vegetation is thick with palmetto, swamp cyrilla, and possum haw, among other varieties. Birds, reptiles, and animals flourish along the Withlacoochee and are readily observable in all their diversity by the silent paddler.

At the GA 37 crossing the river averages a slim 30 feet in width; it expands to 40 feet as it dips into Lowndes County and broadens to 55 to 70 feet below the mouth of the Little. The current is moderate on the Withlacoochee and access is excellent. Signs of habitation are infrequent though swimmers are frequently encountered at bridge crossings and anglers are likely to turn up anywhere. The stream's level of difficulty is Class I with deadfalls being the only hazard to navigation. The course of the Withlacoochee is winding and convoluted. Formation of by-pass islands and oxbow lakes is common.

Section: Southwest of Nashville to Little River

Counties: Berrien, Lowndes, Brooks

Suitable For: Cruising, camping

Appropriate For: Beginners, intermediates, advanced

Months Runnable: Late November to mid-May

Interest Highlights: Scenery, wildlife

Scenery: Beautiful

Difficulty: International Scale I+
Numerical Points 6

Average Width: 30-70 ft.
Gradient: Slow to moderate
Velocity: 1.92 ft./mi.

Runnable Water Level: Minimum 145 cfs
Maximum Up to high flood stage

Hazards: Deadfalls

Scouting: None required

Portages: None required

Rescue Index: Accessible but difficult

Mean Water Temperature (°F)

Jan 52	Feb 53	Mar 59	Apr 65	May 74	Jun 80
Jul 82	Aug 82	Sep 78	Oct 69	Nov 61	Dec 54

Source of Additional Information: Waycross Game and Fish Office (912) 285-6093, Live Oak Canoe Outpost (904) 364-1683

Access Point	Access Code
A	1357
B	1357
C	2357
D	2357
E	2367
F	(11)
G	(11)
H	1357

Access Key
1 Paved Road
2 Unpaved Road
3 Short Carry
4 Long Carry
5 Easy Grade
6 Steep Incline
7 Clear Trail
8 Brush and Trees
9 Launching Fee Charged
10 Private Property, Need Permission
11 No Access, Reference Only

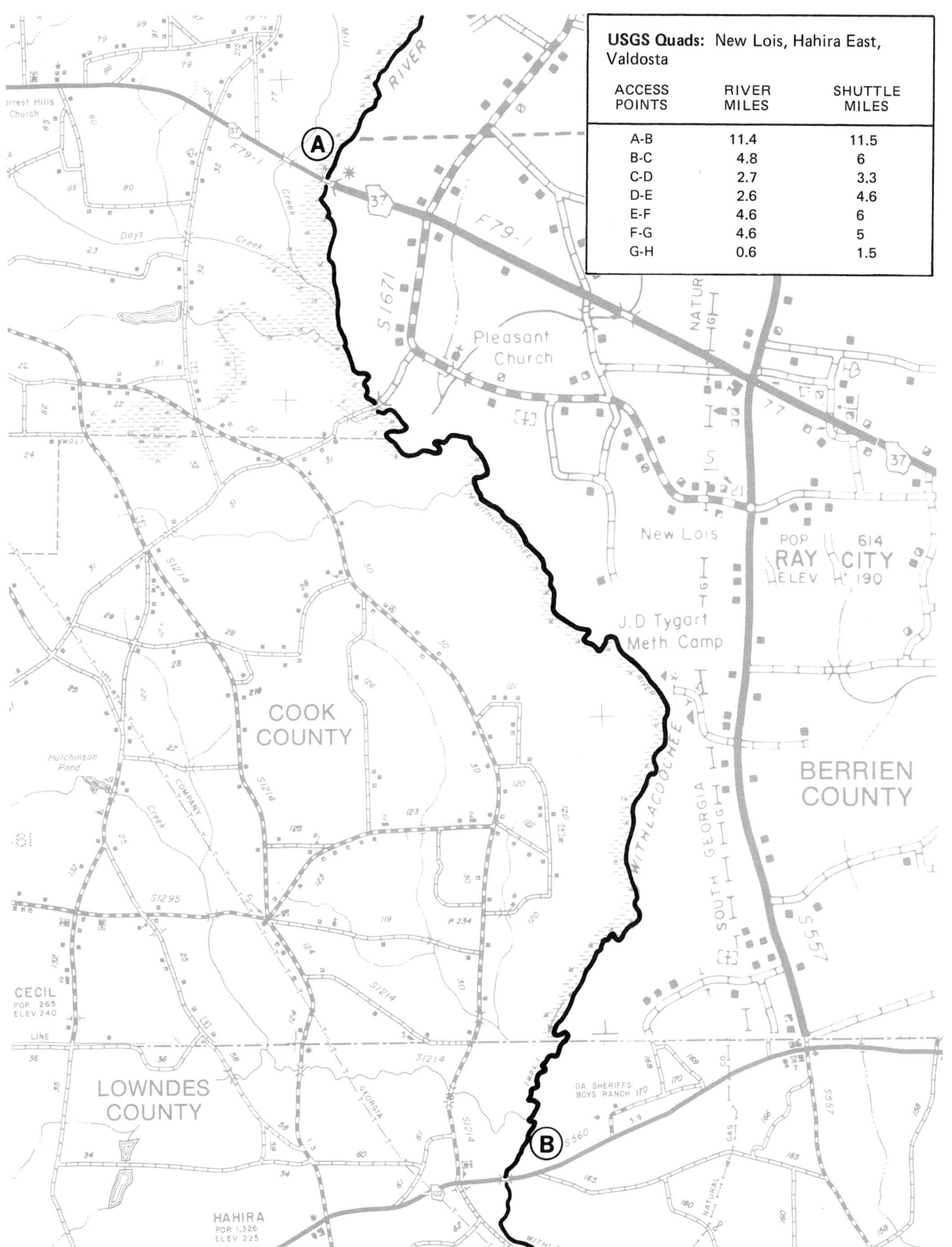

USGS Quads: New Lois, Hahira East, Valdosta

ACCESS POINTS	RIVER MILES	SHUTTLE MILES
A-B	11.4	11.5
B-C	4.8	6
C-D	2.7	3.3
D-E	2.6	4.6
E-F	4.6	6
F-G	4.6	5
G-H	0.6	1.5

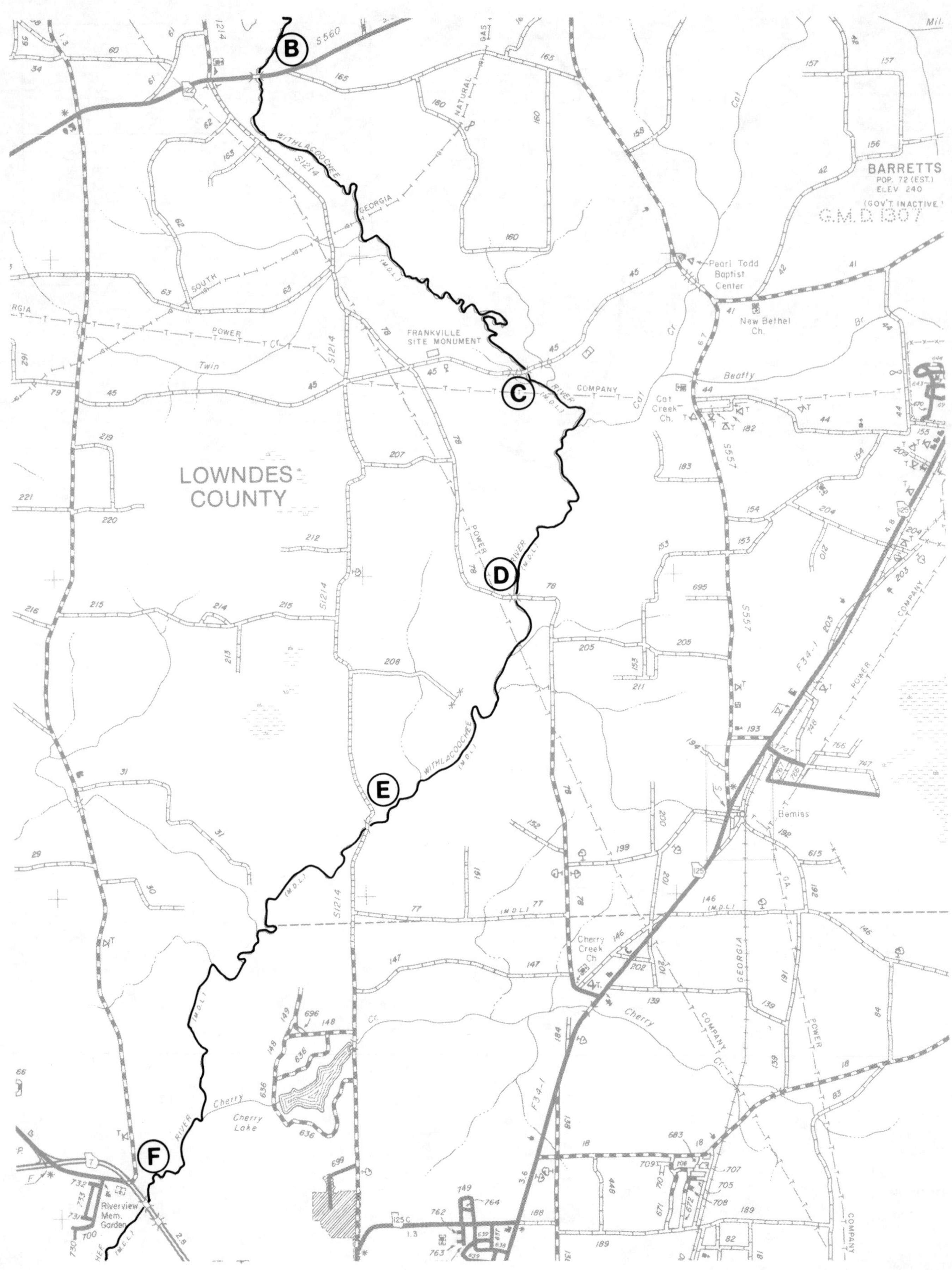
B
C
D
E
F
LOWNDES COUNTY
BARRETTS
POP. 72 (EST.)
ELEV 240
(GOV'T INACTIVE)
G.M.D. 1307
FRANKVILLE SITE MONUMENT
Pearl Todd Baptist Center
New Bethel Ch.
Cat Creek Ch.
Cherry Creek Ch.
Bemiss
Riverview Mem. Garden
Cherry Lake
WITHLACOOCHEE
RIVER
GEORGIA
POWER
COMPANY
SOUTH
NATURAL GAS
Twin
Beatty
Cat
Cherry
Br.
Cr.

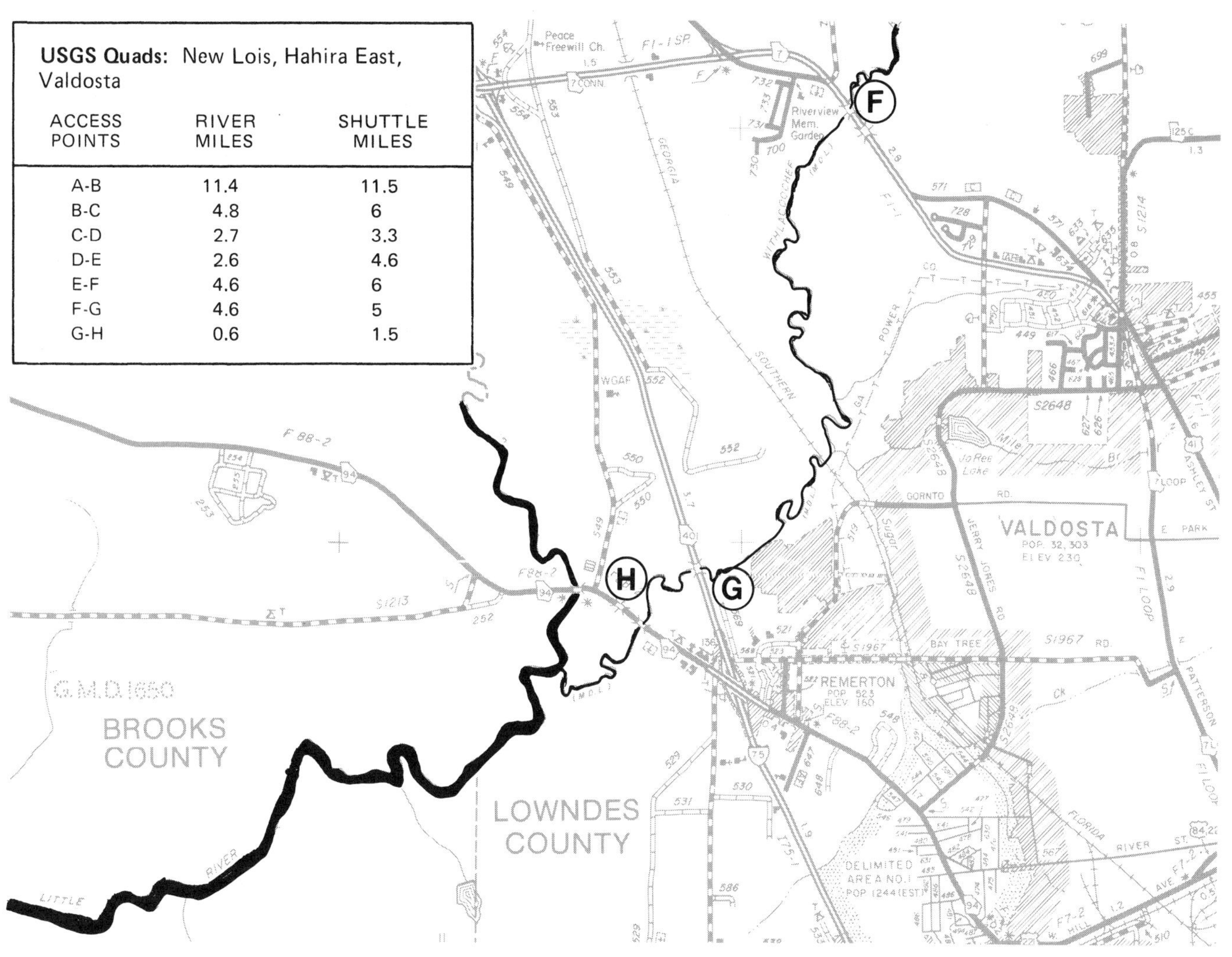
USGS Quads: New Lois, Hahira East, Valdosta

ACCESS POINTS	RIVER MILES	SHUTTLE MILES
A-B	11.4	11.5
B-C	4.8	6
C-D	2.7	3.3
D-E	2.6	4.6
E-F	4.6	6
F-G	4.6	5
G-H	0.6	1.5

Section: Southwest of Nashville to Little River

Counties: Berrien, Lowndes, Brooks

Suitable For: Cruising, camping

Appropriate For: Beginners, intermediates, advanced

Months Runnable: Late November to mid-May

Interest Highlights: Scenery, wildlife

Scenery: Beautiful

Difficulty: International Scale I+
Numerical Points 6

Average Width: 30-70 ft.
Gradient: Slow to moderate
Velocity: 1.92 ft./mi.

Runnable Water Level: Minimum 145 cfs
Maximum Up to high flood stage

Hazards: Deadfalls

Scouting: None required

Portages: None required

Rescue Index: Accessible but difficult

Mean Water Temperature (°F)

Jan 52	Feb 53	Mar 59	Apr 65	May 74	Jun 80
Jul 82	Aug 82	Sep 78	Oct 69	Nov 61	Dec 54

Source of Additional Information: Waycross Game and Fish Office (912) 285-6093, Live Oak Canoe Outpost (904) 364-1683

Access Point	Access Code
A	1357
B	1357
C	2357
D	2357
E	2367
F	(11)
G	(11)
H	1357

Access Key
1 Paved Road
2 Unpaved Road
3 Short Carry
4 Long Carry
5 Easy Grade
6 Steep Incline
7 Clear Trail
8 Brush and Trees
9 Launching Fee Charged
10 Private Property, Need Permission
11 No Access, Reference Only

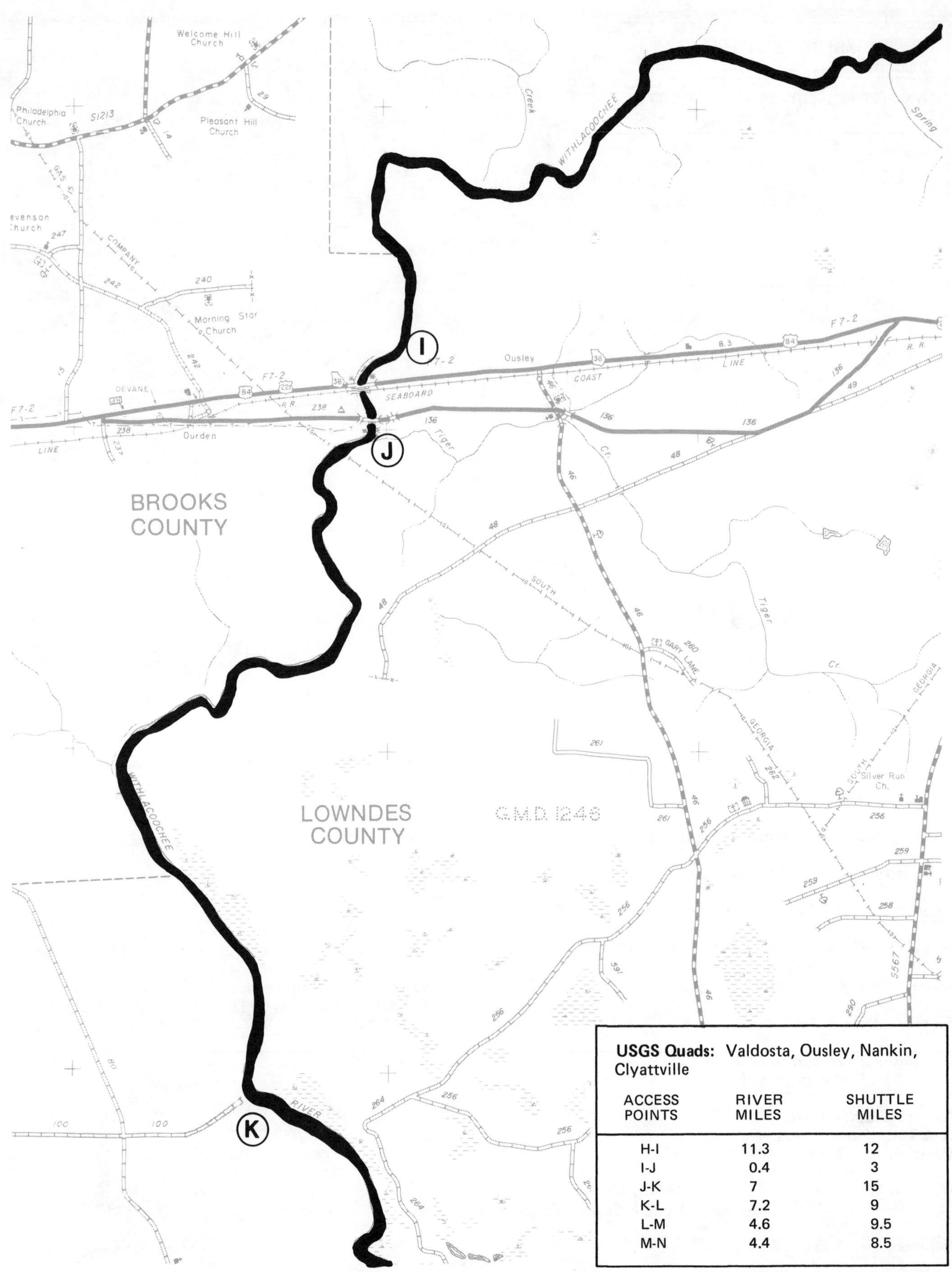

USGS Quads: Valdosta, Ousley, Nankin, Clyattville

ACCESS POINTS	RIVER MILES	SHUTTLE MILES
H-I	11.3	12
I-J	0.4	3
J-K	7	15
K-L	7.2	9
L-M	4.6	9.5
M-N	4.4	8.5

Section: Valdosta (mouth of Little River) to GA 31

Counties: Lowndes, Brooks

Suitable For: Cruising, camping

Appropriate For: Families, beginners, intermediates, advanced

Months Runnable: November through mid-August

Interest Highlights: Scenery, wildlife

Scenery: Beautiful

Difficulty: International Scale I
Numerical Points 4

Average Width: 60-75 ft.
Gradient: Slow to moderate
Velocity: 1.43 ft./mi.

Runnable Water Level: Minimum 180 cfs
Maximum Up to high flood stage

Hazards: Deadfalls

Scouting: None required

Portages: None required

Rescue Index: Accessible but difficult

Mean Water Temperature (°F)

Jan 53	Feb 54	Mar 60	Apr 65	May 75	Jun 81
Jul 83	Aug 81	Sep 78	Oct 70	Nov 62	Dec 55

Source of Additional Information: Waycross Game and Fish Office (912) 285-6093, Live Oak Canoe Outpost (904) 364-1683

Access Point	Access Code
H	1357
I	1357
J	1357
K	2357
L	1357
M	2357
N	1357

Access Key
1 Paved Road
2 Unpaved Road
3 Short Carry
4 Long Carry
5 Easy Grade
6 Steep Incline
7 Clear Trail
8 Brush and Trees
9 Launching Fee Charged
10 Private Property, Need Permission
11 No Access, Reference Only

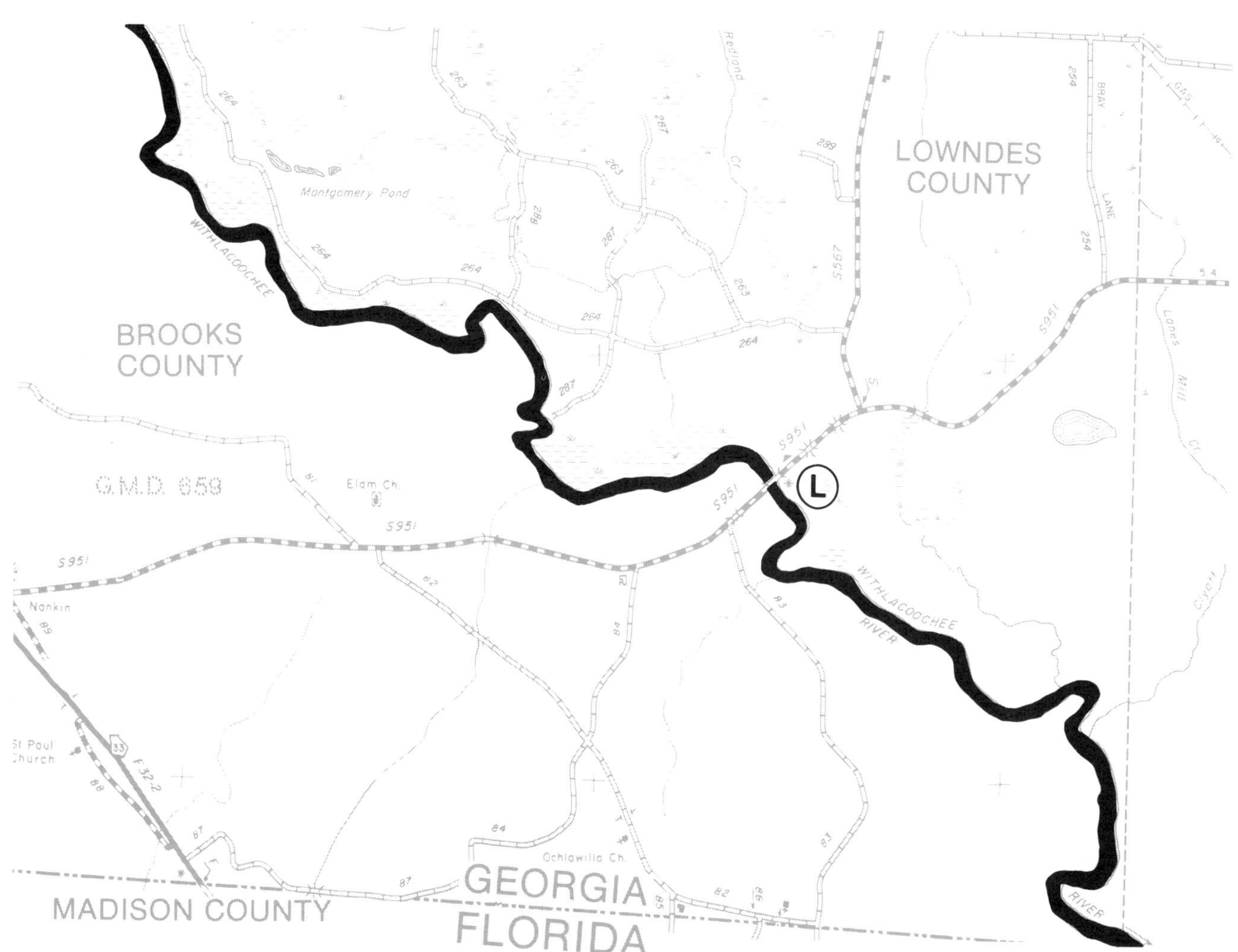

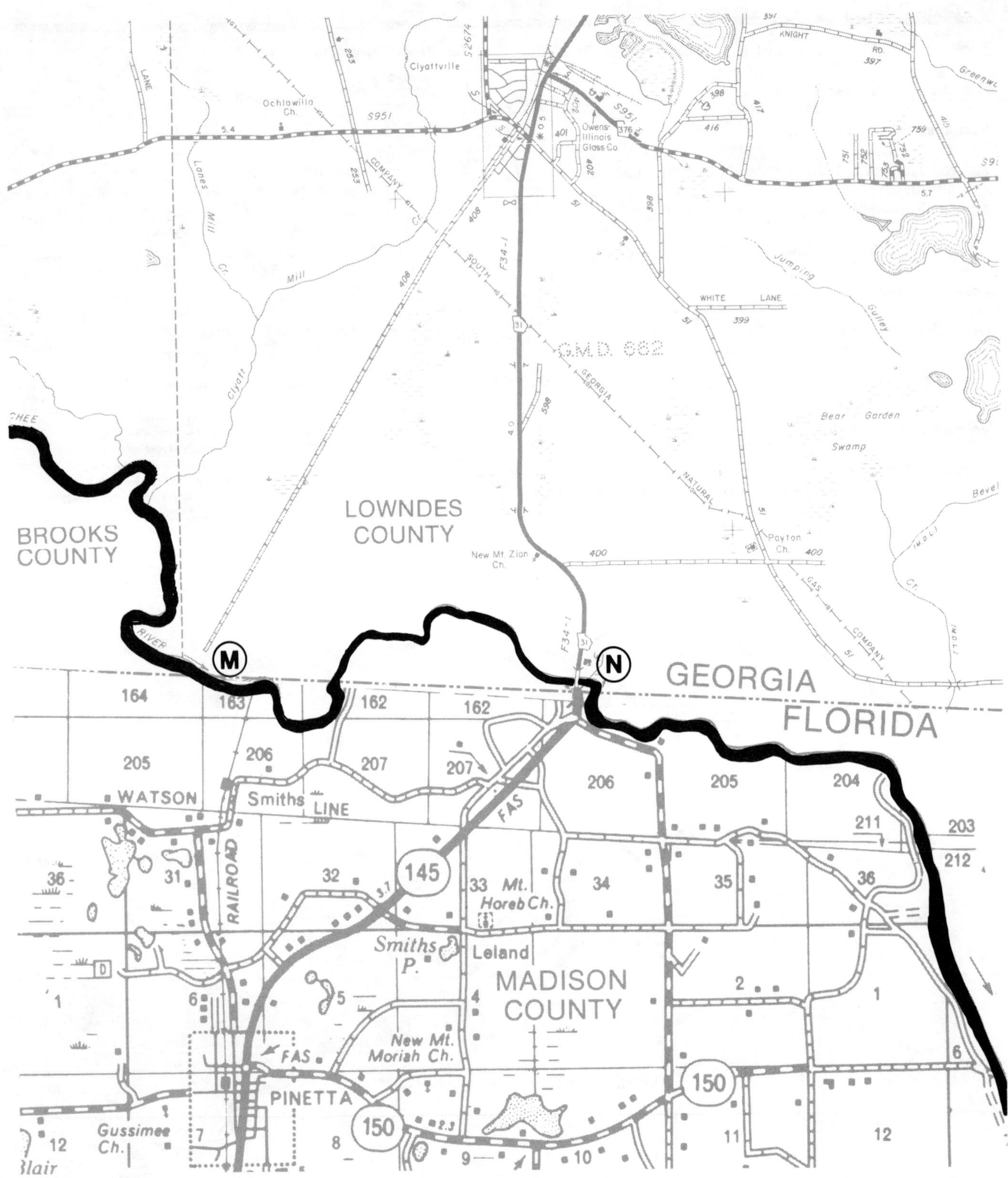

Clyattville
Ochlawilla Ch.
Owens-Illinois Glass Co
KNIGHT RD.
Greenwood
Lanes Mill Cr.
Mill
Clyatt
Jumping Gulley
WHITE LANE
G.M.D. 662
Bear Garden Swamp
LOWNDES COUNTY
BROOKS COUNTY
New Mt. Zion Ch.
Payton Ch.
Bevel
RIVER
M
N
GEORGIA
FLORIDA
WATSON
Smiths
LINE
RAILROAD
FAS
145
Mt. Horeb Ch.
Smiths P.
Leland
MADISON COUNTY
New Mt. Moriah Ch.
PINETTA
150
Gussimee Ch.
Blair

Section: Valdosta (mouth of Little River) to GA 31

Counties: Lowndes, Brooks

Suitable For: Cruising, camping

Appropriate For: Families, beginners, intermediates, advanced

Months Runnable: November through mid-August

Interest Highlights: Scenery, wildlife

Scenery: Beautiful

Difficulty: International Scale I
Numerical Points 4

Average Width: 60-75 ft.
Gradient: Slow to moderate
Velocity: 1.43 ft./mi.

Runnable Water Level: Minimum 180 cfs
Maximum Up to high flood stage

Hazards: Deadfalls

Scouting: None required

Portages: None required

Rescue Index: Accessible but difficult

Mean Water Temperature (°F)

Jan 53	Feb 54	Mar 60	Apr 65	May 75	Jun 81
Jul 83	Aug 81	Sep 78	Oct 70	Nov 62	Dec 55

Source of Additional Information: Waycross Game and Fish Office (912) 285-6093, Live Oak Canoe Outpost (904) 364-1683

Access Point	Access Code
H	1357
I	1357
J	1357
K	2357
L	1357
M	2357
N	1357

Access Key
1 Paved Road
2 Unpaved Road
3 Short Carry
4 Long Carry
5 Easy Grade
6 Steep Incline
7 Clear Trail
8 Brush and Trees
9 Launching Fee Charged
10 Private Property, Need Permission
11 No Access, Reference Only

USGS Quads: Valdosta, Ousley, Nankin, Clyattville

ACCESS POINTS	RIVER MILES	SHUTTLE MILES
H-I	11.3	12
I-J	0.4	3
J-K	7	15
K-L	7.2	9
L-M	4.6	9.5
M-N	4.4	8.5

Withlacoochee River.

Photo courtesy of *Brown's Guide to Georgia.*

Ochlockonee River

The Ochlockonee River rises in Worth County near Gordy and runs southwest draining portions of Colquitt, Thomas, and Grady counties before slipping over the state line into Florida and then to the Gulf of Mexico. Flowing between sandy clay banks of two to five feet, the Ochlockonee is chocolate brown in color, with moderate to sluggish current.

Above GA 188 in Thomas County the Ochlockonee is a maze of deadfalls. Downstream of GA 188 the stream can be run most of the year and is substantially less obstructed. Intimate, pristine, and exotically canopied with cypress, black gum, birch, and willow, the Ochlockonee is an exceptionally pretty stream. As it follows its generally winding and serpentine course through an oak-and-gum-dominated bottom land forest corridor, by-pass islands and oxbow lakes are not uncommon on the river. White sandbars and beaches grace the insides of many bends and provide excellent sites for camping or swimming. Banks are dense and luxurious with vegetation including swamp palm, cyrilla, and Sebastian bush. From time to time tall pines line the streamside, as do sweet bay and water oak. Wildlife, particularly birds, make their presence known through continuous activity.

Passing below the US 19 bridge the watercourse expands into an extensive swamp for about two-thirds of a mile. Below GA 3 the Ochlockonee emerges unexpectedly from the jungle where the surrounding terrain has been completely cleared for a powerline crossing. Here the stark reality of human intervention on otherwise pristine surroundings is brought home with great visual impact.

Continuing downstream and crossing into Florida, the river widens to approximately 60 to 75 feet but otherwise remains essentially unchanged except that it picks up a little sediment as it passes through the Tallahassee hills in southern Grady County. The level of difficulty is Class I throughout; dangers to navigation consist primarily of deadfalls that completely block the stream periodically in all Georgia sections and brush strainers that form in the channel along the side of small islands. Access is good.

Section: Moultrie to Florida border

Counties: Colquitt, Thomas, Grady; Gadsden (FL)

Suitable For: Cruising, camping

Appropriate For: Families, beginners, intermediates, advanced

Months Runnable: November through July and all year during wet years

Interest Highlights: Scenery, wildlife

Scenery: Beautiful

Difficulty: International Scale I
Numerical Points 5

Average Width: 40-60 ft.

Gradient: Slack to slow

Velocity: 2.09 ft./mi.

Runnable Water Level: Minimum 175 cfs
Maximum Up to flood stage

Hazards: Strainers, deadfalls

Scouting: None required

Portages: Around deadfalls

Rescue Index: Accessible but difficult

Mean Water Temperature (°F)

Jan 51	Feb 52	Mar 57	Apr 64	May 72	Jun 77
Jul 81	Aug 80	Sep 75	Oct 66	Nov 60	Dec 53

Source of Additional Information: Albany Game and Fish Office (912) 430-4252

Access Point	Access Code
A	1357
B	2368
C	2357
D	1368
E	1367
F	1357
G	1357
H	1357
I	1357
J	1357
K	1357
L	2357
M	1357

Access Key

1 Paved Road
2 Unpaved Road
3 Short Carry
4 Long Carry
5 Easy Grade
6 Steep Incline
7 Clear Trail
8 Brush and Trees
9 Launching Fee Charged
10 Private Property, Need Permission
11 No Access, Reference Only

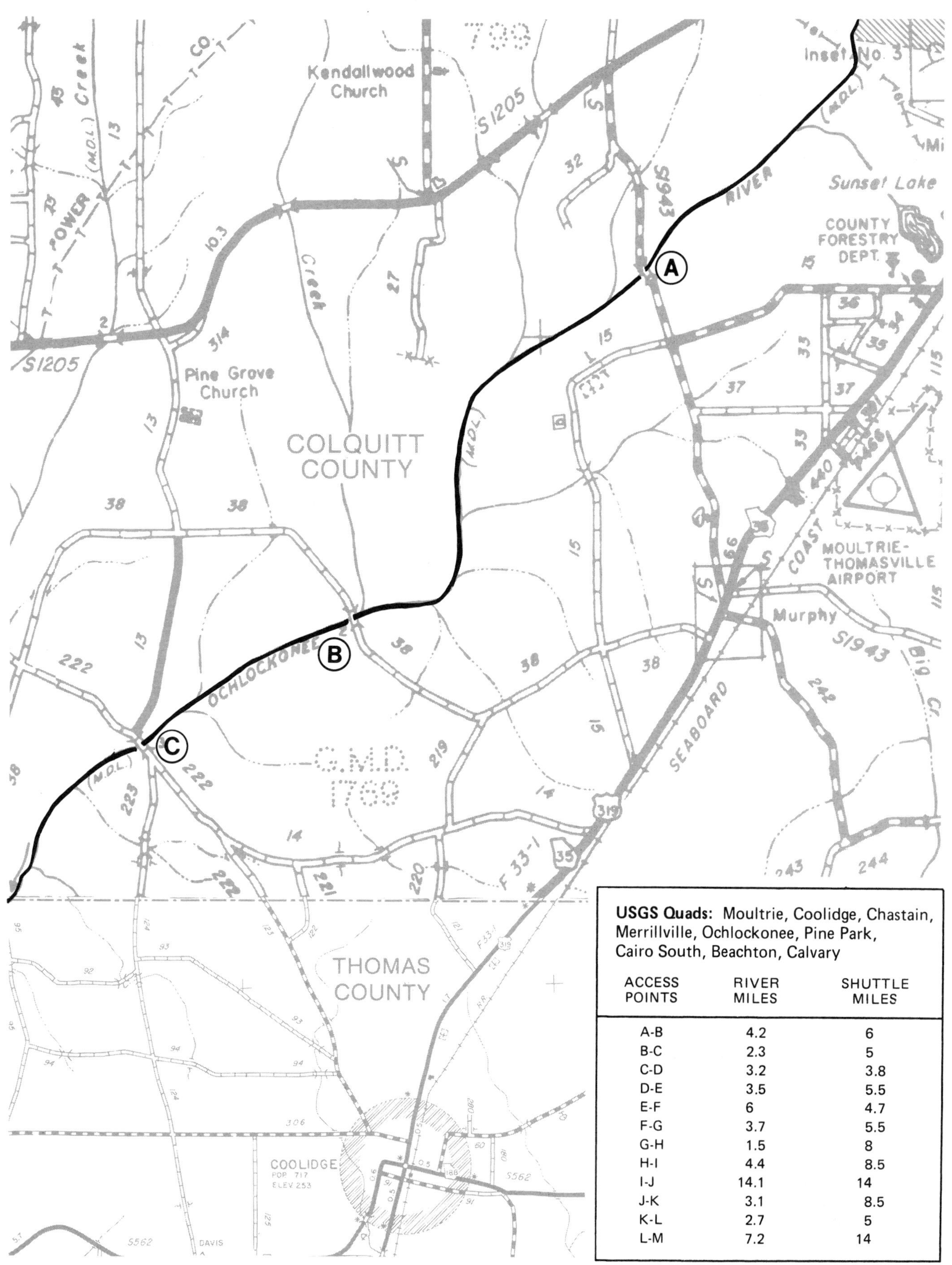

USGS Quads: Moultrie, Coolidge, Chastain, Merrillville, Ochlockonee, Pine Park, Cairo South, Beachton, Calvary

ACCESS POINTS	RIVER MILES	SHUTTLE MILES
A-B	4.2	6
B-C	2.3	5
C-D	3.2	3.8
D-E	3.5	5.5
E-F	6	4.7
F-G	3.7	5.5
G-H	1.5	8
H-I	4.4	8.5
I-J	14.1	14
J-K	3.1	8.5
K-L	2.7	5
L-M	7.2	14

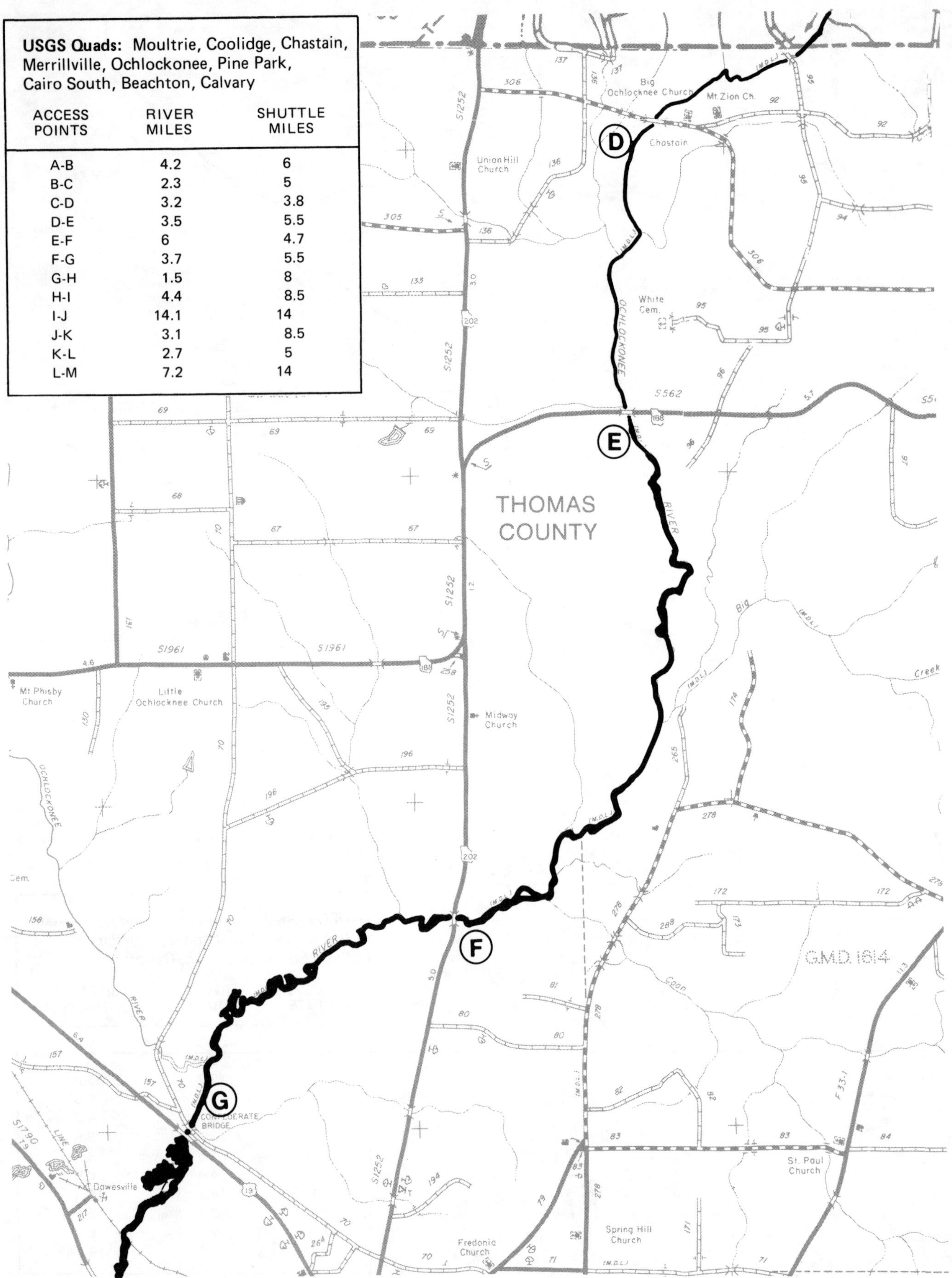

USGS Quads: Moultrie, Coolidge, Chastain, Merrillville, Ochlockonee, Pine Park, Cairo South, Beachton, Calvary

ACCESS POINTS	RIVER MILES	SHUTTLE MILES
A-B	4.2	6
B-C	2.3	5
C-D	3.2	3.8
D-E	3.5	5.5
E-F	6	4.7
F-G	3.7	5.5
G-H	1.5	8
H-I	4.4	8.5
I-J	14.1	14
J-K	3.1	8.5
K-L	2.7	5
L-M	7.2	14

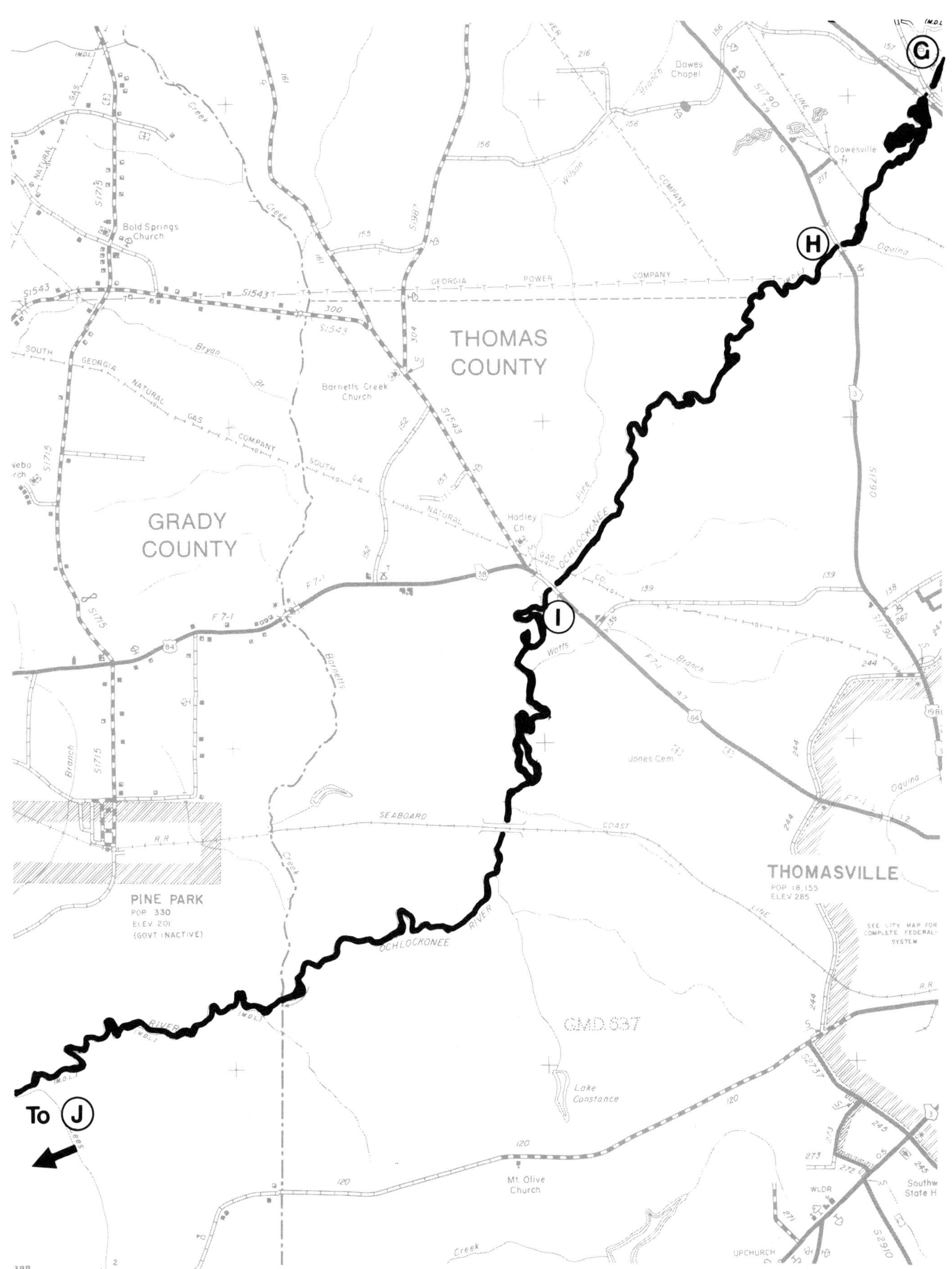
THOMAS
COUNTY
GRADY
COUNTY
THOMASVILLE
POP 18,155
ELEV 285
PINE PARK
POP 330
ELEV 201
(GOVT INACTIVE)
OCHLOCKONEE RIVER
Dawes Chapel
Dawesville
Bold Springs Church
Barnetts Creek Church
Hadley Ch
Jones Cem
Lake Constance
Mt. Olive Church
GEORGIA POWER COMPANY
SOUTH GEORGIA NATURAL GAS COMPANY
SEABOARD COAST LINE R.R.
SEE CITY MAP FOR COMPLETE FEDERAL-AID SYSTEM
G.M.D. 637
To J

Section: Moultrie to Florida border

Counties: Colquitt, Thomas, Grady; Gadsden (FL)

Suitable For: Cruising, camping

Appropriate For: Families, beginners, intermediates, advanced

Months Runnable: November through July and all year during wet years

Interest Highlights: Scenery, wildlife

Scenery: Beautiful

Difficulty: International Scale I
Numerical Points 5

Average Width: 40-60 ft.
Gradient: Slack to slow
Velocity: 2.09 ft./mi.

Runnable Water Level: Minimum 175 cfs
Maximum Up to flood stage

Hazards: Strainers, deadfalls

Scouting: None required

Portages: Around deadfalls

Rescue Index: Accessible but difficult

Mean Water Temperature (°F)

Jan 51	Feb 52	Mar 57	Apr 64	May 72	Jun 77
Jul 81	Aug 80	Sep 75	Oct 66	Nov 60	Dec 53

Source of Additional Information: Albany Game and Fish Office (912) 430-4252

Access Point	Access Code
A	1357
B	2368
C	2357
D	1368
E	1367
F	1357
G	1357
H	1357
I	1357
J	1357
K	1357
L	2357
M	1357

Access Key
1 Paved Road
2 Unpaved Road
3 Short Carry
4 Long Carry
5 Easy Grade
6 Steep Incline
7 Clear Trail
8 Brush and Trees
9 Launching Fee Charged
10 Private Property, Need Permission
11 No Access, Reference Only

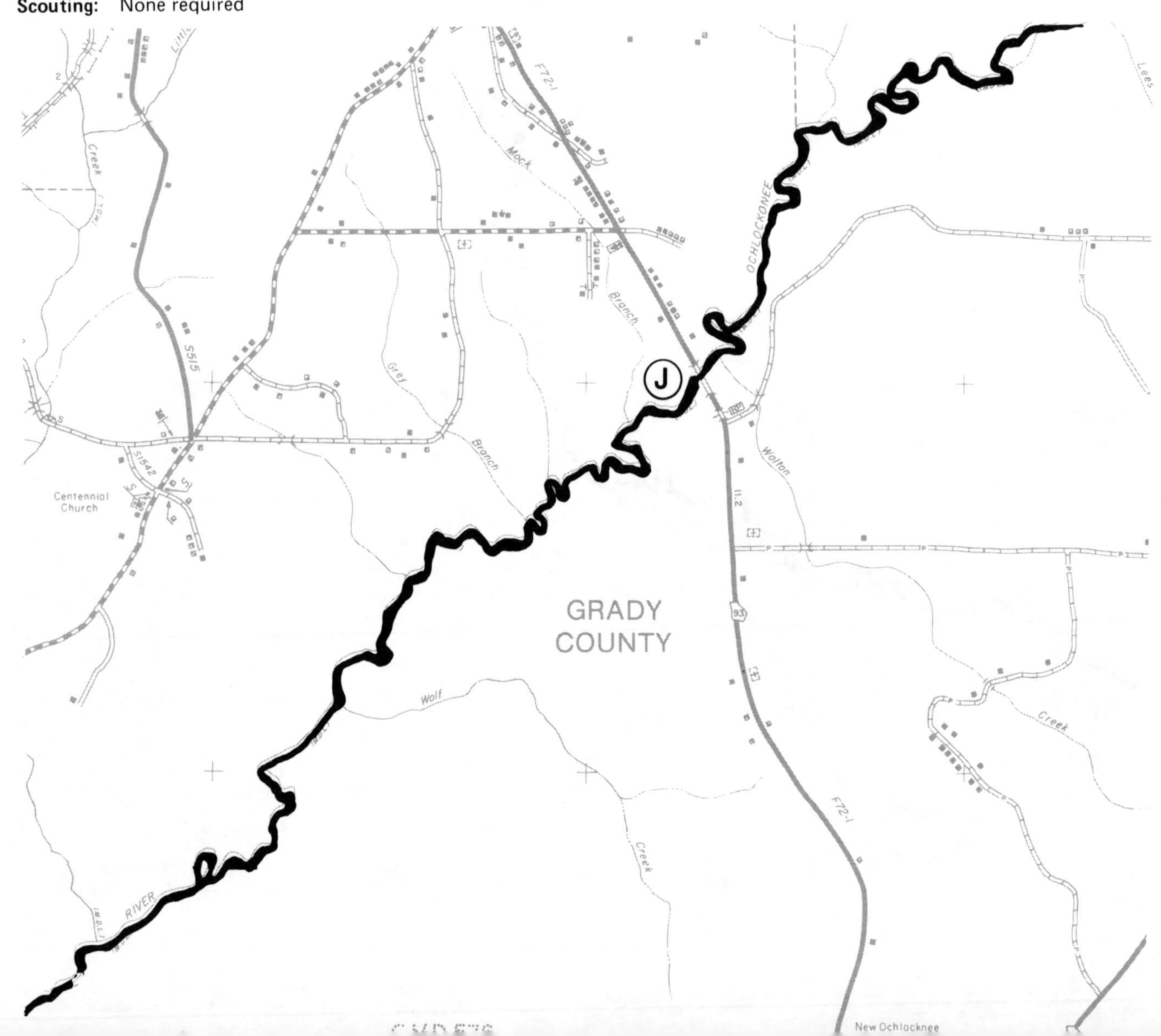

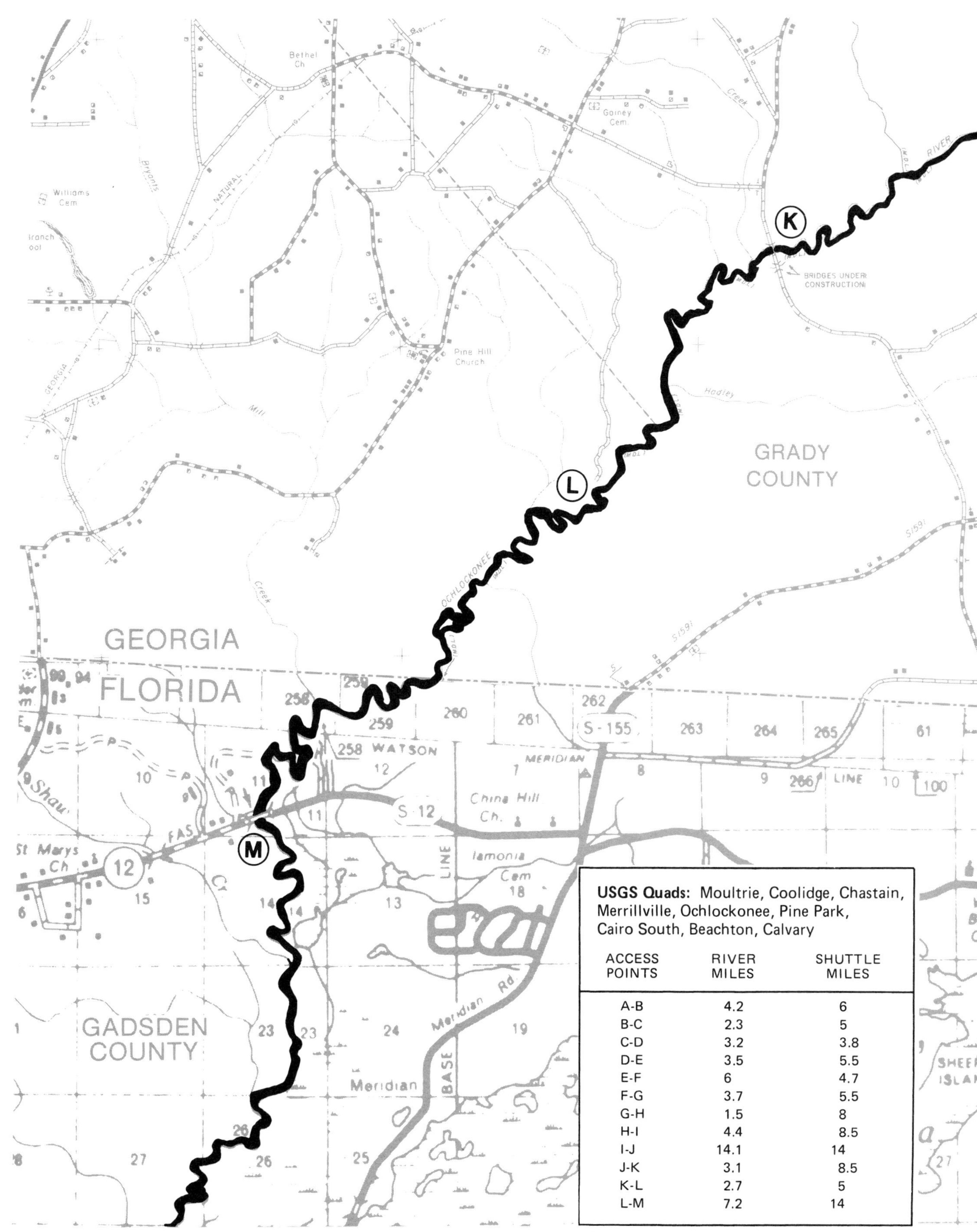

USGS Quads: Moultrie, Coolidge, Chastain, Merrillville, Ochlockonee, Pine Park, Cairo South, Beachton, Calvary

ACCESS POINTS	RIVER MILES	SHUTTLE MILES
A-B	4.2	6
B-C	2.3	5
C-D	3.2	3.8
D-E	3.5	5.5
E-F	6	4.7
F-G	3.7	5.5
G-H	1.5	8
H-I	4.4	8.5
I-J	14.1	14
J-K	3.1	8.5
K-L	2.7	5
L-M	7.2	14

Flint River

After crossing the Fall Line, the Flint River of the western Piedmont (described in the preceding chapter) changes quickly. Four miles below the GA 137 bridge on the Taylor–Crawford county line, the valley farm belt beside the Flint River reverts to forest, which expands almost immediately into a thick corridor on both sides of the stream. As the valley widens, meandering begins and very shortly horseshoe bends and occasional oxbow lakes become common. Seasonally wet bottom lands surrounding the Flint make up the Magnolia Swamp, which slows the flow of the current. As the stream passes east of Reynolds and into Macon County, the banks begin to rise and the swamp is left behind. All through Macon County a tableland wood corridor dominates the terrain, with farm or pastureland occasionally wedging in near the treelined river banks.

About ten miles below Montezuma a single pine grows right in the middle of the river channel. Beyond this pine the river corridor becomes swampy once again as the backwaters of Lake Blackshear are reached. Feeder creeks and backwater sloughs make possible various side explorations here. Wildlife and birds are exceptionally diverse.

Below the Blackshear Dam the Flint continues its journey through the Coastal Plain flowing in long straightaways and broad, seemingly endless bends through a wooded corridor surrounded by fertile farm land. Averaging 210 to 255 feet in width, the current is slower than in the Piedmont sections, and the water is a clear to split-pea green when sediment concentrations are low. Its banks average 5 to 20 feet in height and are lined with pine, sweet gum, sycamore, willow, and ash. Due to the width of the stream and the height of the banks, however, the water is almost totally exposed to the sun.

As the Flint approaches the environs of Albany it is backed up by the Flint River Development Dam on the northeast edge of the city. The lake created is small and rather interesting since a number of swamp marshes and sloughs occur to either side of the main channel. Downstream of the dam, the Flint runs through downtown Albany, where, below the second railroad bridge, a Class II shoal is encountered.

Leaving Albany, the Flint winds through an agricultural plateau punctuated by many small and medium-sized towns. Scenery remains substantially unchanged at streamside and no further shoals are encountered. Above Bainbridge the lake pool of Lake Seminole is encountered, signaling the end of moving water on the Flint. Beyond Bainbridge, in Lake Seminole, the Flint unites with the Chattahoochee to form the Apalachicola River, which continues downstream below the Jim Woodruff Dam to flow into Florida enroute to the Gulf of Mexico.

Level of difficulty on the Flint River below Lake Blackshear is Class I except for the Albany Shoals. Dangers are limited to the dam in Albany and powerboat traffic. Access is good.

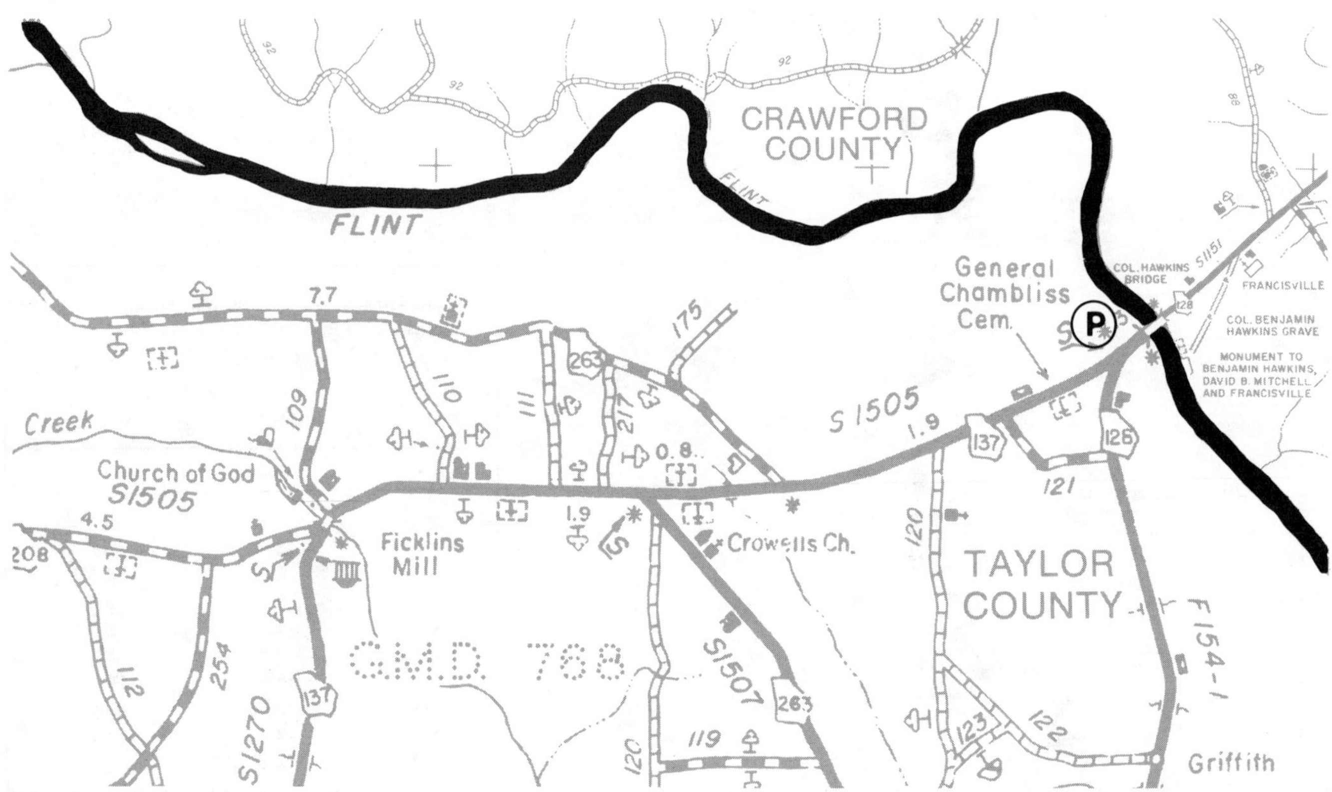

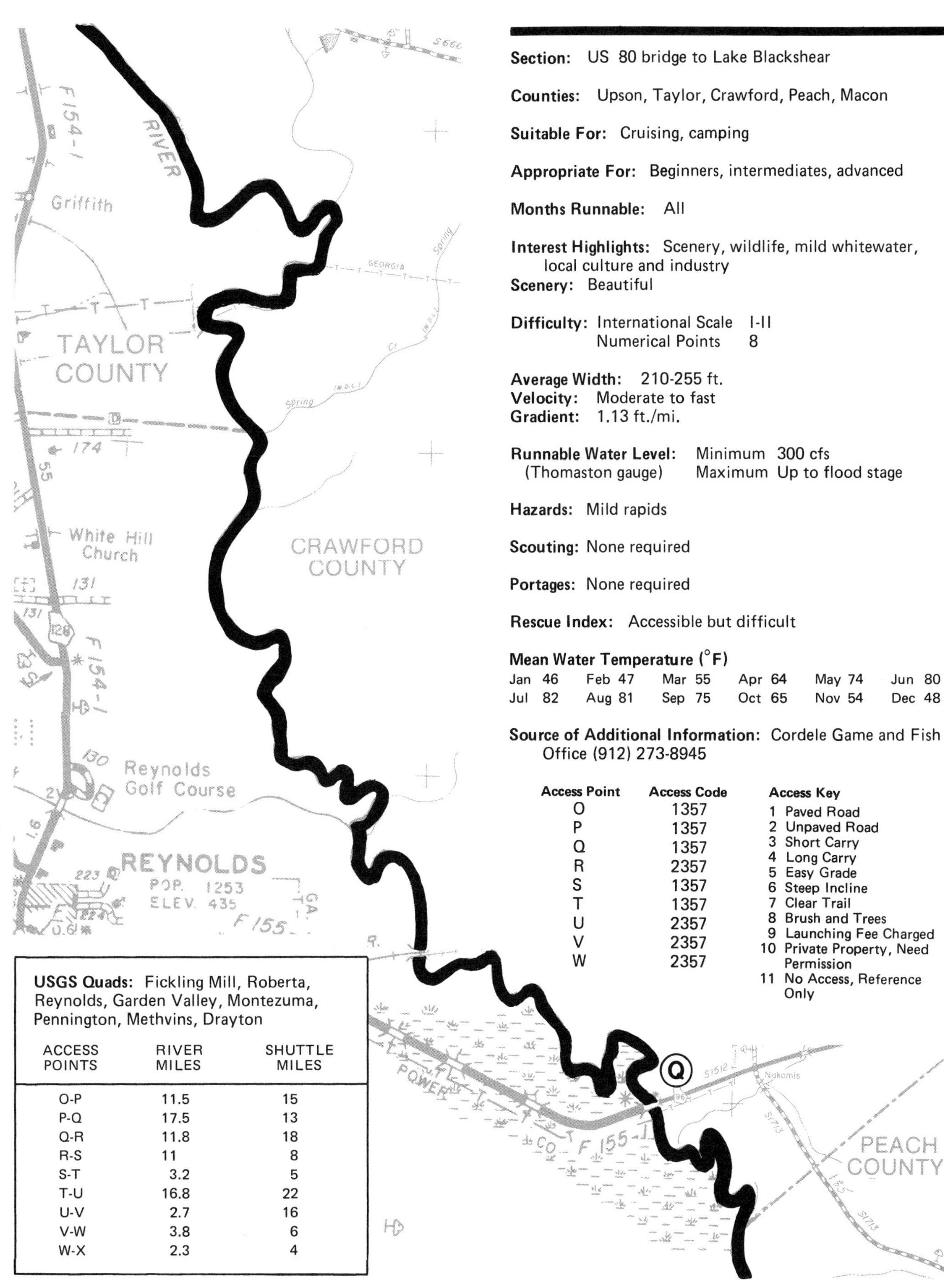

USGS Quads: Fickling Mill, Roberta, Reynolds, Garden Valley, Montezuma, Pennington, Methvins, Drayton

ACCESS POINTS	RIVER MILES	SHUTTLE MILES
O-P	11.5	15
P-Q	17.5	13
Q-R	11.8	18
R-S	11	8
S-T	3.2	5
T-U	16.8	22
U-V	2.7	16
V-W	3.8	6
W-X	2.3	4

Section: US 80 bridge to Lake Blackshear

Counties: Upson, Taylor, Crawford, Peach, Macon

Suitable For: Cruising, camping

Appropriate For: Beginners, intermediates, advanced

Months Runnable: All

Interest Highlights: Scenery, wildlife, mild whitewater, local culture and industry

Scenery: Beautiful

Difficulty: International Scale I-II
Numerical Points 8

Average Width: 210-255 ft.
Velocity: Moderate to fast
Gradient: 1.13 ft./mi.

Runnable Water Level: (Thomaston gauge) Minimum 300 cfs
Maximum Up to flood stage

Hazards: Mild rapids

Scouting: None required

Portages: None required

Rescue Index: Accessible but difficult

Mean Water Temperature (°F)

Jan 46	Feb 47	Mar 55	Apr 64	May 74	Jun 80
Jul 82	Aug 81	Sep 75	Oct 65	Nov 54	Dec 48

Source of Additional Information: Cordele Game and Fish Office (912) 273-8945

Access Point	Access Code
O	1357
P	1357
Q	1357
R	2357
S	1357
T	1357
U	2357
V	2357
W	2357

Access Key
1 Paved Road
2 Unpaved Road
3 Short Carry
4 Long Carry
5 Easy Grade
6 Steep Incline
7 Clear Trail
8 Brush and Trees
9 Launching Fee Charged
10 Private Property, Need Permission
11 No Access, Reference Only

Flint River—*Continued*

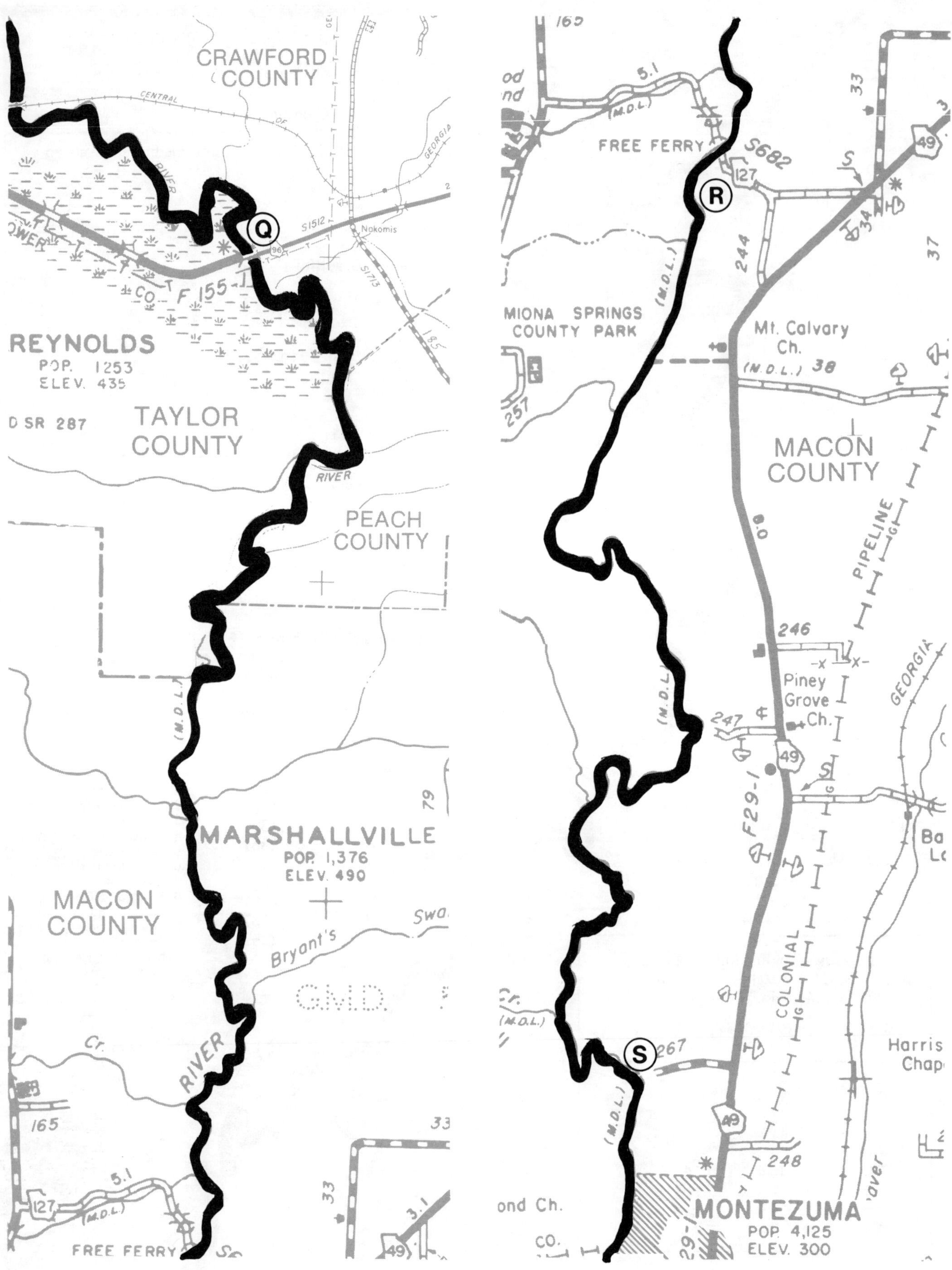

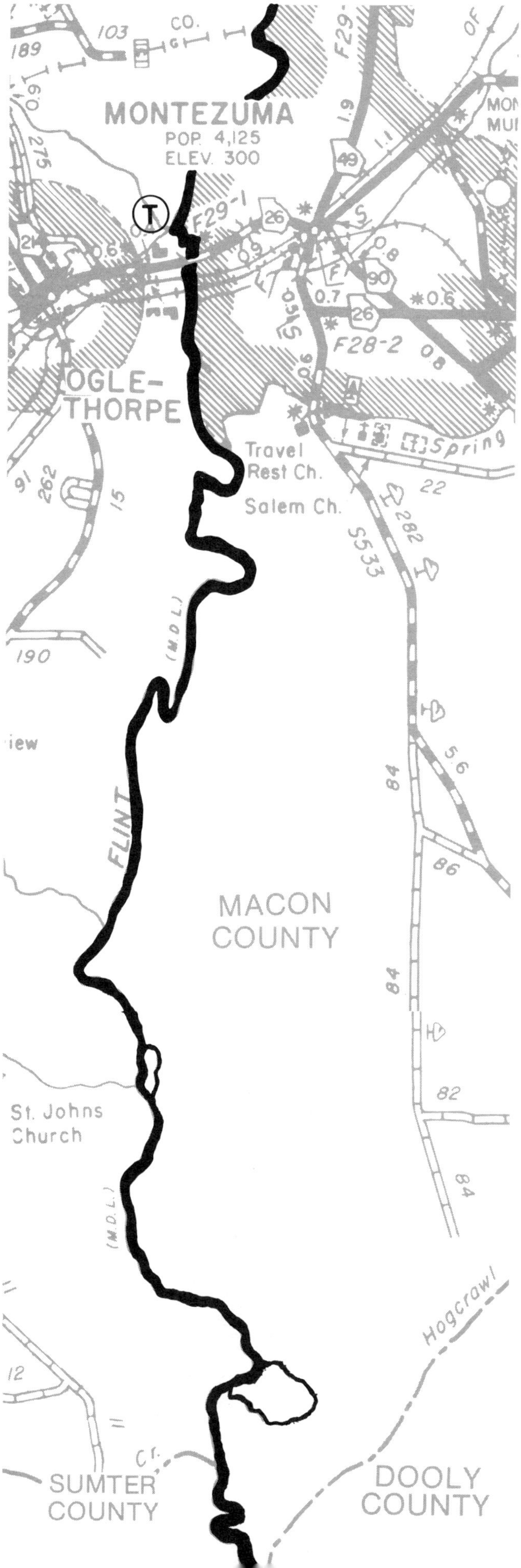

USGS Quads: Fickling Mill, Roberta, Reynolds, Garden Valley, Montezuma, Pennington, Methvins, Drayton		
ACCESS POINTS	RIVER MILES	SHUTTLE MILES
O-P	11.5	15
P-Q	17.5	13
Q-R	11.8	18
R-S	11	8
S-T	3.2	5
T-U	16.8	22
U-V	2.7	16
V-W	3.8	6
W-X	2.3	4
X-Y	3	5

MONTEZUMA
POP. 4,125
ELEV. 300
T
OGLE-
THORPE
Travel Rest Ch.
Salem Ch.
(M.D.L.)
FLINT
MACON
COUNTY
St. Johns Church
Hogcrawl
Cr.
SUMTER COUNTY
DOOLY COUNTY

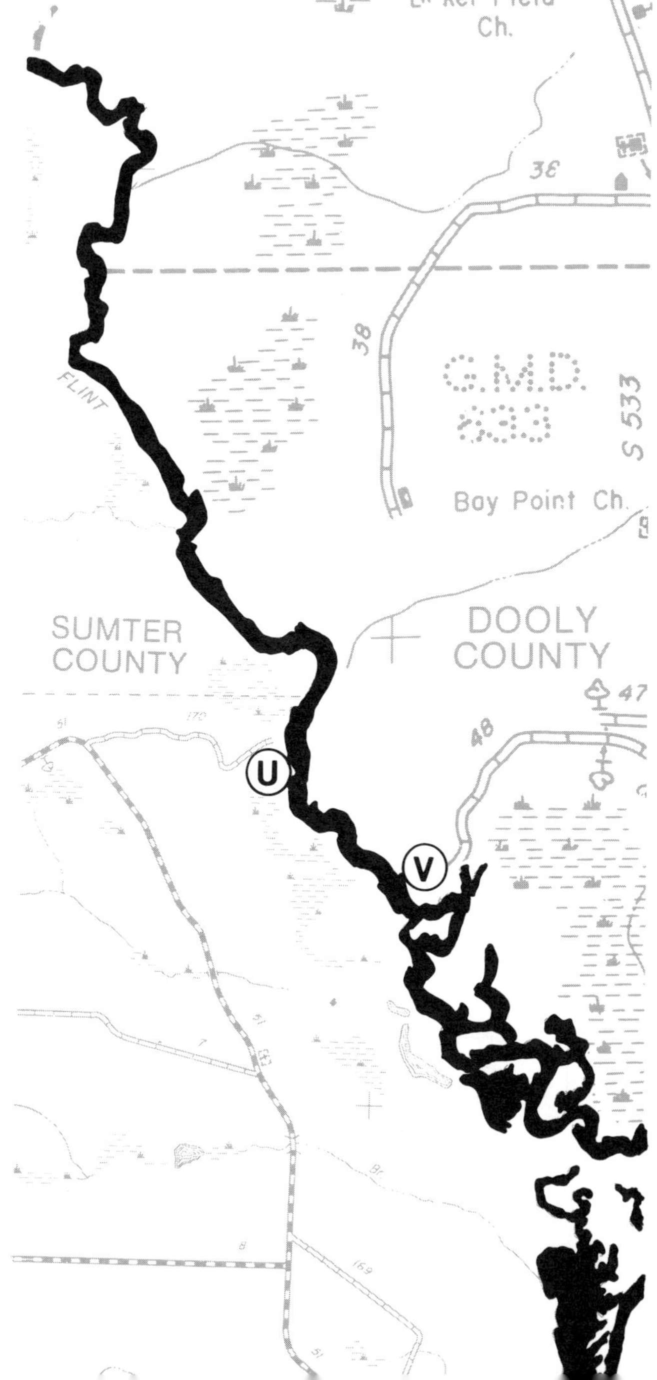

Flint River—*Continued*

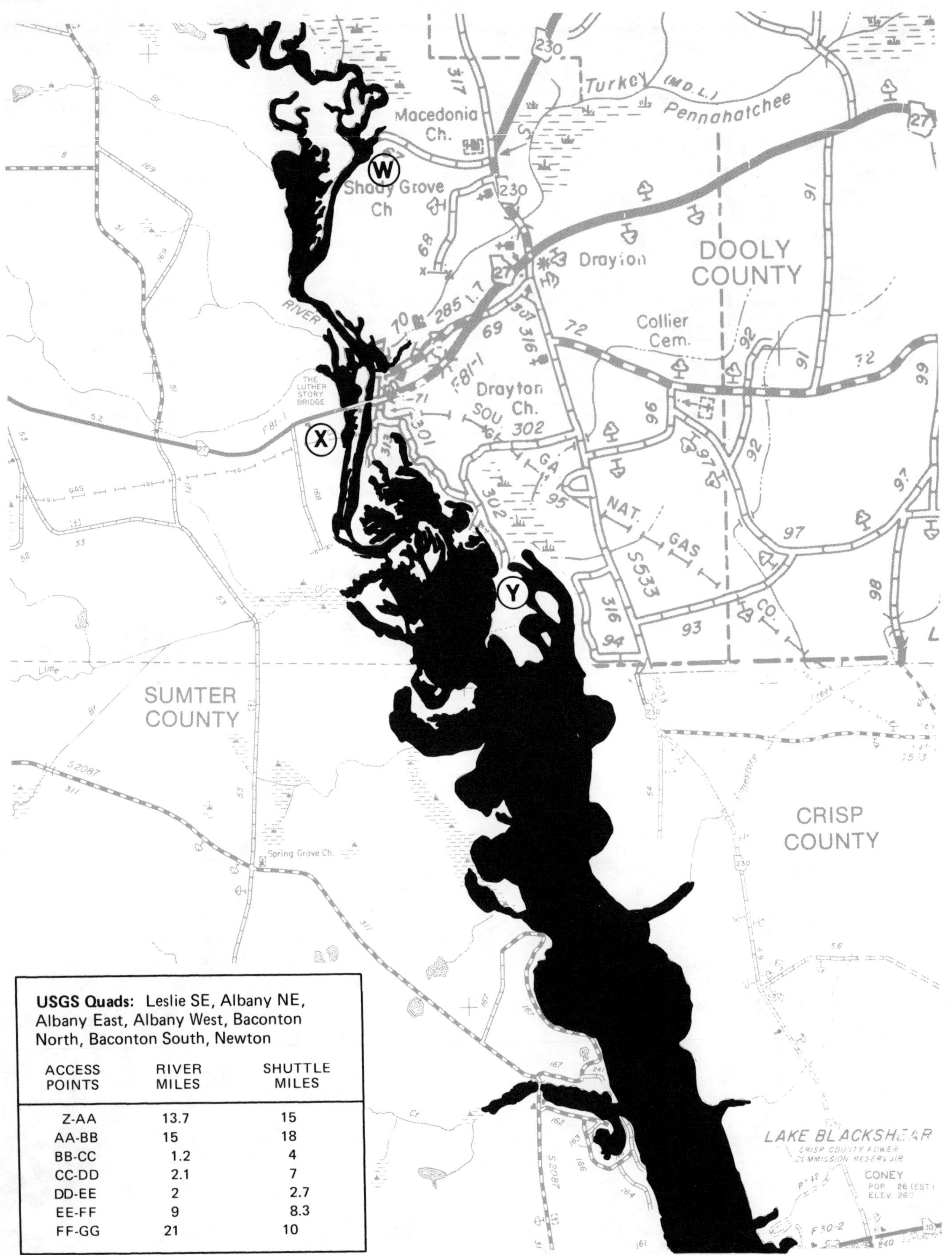

USGS Quads: Leslie SE, Albany NE, Albany East, Albany West, Baconton North, Baconton South, Newton

ACCESS POINTS	RIVER MILES	SHUTTLE MILES
Z-AA	13.7	15
AA-BB	15	18
BB-CC	1.2	4
CC-DD	2.1	7
DD-EE	2	2.7
EE-FF	9	8.3
FF-GG	21	10

Section: Lake Blackshear to Newton

Counties: Lee, Worth, Dougherty, Baker, Mitchell

Suitable For: Cruising, camping

Appropriate For: Families, beginners, intermediates, advanced

Months Runnable: All

Interest Highlights: Scenery, wildlife, local culture and industry

Scenery: Beautiful in spots

Difficulty: International Scale I (II)
Numerical Points 4

Average Width: 230-270 ft.
Velocity: Moderate
Gradient: 1.10 ft./mi.

Runnable Water Level: Minimum Not applicable
Maximum Up to high flood stage

Hazards: Dams, powerboats, mild rapids at Albany Shoals

Scouting: Albany Shoals

Portages: Dam northeast of Albany; Albany Shoals, as necessary

Rescue Index: Accessible to accessible but difficult

Mean Water Temperature (°F)

Jan 51	Feb 52	Mar 58	Apr 66	May 74	Jun 81
Jul 84	Aug 82	Sep 76	Oct 69	Nov 60	Dec 53

Source of Additional Information: Albany Game and Fish Office (912) 430-4252

Access Point	Access Code
Z	2357
AA	1357
BB	1357
CC	2357
DD	(11)
EE	1357
FF	23579
GG	1357

Access Key

1 Paved Road
2 Unpaved Road
3 Short Carry
4 Long Carry
5 Easy Grade
6 Steep Incline
7 Clear Trail
8 Brush and Trees
9 Launching Fee Charged
10 Private Property, Need Permission
11 No Access, Reference Only

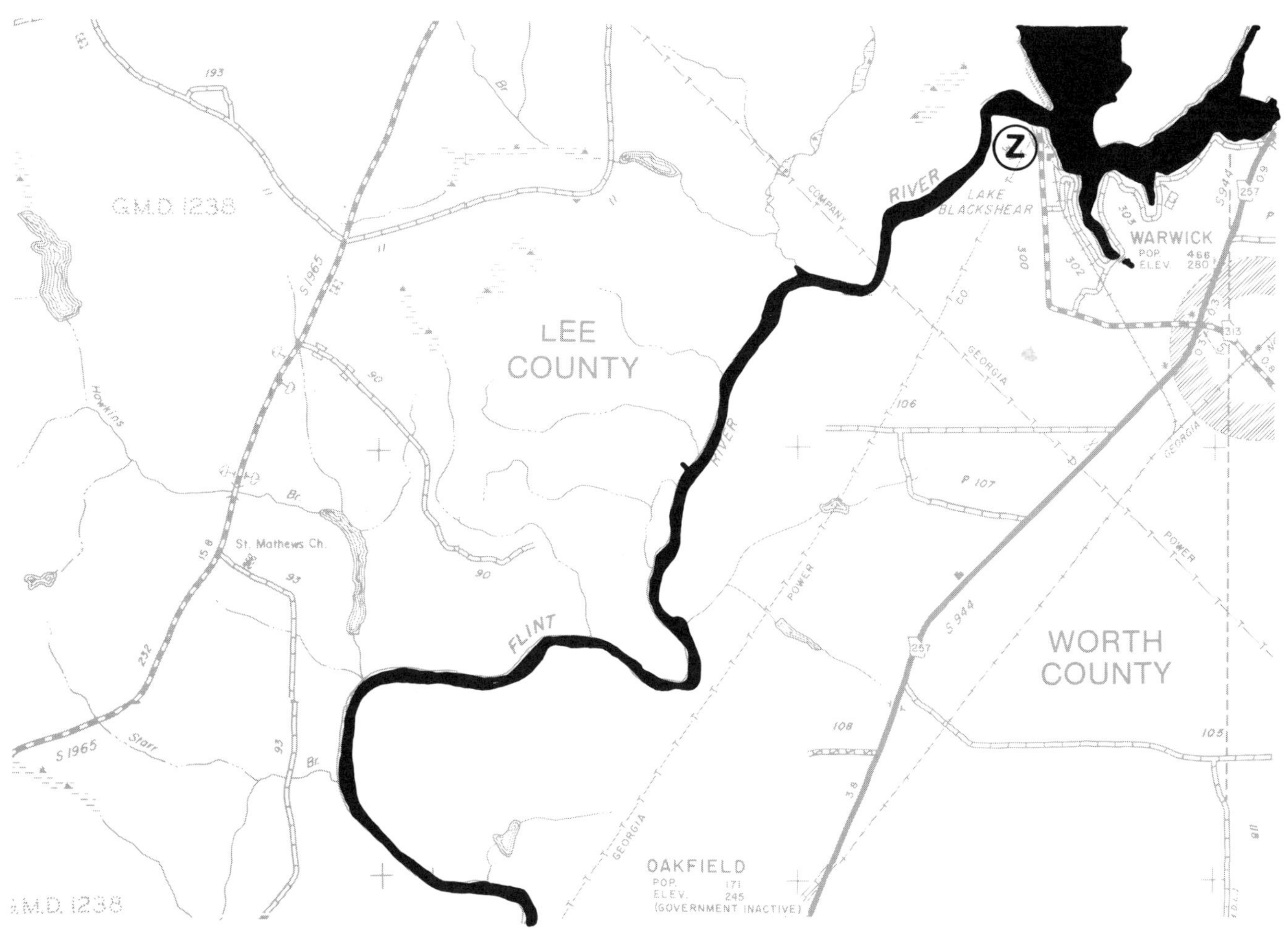

Flint River—*Continued*

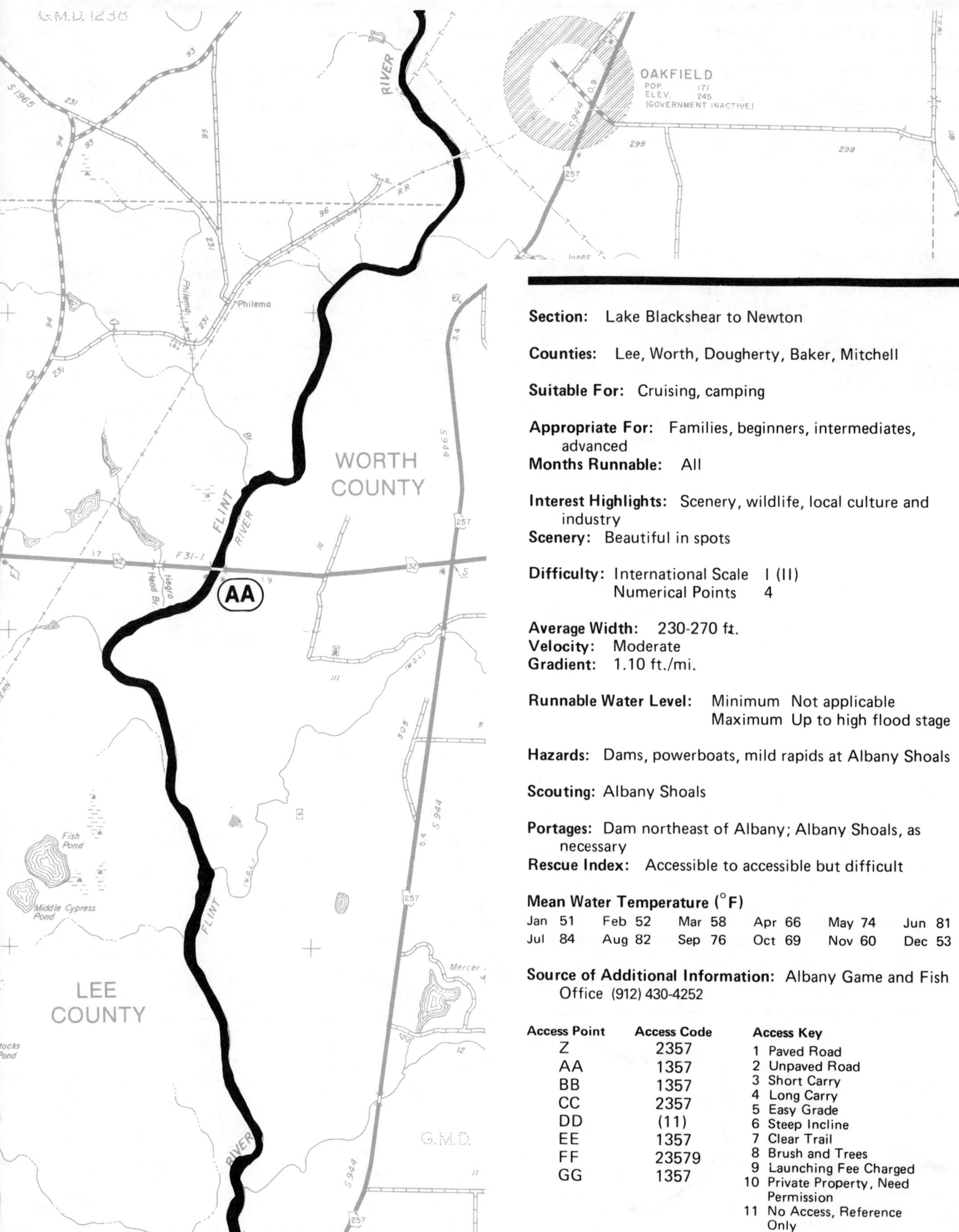

Section: Lake Blackshear to Newton

Counties: Lee, Worth, Dougherty, Baker, Mitchell

Suitable For: Cruising, camping

Appropriate For: Families, beginners, intermediates, advanced
Months Runnable: All

Interest Highlights: Scenery, wildlife, local culture and industry
Scenery: Beautiful in spots

Difficulty: International Scale I (II)
Numerical Points 4

Average Width: 230-270 ft.
Velocity: Moderate
Gradient: 1.10 ft./mi.

Runnable Water Level: Minimum Not applicable
Maximum Up to high flood stage

Hazards: Dams, powerboats, mild rapids at Albany Shoals

Scouting: Albany Shoals

Portages: Dam northeast of Albany; Albany Shoals, as necessary
Rescue Index: Accessible to accessible but difficult

Mean Water Temperature (°F)

Jan 51	Feb 52	Mar 58	Apr 66	May 74	Jun 81
Jul 84	Aug 82	Sep 76	Oct 69	Nov 60	Dec 53

Source of Additional Information: Albany Game and Fish Office (912) 430-4252

Access Point	Access Code
Z	2357
AA	1357
BB	1357
CC	2357
DD	(11)
EE	1357
FF	23579
GG	1357

Access Key
1 Paved Road
2 Unpaved Road
3 Short Carry
4 Long Carry
5 Easy Grade
6 Steep Incline
7 Clear Trail
8 Brush and Trees
9 Launching Fee Charged
10 Private Property, Need Permission
11 No Access, Reference Only

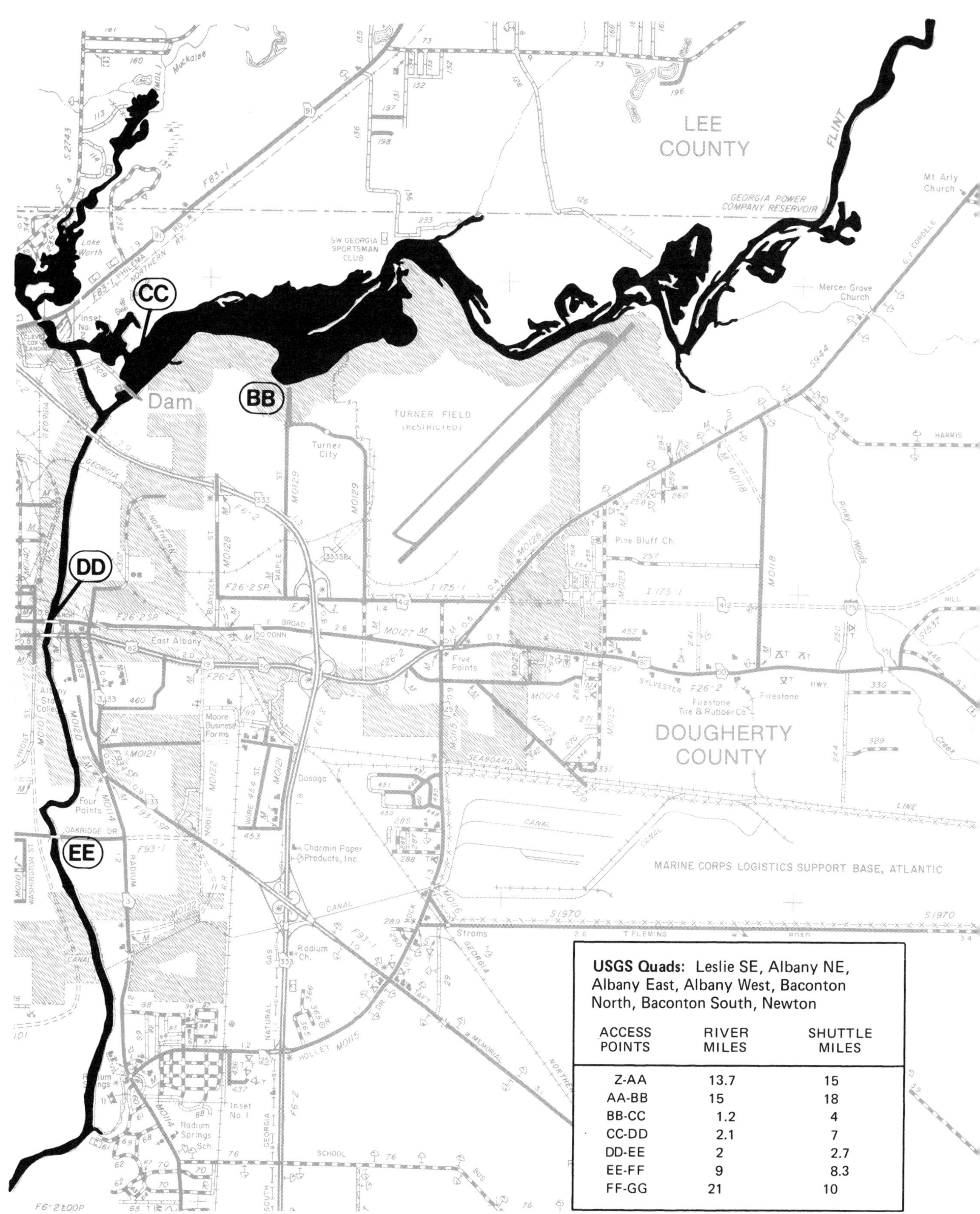

USGS Quads: Leslie SE, Albany NE, Albany East, Albany West, Baconton North, Baconton South, Newton

ACCESS POINTS	RIVER MILES	SHUTTLE MILES
Z-AA	13.7	15
AA-BB	15	18
BB-CC	1.2	4
CC-DD	2.1	7
DD-EE	2	2.7
EE-FF	9	8.3
FF-GG	21	10

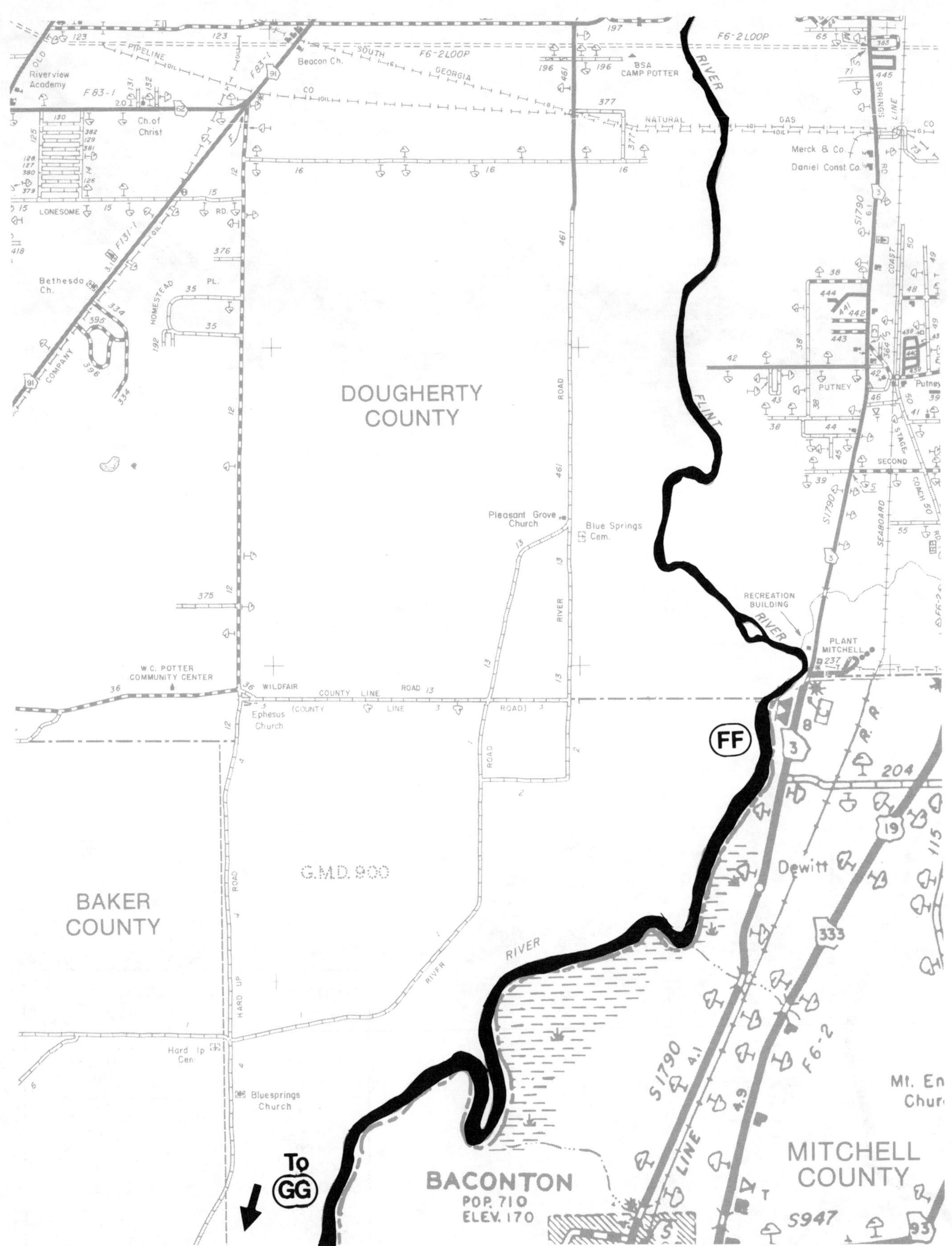
DOUGHERTY
COUNTY
BAKER
COUNTY
MITCHELL
COUNTY
BACONTON
POP. 710
ELEV. 170
G.M.D. 900
FLINT
RIVER
Riverview
Academy
Beacon Ch.
BSA
CAMP POTTER
Ch. of
Christ
Merck & Co.
Daniel Const. Co.
Bethesda
Ch.
PUTNEY
Putney
Pleasant Grove
Church
Blue Springs
Cem.
RECREATION
BUILDING
PLANT
MITCHELL
W.C. POTTER
COMMUNITY CENTER
Ephesus
Church
Dewitt
Hard Up
Cem.
Bluesprings
Church
Mt. En
Chur
FF
To
GG

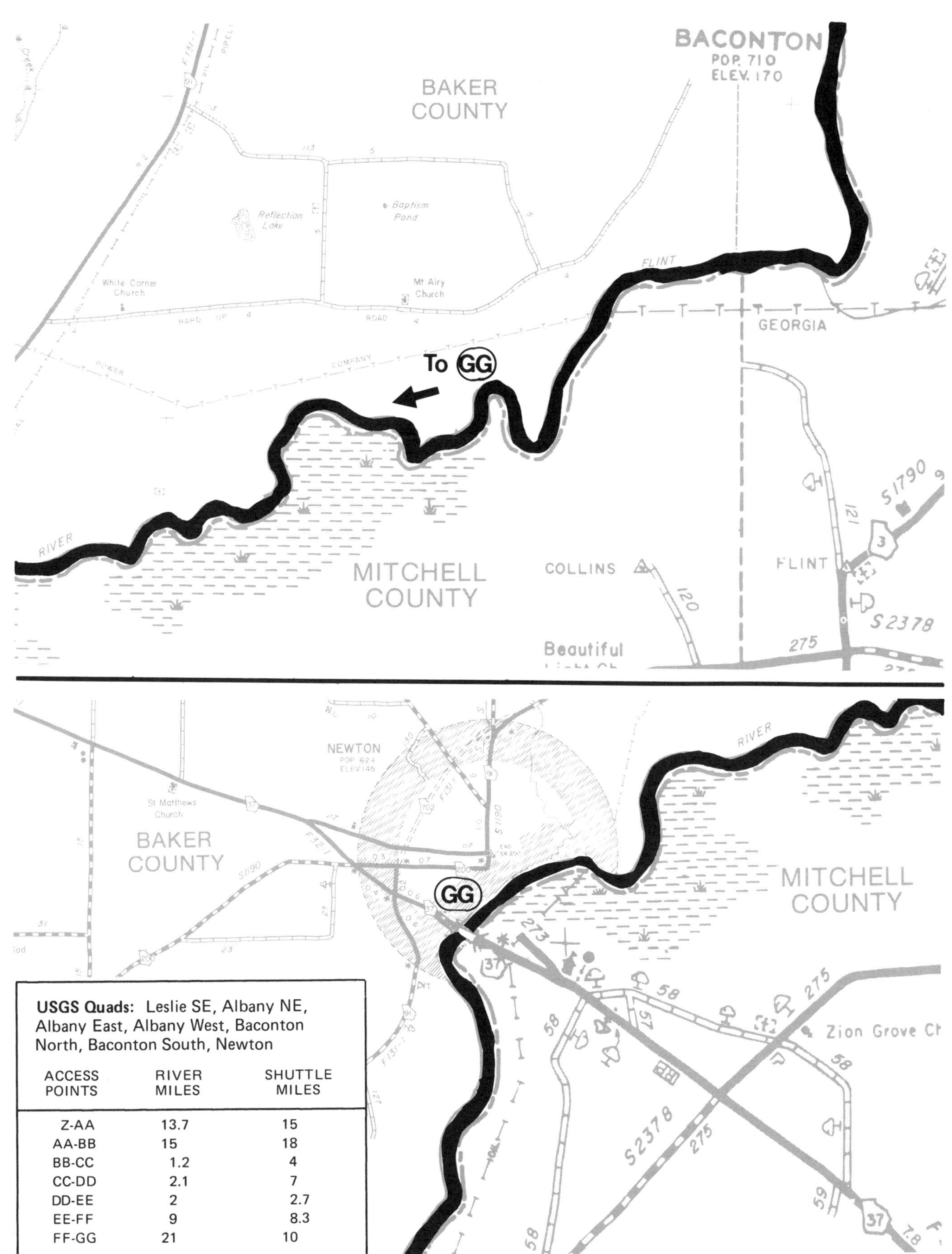

USGS Quads: Leslie SE, Albany NE, Albany East, Albany West, Baconton North, Baconton South, Newton

ACCESS POINTS	RIVER MILES	SHUTTLE MILES
Z-AA	13.7	15
AA-BB	15	18
BB-CC	1.2	4
CC-DD	2.1	7
DD-EE	2	2.7
EE-FF	9	8.3
FF-GG	21	10

Flint River—*Continued*

Section: Newton to Lake Seminole

Counties: Baker, Mitchell, Decatur

Suitable For: Cruising, camping

Appropriate For: Families, beginners, intermediates, advanced

Months Runnable: All

Interest Highlights: Scenery, wildlife, local culture and industry

Scenery: Beautiful in spots

Difficulty: International Scale I (II)
Numerical Points 4

Average Width: 230-270 ft.
Velocity: Moderate
Gradient: 1.10 ft./mi.

Runnable Water Level: Minimum Not applicable
Maximum Up to high flood stage

Hazards: Powerboats

Scouting: None

Portages: None

Rescue Index: Accessible to accessible but difficult

Mean Water Temperature (°F)

Jan 51	Feb 52	Mar 58	Apr 66	May 74	Jun 81
Jul 84	Aug 82	Sep 76	Oct 69	Nov 60	Dec 53

Source of Additional Information: Albany Game and Fish Office (912) 430-4252

Access Point	Access Code
GG	1357
HH	2357
II	1357
JJ	2357
KK	2357
LL	(11)
MM	1357
NN	2357
OO	1357
PP	1357

Access Key
1 Paved Road
2 Unpaved Road
3 Short Carry
4 Long Carry
5 Easy Grade
6 Steep Incline
7 Clear Trail
8 Brush and Trees
9 Launching Fee Charged
10 Private Property, Need Permission
11 No Access, Reference Only

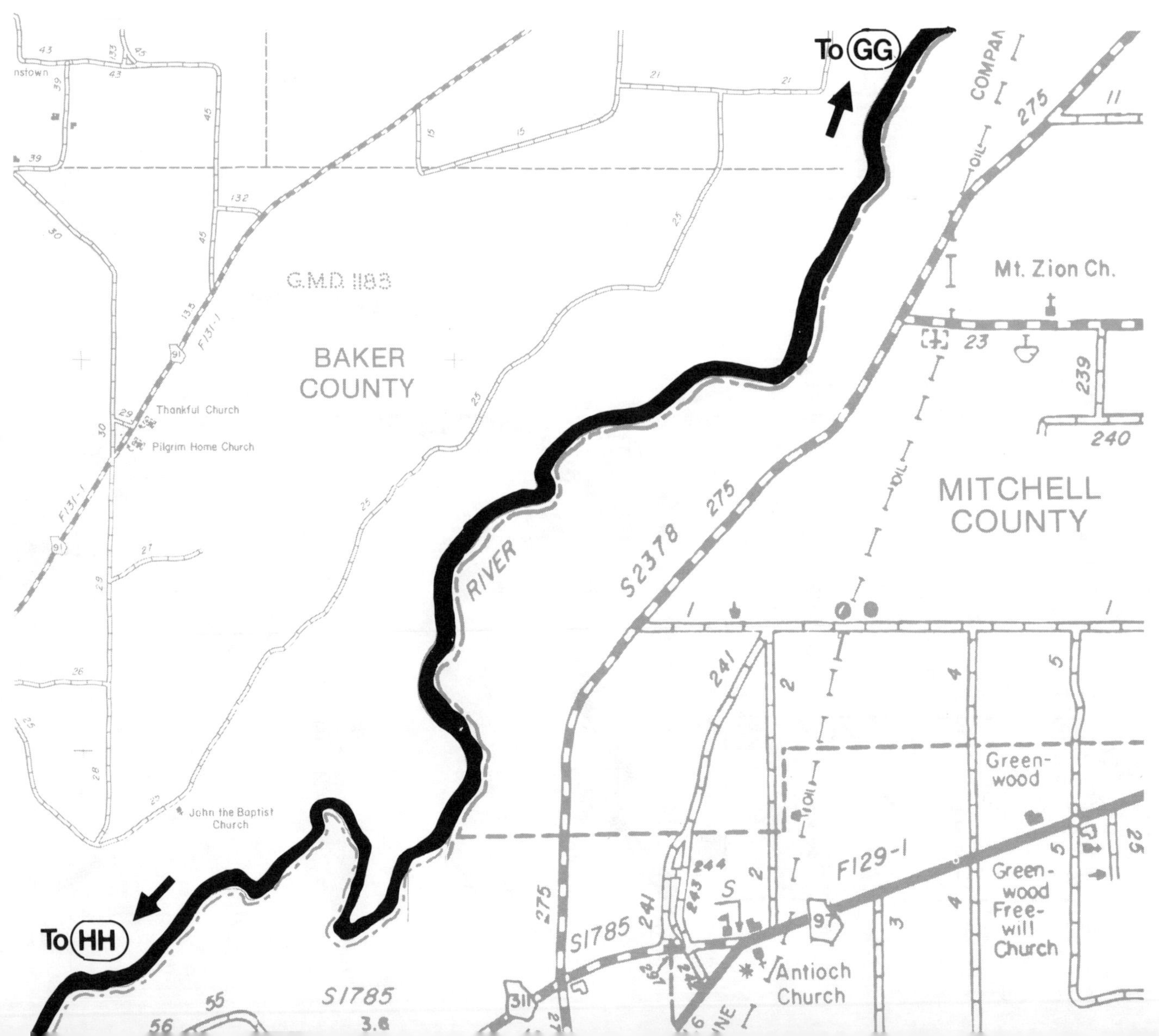

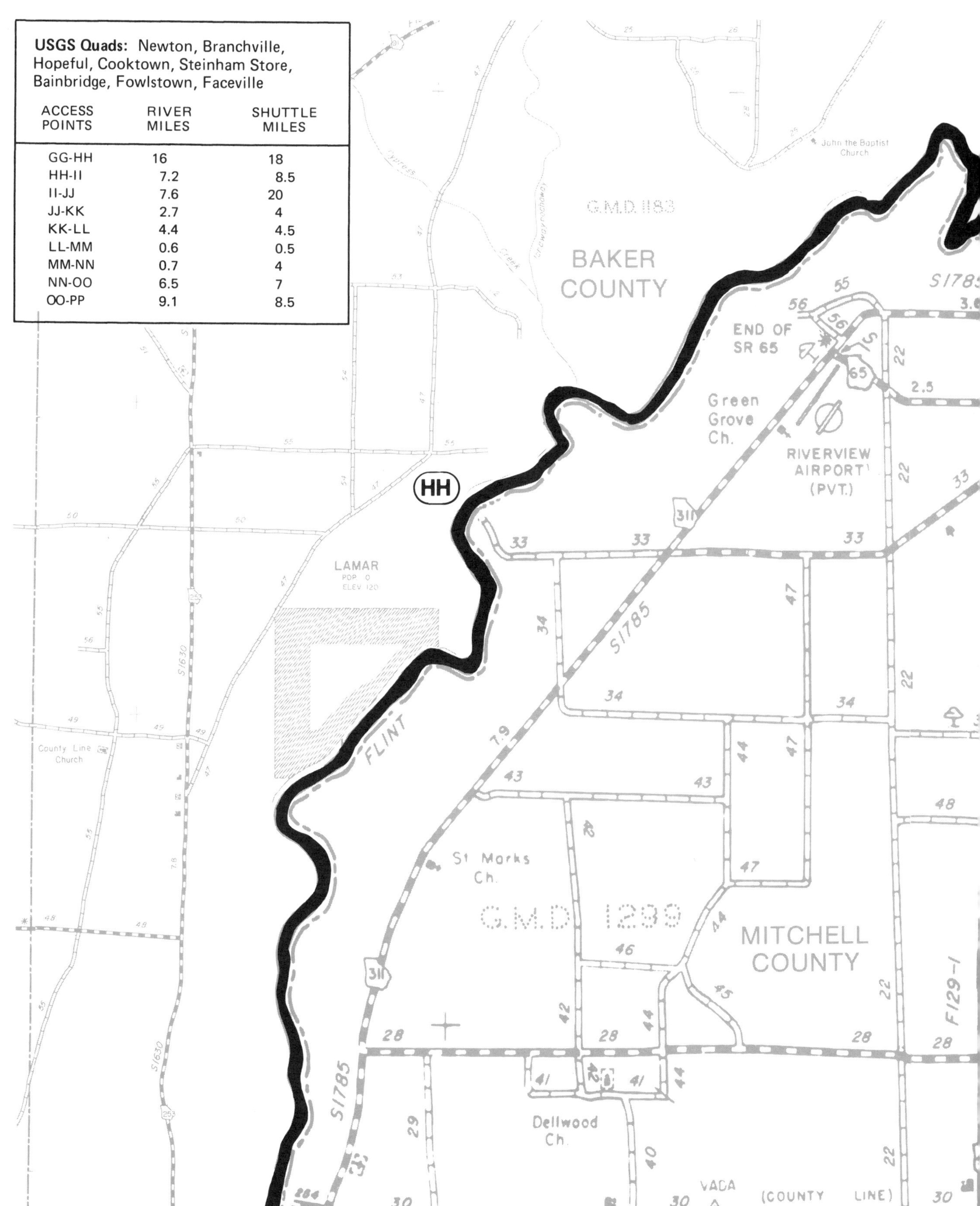

USGS Quads: Newton, Branchville, Hopeful, Cooktown, Steinham Store, Bainbridge, Fowlstown, Faceville

ACCESS POINTS	RIVER MILES	SHUTTLE MILES
GG-HH	16	18
HH-II	7.2	8.5
II-JJ	7.6	20
JJ-KK	2.7	4
KK-LL	4.4	4.5
LL-MM	0.6	0.5
MM-NN	0.7	4
NN-OO	6.5	7
OO-PP	9.1	8.5

Flint River—*Continued*

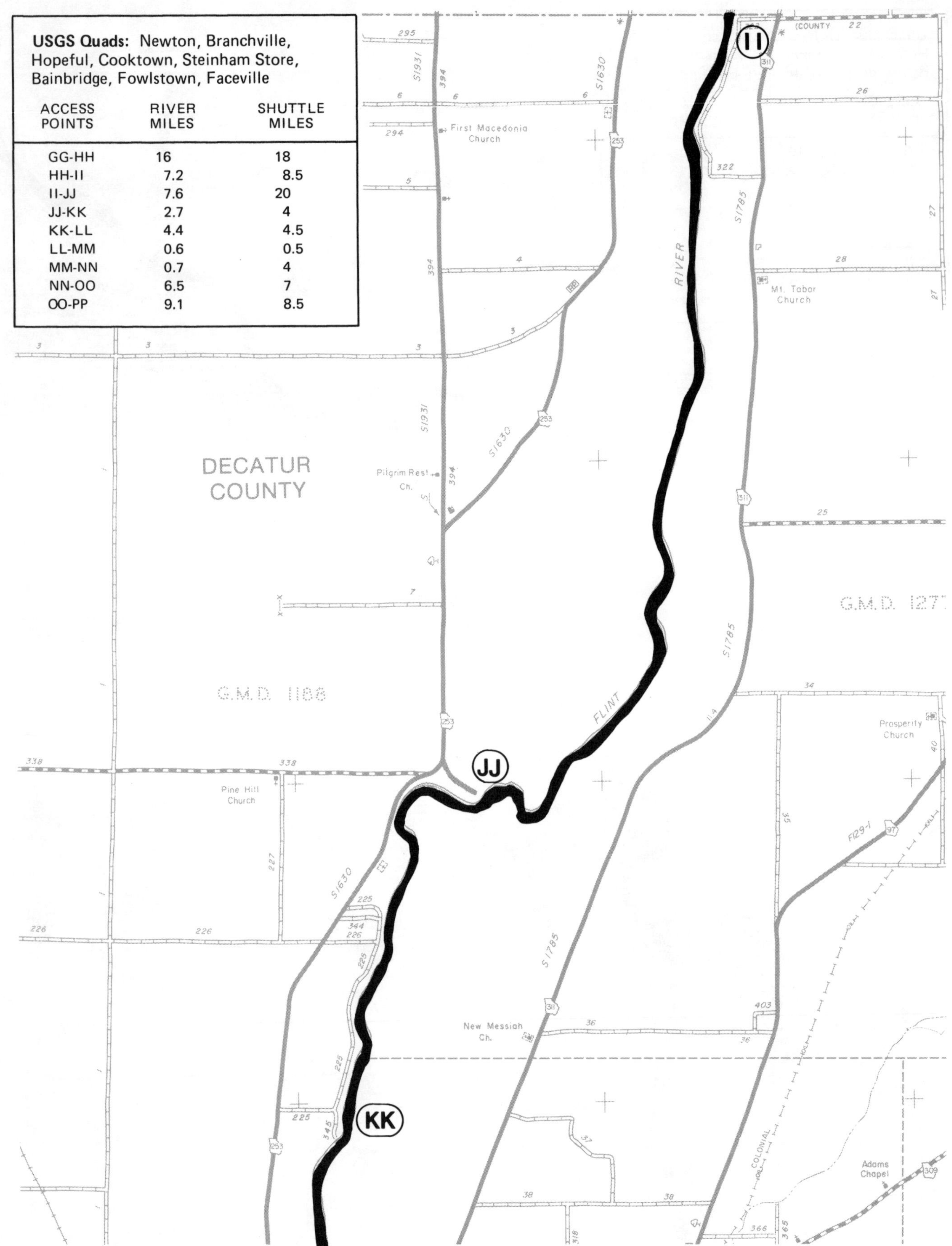

USGS Quads: Newton, Branchville, Hopeful, Cooktown, Steinham Store, Bainbridge, Fowlstown, Faceville

ACCESS POINTS	RIVER MILES	SHUTTLE MILES
GG-HH	16	18
HH-II	7.2	8.5
II-JJ	7.6	20
JJ-KK	2.7	4
KK-LL	4.4	4.5
LL-MM	0.6	0.5
MM-NN	0.7	4
NN-OO	6.5	7
OO-PP	9.1	8.5

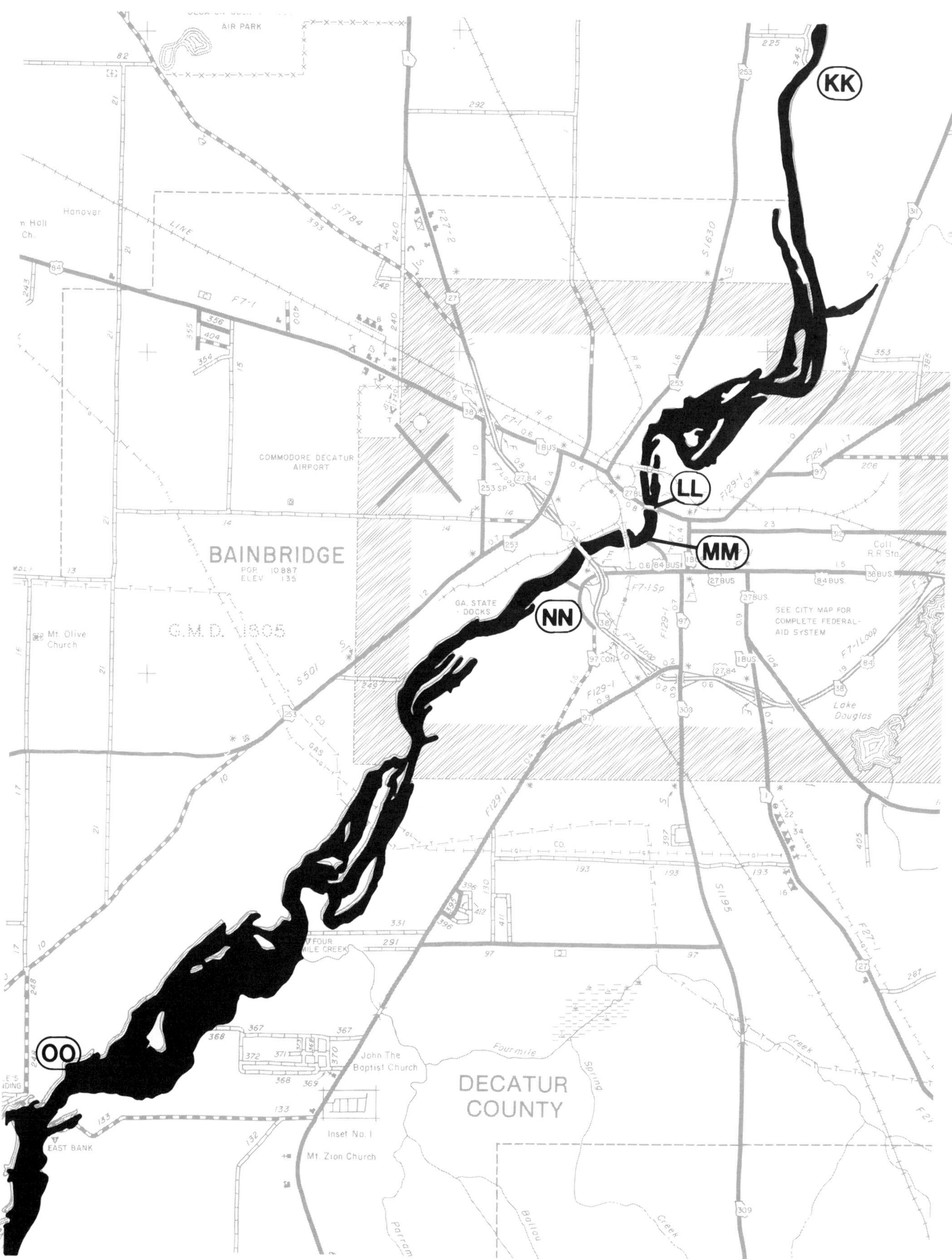
KK
LL
MM
NN
OO
BAINBRIDGE
POP. 10,887
ELEV. 135
G.M.D. 1805
COMMODORE DECATUR AIRPORT
GA. STATE DOCKS
SEE CITY MAP FOR COMPLETE FEDERAL-AID SYSTEM
DECATUR COUNTY
Lake Douglas
Mt. Olive Church
John The Baptist Church
Mt. Zion Church
Hanover
FOUR MILE CREEK
EAST BANK
Inset No. 1
AIR PARK

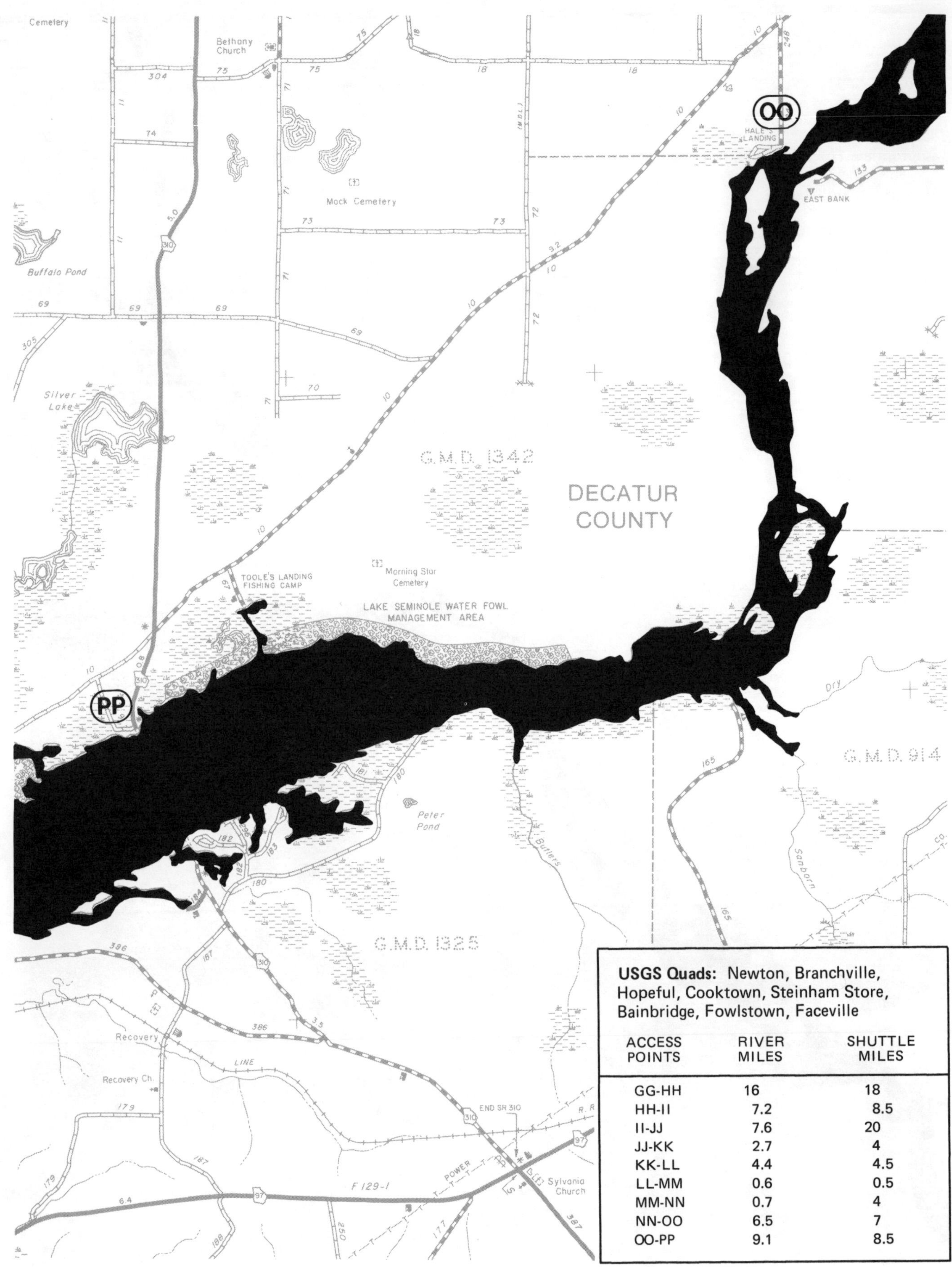

USGS Quads: Newton, Branchville, Hopeful, Cooktown, Steinham Store, Bainbridge, Fowlstown, Faceville

ACCESS POINTS	RIVER MILES	SHUTTLE MILES
GG-HH	16	18
HH-II	7.2	8.5
II-JJ	7.6	20
JJ-KK	2.7	4
KK-LL	4.4	4.5
LL-MM	0.6	0.5
MM-NN	0.7	4
NN-OO	6.5	7
OO-PP	9.1	8.5

Section: Newton to Lake Seminole

Counties: Baker, Mitchell, Decatur

Suitable For: Cruising, camping

Appropriate For: Families, beginners, intermediates, advanced

Months Runnable: All

Interest Highlights: Scenery, wildlife, local culture and industry

Scenery: Beautiful in spots

Difficulty: International Scale I (II)
Numerical Points 4

Average Width: 230-270 ft.
Velocity: Moderate
Gradient: 1.10 ft./mi.

Runnable Water Level: Minimum Not applicable
Maximum Up to high flood stage

Hazards: Powerboats

Scouting: None

Portages: None

Rescue Index: Accessible to accessible but difficult

Mean Water Temperature (°F)

Jan 51	Feb 52	Mar 58	Apr 66	May 74	Jun 81
Jul 84	Aug 82	Sep 76	Oct 69	Nov 60	Dec 53

Source of Additional Information: Albany Game and Fish Office (912) 430-4252

Access Point	Access Code
GG	1357
HH	2357
II	1357
JJ	2357
KK	2357
LL	(11)
MM	1357
NN	2357
OO	1357
PP	1357

Access Key
1 Paved Road
2 Unpaved Road
3 Short Carry
4 Long Carry
5 Easy Grade
6 Steep Incline
7 Clear Trail
8 Brush and Trees
9 Launching Fee Charged
10 Private Property, Need Permission
11 No Access, Reference Only

Flint River.

Photo courtesy of *Brown's Guide to Georgia.*

Spring Creek

Spring Creek has its headwaters in Clay and Calhoun counties and flows directly south draining portions of Early, Miller, Seminole, and Decatur counties before emptying into Lake Seminole. Exotic and beautiful, Spring Creek is vastly different from other Coastal Plains streams. First it is largely spring fed, and when high water subsides following the spring rains, the water in the upper sections is crystal clear and reveals a beautiful array of underwater plant life, spring "boils," and a bottom that is often solid limestone, sometimes pitted by erosion with jagged cutting edges. Fish and molluscks are plentiful and can be observed from a canoe. Cypress and planertrees line the banks, which rise high from the stream thereby eliminating much of the usual wet floodplain flora. Pine and hardwood forests surround the stream. Except in the spring, and in the lake pool of Lake Seminole, the water is too shallow for powerboat traffic, but it is perfect for paddle craft. Limestone outcroppings add to the wilderness beauty of the partially shaded stream, and small shoals and rocky shallows enliven the paddling.

Spring Creek is runnable below US 27 in Miller County. Its level of difficulty is Class I (+) with numerous deadfalls being the primary hazard to navigation. The stream is intimate and diminuitive until the lake pool is encountered near the Seaboard Coast Line rail crossing. From here the run remains interesting as the creek slowly widens to become the Lake Seminole Waterfowl Management Area. Access is good.

Section: Colquitt to Lake Seminole

Counties: Miller, Decatur

Suitable For: Cruising

Appropriate For: Families, beginners, intermediates, advanced

Months Runnable: A-D, November to June; D-G, all

Interest Highlights: Scenery, wildlife, geology of Natural Springs

Scenery: Beautiful to exceptionally beautiful

Difficulty: International Scale I(+)
Numerical Points 6

Average Width: 25-45 ft.

Gradient: Slow to moderate

Velocity: 2.06 ft./mi.

Runnable Water Level: (Iron City gauge) Minimum 125 cfs; Maximum Up to flood stage

Hazards: Deadfalls

Scouting: None required

Portages: None required

Rescue Index: Accessible to accessible but difficult

Mean Water Temperature (°F)

Jan 52	Feb 53	Mar 58	Apr 63	May 70	Jun 75
Jul 78	Aug 77	Sep 73	Oct 66	Nov 61	Dec 54

Source of Additional Information: Albany Game and Fish Office (912) 430-4252

Access Point	Access Code
A	1457
B	2357
C	2357
D	1357
E	2357
F	2357
G	1357

Access Key
1 Paved Road
2 Unpaved Road
3 Short Carry
4 Long Carry
5 Easy Grade
6 Steep Incline
7 Clear Trail
8 Brush and Trees
9 Launching Fee Charged
10 Private Property, Need Permission
11 No Access, Reference Only

USGS Quads: Colquitt, Boykin, Bronson, Desser, Reynoldsville

ACCESS POINTS	RIVER MILES	SHUTTLE MILES
A-B	9.2	8
B-C	4.1	4.5
C-D	6.7	6
D-E	4.8	4.5
E-F	2.2	3.5
F-G	2	3

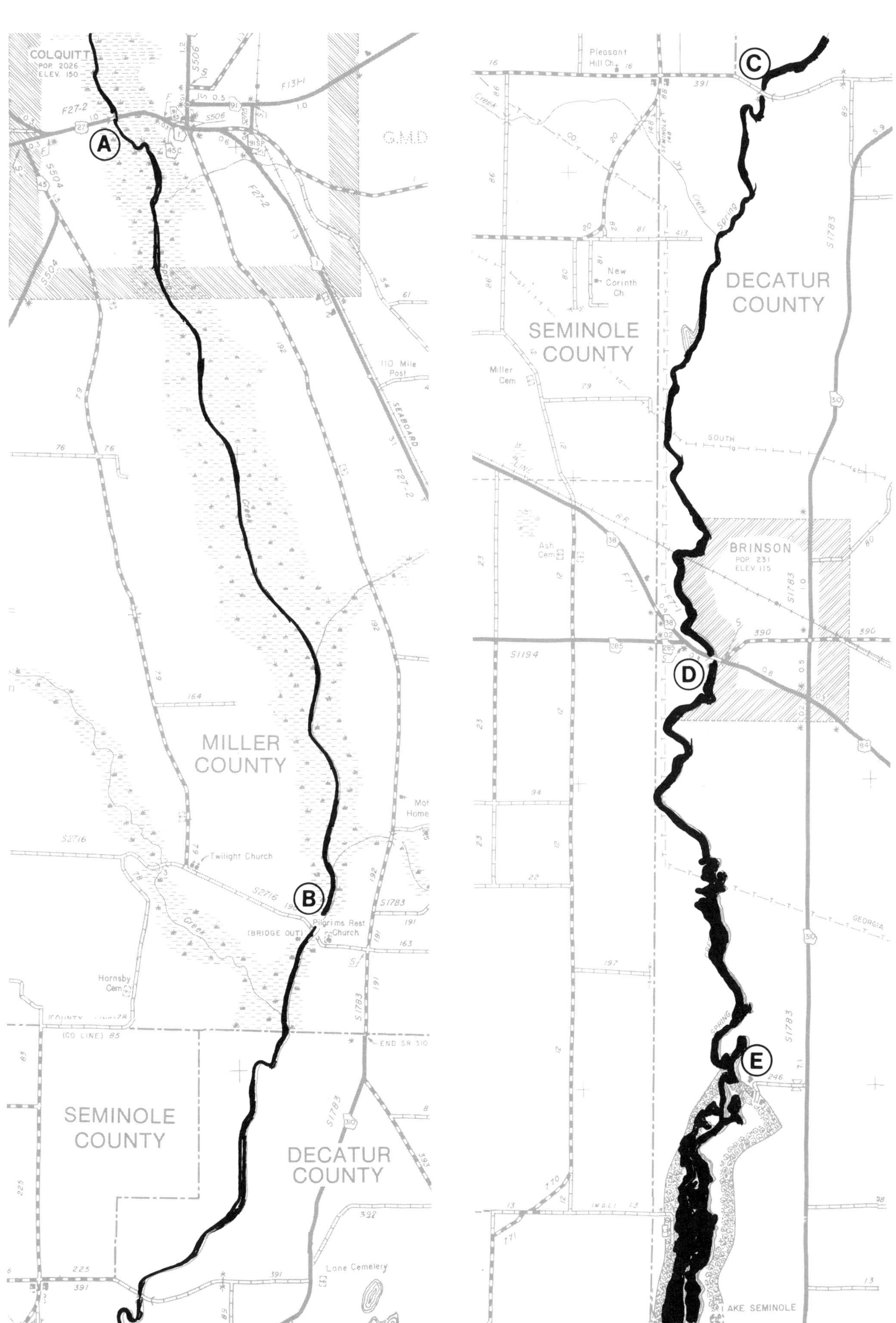
COLQUITT
POP. 2026
ELEV. 150
A
B
Twilight Church
Pilgrims Rest Church
(BRIDGE OUT)
Hornsby Cem
MILLER COUNTY
SEMINOLE COUNTY
DECATUR COUNTY
Lone Cemetery
110 Mile Post
SEABOARD
END SR 310
C
Pleasant Hill Ch.
New Corinth Ch.
SEMINOLE COUNTY
DECATUR COUNTY
Miller Cem
Ash Cem
BRINSON
POP. 231
ELEV. 115
D
E
LAKE SEMINOLE

Spring Creek—*Continued*

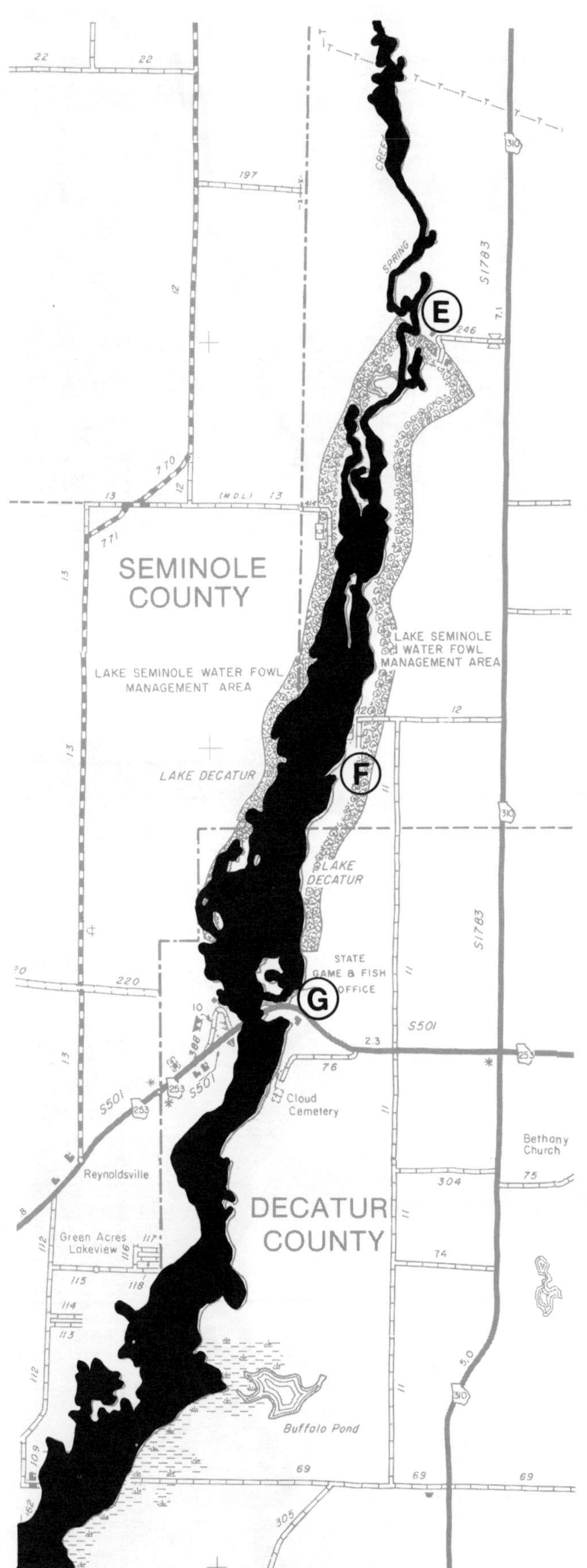

USGS Quads: Colquitt, Boykin, Bronson, Desser, Reynoldsville

ACCESS POINTS	RIVER MILES	SHUTTLE MILES
A-B	9.2	8
B-C	4.1	4.5
C-D	6.7	6
D-E	4.8	4.5
E-F	2.2	3.5
F-G	2	3

Section: Colquitt to Lake Seminole

Counties: Miller, Decatur

Suitable For: Cruising

Appropriate For: Families, beginners, intermediates, advanced

Months Runnable: A-D, November to June; D-G, all

Interest Highlights: Scenery, wildlife, geology of Natural Springs

Scenery: Beautiful to exceptionally beautiful

Difficulty: International Scale I(+)
Numerical Points 6

Average Width: 25-45 ft.
Gradient: Slow to moderate
Velocity: 2.06 ft./mi.

Runnable Water Level: Minimum 125 cfs
(Iron City gauge) Maximum Up to flood stage

Hazards: Deadfalls

Scouting: None required

Portages: None required

Rescue Index: Accessible to accessible but difficult

Mean Water Temperature (°F)

Jan 52	Feb 53	Mar 58	Apr 63	May 70	Jun 75
Jul 78	Aug 77	Sep 73	Oct 66	Nov 61	Dec 54

Source of Additional Information: Albany Game and Fish Office (912) 430-4252

Access Point	Access Code
A	1457
B	2357
C	2357
D	1357
E	2357
F	2357
G	1357

Access Key
1 Paved Road
2 Unpaved Road
3 Short Carry
4 Long Carry
5 Easy Grade
6 Steep Incline
7 Clear Trail
8 Brush and Trees
9 Launching Fee Charged
10 Private Property, Need Permission
11 No Access, Reference Only

Southern Georgia "blackwater" stream.

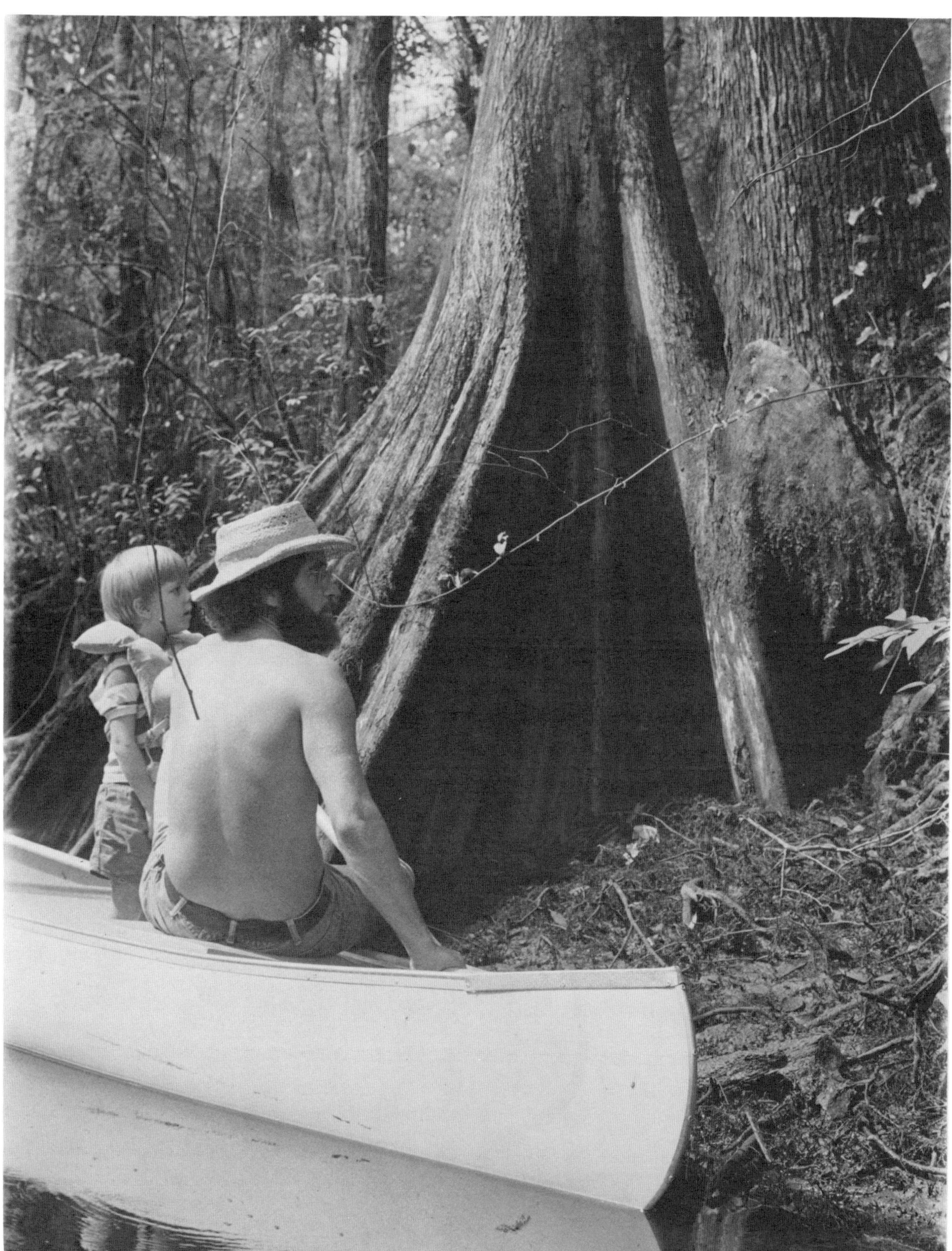

Photo courtesy of *Brown's Guide to Georgia*.

Chattahoochee River

Flowing south from Columbus, in Muscogee County, the Chattahoochee River continues to be impounded frequently as it winds through farm plateau sprinkled with industry throughout the Coastal Plain. Its banks average four to eight feet here and are treelined. Towboats and other industrial traffic move up and down the 300-foot-wide stream. From Columbus the Chattahoochee moves down to the Walter F. George Reservoir and from there to Lake Seminole where it meets the Flint to form the Apalachicola River. The level of difficulty from Columbus to Lake Seminole is Class I; powerboat traffic is the primary hazard to navigation. Access is good. (The Chattahoochee flowing through the western Piedmont is described in the preceding chapter. The river above Lake Sidney Lanier is found in *Northern Georgia Canoeing: A Canoeing and Kayaking Guide to the Streams of the Cumberland Plateau, Blue Ridge Mountains and Eastern Piedmont*, a companion book.)

USGS Quads: Columbus, Fort Mitchell, Fort Benning, Union, Omaha, Twin Springs, Georgetown, Eufaula North, Eufaula South

ACCESS POINTS	RIVER MILES	SHUTTLE MILES
GG-HH	12.4	18
HH-II	11.2	15
II-JJ	13.4	26
JJ-KK	4.5	8
KK-LL	1.2	2

Section: South Columbus to Walter F. George Reservoir

Counties: Muscogee, Chattahoochee, Stewart

Suitable For: Cruising, camping

Appropriate For: Beginners, intermediates, advanced

Months Runnable: All

Interest Highlights: Scenery, local culture and industry

Scenery: Pretty in spots to beautiful in spots

Difficulty: International Scale I
Numerical Points 4

Average Width: 300-330 ft.
Velocity: Slack
Gradient: 0 ft./mi.

Runnable Water Level: Minimum Not applicable
Maximum Not applicable

Hazards: Powerboats

Scouting: None

Portages: None

Rescue Index: Accessible to accessible but difficult

Mean Water Temperature (°F)

Jan 50	Feb 51	Mar 54	Apr 62	May 70	Jun 78
Jul 82	Aug 81	Sep 77	Oct 69	Nov 60	Dec 53

Source of Additional Information: Manchester Game and Fish Office (404) 846-8448

Access Point	Access Code
GG	1357
HH	1357
II	1357
JJ	2357
KK	1357
LL	2358

Access Key
1 Paved Road
2 Unpaved Road
3 Short Carry
4 Long Carry
5 Easy Grade
6 Steep Incline
7 Clear Trail
8 Brush and Trees
9 Launching Fee Charged
10 Private Property, Need Permission
11 No Access, Reference Only

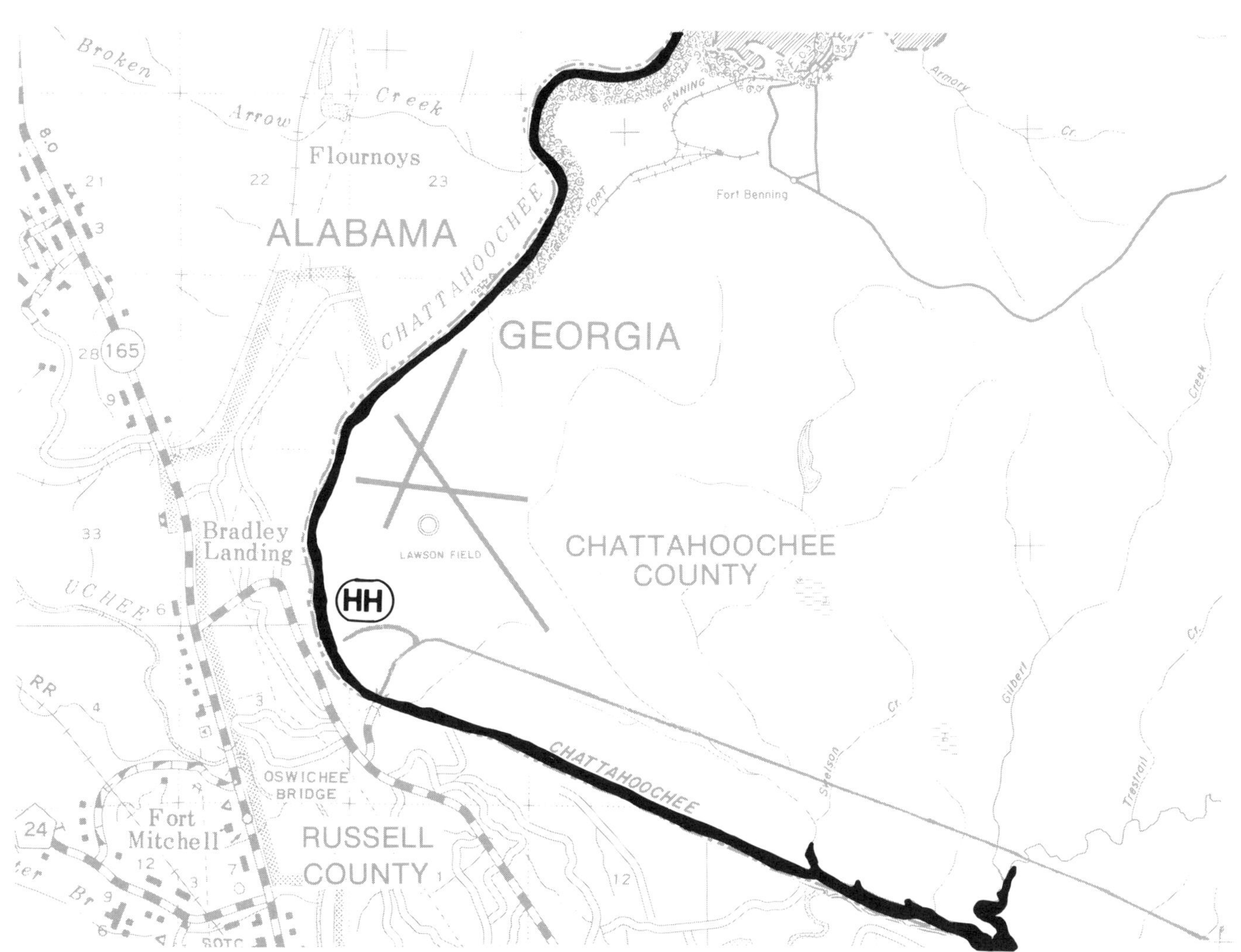

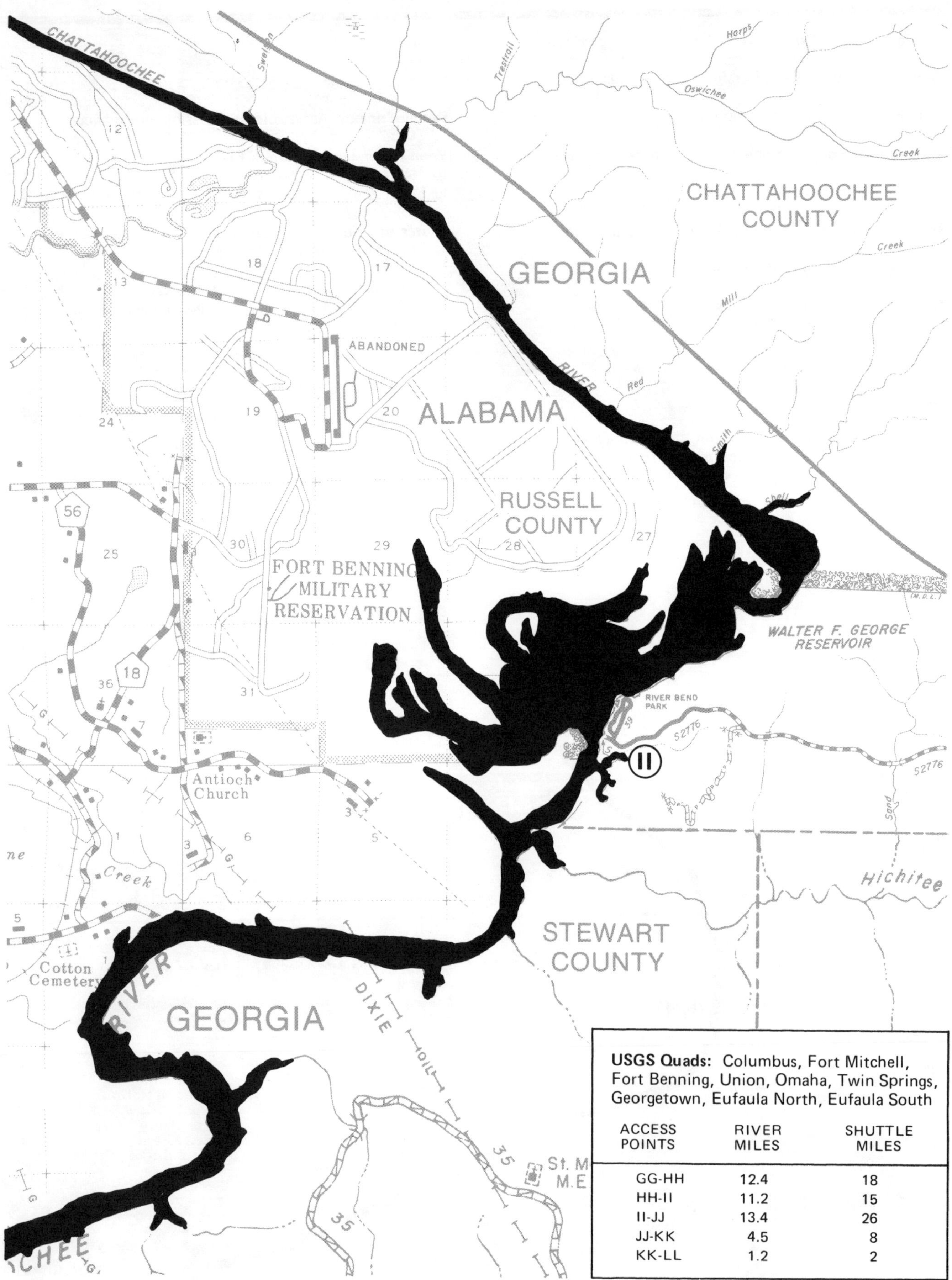

USGS Quads: Columbus, Fort Mitchell, Fort Benning, Union, Omaha, Twin Springs, Georgetown, Eufaula North, Eufaula South

ACCESS POINTS	RIVER MILES	SHUTTLE MILES
GG-HH	12.4	18
HH-II	11.2	15
II-JJ	13.4	26
JJ-KK	4.5	8
KK-LL	1.2	2

Section: South Columbus to Walter F. George Reservoir

Counties: Muscogee, Chattahoochee, Stewart

Suitable For: Cruising, camping

Appropriate For: Beginners, intermediates, advanced

Months Runnable: All

Interest Highlights: Scenery, local culture and industry

Scenery: Pretty in spots to beautiful in spots

Difficulty: International Scale I
Numerical Points 4

Average Width: 300-330 ft.
Velocity: Slack
Gradient: 0 ft./mi.

Runnable Water Level: Minimum Not applicable
Maximum Not applicable

Hazards: Powerboats

Scouting: None

Portages: None

Rescue Index: Accessible to accessible but difficult

Mean Water Temperature (°F)

Jan 50	Feb 51	Mar 54	Apr 62	May 70	Jun 78
Jul 82	Aug 81	Sep 77	Oct 69	Nov 60	Dec 53

Source of Additional Information: Manchester Game and Fish Office (404) 846-8448

Access Point	Access Code
GG	1357
HH	1357
II	1357
JJ	2357
KK	1357
LL	2358

Access Key
1 Paved Road
2 Unpaved Road
3 Short Carry
4 Long Carry
5 Easy Grade
6 Steep Incline
7 Clear Trail
8 Brush and Trees
9 Launching Fee Charged
10 Private Property, Need Permission
11 No Access, Reference Only

Chattahoochee River—*Continued*

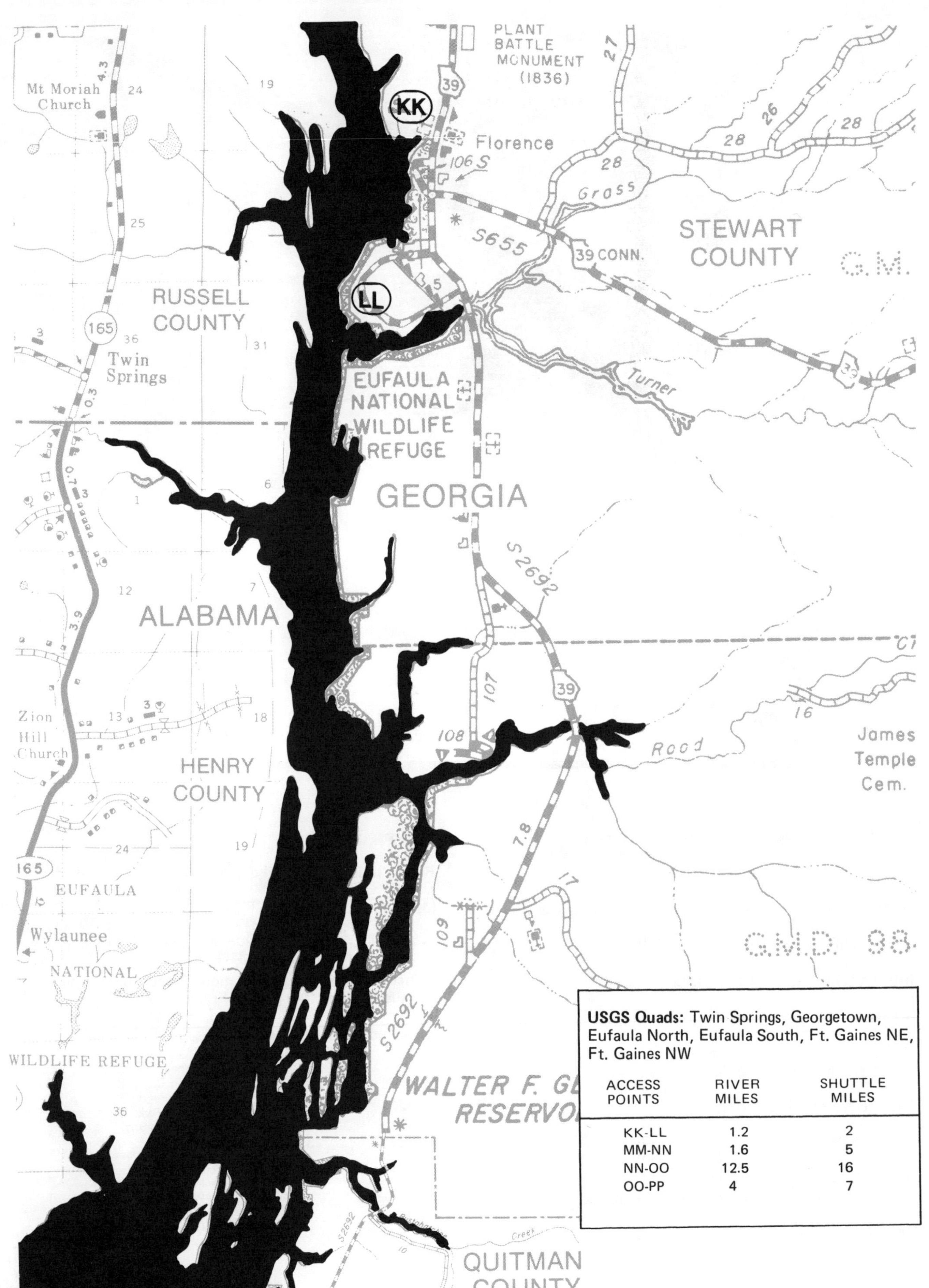

USGS Quads: Twin Springs, Georgetown, Eufaula North, Eufaula South, Ft. Gaines NE, Ft. Gaines NW

ACCESS POINTS	RIVER MILES	SHUTTLE MILES
KK-LL	1.2	2
MM-NN	1.6	5
NN-OO	12.5	16
OO-PP	4	7

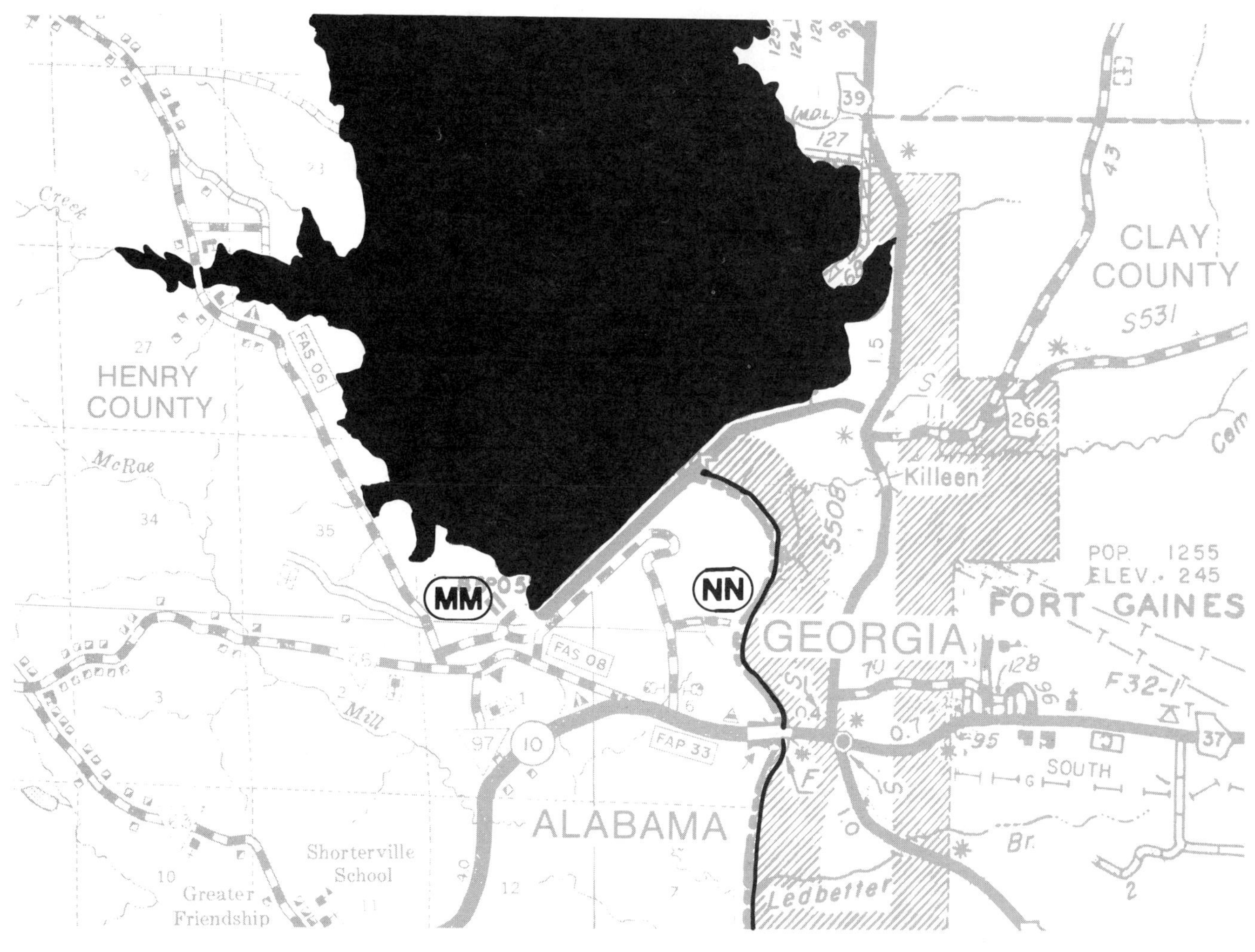

Section: Walter F. George Dam to Lake Seminole

Counties: Clay, Early, Seminole

Suitable For: Cruising, camping

Appropriate For: Beginners, intermediates, advanced

Months Runnable: All

Interest Highlights: Scenery, local culture and industry

Scenery: Pretty in spots

Difficulty: International Scale I
Numerical Points 4

Average Width: 320-340 ft.
Velocity: Slack
Gradient: 0 ft./mi.

Runnable Water Level: Minimum Not applicable
Maximum Not applicable

Hazards: Powerboats

Scouting: None

Portages: George Andrews Dam southwest of Hilton

Rescue Index: Accessible to accessible but difficult

Mean Water Temperature (°F)

Jan 51	Feb 52	Mar 56	Apr 63	May 72	Jun 79
Jul 82	Aug 81	Sep 77	Oct 69	Nov 60	Dec 54

Source of Additional Information: Manchester Game and Fish Office (404) 846-8448

Access Point	Access Code
KK	1357
LL	2358
MM	2357
NN	1357
OO	2357
PP	1357

Access Key
1 Paved Road
2 Unpaved Road
3 Short Carry
4 Long Carry
5 Easy Grade
6 Steep Incline
7 Clear Trail
8 Brush and Trees
9 Launching Fee Charged
10 Private Property, Need Permission
11 No Access, Reference Only

Chattahoochee River—*Continued*

Section: Walter F. George Dam to Lake Seminole

Counties: Clay, Early, Seminole

Suitable For: Cruising, camping

Appropriate For: Beginners, intermediates, advanced

Months Runnable: All

Interest Highlights: Scenery, local culture and industry

Scenery: Pretty in spots

Difficulty: International Scale I
Numerical Points 4

Average Width: 320-340 ft.
Velocity: Slack
Gradient: 0 ft./mi.

Runnable Water Level: Minimum Not applicable
Maximum Not applicable

Hazards: Powerboats

Scouting: None

Portages: George Andrews Dam southwest of Hilton

Rescue Index: Accessible to accessible but difficult

Mean Water Temperature (°F)

Jan 51	Feb 52	Mar 56	Apr 63	May 72	Jun 79
Jul 82	Aug 81	Sep 77	Oct 69	Nov 60	Dec 54

Source of Additional Information: Manchester Game and Fish Office (404) 846-8448

Access Point	Access Code
MM	2357
NN	1357
OO	2357
PP	1357
QQ	2357
RR	2368
SS	1357

Access Key
1 Paved Road
2 Unpaved Road
3 Short Carry
4 Long Carry
5 Easy Grade
6 Steep Incline
7 Clear Trail
8 Brush and Trees
9 Launching Fee Charged
10 Private Property, Need Permission
11 No Access, Reference Only

USGS Quads: Ft. Gaines, Columbia NE, Columbia, Gordon, Saffold, Bascom, Steam Mill, Fairchild, Sneads

ACCESS POINTS	RIVER MILES	SHUTTLE MILES
MM-NN	1.6	5
NN-OO	12.5	16
OO-PP	4	7
PP-QQ	5.8	9
QQ-RR	2	5
RR-SS	2.1	3

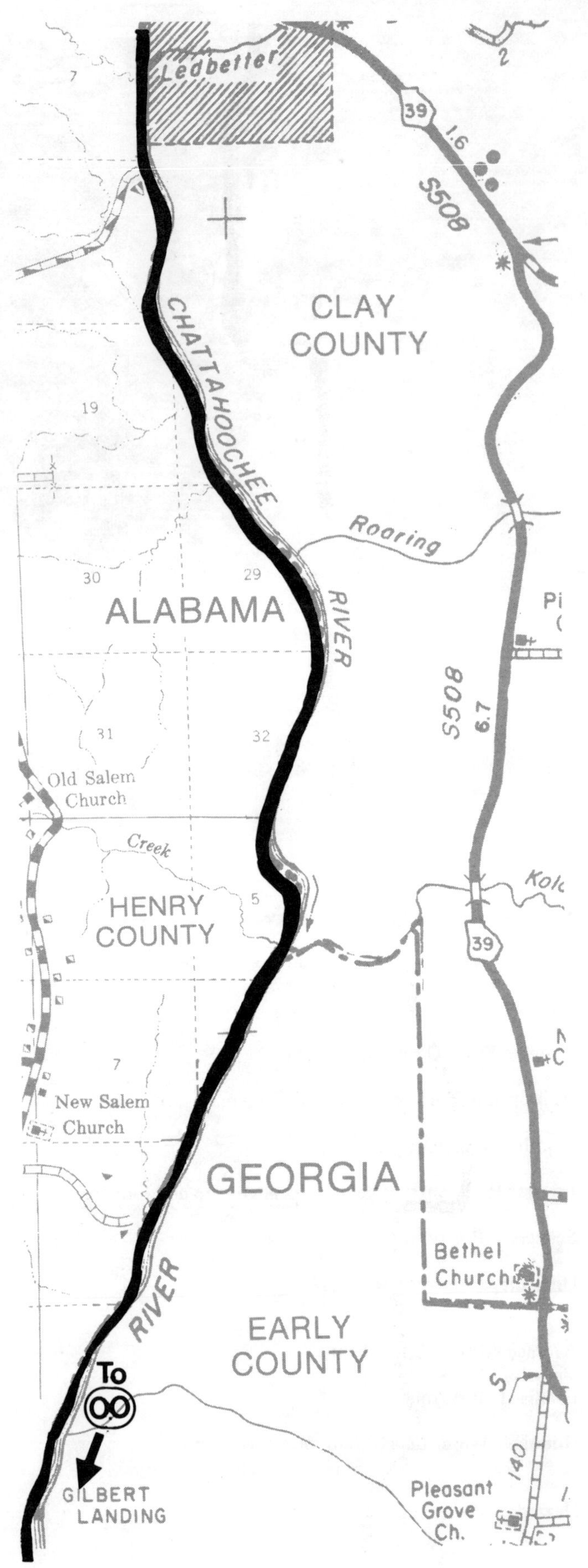

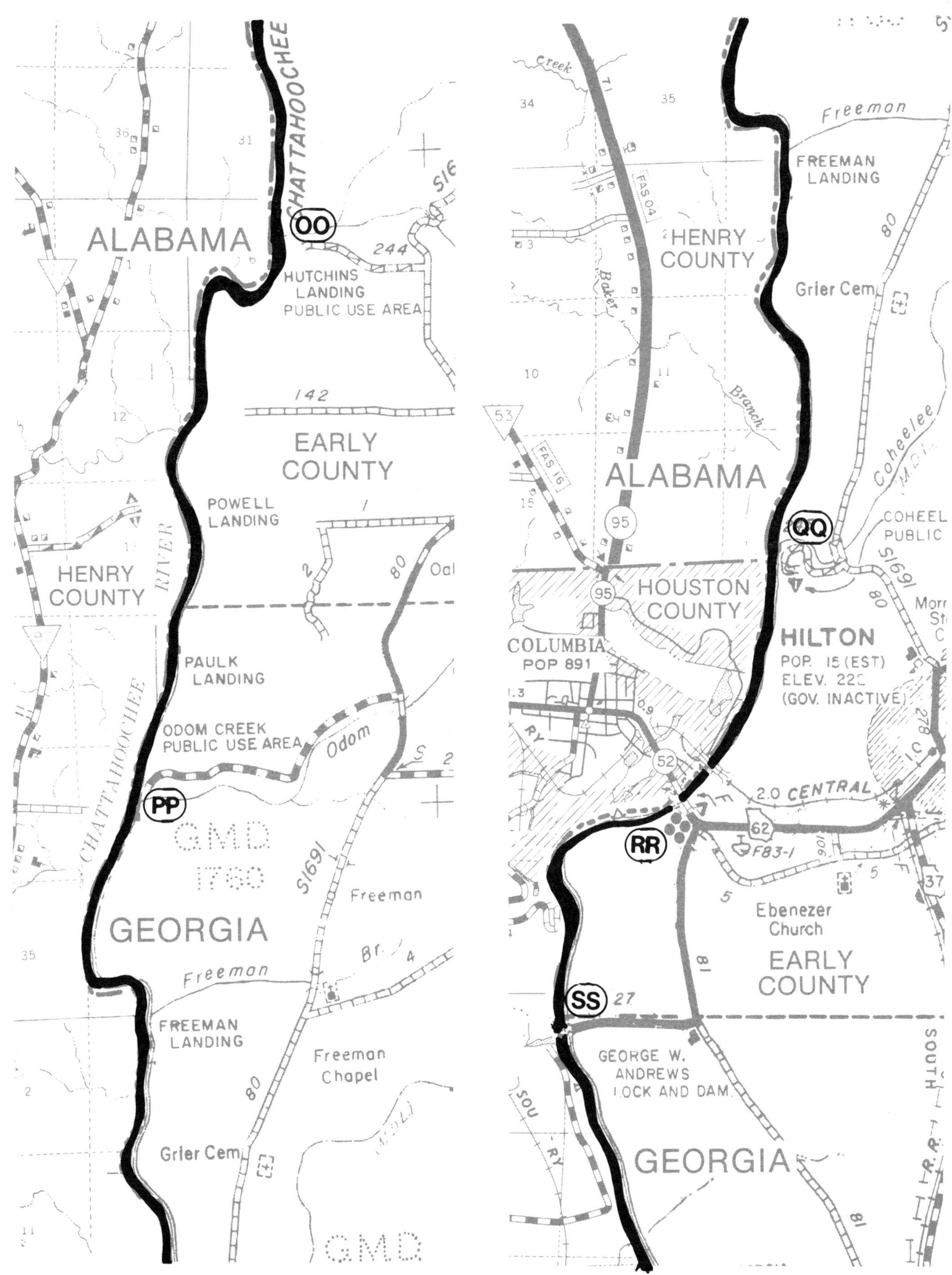

CHATTAHOOCHEE
OO
ALABAMA
244
HUTCHINS
LANDING
PUBLIC USE AREA
142
EARLY
COUNTY
POWELL
LANDING
HENRY
COUNTY
RIVER
PAULK
LANDING
ODOM CREEK
PUBLIC USE AREA
Odom
PP
CHATTAHOOCHEE
GMD
1760
S1691
Freeman
GEORGIA
Freeman
FREEMAN
LANDING
Freeman
Chapel
Grier Cem
G.M.D.
Creek
Freeman
FREEMAN
LANDING
HENRY
COUNTY
Baker
Grier Cem
Branch
ALABAMA
Coheelee
QQ
COHEEL
PUBLIC
HOUSTON
COUNTY
HILTON
POP. 15 (EST)
ELEV. 22
(GOV. INACTIVE)
COLUMBIA
POP 891
2.0 CENTRAL
RR
F83-1
Ebenezer
Church
EARLY
COUNTY
SS
GEORGE W.
ANDREWS
LOCK AND DAM
GEORGIA
SOUTH

Chattahoochee River—*Continued*

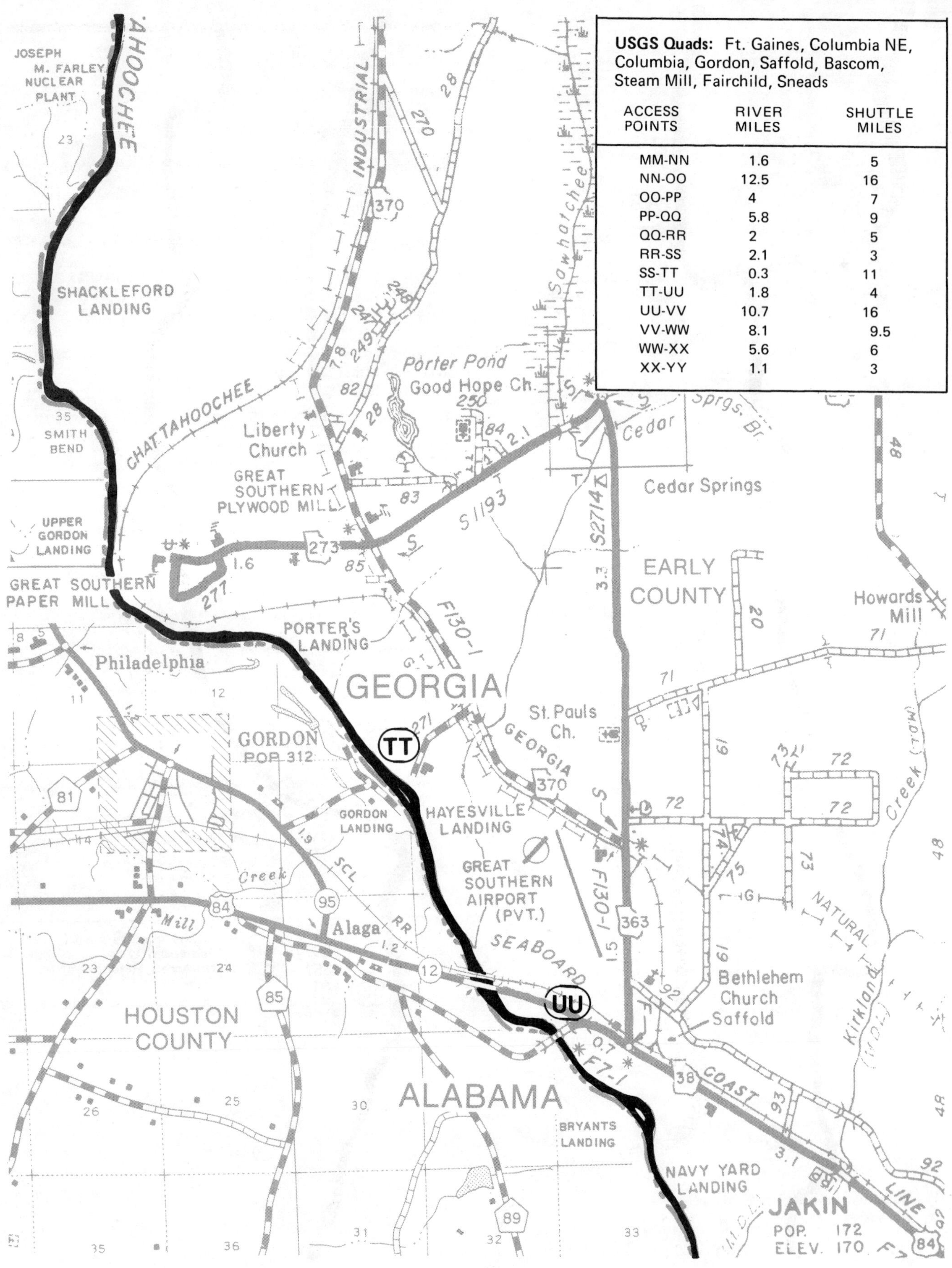

USGS Quads: Ft. Gaines, Columbia NE, Columbia, Gordon, Saffold, Bascom, Steam Mill, Fairchild, Sneads

ACCESS POINTS	RIVER MILES	SHUTTLE MILES
MM-NN	1.6	5
NN-OO	12.5	16
OO-PP	4	7
PP-QQ	5.8	9
QQ-RR	2	5
RR-SS	2.1	3
SS-TT	0.3	11
TT-UU	1.8	4
UU-VV	10.7	16
VV-WW	8.1	9.5
WW-XX	5.6	6
XX-YY	1.1	3

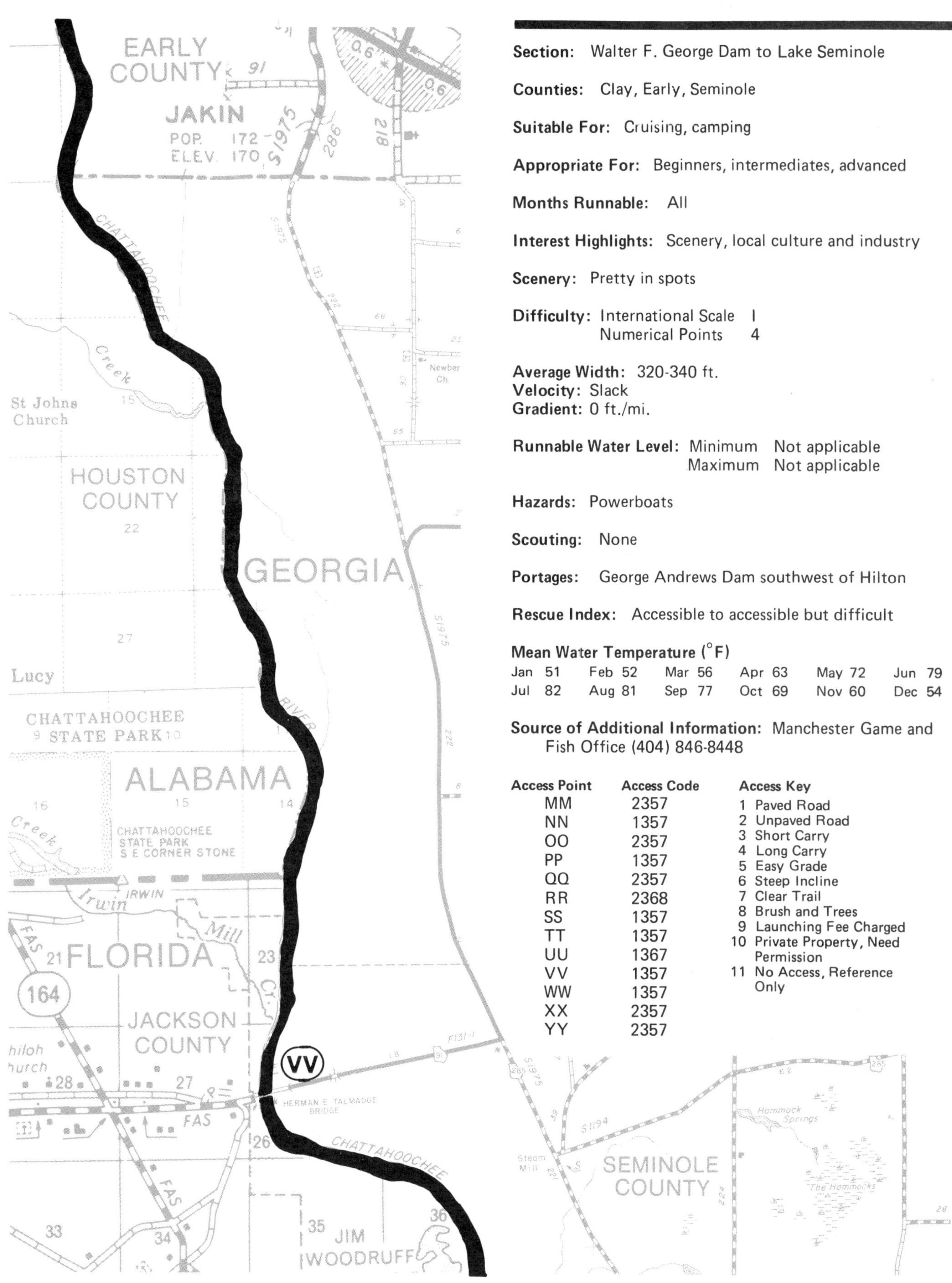

Section: Walter F. George Dam to Lake Seminole

Counties: Clay, Early, Seminole

Suitable For: Cruising, camping

Appropriate For: Beginners, intermediates, advanced

Months Runnable: All

Interest Highlights: Scenery, local culture and industry

Scenery: Pretty in spots

Difficulty: International Scale I
Numerical Points 4

Average Width: 320-340 ft.
Velocity: Slack
Gradient: 0 ft./mi.

Runnable Water Level: Minimum Not applicable
Maximum Not applicable

Hazards: Powerboats

Scouting: None

Portages: George Andrews Dam southwest of Hilton

Rescue Index: Accessible to accessible but difficult

Mean Water Temperature (°F)

Jan	51	Feb	52	Mar	56	Apr	63	May	72	Jun	79
Jul	82	Aug	81	Sep	77	Oct	69	Nov	60	Dec	54

Source of Additional Information: Manchester Game and Fish Office (404) 846-8448

Access Point	Access Code
MM	2357
NN	1357
OO	2357
PP	1357
QQ	2357
RR	2368
SS	1357
TT	1357
UU	1367
VV	1357
WW	1357
XX	2357
YY	2357

Access Key

1 Paved Road
2 Unpaved Road
3 Short Carry
4 Long Carry
5 Easy Grade
6 Steep Incline
7 Clear Trail
8 Brush and Trees
9 Launching Fee Charged
10 Private Property, Need Permission
11 No Access, Reference Only

Chattahoochee River—*Continued*

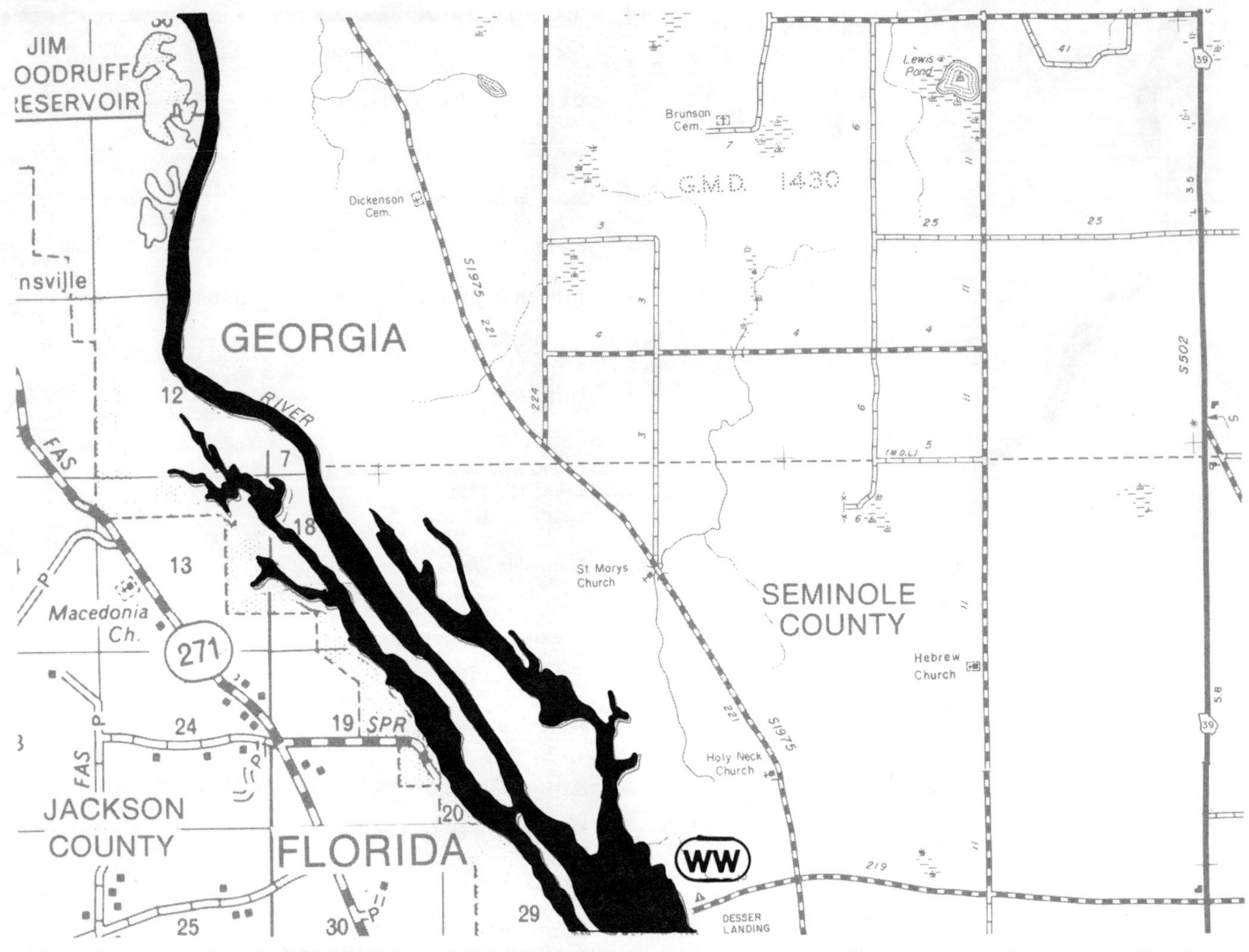

Section: Walter F. George Dam to Lake Seminole

Counties: Clay, Early, Seminole

Suitable For: Cruising, camping

Appropriate For: Beginners, intermediates, advanced

Months Runnable: All

Interest Highlights: Scenery, local culture and industry

Scenery: Pretty in spots

Difficulty: International Scale I
Numerical Points 4

Average Width: 320-340 ft.
Velocity: Slack
Gradient: 0 ft./mi.

Runnable Water Level: Minimum Not applicable
Maximum Not applicable

Hazards: Powerboats

Scouting: None

Portages: George Andrews Dam southwest of Hilton

Rescue Index: Accessible to accessible but difficult

Mean Water Temperature (°F)

Jan 51	Feb 52	Mar 56	Apr 63	May 72	Jun 79
Jul 82	Aug 81	Sep 77	Oct 69	Nov 60	Dec 54

Source of Additional Information: Manchester Game and Fish Office (404) 846-8448

Access Point	Access Code
MM	2357
NN	1357
OO	2357
PP	1357
QQ	2357
RR	2368
SS	1357
TT	1357
UU	1367
VV	1357
WW	1357
XX	2357
YY	2357

Access Key
1 Paved Road
2 Unpaved Road
3 Short Carry
4 Long Carry
5 Easy Grade
6 Steep Incline
7 Clear Trail
8 Brush and Trees
9 Launching Fee Charged
10 Private Property, Need Permission
11 No Access, Reference Only

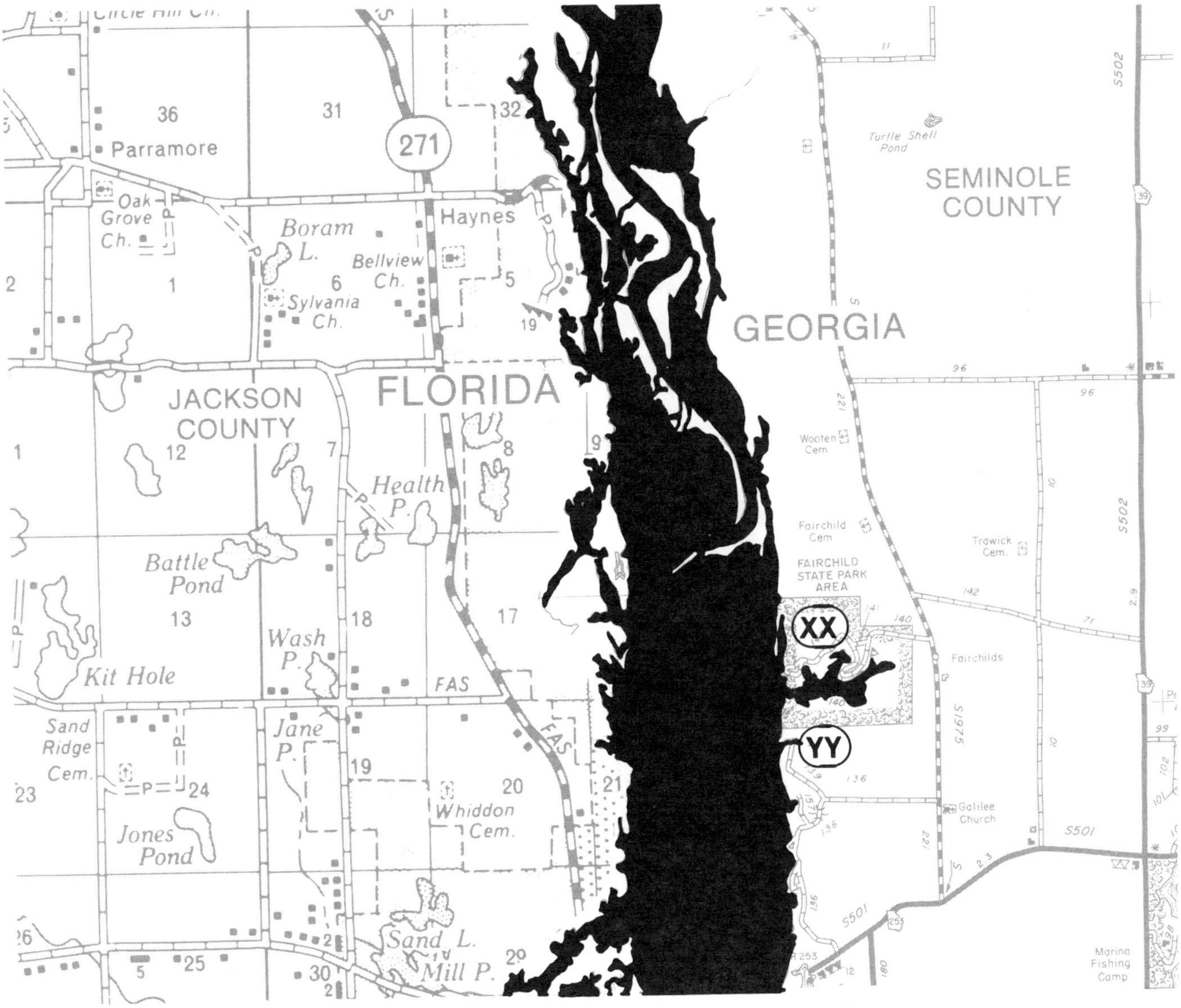

USGS Quads: Ft. Gaines, Columbia NE, Columbia, Gordon, Saffold, Bascom, Steam Mill, Fairchild, Sneads

ACCESS POINTS	RIVER MILES	SHUTTLE MILES
MM-NN	1.6	5
NN-OO	12.5	16
OO-PP	4	7
PP-QQ	5.8	9
QQ-RR	2	5
RR-SS	2.1	3
SS-TT	0.3	11
TT-UU	1.8	4
UU-VV	10.7	16
VV-WW	8.1	9.5
WW-XX	5.6	6
XX-YY	1.1	3

Chattahoochee River near Atlanta.

Photo courtesy of *Brown's Guide to Georgia.*

Savannah River Wildlife Refuge.

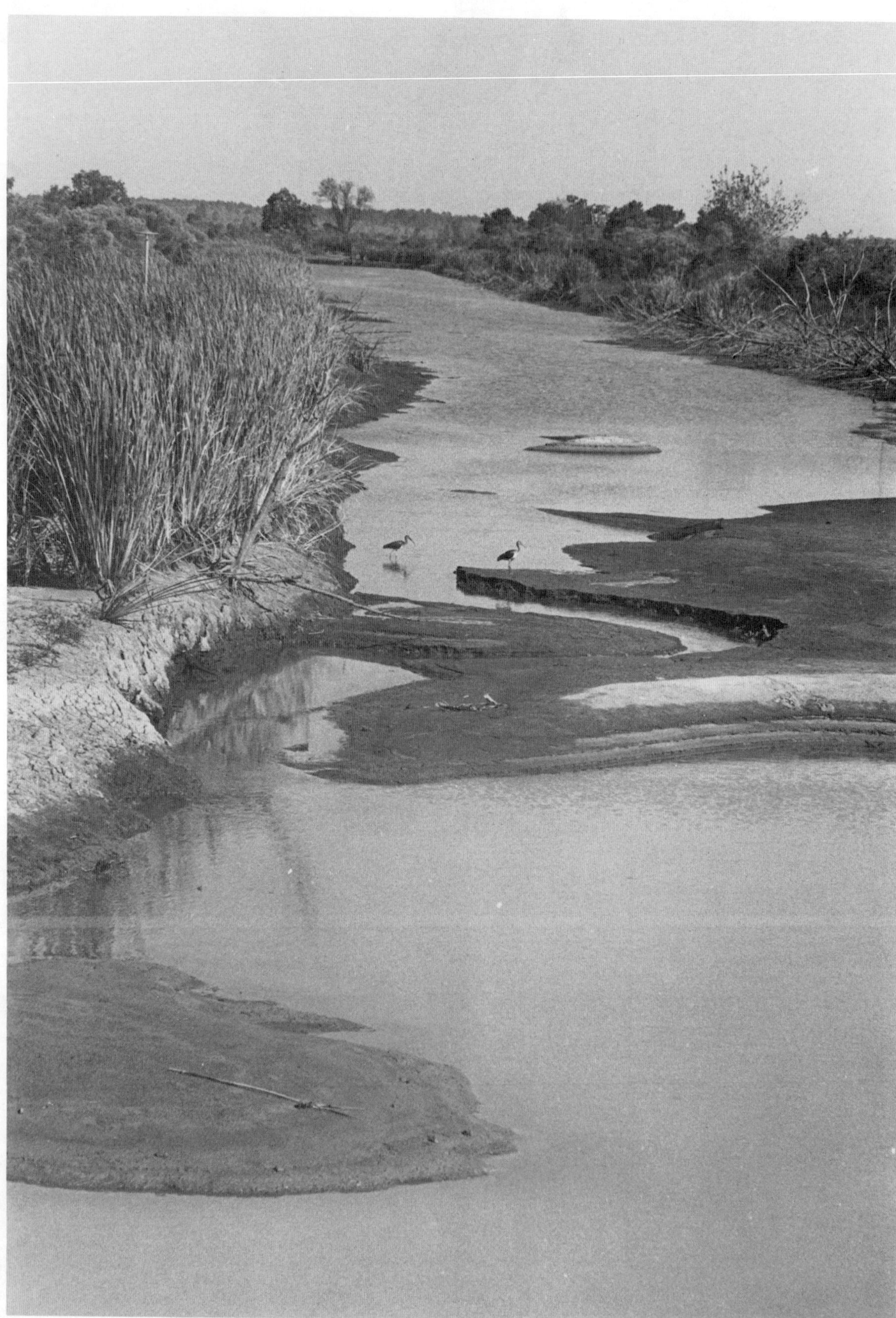

Photo courtesy of *Brown's Guide to Georgia.*

Chapter 6

Waters of Special Mention

Typical bottomland in the Coastal Plain.

Photo courtesy of *Brown's Guide to Georgia.*

Okefenokee Swamp

If Georgia consisted only of the Chattooga River and the Okefenokee Swamp it would still be a water wonderland beautiful and exciting beyond all expectation. As it is, of course, Georgia is rich in watercourses from top to bottom and offers paddlers an almost inexhaustable opportunity for exploration. Even so, the Chattooga and the Okefenokee occupy positions of exhalted prominence not only in Georgia, but among the natural treasures of the entire United States.

The Okefenokee is particularly special. It is unique, a self-contained microcosm of ongoing evolution, an incredible miniature ecosystem in which the drama of the survival of the fittest is performed countless times each day. But more than an ordeal in survival, the Okefenokee is a joyous celebration of everything right and beautiful in nature and a living testimony to man's ability to preserve rather than to destroy when he is stirred out of his ignorance and complacency.

Dark and mysterious, bright and colorful, quiet and expectant, shrill and cacaphonous, the Okefenokee is a study in contrasts. It epitomizes the swamps of imagination and Hollywood while revealing environments and wonders that transcend all expectations. The Okefenokee, says Franklin Russell, "is a fascinating realm that both confirms and contradicts popular notions of a swamp. Along with stately cypresses, peat quagmires, and dim waterways, the Okefenokee has sandy pine islands, sunlit prairies, and clear lakes."

The swamp is situated in southeastern Georgia near the Florida border. It extends about thirty-eight miles from north to south and approximately twenty-five miles from east to west at its widest part. Covering some 430,000 acres, the Okefenokee is one of the largest, oldest, and most primitive swamps in America. Most of the Okefenokee is under the protection of the Okefenokee National Wildlife Refuge, established in 1937, that occupies ninety percent of the swamp's area. Actually a vast peat bog, the Okefenokee was formed more than 250,000 years ago when the Atlantic Ocean covered an area seventy-five miles inland from the present coastline. The pounding surf and the continuing currents created an elongated sandbar with a large lagoon on its landward side. When the ocean receded, the sandbar became a ridge. The lagoon drained leaving a sandy basin that became the bed of the Okefenokee, which is now more than one hundred feet above sea level. Today, the entire swamp, except for the islands, is covered with a bed of peat underlain by a huge, saucer-shaped, sand-floored depression. The peat bed exceeds twenty feet in depth in some places and a mere six inches in others.

Being higher than much of the surrounding area, the Okefenokee depends on local rainfall to maintain its water level. Draining away from a series of ridges in the center of the swamp, the waters of the Okefenokee are in constant circulation. Moving slowly through the prairies and around the hammocks and islands, the waters of the swamp are colored a burgundy red by tannic acid released into the water as swamp vegetation decomposes. Both the fabled Suwannee and the beautiful but less celebrated St. Marys rivers originate in the Okefenokee.

Much of the swamp consists of "prairies," expansive shallow lakes clogged with aquatic plant life. Open water in the Okefenokee is surprisingly scarce. All of the lakes (about 60), gator holes, and waterways combined cover less than a thousand acres.

Known throughout the world for its unusual and diversified wildlife, the swamp is home for 225 species of birds, 43 species of mammals, 58 species of reptiles, 32 species of amphibians, and 34 species of fish. Except at noon when an eerie quiet descends over the swamp, the shrill cries of wood ducks and the hoarse squawks of egrets and herons can be heard resounding everywhere. Turkey vultures ride the hot air currents high overhead while flocks of white ibis glide along just above the tree tops. Old bull alligators bellow their challenges undisturbed by the beat of woodpeckers hammering on dead trees, while choruses of frogs turn the night into a guttural symphony. In the tangled jungle, raccoon, otter, bobcat, opossum, and white-tailed deer hold court among the pond cypress, bay, black gum, and swamp cyrilla.

The Okefenokee defies summary; no description can do justice to what even unbelieving eyes can scarcely comprehend. "It is possible," cites Franklin, "to describe the Okefenokee as a peat-filled bog . . . but this reduces the swamp to an unpleasant image of immense dreariness. It is possible to count the islands, about 70, and say that they cover 25,000 acres, but this says nothing of their having been the sites of bitter battles between bears and cougars, of their having sprouted crops of corn and vegetables and great whispering plantations of slash pines surrounded by the stark grandeur of water loving cypresses.

"It is possible," he continues, "to talk about 60,000 acres of prairies, the flooded open areas choked with water lilies and neverwets, pipeworts and ferns, with maiden canes and sedges and moss, but this is only one facet of the great swamp. This is to say nothing of the wildlife, the reptiles, the waterfowl, or even the hammocks, those dense labyrinths of twisted growth, odd collections of hardwoods, water oaks, live oaks, and magnolias clustered together."

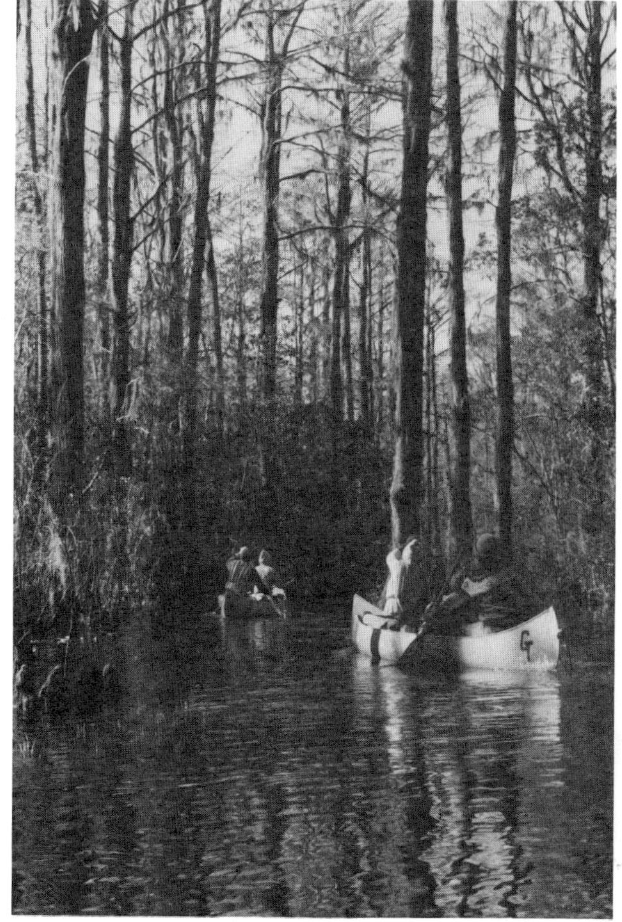
Photo courtesy of *Brown's Guide to Georgia.*

Okefenokee Swamp.

Paddling in the Okefenokee

Though the natural panorama of the Okefenokee defies verbal description, first hand, physical exploration of the swamp can be undertaken for the asking. The Okefenokee National Wildlife Refuge wilderness canoeing program includes a system of thirteen designated trails that provide the opportunity to spend from two to six days in the swamp. The trails are well marked; guides are neither required nor needed, but a permit must be obtained well in advance for the use of these trails. For paddlers interested in a one day (or shorter) outing, circuit trips are available in specified areas that depart from and return to the same access point. Permits are not required for one day outings.

Partially covered overnight camping shelters are provided at Maul Hammock, Big Water, Bluff Lake, and Cedar Hammock. These consist of 20' x 28' platforms built above the water. For the maximum allowable group size, twenty persons, this space equates to a 4' x 7' section of platform for each individual. It should be remembered, in planning, however, that community space for eating, cooking, storage, loading and unloading must be provided for. With this in mind, it is suggested that fourteen persons (or fewer) represents a more ideal group size. Other campsites are located on dry islands within the swamp.

Because of sanitation problems, each group is required to carry a portable toilet with disposable plastic bags. Human waste must be carried out of the swamp and disposed of at the end of the trip. This regulation essentially applies to waste generated in route since chemical flush toilets are available at each overnight stop. Portable toilets and associated gear are the responsibility of the paddler and are not provided by the refuge management.

Portions of all the canoe trails are open to the general public (paddlers on one day trips, tour boats, etc.), and trippers staying longer can expect to encounter other refuge visitors on these sections of the trails. On those parts of the trails requiring a permit, however, only other paddle groups in transit will normally be encountered. The existing system of scheduling allows only one group at each campsite on any given night.

Fluctuating water levels affect the difficulty of the paddling. Some trails may be closed or difficult to travel during certain times of the year because of low water. These difficulties, according to the refuge management, should be viewed "as an integral part of the wilderness experience." Paddlers should read all regulations carefully and not be reluctant to ask questions before departing. This simple precaution may eliminate considerable discomfort and unnecessary problems.

The spring months (March through early May) with their mild temperatures, high water levels, and profusion of wildflowers, are the most popular period for canoeing in the Okefenokee. If you are planning a trip for this period, make reservations one year in advance to avoid disappointment. Reservations for the spring of the *following calendar year* are accepted each year after March 1st. For other periods of the year scheduling is not quite so tight but still warrants advance planning of at least several months. On receipt of inquiry or permit application, the refuge management will forward an information packet containing information on the history, geology, wildlife, and management of the refuge as well as paddling trip regulations and suggestions for a more pleasant and successful outing. Refuge management advises that first-time visitors carefully digest this information *before making their reservations.*

All paddlers should remember that temperatures and biting insects can be vary harsh in the Okefenokee, particularly during the summer months. Temperatures can fall into the teens during January and February. Most of the swamp is bathed in direct sunlight and shade is often at a premium. In stormy weather this same lack of cover creates uncomfortable moments when heavy rain, high wind, and lightning assault the paddler. The bottom line is that the Okefenokee offers a true wilderness experience. Careful planning and preparation are key elements of a successful trip.

Paddling Trip Information

Quality Control. Each canoe trail will be limited to one party daily, and each party will be limited to a maximum of ten canoes or twenty persons. Canoeists are responsible for keeping trails free from litter. This means that litter must be held until after you leave the swamp; litter left by previous parties should be retrieved. Motors are not permitted on canoe trips.

Wildlife. Wildlife abounds in the Okefenokee every month of the year. Sandhill cranes, ducks, and other migratory birds are most numerous from November through March. Otter are commonly seen during cold weather when alligators are relatively inactive. Alligators are active in the summer and are observed sunning on banks mostly during spring and fall.

In general, mosquitoes are no problem except after dark from April through October. They are rarely encountered during the daytime. Deerflies, although a biting menace at times during the summer, are not as bad deep in the swamp. There is no need to fear snakes or alligators as long as normal precautions are taken and animals or nests are not molested.

Fishing. Sport fishing is permitted during posted hours in accordance with Georgia State Law and refuge regulations. Live minnows are not permitted as bait in Okefenokee waters. Bass fishing is best in early spring and late fall, but a lot depends on water levels, moon phase, weather, and the skill of the angler.

Suggested Supplies. (1) Rope for pulling canoe. (2) Drinking water. (3) Insect repellent. (4) Mosquito netting. (5) Rain gear. (6) First aid kit. (7) Snake bite kit. (8) Extra batteries. (9) Litter bags. (10) Pop tent or jungle hammock and sleeping bag. Canoes, other camping equipment, and services are available for rent from the concessionaire, Suwannee Canal Recreation Area, Folkston, Georgia 31537. Phone: (912) 496-7156.

Designated Canoe Trips.

1. Kingsfisher—Maul Hammock—Big Water—Stephen Foster; 3 days, 31 miles.
2. Kingfisher—Bluff Lake—Floyds Island—Stephen Foster (via Floyds Prairie); 3 days, 24 miles.
3. Kingfisher—Bluff Lake—Floyds Island—Stephen Foster (via Suwannee Canal Run); 3 days, 27 miles.
4. Suwannee Canal—Cedar Hammock—Suwannee Canal; 2 days, 12 miles.
5. Suwannee Canal—Suwannee Canal Run—Stephen Foster; 2 days, 17 miles.
6. *Suwannee Canal—Cedar Hammock—Floyds Island—Stephen Foster (via Floyds Prairie); 3 days, 24 miles.
7. Suwannee Canal—Cedar Hammock—Floyds Island—Stephen Foster (via Suwannee Canal Run); 3 days, 27 miles.
8. Stephen Foster—Cravens Hammock—Stephen Foster; 2 days, 18 miles.
9. *Suwannee Canal—Cedar Hammock—Floyds Island—Suwannee Canal; 3 days, 29 miles.
10. *Suwannee Canal—Cedar Hammock—Floyds Island—Bluff Lake—Kingfisher; 4 days, 32 miles.
11. *Kingfisher—Maul Hammock—Big Water—Floyds Island—Bluff Lake—Kingfisher; 5 days, 43 miles.
12. Kingfisher—Bluff Lake—Kingfisher; 2 days, 15 miles.
13. Kingfisher—Maul Hammock—Big Water—Stephen Foster—Floyds Island—Bluff Lake—Kingfisher; 6 days, 55 miles.

Note: A short portage across Floyds Island is required on all trips crossing this island. The state charges a camping fee at Stephen Foster State Park and there are boat launching fees at Stephen Foster and the Suwannee Canal Recreation Area. Mileages shown are total for each trip.

*Starting point and destination may be reversed, but only by permit.

Permits. Canoe trips into the Okefenokee wilderness may be arranged in advance or on a first-come, first-served basis. For reservations write or phone

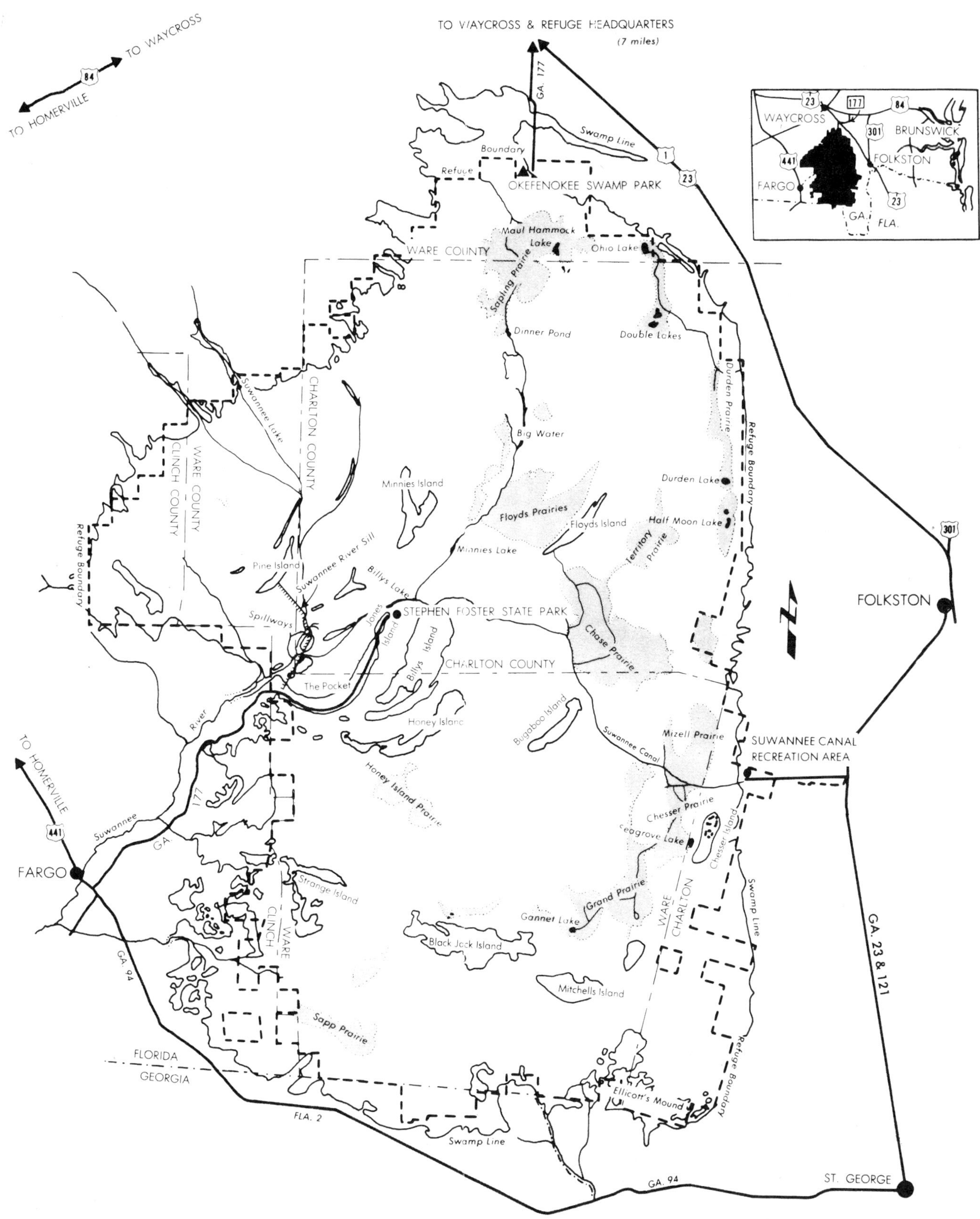

TO WAYCROSS & REFUGE HEADQUARTERS
(7 miles)
TO WAYCROSS
TO HOMERVILLE
84
GA. 177
Swamp Line
Boundary
Refuge
1
23
OKEFENOKEE SWAMP PARK
WAYCROSS
177
84
301
BRUNSWICK
441
FOLKSTON
FARGO
23
GA.
FLA.
Maul Hammock Lake
Ohio Lake
WARE COUNTY
Sapling Prairie
Dinner Pond
Double Lakes
Durden Prairie
Refuge Boundary
Suwannee Lake
CHARLTON COUNTY
WARE COUNTY
CLINCH COUNTY
Big Water
Minnies Island
Durden Lake
Floyds Prairies
Floyds Island
Half Moon Lake
Territory Prairie
301
Refuge Boundary
Pine Island
Suwannee River Sill
Minnies Lake
Billys Lake
Spillways
Jones Island
STEPHEN FOSTER STATE PARK
Billys Island
Chase Prairie
FOLKSTON
CHARLTON COUNTY
The Pocket
River
Honey Island
Bugaboo Island
Suwannee Canal
Mizell Prairie
SUWANNEE CANAL
RECREATION AREA
TO HOMERVILLE
441
Honey Island Prairie
Suwannee
177
GA.
Chesser Prairie
Seagrove Lake
Chesser Island
FARGO
Strange Island
Grand Prairie
Gannet Lake
WARE
CHARLTON
CLINCH
WARE
Swamp Line
GA. 23 & 121
Black Jack Island
GA. 94
Mitchells Island
Sapp Prairie
Refuge Boundary
FLORIDA
GEORGIA
Ellicott's Mound
FLA. 2
Swamp Line
GA. 94
ST. GEORGE

well in advance of planned trip to: Refuge Manager, Okefenokee National Wildlife Refuge, Route 2, Box 338, Folkston, Georgia 31537: phone (912) 496-3331. The following information should be submitted with your written request for a permit:

1. Date trip is planned.
2. Choices of canoe trails.
3. Expected number of canoes in party. A maximum of ten canoes (twenty persons) is permitted.
4. Name of person in charge.
5. Names and addresses of all participants.

Physical Conditions. The swamp terrain is flat; there is no fast water and very little dry land. Your paddle will be used every inch of the way as you wind through cypress forests or cross open "prairies" exposed to the sun and wind. *You may have to get out of your canoe and push across peat blowups or shallow water.* Water levels in the Okefenokee Swamp sometimes become too low to permit use of certain trails; when this occurs, parties holding reservations will be notified.

Okefenokee Swamp.

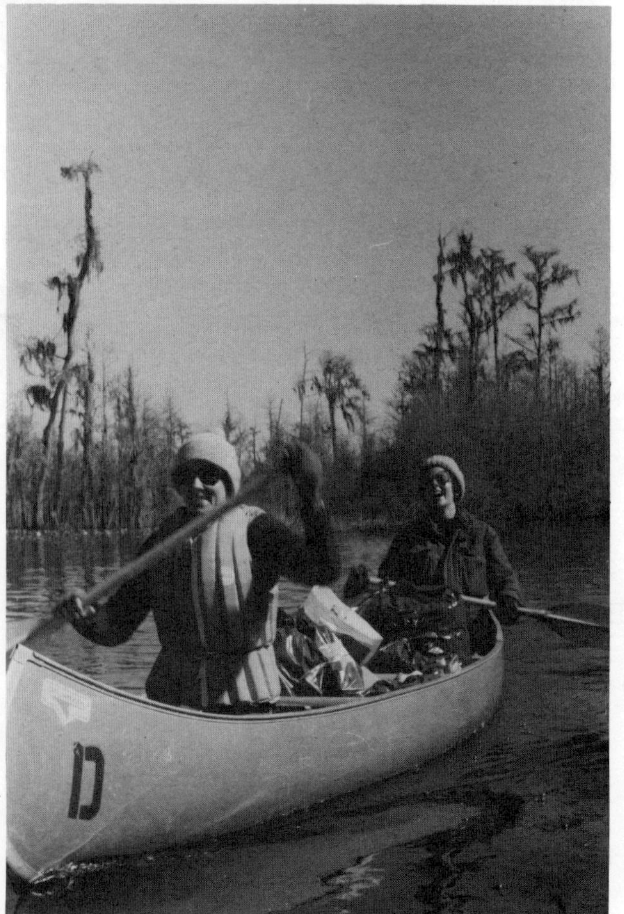

Photo courtesy of *Brown's Guide to Georgia.*

Weather. Daytime temperatures are mostly mild. However, during June, July, August, and September the swamp can be hot and humid with temperatures ranging above 90°F. Winter days range from below 40°F to 80°F, but much of the time tempertures are in the fifties and sixties. Summer nights are warm, and winter nighttime temperatures can be near or below freezing. Record lows have dipped to 18°F. The rainy season is normally from June through September. Many summer afternoons are drenched with localized thundershowers. Lightning is probably the most dangerous feature of an Okefenokee experience.

Safety. Each traveler is required by law to have a Coast Guard approved life preserver in his or her possession. Each canoe must contain a compass and a flashlight. Each canoeist must register when entering and leaving the swamp. Due to danger from alligators, pets may not be taken into the swamp. For the same reason, swimming is not permitted. The minimum party size for safety is two persons. Parties will not be permitted to launch later than 10:00 a.m. to ensure that the overnight stop is reached before dark.

Camping. Overnight camping is permitted only at a designated overnight stop. You must register at each stop. Since firm land is not available at all overnight stops, a 20' x 28' wooden platform is provided. Pop tents are recommended. No nails should be used and no trees or limbs should be cut. Open fires are not permitted except at specified areas, so gasoline, bottled gas, or similar types of stoves will be required if you plan to cook meals. You must remain at the designated overnight area between sunset and sunrise. You may camp only one night per rest stop. Portable toilets with disposable bags are required even though overnight camp sites are outfitted with chemical toilets.

General Trip Canoeing Regulations

1. Overnight canoeing trips by reservation and permit only.
2. Canoeists must camp *only* at assigned camp sites and *only* on assigned dates.
3. Canoeists must use *only* assigned trails and must travel *only* in assigned directions.
4. Canoeists must sign in and out of the refuge and in and out at each overnight stop.
5. All camp sites and trails must be maintained litter free. Litter may be disposed of at exits.
6. Portable toilets are still required. Chemical toilets at overnight stops must be kept clean and used according to posted instructions. Advise ranger if toilet is inoperable or out of supplies.
7. Human waste materials from portable toilets must be disposed of off the refuge. Do not use garbage cans, chemical toilets, or the swamp for disposal.
8. Maximum canoe party size is ten canoes or twenty people. Minimum canoe party size is two people.
9. Pets are not allowed under any circumstances.
10. Each canoeist must have a Coast Guard approved life saving device.
11. Each canoe must contain a compass and flashlight.
12. No swimming.
13. All launches *must be* prior to 10:00 a.m.
14. Use no nails on camping platforms and cut no vegetation. Platforms, all of which are half covered, are suitable for pop-up tents.
15. Open fires are limited to island stops and at certain locations at these stops. Gasoline stoves are recommended.
16. Vehicles parked overnight at entrances or exits are left at the owner's risk and must display the parking placard issued with canoeing permit. Vehicles must be parked in designated area at each entrance or exit.
17. No motors permitted on reserved canoe trips.
18. Equipment reservations, rentals, and canoe shuttles must be made directly with concessionaires. Equipment must be picked up from and returned to concessionaires.
19. Color-coded markers designate specific trails and white-topped posts provide guidance between markers.
20. **Commercial guiding is absolutely illegal unless carried out by Suwannee Canal Recreation Area, Stephen C. Foster State Park, and Okefenokee Swamp Park personnel. Refuge visitors should require guides to display approved guide licenses.**
21. Day-use only canoeing is allowed without a permit but only to those points marked "Permit Required Beyond This Point."
22. Vehicle shuttle is not provided by refuge personnel and must be arranged by canoeists.
23. Know and understand *all* refuge regulations. Violators will be cited *without* warning.

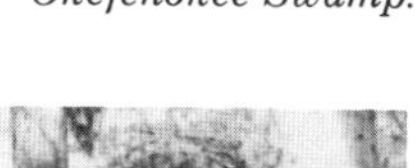

Okefenokee Swamp.

The Georgia Coast

No paddling guide for Georgia would be complete without some mention of the vast, largely wild, Atlantic coastal waters. Ranging for almost one hundred miles from the mouth of the Savannah River at the South Carolina boundary to the mouth of the St. Marys River at the Florida state line, the Georgia coast represents one of the largest areas of generally undeveloped coastline on the Atlantic Seaboard. Comprising thousands of islands measuring anywhere from half an acre to twenty-three miles long (Cumberland Island), the coast appears at first glance to be tangled labyrinth of marshes, rivers, sounds, and vast networks of convoluted tidal creeks. On closer inspection, however, it is observed that thirteen islands extend into the Atlantic to form a barrier between the sea and the Georgia coast. At the mouth of the Savannah is Tybee Island. Moving south the next barrier island is Wassaw followed by Ossabaw Island at the mouth of the Ogeechee River. Next, shielding the mouth of the short Newport River are Wahoo and St. Catherines islands with Blackbeard and Sapelo islands to their south. At the mouth of the Altamaha is St. Simons Island, site of Sea Island Resort and the most developed of the barrier islands. Continuing south, Jekyll Island protects the mouth of the Little Satilla (of Glynn County) and Cumberland Island stretches from the terminus of the Satilla River to the mouth of the St. Marys River.

The sea sides of the barrier islands are largely beach bordered by dunes while the inland sides of the islands taper off into expansive grassy marshes. Between the barrier islands and the coast runs the Intercoastal Waterway, which, as it passes through Georgia, is also called the Cumberland River. To either side of the Cumberland River countless sloughs, small rivers, and tidal creeks wind in intricate fashion among the marshes, islands, and hammocks connecting the major sounds and rivers with the Intercoastal Waterway and the ocean. It is these smaller watercourses that provide the best avenue of exploration for the paddler. Free of commercial powerboat traffic, a canoeist can travel the sloughs and creeks to his or her heart's content, absorbing the beauty and ecology of the estuaries and sounds, small islands, and marshes. Grasses thrive in even the most brackish marshes while shrubs and trees, being more sensitive to high saline concentrations, are found on islands above the high-water mark and where fresh water from emptying rivers and creeks dilutes the salt concentrations to a tolerable level. No amphibians occupy the salt marshes. Birds, including the willet, great blue heron, and snowy egret feed in the marsh but do not nest there. Raccoons, mink, and rice rats are common to the marshes and dwell among the innumerable tidal creeks that serve as nurseries for young fish, shrimp, and crabs.

Dry land can be found by paddling upstream on the fresh-water rivers and creeks that end their journey at the Georgia Coast and also on some of the larger of the many islands. Flora on the islands is often exotic with cypress, gum, and sprawling live oak draped with Spanish moss.

Counting the coastal islands of South Carolina, the Atlantic barrier islands have flown the flags of Spain, France, England, the Confererate States of America and the United States of America. Today, though largely undeveloped, many of the coast and barrier islands are administered as state or federal game preserves and wildlife refuges. Of the remainder, several are occupied by military installations and some remain in private hands. Access to many islands is diligently controlled. Paddlers planning extended trips should obtain Small Craft Nautical Strip Navigation Charts, pinpoint anticipated campsites, and obtain permission in advance to camp from the managing authority or owner. A series of seven charts covers the entire Georgia coast (Charts number 11506 through 11512) and are available from local coastal marinas for around $4.00. Also available, at the same price, is a master chart or key that illustrates the respective area covered by the individual charts.

Paddling among the tidal islands and marshes can be exceptionally enjoyable but it requires comprehensive planning. First, camping is limited and restricted as mentioned above. Second, access to the coastal tidewaters is scarce and shorter trips, except those departing from and returning to the same point, are limited in number. On longer trips (in excess of one day), reprovisioning is often not possible. Tidal currents can be tricky and strong

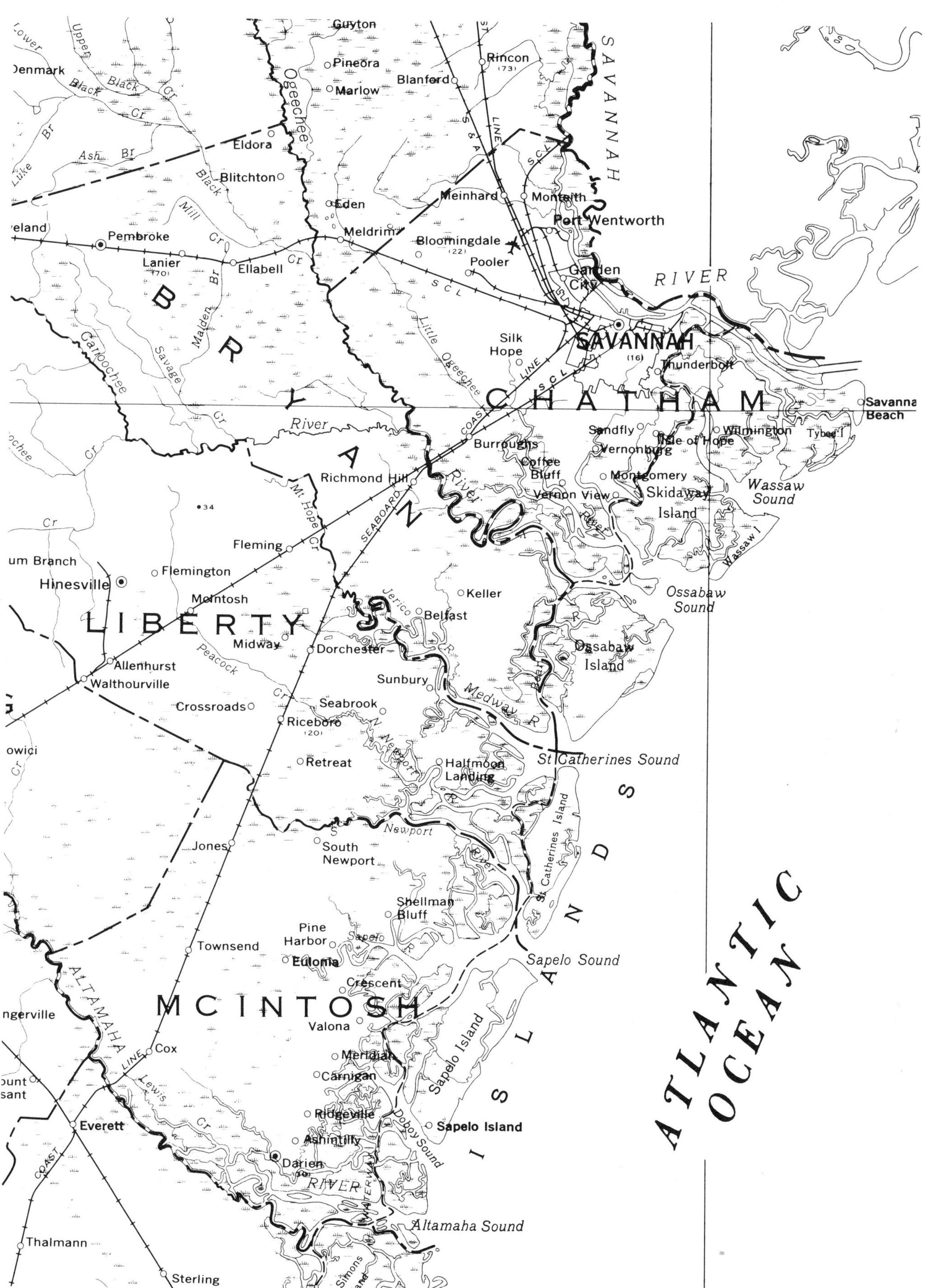
Guyton
Pineora
Marlow
Rincon
Blanford
Denmark
Eldora
Blitchton
Eden
Meinhard
Monteith
Port Wentworth
Meldrim
Bloomingdale
Pooler
Pembroke
Lanier
Ellabell
Garden City
SAVANNAH
Silk Hope
Thunderbolt
BRYAN
CHATHAM
Savannah Beach
Sandfly
Isle of Hope
Wilmington
Tybee I
Vernonburg
Burroughs
Coffee Bluff
Montgomery
Vernon View
Skidaway Island
Wassaw Sound
Richmond Hill
Fleming
Hinesville
Flemington
McIntosh
LIBERTY
Keller
Belfast
Ossabaw Sound
Ossabaw Island
Midway
Dorchester
Allenhurst
Walthourville
Sunbury
Crossroads
Seabrook
Riceboro
Retreat
Halfmoon Landing
St Catherines Sound
St Catherines Island
Jones
South Newport
Shellman Bluff
Pine Harbor
Townsend
Eulonia
Sapelo Sound
Crescent
MCINTOSH
Valona
Cox
Meridian
Carnigan
Sapelo Island
Everett
Ridgeville
Ashintilly
Darien
Altamaha Sound
Thalmann
Sterling
ISLANDS
ATLANTIC OCEAN
SAVANNAH RIVER

especially in the various sounds that lead to the open sea between the barrier islands. Travel by canoe on the seaward side of the barrier islands is possible but risky. Would-be trippers should practice launching and beaching an empty canoe at a public beach before attempting even short trips. Weather conditions should be carefully evaluated before paddling off shore in the Atlantic. Calm seas and slack to moderate winds are essential. On extended trips paddlers should carry a transistor radio and monitor weather forecasts and, in all cases, travel in groups of no fewer than three craft. Emergency routes to protected waters and possible beaching sites should be anticipated and marked on charts. Except in glassy seas (perfectly calm), paddlers should run a zig-zag pattern to quarter waves and swells. Always wear a PFD and paddle within easy swimming distance of shore. Consider tidal conditions, particularly when entering or crossing a sound and plan your trip accordingly. On extended floats file an itinerary with the local Coast Guard authority before departing.

Altamaha River delta at low tide. (See page 162 for the same area at high tide.)

Photo courtesy of *Brown's Guide to Georgia.*

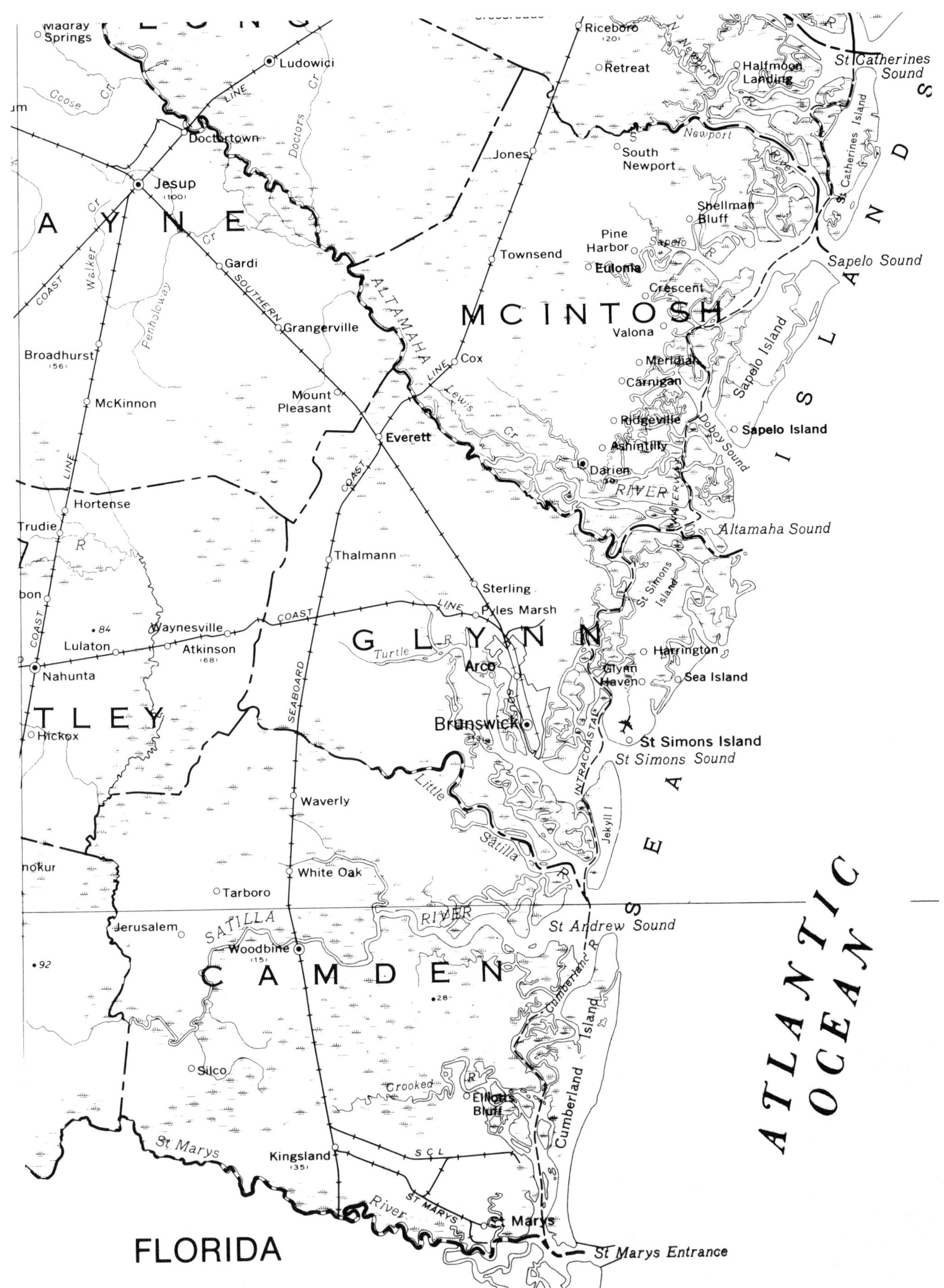
Springs
Ludowici
Riceboro
Retreat
Halfmoon Landing
St Catherines Sound
Goose Cr
Doctors Cr
Doctortown
Jones
South Newport
Newport
St Catherines Island
Jesup
Shellman Bluff
A Y N E
Walker Cr
Gardi
Townsend
Pine Harbor
Eulonia
Sapelo Sound
Crescent
M C I N T O S H
Grangerville
ALTAMAHA
Valona
Sapelo Island
Broadhurst
Cox
Meridian
Carnigan
McKinnon
Mount Pleasant
Lewis Cr
Ridgeville
Sapelo Island
Everett
Ashintilly
Doboy Sound
Darien
RIVER
Hortense
Altamaha Sound
Trudie
Thalmann
St Simons Island
Sterling
Pyles Marsh
Waynesville
Lulaton
Atkinson
G L Y N N
Harrington
Nahunta
Arco
Glynn Haven
Sea Island
Brunswick
T L E Y
Hickox
St Simons Island
St Simons Sound
INTRACOASTAL
Little Satilla
Waverly
Jekyll I
White Oak
Tarboro
ATLANTIC OCEAN
Jerusalem
SATILLA RIVER
St Andrew Sound
Woodbine
C A M D E N
Cumberland R
Cumberland Island
Silco
Crooked R
Ellicotts Bluff
Cumberland Island
St Marys
Kingsland
S C L
St Marys River
ST MARYS
St Marys
FLORIDA
St Marys Entrance

Canoe-camping.

Photo courtesy of *Brown's Guide to Georgia.*

Appendixes

Appendix A

Commercial Raft Trips and Expeditions

Several commercial raft outfitters operate in the state of Georgia. All operate on whitewater streams of varying difficulty and are reputable, safety conscious, and professional. There are, however, several companies that will rent rafts or other inflatables for use on rated whitewater to individuals who are totally ignorant and naïve about the dangers involved. These companies normally do not run guided trips but rather send unsuspecting clients down the river on their own to cope with whatever problems or hazards materialize. It is our position that safe enjoyment of whitewater requires education and experience, and that attempting to paddle whitewater in any type of craft, privately owned or rented, without the prerequisite skills or without on-river professional guidance is dangerous in the extreme. That various companies will rent boats or rafts to the unknowing only proves that some people are unscrupulous, not that whitewater paddling is safe for the unaccompanied beginner.

All the reputable raft companies in Georgia operate guided excursions only, where professional whitewater guides accompany and assist their clients throughout the run. This type of experience has an unparalleled safety record in the United States and represents an enjoyable and educational way of exposing the newcomer to this whitewater sport. Through professional outfitters, thousands of people every year are turned on to the exhilaration of paddling. Spouses and friends of paddlers, who are normally relegated to enjoying our beautiful rivers vicariously through the stories of their companions, are made welcome and provided the thrill of experiencing the tumbling cascades firsthand.

Choosing a commercial outfitter is made somewhat easier by the Eastern Professional River Outfitters' Association (EPRO), the professional organization for commercial river runners in the eastern United States and Canada. Through its devotion to safety and its strict membership admission requirements, EPRO ensures that its members companies epitomize the highest standards in professional river outfitting. EPRO members operating guided raft trips in Georgia include:

Buckhorn Mountain Shop, 2341 Thompson Bridge Road, Gainesville, GA 30501. Phone: (404) 536-0081.
Guided trips and clinics on Georgia rivers. Guided raft trips on the Ocoee River; canoe and kayak clinics on the Chattooga River.

High Country Outfitters, Inc., 6300 Powers Ferry Road, Atlanta, GA 30339. Phone: (404) 955-1866.
Clinics and guided trips on Georgia rivers.

Nantahala Outdoor Center, US 19 West, Box 41, Bryson City, NC 28713. Phone: (704) 488-6900.
Guided raft trips on the Ocoee and Chattooga rivers.

Southeastern Expeditions, 1955 Cliff Valley Way NE, Suite 220-B, Atlanta, GA 30329. Phone: (404) 329-0433 (Atlanta) or (404) 782-4331 (Clayton).
Guided raft trips on the Chattooga and Ocoee rivers.

Wildwater, Ltd., Box 100E, Long Creek, SC 29658. Phone: (803) 647-9587.
Guided raft trips on the Chattooga and Ocoee rivers.

Educational Field Trips

Wilderness Southeast, 711 Sandtown Road, Savannah, Georgia 31410. Phone: (912) 897-5108.
Nonprofit outdoor school in southern Georgia.

Wolfcreek Wilderness, Inc., P.O. Box 596, Blairsville, GA 30512. Phone: (404) 745-6460.
Nonprofit outdoor school.

Commercial River Outfitters (Canoe Liveries)

Blue Ridge Mountain Sports
Lenox Square
3395 Peachtree Rd. NE
Atlanta, GA 30326
(404) 266-8372

Buckhorn Mountain Shop
2341 Thompson Bridge Rd.
Gainesville, GA 30501
(404) 536-0081

The Diving Locker
1490 Baxter St.
Athens, GA 30601
(404) 546-5877

High Country Outfitters, Inc.
6300 Powers Ferry Rd.
Atlanta, GA 30339
(404) 955-1866

Ogeechee Canoe Outpost
Safari Campground
GA Hwy 204
Savannah, GA 31402
(912) 925-9527

Suwannee Canal Recreation Area, Inc.
Route 2
Okefenokee National Wildlife Refuge
Folkston, GA 31537 (912) 496-7156

Live Oak Outpost
Highway 129
Route 1, Box 98
Live Oak, FL 32060
(904) 364-1683

Some state parks rent canoes for use at their locations only. See the state park information in another part of this Appendix.

Canoeing Organizations

Georgia

Local canoe clubs render an invaluable service to paddlers of all skill levels. Georgia clubs provide well-rounded programs including competition, whitewater and flatwater scheduled cruises, clinics, conservation programs, social outings, winter pool sessions, and regular meetings. In addition most clubs publish monthly or bimonthly newsletters. Dues vary as do services to members but the general range is $5.00 to $12.00 a year.

Atlanta Whitewater Club
P.O. Box 33
Clarkston, GA 30021

Georgia Canoeing Association
Box 7023
Atlanta, GA 30309

Neighboring States

Tennessee Scenic Rivers Association
P.O. Box 3104
Nashville, TN 37219

Tennessee Valley Canoe Club
P.O. Box 11125
Chattanooga, TN 37401

Chota Canoe Club
P.O. Box 8270, University Station
Knoxville, TN 37916

Bluff City Canoe Club
P.O. Box 4523
Memphis, TN 38104

Tennessee Eastman Recreation Club
Gordon Newland Building, 150-B
P.O. Box 511
Kingsport, TN 37662

East Tennessee Whitewater Club
P.O. Box 3074
Oak Ridge, TN 37830

Sewanee Canoe and Outing Club
The University of the South
Sewanee, TN 37375

Jackson Rapids Transit
P.O. Box 3034
Jackson, TN 38301

Birmingham Canoe Club
P.O. Box 951
Birmingham, AL 35201

Carolina Canoe Club
Box 9011
Greensboro, NC 27408

National

American Canoe Association
P.O. Box 248
Lorton, VA 22079

American Whitewater Affiliation
P.O. Box 321
Concord, NH 03301

U.S. Canoe Association
P.O. Box 9
Winamac, IN 46996

Appendix C

Where to Buy Maps

As indicated in the introductory material, maps included in this book are intended to supplement rather than replace U.S. Geological Survey topographic quadrangles and county road maps. Maps can be purchased from the following locations.

United States Geological Survey (USGS)

Topographic Quadrangles

Eastern U.S.

Distribution section
U.S. Geological Survey
1200 South Eads Street
Arlington, VA 22202

Georgia

Department of Natural Resources Map Sales
Fourth Floor, Agriculture Building
19 Martin Luther King Drive
Atlanta, GA 30334
Phone (404) 656-3214

Albany

Albany Metropolitan Planning Commission
225 Pine Ave.
Zip 31703

Atlanta

Lowe Engineers, Inc.
1920 Monroe Dr. NE
Zip 31703

Atlanta General Microfilm Map Co.
3060 Pharr Court North, C
Zip 31702

Mayes, Sudderth & Etheredge, Inc.
1775 The Exchange
Zip 31705

John J. Harte Associates, Inc.
3290 Cumberland Club Drive
Zip 31703

Augusta

Augusta Blueprint & Microfilm, Inc.
No. 6 Eighth St.
Zip 30904

Besson & Pope Consulting Engineers
1005 Emmett St., Suite B
Zip 30903

Brunswick

Coastal Area Planning & Development Commission
Zip 31520

Columbus

White's Book Store
Cross Country Plaza
Zip 31906

Wickham's Outdoor World
Cross Country Plaza
Zip 31906

Dalton

North Georgia Area Planning & Development Commission
212 North Pentz St.
Zip 30720

Decatur

Reeder & McGaughey, Inc.
2024 Lawrenceville Hwy.
Zip 30033

Jonesboro

Hoffman, Butler & Associates, Inc.
Arrowhead Professional Park
409 Arrowhead, Building A
Zip 30236

Marietta

Aerial Surveys
107 Church St. NW
Zip 30062

Morrow

Reeder & McGaughey, Inc.
1221 Southlake Mall
Zip 30260

Savannah

Savannah Blue Print Company
11 East York St.
Zip 31404

Stockbridge

Lewis Hurd Engineers
May's Corner, US 23N
Zip 30281

Toccoa

Harris Sporting Goods
Grant Plaza
Zip 30577

County Road Maps

In addition to the addresses listed, county maps are also usually available at county office buildings and local highway departments.

Georgia

Department of Transportation
Map Room, Room 10
Number 2, Capital Square
Atlanta, GA 30334

Tennessee

Department of Transporation
Research and Planning
Room 400 Doctors Building
706 Church Street
Nashville, TN 37203
ATTN: Map Sales

North Carolina

Department of Transportation
Division of Highways
Raleigh, NC 27611
ATTN: Map Sales

Virginia

Department of Highways and Transportation
1221 East Broad Street
Richmond, VA 23219
ATTN: Map Sales

South Carolina

Department of Highways and Public Transportation
ATTN: Map Sales
P.O. Box 191
Columbia, SC 29202

Alabama

State of Alabama Highway Department
Bureau of State Planning
ATTN: Map Room
Montgomery, AL 36130

Florida

Department of Transportation
ATTN: Maps and Publications
Mail Station 13
Haydon Burns Building
Tallahassee, FL 32301

Lake Maps

U.S. Army Corps of Engineers
Public Affairs Office
30 Pryor Street, S.W.
Atlanta, GA 30303

Appendix D

Georgia Fish and Wildlife

The following compilations of fish and animal life have been adapted from *The Natural Environments of Georgia,* by Charles H. Wharton, published jointly by the Geologic and Water Resources Division and Resource Planning Section of the Office of Planning and Research, Georgia Department of Natural Resources, Atlanta, Georgia, in 1978.

Georgia Department of Natural Resources Game and Fish Offices

Calhoun Game & Fish Office
P.O. Box 786
Calhoun, GA 30701
(404) 629-8674

Gainesville Game & Fish Office
Route 13, Box 322A
Gainesville, GA 30501
(404) 532-5302

Thomson Game & Fish Office
P.O. Box 204
Thomson, GA 30824
(404) 595-4211

Walton Game & Fish Office
Route 2
Social Circle, GA 30279
(404) 557-2227

Manchester Game & Fish Office
P.O. Drawer 152
Manchester, GA 31816
(404) 846-8448

Macon Game & Fish Office
Rt. 1, Box 86
Dry Branch, GA 31020
(912) 744-3228

Metter Game & Fish Office
P.O. Box 358
Metter, GA 30439
(912) 685-2145

Cordele Game & Fish Office
Rt. 3
Cordele, GA 31015
(912) 273-8945

Albany Game & Fish Office
2024 Newton Rd.
Albany, GA 31705
(912) 439-4252

Waycross Game & Fish Office
P.O. Box 711
Waycross, GA 31501
(912) 285-6093

Brunswick Game & Fish Office
P.O. Box 1097
Brunswick, GA 31520
(912) 264-7237

Demeries Creek Game & Fish Office
P.O. Box E
Richmond Hill, GA 31324
(912) 727-2111

Game Fish

Altamaha River

hickory shad
American shad
redfin or grass pickerel
chain pickerel
muskellunge
channel catfish
white bass
striped bass
striped-white bass hybrid
flier
redbreast sunfish
warmouth
bluegill
dollar sunfish
redear sunfish
spotted sunfish (stumpknocker)
largemouth bass
black crappie

Chattahoochee River

brown trout
rainbow trout
brook trout
redfin or grass pickerel
chain pickerel
muskellunge
channel catfish
white bass
striped bass
striped-white bass hybrid
rock bass
flier
redbreast sunfish
warmouth
bluegill
dollar sunfish
longear sunfish
redear sunfish
spotted sunfish (stumpknocker)
redeye bass
smallmouth bass
largemouth bass
spotted bass
white crappie
black crappie
sauger
walleye

Oconee River

American shad
redfin or grass pickerel
chain pickerel
muskellunge
channel catfish
white bass
striped bass
striped-white bass hybrid
redbreast sunfish
warmouth
bluegill
dollar sunfish
redear sunfish
spotted sunfish (stumpknocker)
redeye bass
spotted bass
largemouth bass
white crappie
black crappie
walleye

Ogeechee River

hickory shad
American shad
redfin or grass pickerel
chain pickerel
muskellunge
channel catfish
striped bass
flier
redbreast sunfish
warmouth
bluegill
dollar sunfish
redear sunfish
spotted sunfish (stumpknocker)
largemouth bass
black crappie

Savannah River

hickory shad
American shad
brown trout
rainbow trout
brook trout

redfin or grass pickerel
chain pickerel
muskellunge
channel catfish
flathead catfish
white bass
striped bass
striped-white bass hybrid
flier
redbreast sunfish
warmouth
bluegill
dollar sunfish
redear sunfish
spotted sunfish (stumpknocker)
redeye bass
smallmouth bass
largemouth bass
white crappie
black crappie
sauger
walleye

Vertebrate Fauna of the Piedmont

A. Salamanders

Small-mouthed salamander
Eastern four-toed salamander
Georgia red-backed salamander
Eastern mud salamander*
Southern two-lined salamander*
Three-lined salamander*
Northern red salamander*
Red-backed salamander
Red-spotted newt
Mole salamander
Marbled salamander*
Slimy salamander
Spotted salamander
Spotted dusky salamander*

B. Frogs and Toads

Eastern chorus frog
Northern spring peeper
Northern green frog
Pickeral frog
American toad*
Green tree frog*
Bird-voiced tree frog
Eastern bird-voiced tree frog*
Bronze frog*
Southern leopard frog*
Upland chorus frog
Eastern narrow-mouthed toad
Bullfrog*
Gray tree frog
Fowler's toad

C. Turtles

Three-toed box turtle
Eastern painted turtle*
Barbour's map turtle*
River cooter*
Yellow-bellied turtle*
Gulf coast spiny softshell turtle
Snapper*
Loggerhead musk turtle*
Florida snapper*
Gulf coast smooth softshell turtle*

D. Lizards

Northern fence lizard
Slender glass lizard
Green anole lizard
Five-lined skink
Ground skink
Southeastern five-lined skink
Six-lined race runner

E. Snakes

Yellow-bellied water snake*
Midland banded water snake*
Midwest worm snake
Eastern worm snake
Northern black racer
Black king snake
Northern pine snake
Northern copperhead
Red-bellied water snake*
Brown water*
Southern ringneck snake
Gray rat snake*
Scarlet king snake
Eastern cottonmouth*
Timber rattlesnake
Southern ground snake
King snake
Eastern ribbon snake
Southern ribbon snake
Red-bellied snake
Eastern hognose snake
Rough green snake
Mole snake
Corn snake
Coachwhip snake
Northern scarlet snake
Garter snake
Crowned snake

F. Mammals

Silver-haired bat
Harvest mouse
Meadow vole
Meadow jumping mouse
Groundhog
Eastern chipmunk
White-footed mouse
Seminole bat
Beaver*
River otter*
Cotton mouse
Southeast shrew
Hoary bat
Least shrew
Eastern pipistrelle
Big brown bat
Evening bat
Red bat
Cotton rat
Muskrat*
Mink*
Golden mouse
Black bear
Opossum
Swamp rabbit*
Raccoon*
Short-tailed shrew
Gray squirrel
Eastern mole
Southern flying squirrel
Pine vole
Long-tailed weasel
Bobcat
White-tailed deer
Old-field mouse
Fox squirrel
Red fox
Gray fox
Spotted skunk
Striped skunk
Cottontail rabbit

Vertebrate Fauna of the Coastal Plain

A. Salamanders

Dwarf water hog salamander*
Alabama water hog salamander*
Greater siren salamander*
Eastern-lesser siren salamander*
Broad-striped siren salamander*
Narrow-striped mud salamander*
Slender dwarf siren salamander*
One-toed amphiuma salamander*
Two-toed amphiuma salamander*
Three-toed amphiuma salamander*
Margined salamander*
Georgia blind salamander*
Southern red salamander*
Dwarf four-toed salamander*
Southern dusky salamander*
Brimley's dusky salamander*
Gulf coast mud salamander*
Rusty mud salamander*
Tiger salamander
Frosted flatwoods salamander

Western reticulated salamander
Mabee's salamander
Striped newt*
Central newt*
Mole salamander
Marbled salamander*
Slimy salamander*
Spotted salamander*
Spotted dusky salamander*

B. Frogs and Toads

Southern spring peeper
Pig frog*
River frog*
Florida cricket frog*
Southern cricket frog*
Carpenter frog*
Brimley's chorus frog
Southern chorus frog
Little grass frog
Southern toad
Squirrel tree frog
Anderson's tree frog
Gopher frog
Dusky gopher frog
Ornate chorus frog
Pine woods tree frog
Oak toad
Barking tree frog
Eastern spadefoot toad
Green tree frog*
Bird-voiced tree frog*
Bronze frog*
Southern leopard frog*
Upland chorus frog
Eastern narrow-mouthed toad
Bullfrog*
Gray tree frog
Fowler's toad

C. Turtles

Diamond back terrapin
Alligator snapper*
Stinkpot*
Striped mud turtle*
Eastern mud turtle*
Southern painted turtle*
Florida cooter*
Mobile cooter*
Red-eared turtle*
Chicken turtle*
Florida softshell turtle*
Spotted turtle*
Eastern box turtle
Florida box turtle
Gulf coast box turtle
Gopher turtle
Loggerhead musk turtle*
Barbour's map turtle*
River cooter*
Yellow-bellied turtle*
Gulf coast spiny softshell turtle*
Snapper*
Florida snapper
Gulf coast smooth softshell turtle*

D. Lizards

Eastern glass lizard
Island glass lizard
Striped red-tailed lizard
Red-tailed skink
Southern fence lizard
Slender glass lizard
Green anole
Five-lined skink
Ground skink
Broad-headed skink
South eastern five-lined skink
Six-lined race runner

E. Snakes

Glossy water snake*
Green water snake*
Florida green water snake*
Southern banded water snake*
Florida banded water snake*
Gulf glossy water snake*
Black swamp snake*
Striped swamp snake*
Rainbow snake*
Eastern mud snake*
Florida cottonmouth*
Canebrake rattlesnake
Florida brown snake
Florida red-bellied snake
Southern hognose snake
Yellow rat snake
Southern copperhead
Dusky pigmy rattlesnake
Southern black racer
Indigo snake
Florida pine snake
Coral snake
Eastern diamond rattlesnake
Yellow-lipped snake
Red-bellied water snake*
Brown water snake*
Midland brown snake
Southern ringneck snake
Gray rat snake
Scarlet king snake
Eastern cottonmouth*
Southern ground snake
King snake
Eastern ribbon snake
Southern ribbon snake
Red-bellied snake
Eastern hognose snake
Rough green snake
Mole snake
Corn snake
Coachwhip snake
Northern scarlet snake
Crowned snake
Garter snake*
Smooth earth snake

F. Mammals

Southeastern myotis
Florida yellow bat
Brazilian free-tailed bat
Star-nosed mole*
Round-tailed muskrat*
March rabbit*
Southeastern pocket gopher
Colonial pocket gopher
Cumberland Island pocket gopher
Nine-banded armadillo
Big-eared bat
Eastern wood rat
Mountain lion (cougar)
Mahogany bat
Beaver*
River otter*
Southeastern shrew
Hoary bat
Cotton mouse
Least shrew
Little brown myotis
Eastern pipistrelle
Big brown bat
Red bat
Evening bat
Cotton rat
Rice rat*
Muskrat*
Mink*
Golden mouse
Black bear
Opossum
Swamp rabbit*
Raccoon*
Short-tailed shrew
Eastern mole
Gray squirrel
Southern flying squirrel
Pine vole
Long-tailed weasel
Bobcat
White-tailed deer
Old-field mouse
Fox squirrel
Red fox
Gray fox
Eastern spotted skunk
Striped skunk
Cottontail rabbit

*Likely to be encountered on or around streams

Appendix E

Camping Sites

The following camp sites have been selected from listings of the Georgia State Bureau of Industry and Trade and the U.S. Forest Service.

NEAREST TOWN	CAMP NAME	DIRECTIONS & ADDRESS	FACILITIES	SEASON
Calhoun A-1	Hidden Creek (Chattahoochee Nat. Forest)	7¾ mi. W on GA 156; 2 mi. NW on FS Rd. 231; 3¼ mi. N on FS Rd. 228; 1 mi. N on FS Rd. 955. Armuchee Ranger Dist. (404) 638-1085	16 sites; no hookups; pit toilets; picnic tables; fire area	April 1 to October 31 Maximum: 14 days
	Little Creek Campsites	Exit 130 (GA 156) on I-75; 0.1 mi. E on GA 156; 0.1 mi. N on county road. (404) 629-2157	50 sites; 4 full hookups; 36 water & electric; 10 no hookup; 10 pull-throughs; flush toilets; hot showers; dump facility; laundry; phone; 40 picnic tables	Year Round
Chatsworth	Fort Mountain State Park	US 76 & US 441; 7 mi. SE on US 76. (404) 695-2621	114 sites; 114 water & electric; flush toilets; hot showers; picnic tables; fire area	Year Round Maximum: 14 days
	Lake Conasauga	14 mi. E on US 76, 3 mi. NW on FS Rd. 18; 10 mi. N on FS Rd. 68. Cohutta Ranger Dist. 401 Old Ellijay Rd., Chatsworth, Ga. 30705. (404) 695-6736	17 sites; 32' max. RV length; 17 no hookup; flush toilets; picnic tables; fire area	May 25 to Sep. 10 Maximum: 14 days
	Wood Ring Branch Public Use Area	20 mi. S on US 411 and follow signs	15 sites; 15 no hookups; pit toilets; 15 picnic tables; fire area; grills	Year Round Maximum: days
Rossville	Holiday Inn Travel-Park	US 41 & I-75; (Southbound exit 1-Northbound exit 1B); ½ mi. W on US 41N; ½ mi. S on Mack Smith Rd. (404) 891-9766	171 sites; 74 full hookups; 79 water & electric (20 & 30 amp receptacles); 18 no hookups; flush toilets; hot showers; dump stations; laundry; public phone; full service store/RV supplies; LP-gas refill; ice; 171 picnic tables; church service	Year Round, full facility Memorial Day thru Labor Day
Summerville	James H. Floyd State Park	US 27 & GA 100; 3 mi. E on Marble Springs Rd. (404) 857-5211	20 sites; 20 no hookups; no motorcycles, flush toilets; picnic tables; fire area	Year Round Maximum: 14 days
Blairsville A-2	Canal-Lake Campground	US 129 & US 76; 2 mi. N on US 129/US 19; 1½ mi. NW on county road. (404) 745-2648	24 sites; 4 hookups; 13 water & electric, 7 no hookups; 24 pull-thrus, flush toilets; hot showers; dump facility, laundry; public phone; grocery; gas; ice; 11 picnic tables; fire rings; grills; wood	Year Round; full facility Apr. 16 thru Nov. 30
	Lake Winfield Scott (Chattachoochee Nat. Forest)	10¼ mi. S on US 19; 6½ mi. W on GA 180. Brasstown Ranger Dist. (404) 745-6259	23 sites; 32' max. RV length; 23 no hookups; flush toilets; hot showers; picnic tables; fire area	May 1 to Sept. 15 Maximum: 14 days
	Trackrock Campground	US 129 & US 76; 2¾ mi. S on US 129; 4 mi. E on county road. (404) 745-2420	77 sites; 25 full hookups; 52 water & electric (15 amp receptacles) 10 pull-thrus; flush toilets; hot showers; dump facility; laundry; public phone; LP gas refill; ice; 77 picnic tables; grills; wood	Year Round; full facility Memorial Day to Labor Day.
	Vogel State Park	US 76 & US 129-19; 11 mi. S on US 129-19. (404) 745-2628	85 sites; 85 water & electric; flush toilets; hot showers; dump facility; picnic tables; fire area	Year Round Maximum: 14 days
Blue Ridge	Lake Blue Ridge Campground	US 76 & GA 5; 2 mi. E on US 76; 2 mi. S on FS Rd. 605 Toccoa Ranger District (404) 632-2031	52 sites; 22' max RV length; 52 no hookups; flush toilets; ice; picnic tables; wood	May 24 to Sep. 10 Maximum: 14 days
Dahlonega	Cooper Creek (Chattahoochee Nat. Forest)	23½ mi. N on GA 60; 3½ mi. N on FS Rd 236. Toccoa Ranger District (404) 632-2031	20 sites; 32' max RV length; 20 no hookups; flush toilets; picnic tables; fire area	Apr. 1 to Dec. 10 Maximum: 14 days
	Dockery Lake (Chattahoochee Nat. Forest)	11½ mi N on GA 60; ¾ mi. NE on FS Rd. 654. Chestatee Ranger Dist. (404) 864-2541	11 sites; 32' max RV length; 11 no hookups; flush toilets; picnic tables; fire area	May 1 to Oct. 31 Maximum: 14 days
	Frank Gross (Chattahoochee Nat. Forest)	27 mi. N on GA 60; 5 mi. SW on FS Rd. 69. Toccoa Ranger Dist.; (404) 632-2031	11 sites; 11 no hookups; flush toilets; picnic tables; fire area	May 1 to Dec. 10 Maximum: 14 days
	Mulky (Chattahoochee Nat. Forest)	25½ mi. N on GA 60; 4¾ mi. NE on FS Rd. 4. Toccoa Ranger Dist. (404) 632-2031	10 sites; 10 no hookups; pit toilets; picnic tables; fire area	Apr. 1 to Dec. 10 Maximum: 14 days
	Waters Creek (Chattahoochee Nat. Forest)	12¼ mi. NE on US 19; 1 mi. NW on FS Rd. 34. Chestatee Ranger Dist. (404) 864-2541	10 sites; 10 no hookups; pit toilets; picnic tables; fire area	May 1 to Oct. 31 Maximum: 14 days
	Deep Hole	27 mi. N on GA 60. Toccoa Ranger Dist. (404) 632-2031	Camping, hiking, fishing	
Ellijay	Doll Mountain Campground on Carters Lake (Corp of Engineers)	5 mi. S on GA 5; 5 mi. W on Flat Creek Rd.; 5 mi. N to Doll Mountain sign; 1 mi. E to park entrance.	22 sites; 22 no hookups; no motorcycles; flush toilets; hot showers; 22 picnic tables; fire area; grills	Year Round Maximum: 14 days
Hiawassee	Eagle Mountain Trout Farms & Campground	US 76 & GA 75; 2 mi. N on GA 75, 3 mi. E on County Rd. (404) 896-2323	100 sites; 75 water & electric (20 amp receptacles); 25 no hookups; 30 pull-thrus; flush toilets; hot showers; dump facility; phone available; ice; 75 picnic tables; wood	Year Round; full facility Mar. 2 to Nov. 30
	Georgia Mountain Campground	GA 17 & US 76; ¼ mi. E on US 76. (404) 896-2600	90 sites; 90 water & electric; flush toilets; hot showers; public phone; ice	Apr. 1 to Nov. 1
	Lake Chatuge (Chattahoochee Nat. Forest)	2½ mi. W on US 76; 1 mi. S on GA 288. Brasstown Ranger Dist. (404) 745-6259	32 sites; 32 no hookups; flush toilets; hot showers; picnic tables; fire area;	May 1 to Sept. 15 Maximum: 14 days

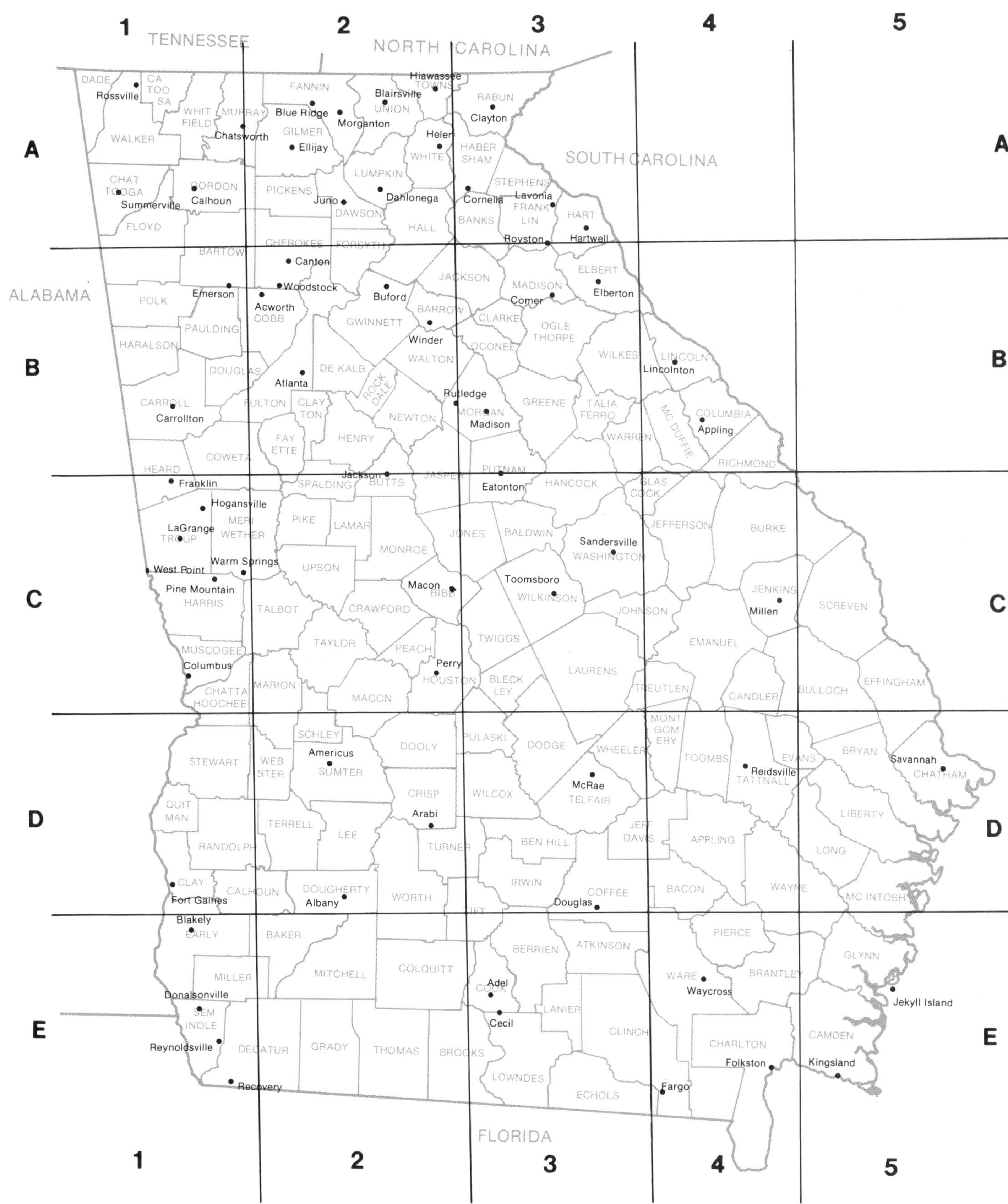
1
2
3
4
5
A
B
C
D
E
TENNESSEE
NORTH CAROLINA
SOUTH CAROLINA
ALABAMA
FLORIDA
DADE
Rossville
CA TOO SA
WALKER
WHIT FIELD
MURRAY
Chatsworth
FANNIN
Blue Ridge
Morganton
GILMER
Ellijay
Blairsville
UNION
Hiawassee
TOWNS
RABUN
Clayton
Helen
WHITE
HABER SHAM
LUMPKIN
Dahlonega
PICKENS
Juno
DAWSON
CHAT TOOGA
Summerville
GORDON
Calhoun
FLOYD
Cornelia
STEPHENS
Lavonia
FRANK LIN
HART
Hartwell
BANKS
HALL
Royston
CHEROKEE
FORSYTH
BARTOW
Canton
Woodstock
Emerson
Acworth
COBB
POLK
PAULDING
HARALSON
Buford
JACKSON
MADISON
Comer
ELBERT
Elberton
GWINNETT
BARROW
Winder
CLARKE
OGLE THORPE
OCONEE
WALTON
WILKES
LINCOLN
Lincolnton
DOUGLAS
Atlanta
DE KALB
ROCK DALE
CARROLL
Carrollton
FULTON
CLAY TON
Rutledge
MORGAN
Madison
GREENE
TALIA FERRO
MC DUFFIE
COLUMBIA
Appling
NEWTON
FAY ETTE
HENRY
WARREN
COWETA
RICHMOND
HEARD
Franklin
Jackson
SPALDING
BUTTS
JASPER
PUTNAM
Eatonton
HANCOCK
GLAS COCK
Hogansville
MERI WETHER
LaGrange
TROUP
PIKE
LAMAR
MONROE
JONES
BALDWIN
Sandersville
WASHINGTON
JEFFERSON
BURKE
Warm Springs
West Point
Pine Mountain
HARRIS
UPSON
TALBOT
Macon
BIBB
CRAWFORD
Toomsboro
WILKINSON
JOHNSON
JENKINS
Millen
SCREVEN
TAYLOR
PEACH
TWIGGS
EMANUEL
MUSCOGEE
Columbus
Perry
HOUSTON
BLECK LEY
LAURENS
CHATTA HOOCHEE
MARION
MACON
TREUTLEN
CANDLER
BULLOCH
EFFINGHAM
SCHLEY
STEWART
WEB STER
Americus
SUMTER
DOOLY
PULASKI
DODGE
WHEELER
MONT GOM ERY
TOOMBS
Reidsville
TATTNALL
EVANS
BRYAN
Savannah
CHATHAM
QUIT MAN
CRISP
WILCOX
McRae
TELFAIR
Arabi
TERRELL
LEE
RANDOLPH
TURNER
BEN HILL
JEFF DAVIS
APPLING
LIBERTY
LONG
CLAY
Fort Gaines
CALHOUN
DOUGHERTY
Albany
WORTH
IRWIN
COFFEE
Douglas
BACON
WAYNE
MC INTOSH
Blakely
EARLY
BAKER
TIFT
BERRIEN
ATKINSON
PIERCE
GLYNN
MILLER
MITCHELL
COLQUITT
Adel
COOK
WARE
Waycross
BRANTLEY
Jekyll Island
Donalsonville
SEM INOLE
Cecil
LANIER
CLINCH
Reynoldsville
DECATUR
GRADY
THOMAS
BROOKS
CHARLTON
Folkston
CAMDEN
Kingsland
LOWNDES
ECHOLS
Fargo
Recovery

NEAREST TOWN	CAMP NAME	DIRECTIONS & ADDRESS	FACILITIES	SEASON
Helen	Andrews Cove (Chattahoochee Nat. Forest)	6 mi. N on GA 75; Chattoga Ranger Dist. (404) 754-6221	11 sites; 11 no hookups; flush toilets; picnic tables; fire area	May 1 to Sep. 10 Maximum: 14 days
	Hickory Nut Mountain Campground	GA 17-75 & GA 356; 4½ mi. E on GA 356; ½ mi. N. (404) 878-2772	80 sites; 10 full hookups; 60 water & electric (15 amp receptacles); 10 no hookups; flush toilets; hot showers; dump facility; laundry; public phone; limited grocery; ice; 80 picnic tables	Year Round
	Unicoi State Park	GA 356 & GA 75; 1 mi N on GA 356.	100 sites; 54 water & electric; 46 no hookups; no motorcycles; flush toilets; hot showers; dump facility; public phone; picnic tables; fire area	Year Round Maximum: 14 days
Juno	Amicalola Falls State Park	GA 136 & GA 183; 5 mi NW on GA 183. (404) 265-2285	25 sites; 23 water & electric; 2 no hookups; no motorcycles; flush toilets; hot showers; picnic tables; fire area	Year Round Maximum: 14 days
Morganton	Morganton Point	US 76 SE from Blue Ridge 6 mi; SW at Morganton on County Road 616 1 mi. Toccoa Ranger District (404) 632-2031		
Clayton A-3	Black Rock Mountain State Park	US 76 & US 441; 3 mi. N on US 441-23. (404) 746-2141	50 sites; 32 water & electric; flush toilets; hot showers; laundry; public phone; grocery; ice; picnic tables; fire area; wood	Year Round Maximum: 14 days
	Rabun Beach (Chattahoochee Nat. Forest)	6½ mi. S on US 441; ¼ mi. W on County Rd. 10; 1½ mi. S on GA 15. Tallulah Ranger Dist. (404) 782-3320	95 sites; 32' max RV length; 95 no hookups; flush toilets; hot showers; dump facility; picnic tables; fire area; wood	Year Round Maximum: 14 days
	Tallulah River (Chattahoochee Nat. Forest)	8 mi. SW on US 76; 4¼ mi. N on County Rd. 70; 1¼ mi. NW on FS Rd. 70. Tallulah Ranger Dist. (404) 782-3320	16 sites; 16 no hookups; flush toilets; picnic tables; fire area	Year Round Maximum: 14 days
	Tate Branch (Chattahoochee Nat. Forest)	9 mi. NW on US 76; 4¼ mi. N on County Rd. 70; 4 mi. NW on FS Rd. 70. Tallulah Ranger Dist. (404) 782-3320	11 sites; 11 no hookups; pit toilets; picnic tables; fire area	Apr. 1 to Oct. 29 Maximum: 14 days
Cornelia	Lake Russell (Chattahoochee Nat. Forest)	½ mi. NE on US 123; 1 mi. SE on FS Rd. 63; 2¾ mi. SE on FS Rd. 59. Chattoga Ranger Dist. (404) 754-6221	51 sites; 32' max RV length; 51 no hookups; flush toilets; picnic tables; fire area	May 1 to Sep. 10 Maximum: 14 days
Hartwell	Hart State Park	US 29 & GA 51; 4 mi. W on GA 51; 3 mi. N on GA 8. (404) 376-8756	100 sites; 100 water & electric; flush toilets; hot showers; laundry; picnic tables; fire area	Year Round Maximum: 14 days
Lavonia	Tugaloo State Park	I-85 & GA 328; 4 mi. N off GA 328. (404) 356-4361	138 sites; 138 water & electric; flush toilets; hot showers; dump facility; laundry; picnic tables; fire area.	Year Round Maximum: 14 days
Royston	Victoria Bryant State Park	I-29 & GA 17; 4 mi. W on I-29 & GA 327. (404) 245-6270	25 sites; 25 water & electric; flush toilets; hot showers; dump facility; laundry; public phone; ice; picnic tables; fire area; wood.	Year Round Maximum: 14 days
Carrollton B-1	John Tanner State Park	US 27 & GA 166; 6 mi. W on GA 166. (404) 832-7545	80 sites; 80 water & electric; flush toilets; hot showers; dump facility; laundry; public phone; ice; picnic tables; fire area.	Year Round Maximum: 14 days
Emerson	Allatoona Pass Campground (Allatoona Lake Corps of Engineers)	S on 293; 1½ mi. E on Allatoona Rd; follow signs.	11 sites; 11 no hookups; pit toilets; 11 picnic tables; grills	Year Round Maximum: 14 days
Acworth B-2	Clark Creek North (Allatoona Lake Corps of Engineers)	3 mi. N on Bethany-Beach Rd; W over Clark Creek bridge. (404) 974-9112	24 sites; 24 no hookups; pit toilets; 24 picnic tables; grills.	May 1 to Dec. 1 Maximum: 14 days
	Clark Creek South (Allatoona Lake Corps of Engineers)	3 mi. N on Bethany-Beach Rd; W to park entrance before Clark Creek bridge. (404) 974-9113	40 sites; 40 no hookups; pit toilets; 40 picnic tables; fire area; grills	May 1 to Dec. 1 Maximum: 14 days
	Glade Farm Campground (Allatoona Lake Corps of Engineers)	5 mi. N on Glade Rd. (Bartow Rd.) W on King's Camp Rd. (404)	37 sites; 37 no hookups; pit toilets; 27 picnic tables; grills	Year Round Maximum: 14 days
	McKinney Campground (Allatoona Lake Corps of Engineers)	5 mi. N on Glade Rd; ¾ mi. W on King's Camp Rd. (404) 974-9109	74 sites; 74 no hookups; pit toilets; 74 picnic tables; grills	Year Round Maximum: 14 days
Atlanta	Stone Mountain Park	I-85 & I-285; 5½ mi. S on I-285 (exit 30-B); 7½ E on US 78 (Stone Mountain Freeway) (404) 469-5084 (404) 469-9831	461 sites; 115 full hookups; 278 water & electric (20 & 30 amp receptacles); 68 no hookups; 20 pull-thrus; flush toilets; hot showers; dump station; laundry; public phone; grocery/RV supplies; LP-gas refill; ice; picnic tables; grills; wood	Year Round Maximum: 14 days
Buford	Big Creek Campground (Corps of Engineers)	GA 20 & US 53; 6 mi. N off US 23	21 sites; 21 no hookups; flush toilets; picnic tables; fire area	May 14 to Sept. 10
	Chestnut Ridge Park (Corps of Engineers)	US 23 & GA 20; 7 mi. N off US 23. (404)	44 sites; 44 no hookups; flush toilets; picnic tables; fire area	May 14 to Sept. 10
	Keith Bridge Campground (Corps of Engineers)	US 19 & GA 53; 14 mi. SE on GA 53 (Cumming) (404)	40 sites; 40 no hookups; flush toilets; picnic tables; fire area.	May 14 to Sept. 10
	Lake Lanier Islands Campground	GA 365 (exit 2) & GA 347; 4½ mi. W on GA 347 (404) 945-6706	252 sites; 52 full hookups; 178 water & electric (20 & 30 amp receptacles) 22 no hookups; 55 pull-thrus; flush toilets; hot showers; dump facility; laundry; public phone; grocery/RV supplies; LP-gas refill; marine gas; ice; 252 picnic tables; grills; wood	Year Round full facility Memorial Day to Labor Day Maximum: 14 days

NEAREST TOWN	CAMP NAME	DIRECTIONS & ADDRESS	FACILITIES	SEASON
Buford (Cont'd.)	Little Hall Park (Corps of Engineers)	US 19 & GA 306; 123 mi. NE on GA 306 (Cumming) (404)	48 sites; 48 no hookups; flush toilets; picnic tables; fire area	May 14 to Sept. 10
	Old Federal Road Park (Corps of Engineers)	US 23 & GA 20; 10 mi. N off US 23	49 sites; flush toilets; picnic tables; fire area.	May 14 to Sept. 10
	Robinson Campground	US 23 & GA 20; 20 mi. N on US 23; 15 mi. W on GA 53.	40 sites; 40 no hookups; flush toilets; picnic tables; fire area	May 14 to Sept. 10
	Sawnee Campground (Corps of Engineers)	US 23 & GA 20; 6 mi. W off GA 20.	68 sites; 68 no hookups; flush toilets; picnic tables; fire area.	May 14 to Sept. 10
	Shady Grove Park (Corps of Engineers)	US 19 & GA 369; 5 mi. W on GA 369; 5 mi. S (Cumming).	32 sites; 32 no hookups; flush toilets; picnic tables; fire area.	May 14 to Sept. 10
	Shoal Creek Camping Area (Corps of Engineers)	5 mi. NW of town.	89 sites; 89 no hookups; flush toilets	May 14 to Sept: 10
	Toto Creek Campground (Corps of Engineers)	US 19 & GA 136; 8 mi. E on GA 136 (Dawsonville).	25 sites; 25 no hookups; flush toilets; picnic tables; fire area.	May 14 to Sept. 10
	Two Mile Creek (Corps of Engineers)	US 19 & GA 369; 9 mi. E on GA 369; 4 mi. S (Cumming).	38 sites; 38 no hookups; flush toilets; picnic tables; fire area.	May 14 to Sept. 10
	Van Pugh Campground (Corps of Engineers)	US 23 & GA 20; 6 mi. N on US 23.	69 sites; 69 no hookups; flush toilets; picnic tables; fire area.	May 14 to Sept. 10
Canton	Sweetwater Campground (Allatoona Lake Corps of Engineers)	5½ mi. W on GA 20; 2 mi. S at Sweetwater Corner Store. (404) 382-4700 (Allatoona Lake Corps of Engineers)	70 sites; 70 no hookups; flush/pit toilets; 70 picnic tables; grills	Year Round Maximum: 14 days
Winder	Fort Vargo State Park	GA 81 & US 29; 1 mi. S on GA 81.	33 sites; 33 water & electric; flush toilets; hot showers; picnic tables; fire area.	Year Round Maximum: 14 days
Woodstock	Victoria Campground (Allatoona Lake Corps of Engineers)	S on GA 5; 6 mi. W on GA 92; 2 mi. N on GA 205; 2.2 mi. W. (404) 382-4700 (Allatoona Lake Corps of Engineers)	10 sites; 10 no hookups; pit toilets; 10 picnic tables; grills.	Year Round Maximum: 14 days
Comer B-3	Watson Mill Bridge (State Park)	1¼ mi. S on GA 22.	25 sites; 25 water & electric; 25 no hookups; flush toilets; hot showers; 25 picnic tables; grills.	Year Round
Elberton	Bobby Brown State Park	GA 72 & GA 77; 18 mi. SE off GA 79 on shore of Clark Hill Lake (404) 283-3313	59 sites; 59 water & electric; no motorcycles; flush toilets; cold showers; dump facility; laundry; picnic tables; fire area; wood.	Year Round Maximum: 14 days
Madison	Koa-Madison/Talisman	I-20 & US 441 (exit 51); 1¾ mi. S on US 441. (404) 342-1799	74 sites; 11 full hookups; 49 water & electric (20 amp receptacles); 14 no hookups; 27 pull-thrus; flush toilets; hot showers; dump station; laundry; public phone; grocery/RV supplies; ice; 30 picnic tables; wood.	Year Round full facility May 15 to Sep. 15
Rutledge	Hard Labor Creek State Park	2 mi. N of town off US 278. (404) 557-2863	105 sites; 105 water & electric; flush toilets; hot showers; dump facility; public phone; grocery; ice; picnic tables; fire area; wood.	Year Round Maximum: 14 days
Appling B-4	Keg Creek State Park	I-20 & US 221; 8 mi. N on US 221; 2 mi. NW on GA 104; 1 mi. E.	25 sites; 15' max. RV length; 25 no hookups; no motorcycles; flush toilets; hot showers; picnic tables; fire area.	Year Round Maximum: 14 days
	Mistletoe State Park	I-20 (exit 60); 12 mi. N. (404) 541-0321	107 sites; 107 water & electric; flush toilets; hot showers; dump facility; laundry.	Year Round Maximum: 14 days
Lincolnton	Elijah Clark State Park	US 378 & GA 47; 7 mi. NE on US 378 to shore of Clark Hill Lake. (404) 359-3458	141 sites; 125 water & electric; flush toilets; hot showers; dump facility; laundry; picnic tables; fire area.	Year Round Maximum: 14 days
Columbus C-1	Hills of Harris Campground	US 27 & GA 103; 15 mi. N on GA 103 (Fortson). (404) 327-9245	80 sites; 10 full hookups; 40 water & electric (20 amp receptacles); 30 no hookups; 5 pull-thrus; flush toilets; hot showers; dump facility; public phone; limited grocery; ice; 15 picnic tables; wood; church services.	Year Round; full facility May through Oct.
	Lake Pines Campground	I-185 & US 80; 8½ mi. E on US 80; ¼ mi. S on Garrett Rd. (404) 561-9122	80 sites; 60 water & electric; (15-20 amp receptacles); 20 no hookups; 20 pull-thrus; flush toilets; hot showers; dump facility; laundry; public phone; limited grocery; LP-gas; refill; ice; 80 picnic tables; wood.	Year Round
Franklin	Brush Creek Access (West Point Lake Corps of Engineers)	5 mi. S on GA 219 and follow signs.	37 sites; 14 water & electric; 23 no hookups; flush/pit toilets; hot showers; dump facility; 37 picnic tables; grills.	Year Round Maximum: 14 days
Hogansville	Flat Creek Ranch Campground	I-85 & GA 54/100 (exit 6); 1/10 mi. W on GA 54/100; 2 mi. SW on Bass Cross Rd.; ½ mi. S on Mountville Rd. (404) 637-4862	100 sites; 30 full hookups; 70 water & electric (20 amp receptacles); 30 pull-thrus; flush toilets; hot showers; dump facility; laundry; public phone; limited grocery; ice; 25 picnic tables.	Year Round
LaGrange	Autry Park (West Point Lake Corps of Engineers)	20 mi. W on GA 109; N on Alt 109; E on Antioch Rd. to Gene Autry Rd. (404) 645-2937 West Point Lake Corps of Engineers	126 sites; 126 no hookups; flush/pit toilets; dump facility; 126 picnic tables; grills.	Year Round Maximum: 14 days
	Holiday Park (West Point Lake Corps of Engineers)	10 mi. W on GA 109; over Chattahoochee River and follow signs. (404) 645-2937 West Point Lake Corps of Engineers	185 sites; 49 water & electric; 134 no hookups; flush/pit toilets; hot showers; dump facility; 185 picnic tables; grills.	Year Round Maximum: 14 days
	State Line Park (West Point Lake Corps of Engineers)	14 mi. W on GA 109 to GA 109 spur; then New State Line Rd. Off and follow signs. (404) 645-2937 West Point Lake Corps of Engineers	125 sites; 30 water & electric; 95 no hookups; flush/pit toilets; hot showers; dump facility; 125 picnic tables; grills.	Year Round Maximum: 14 days

NEAREST TOWN	CAMP NAME	DIRECTIONS & ADDRESS	FACILITIES	SEASON
Pine Mountain	Franklin Roosevelt State Park	GA 18 & US 27; 5 mi. SE on US 27.	100 sites; 50 water & electric; 50 no hookups; no motorcycles; flush toilets; hot showers; dump facility; public phone; limited grocery; ice; picnic tables; fire area.	Year Round Maximum: 14 days
Warm Springs	Franklin D. Roosevelt State Park	US 27 alt. & GA 85 W; 3 mi. S on GA 85 W; 9 mi. W on on GA 190. (404) 663-4858	140 sites; 100 water & electric; 40 no hookups; 35 pull-thrus; flush toilets; hot showers; dump station; public phone; limited grocery; ice; 140 picnic tables; grills	Year Round Maximum: 14 days
West Point	Amity Park (West Point Lake Corps of Engineers	7 mi. N on New State Line Rd. and follow signs. (404) 645-2937 West Point Lake Corps of Engineers	97 sites; 48 water & electric; 59 no hookups; flush/pit toilets; hot showers; 97 picnic tables; grills.	Year Round Maximum: 14 days
	Bird Creek Access (West Point Lake Corps of Engineers)	8 mi. N on GA 29 and follow signs. (404) 645-2937 West Point Lake Corps of Engineers	72 sites; 72 no hookups; flush/pit toilets; hot showers; dump facility; 72 picnic tables; grills	Year Round Maximum: 14 days
	East Lake Park (West Point Lake Corps of Engineers)	3 mi. N on GA 29 and follow signs. (404) 645-2937 West Point Lake Corps of Engineers	72 sites; 46 water & electric; 26 no hookups; flush/pit toilets; hot showers; dump facility; 82 picnic tables; grills	Year Round Maximum: 14 days
Jackson C-2	High Falls State Park	GA 36 & I-75; Exit I-75 on High Fall Rd; 1½ mi. E.	142 sites; 142 water & electric; flush toilets; hot showers; dump facility; laundry; ice; picnic tables; fire area.	Year Round Maximum: 14 days
	Indian Springs State Park	I-23 & GA 42; 4 mi. SE on GA 42. (404) 775-7241	125 sites; 125 water & electric; no motorcycles; flush toilets; hot showers; dump facility; public phone; grocery; picnic tables; fire area.	Year Round
	I-75 South Travel Trailer Park	I-75 & GA 16 (exit 67); 1/10 mi. W on GA 16. (404) 228-3399	44 sites; 44 full hookups; (20 & 30 amp receptacles); 42 pull-thrus; flush toilets; hot showers; laundry; public phone; full service store/RV supplies; LP Gas & refill; gas; ice; 12 picnic tables	Year Round; full facility May 15 to Sept. 30
Macon	Tobesofkee Recreation Area	GA 74 & I-75; 8 mi. W on GA 74; 2 mi. S. (912) 474-8770	110 sites; 30' maximum RV length; 110 water & electric; no motorcycles; flush toilets; hot showers; dump facility; laundry; public phone; grocery; ice; picnic tables; fire area; wood	Year Round
Perry	Safari Camp	I-75 & GA 127 (exit 42); 1/10 mi. W on GA 127. (912) 987-4562	120 sites; 64 full hookups; 31 water & electric (15 amp receptacles); 25 no hookups; 80 pull-thrus; flush toilets; hot showers; dump facility; laundry; public phone; limited grocery; LP-gas refill; ice; 120 picnic tables	Year Round Maximum: 14 days full facility Apr. thru Oct.
Eatonton C-3	Lake Sinclair (Oconee National Forest)	10 mi. S on US 129; 1 mi. SE on GA 212; 1 mi. E on CR 1062; ¼ mi. N on FS Rd 1105. (404) 468-6990.	25 sites; 32' maximum RV length; 25 no hookups; flush toilets; picnic tables; fire area.	Apr. 1 to Nov. 1 Maximum: 14 days
Sanders-ville	Hamburg State Park	GA 24 & GA 15; 16 mi. N on GA 15 & GA 248 (Mitchell). (912) 552-2393	30 sites; 30 water & electric; flush toilets; hot showers; picnic tables; fire area	Year Round Maximum: 14 days
Toomsboro	Swamplanders Camp Ground	GA 112 & GA 57; ¼ mi. W on GA 57; ¼ mi. S on country road	30 sites; 1 full hookup; 29 water & electric (20 amp receptacles); flush toilets; hot showers; dump facility; 6 picnic tables	Year Round
Millen C-4	Magnolia Springs State Park	US 25 & GA 23; 5 mi. N on US 25. (912) 982-1860	100 sites; 100 water & electric; flush toilets; hot showers; dump facility	Year Round Maximum: 14 days
Fort Gaines D-1	Cotton Hill Park (Corps of Engineers)	6 mi. N on GA 39.	37 sites; 37 no hookups; 37 picnic tables; grills.	Year Round
Albany D-2	Chehaw Park (City-County Park)	US 19 & GA 91; 5 mi. NE on GA 91. (912) 432-2371	125 sites; 75 water & electric; 50 no hookups; no motorcycles; flush toilets; hot showers; dump facility; laundry; picnic tables; fire area.	Year Round
Americus	Pet Rock Campground	US 280 & US 19 (west jct); 2½ mi. W on US 280; 1/3 mi. N on dirt road. (912) 924-6564	38 sites; 23 full hookups; 15 water & electric (15 amp receptacles); 38 pull-thrus; flush toilets; hot showers; dump facility; phone available; LP-gas refill; 10 picnic tables.	Year Round
Arabi	Arabi Campsites	I-75 (exit 30-Arabi); ¼ mi. W on Deer Creek Rd. (912) 273-6464	75 sites; 24 full hookups; 51 water & electric (20 amp receptacles); 36 pull-thrus; flush toilets; hot showers; dump facility; laundry; public phone; limited grocery; LP-gas refill; ice; 50 picnic tables; wood.	Year Round full facility Apr. to Oct.
Douglas D-3	General Coffee State Park	US 441 & GA 32; 5 mi. E on GA 32. (912) 384-7082	50 sites; 25 water & electric; flush toilets; hot showers; laundry; picnic tables; fire area.	Year Round Maximum: 14 days
McRae	Little Ocmulgee State Park	US 441 & US 280; 1 mi. N on US 441-319. (912) 868-2832	59 sites; 59 water & electric; flush toilets; hot showers; dump facility; public phone; ice; picnic tables; fire area; wood.	Year Round Maximum: 14 days
Reidsville D-4	Gordonia Alatamaha State Park	City limits on US 280.	25 sites; 25 water & electric; flush toilets; hot showers; dump facility; laundry; public phone; picnic tables; fire fire area; wood.	Year Round Maximum: 14 days
Savannah D-5	Richmond Hill State Park	I-16 & US 17; 25 mi. S on US 17; exit at terminus of GA 67 Spur. (912) 727-2242	75 sites; 30 water & electric; 45 no hookups; flush toilets; hot showers; dump facility; picnic tables; fire area.	Year Round Maximum: 14 days
	Skidaway Island State Park	I-16 & US 17; 5 mi. SE on I-16 to Loop 26 to Skidaway Rd. (912) 352-8599	100 sites; 100 water & electric; no motorcycles; flush toilets; picnic tables; fire area.	Year Round Maximum: 14 days
Blakely E-1	Kolomoki Mounds State Park	US 27 & GA 62; 6 mi. N on US 27.	32 sites; 32 water & electric; no motorcycles; flush toilets; hot showers; laundry; public phone; ice; picnic tables; fire area.	Year Round Maximum: 14 days
Donalsonville	Seminole State Park	US 84 & GA 39; 16 mi. S on GA 39. (912) 861-3137	50 sites; 50 water & electric; flush toilets; hot showers; dump facility; laundry; ice; picnic tables; fire area; wood.	Year Round Maximum: 14 days
Recovery	Hutchinson's Ferry Landing	GA 97 & GA 310; 3 mi. W on GA 310.	sites; flush toilets; picnic tables; fire area.	

NEAREST TOWN	CAMP NAME	DIRECTIONS & ADDRESS	FACILITIES	SEASON
Reynoldsville	Butler's Ferry Landing (Corps of Engineers)	GA 253 & GA 45; 10 mi. SW on GA 253.	sites; flush toilets; dump facility; picnic tables; fire area.	
Adel E-3	Reed Bingham State Park	I-75 & GA 37; 6 mi. W on GA 37. (912) 896-7788	85 sites; 85 water & electric; flush toilets; hot showers; dump facility; laundry; public phone; picnic tables; fire area.	Year Round Maximum: 14 days
Cecil	Safari Tall Pines Campground	I-75 (exit 8); 1/10 mi. on W Old Coffee Rd. (912) 794-2323	92 sites; 8 full hookups; 32 water & electric (20 amp receptacles); 52 no hookups; 92 pull-thrus; hot showers; laundry; public phone; limited grocery/RV supplies; LP-gas refill; ice; 92 picnic tables	Year Round
Fargo E-4	Stephan C. Foster State Park	GA 177 & GA 94; 18 mi. NE on GA 177. (912) 637-5274	69 sites; 69 water & electric; no motorcycles; flush toilets; hot showers; dump facility; ice; picnic tables; fire area.	Year Round Maximum: 14 days
Folkston	Koa-Okefenoke	US 301 & GA 121; 7 mi. S on GA 121. (912) 496-7414	37 sites; 4 full hookups; 18 water & electric (15, 20 & 30 amp receptacles); 15 no hookups; 17 pull-thrus; flush toilets; hot showers; dump facility; laundry; public phone; grocery/RV supplies; LP-gas refill; ice; 16 picnic tables.	Year Round
Waycross	Laura S. Walker State Park	US 82 & US 84; 10 mi. SE on US 84 off GA 177. (912) 283-0410	44 sites; 44 water & electric; flush toilets; hot showers; dump facility; laundry; public phone; ice; picnic tables; fire area.	Year Round Maximum: 14 days
Jekyll Island E-5	Cherokee Campground	4 mi. N on Beachview Drive. (912) 635-2592	225 sites; 100 full hookups; 100 water & electric (20 & 30 amp receptacles); 25 no hookups; 24 pull-thrus; flush toilets; hot showers; dump facility; laundry; public phone; grocery/RV supplies; LP-gas refill; gas; ice; 225 picnic tables.	Year Round
Kingsland	Crooked River State Park	US 17 & GA 40; 12 mi. E on GA 40. (912) 882-5256 or (912) 882-3518	63 sites; 63 water & electric; flush toilets; hot showers; dump facility; grocery; ice; picnic tables; fire area.	Year Round Maximum: 14 days

Glossary of Paddling Terms

Blackwater stream. A river with waters dyed a reddish color by tannic acid from tree roots and rotting vegetation.

Bottom. The stream bottoms described in this book allude to what the paddler sees as opposed to the geological composition of the river bed. From a geologist's perspective, for example, a river may flow over a limestone bed. The paddler, however, because of the overlying silt and sediment, perceives the bottom as being mud.

Bow. The front of a boat.

Broaching. A boat that is sideways to the current and usually out of control or pinned to an obstacle in the stream.

By-pass. A channel cut across a meander that creates an island or oxbow lake.

cfs. Cubic feet per second; an accurate method of expressing river flow in terms of function of flow and volume.

C-1. One-person, decked canoe equipped with a spray skirt; frequently mistaken for a kayak. The canoeist kneels in the boat and uses a single-bladed paddle.

C-2. A two-person, decked canoe; frequently mistaken for a two-person kayak.

Chute. A clear channel between obstructions that has faster current than the surrounding water.

Curler. A wave that curls or falls back on itself (upstream).

Cut-off. *See* **By-pass.**

Deadfalls. Trees that have fallen into the stream totally or partially obstructing it.

Decked boat. A completely enclosed canoe or kayak fitted with a spray skirt. When the boater is properly in place, this forms a nearly waterproof unit.

Downstream ferry. A technique for moving sideways in the current while facing downstream. Can also be done by "surfing" on a wave.

Downward erosion. The wearing away of the bottom of a stream by the current.

Drainage area. Officially defined as an area measured in a horizontal plane, enclosed by a topographic divide, from which direct surface runoff from precipitation normally drains by gravity into a stream above a specified point. In other words, this is an area that has provided the water on which you are paddling at any given time. Accordingly, the drainage area increases as you go downstream. The drainage basin of a river is expressed in square miles. (Also known as a "watershed.")

Drop. Paddler's term for **gradient.**

Eddy. The water behind an obstruction in the current or behind a river bend. The water may be relatively calm or boiling and will flow upstream.

Eddy line. The boundary at the edge of an eddy between two currents of different velocity and direction.

Eddy out. *See* **Eddy turn.**

Eddy turn. Maneuver used to move into an eddy from the downstream current.

Eskimo roll. The technique used to upright an overturned decked canoe or kayak, by the occupant, while remaining in the craft. This is done by coordinated body motion and usually facilitated by the proper use of the paddle.

Expert boater. A person with extensive experience and good judgment who is familiar with up-to-date boating techniques, practical hydrology, and proper safety practices. An expert boater never paddles alone and always uses the proper equipment.

Fall Line. The line between the Piedmont and Coastal Plain where the land slopes sharply.

Falls. A portion of river where the water falls freely over a drop. This designation has nothing to do with hazard rating or difficulty. *See* **Rapids.**

Ferry. Moving sideways to the current facing either up- or downstream.

Flotation. Additional buoyant materials (air bags, styrofoam, inner tubes, etc.) placed in a boat to provide displacement of water and extra buoyancy in case of upset.

Grab loops. Loops (about 6 inches in diameter) of nylon rope or similar material attached to the bow and stern of a boat to facilitate rescue.

Gradient. The geographical drop of the river expressed in feet per mile.

Hair. Turbulent whitewater.

Haystack. A pyramid-shaped standing wave caused by deceleration of current from underwater resistance.

Headward erosion. The wearing away of the rock strata forming the base of ledges or waterfalls by the current.

Heavy water. Fast current and large waves usually associated with holes and boulders.

Hydraulic. General term for souse holes and back-rollers, where there is a hydraulic jump (powerful current differential) and strong reversal current.

K-1. One-person, decked kayak equipped with spray skirt. In this book, this category does not include non-decked kayaks. The kayaker sits in the boat with both feet extended forward. A double-bladed paddle is used.

Keeper. A souse hole or hydraulic with sufficient vacuum in its trough to hold an object (paddler, boat, log, etc.) that floats into it for an undetermined time. Extremely dangerous and to be avoided.

Lateral erosion. The wearing away of the sides or banks of a stream by the current.

Ledge. The exposed edge of a rock stratum that acts as a low, natural dam or as a series of such dams.

Left bank. Left bank of river when facing downstream.

Lining. A compromise between portaging and running a rapids. By the use of a rope (line), a boat can be worked downstream from the shore.

Logjam. A jumbled tangle of fallen trees, branches, and sometimes debris that totally or partially obstructs a stream.

Low-water bridge. A bridge across the river that barely clears the surface of the water or may even be awash; very dangerous for the paddler if in a fast current.

Meander. A large loop in a river's path through a wide floodplain.

PFD. Personal flotation device, e.g., lifejacket.

Painter. A rope attached to the end of a craft.

Pillow. Bulge on surface created by underwater obstruction, usually a rock. Remember: these pillows are stuffed with rocks.

Pool. A section of water that is usually deep and quiet; frequently found below rapids and falls.

Rapids. Portion of a river where there is appreciable turbulence usually accompanied by obstacles. *See* **Falls.**

Riffles. Slight turbulence with or without a few rocks tossed in; usually Class I on the International Scale of River Difficulty.

Right bank. The right bank of the river as you progress downstream.

Rock garden. Rapids that have many exposed or partially submerged rocks necessitating intricate maneuvering or an occasional carry over shallow places.

Roller. *Also* **curler** or **backroller;** a wave that falls back on itself.

Run. *See* **Section** and **Stretch.**

Scout. To look at rapids from the shore to decide whether or not to run them, or to facilitate selection of a suitable route through the rapids.

Section. A portion of river located between two points. *Also* **Stretch** and **Run.**

Shuttle. Movement of at least two vehicles, one to the take-out and one back to the put-in points. Used to avoid having to paddle back upstream at the end of a run.

Slide rapids. An elongated ledge that descends or slopes gently rather than abruptly, and is covered usually with only shallow water.

Souse hole. A wave at the bottom of a ledge that curls back on itself. Water enters the trough of the wave from the upstream and downstream sides with reversal (upstream) current present downstream of the trough.

Spray skirt. A hemmed piece of waterproof material resembling a short skirt, having an elastic hem fitting around the boater's waist and an elastic hem fitting around the cockpit rim of a decked boat.

Standing wave. A regular wave downstream of submerged rocks that does not move in relation to the riverbed (as opposed to a moving wave such as an ocean wave).

Stern. The back end of a boat.

Stopper. Any very heavy wave or turbulence that quickly impedes the downriver progress of a rapidly paddled boat.

Stretch. A portion of river located between two points. *See* **Section** and **Run.**

Surfing. The technique of sitting on the upstream face of a wave or traveling back and forth across the wave when ferrying.

Surfing wave. A very wide wave that is fairly steep. A good paddler can slide into it and either stay balanced on its upstream face or else travel back and forth across it much in the same manner as a surfer in the ocean.

Sweep. The last boat in a group.

TVA. Tennessee Valley Authority.

Technical whitewater. Whitewater where the route is often less than obvious and where maneuvering in the rapids is frequently required.

Thwart. Transverse braces from gunwale to gunwale.

Trim. The balance of a boat in the water. Paddlers and duffel should be positioned so the waterline is even from bow to stern and the boat does not list to either side.

Undercut rock. A potentially dangerous situation where a large boulder has been eroded or undercut by water flow and could trap a paddler accidentally swept under it.

Upstream ferry. Similar to **downstream ferry** except the paddler faces upstream. *See also* **Surfing.**

Alphabetical Index

Alabaha River, 170
Alapaha River, 206
Alcovy River, 36
Altamaha River, 160
Big Creek, 64
Brier Creek, 92
Canoochee River, 114
Chattahoochee River, of the Western Piedmont, 76; of the Coastal Plain, 252
Coast, Georgia, 272
Dog River, 68
Flat Shoal Creek, 70
Flint River, above the Fall Line, 56; below the Fall Line, 232
Lazer Creek, 54
Little River, 212
Little Ocmulgee River, 142
Little Satilla River, 172
Mulberry Creek, 72
Ochlockonee River, 226
Ocmulgee River, above Macon, 50; below Macon, 144; Little, 142
Oconee River, 132
Ogeechee River, 118
Ohoopee River, 157
Okefenokee Swamp, 266
St. Marys River, 190
Satilla River, 176; Little, 172
Savannah River, 98
South River, 44
Spring Creek, 248
Suwannee River, 200
Sweetwater Creek, 66
Tallapoosa River, 86
Towaliga River, 48
Withlacoochee River, 218
Yellow River, 40

Canoe–Camping Streams

Alapaha River, 206
Altamaha River, 160
Chattahoochee River (below Sweetwater Creek), 82–85, 252–263
Flint River, above the Fall Line, 56; below the Fall Line, 232
Little River of Southern Georgia, 212
Little Satilla River, 172
Ochlockonee River, 226
Ocmulgee River, above Macon, 50; below Macon, 144
Oconee River, 132
Ogeechee River, 118
Ohoopee River, 157
St. Marys River, 190
Satilla River, 176; Little, 172
Savannah River, 98
Suwannee River, 200
Tallapoosa River, 86
Towaliga River, 48
Withlacoochee River, 218

Whitewater Streams

Alcovy River, 36
Chattahoochee River (Sweetwater Creek to West Point Lake), 82–84
Dog River, 68
Flat Shoal Creek, 70
Flint River (Woolsey to Lake Blackshear), 56–63, 232–235
Lazer Creek, 54
Mulberry Creek, 72
South River, 44
Sweetwater Creek, 66
Towaliga River, 48

CANOEING STREAMS OF SOUTHERN GEORGIA

STREAM INDEX

Page	*River Name*
36	Alcovy River
40	Yellow River
44	South River
48	Towaliga River
50	Ocmulgee River
54	Lazer Creek
56	Flint River
64	Big Creek
66	Sweetwater Creek
68	Dog River
70	Flat Shoal Creek
72	Mulberry Creek
76	Chattahoochee River
86	Tallapoosa River
92	Brier Creek
98	Savannah River
114	Canoochee River
118	Ogeechee River
132	Oconee River
142	Little Ocmulgee River
144	Ocmulgee River
157	Ohoopee River
160	Altamaha River
170	Alabaha River
172	Little Satilla River
176	Satilla River
190	St. Marys River
200	Suwannee River
206	Alapaha River
212	Little River
218	Withlacoochee River
226	Ochlockonee River
232	Flint River
248	Spring Creek
252	Chattahoochee River
266	Okefenokee Swamp
272	Georgia Coast

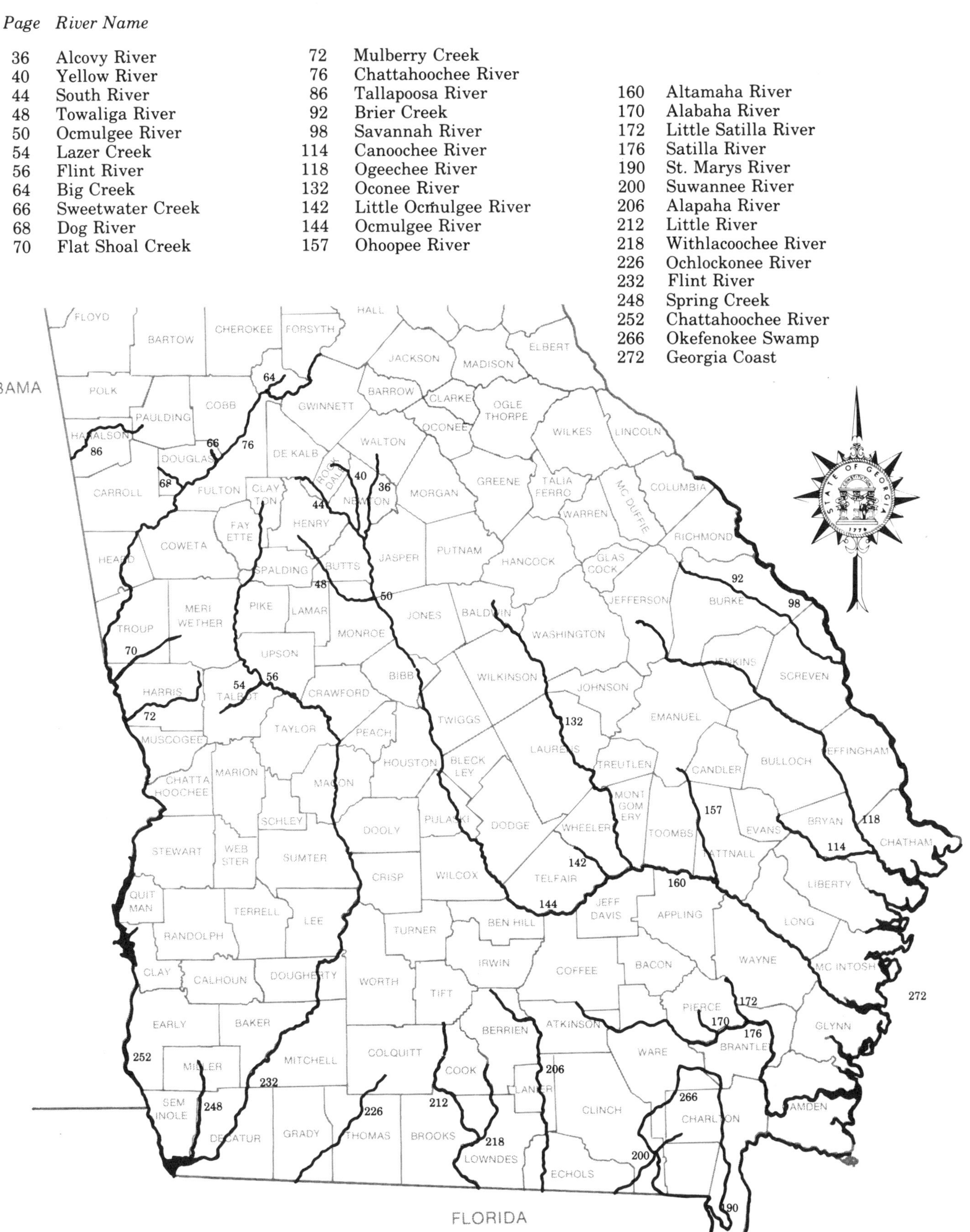

Other Menasha Ridge Press Books

A Hiking Guide to the Trails of Florida, Elizabeth F. Carter

The Squirt Book: The Manual of Squirt Kayaking Technique, James E. Snyder, illustrated by W. Nealy

Chattooga River (Section IV) Flip Map, Ron Rathnow

Nantahala River Flip Map, Ron Rathnow

New River Flip Map, Ron Rathnow

Ocoee River Flip Map, Ron Rathnow

Youghiogheny River Flip Map, Ron Rathnow

Kayak: The Animated Manual of Intermediate and Advanced Whitewater Technique, William Nealy

Kayaks to Hell, William Nealy

Whitewater Home Companion, Southeastern Rivers, Volume I, William Nealy

Whitewater Home Companion, Southeastern Rivers, Volume II, William Nealy

Whitewater Tales of Terror, William Nealy

Carolina Whitewater: A Canoeist's Guide to the Western Carolinas, Bob Benner

A Paddler's Guide to Eastern North Carolina, Bob Benner and Tom McCloud

Wildwater West Virginia, Volume I, The Northern Streams, Paul Davidson, Ward Eister, and Dirk Davidson

Wildwater West Virginia, Volume II, The Southern Streams, Paul Davidson, Ward Eister, and Dirk Davidson

Diver's Guide to Underwater America, Kate Kelley and John Shobe

Shipwrecks: Diving the Graveyard of the Atlantic, Roderick M. Farb

Boatbuilder's Manual, Charles Walbridge, editor

Smoky Mountains Trout Fishing Guide, Don Kirk

Fishing the Great Lakes of the South: An Angler's Guide to the TVA System, Don and Joann Kirk

A Fishing Guide to Kentucky's Major Lakes, Arthur B. Lander, Jr.

A Guide to the Backpacking and Day-Hiking Trails of Kentucky, Arthur B. Lander, Jr.

A Canoeing and Kayaking Guide to the Streams of Florida, Volume I, North Central Peninsula and Panhandle, Elizabeth F. Carter and John L. Pearce

A Canoeing and Kayaking Guide to the Streams of Florida, Volume II, Central and South Peninsula, Lou Glaros and Doug Sphar

Appalachian Whitewater, Volume I, The Southern Mountains, Bob Sehlinger, Don Otey, Bob Benner, William Nealy, and Bob Lantz

Appalachian Whitewater, Volume II, The Central Mountains, Ed Grove, Bill Kirby, Charles Walbridge, Ward Eister, Paul Davidson, and Dirk Davidson

Appalachian Whitewater, Volume III, The Northern Mountains, John Connelly and John Porterfield

Northern Georgia Canoeing, Bob Sehlinger and Don Otey

Southern Georgia Canoeing, Bob Sehlinger and Don Otey

A Canoeing and Kayaking Guide to the Streams of Kentucky, Bob Sehlinger

A Canoeing and Kayaking Guide to the Streams of Ohio, Volume I, Richard Combs and Stephen E. Gillen

A Canoeing and Kayaking Guide to the Streams of Ohio, Volume II, Richard Combs and Stephen E. Gillen

A Canoeing and Kayaking Guide to the Streams of Tennessee, Volume I, Bob Sehlinger and Bob Lantz

A Canoeing and Kayaking Guide to the Streams of Tennessee, Volume II, Bob Sehlinger and Bob Lantz

Emergency Medical Procedures for the Outdoors, Patient Care Publications, Inc.

Guide and Map to the Uwharrie Trails, G. Nicholas Hancock

Harsh Weather Camping, Sam Curtis

Modern Outdoor Survival, Dwight R. Schuh

Menasha Ridge Press, Post Office Box 59257, Birmingham, Alabama 35259-9257